A Companion to American Technology

BLACKWELL COMPANIONS TO AMERICAN HISTORY

This series provides essential and authoritative overviews of the scholarship that has shaped our present understanding of the American past. Edited by eminent historians, each volume tackles one of the major periods or themes of American history, with individual topics authored by key scholars who have spent considerable time in research on the questions and controversies that have sparked debate in their field of interest. The volumes are accessible for the non-specialist, while also engaging scholars seeking a reference to the historiography or future concerns.

Published

A Companion to the American Revolution
Edited by Jack P. Greene and J.R. Pole

A Companion to 19th-Century America
Edited by William L. Barney

A Companion to the American South
Edited by John B. Boles

A Companion to American Indian History
Edited by Philip J. Deloria and Neal Salisbury

A Companion to American Women's History
Edited by Nancy Hewitt

A Companion to Post-1945 America
Edited by Jean-Christophe Agnew and Roy Rosenzweig

A Companion to the Vietnam War
Edited by Marilyn Young and Robert Buzzanco

A Companion to Colonial America
Edited by Daniel Vickers

A Companion to 20th-Century America
Edited by Stephen J. Whitfield

A Companion to the American West
Edited by William Deverell

A Companion to American Foreign Relations
Edited by Robert Schulzinger

A Companion to the Civil War and Reconstruction
Edited by Lacy K. Ford

A Companion to American Technology
Edited by Carroll Pursell

A Companion to African-American History
Edited by Alton Hornsby

In preparation

A Companion to American Immigration
Edited by Reed Ueda

BLACKWELL COMPANIONS TO HISTORY

Published

A Companion to Western Historical Thought
Edited by Lloyd Kramer and Sarah Maza

A Companion to Gender History
Edited by Teresa A. Meade and Merry E. Wiesner-Hanks

BLACKWELL COMPANIONS TO BRITISH HISTORY

Published

A Companion to Roman Britain
Edited by Malcolm Todd

A Companion to Britain in the Later Middle Ages
Edited by S.H. Rigby

A Companion to Stuart Britain
Edited by Barry Coward

A Companion to Eighteenth-Century Britain
Edited by H.T. Dickinson

A Companion to Early Twentieth-Century Britain
Edited by Chris Wrigley

In preparation

A Companion to Tudor Britain
Edited by Robert Tittler and Norman Jones

A Companion to Britain in the Early Middle Ages
Edited by Pauline Stafford

A Companion to Nineteenth-Century Britain
Edited by Chris Williams

A Companion to Contemporary Britain
Edited by Paul Addison and Harriet Jones

BLACKWELL COMPANIONS TO EUROPEAN HISTORY

Published

A Companion to the Worlds of the Renaissance
Edited by Guido Ruggiero

A Companion to the Reformation World
Edited by R. Po-chia Hsia

In preparation

A Companion to Europe Since 1945
Edited by Klaus Larres

A Companion to Europe 1900–1945
Edited by Gordon Martel

BLACKWELL COMPANIONS TO WORLD HISTORY

In preparation

A Companion to the History of the Middle East
Edited by Youssef M. Choueiri

A COMPANION TO AMERICAN TECHNOLOGY

Edited by

Carroll Pursell

Blackwell
Publishing

BLACKWELL PUBLISHING
350 Main Street, Malden, MA 02148-5020, USA
108 Cowley Road, Oxford OX4 1JF, UK
550 Swanston Street, Carlton, Victoria 3053, Australia

First published 2005 by Blackwell Publishing Ltd

Library of Congress Cataloging-in-Publication Data

A companion to American technology / edited by Carroll Pursell.
    p.   cm. — (Blackwell companions to American history ; 13)
    Includes bibliographical references and index.
    ISBN 0–631–22844–6 (hardback : alk. paper)
    1. Technology—United States—History.   I. Pursell, Carroll W.   II. Series.

    T21.C65 2004
    609′.73—dc22

                                                            2004019638

A catalogue record for this title is available from the British Library

Set in 10/12.5 pt Galliard
by Integra Software Services Pvt. Ltd, Pondicherry, India
Printed and bound in the United Kingdom
by TJ International, Padstow, Cornwall

For further information on Blackwell Publishing, visit our website:
www.blackwellpublishing.com

Contents

Notes on Contributors

Henry Adams was recently singled out by *Art News* as one of the foremost experts in the American field. Dr Adams has produced over two hundred publications, including scholarly and popular articles, books, catalogues, and exhibitions catalogues. His major books and exhibition catalogues include *John La Farge* (1987), *Thomas Hart Benton: An American Original* (1989), *Thomas Hart Benton: Drawing from Life* (1990), *Albert Bloch: The American Blue Rider* (1997), and *Viktor Schreckengost and 20th-Century Design* (2000). In 1989, in partnership with filmmaker Ken Burns, he produced a documentary on Thomas Hart Benton, which was broadcast nationally on PBS to an audience of 20 million. He currently serves as Professor of American Art at Case Western Reserve University.

Molly W. Berger is an Instructor of History in the Department of History at Case Western Reserve University. She also serves as Assistant Dean in the College of Arts and Sciences. Dr Berger is currently writing *The Modern Hotel in America, 1829–1929*, a cultural history about nineteenth-century American urban luxury hotels that explores ideas about technology, democracy, and urban growth. The book is forthcoming from Johns Hopkins University Press.

Roger E. Bilstein is Professor of History, Emeritus, University of Houston-Clear Lake, where he was a Charter Faculty Member at the time of its establishment in 1974 as an upper-division, suburban campus for juniors, seniors, and graduate students. He is the co-author/editor or sole author of nine books and monographs, including *Flight in America: From the Wrights to the Astronauts* (3rd edition, 2000) and *Enterprise of Flight: The American*

Aviation and Aerospace Industry (2nd edition, 2001). The official NASA history *Stages to Space: A Technological History of the Apollo/Saturn Launch Vehicles* (1980), received the history award for 1979 from the American Institute of Aeronautics and Astronautics and was released in a second edition by the University of Florida Press in 2003. His latest book is *Testing Aircraft, Exploring Space: An Illustrated History of NACA and NASA* (2003). He is also the author of several dozen articles and book chapters.

Gail Cooper is an Associate Professor in the history department at Lehigh University. She is the author of *Air-conditioning America* (1998). In addition, she served as historical consultant for the exhibit *Keep Cool!* at the National Building Museum in Washington, DC. She is particularly interested in the history of manufacturing, and has written on the connections between gender and technology.

James M. Edmonson is Chief Curator of the Dittrick Medical History Center and Museum of Case Western Reserve University, and is Adjunct Associate Professor in the Department of History. A graduate of the College of Wooster, he received an MA and PhD in the history of technology at the University of Delaware. While at Delaware he was a Hagley Fellow and a Fulbright-Hays Fellow in Paris, France, and his dissertation, *From mécanicien to ingénieur: Technical Education and the Machine Building Industry in Nineteenth Century France* (1986) received the Sypherd Prize for outstanding dissertation in the humanities. Since becoming Chief Curator at the Dittrick he has written on medical museology, surgical instrumentation, endoscopy, and medical patents. His publications include *Nineteenth*

Century Surgical Instruments (1986) and *American Surgical Instruments* (1997), as well as introductions for reprint editions of Charles Truax, *The Mechanics of Surgery* (1988) and George Tiemann & Co., *American Armamentarium Chirurgicum* (1989). He has served as consultant to the Warren Anatomical Museum of Harvard University, the New York Academy of Medicine, and the National Library of Medicine.

Deborah Fitzgerald is Professor of the history of technology in the Program in Science, Technology and Society at MIT. Her work includes the book *The Business of Breeding: Hybrid Corn in Illinois, 1890–1940* (1990), and *"Every Farm a Factory": The Industrial Ideal in American Agriculture* (2003), which won the Theodore Saloutos Prize for the best book in agricultural history in 2003 from the Agricultural History Society. She has published essays and articles on deskilling in agriculture, the Rockefeller Foundation's agricultural experiences, and the modernization of agricultural practice and thinking. Fitzgerald is an advisory editor for *Technology and Culture*. She is currently president of the Agricultural History Society, and has served on the Executive Council, the Secretary search committee, and the Dexter Prize committee for the Society for the History of Technology. She has been awarded two National Science Foundation Fellowships. With Harriet Ritvo, Fitzgerald received a Sawyer Seminar Grant from the Mellon Foundation to run a seminar "Modern Times, Rural Places," at MIT in 2001–2004. She is currently working on the industrialization of food in America.

Douglas Gomery teaches media history at the University of Maryland and is Resident Scholar of the Library of American Broadcasting. His *Who Owns the Media?* won the Picard Award in 2002. He has published 11 more books, and over 1,000 articles in journals, magazines, and reference works.

Robert B. Gordon is professor at Yale University in the departments of Geology and Geophysics and Mechanical Engineering, and

the Council on Archaeological Studies. His current research focuses on archaeometallurgy and industrial ecology. Among his books are *Toward a New Iron Age?* with B.J. Skinner, W.D. Norhaus, and T. Koopmans (1987), *Texture of Industry* with Patrick Malone (1994), *American Iron* (1996) and *A Landscape Transformed* (2000).

Chris Hables Gray is an Associate Professor of the Cultural Studies of Science and Technology and of Computer Science at the University of Great Falls in Montana. He is the author of numerous articles and *Postmodern War* (1997), *Cyborg Citizen* (2001) and *Peace, War, and Computers* (New York: Routledge, 2005) and edited *The Cyborg Handbook* (1995) and *Technohistory* (1996). He is also Core Faculty of the Graduate College of the Union Institute and University and is a professor at Goddard College. A former NASA and Eisenhower fellow, he is currently writing on information theory, anarchism, and art.

Rebecca Herzig teaches courses on the history and sociology of science, technology, and medicine in the Program in Women and Gender Studies at Bates College. She is the author of two forthcoming books: *Suffering for Science: Will, Reason, and Sacrifice in Nineteenth-Century America* and, with Evelynn Hammonds and Abigail Bass, *The Nature of Difference: A Reader on Science, Race, and Gender*.

Roger D. Launius is Chair of the Division of Space History at the Smithsonian Institution's National Air and Space Museum in Washington, DC. Between 1990 and 2002 he served as chief historian of the National Aeronautics and Space Administration. He has written or edited more than twenty books on aerospace history, including *Space Stations: Base Camps to the Stars* (2003), which received the AIAA's history manuscript prize, *Flight: A Celebration of 100 Years in Art and Literature* edited with Anne Collins Goodyear, Anthony M. Springer, and Bertram Ulrich (2003), *Taking Off: A Century of Manned Flight* edited with Jonathan

Coopersmith (2003), and *Reconsidering a Century of Flight*, edited with Janet R. Daly (2003).

Betsy Mendelsohn studies how law, science and technology have interacted to shape environmental quality in the United States. She is finishing a book about how Chicago managed surface water to meet its needs for clean water, drainage, sewerage, navigation, and secure property boundaries. Her next book describes how science and law interacted to resolve environmental conflicts during the period 1850–1940. She earned her history PhD from University of Chicago as a US Environmental Protection Agency graduate fellow. She is the co-chair of Envirotech, a special interest group of the Society for the History of Technology, and is a postdoctoral fellow in the history of environment and technology at the University of Virginia's School of Engineering and Applied Science, Department of Science, Technology and Society.

Arwen P. Mohun teaches in the History Department of the University of Delaware. She is the author of *Steam Laundries: Gender, Work, and Technology in the United States and Great Britain, 1880–1940* (1999). With Nina Lerman and Ruth Oldenziel, she edited *Gender and Technology: A Reader* (2003). Her published work also includes *His and Hers: Gender, Technology, and Consumption* edited with Roger Horowitz (1998). Risk and technology in industrializing America is the focus of her current research.

David E. Nye is the author of many books on technology and American culture, including most recently *America as Second Creation: Technology and Narratives of New Beginnings* (2003) and *Narratives and Spaces: Technology and the Construction of American Culture* (1998).

Carroll Pursell is Adeline Barry Davee Distinguished Professor of History Emeritus at Case Western Reserve University, and Adjunct Professor of Modern History at Macquarie University in Sydney, Australia. He is a past president of the Society for the History of Technology and author of *The Machine in America* (1995).

Bruce E. Seely is Professor of History and Chair of the Department of Social Sciences at Michigan Technological University. He is the author of a number of books and articles on the history of American highways and transportation, on the history of engineering education and research, and on the history of the iron and steel industry. His professional activities include extensive service to the Society for the History of Technology. He has served as Program Director for Science and Technology Studies at the National Science Foundation. He is also a founding co-editor-in-chief of the journal, *Comparative Technology Transfer and Society*.

M. Joshua Silverman is a Program Manager for the US Department of Energy's Office of Environment, Safety and Health. He manages a federal program addressing the health legacy of American nuclear weapons production. His research focuses on changing risk management and environmental safety practices in American nuclear weapons production.

Bruce Sinclair is a Senior Fellow at the Dibner Institute at MIT. He taught for a number of years at the University of Toronto, where he was director of the Institute for the History and Philosophy of Science and Technology, and then moved to the Georgia Institute of Technology, when he was appointed Melvin Kranzberg Professor of the History of Technology. Long active in the Society for the History of Technology, he won its Dexter Prize, served as its president, and was awarded its da Vinci Medal.

Joel A. Tarr is the Richard S. Caliguiri Professor of History and Policy at Carnegie Mellon University. His main research interests are in the history of urban environmental pollution and urban technological systems. Most recently, he is the author of *The Search for the Ultimate Sink: Urban Pollution in Historical Perspective* (1996) and the editor of *Devastation* *and Renewal: An Environmental History of Pittsburgh and Its Region* (2004). He has served as president of both the Urban History Association and the Public Works Historical Society.

James C. Williams is Professor Emeritus of History at de Anza College, was formerly the Treasurer of the Society for the History of Technology and is currently Vice President of the International Committee for the History of Technology. He is the author of *Energy and the Making of Modern California* (1997).

Jeffrey R. Yost is the Associate Director of the Charles Babbage Institute, University of Minnesota. He served as the principal investi-

gator on a recently completed National Science Foundation sponsored project, "Building a Future for Software History," was co-principal investigator on the NSF-sponsored "Computer as a Scientific Instrument," published a book on the history of scientific computing, *A Bibliographic Guide to Scientific Computing, 1945–1975* (2002), and is currently completing a book on the history of strategic management and technological change in the computer industry. He serves as the editor of the scholarly journal *Iterations: An Interdisciplinary Journal of Software History*, and has published a number of articles on the business, technical, and cultural and intellectual history of computing, software, and networking.

Introduction

CARROLL PURSELL

Americans live lives saturated with technology. They are certainly not unique in that, but this is no reason not to accept responsibility for attempting to discover how that happened, what shape it takes, and what it means. This *Companion* is designed to give us a place to start on that voyage of self-discovery.

First let us deal with the problem of definition. Those of us who study technology for a living are often challenged to define what that is. In fact, no single definition has been imposed upon the authors because, in my opinion at least, no single definition is possible. This is not because defining technology is difficult – indeed, the problem is the opposite: it is all too easy. Such chestnuts as "applied science" or "the tools with which we make things" spring to mind, but are immediately seen as too partial to serve.

As Leo Marx has famously pointed out, the word itself is of fairly recent origin. For most of American history such phrases as the *mechanical*, the *practical* or *industrial arts* stood for the stock of tools we used and the knowledge of how to use them. *Technology*, as both a word and a concept, replaced these older terms, in Marx's estimation, sometime between the two world wars. During the period roughly from 1880 to 1920, he claims, both the character and representation of "technology" changed dramatically, eliding the accustomed identification of the older terms with real and specific tools and processes.

These tools and processes were displaced by great systems of power and production, in railroads and chemical, electrical and other industries, which were "large-scale, complex, hierarchical, centralized."[1] A telling case in point is the contrasting ways in which the Ford company represented its automobiles to the public. At the 1915 Pan-Pacific Exposition in San Francisco, Ford set up an actual assembly line so that viewers could see for themselves the miraculous way in which the Model T was produced. A quarter century later, at the New York World's Fair of 1939–40, the emphasis had shifted from the artifact and how it was made to the *image* of the happy, fulfilled lifestyle which could be yours if you bought a Ford.

The cutting loose of the representation from the things themselves also marked an ideological shift from the Enlightenment notion of first defining the good life or the just society through rational argument and political debate, and then using particular tools to help create those ideals, to a modern urge to define that good life and just society in terms of technological progress. In other words, this new floating signifier *technology* became the end and not the means of our lives. All this is a powerful reminder that what words we use, and what we mean by them, is critical to our political and social, as well as personal being.

A problem closely related to that of definition is the way in which I have chosen to organize this book as shown in the Table of Contents. *Beginnings* seems straightforward enough. Most of the chapters that follow concentrate on the twentieth century but Americans had technology long before then of course. Indeed, the idea that we somehow live in a "technological age" whereas previous generations did not is not only nonsense but profoundly ahistorical. One can argue in fact that since our use of technology is one of the major ways of separating us from other animals, humankind has always lived in a technological age. In discussing the Technology of Colonial North America, Robert Gordon begins with that of the indigenous Americans, moves through that of the Spanish settlers, before focusing on the more familiar stories of Northern European activities. For the 1800s, James Williams chronicles the changes of the "Long Century," encompassing the Industrial Revolution in America and its spread across the continent, setting the stage for the so-called Second Industrial Revolution of the twentieth century.

Sites of Production seems somewhat less straightforward. Factories and farms; yes of course. Cities and the environment are where we expect to find factories and farms so they may be accepted as well. The home is more often thought of as a site of consumption than of production, though, of course, a great deal of consumption (of coal, steel, fertilizers, pesticides, petroleum and so forth) goes on in factories and on farms. How though do we justify government and medicine as topics of production? These last two tip us off that sites of production are also sites of contest.

The essay on Manufacturing Technology covers the familiar subjects of Armory Practice and Mass Production, but also shows the ways in which the latter influenced the way in which ships and houses came to be made. As Deborah Fitzgerald's essay on Agriculture reveals, the ideal of the "Factory Farm" provided both a roadmap for agricultural change and a model of what the modern farm should look like. Gail Cooper's essay on House and Home chronicles the way in which houses are networked into systems of utility, and the gradual integration of appliances into the home. The "house," in other words, has become a part of technological systems from electrical grids to electric toasters. Cities are "home" to millions of people and, according to Joel Tarr, are shaped and serviced in much the same way as Cooper's homes. From walking cities to "edge" cities, technology has played a critical role in the way urban geography and urban life have been formed, not always by design.

In writing on the Environment, Betsy Mendelsohn includes under that term both wilderness and urban neighborhood air quality. Our own particular "environments" are ones in which we necessarily consume not only food but air and sensory perceptions. Work environments, whether the factory floor or the office cubicle, are places where we both consume and produce. Governments at all levels play a critical part in production: setting the rules, defining the playing field, offering incentives or dis-incentives. The most passionate libertarian walks the streets, flies in and out of airports, lives under the shadow of the law. In a democracy, governments are the chosen instruments with which we produce the conditions of our lives. As James

Edmonson points out, medical technology at the very least *re*produces good health and well-being. The "mechanical fix," he asserts, tends to be preferred to preventative medicine.

The Body, according to Chris Hables Gray, is "one of the main sites of technological innovation in America." Whether or not that should be so, of course, is hotly debated. Technology moves the body about (cars, for example), decorates them, reshapes them, and makes them perform more to our liking. Tattoos, birth control pills, cloning, and penal implants can all cause an argument and, in some cases, perhaps sway an election. Even the very notion of gender, or at least its malleability, is controversial. Rebecca Herzig notes that so basic a technology as the water closet (more commonly called a toilet in the US) is gendered in ways that most people accept without thinking unless the line at the "ladies" room is impossibly long. It is one of those technological spaces which compel us to make the "right" decision about our own gender identification or risk not only the wrath of our colleagues but the majesty of the law. And finally, Arwen Mohun analyses the ways in which class is shaped by and determines technological choices. Matters of skill or unskill, for example, are deflected by notions of class and the extent and form of technological alienation are closely tied to class. It is ironic that in a country where *everyone* considers themselves "middle class," historians have concentrated more on the relationship between machines and the working class than any other.

Sites of Contest itself becomes clear as a subheading only when we see the topics that have been subsumed under it. The body and gender are both, most scholars would argue, socially constructed and labor is, as always, very much about class which too is socially constructed. Originally an essay on race and technology was planned, but finally proved impossible to include. Race, too, we now understand is socially constructed. What most scholars mean by that term, I think, is that race, class, gender and the body (and other things as well, like sexuality and ethnicity) are categories that, while more or less agreed upon by societies in any particular time and place, lack the kind of essentialist quality that is so often attributed to them. All of these are contingent as well as contested, but they are also sites where meaning in produced.

Technological Systems seems to put us back on a more solid footing – we are talking about things, and in the case of this book the very most obvious, ubiquitous, and iconic things at that. Although not an American invention, the automobile is intimately connected not only to the nation's economy but to its very self-conception. As Bruce Seely shows, the car along with the highway is an American totem of great power. Despite excited predictions that the airplane would replace the car as a mode of personal travel, Roger Bilstein shows that commercial and military applications quickly took precedent in aviation development. Rockets and space flight, on the other hand, grew largely out of the circumstances of America's international rivalries, according to Roger Launius. M. Joshua Silverman emphasizes the dual nature of the promise and practice of nuclear technology: energy and medical treatments, for example, on the one hand, but toxic wastes and weapons of mass destruction, on the other. Douglas Gomery describes how television took a half century to materialize, but then became a major factor in the way Americans spend their time and understand their

world. Along with the car and television, the computer has a ubiquitous and totaliz-
ing influence on American life. Jeffrey Yost emphasizes the "ironic" nature of the
complexities of the computer's development.

Producing and Reading Technological Culture seems almost as unproblematic but
hides a few complexities. It would be wrong, I think, to read it as meaning that
engineers produce the culture and painters, let us say, or novelists, do the interpreting.
Engineers stand ready and willing to interpret our technological culture (they do it
all the time in fact), and cultural production is the very purpose of Hollywood and
academic departments of humanities, of High Art and Popular Art.

Bruce Sinclair traces the practice and the public understanding of engineers from
the manly heroes of the early twentieth century to the "nerds" and "geeks" of a century later. Dilbert is a sympathetic and competent engineer, but more anti-hero than
hero; more "everyman" than elite. Molly Berger looks closely at the ways in which
our popular culture figures both engineers and technology in general. She finds that
while many "popular" expressions of culture would appear to express a bottom-up
picture of technology, they are often commodities produced by particular people for
particular purposes. The High Art of paintings, sculptures, photographs and the like,
links the complications of defining technology with the equally slippery definitions of
"art." Henry Adams, in his essay, calls for a new art history which places art in not
just a social context, but one of technological development as well. And finally, David
Nye discusses the tradition of questioning our technology even as we elaborate it. Since
the late eighteenth century, he shows – that is from the dawn of the industrial age –
there have been individuals and groups which have asked the hard political, social,
and moral questions of technology as a whole as well as its various components.

In fact none of these categories will withstand too close an inspection. It is an
article of faith among historians that everything including the word "technology"
and everything signified by it is contingent and contested. *Contingent* because, as
historians, we insist that things change through time and the understanding of any
one historical moment is not frozen in time but was something else before and
became something else as time moved on. Not only did the means of travel change
with the coming of the automobile, but the very idea and meaning of travel as well.
It was one thing to be an "engineer" in the early nineteenth century, but quite another at
the end of the twentieth. What it took to be manly – a concept long associated with the
possession and use of technologies – in one period did not prove adequate in another.

All this is also *contested* because at any one time there were competing measures of
masculinity and while one is usually hegemonic at any point in time, it is never
universally accepted. The definition of the word *technology*, as we have seen, is still
contested: it will not be obvious to everyone that *the body* deserves a place in a book
such as this or that wearing glasses makes us cyborgs. One very important contest
being fought out in our own time is whether the factory model of farming is either
efficient or constructive of the kind of society in which we want to live. (And the
Good Society, of course, is a concept that has always been fought over and redefined –
while, it should be pointed out, the role of particular technologies in furthering or
eroding one's own idea of the Good Society is an important part of that debate.)

The history of technology, as a self-conscious academic field, is hardly a half-century old.[2] It came together during the post-*Sputnik* years when rapid technological change was devoutly desired to keep the Americans ahead of the Soviet Union. Both the economy and defense seemed to be based on Americans' ability to invent, engineer, and impose their technologies on themselves, their allies, and the nations of Africa and Asia, newly emerging from the often violent decay of the great European empires. Understanding what Americans had done right in the past seemed useful to shaping sound policies for the future.

A second critical context of the emergence of this new field was that it tended to take place in engineering schools. As a profession, engineers had always suffered from a belief that they were not sufficiently appreciated; that the American public at large, while basking in a technological modernity, did not recognize where and from whom this all came about. Not surprisingly many early historians of technology had some engineering background, either through training or practice. This meant that such scholars had a close and insiders' knowledge of the machines and tools they wrote about, but it also meant that they were sometimes inclined by training, practice, and employment to have a basically uncritical view of what it all meant. Progress was the measure of civilization, and technology was the engine of that progress.

Being centered in engineering colleges also meant that women were not often found in their ranks. Both the subject ("toys for boys") and the engineering departments which provided the employment for these scholars were not welcoming to women. This was importantly true also of the larger historical profession, and of academia as a whole, but the history of technology seemed particularly masculine. All this constituted a serious limitation on who would be likely to take up the subject, but also worked to limit what subjects were taken up at all.

Over the past half century, however, many of these limitations have been swept aside and new scholars as well as new topics have become a part of the shared enterprise of understanding the history of technology.[3] This book is a snapshot in time of what we now know, and in what we are interested.

NOTES

1   Leo Marx, "The Idea of 'Technology' and Postmodern Pessimism," *Does Technology Drive History? The Dilemma of Technological Determinism*, eds Merritt Roe Smith and Leo Marx (Cambridge: MIT Press, 1994), p. 241. See also Lewis Mumford, "Authoritarian and Democratic Technics," *Technology and Culture*, 5 (Winter 1964), 1–8.
2   See Bruce E. Seely, "SHOT, the History of Technology, and Engineering Education," *Technology and Culture*, 36 (October 1995), 739–72 and John A. Staudenmaier, "Rationality, Agency, Contingency: Recent Trends in the History of Technology," *Reviews in American History*, 30 (March 2002), 168–81.
3   Carroll Pursell, "Seeing the Invisible: New Perspectives in the History of Technology," *Icon*, 1 (1995), 9–15.

Part I

Beginnings

CHAPTER ONE

Technology in Colonial North America

ROBERT B. GORDON

Technology, in the definition favored by those who study its history, encompasses the skills and tools people need to make and do things. It is, and has been since earliest human experience, a part of everyone's life. Knowledge gained through experience, experiment, and in recent times the application of natural science, has expanded opportunities for the use of techniques to achieve aspirations and express cultural values. Because of the distinctly different choices people worldwide have made in the techniques they have used in their everyday lives and enterprises, technology is a record of cultural choice.

European immigrants to North America gradually adapted the techniques of their homelands to their new environment to provide themselves with food and shelter, and to earn a place for themselves in the North Atlantic trade networks that would allow them to prosper. The natural resources available in North America and the choices colonists made about the technologies they would use to exploit these resources defined regional cultural patterns that persisted far beyond the colonial period.

History

Native Americans' Technology

The immigrants from Asia who populated North America thousands of years before Europeans arrived developed specialized techniques for hunting the continent's varied and abundant wildlife, their primary source of food and an important source of materials for clothing. These Native Americans used agriculture largely to supplement the food they got from hunting and fishing. Those who lived near waterways developed sophisticated skills as builders of small boats. None built roads, or used wheeled vehicles. They relied on human or animal power for all purposes, even to propel their watercraft.

Although Native Americans in the southwest opened turquoise mines as early as AD 900 to supply demand from their Mexican cousins, they made only sparse use of North America's abundant mineral resources, such as the copper found in northern Michigan. Unlike the native settlers of South America, those in the northern continent never smelted metal from ore. In their early contacts with Europeans, they supplied French adventurers with animal pelts, and taught British colonists on the east coast food-production skills vital to their survival. Native Americans quickly learned the use of firearms through their contacts with Europeans, and soon developed the mechanical skills to make repair parts for their gunlocks.

Native Americans' low population density, further reduced by new diseases, combined with their limited use of the continent's natural resources left North America open for colonists to apply European technologies on a scale unimaginable in their home countries. Europeans brought dramatically different systems of land tenure and management to the New World, and commenced road building, pyrotechnology (metallurgy, glassmaking), and the application of inanimate power (principally from falling water). By the end of the colonial period they had applied technology to achieve a material culture comparable in quality to that of all but the richest Europeans, and had initiated the rapid industrialization that would transform the entire continent in the nineteenth century.

European Background

Sixteenth-century Europe saw the rise of industrial capitalism and the belief that people had both a right and duty to fully exploit natural resources wherever they might be found. Vannoccio Biringuccio explained in his *Pirotechnica* published in 1540 "I say and conclude that the gifts of such copious blessings conceded by heaven should not be left to our descendents in future centuries...we should denounce [those who fail to exploit minerals] and severely reprove them in the same terms that farmers would deserve if, when the fruits of the earth are ripe, instead of gathering them, they should leave them to rot and waste in the fields...." Spanish adventurers diligently applied this concept of exploitation in Central and South America. French, British, Portuguese, and others applied it in their North Atlantic fisheries, and to the fur and timber resources of the adjacent land.

Although the Spanish and Dutch were the first Europeans to settle in North America, and Germans, French, Swedes, and others followed. Immigrants from Britain predominated in all but the extreme southeast, the distant southwest, and Quebec. The early sixteenth century saw the start of rapid population growth in Britain that would double the country's population by the end of the seventeenth century. Rapid growth overtaxed Britain's ability to house and employ everyone. Prices rose, landlords enclosed commons, increased agricultural productivity released men for industrial work if they could find it, while the gentry invested in manufactures. The crown, always in need of new revenue, fostered commercial expansion, principally through international trade. The mercantile concept, with its emphasis on a favorable balance of trade for the mother country, turned investors' interest to the Atlantic Coast of North America. Here the British could apply European techniques of fishing, mining, and metallurgy to resources far more abundant than any they knew at home. When they ventured to North America, they had centuries of experience with the application of waterpower to tasks such as grinding grain and blowing furnaces (but, curiously, not to sawing wood). They had learned and surpassed Spanish deep-water shipbuilding and navigation, and continental ordnance. Their agriculture emphasized husbandry without extreme specialization.

The Puritans who migrated to New England in the early seventeenth century held beliefs different from the values held in Spain and Italy, as expressed by Biringuccio. They endowed work with religious and social purpose as well as material gain. They believed in stewardship and a duty to improve one's holdings, and insisted that the common good must take precedence over personal gain.

The Sixteenth Century

The Spanish, already established in Mexico, settled in St Augustine, Florida, in 1565 and in Santa Fe, New Mexico, in 1609. Spanish technology had its greatest influence in the southwest and the extreme southeast in the seventeenth century. The French, established along the Gulf Coast, had applied European military technology in the forts they built in Florida, such as Fort Caroline, erected in 1564. Since the French built with timber, their fortifications lacked the permanence of later Spanish stonework forts and do not survive for our inspection.

The lure of gold attracted British as well as Spanish adventurers to the New World. Martin Frobisher returned from a voyage to find the Northwest Passage in 1540 with a dark, glittering rock from Baffin Island. London adventurers chose to believe the claim by Italian alchemist Agnello that Frobisher's rock was gold ore rather than the assays of others that showed no precious metal content. On two subsequent expeditions Frobisher's men mined 1,500 tons of worthless rock, and failed to plant the colony that Queen Elizabeth wanted established in America. Instead of gold, it was the more prosaic fisheries of the northwest Atlantic and the fur-bearing animals trapped on the adjacent land that earned profits for sixteenth-century European adventurers in the New World.

The Seventeenth Century

The Spanish spread settlements through the southwest, establishing Sante Fe in 1609, and extending them into Texas and California in the eighteenth century. Documentation of Spanish technology in the southwest remains sparse. Excavation of a pueblo near Albuquerque has uncovered evidence of copper smelting carried on before the Puebelo Revolt of 1680 in which all the Spanish colonists were killed or expelled. The Spanish technological presence in the southeast is still on display in fortifications they built for the defense of Florida. Work on the four-bastion Castillo de San Marcos, designed by Ignacio Daza for the defense of Saint Augustine, began in 1672. The Castillo's walls of coquina stone finished with stucco had a surrounding ditch crossed by a drawbridge defended by a portcullis. Characteristic Spanish features were the bartizans (lookout towers) placed on the salient of each bastion, and the prominent place given to the fort's chapel.

French military architects adapted the European four-bastion form to local circumstances and materials in numerous fortifications built around the American east and south coasts. The French constructed Fort Pentagoet (1635) in Maine of earth and stone. On the Gulf Coast in Mississippi they used squared timber for Fort Maurepas (1699). In the eighteenth century, the Spanish did little further fortification; however, the British competed with the French in fort-building at strategic locations on the coast and on the inland waterways.

Northern Europeans who ventured to Newfoundland and Labrador early in the sixteenth century preserved fish in camps along the coast by drying and salting, and found a ready market for their product in the Catholic countries of Europe. Two companies of British merchant adventurers, organized in 1606, sponsored colonies in Maine and Virginia. The colonists at Sagadahoc, Maine, were to exploit the fish and fur trades. They failed to appreciate the difficulties of winter survival without thorough preparation, and their enterprise lasted only a year. The settlement in Virginia fared only slightly better. Here the colonists, who were expected to establish industries that would produce goods such as glass and iron for export, did not grow enough food for themselves, or establish constructive relations with the Native Americans. Their industrial enterprises failed to achieve either adequate quality or quantity to be economically viable. Virginia eventually became a stable colony after 1614, when the colonists discovered the profits to be made by exporting tobacco to Britain.

Unlike the adventurers sent to Virginia, the settlers in the Massachusetts colonies included merchants and men with experience in manufacturing as well as ministers and members of the gentry. While they had strong feelings about cleansing the British church from Roman Catholic influence, they also represented the new British mercantile economy. New England offered them the chance to put their mercantile ideas to the test. Accordingly, the Massachusetts Bay Company recruited artisans with the skills needed to process the material resources of North America: sawyers, carpenters, smiths, millwrights, and the like. Although the founders of the early colonies brought ideas of common ownership with them, they soon discovered these principles were inimical with the need to produce food for sustenance and products for export. Massachusetts began the sale of private land in 1627. An unforeseen consequence was that the availability of land encouraged artisans to give up their trades to enter farming on their own accounts. Towns soon had to recruit, and offer subsidies to induce smiths, millers, and other artisans to settle and provide their essential services.

Decreased immigration in the early 1640s created a balance of payments problem in New England. The Massachusetts Bay colony offered land grants, tax abatements, exemptions from militia duty, and 21-year monopolies to entrepreneurs who would undertake new industries or shipbuilding. It sent John Winthrop, Jr, to Britain to raise capital and hire artisans for a modern, integrated ironworks that would produce metal for export. However, the proprietors of these early industrial ventures faced numerous difficulties, including insufficient capital, inadequate skills and experience, and poorly developed market mechanisms. Agriculture offered the best comparative advantage, distantly followed by industries that could make use of the continent's abundant natural resources. Imported goods, often of superior quality, could be had for less than those made in the colonies. Successful exporting called for the services of skilled agents abroad. Proprietors' difficulties in coping with these problems soon led most of the subsidized enterprises into financial failure.

From 1650 onward New England merchants, joined later by entrepreneurs in the middle colonies, profited by exporting barrel staves, timber, and other wood products, fish; and provisions to the southern colonies and the West Indies. Planters in the West Indies soon depended entirely on the North American colonies for flour, rice, corn, peas, salt fish, cattle, shingles, staves for sugar casks, and lumber delivered by American-made ships. Colonial merchants organized supply networks for production in inland communities through creation of markets and, in some cases, direct investment in production facilities such as sawmills. Thus, even remote communities were removed from the need for self-sufficiency and incorporated into organizations that applied technology to specialized production by the end of the seventeenth century. Additionally, entrepreneurs in New England and the middle-Atlantic colonies found economic opportunity in processing raw sugar imported from the West Indies. They began distilling rum in the 1650s. Over the following decades Boston, Newport, New York, and Philadelphia developed numerous distilleries. Rum exports made a large contribution to the colonial balance of trade.

The New England colonists started hunting the world's largest mammals when they captured whales along the coast. To export their whale oil, fish, and furs, they began building oceangoing ships that could also enter their own coastal trade and for trade with the West Indies. War-induced demand opened the opportunity of selling ships in Europe after 1680. Shipbuilding had important backward linkages since shipwrights needed timber, iron fastenings, sailcloth, and cordage that colonial makers could produce. Shipyard demand stimulated colonial industries that had previously failed due to lack of local markets and the difficulties of successful export trade.

The Eighteenth Century

The economies of the southern colonies throve through concentration on monoculture: tobacco in Virginia and rice in South Carolina. Trade with the West Indies and military expenditures for the Seven Years War stimulated the economies of New England and the middle-Atlantic colonies through the mid-eighteenth century. As the middle colonies added industrial-scale food processing and ironmaking, their artisans expanded their use of mechanical arts and pyrotechnology. New Englanders diversified industrial production of goods for export. Despite periods of economic slackness, non-farm, artisanal and industrial work occupied an increasing proportion of people's time outside the southern colonies as the century advanced.

Trade with the West Indies and Europe required a network of support services. New England merchants such as the Brown family in Rhode Island commissioned shipwrights to build vessels for their own use and for sale in Europe. By 1750, New Hampshire yards were producing 20–30 ships a year. Shipwrights in turn required timber, cordage, iron, pitch, and sailcloth produced by local industries. Merchants stimulated industry by accepting these products in payment of loans. Whale oil and potash made by frontier farmers became major colonial exports from New England to Britain by mid-century.

Farm sizes decreased after 1730 as farm families in New England and the middle colonies invested in equipment such as wool cards and looms, and put more time into home industries such as weaving, shoemaking, and broom-making. Towns tended to specialize in particular products. Specialization implied dependence on markets for the exchange of goods and services. By 1750 New England farmers routinely traveled to other towns to reach markets for their products. A sample of some 200 trips made by farmers in central Massachusetts showed that in 1750–75 the most frequent trips were about 20 miles, and ranged from 5 to 175 miles. The distribution remained the same for 1775–90. Local merchants encouraged home industry with the putting-out system, which also increased the division of labor. These entrepreneurs might purchase wool to distribute to homes for spinning or weaving, or precut shoe parts for home sewing into finished shoes. Later they collected and paid for the finished products.

Growing affluence stimulated consumer demand for the services of cabinetmakers, tinsmiths, and silversmiths. Connecticut had 13 silversmiths before 1750; the number soon rose to 125. By 1768 makers in Lynn were turning out 80,000 pairs of shoes per year. Colonial iron production so impacted the British economy that the mother country passed the Iron Act in 1750. It encouraged export of the pig and bar iron that British manufacturers wanted and required colonial governors to suppress any new enterprises that attempted to make finished iron products. In the southern colonies no communities achieved comparable production of manufactured goods, and even individual artisans found limited opportunities, partly because of the dispersion of population on plantations. Wealthy southerners bought imported goods or traded with the northern colonies.

By 1785 southern New England and the middle-Atlantic states were ready to enlarge manufacturing of textile, wood, and metal products in factories with power-driven machinery, thereby initiating the industrialization that would gather momentum in the early republic, and by the mid-nineteenth century give the northern states an enormous economic advantage over the still-agricultural south. One stimulant to industrialization was the network of regional, integrated produce markets in place within a few years of the Revolution that delivered agricultural products to the towns and cities where factories would be established. Farm productivity had so increased that farmers had surplus funds to invest. They, along with merchants, put the new savings into the growth opportunities of the day: textile mills; turnpike roads; and the mechanized production of tools and household products.

Colonial Artisans and Industries

Technology entered everyone's home life in the colonies of British North America, and most people used some agricultural implements regardless of whatever else they did. Artisans who had forsaken full-time farming typically specialized in particular crafts and techniques. Some, such as metalsmiths, could work alone, or part time, in

Table 1.1   Work of colonial artisans

Domestic
Cheesemaking
Cidermaking
Potash making
Spinning and weaving

Artisans working alone or with assistants
Blacksmiths
Cabinetmakers and turners
Coopers
Gunsmiths and Metalsmiths
Potters
Quarrymen
Shoemakers
Spinners and weavers
Tanners
Wheelwrights

Artisan's work requiring assistants
Bridge building
Coaling wood
House and barn construction
Mill building

Work requiring mechanical power systems
Grist, fulling, oil, saw milling
Blast furnace smelting and fining iron

Work requiring industrial organization and physical plant
Blast furnace smelting
Distilling
Glassblowing
Papermaking
Ropemaking
Shipbuilding

their own shops with or without partners, or at home. At the other extreme, glassblowing and ironmaking required team efforts with a physical plant that would ordinarily be beyond the means of individuals. The list of some of the colonial industries in Table 1.1 shows the range of work undertaken by colonial artisans.

Metalsmiths

The increase in colonial wealth by the mid-seventeenth century opened opportunities for artisans supplying luxury goods, primarily to the urban wealthy, but also to reasonably prosperous town and country dwellers. Boston had one silversmith for every 240 inhabitants in 1690. Metalsmiths made gold, silver, pewter, or brass goods. An advanced smith might undertake assaying or refining, but most worked with imported or recycled metal, often supplied by the customer. Success depended first on having the requisite skill in metal forming, casting, joining, and engraving. Technical skill alone did not suffice, however. A smith needed business acumen, and had to build a reputation with a network of customers. Reputation in the community was particularly important for gold and silversmiths since customers entrusted them with precious metals for fabrication.

A skilled smith in colonial America could achieve a position of social equality with leading merchants and statesmen in society. Jeremiah Drummer, the son of one of the largest landowners in Massachusetts established himself as a silversmith in late seventeenth-century Boston without loss of social standing. Customers expected him to keep up with the latest fashions, and to remake their silverware accordingly. The large collections of colonial silverware now in museums give us an unusually good record of these artisans' skills and the tastes of their customers. Smiths in the larger towns, such as Boston, introduced division of labor with particular smiths specializing in specific branches of the trade, such as casting or engraving. Work would then pass through several shops on its way to completion.

Gunsmith

The colonial gunsmith catered to the needs of men in all classes of colonial society since nearly everyone at one time or another participated in hunting, the militia, and the occasional military adventure away from home. The gunsmith worked with iron, steel, wood, brass, and sometimes silver. He might have a water-powered hammer or grindstone, but most worked entirely with hand-operated tools as they carried out tasks ranging from heavy forging, through heat-treating delicate springs, to shaping the complex curves of gunstocks. The decorative brass and silver inlay work on the frontiersman's rifle could equal the work of the best urban artisans.

Since colonists found their European firearms ill-suited to American conditions once they moved inland from the immediate coastal areas, gunsmiths everywhere modified European designs to suit the needs of their customers. However, Huguenot artisans, joined later by Germans and Swiss, working near Lancaster, Pennsylvania, in the eighteenth century carried this process of adaptation a huge step forward when they developed the long, precision, handsomely proportioned and decorated weapon now popularly known as the Kentucky rifle. William Penn had granted land near Lancaster to Huguenot refugees arriving from Europe from 1710 onward. Here the Ferree and LeFevre families each produced a line of distinguished gunsmiths. They created a uniquely American technology beginning in the 1720s with rifles that gave their owners an accurate, light, and easily reloaded rifle particularly suited to the needs of frontiersmen. The long, slim, fully stocked barrel sweeping into a gracefully curving, richly decorated curly maple butt have made surviving Kentucky rifles highly prized by collectors and art galleries today.

It took a Pennsylvania gunsmith working with an apprentice about a week to make a good, plain rifle, two days on the stock and the rest on the metal parts and assembly. He shaped a flat iron plate into a tube and welded the seam to make the barrel. After reaming and straightening, he cut the rifling in the bore with the aid of a machine he made himself. Finally, he browned the outside of the barrel to give it a pleasing finish. Most Pennsylvania gunsmiths made their own locks by forging and filing the individual parts. Often the springs were cut out of an old sword or bayonet, shaped by filing, and then hardened to the requisite temper.

For stocking material the gunsmith selected maple grown on a mountainside since trees on thin, rocky soils had a closer grain and better curl than those from lowland soil. He used planes, chisels, and rasps to shape the stock. This work was unlike cabinetmaking because every surface of the gunstock was curved. He let brass or silver decorative work into the stock. Oil rubbed into the wood gave it a smooth, mellow finish. Owners highly prized the finished product. A gunsmith's trade grew with his reputation for the quality of his work.

The Kentucky rifle proved enormously successful in the Appalachian frontier county. The mountain riflemen soon acquired a reputation for prowess in hunting and Indian fighting known throughout the colonies. At the opening of war in 1775, Washington and his fellow officers called on Pennsylvanian rifle companies to demonstrate the prowess of the Continental Army facing the British in Boston. They failed to realize that a technology perfectly adapted to one particular need is not necessarily useful in another setting, or the need to devise tactics that exploit the advantages of a particular technology in warfare. The riflemen made a great show of precision shooting until the British sentries learned not to expose themselves, and thereafter could accomplish little in the siege warfare underway at Boston. Later, in fighting inside Quebec City, the riflemen's long weapons proved a positive disadvantage and led to most being captured. By the summer of 1777, American commanders better understood how to use this unique weapon. At the battles of Freeman's Farm and Bemis Heights, Daniel Morgan's riflemen acted as light infantry and, firing from concealed positions, caused havoc in the ordered ranks of British soldiers.

Millwrights and Millers

New England and the middle-Atlantic colonies had excellent water power resources. The abundance of small water privileges that could be developed with modest capital allowed colonists to erect power-driven mills near their communities. Most had grist and saw mills; many also had fulling, snuff, and oil mills. The seaport cities, however, lacked waterpower sites. Hence, breweries in Philadelphia had to use horse gins to grind their malt and New Haven citizens trekked two miles to the falls of the Mill River north of town to get their grain ground.

Colonists made water-powered mills one of the principal adaptations of mechanical technology to the natural resources of North America. Wherever settlers moved into new land, they made erection of a gristmill their first-community enterprise. As soon as possible, they added a sawmill so they could side and floor their buildings with sawn planks. Sawing could be a part-time occupation for farmers in the winter and early spring, when streams were in spate and there was little to do in the fields. The Dutch had a sawmill operating in New Amsterdam by 1623, and New Englanders had them by 1634. Within a decade, mills in Massachusetts, New Hampshire, Maine, and the Connecticut River valley were turning out sawn products for domestic use and export.

The millwright who erected a gristmill needed practical knowledge of hydraulics, waterwheel construction, and gearing for a power train. Millstones had to be procured from distant quarries (the best were imported). The miller had to know how to align the stones and set the spacing between them so that they cut rather than mashed the grain. From time to time he had to dress the stones by re-cutting the grooves that gripped the grain as the stones rotated. All these were skilled tasks. Watching a miller and his machinery at work introduced children to mechanical and hydraulic technology in a way that would contribute to the development of Yankee ingenuity.

Grist millers developed a mercantile function as well as a technological one. Since they were paid in kind and had grain to place on the market, they began trading, which led them to act as merchants and as agents for farmers. A concentration of grist, fulling, paper, saw, and snuff mills along the Brandywine formed the basis of the economy of Wilmington, Delaware. In this way, millers contributed both to the diffusion of technological sophistication and to the development of domestic and overseas marketing networks.

Glassblower

The Virginia Company had a glassworks underway at Jamestown by 1609. It intended to utilize the abundant American wood fuel and sand resources to supplement the then inadequate production of British glassworks for the home market, but achieved only marginal success. Other seventeenth-century glassmaking attempts at Salem, Massachusetts (1639–43), New York City (c. 1645), and Philadelphia (c. 1683) also achieved little. Successful colonial glassmaking began with Caspar and Richard Wistar's glassworks in Salem County, New Jersey (1739–77); it produced window glass and bottles until the Revolution. The Bayard works in New York, Stiegel's in Pennsylvania, and the Germanstown works in Quincy, Massachusetts, joined in producing utilitarian products for the domestic market in the eighteenth century.

No one managed to mechanize any of the glassblowers' work until the 1830s, when artisans first used full-size bottle molds. The colonial blower gathered molten glass on the end of a blowpipe and, while it remained hot enough to flow under air pressure applied by his lungs and rotation of the pipe, shaped it into a bottle. In the crown method used to make window glass the blower collapsed the molten glass bubble into a thin disk from which other artisans subsequently cut the glass panes. The center "bullseyes" could be used for small windows through which one did not need to see. The combined need for lung power, strength to twirl the heavy iron blowpipe weighted at the end with hot glass, manipulative dexterity, and judgment of temperature made glassblowing a physically demanding, highly skilled, specialized occupation.

A glassblower could not work as an independent artisan because of the size and complexity of the physical plant he used. Glass was melted in clay crucibles placed in a specialized wood-burning furnace. Workers had to gather the sand, soda ash, and fuel. A melter blended the ingredients, supervised the filling of the crucibles, and kept the furnace at the proper temperature. Assistants handling the blowpipes gathered the glass for the blower. Consequently, a glassblower depended on an owner-manager to erect, staff, and manage the glasshouse. Glassblowers for the colonies had to be recruited in Europe. Potential recruits were often reluctant to come since this could mean working for an unknown proprietor. There would be additional doubts about the nature of the sand (which affected the quality of the glass) available in a strange location. The proprietors of the United Glass Company of Wistarburg, New Jersey, were unique in offering their four blowers a partnership that included a share of the profits.

None of the colonial works successfully challenged the cheaper, better-quality glassware imported from Europe. Their experience shows that, even with rich natural resources at hand, major difficulties stood in the way of colonial enterprises that required the sustained application of specialized skills by groups of artisans (as distinct from individual craftsmen). However, additional works established after 1781 gradually attained profitability while improving the quality of their products.

Shipwrights

By colonial times, shipbuilders had settled on a well-established technique for constructing vessels for the North Atlantic trade. They started with a keel to which they fastened frames (ribs), planking, ceiling, and decks to form the hull. Colonial shipwrights shaped timber for the keel and frames by hand with broadax and adze. They utilized the naturally curved shape of trees at branches and roots to make "compass timbers" for the curved, structural members of large ships. Since sawmills had to be located upland at waterpower sites, gangs of sawyers working with pit saws cut the hull and deck planking. Builders of small boats used sawn planks and timber keels, and shaped the ribs either by sawing or steaming and bending. Shipwrights fastened large timbers and planks together with treenails (tapered wooden pins) that they drove into holes bored with hand augers. They fastened smaller pieces with iron or, later, copper nails and bolts.

Since a shipwright worked primarily with hand tools, he did not need a large investment in equipment to set up business. He did need a plot of level land near a navigable waterway, but did not need permanent shipways. For all but small-boatmaking, he needed to assemble and organize a workforce, and arrange for the delivery of timber and other materials at his yard. Usually the master shipwright designed the vessels his yard built. He might retain the services of a draftsman or artist to draw plans, but usually worked from a concept, carried in his head, of the ship he wanted.

While most seamen could assemble some sort of boat in an emergency, building quality ships required experience usually learned through apprenticeship. A yard of any size needed the services of a variety of artisans. Shipwrights and their apprentices and helpers constructed the hull. Joiners built cabins, rails, and other wood fittings. Caulkers drove oakum into the seams between the hull and deck planks to make them watertight. Blacksmiths made fasteners and fittings. Riggers set up the spars and rigging. Since they worked outside with no protection from the weather, shipwrights usually stopped work in the winter, and then needed to find other employment.

When the flow of immigrants to Massachusetts subsided after 1639, the flow of money they brought with them also diminished. The Massachusetts government encouraged shipbuilding as a way to revive the colony's economy. It offered free land for shipyards, and exempted shipwrights from militia duty. As with other government-subsidized industries sponsored in the mid-seventeenth century, problems with product quality soon arose. The rapid expansion of the industry drew inexperienced artisans into the trade. Additionally, newly arrived British shipwrights were unfamiliar with the properties of American varieties of oak. Many built ships of red oak, which is not resistant to rot, instead of the white oak they should have used. When rapid deterioration of Massachusetts-built ships led buyers to look elsewhere, the colonial government found it needed to establish rules and inspections to insure the quality of new vessels, thereby establishing another technological component to governance.

When tobacco prices slumped, Virginians looked to shipbuilding to diversify their economy. Lack of sawmills and ironworks needed to supply essential materials to the shipyards frustrated these attempts through the seventeenth century. However, when in 1685 British shipwrights began building vessels in Philadelphia, they could draw on Pennsylvania's mills and forges for essential materials. Their production increased rapidly in the next decades. Shipyards lined eight blocks of the town's original waterfront until congestion forced them to move south of the city to a community named Southwark, after the London suburb that specialized in shipbuilding.

Ironmakers

Iron ore is abundant, but smelting it is labor- and energy-intensive work. Since through colonial times nearly all ironworks used charcoal fuel, abundant forests gave North American ironmakers a comparative advantage over Britain and Europe, where the cost of hauling wood from distant sources was already a burden in the seventeenth century. Virginians began building an integrated ironworks (a blast furnace to make pig iron and a finery forge to convert the pig to bar iron) at Falling Creek near Richmond in 1621, but abandoned the enterprise after Native Americans massacred the artisans. John Winthrop, Jr, and his fellow proprietors encountered the difficulties common to state-subsidized colonial enterprises in Massachusetts when they launched an integrated ironworks intended to export castings, bar iron, and nail rod to Britain. They chose a poor site for their first blast furnace, near Braintree, abandoned it, and moved to Saugus, now a National Historical Site, where they completed their works in about 1647. They had difficulty keeping a reliable staff of artisans and maintaining the quality of their products. Ensuing financial and legal problems forced them to close the Saugus works in 1652. A similar venture undertaken for the New Haven Colony by Winthrop failed for the same reasons in 1680.

These seventeenth-century attempts to copy British ironworks in America showed that, while colonists could duplicate and operate the British equipment, they could not easily master the more subtle problems of quality control and the organization of a reliable work force and supply network. They turned to bloomery forges, where one or two artisans could make bar iron directly from the ore on a part-time basis to meet local demand. European political developments in the early eighteenth century helped the American colonists enter the international iron trade and within 50 years become a major player in it.

As the eighteenth century opened, British manufacturers could buy Swedish iron cheaper than that made in Britain. However, when Parliament restrained trade with Sweden in 1717, many manufacturers decided to invest in American ventures. Colonists in the middle-Atlantic states, where the embayed coastal plain had abundant, easily mined bog ore and convenient access to shipping, quickly grasped this new economic opportunity. The Maryland legislature encouraged them with acts in 1719 that allowed ironmasters to acquire land by condemnation, and a 1721 law exempting ironworkers from highway labor. The next year, British investors financed construction of a blast furnace and finery for the Principio works, located near the head of Chesapeake Bay. They inaugurated a new era of American ironmaking that would make the British North American colonies the world's third largest iron producers by 1770. The Principio entrepreneurs added a blast furnace on Augustine Washington's land at Accokeek, Virginia, and by 1736 had a furnace, mine, store, gristmill, and plantation at Accokeek; a forge and plantation at North East, Maryland; and a furnace, forge, store, gristmill, and smithy at Principio. Together with the Baltimore Company, started by Maryland investors in 1731, they were the largest American ironmakers in the years before 1760.

Charles Reed, a Burlington, New Jersey merchant, typified the new entrepreneurial spirit. With partners from Philadelphia and New York City, he bought over 10,000 acres of forest and wetland in southern New Jersey, and put up Etna, Taunton, and Batsto blast furnaces and Atsion Forge between 1765 and 1768. Reed and partners, acting as "latchkey entrepreneurs," built complete plants that they then sold to others ready to operate. Pennsylvanians often found their own capital for ironworks. They began with Thomas Rutter's bloomery, Pool Forge, built near Pottstown in 1716. A few years later Rutter and Thomas Potts started the Colebrookdale Furnace, and by 1730 other entrepreneurs had ten additional forges and furnaces in operation financed with shares held by as many as nine families.

French colonists in Quebec recognized a potential market for American iron in France. In 1729, F.P. de Franceville, a Montreal merchant, acquired the right to exploit the bog iron ore, forest, and waterpower for the Forges of Saint Maurice at a site near Three Rivers. The French artisans brought over to build the furnace and forges failed to adapt their traditional ideas to the American environment and, as the Saugus artisans had 80 years earlier, sited their works badly. Successive proprietors at Three Rivers experienced the difficulties of operating a colonial work that had earlier defeated the Saugus and East Haven entrepreneurs, thereby leaving the mid-Atlantic colonies supreme in the Atlantic iron trade.

New Englanders eventually joined the eighteenth-century revival of ironmaking along lines of their own by gradually specializing in iron products rather than pig and bar for export. John Forbes of Canaan, Connecticut, began making tools, chain, wagon parts, and nails with a bloomery and forge shop in 1746. Conclusion of the colonial wars with France brought increased demand for iron and forged products that an ordinary smith could not easily make. Millwrights needed parts for new grist, saw, fulling, paper, and oil mills as well as repair parts for older ones. Shipbuilders wanted larger anchors as they ventured into making bigger vessels. By 1760, Forbes and his son had transformed their business from serving a local market to industrial production by expanding sales throughout southern New England, and concentrating on specialized products such as sawmill gudgeons and cranks, grist mill spindles and rynds, spindles for paper mills, screws for clothiers and paper presses, gears, massive ship's anchors, logging chains, gun barrels, trip and helve hammers for other iron-works, and nail rod. They hired commission men to sell their products in major East-Coast cities, and standardized specifications for mill machinery to facilitate sales to distant customers. By 1779 Samuel Forbes with partner John Adam, Jr, began making parts for mill machinery to numerical dimensions specified in customers' drawings, anticipating one of the techniques that mechanics would later use to make Connecticut the cradle of the American system of manufactures. Eli Whitney turned to Forbes & Adam in 1798 for gun barrels and the machinery he needed to begin mechanized musketmaking for the federal government.

Although the products of the colonial iron industry never approached the value of the exports of agricultural products, their impact on the British economy provoked regulation in 1750. More importantly, the ironworks gave the colonies vital capacity to produce ordnance during the Revolution. Because operation of a blast furnace required organization of a workforce that worked in shifts around the clock and a network of suppliers who would assure a steady flow of materials to the furnace, iron-works were precursors to the industrial organization of the American manufacturing industries that blossomed in the early republic.

Applied Science and Innovation

The need to adapt European technology to American conditions called forth the inventive capacity of colonists almost as soon as they arrived in the New World. Although increased affluence and better access to the press beginning in the late seventeenth century encouraged publication of a flow of crank and crackpot ideas that revealed the limits of popular understanding of natural science, and aspects of colonial agricultural practice were mired in ignorance, colonial intellectuals gradually expanded their interest in applied science and technology. The leaders who brought bands of colonists to the northern and middle colonies of British North America, such as John Davenport or Henry Whitfield, were men of learning and substance. They and their followers made education and curiosity about the natural world part of colonial culture. Weather, soil and water resources, and the sea touched nearly every colonist's life; everyone through the colonial period of necessity lived closer to nature than later generations could imagine. The tradition of liberal education – Harvard College in Massachusetts was founded in 1636; William and Mary in Virginia in 1693 – led men to a close study of their environment.

New York Governor Francis Lovelace initiated the first regular inter-colonial postal service with monthly round trips by a rider to Boston in 1673. As the regular service among the other colonies initiated in the 1690s along with overseas mails gradually improved, colonial intellectuals such as Benjamin Franklin and Jared Eliot exchanged observations and ideas in both pure and applied science with each other and with colleagues in Britain. Library collections of their papers, along with those of the entrepreneurial innovators of the late eighteenth century such as Oliver Evans and Eli Whitney, are a valuable resource for understanding applied science and innovation in America's early centuries. However, many talented artisans, such as Joseph Jenks, left few written records, so we rely on artifacts for much of what we know of their work.

Joseph Jenks, Artisan

John Winthrop, Jr, recruited Joseph Jenks (c. 1599–1683), a Londoner and cutler who had immigrated to Maine sometime before 1641, for his Saugus ironworks. While the Saugus enterprise contributed little to the seventeenth-century colonial economy, it played an important role in launching the careers of artisans such as Jenks. Jenks secured a patent from the Massachusetts General Court to erect mills for making scythes and other edge tools, and set up shop adjacent to the Saugus furnaces. He began supplying blades to the numerous sawmills being erected throughout the forested areas of the northeast, thereby freeing sawmill operators from their total dependence on imported British blades. He received additional patents for a fire engine and a mowing machine, undertook coining for colonial governments, and kept a stream of products and innovations flowing from his shop until his death. His sons and apprentices carried Jenks's innovations and technique to Rhode Island and, eventually, more distant colonies.

Jared Eliot, Minister, Doctor, and Applied Scientist

Jared Eliot (1685–1763), son of the Harvard-educated minister of Guilford, Connecticut, received a liberal preparatory education in the neighboring town of Killingworth and graduated from Yale in the class of 1704. He became minister of the Killingworth church in 1707, and his congregation, pleased with his preaching, retained him throughout his lifetime. Between 1710 and 1717, Eliot enlarged his education by studying medicine with Joshua Hobart, the minister at Southold on Long Island. (The difficulties of inland travel were such that the 20-mile journey across Long Island Sound was relatively easy.) Frequent trans-Atlantic voyages made regular correspondence with other intellectuals possible for the colonists by the mid-eighteenth century. Eliot, as did Benjamin Franklin, exchanged letters with the Quaker merchant Peter Collinson in London, who sent reports of matters discussed at the meetings of the Royal Society to his colonial friends.

Eliot closely observed the techniques used by colonial farmers as he traveled about on pastoral and medical missions, and found many faulty. He launched a long series of agricultural experiments on his parent's farm in Guilford and his own fields in Killingworth beginning about 1742. He believed that experiment rather than theory was the only sure way to improve practice, and that agriculturists needed to exchange ideas and observations so that the best practice could be sifted out of the experiments tried by others.

In his six *Essays on Field Husbandry* published between 1747 and 1760 Eliot presented the results of his experiments and those of his correspondents. Because colonial farmers had already depleted their soil of essential nutrients, much of Eliot's work focused on the techniques of using manures, lime, seaweed, and legumes to restore soil fertility. He explored the technology of making silk, and how a silk industry would fit into the New England social and economic life. His investigations of how nutrients reach soil particles led him to design a mechanical drill that would plant and fertilize field crops as a team pulled it across a field. Benoni Hyliard, a Killingworth wheelwright and typical ingenious Yankee, built the drills Eliot used and sent them to his friends in other colonies.

Eliot was a keen observer of all kinds of natural phenomena. While watching a brook, he noted how the flowing water carrying sand grains could sort them into deposits of different mineral content. Upon taking some of the dark grains home, he found that a magnet would pick them up. Jared realized that the black sand might be an iron ore purer than the bog ore then commonly used in southern New England, and that iron made from pure ore might be converted to good quality steel, then very much in demand. Jared and his son Aaron successfully smelted iron from black sea sand at Aaron's ironworks, and converted some into steel. A sample sent to the Society for the Encouragement of Arts in London earned Jared a gold medal.

Benjamin Franklin, Colonial Polymath

Benjamin Franklin [1706–90] left his native Massachusetts, spent 2 years in Britain, and returned to Philadelphia in 1726, where he worked as a printer and cultivated an interest in natural science that led to his election to fellowship in the Royal Society of London in 1756. Franklin approached natural science through solving practical problems. Colonial governments were troubled in the 1720s by the ease with which any printer could duplicate their paper currency. Franklin solved this problem for New Jersey with the copperplate printing technique hitherto unused in America. Other printers found it near impossible to duplicate the elaborate patterns Franklin could carve on his printing plates. His service on the committee appointed to deal with the pollution of Dock Creek in Philadelphia led him to recognize the importance of the management of water resources. In founding the American Philosophical Society in 1743, he included increasing knowledge of drainage and water-pumping machinery among its objectives. The Philosophical Society, which continues as a learned organization today, succeeded in its mission of stimulating exchange of knowledge among inquiring minds throughout the colonies.

Residents in colonial cites and towns had consumed much of their nearby wood supplies by the 1740s, and bore the expense of having wood hauled in from distant forests. A typical colonial home used about 30 cords of firewood each year for heating and cooking. Franklin's curiosity led him to examine the flow of air and combustion gases in fireplaces. He discovered that the excess air that a conventional fireplace allowed to reach the fire carried most of the heat from the burning wood up the chimney instead of into the room it was supposed to be warming. His Franklin stove (actually a modified fireplace) increased fuel efficiency. He included an explanation of the principles of convection heating in the sales literature for his stoves with the idea that his colonial customers would read and be interested in how natural science could be applied to useful improvements.

Franklin applied science in the design of his armonica, a musical instrument widely popular in Europe for several years, and in creating bifocal glasses. On his voyages across the Atlantic, Franklin made observations of the Gulf Stream that would later prove of great value to navigators. He investigated the circulation of storms, the disabilities associated with lead poisoning and, most notably, the protection of buildings from lightning strikes. Franklin began experiments on electricity in 1748, which he reported to Collinson, and originated the concept of positive and negative electric charge that remains the cornerstone of electrostatics today. After his famous 1752 experiment with a kite flying in a thunderstorm, he designed metal conductors that would safely carry a lightening discharge to earth. While in London in the 1760s Franklin served as a consultant on the protection of notable buildings, including Saint Paul's cathedral and the Royal powder magazines. He knew that a sharp point on a lightening rod would discharge electricity faster than a blunt one, a view contrary to that held by many others, however. When he recommended sharp-pointed conductors for the new rod system to be placed on Kew Palace, King George, annoyed by Franklin's patriot sympathies, demanded that blunt ones be used. The resulting dispute led to the resignation of Sir John Pringle as the president of the Royal Society and to the widespread circulation of the verse,

When you, great George, for safety hunt,
And sharp conductors change for blunt,
Franklin a wiser course pursues,
And all your thunder fearless views,
By keeping to the point.

Oliver Evans and Eli Whitney

French officers serving with the Continental Army brought new ideas of rationality, uniformity, and mechanization to America. With the revival of industry and commerce after the war, innovators such as Oliver Evans and Eli Whitney drew on the pre-war base of colonial applied science, technology, and basic industry to put these new ideas to use in making and doing things. Freedom from the restraints on innovation arising from restrictive rules, guilds, prejudice, and property rights common in Europe aided them.

Oliver Evans, son of a Delaware farm family, devised materials-handling systems for gristmills in the 1780s that automated movement of grain through the milling process. Successive editions of his *Young Mill-wright and Millers Guide*, first published in 1795, gave American artisans practical guidance on hydraulics and mill mechanisms through the mid-nineteenth century. Eli Whitney's cotton gin had a profound effect on the agriculture and regional economy of the South. After graduating from Yale in 1792, Whitney, while visiting Georgia, heard about the difficulty planters had removing the tenacious green seeds from the short-staple cotton that they could grow in upland fields. Whitney's gin removed these seeds efficiently. Southern cotton growers profited immensely from the gin and the mechanized cotton spinning mills in New England that dramatically increased demand for their product as the nineteenth century opened.

Issues in Interpretation

Technology played a central role in the everyday lives of European colonists in North America. Adaptation of European techniques to their new environment enabled them to achieve standards of living comparable to, or better than, those they left behind in the Old World, and prepared the way for the rapid expansion of the American economy in the early republic. Their success can help us better understand the processes of technology transfer, and its social and environmental consequences.

Artisans and the Application of Skill and Technique

Through the colonial period natural science could not adequately codify artisans' knowledge. Jared Eliot could accurately describe the visible processes carried out at his son's ironworks, but floundered badly in trying to explain the chemical changes they effected. Colonial leaders knew that successful transfer of technique depended on bringing experienced artisans, not just theories or written instructions, across the Atlantic, and offered inducements to attract artisans with the skills that their communities needed. Nevertheless, difficulties arose in the transfer of technique when artisans encountered unfamiliar natural resources, such as the red oak Massachusetts shipwrights used instead of white. Or, glassblowers might find locally available sand different in subtle ways from that they used in the old country. Difficulties also arose in organizing the talents of individual artisans into a production process that required teamwork, or, as in tending a blast furnace, disciplined attendance over many weeks or months.

Tools were common in everyday life in almost every colonial household, and by the late eighteenth century almost every village on a watercourse had mills. Young people gained experience with the mechanical arts early in life. The widespread interest in tinkering helped lay the foundation for rapid industrialization in the early republic. Artisans skilled in working with both their hands and minds gained a prominent place in colonial society, quite unlike the low prestige accorded them today. The American pattern axe and the Kentucky rifle were strikingly successful innovations made by artisans responding to the American environment with a high standard of skill. However, the unskilled sometimes made their presence felt. South Carolinians had added naval stores to their exports to Britain in the late seventeenth century, but lost this market to Baltic suppliers because of the poor quality of their products arising from the inexperience of colonial artisans, who were more successful at achieving quantity rather than quality production.

Colonial artisans identified with their fellows, and commonly appeared at parades and other public events as, for example, carpenters or wheelwrights. Artisans' specialization was one of the factors that made exchange of services, either for cash or in kind, essential in the colonial economy outside of the most remote frontiers. Judith McGaw found that lists of tools in eighteenth-century probate inventories for households in the middle-Atlantic region contained no standard array of equipment, and varied greatly between households. The American colonists, contrary to popular myth, were not self-sufficient. Instead, they relied on markets for necessities. Thus, McGaw found that while everyone had candles, few households had candle molds. Weaving equipment was present in less than 5 percent of homes, and woodworking tools were typically specialized.

Cultural, Regional, and Ethnic Differences

Regional differences in technologies chosen by the early colonists of the southwest, South, middle colonies, and New England arose in part not only from the particular natural resources available, but also from the different cultures and values of the European settlers. These regional differences established economic and social structures that would persist for the next two centuries.

In 1731, the Canary Islander settlers of San Antonio brought to Texas a system of arid land irrigation based on municipal control that lasted into the twentieth century. The founders of South Carolina, many of whom came from colonies in the West Indies, chose rice cultivation with labor by indentured servants as the basis of their economy. After 1700, they increasingly relied on the knowledge and skills of slaves brought from the rice-growing regions of West Africa. Because rice offered them economies of scale, South Carolinians concentrated production in large units – plantations – that could be managed by professional overseers, leaving the owners free to reside elsewhere during oppressive parts of the year. Virginians chose tobacco cultivation as the best adaptation to their soil and climate and, like the South Carolinians, adopted the plantation system. During periods of depressed tobacco prices, Virginians diversified their plantation products to include meat and grain. Plantation owners in the lower South eschewed diversification, and relied on outlying districts for meat and grain. Through their technological specialization they achieved the highest levels of colonial wealth, and the greatest inequality in wealth distribution.

Slaves in the upper South undertook technological as well as agricultural tasks. Thus, at ironworks slaves began as laborers in the early eighteenth century and by the end of the century carried out all of the skilled tasks at most Southern forges and furnaces. Owners reserved only managerial responsibilities for whites. They might buy slaves or rent them from their owners. Managers often paid their slaves cash for piecework once they exceeded an agreed upon output.

Middle-Atlantic colonies had the greatest ethnic diversity – British, Dutch, and German with lesser additions of French, Swedes, Scots, and Irish – and profited from the selection of the most useful components of the technologies that each ethnic group brought to the New World. McGaw's study of probate inventories shows that German farmers had many more tools for spreading dung on their fields, as well as grain fans and scythes with cradles, than did their British neighbors. German families used stoves for cooking and heating while British families stuck to their traditional, wasteful open fireplaces, and had much less interest in preserving the fertility of their land. By the mid-eighteenth century export-led growth engendered diversity in the rural economy, with processing and manufacturing industries dispersed in numerous towns. Inequalities in the distribution of wealth were small.

New Englanders substituted animal and mechanical sources of power for human labor wherever possible, and made only the slightest use of slaves. They had the lowest level of personal wealth, but a low level of inequality in wealth distribution. Their particular combination of diversified entrepreneurship, high rate of saving, commitment to education, and emphasis on the use of waterpower created the most favorable opportunities for rapid industrial development after the Revolution.

Advent of Mechanized Manufacturing

By 1780, southern New England and the middle-Atlantic states had in place the culture, supportive primary industries, and government institutions needed to carry industrialization into manufacturing in factories with power-driven machinery. Moderated population growth, higher agricultural productivity, and accumulation of mobile capital from trade and agriculture helped entrepreneurs turn to manufacturing. They could draw on experienced millwrights to build efficient waterpower systems to run the machines that reduced the brute physical labor of heavy tasks, or the endlessly repetitive tasks of spinning and weaving. Eli Whitney's armory in Hamden, Connecticut and the Almy, Brown and Slater mill in Pawtucket, Rhode Island, serve as examples of the new manufactories.

Although probably larger in legend than in fact, the Whitney Armory symbolizes the emerging characteristic of the so-called American system of manufacture that achieved worldwide adoption by the mid-nineteenth century: division of labor, interchangeable parts, and production with power-driven machinery. Whitney drew heavily on established skills and knowledge of the already established colonial industrial base, such as the Forbes & Adam partnership that supplied much of the heavy equipment he needed for production of muskets for the federal government.

Samuel Slater learned the construction of Arkwright spinning machinery in his native Britain. Moses Brown hired the newly arrived Slater in 1789 to mechanize production in his Pawtucket mill (now preserved as a historic site). Slater, as had Whitney, drew on the colonial base of skills and supporting industry, in this case Pawtucket iron founder and machinist Oziel Wilkinson and his son David, who made the machinery, and millwright Sylvanus Brown who set up the waterpower system. Slater's organizational acumen arranged the orderly flow of materials from distant sources to completed products. Within a year the partners had drawing, carding, roving, and spinning machines at work making yarn that they passed on to handloom weavers for conversion into cloth.

Environmental Consequences

A region's natural resources create opportunities for, and set limits on, people's use of technology. Technological knowledge creates opportunities to use these resources, but choices then have to be made of how to use this knowledge. Separating capacity from choice in the historical record of colonial America is beset with difficulties and will continue to exercise future historians and archaeologists. There is increasingly abundant evidence of Native Americans' full exploitation of animal and fishery resources. We know that Europeans found bountiful opportunities in America to apply their belief that resources were put on earth for humans to use. However, the very abundance of land, forest, and minerals undermined the Puritan commitment to stewardship, while other colonists, particularly in the South, never encumbered themselves with this concept.

The written record of colonial environmental change outside of deforestation and soil depletion remains sparse. Recent archaeological studies increasingly reveal evidence of watercourses altered to meet the needs of mills, and of millponds silted in by soil eroded from badly managed fields. Displacement of anadromous fish by milldams became an issue late in the early republic as mill proprietors dammed the larger streams for waterpower.

Sparse population limited gross environmental consequences arising from the colonists' abandonment of early commitment to stewardship of the land. However, local environmental degradation could be severe in colonial towns and cities. Within 17 years of Philadelphia's founding in 1682, residents considered the pollution of Dock Creek, the estuary that accommodated the city's early shipping, unacceptable. Tankards and slaughterhouses discharged their wastes directly into the creek, where, the silt washed off unpaved streets, and accumulated. Municipal efforts at remediation accomplished little. Outbreaks of epidemics in infectious diseases in the 1730s led citizens to blame the smells and standing water at the tankards. By 1747 the city had a committee looking for solutions. Limited understanding of hydrology and disease hampered its work, and the city proved unable to find money to pay for the remedies proposed. This failure to address an important issue led the city to a cover-up: it built a roof over the creek to get it out of sight.

BIBLIOGRAPHY

Brands, H.W. *The First American, the Life and Times of Benjamin Franklin* (New York: Doubleday, 2000).
Carney, J.A. *Black Rice, the African Origins of Rice Cultivation in the Americas* (Cambridge: Harvard University Press, 2001).

Eliot, J. *Essays Upon Field Husbandry in New England and Other Papers 1748–1762*, eds Carman, H.J., Tugwell, R.G., and True, R.H. (New York: Columbia University Press, 1934).

Goldenberg, J.A. *Shipbuilding in Colonial America* (Charlottesville: University Press of Virginia, 1976).

Malone, Patrick M. *The Skulking Way of War: Technology and Tactics Among the New England Indians* (Lanham: Madison Books, 1991).

McCusker, J.J. and Menard, R.R. *The Economy of British North America, 1607–1789* (Chapel Hill: University of North Carolina Press, 1985).

McGaw, J. *Early American Technology* (Chapel Hill: University of North Carolina Press, 1994).

Newell, M.E. *From Dependency to Independence, Economic Revolution in Colonial New England* (Ithaca: Cornell University Press, 1998).

O'Shaughnessy, A.J. *An Empire Divided: The American Revolution and the British Caribbean* (Philadelphia: University of Pennsylvania Press, 2000).

Quimby, I.M.G. *The Craftsman in Early America* (New York: Norton, 1984).

Robinson, W.B. *American Forts* (Urbana: University of Illinois Press, 1977).

Rothenberg, W.B. *From Market Place to Market Economy* (Chicago: University of Chicago Press, 1992).

Steele, I.K. *The English Atlantic* (New York: Oxford University Press, 1986).

CHAPTER TWO

The American Industrial Revolution

JAMES C. WILLIAMS

Halfway through the twentieth century, American sociologist Henry Pratt Fairchild (1950) observed that United States Census enumerators in 1900 counted 23 persons who had been alive when the first Census was taken in 1790. He speculated about the extraordinarily fascinating times through which these centenarians had lived: "This little handful of individuals had not only shared in the growth of one of the greatest nations in history, from its birth to its late adolescence, but, even more, their lifetime had also covered a century [in] which...the availability of vast stretches of unexploited land [converged] with brand-new, and incredibly efficacious, instrumentalities for getting things out of the land and fitting them for human use" (pp. xi, xvi–xvii). They had lived, Fairchild rightly declared, through an age of striking technological change.

The great societal transformation known as the Industrial Revolution began in Great Britain, where canals built during the late eighteenth century vastly improved transportation. This accelerated the change from a traditional agrarian and artisan society to one based on manufacturing and machine-made goods, a change already underway in textile production. At the same time, coal replaced wood as fuel, technological innovations occurred in iron production and use, improvements in precision machining of wood and metal set the foundation for the machine tool industry, and James Watt (1736–1819) invented a steam powered engine in 1769 that eventually freed manufacturers from relying on waterpower and opened up enormous opportunities in locomotion.

Despite the War of Independence and subsequent hostile relations between Great Britain and the new United States, the Americans shared in the benefits of Britain's technological changes. As colonists, they had years of experience importing tools, machines, and the people who made and used them. Therefore, even though British legislation in 1785 prohibited the export of textile machinery, steam engines, and other new machines, "the Americans were well positioned," note historians Hindle and Lubar (1986, p. 25), "to import the Industrial Revolution from their former mother country." All they needed was the motivation to do so, which their location and geopolitical situation in the world readily provided.

America in 1800

In 1800, the United States was a quiet, pre-industrial nation comprised largely of white subsistence farmers, who were hostile to aristocracy, supportive of equality, and independent of character. It operated under a new and untested political system, an experiment in democratic republicanism that some Europeans thought was teetering and which the Federalists from whom Thomas Jefferson (1743–1826) had just captured the presidency already felt had collapsed. Yet, the country was remarkably rich in natural resources which had a potential that was, if not infinite, huge, and the ambitions and energies of many of its people churned as if awaiting some great thing.

Between 1795 and 1797, the Duc de La Rochefoucauld-Liancourt spent 30 months in America, visiting from Pennsylvania to New England. Wherever he went, he met people on the move, discovering that the idea of being permanently attached to a piece of land, so highly valued by European peasants, here signified a lack of spirit. He concluded that the United States was "a country in flux.... [T]hat which is true today as regards its population, its establishments, its prices, its commerce will not be true in six months" (as cited in Appleby 2000, p. 6). Historian Joyce Appleby declares that for the generation of Americans born after the War of Independence and the adoption of the Constitution, "national goals cemented...personal ambitions to an imagined national enterprise that vindicated democracy in a world of monarchies." The energies of these Americans and their children led Michel Chevalier, a French visitor in the 1830s, to report that in the United States "all is circulation, motion, and boiling agitation...Experiment follows experiment; enterprise follows enterprise" (as cited in Appleby 2000, p. 7).

Chevalier visited the United States in the midst of a market revolution that stemmed from a focus on economic growth, which most Americans believed essential to national survival. Nationalist leaders such as Alexander Hamilton fostered this by strengthening public credit and trade during the 1790s, whereas the egalitarian Jefferson fostered it by seeking to expand the agrarian foundation of the country. Historian Pursell (1995, p. 36) remarks: "The calculus of success was implicit. To preserve...liberty and ensure prosperity, the economy had to grow." Economic growth depended on population increase, which a remarkably high fertility rate plus immigration provided over the next 100 years, and it required the progressive exploitation of natural resources, the availability of which steady and rapid expansion across the continent seemed to guarantee in perpetuity. Since the technologies available to use them defined natural resources, America's "well-being and very survival depended on a powerful technological base."

Transportation and Communication

Time, distance, rivers, mountains, and topography greatly occupied Americans living in 1800. The country occupied an area roughly 1,000 miles by a thousand miles, its boundaries stretching from the Atlantic Ocean to the Mississippi River and from the Great Lakes and St Lawrence River almost to the Gulf of Mexico. Four nations the size of France, Europe's largest, could fit into it and have room left over. Five million three hundred thousand non-Native Americans, of which 17 percent were enslaved, occupied the thinly populated country. Two-thirds of them lived within 50 miles of the Atlantic tidewater, while only a half million lived west of the Appalachian

Mountains. Surrounded by the empires of Spain and Great Britain, historian Ambrose (1996, pp. 51–2) observes: "it was not clear the country could hold on to its existing territory between the Appalachians and the Mississippi...." The Whiskey Rebellion in the 1790s had shown that Americans living west of the Appalachians "were already disposed to think of themselves as the germ of an independent nation that would find its outlet to the world marketplace...by the Ohio and Mississippi river system to the Gulf of Mexico." During his presidency, Thomas Jefferson, had to nip secessionist plots in the bud, lest they destroy the nascent republican experiment.

The problem, of course, was that nothing moved over land faster than the speed of a horse. As Ambrose (1996, p. 52) puts it: "No human being, no manufactured item, no bushel of wheat, no side of beef..., no letter, no information, no idea, order, or instruction of any kind moved faster. Nothing ever had moved any faster...." Roads were poor and often impassable in the rainy season. By stagecoach from the nation's largest city, Philadelphia, to its second largest city, New York, a distance of 90 miles took two days. One needed to travel three more days to cover the additional 175 miles to the third largest city, Boston. Thomas Jefferson wrote in 1801: "Of eight rivers between here [Monticello, Virginia] and Washington, five have neither bridges nor boats." A 225-mile trip from Monticello to Philadelphia consumed ten days (quoted in Ambrose 1996, p. 52).

When it came to the West, only four roads crossed the Appalachians into western Pennsylvania and Kentucky and Tennessee, and once they entered the mountains they became little more than trails. By any route, it took six weeks or more to travel from the Mississippi River to the Atlantic Seaboard. "Until the end of the 1820s," writes the historian Appleby (2000, pp. 62–3), "only those living on the nation's rivers could be sure of long-distance transportation, and then only in one direction." As long as people beyond the Atlantic tidewater depended on rivers and roads for transportation, only grain transformed into whiskey could pay for its freight overland to the East. Moreover, west of the Appalachians few crops earned a profit when sent downriver to New Orleans.

The cost of mailing a letter through the newly established post office clearly shows the enormous expense of travel and communication: "For every letter composed of a single sheet of paper, not exceeding 40 miles, 8 cents; over 40 miles and not exceeding 90 miles, 10 cents; over 90 miles..., 12½ cents; over 150 miles..., 17 cents; over 300 miles..., 20 cents; over 500 miles, 25 cents" (quoted in Pratt 1950, xii). Considering the value of a penny in 1801 compared to today, even prosperous Americans did not indulge in trivial letter writing. No wonder Americans in the Ohio and Mississippi river valleys contemplated an independent future. If the United States were to survive, much less grow and prosper, Americans simply had to overcome the great distances that marked their far-flung territory.

Roads, Canals, and Engineering

As with many aspects of the Industrial Revolution, Americans followed the British example in transportation technology. Beginning in the 1790s, state governments chartered private turnpike companies to build improved roads. The first, the Philadelphia and Lancaster Turnpike Company, opened in 1794 and was an immediate financial success. Subsequently, scores of such corporations formed, and by 1820 all the cities along the northern and middle-Atlantic corridor were connected by improved roads. Even Congress responded to the pestering of Americans west of the Appalachians by approving construction of the National Road. Started in Maryland in 1808, the 80-foot-wide stone-covered road reached the Ohio River in 9 years and, eventually, Vandalia, Illinois, in 1852. Soon thereafter, however, all the segments of the National Road had been turned back over to the states. Roads and turnpikes remained a local responsibility until the twentieth century, and few of them were macadamized or otherwise surfaced.

As in Britain, canals soon rivaled roads and turnpikes. Among the first was the 27-mile Middlesex Canal connecting the Charles and Merrimack rivers in Massachusetts. Work started in 1793, construction was overseen by sometime cabinetmaker and man of learning, Laommi Baldwin (1744–1807). He and his crew had done little surveying, never built a canal (few, if any, had seen one), and possessed only traditional hand tools; however, they agreed with Secretary of War Henry Knox (1750–1806), a Bostonian and great supporter of the project, that surveying and such was "more a matter of accurate perceptions and judgments than of science" (quoted in Morrison 1974, p. 20). Unfortunately, their first survey resulted in a vertical error of forty-one and a half feet in one six-mile stretch, and workers confronted a wide range of other insoluble problems: how to expeditiously dig a ditch, dispose of the earth they dug, seal the ditch so water would not seep through the bottom and sides, design a canal lock, lay up brick or stone with mortar that held under water, and design machinery for opening and closing the locks. "They found, in sum," observes historian Morrison (1974, p. 21), "that they did not know anything about building a canal."

Baldwin sought to depend on "the morals and steadiness of our own people," a workforce comprised mostly of farmers. But he quickly realized that he needed help. In Philadelphia, he found William Weston (1753–1833), an Englishman supervising construction of a shorter canal to connect Pennsylvania's Susquehanna and Schuylkill Rivers. Weston had learned most of what he knew about canal construction from James Brindley (1716–62), who completed the Duke of Bridgewater's famous canal in Britain in 1761. Eager to visit Boston, Weston looked at the Middlesex Canal project in early 1794. In just two weeks, he used a telescopic leveling instrument to accurately survey the entire canal route, advised on building materials, instructed how to seal the canal by puddling the bottom and sides with clayey soil, and drew up designs for locks and valve gate machinery. Nevertheless, trial and error guided the Middlesex Canal builders as they translated what knowledge Weston gave them about canal building into the actual construction of one. Over a dozen years later at a cost of over three times the original estimates, they finally completed the 20-lock canal.

In 1808, the year the Middlesex Canal was opened, Jesse Hawley, a flour merchant in the Finger Lakes region of upstate New York, wrote a series of articles calling for the building of an east-west canal from the Hudson River to Lake Erie along the one relatively low-level route on the entire east coast, north of Georgia, which runs through the eastern mountains to the enormous interior of the country. The same year, Secretary of the Treasury Albert Gallatin (1761–1849), who, like President Jefferson, believed in the importance of transportation and communication to the young nation, submitted to Congress a *Report on the Subject of Public Roads and Canals*, a transportation master plan. In it he argued that the federal government should invest $20 million over 10 years on roads, canals, and river navigation improvements. Moreover, he emphasized that financing these projects ought to be the responsibility of governments because the projects themselves provided so much for the public good.

Economic hard times and war with Britain between 1812 and 1815 interrupted Hawley's vision as well as Gallatin's, but New Yorkers and their governor, De Witt Clinton (1769–1828), soon put it back on course. Seized by what was widely scoffed at as an impossible dream, New York State in 1817, entirely out of its own funds, flung itself into a project so dramatic, visionary, and immense that the world was astonished: the excavation and construction of the 363-mile long Erie Canal. Nothing like it had ever been attempted before, and its completion 7 years later in 1825 revolutionized North American geography. Oceangoing vessels could navigate to Albany on the Hudson River and transship their passengers and cargoes to canal boats, which journeyed right on to the lake port of Buffalo, on Lake Erie. Even though the canal cost $7 million to construct and had an average towage speed of less than two miles per hour, freight could be shipped at one-twentieth of the overland price. New York State became the highway of the westward movement, and New York City, sitting at the entry point to this great water-transport network, became the preeminent seaport, metropolis, and eventually financial capital of the continent.

"The Artificial River," as historian Sheriff (1996), describes the Erie Canal, was 4-feet deep, 28-feet wide at bottom and 40-feet wide on the surface. Its 14-foot wide towpaths stood about three feet above the channel's surface, it traveled on aqueducts over 18 valleys, and it contained 84 locks, which raised the water 62-feet up from Lake Erie to the summit and then 630-feet down to the Hudson River. The engineering task was enormous and the results spectacular, and several sites along its length quickly became famous landmarks. Historian Nye (1994, p. 34) suggests that two of them – the giant staircase of five locks in Lockport that carried boats up and over the Niagara escarpment and the 802-foot stone aqueduct that carried the canal over the Genessee River at Rochester – are among the first examples of Americans' embrace of the "technological sublime," that essentially religious, passionate experience aroused by confronting impressive objects.

One might expect that only formally trained engineers could accomplish such a task, as the Middlesex Canal, the Erie Canal's engineers had little or no practice in building anything. They learned on the job, perfecting their skills at surveying, discovering how to use limestone-based hydraulic cement in place of puddling, and inventing new machines, such as stump pullers and turf cutters. As Morrison (1974, p. 41) observes, the canal project became "the first – and quite possibly the best – school of general engineering in this country." The military academy at West Point offered the only formal engineering education in the United States but had only been established in 1811 and did not graduate its first civil engineer until 1818. The country's first private school of civil engineering, Rensselaer Polytechnic Institute near Albany, New York, was not founded until 1824, the year before the canal was completed. So, the Erie Canal actually educated a generation of civil engineers, who fanned out across the country to build many more canals and a multitude of other projects.

Although Americans built fewer than one hundred miles of canals before 1815, they invested over $125 million on 3,326 miles of canals during the next 25 years, the money for which largely came from governmental bodies. Through canal building, the nation took a giant step toward tying together its enormous continental domain. These artificial rivers greatly extended technology's transformational impact on the environment by adding enormously to what historian Cronon (1991, p. xix) calls "second nature," the "artificial nature that people erect atop first nature … the original, prehuman nature.…" The new routes of travel available from east to west soon came to seem "natural," and the Great Lakes Basin and other previously inaccessible areas quickly teemed with settlers.

Steamboats

Through most of the nineteenth century, horses and mules towed canal boats, but steam engines took hold on America's rivers. "The notion of steam propulsion for boats was nearly as old as the steam engine itself," writes Pursell (1995, p. 75), "but the proper proportions of engine to boat and the best way to apply the power – whether by water forced out the back in a jet, screw propellers, paddle wheel…, or by banks of oars or poles – was not obvious." A number of inventors worked hard to make the steamboat a technical as well as a commercial success (Hindle 1981). During the 1790s, the most promising of them were John Fitch (1743–98), John Rumsey (1743–92), and John Stevens III (1749–1838), but they fell into a legal battle over their patents and who among them would receive royalties from the others. Thus it fell to Stevens's brother-in-law, Robert R. Livingston (1746–1813) and Robert Fulton (1765–1815) to launch the first successful steamboat operation.

In 1801, Livingston, newly appointed ambassador to France, met Fulton, a Pennsylvanian living in Paris. They signed a contract to build and operate a boat on the Hudson River between New York and Albany. Fulton had built a boat in France in 1803, using side paddle wheels and a Watt-type steam engine with a separate condenser, none of which infringed on the patents of Fitch, Rumsey, or Stevens. Following the boat's successful testing, Livingston used his political connections to secure a steam transport monopoly in New York, and Fulton launched a second, similar boat, *The Clermont*, in 1807. Technically and financially successful, the two men extended steamboat commerce from the Hudson River into Long Island Sound, and in 1811, they inaugurated steamboat service on the Mississippi River. Not surprisingly, however, other entrepreneurs entered the game, and competition spawned lawsuits over river traffic monopolies. In 1824, the United States Supreme

Court ended the Livingston–Fulton control of steamer service on the Hudson by establishing the precedent in *Gibbons v. Ogden* that only Congress could regulate commerce between the states.

Between 1816 and 1818, Henry M. Shreve (1785–1841) in Louisiana employed a high-pressure steam engine based on the one invented in 1805 by Philadelphian Oliver Evans (1755–1819). As high-pressure engines replaced the Bolton and Watt-type low-pressure engines, much faster steamboats extended along the Atlantic tidewater, to the Great Lakes, and to the western rivers. They drastically cut river travel time and shipping costs both downstream and upstream; on the western rivers, where river travel occurred only on flat-bottomed keelboats poled by hand and upstream passage was virtually nonexistent, their impact was revolutionary. By 1855, there were 727 steamboats on the Mississippi River system, and at least fifty plied rivers in California. Western boats, designed for shallow, snag-infested river bottoms, principally carried freight and appeared a bit ungainly with two or three above decks for passengers. One contemporary described them disdainfully "as an engine on a raft with $11,000 worth of jig-saw work" (quoted in Pursell 1995, p. 77).

Although standard-design high-pressure wood-fueled engines driving stern or side paddle wheels moved steamboats along at speeds reaching 20 knots, the speed plus navigational obstructions took a tragic toll on both steamboats and passengers. Five hundred and twenty boats were lost by 1850 to snags, various navigational accidents, and boiler explosions. Bursting boilers, 42 of which killed 273 people between 1825 and 1830, resulted both from efforts to make speed and from deficiencies in boiler construction and poor maintenance. Following a severe explosion near Memphis, Tennessee in 1830 that killed almost 60, Congress authorized the federal government to give its first grant for scientific research to the Franklin Institute in Philadelphia to discover the cause of boiler explosions. In 1836, the Institute submitted a report calling for federal boiler inspectors; following another explosion killing 140 people in Charleston, it became law. This set, remarks historian Cowan (1997, p. 111), "the precedent on which all succeeding federal safety-regulating legislation would be based."

Railroads

Equally dramatic and historic to canal building and steamboats in North America was the application of steam power to land travel, and the construction of thousands of miles of railroads connecting the east coast with the interior. The first railroading began in Britain in 1825, but its most extraordinary development occurred in the United States. Americans borrowed and improved on British technology immediately. In January 1831, the Charleston and Hamburg Railroad in South Carolina became the first in the nation to begin regular service, and its locomotive, the *Best Friend of Charleston*, built at the West Point Foundry in New York in 1830, was the first one built entirely in the United States. Several foundries and machine shops, such as Philadelphia's Matthias Baldwin Engine Works and Norris Locomotive Works, were set up to produce locomotives while other firms turned to build other railroad equipments. By 1840, America's 3,326 miles of trackage far surpassed the less than

2,000 miles in all of Europe. What is more, Austria, some German states, Russia, and even Britain began importing American locomotives.

Although almost all the railroads constructed during the 1830s were east of the Appalachian Mountains, the need to conquer distance in so enormous a country was urgent, and a continental expanse free of boundary and tariff restrictions lay open for development. Especially in the Midwest and West, land was cheap and much of it was flat, making railroad construction easier than in Europe, and the American economy was more innovative and less hampered by monopolies and long-established customs. The result was a veritable detonation of railroads, building feverishly all over the countryside.

By 1860, so frantic was the pace of railroad construction, that trackage totaled more than 30,000 miles, whereas canals, even though many new ones had been built, were fewer than 9,000 miles in total extent. There was not enough private capital in the country to provide the transportation network that was wanted, so following the precedent established for funding roads and canals, state governments and local communities responded by making generous grants to railroad projects, devising attractive charters to make construction profitable, and sometimes building the railroads themselves. During the 1850s, the federal government joined in this public funding, giving the Illinois Central land grants that ultimately totaled four million acres. It also sponsored a series of surveys to determine the best transcontinental rail routes, and during the Civil War in 1862 the northern controlled Congress chartered the Union Pacific and Central Pacific railroads with a lavish land grant and loan guarantee program. It continued to provide similar support for other railroad projects through the end of the century.

Dominating the railroad system by the 1850s were the great east–west trunk lines, such as the New York Central, the Pennsylvania, the Erie, and the Baltimore & Ohio, which headed out westward from the Atlantic seaboard in a more or less straight line to Chicago. Beyond that city, railroad builders threw out a complex network, which gave an electrifying stimulus to the growth of the rapidly expanding farm empire, which had already, with canals, begun focusing on Chicago as its "natural" outlet to the East. In the incredible surge of railroad building nationwide, some 2,500 miles of track were laid in the state of Illinois alone during the 1850s. This made Chicago even more the place to which farmers sent their crops, for there they could market them to the East through the trunk railroads running to New York and other north-eastern cities, or put them on lake steamers, which continued to carry a heavy traffic. The volume of wheat arriving in Chicago by rail mounted dramatically, and by 1860, writes Cronon in *Nature's Metropolis* (1991, p. 68), "eastern investors and Chicago railroad managers had succeeded in imposing a new geography on the western landscape. Almost all the new lines west of Lake Michigan focused on the city, extending from it like the spokes of a great wheel and dividing the region into a series of pie-shaped wedges, each more or less within the territory of a single Chicago-based railroad." By the 1870s, construction of transcontinental railroads from the Middle West to the Pacific Coast connected Chicago as well to all the states along the Pacific Coast.

While Chicago became the great metropolis of interior North America, railroads stimulated industry everywhere, particularly the iron and steel industry. Between 1800 and 1860, iron consumption increased fivefold and the rolling of rails was perfected. The most important technical innovation in the industry, however, was the adoption of the Bessemer-Kelley steel-making process that burned carbon out of molten iron by blowing highly pressurized cold air through it. Developed in 1855 by Henry Bessemer (1813–98) in Britain and perhaps simultaneously in the United States by Kentucky ironmaster William Kelly (1811–88), the process was capitalized on by the entrepreneur Andrew Carnegie (1835–1919). During the last quarter of the nineteenth century, Carnegie's adoption of Bessemer process, mainly to produce steel rails for the competitive and impatient railroad industry, led to what historian Thomas Misa (1995) calls the "reckless mass production" of rails. Unfortunately, as railroads began using larger locomotives and carrying heavier loads, Carnegie's sacrifice of quality for quantity, resulted in railroad companies having to rebuild their trackage.

The Magic of the Railroads

"Railroads were more than just natural," observes Cronon (1991, p. 72): "their power to transform landscapes partook of the supernatural, drawing upon a mysterious creative energy that was beyond human influence or knowledge." To Americans of the nineteenth century they were the most stunning, fascinating symbol of the American Industrial Revolution. Even more than the Erie Canal, the railroad became a sublime and romantic symbol of humankind's conquest of nature, especially of technology's dramatic alteration of space and time. Railroads ran across the countryside at extraordinary speeds never before attained on land, pulling incredible loads day and night. By the 1850s, it took not two weeks to travel from Chicago to New York City, but, astonishingly, only two days. As a result, Americans began thinking of their country in quite new perceptual terms, for with speed of transport it shrank drastically in people's minds.

The railroad embedded itself in the psyches of the American people and into the national culture. When people watched steam locomotives snorting by on the plains, they were watching an awesome wonder on the stage of national life: a physical object, constructed of iron and steel, which had incredibly leaped into life and motion, like some magical genie coming alive right before one's eyes. They endowed railroads and their locomotives with personality. The hooting sound of the locomotive's steam whistle could be heard for miles, wafting over the plains. Farmers and their families in their remote homes drew comfort from the regularly recurring signal, coming to them through the dark night, that out there, bustling along, was life, and life connected with the far away city and all the world beyond. City dwellers came to see the railroad as the engine of their communities, a grand icon of economic and cultural progress. Writers, remarks Cronon (1991, p. 73), who

> waxed poetic about the railroad were surely right to regard it as much more than just a machine. It touched all facets of American life in the second half of the nineteenth

century, insinuating itself into virtually every aspect of the national landscape. . . . The railroad left almost nothing unchanged: that was its magic. To those whose lives it touched, it seemed at once so ordinary and extraordinary – so second nature – that the landscape became unimaginable without it.

Telegraph

Telegraph lines soon accompanied the signatures left by railroads across the land. Artist and professor Samuel F.B. Morse (1791–1872) conceived of the electromagnetic telegraph in 1832, while aboard a ship returning to the United States from London. He worked on the idea for several years during the hours and days he could grasp between his teaching duties at New York University, securing scientific and mechanical assistance when he needed it (Hindle 1981). After he patented and demonstrated his communication device and the code to transmit words, Morse and partners whom he had enlisted along the way, convinced Congress in 1842 to fund the building of an experimental line between Baltimore and Washington. The line, completed 2 years later, was not much of a success. The government turned its back on further support and few customers paid to send messages. Nonetheless, Morse and his partners persisted, arranging to commercialize the telegraph with entrepreneurs in the private sector. Line extensions had reached some 1,200 miles by 1846, when the outbreak of the Mexican War created a national hunger for news. "By 1850 the telegraph was more than just accepted," observes Lubar (1993, p. 83), "it was the rage."

Businesses soon grasped the advantages of telegraphic communication. Perhaps it was prophetic that Morse's first line in 1842 had followed the Baltimore & Ohio Railroad's tracks, for railroads were among the first to exploit the new device. Telegraph communication soon became essential to the management of rail traffic, and as railroads expanded and stretched across the nation, so did telegraph lines. The first transcontinental telegraph was completed before the first transcontinental railroad during the 1860s, as was a viable transatlantic cable. Meanwhile other businesses discovered its value. Dealers in commodities, financial institutions, and news used it heavily, and the telegraph became a technological icon of wealth and information. Along with the railroad, Morse's telegraph had conquered space and time and seemed to have a sublime moral influence as well. In 1881, *Scientific American* argued that the telegraph made possible "kinship of humanity." "The touch of the telegraph key," brought a international reaction to the assassination of President James A. Garfield (1831–81) "that welded human sympathy and made possible its manifestation in a common, universal, simultaneous heart throb" (quoted in Marvin 1988, p. 199).

Manufacturing

While the United States experienced a transportation and communication revolution during the nineteenth century, it also underwent a transformation in the way its people made things. Particularly in the northern states, manufacturing took hold in the form of the factory system imported from Britain, but it was not universally welcomed. "The promise of labor-saving devices strongly appealed to a nation concerned with establishing independence, safeguarding moral purity, and promoting industry and thrift among her people," observes historian Kasson (1976, p. 50). Technological progress in transportation and communication seemed to overcome the country's regional fragmentation, but "the union of technology and republicanism, while settling some issues, raised others.... [Could] her manufacturing towns,... avoid the blight and degradation of their English counterparts."

Apprehension about this was strongest among the egalitarian followers of Thomas Jefferson. While they looked to new mechanical technologies as a means of achieving a virtuous and prosperous republican society, they nevertheless felt that virtue and liberty were grounded in agrarian life. Thus, they worried about the evils of factory towns and the corrupting influence such places could have on the political economy. Hamiltonian nationalists, on the other hand, quickly embraced manufacturing as crucial to liberty and national health. They set out to allay their fellow citizens' anxieties by ensuring that manufacturers operated under a strict system of moral supervision, which would protect the health and virtue of their workers as well as republicanism. Such factories would result in a middle landscape between the city and the wilderness, where the virtue of Jefferson's agrarian world and the civilizing process of progress would coexist. Not surprisingly, this vision of the republican factory first emerged in New England, where waterpower, an available labor supply of farmwomen and children, and an enterprising, industrious, and moralist Yankee culture existed together.

Lowell System

Beginning in Waltham, Massachusetts, in 1813, a group of merchants known as the Boston associates formed the Boston Manufacturing Company and established what was probably the first true factory in America: a textile mill in which all the processes were power operated. The associates soon located mills in several other New England towns, the most famous of which was Lowell, Massachusetts, where they ultimately transformed an unsettled tract of land on the Merrimack River, 25 miles north of Boston, into a water-powered industrial city. When the first Lowell mills opened in 1822, raw cotton was turned into finished cloth in four-storey-high factories in which every process that could be had been mechanized and integrated – spinning, dying, bleaching, and weaving. The large corporate-owned mills were run not by the owners but entirely by salaried managers, who oversaw the workforce.

The patriarchal Boston associates sought to establish in Lowell an ideal factory community that would provide a virtuous institutional environment for their workers and thereby avoid the poverty and degradation associated with factory towns. Drawing on social thinking of their time, they organized the Lowell mills on the model of "total institutions," such as asylums, which fully cared for the morals and virtues of its people. Rather than establishing a workforce of permanent factory operatives, they hired young, single women from the surrounding countryside. In theory, each would work until she earned a dowry, left for marriage, and was replaced by another single girl. In addition to earning a wage, "Lowell girls" were housed in dormitories, supervised by matrons, and provided compulsory religious services. The Lowell factory system was to be, in Kasson's words (1976, p. 70), "a beacon of republican prosperity and purity upon the American landscape."

By 1855, thanks to rapid expansion permitted by the virtue of corporate ownership, Lowell boasted 52 mills employing over 12,000 workers. Its success caused the factory system to surge into other industries, from boots and shoes and papermaking to diary products and meatpacking. But, Lowell's growth also contributed to the failure of the Boston associates' attempt to smoothly weave the machine into the republican garden (Marx 1964, 158–60). From the start, they provided no housing at all for the Irish-Catholic immigrants who built the canals and mills and who lived in thrown together shanties, and over time the "Lowell girls" found themselves treated less and less well. As Lowell grew, explains Cowan (1997, pp. 87–8),

> Parents could not control their children's labor, and they could not negotiate with their children's employers . . . [M]anagers stopped being able to control where workers lived and how frequently they went to church. The Lowell system created a new kind of wage laborer: a person who contracted individually with her or his employer and who lacked either an older family member or any other form of communal support system to help with the negotiations.

During the 1830s, managers increased workloads, wages declined, and workers began to fight wage slavery. But immigration, particularly the massive influx from Ireland during that country's potato famine, gave managers a new source of labor. Nativist prejudices soon took aim at factory workers; wages continued declining and a permanent working class took shape. With the advance of industrial capitalism, the early emphasis on virtue in adopting the factory system into republican society gave way to a more technocratic vision of progress.

The American System of Manufactures

One of the most distinctive ways in which Americans gave shape to the Industrial Revolution was in the way they produced goods. During the 1850s, British observers of American products, tools, and manufacturing techniques saw novel and original methods, which historians have since referred to as "the American system of manufactures" (Rosenberg 1969; Mayr and Post 1981; Hounshell 1984, pp. 15–17). Traditionally, observes Pursell (1995, p. 87), manufactured goods "were made one at time by skilled craftspeople, who, perhaps with the help of an apprentice, saw the entire process through to its end." The American system, however, sought "to achieve uniformity of product by the transfer of skills from workers to machines." Jigs, gauges, fixtures, dies, and special tools produced "a large number of similar parts, the accurate dimensions of which were determined by the design and setting of the machine tool, rather than [by] the skill and experience of the worker."

The American system of manufactures, sometimes called armory practice, emerged from methods used in the American arms industry to produce guns with interchangeable parts made by special purpose machines and a relatively unskilled workforce. Historian Hounshell (1984, p. 27) remarks: "The United States War Department . . . found the idea of interchangeability irresistible." To achieve it, the government lavished an extraordinary sum of money over many years on its own armories and on private arms contractors. The first of those private contractors, Eli Whitney (1765–1825), inventor of the cotton gin, is often credited with the idea of interchangeability, but we know now that even though he thought about making muskets with interchangeable parts, he never achieved it. Credit goes to John H. Hall (1781–1841), who planned out and installed a series of machines at the federal arsenal in Harpers Ferry, Virginia, during the 1820s, and to Elisha K. Root (1808–65), who developed a similar system at Samuel Colt's (1814–62) private arms factory in Hartford, Connecticut (Smith 1977). Other contributors to the process included Simeon North (1765–1852), who developed the first metal milling machine in 1816, and Thomas Blanchard (1788–1864), who patented a special purpose lathe in 1822 that could cut irregular shapes, such as gunstocks (Cooper 1991).

British visitors to the United States during 1850s were particularly fascinated with small arms production. They put the system to the test at the Springfield Armory in Massachusetts, where they selected ten muskets made between 1844 and 1853, tore them down, and thoroughly mixed up their parts. When regular armory workers reassembled the weapons, they fit together and worked perfectly. It was a technical triumph, but achieving product uniformity was an expensive luxury for most manufacturers. While many of the special tools developed for the arms industry, such as the concept of Blanchard's copying lathe, transferred to the production of other products, advances in mechanized production took time. The few manufacturers who invested in machine tools found themselves working with the toolmakers to improve the tools and solve production problems. Over time, the machine toolmakers used the improved tools to solve production problems in other industries. Since all manufacturers depended on similar metalworking techniques, common needs converged at the machine tool industry itself.

Following an uneven trajectory, then, mechanization and uniformity in manufacturing, the hallmarks of the American system, ultimately transformed a multitude of traditional handicrafts. Clock-making is a good example. In 1802, long before armory practice was perfected, Eli Terry (1772–1852), a clockmaker in Connecticut, harnessed waterpower for clock-making and began designing special purpose tools for making the wooden workings of his clocks. Two decades later, Seth Thomas (1785–1865) licensed Terry's methods and soon he and other clock manufacturers were producing machine-made clocks. In time, production of high-quality sheet brass led to the adoption of machine-made brass clock wheels and gears. By 1850, the price of a clock had fallen over a half century from $50 to $1.50, and the average clock factory produced as many as 150,000 clocks annually (Hindle and Lubar 1986, pp. 219–26).

After mid-century, sewing machine manufacturers began adopting armory practice techniques, benefiting from diffusion of know-how when individual mechanics migrated from the firearms industry. William H. Perry came from Samuel Colt's small arms factory to the Wheeler and Wilson Manufacturing Company in 1856, and Henry M. Leland (1843–1932) moved from the Springfield Armory to Brown & Sharpe Manufacturing Company in 1872, when the latter was manufacturing tools as well as Willcox & Gibbs sewing machines, both introducing armory practice. (Leland later went on to found the Cadillac Motor Car Company.) Ironically, the leading sewing machine company, Singer, continued to use general-purpose machine tools and hand labor; its market success came through advertising and other marketing techniques.

Toward the end of the century, bicycle makers were the first manufacturers to go beyond traditional armory practice. Particularly outside New England, they abandoned traditional drop-forge metalworking techniques in favor of pressing bicycle parts from sheet steel. By the 1890s, entire bicycles were being fabricated from pressed steel. Meanwhile, it became apparent that larger operations could be much more productive than small ones in terms of the investment and the number of people employed. Larger operations could afford larger equipment, the use of more power, and the most up-to-date technical innovations. Greater mechanization meant labor saving, and this meant cheaper products. Thus, economies of scale permitted private manufacturers to make the investments necessary to achieve product uniformity. Shortly after the century ended, Henry Ford (1863–1947) combined the pressed steel production techniques of bicycle makers with the best of the American system of manufactures and introduced the term "mass production" into people's vocabulary.

Agriculture

The factory system, once begun, could only result in the destruction of local crafts in small towns and expand the urban world. Transportation and communication technologies further undermined craft-based communities while they transformed landscape, space, and time. Technology, through the agency of the inventor-mechanic-engineer-entrepreneur, marginalized the farmer-citizen in whom Jefferson entrusted the nation's virtue. While the Industrial Revolution overwhelmed agrarianism, at the same time it brought about an agricultural revolution.

At the outset of the nineteenth century, 80 percent of Americans worked in agriculture. They used traditional hand tools such as hoes, scythes, and pitchforks, and draft animals assisted them in plowing and hauling. Clearing land of forests was their biggest task, however. Using only axes, levers, and teams of oxen or horses, the job of removing stumps consumed far more work than all other tasks combined. In 1841, it took as much as 13 days for one man to clear an acre of stumps, and during the course of the century almost 150 million acres of land were cleared. Although people marketed scores of clever inventions, as late as 1890 the only truly effective aid to removing stumps from a field was blasting powder. But if technology did not come to the farmer's rescue in clearing land, new and improved tools and machines for plowing, planting, harvesting, hauling, and preparing foodstuffs for market made American farmers remarkably productive.

On the prairies that dominated the vast center of the country, stumps gave way to rock-hard soil. With traditional iron-tipped wooden plows or plows made entirely of wrought iron, Pursell (1995, p. 110) tells us, "it took three to five yoke of oxen and two people an entire day to turn just one-half acre of prairie sod." Then in 1837, in Illinois, John Deere (1804–86) introduced a plow with a share of steel attached to the moldboard. Within two decades, he was producing and shipping by rail 10,000 plows a year from a factory he erected in the town of Moline, and now he was making steel plows with steel moldboards as well as steel shares. The Deere plow was a real prairie sod buster, the matted roots in the soil sliced cleanly by the polished steel share and the moist sod turned by the moldboard without sticking, as it did to wood or iron. In 1868, James Oliver (1823–1908) invented the chilled-iron plow, which also had the virtue of nonstick surfaces, and out in California, local mechanics introduced the steel gangplow, several plow shares grouped together with which scores of acres a day could be prepared for sowing grain.

With more and more land being planted with hay and grain, harvesting by scythe proved a bottleneck. Gathering hay by rakes pulled by horses began dispensing with the pitchfork during the 1830s, and one person and a horse could bring in 20–30 acres of hay per day by the 1870s. But replacing the scythe with a machine for cutting the hay, wheat, or other grains proved much more difficult. Several inventors attacked the problem, and after 1850, Cyrus McCormick's (1809–84) horse-drawn reaper swept across the country. His reaper, with a bar of stationary metal fingers to hold the grain stalks while a reciprocating horizontal blade moved through the bar and cut them, could harvest 12 acres a day on flat land. It quickly began to replace harvest hands, and by 1861, just as the Civil War drained the Midwest countryside of young men, almost 70 percent of the region's wheat was mechanically harvested.

Meanwhile, other inventors had introduced the cylindrical thresher, first powered by animals and after mid-century increasingly by steam engines. Not surprisingly, inventors tried to combine reaping and threshing. Hiram Moore developed the first combine in Kalamzoo, Michigan, in 1836. He had mixed results with the machine because of Michigan's damp climate, and in 1854 sold a half-interest in it to a Californian, George Leland. In California, where hot summer air thoroughly dried the wheat and where ranches as large as 60,000 acres appeared to demand new harvesting technology, the combine was perfected. Soon several companies produced wheat combines, some of them so large that 20- to 40-horse teams had to pull them. The combine soon spread to wheat farms everywhere (Williams 1997, pp. 32–4).

Mechanics and inventors surfaced in every state. Hank Monk, Mark Twain's fictional hero in *A Connecticut Yankee in King Arthur's Court* (1963, p. 15), represented them: "I could make anything a body wanted – anything in the world, it didn't make any difference what; and if there wasn't any quick, new-fangled way to make a thing, I could invent one – and do so as easy as rolling off a log." Agricultural societies sponsored fairs in every corner of the country, giving prizes to the inventors of the best hay rakes, windmills, barley crushers, grinders, grape presses, and other farm machinery. Over the course of the nineteenth century, land given over to farming in the United States quadrupled, thanks to generous government policies, and although only 40 percent of Americans were still engaged in farming by 1900, the actual number of farmers climbed from about 4 million to almost 30 million. Even if draft animals still powered most farm equipment, a large proportion of farm work had been mechanized, industrialized farming had been introduced to the nation, and government had begun support of agricultural education and scientific experiment stations. A great transformation occurred, as farmers and their new technologies pushed aside natural ecosystems and brought in the few crops, European in origin (save corn), that henceforth would replace the original diversity of the landscape.

Networks and Systems Emerge

As the nineteenth century dissolved into the twentieth, the United States completed its passage from a pre-industrial, rural and agricultural society to an industrial and increasingly urban society. In doing so, its people discovered they were dependent less on the vagaries of nature than on the successful functioning of technological networks and systems in transportation, communication, energy, and urban services. Their lives increasingly were embedded in technological systems that were simply second nature to them.

The telegraph and the railroad were perhaps the first such technological systems. Toward the end of the century, the telegraph connected the entire country together. "The elongated spider's web of electric wires that carried telegraph signals," suggests Cowan (1997, pp. 151, 153), "really looked like a network." Railroads, newspapers, the stock market, government, and even families keeping in touch with one another had come to depend on it. "By 1880, if by some weird accident all the batteries that generated electricity for telegraph lines had suddenly run out, the economic and social life of the nation would have faltered." Similarly, over 150,000 miles of main line railroad tracks linked every corner of the country by 1890, and thousands of miles more were being laid each year. Railroad ownership became consolidated and the rail system became physically integrated, resulting in standard gauge tracks, standard car sizes, standard automatic couplers, and in 1883 even an industry- and, by default, a nation-wide standard railroad time, which Congress would finally make official 35 years later.

Energy in pre-industrial America came from human labor, animal power, waterpower, and wood. Controlled locally and by individuals, it inspired what Mumford (1964) aptly labeled "democratic technology." As the nineteenth century progressed, however, control over energy resources changed. In the American south, the white society systemized its already enslaved black human labor into work rhythms that were more like a modern assembly line than were the factories of the time. Outside the south, American industry turned to coal for heat, raising steam, and smelting metals, and large-scale energy systems began to emerge. Through vertical integration, Carnegie Steel owned and controlled its own coal and iron mines as well as the rail and steamship lines that delivered the coal and ore to its mills. In California, which possessed almost no good coal, an international energy system emerged during the 1870s: entrepreneurs exported California's high-quality wheat to Britain and America's Atlantic seaboard in exchange for imported high-grade coal (Williams 1997, pp. 46–8). But the development of petroleum for lighting and fuel created a much larger energy system. Within a decade after prospectors dug the first oil well in Titusville, Pennsylvania (1859), entrepreneurs began constructing iron pipelines to deliver petroleum from the oil fields to rail loading points and eventually to the refineries themselves. John D. Rockefeller (1839–1937) and his Standard Oil Trust played a leading role in the integration of petroleum transportation systems into a network of pipelines and rail tank cars.

Other late nineteenth-century technological systems included telephonic communication and electricity. Bell Telephone, controlling the patents issued in 1876 to Alexander Graham Bell (1847–1922), created from the start an integrated and standardized system by manufacturing the telephone instruments, which they leased only to local companies that operated under a license to Bell. After their patent protection expired in 1893, thousands of independent companies entered the business, which profoundly expanded the telephone network, but the Bell system was well-established. "By 1920," writes Cowan (1997, p. 162), "there were 13 million telephones…, 123 for every 1,000 people. Eight million of those 13 million phones belonged to Bell and 4 million to independent companies that connected to Bell lines." Meanwhile, developments in electricity through the work of Thomas Edison (1847–1931), Nikola Tesla (1856–1943), Frank Sprague (1857–1934), and others created yet another network of wires. As electricity was applied to street lighting, street railways, and commercial and domestic lighting as well as other uses, a sophisticated technological system took shape that involved a variety of technological components to generate, transmit, and deliver electricity. Its complexity precluded a single national system, but regional systems, some with distinct variations were identifiable by 1900 (Hughes 1983).

Finally, water and waste disposal systems evolved as Americans became more urbanized (Tarr 1996; Melosi 2000). Water supply and waste disposal during the first half of the nineteenth century had a very local focus. Potable water came from wells, rainwater cisterns, and nearby streams and ponds. Kitchen garbage and other household waste were thrown into the street or into vacant lots where pigs rooted it out. Human waste and most wastewater went into privy vaults and cesspools. Gutters or open channels down the center of streets carried off rainwater. Such methods were satisfactory for small cities, but growth brought insufficient and often contaminated water supplies and an intolerable waste situation. In 1799, Philadelphia became the first American city to construct a waterworks to pump potable water from a nearby river, and by the time of the Civil War, the country's 16 largest cities plus another 120 communities had waterworks. By 1880, the number reached almost 600, and, by 1902, municipal indebtedness incurred to build water systems had reached $1.4 billion.

Unhappily, cities were slower to provide for methods of removing garbage and wastewater. As more and more city residents piped fresh water into their homes between 1800 and 1850, per capita water consumption increased dramatically from 2–3 gallons to 50–100 gallons per day. Consumption kept climbing during the second half of the century with household installation of modern sinks, bathtubs, and, worse, flush toilets. Overflowing privy vaults and cesspools across urban America made removing wastewater crucial, and after 1850 cities began constructing wastewater systems. Planners and engineers believed that disease came from filth and that running water purified itself, so they constructed massive combined waste and storm sewerage systems to carry sewage away from cities and deposit it in running waterways before it could decay. Unfortunately, the raw sewage polluted water supplies, and it was thanks only to bacteriological research and, in the 1890s, to chlorination, that water supplies polluted by raw sewage could be made potable. With large, inflexible systems in place, dealing with ever-widening regional pollution and industrial waste disposal was left to twentieth-century planners and engineers.

Conclusion

In the course of 100 years, the Industrial Revolution transformed every aspect of American life. A thinly populated agrarian society evolved into a bustling country of vibrant urban-industrial centers and expansive agricultural regions linked together by vast transportation and communication networks. Equally dramatic was the United States' population growth, from 5.2 to 76 million people, a larger and larger proportion of which, even as the continent was put to the plow, flocked away from farms and into the cities to work in factories and commercial enterprises. With their exodus came a loss of independence that characterized the self-sufficient farmer and, for many independent craftspeople, the satisfactions of their trade. Thus, the social environment changed as these large groups, which had a great sense of personal worth and autonomy, were slowly diminished.

Nevertheless, almost from the start of the nineteenth century fewer and fewer Americans agonized over what industrialization might do to national life. Victory in the War of 1812 guaranteed the existence of the Republic. Afterwards the attitude of Americans who had earlier wanted to keep America's way of life simple and largely agrarian so as to keep the ordinary citizenry virtuous and independent gave way to something new: a rising intoxication with the possibilities that a swiftly developing industrial economy could fulfill dreams and bring a more abundant life for every individual. "Indeed," writes American historian Kelley (1990, p. 187), "new productivity, it was believed, could also make people more optimistic, compassionate, and concerned for others."

Technological progress came to be seen as a powerful tool of republicanism, enhancing the idea that America meant prosperity and relative affluence for the common person. An outpouring of speeches, sermons, pamphlets, and books described textile mills as sublime instruments of a better life, locomotives as fabulous creations, and mechanization as the path to cornucopia. These were "the images of the new America," writes Kelley (1990, p. 187). "The most famous orator in the United States in the pre-Civil War generation – who would speak before President Abraham Lincoln (1809–65) at Gettysburg – the Harvard classics professor, leading Whig, and editor of the *North American Review* Edward Everett (1794–1865), spent a lifetime crying the marvels and beauties of industrialism. Republicanism and technology, he insisted, combined to put America, with its unusual freedom of economic life, in a position of promise offered by no other nation in the world."

Even America's great Civil War, which tore the nation asunder, advanced rather than slowed the technological enthusiasm that enraptured Americans. The newly industrializing society seemed to enmesh people happily into dependency on technological networks and systems. While people no doubt felt liberated from the drudgery of isolated rural and small town life, they soon were encased in the regimes of urban-industrial society. In a powerful example of how dependent on technological networks and systems people became, Cowan suggests in her *Social History of American Technology* (1997, pp. 150–51) how a woman might provide food for her two-year-old child in a pre-industrial society compared to an industrial one. In the former, she could gather berries and nuts, dig for shellfish, or "work with a small group of other people to plant corn, tend it, harvest, and shuck it." She could then "dry it, grind it into meal, mix it with water, and bake it into a bread for the child to eat." While providing for her child she would be dependent on cooperating with a few other people, but she would have known them all and could have done all the things they did if "necessity had demanded."

In an industrialized world, however, "an average woman's situation is wholly different." To get bread for one's child, a "woman is dependent on thousands of other people, virtually all of them unknown to her." Grain is grown and harvested on mechanized farms fueled by petroleum-driven machines. It is stored "perhaps for several years" in large commercial granaries, turned into flour at a large corporate mill using electric powered rollers, transported (and transported and transported) by petroleum-fueled conveyances "to a baking factory, where dozens of people (and millions of dollars of machinery)... turn the flour into bread." Then more transport "to a market, where the woman could purchase it" after first driving herself there in a manufactured, petroleum-fueled automobile – "all of this before a slice of it could be spread with peanut butter to the delight of a two-year old."

In a century, Americans had gone from an agrarian society in which self-sufficiency was more or less the norm and people worried over droughts, floods, insect infestations, and good or bad weather to an urban-industrial society in which they were much more dependent on technological systems and networks over which they had no control. Exchanging one sort of dependency for another, perhaps, suggests Cowan (1997, p. 151): "nature for technology." One cannot help but wonder if this is what the 23 centenarians who so fascinated Henry Pratt Fairchild might have thought about the remarkable technological revolution that America underwent during the nineteenth century.

BIBLIOGRAPHY

Ambrose, Stephen E. *Undaunted Courage: Meriwether Lewis, Thomas Jefferson, and the Opening of the American West* (New York: Simon & Schuster, 1996).

Appleby, Joyce. *Inheriting the Revolution: The First Generation of Americans* (Cambridge: Harvard University Press, 2000).

Cooper, Carolyn C. *Shaping Invention: Thomas Blanchard's Machinery and Patent Management in Nineteenth Century America* (New York: Columbia University Press, 1991).

Cowan, Ruth Schwartz. *A Social History of American Technology* (New York: Oxford University Press, 1997).

Cronon, William. *Nature's Metropolis: Chicago and the Great West* (New York: W.W. Norton, 1991).

Fairchild, Henry Pratt. *The Prodigal Century* (New York: Philosophical Library, 1950).

Hindle, Brooke. *Emulation and Invention* (New York: New York University Press, 1981).

Hindle, Brooke and Steven Lubar. *Engines of Change: The American Industrial Revolution, 1790–1860* (Washington, DC: Smithsonian Institution Press, 1986).

Hounshell, David A. *From the American System to Mass Production, 1800–1932: The Development of Manufacturing Technology in the United States* (Baltimore: Johns Hopkins University Press, 1984).

Hughes, Thomas P. *Networks of Power: Electrification in Western Society, 1880–1930* (Baltimore: Johns Hopkins University Press, 1983).

Kasson, John F. *Civilizing the Machine: Technology and Republican Values in America, 1776–1900* (New York: Grossman Publishers, 1976).

Kelley, Robert. *The Shaping of the American Past*, vol. I, 5th edn (Englewood Cliffs, NJ: Prentice-Hall, 1990).

Lubar, Steven. *InfoCulture: The Smithsonian Book of Information Age Inventions* (Washington, DC: Smithsonian Institution Press, 1993).

Marvin, Carolyn. *When Old Technologies Were New: Thinking About Communications in the Late Nineteenth Century* (New York: Oxford University Press, 1988).

Marx, Leo. *The Machine in the Garden: Technology and the Pastoral Ideal in America* (New York: Oxford University Press, 1964).

Mayr, Otto and Robert C. Post, eds. *Yankee Enterprise: The Rise of the American System of Manufactures* (Washington, DC: Smithsonian Institution Press, 1981).

Melosi, Martin. *The Sanitary City: Urban Infrastructure in America from Colonial Times to the Present* (Baltimore: Johns Hopkins University Press, 2000).

Misa, Thomas J. *A Nation of Steel: The Making of Modern America* (Baltimore: Johns Hopkins University Press, 1995).

Morrison, Elting E. *From Know-how to Nowhere: The Development of American Technology* (New York: Basic Books, 1974).

Mumford, Lewis. "Authoritarian and democratic technics," *Technology and Culture*, 5 (January 1964): 1–8.

Nye, David. *American Technological Sublime* (Cambridge: MIT Press, 1994).

Pursell, Carroll. *The Machine in America: A Social History of Technology* (Baltimore: Johns Hopkins University Press, 1995).

Rosenberg, Nathan, ed. *The American System of Manufactures* (Edinburgh: Edinburgh University Press, 1969).

Sheriff, Carol. *The Artificial River: The Erie Canal and the Paradox of Progress, 1817–1862* (New York: Hill and Wang, 1996).

Smith, Merritt Roe. *Harpers Ferry Armory and the New Technology: The Challenge of Change* (Ithaca, NY: Cornell University Press, 1977).

Tarr, Joel A. *The Search for the Ultimate Sink: Urban Pollution in Historical Perspective* (Akron, OH: The University of Akron Press, 1996).

Twain, Mark. *A Connecticut Yankee in King Arthur's Court* (New York: Signet, 1963 [1889]).

Williams, James C. *Energy and the Making of Modern California* (Akron, OH: The University of Akron Press, 1997).

Wosk, Julie. *Breaking Frame: Technology and the Visual Arts in the Nineteenth Century* (New Brunswick, NJ: Rutgers University Press, 1992).

PART II

SITES OF PRODUCTION

CHAPTER THREE

The Technology of Production

CARROLL PURSELL

Save for the recent tendency to equate the word "technology" with microchips, and the gadgets (computers, palm pilots, mobile phones) that they serve, the word perhaps most readily calls to mind the great machines and factories that, for well over a century, have flooded the world with the capital and consumer goods that fill our lives. The Industrial Revolution, though accompanied by a Transportation Revolution of canals, turnpikes and railroads, most powerfully conjures up William Blake's "dark satanic mills," powered first by water but then by great steam engines and always filled with powerful, noisy, untiring, and uncaring machines. These technologies of production, and the way they have been organized into mills and factories, mines, shipyards, and construction sites, are among the most studied parts of the history of technology.

The reason is only partly that they appear to be the source of all the rest of the technologies that surround us, and that their very scale has, since the late eighteenth century, conjured up spectacles that suggest the sublime. It is also because production seems the very essence of technology: profoundly active, public, and progressive – and as such, deeply masculine. If the polar opposite of production is consumption, which is thought of as passive, private, and somehow circular rather than straight ahead, that makes it also feminine and somehow less worthy of serious historical attention. The fact is, of course, that production entails a vast amount of consumption, and out of consumption comes important productions. The malleability of these terms was dramatically, and somewhat comically, highlighted by the suggestion during the administration of George W. Bush that, in the face of disappearing manufacturing jobs, the making of hamburgers at fast food establishments should be reclassified as manufacturing since hamburgers were, undoubtedly, "made."

Over the years since the beginnings of the Industrial Revolution, production has become increasingly carried on by powered machinery, often incorporating the skills which were once the sole possession of experienced workers. This historical process is sometimes thought of as part of "industrialization," a transformation which can be seen outside the factory in the areas of agriculture, construction, and similar productive activities. In all of these areas, however, it was seldom true that new machines and processes entirely displaced the old. Instead, as in other areas of technological change, the new joined the old as part of a menu of available practices. Down to today, mass production coexists with newer forms such as lean production, but also with older forms such as custom and batch production. Better methods may tend to drive out older ones, but no one method is always "best" for all purposes.

Traditional methods of production, what were often called "European" by American producers in the nineteenth century, typically involved skilled artisans using hand tools and producing items one at a time. Here and there, by the end of the eighteenth century, people like Honore Blanc in France and Christopher Polhem in Sweden had made some progress in producing firearms or clocks from uniform and perhaps even interchangeable parts, and British shops were turning out blocks for the Royal Navy in large numbers from nearly identical components. Not until this technique was applied in the United States, however, did it find perfection and wide acceptance.

Eli Whitney has been popularly given credit for the innovation of "interchangeable parts," but careful research has shown this to be a misattribution. When he received his contract for 10,000 muskets in 1798 he had no factory, no machinery, no workers, no experience, and no notion of how to go about making guns. He finally delivered the last of his muskets, 9 years late, and recent tests have shown that their parts were in fact not interchangeable. Despite vague references to "machinery moved by water," there is no evidence of what might have been novel about his production methods.

As it turns out, the technique of assembling firearms from interchangeable parts produced in large numbers by machines came to be known as "Armory practice" and was developed, in fact, through the efforts of the federal Ordnance Bureau working with the national armories. The Springfield arsenal, for example, by 1799 was using machines that were said to dramatically cut the time needed to make a musket. In 1811, John Hall took out a patent for the production of guns made up of interchangeable parts and by 1817 he was installing his machines in the Federal arsenal at Harper's Ferry, Virginia. An official commission visiting the facility 10 years later claimed that his work there was unique and far advanced. Such machines as Thomas Blanchard's copying lathe, which used a model gun stock as a pattern to produce any number of others, was typical and its principles can still be found in key-making machines at local hardware stores.

By the mid-nineteenth century, this so-called Armory practice, the assembly of devices from uniform (if not always quite identical) parts made by single-purpose machine tools, had spread far beyond the manufacture of small arms. Indeed, so much had it established itself in areas of civilian production that it was universally termed the "American" system of manufacture. Many manufacturers continued to reply on what came to be called the "European" method, that is the reworking of each part, usually through hand filing, to fit its neighbor, but by the end of the century such diverse products as clocks, typewriters, bicycles, sewing machines, and even reapers were manufactured by firms using some or many of the elements of Armory practice.

This spread came about in several ways. First, the Ordnance Department contracted with private shops to produce weapons with interchangeable parts, thus forcing them to adopt Armory practice. Second, and perhaps most important, the makers of machine tools, who produced for a wide range of industries, spread the word of production innovations in one industry to firms in another. The economic historian Nathan Rosenberg

(1962) has identified the machine tool industry as the critical link in this process of diffusion. And finally, individual workers moved not only from one show to another, but from industry to industry. No better example of this can be found than in the person of Henry M. Leland, who worked at the Springfield Armory, moved to the shops of the machine tool maker Brown & Sharp (which also manufactured Willcox & Gibbs sewing machines), then went on to establish both the Cadillac Motor Car Co. and the Lincoln Motor Co.

However, the spread of the American System was hardly a triumphant march from pre-modern to modern production. Certain firms, like Singer for sewing machines and McCormick for reapers, dominated their fields through aggressive and innovative advertising and sales and brand manipulation rather than progressive technical change. Hand-fitting lives on even today and even in such bastions of mass production as the Detroit automobile industry. The increased production, lower unit costs and workforce deskilling and discipline made possible by the American System, however, proved a powerful incentive for its adoption.

In most areas of industry, including those which did not turn out devices assembled from many small parts, the shift from hand to machine production was rapid in the nineteenth century. An 1898 report from the US Commissioner of Labor declared flatly that "scarcely an article now in use is the exact counterpart of the one serving the same purpose fifty years ago." The same held for the way in which the articles were made, so radical was the shift from hand to machine production. It was simple enough to find out about current methods, but to discover how things were made previously, investigators had to look away from the centers of production and into the past. That is, the old hand methods persisted in the periphery away from the metropole and their knowledge among the elderly workers who had been displaced or retired.

In some cases these changes simply made use of old technologies. Ten men, it was reported, now took only 10 hours to unload a boatload of coal, whereas previously it had taken 12 men a total of 120 hours. At that time the coal was loaded into baskets and carried to wheelbarrows. Under the new method an endless belt with buckets attached was lowered into the hold of the boat and the coal was scooped up to "a receiving bin, where automatic cars were stationed to receive and carry it to the storage bins." The endless chain of buckets was, of course, Oliver Evans' old flourmill device from a century before. Most cases of change involved the fabrication of items like mens' boots, where division of labor, specialized shops, and machines reorganized work and made it more productive.

Two critical areas of fabrication took hold first in the manufacture of bicycles, and then of automobiles. One was the shaping of sheet metal through stamping and punch pressing which produced fenders, pedals, and a good number of other bicycle parts. The second was the employment of electric resistance welding to join the seams of individual parts as well as connect parts into larger components. Joined with Armory practice, these two production techniques carried over into the nascent automobile industry.

It was, of course, Henry Ford who, by ardently adopting both Armory practice and the techniques of stamping and welding, and then critically adding to these the moving assembly line, moved American manufacturing into the age of mass production. In the article on "Mass Production" which appeared in the 1925 edition of the *Encyclopedia Brittanica* over Ford's name (though not written by him), the new manufacturing principle was famously defined as "the focusing upon a manufacturing project of the principles of power, accuracy, economy, system, continuity, speed, and repetition. To interpret these principles," he continued, "through studies of operation and machine development and their coordination, is the conspicuous task of management. The normal result," he concluded, "is a productive organization that delivers in continuous quantities a useful commodity of standard material, workmanship and design at minimum cost."

Ford's goal, unlike that of earlier industrialists, was to produce the largest number of units at the lowest possible cost and to constantly lower the retail price as the costs dropped: in other words, profits through volume production rather than high prices. Toward this end he pushed his engineers to adopt dedicated machine tools along with the jigs and fixtures which would make possible uniformity of parts. He also contracted with a firm that was a leading supplier of stamped sheet steel for the bicycle industry. And finally, of course, in 1913 he introduced the moving assembly line, the last key element of mass production.

Ford claimed that his inspiration for the assembly line was the "disassembly line" found in the giant slaughterhouses of Chicago and Cincinnati. There, overhead chains moved animal carcasses through the plant as heads, legs, viscera and other parts were removed. Workers stood immobile using one tool to perform one task, over and over. On April 1, 1913, Ford's first moving assembly line was put into operation making magnetos. Within a year-and-a-half the experiment, having proven wonderfully effective, was used throughout the plant including in the iconic case of final assembly. Production of Model Ts stood at 82,388 the year before the assembly line, rose to 189,088 in 1913, reached 230,788 in 1914 and two million in 1923. Production gains of 50 percent to a factor of ten were experienced as soon as assembly lines were installed in the various sections of the plant.

Nicely compatible with Fordism was Taylorism, called by its originator Scientific Management. Frederick Winslow Taylor was born to a wealthy family in 1856 and had an engineering degree from Stevens Institute of Technology. While working for the Bethlehem Steel Co. from 1898 to 1901 he perfected his system of fitting workers to machines in what he considered the most efficient ways. It was his observation (reinforced, no doubt, by his class prejudice) that labor worked well below its productive potential. There were, he said, in each occupation many different tools in use and many ways in which things were done by individual workers. (The contemporary observer might see something like this still at a construction site, a service station, or a college classroom!) Using a stopwatch and special forms, Taylor insisted that he could calculate on purely scientific grounds, the "one best tool" for each job and the "one best way" of accomplishing it.

Scientific Management went far beyond the Armory Practice of designing skill into machines so that semi-skilled workers could operate them. Machinery was redesigned (later ergonomics became a part of this effort) and machines were rearranged to save steps, time, and effort. Critically, the layer of managers between owners and workers was greatly expanded and workers were retrained to use the new methods and tools. From Taylor's classic statement of his system, *The Principles of Scientific Management* (1911), came the story of Schmidt the pig-iron handler at Bethlehem. Workers were observed to be carrying and stacking 12½ tons of pig iron per day. Using his "scientific" methods Taylor calculated that they should be able to handle 47–8 tons per day. Schmidt was singled out for the experiment, taught to carry the iron "scientifically," and given a raise from $1.15 to $1.85 a day. The experiment was a success, and Schmidt carried the extra tons.

Taylor's rigid belief in the "one best way" extended beyond specific jobs to industry as a whole and, indeed, to all of American society. He insisted on having his method followed down to the last letter but, of course, had no way to enforce it. His many followers and admirers introduced changes of which he did not approve, but which, taken together, gave "the efficiency movement" a wide currency in manufacturing. Frank Gilbreth, for example, gained fame by breaking human movements down into units he called *therbligs*, after himself. He took motion pictures of workers performing set tasks, with a small clock in the corner of the frame, then ran them slowly back to count and measured the therbligs. He gained even greater fame after his death as the Father in the best-selling book *Cheaper by the Dozen*. His widow, Lillian Gilbreth, tried to carry on his consultancy but was relegated to being the advocate of the "Kitchen Efficient," an attempt to make the home more efficient of time and effort for housewives.

What Thomas P. Hughes (1989) has memorably termed "The Second Discovery of America" was triggered, to no small degree, by the "miracle" of mass production and its ability to transform the nation into what another historian long ago called a "people of plenty." The new Soviet Union, searching for a way to catapult Russia into the modern world, seized upon "Taylorismus+Fordismus" as a way of emulating American production without recourse to capitalism. A defeated Germany saw the combination as an equally non-ideological way of rebuilding that country without falling into the arms of either the Right or the Left. While American manufacturers of everything from houses to ships, and from furniture to textiles tried to take practical steps to emulate the great automobile plants, many people, both here and abroad who had no connection to mills or factories saw Fordism and Taylorism as metaphors as well as blueprints.

But the American experience was, according to Hughes, not simply a "second industrial revolution" but a "cultural transformation." For much of the rest of the world America seemed not just rich and prosperous but to have its own cultural modernism. High modernism, of course, was European: Stravinsky, Picasso, and the Bauhaus school of architects and designers. But the United States had its photographs by Alfred Stieglitz, its paintings by Charles Sheeler, and above all its jazz. Indeed Joel Dinerstein (2003) has put forward the claim that it was African-American cultural forms between the wars, particularly in music and dance, that first captured the rhythms and logic of a machine civilization and interpreted it for the nation as a whole.

Even as mass production was being touted around the world, as well as around the nation, as a modern miracle of efficiency, there was a persistence of older and still viable forms. As a case in point, historian David Hounshell (1984) has observed that "there was no Henry Ford in the furniture industry." Even before River Rouge there were a handful of furniture factories which used something very like classical mass production. With Ford's trumpeted success, mass production became the ideal for furniture makers, as it did for most other manufacturers. And finally, with the advent of "modern" furniture designs, new materials such as aluminum, plastics, and laminated wood made innovative fabrication techniques not only possible but, on occasion, necessary. Nonetheless, Philip Scranton's phrase "flexible," or "batch/custom" production better describes how these manufacturers worked.

Machines to shape wood were among America's most successful innovations of the nineteenth century and using them, some of which were made in-house for very specific purposes, the Singer Manufacturing Co. was turning out two million sewing machine cabinets a year from one plant. Singer, however, had the advantage of being its own market and could therefore specialize to a degree denied to other furniture makers. The industry as a whole turned out tables and chairs, stools and desks, bookcases, hat racks, and a myriad of other pieces. To further complicate matters, each type, chairs for example, came in any number of styles and had special uses: desk chairs, rocking chairs, high chairs, and so forth. And finally, each of these were made in a wide variety of styles from Louis XIV to Craftsman. In 1929, one North Carolina firm had 1,200 designs in production, "most of which are changing rapidly" according to its president. This was a far cry from Henry Ford's Model T which the customer could have in any color so long as it was black.

Probably no two firms worked to the same plan, but overall the industry gave evidence of something very like what, in the late twentieth century, was called "lean" production. A list of innovations made use of included, power hand tools, lines of rollers along which pieces moved as they were worked on, including at some points turntables so that workers could easily get at all sides, sloping floors and overhead cranes to move materials, machine tools grouped by function. Strict inventory control, worker "quality" discussion groups, and improved packaging for rail shipment were all introduced. It did not look quite like River Rouge, but neither was the industry in any way primitive nor backward.

The interwar triumph of machine production, in the popular mind closely identified with Fordism and Taylorism, was celebrated for its efficiency: its apparent ability to produce ever-larger quantities of consumer goods for the masses with ever-fewer workers. The process was said to be "labor saving." For a century it had been claimed that only onerous and unpleasant labor was "saved," and that any resulting unemployment was bound to be only temporary: in a common comparison, buggy-whip makers might be out of work but a vastly larger army of auto workers had found new employment. The nation congratulated itself that unlike in Europe, workers disemployed in one trade moved freely to others and did not resort to Luddite spasms of machine-breaking.

With the coming of the Great Depression in 1929, however, unemployment became the signal feature of the American economy. A 1934 study, *Mechanization in Industry*, reported that between 1899 and 1929, installed horsepower per American industrial workers had increased 130.3 percent. In an economy which tied the ability of most Americans to consume with wages from jobs, growing unemployment created both personal tragedies and public crisis. As historian Amy Bix has written, "the displacement [of labor] issue underlined how much the rapid evolution of production machinery had come to determine prospects for both individuals and the nation" (Bix p. 9). In the end, only the re-employment of workers in defense industries and the siphoning off of an increasing number of men into the armed services returned the economy to healthy growth.

With the coming of war to Europe in the Fall of 1939, the crisis of American production was suddenly measured in terms of too little rather than too much. World War I had uncovered a fundamental disconnect between the way the economy was organized (by products like steel or textiles) and the way the military organized itself (by functions like coast defense or transport). Between the wars, industrial and military personnel worked together to plan mobilization scenarios, often with military officers being assigned to particular corporations. With the build up for defense in World War II, such cooperation, if not the details of the particular plans, proved valuable. During the conflict the government spent $315.8 billion with contracts being let with 18,539 business firms. Significantly, two-thirds of those contracts went to just 100 firms and of those, 30 received almost half. Among the top 20 contractors there were four automobile manufacturers, nine airplane manufacturers, two steel companies, Henry J. Kaiser Co., the Sperry Corp., and such household names as du Pont, General Electric (GE), and AT&T. To orchestrate this spending, a War Production Board was set up in 1942 and by the beginning of that year, 255 dollar-a-year men (who served without compensation) had moved from business into the Office of Production Management.

Manufacturing production was clearly a key to the successful prosecution of the war, and by and large that meant quickly building more factories, converting old ones to weapons production, buying new machines, recruiting and training more workers, and dividing up scarce raw materials such as coal and aluminum. Technological improvements in production on the line were minimal with classic mass production techniques bearing the brunt of the load. Nevertheless, the notion that surely American inventive genius could find parts of the system to improve led to the establishment of an Office of Production Research and Development in 1942. The mission of the new Office was to serve as the industrial research arm of the War Production Board, but it never really settled into its work, spending only $13 million during the entire war. In part, this was because neither private corporations nor the scientific establishment which served them were enthusiastic about tax-supported research and development which had the potential of making obsolete proprietary machines and methods which, in any case, represented an enormous fixed investment. Significant exceptions to this record were the Office's support for penicillin and alcohol production.

One innovation that aided wartime production, and became a factor in the postwar rise of Japanese manufacturing to world prominence, was Statistical Quality Control (SQC). This technique had been steadily developing in the United States and Great Britain during the interwar years, and was commonly understood to be the application of statistical methods to guarantee that production measured up to standards. Under the regime of Armory Practice, jigs, gauges, and fixtures were used to not only produce but measure finished products. They were an absolutely necessary part of the technological system that produced uniformity of parts and if not rigorously applied, manufacturers ran the risk of producing vast numbers of defective parts. The larger the number of items produced, of course, the more time-consuming and onerous this constant checking became. A statistical method of checking for quality was obviously to be preferred, but the precise technique had to be carefully developed and taught to (often female) inspectors.

W. Edwards Deming was arguably the most famous of the SQC advocates, especially as a result of his carrying the technique to Japan, beginning in 1947. Another pioneer was Lowell Mellen, a management consultant with only a high school education who worked on production problems during the war and soon thereafter formed a company called Training Within Industry Inc. which pioneered such management techniques as written suggestions from workers and plans of "continuous improvement," which approached the famous "quality circles" of Japanese workers. A third American, who carried his techniques to Japan after the war, was Joseph Juran, who had worked to re-orient quality control away from a rigid dependence upon statistics toward a program based more on winning workers' involvement and cooperation.

In World War II, as in World War I, the federal government sought to quickly increase the pace of building both cargo and warships. There were 19 private shipyards in the country before the war and with government aid, 21 emergency shipyards were added. Among these were those of Henry J. Kaiser, a construction contractor whose firm was one of the Six Companies to build Hoover Dam. Kaiser had partnered with the construction firm Bechtel on that project and in 1938 they began to think in terms of taking advantage of what looked like a reviving shipbuilding industry. Most shipyards were on the East Coast and Kaiser had no knowledge of the industry, but his employees got the job of building a new yard for the recently organized Seattle-Tacoma Shipbuilding Co. in Washington State.

In 1939 the Six Companies joined with the new Washington firm to win a $9 million contract from the Maritime Commission to build five C-1 cargo ships. As Mark Foster has written, "Six Companies people constructed the shipways, watched the shipbuilding – and learned" (Foster 1989, p. 69). In December, 1940, Kaiser became directly involved in shipbuilding with a shared contract to provide ships for Britain. Then in January, 1941, a new American program to build Liberty Ships was announced. In December the first dirt had been moved for a new yard in Richmond, California, and four months later the first keel was laid down. In January, construction began on a new shipyard at Portland, Oregon as well. Construction on both yards began well before blueprints were ready, since capacity was a magnet for further orders.

Over the next 4 years, these Kaiser shipyards employed nearly 200,000 workers. The fact that most of them had no experience in shipbuilding, and many had never worked in manufacturing before, suggested that production would be organized and carried out differently in these yards. This ignorance, of course, was reflected at the highest levels where Kaiser and his closest associates were also learning as they went.

Partners who did know the traditional way to build ships were horrified and soon dropped out. This traditional way was to "lay a ship's keel, then send hundreds of workers swarming into cramped quarters to perform many different functions" (Foster 1989, p. 83).

In part to eliminate this bottleneck British and some East Coast yards had experimented with subassemblies during the 1930s. When Kaiser seized upon this innovation they were able to apply it to full advantage because, building their yards from scratch, they had plenty of room to lay out appropriate areas for subassemblies as well as ways for laying the keel to which the former would be eventually brought. The use of subassemblies was a critical part of Kaiser's ability to produce ships quickly (one was put together out of subassemblies in 4 days, 15 hours and 26 minutes), but other innovations, more obviously their own, helped as well.

One of Kaiser's close associates had even gone to visit a Ford assembly plant in late 1940. While obvious features of mass production, like the moving assembly line, were clearly inappropriate for shipbuilding, other parts were adapted. Workers, for example, while unionized, could be taught new quicker techniques in a shorter time than was taken by the older East Coast yards. Also, Kaiser realized that for most purposes, welding was as good as riveting, and easier to teach to the thousands of women who flocked to his yards. It was also less physically demanding, especially since work to be done was positioned so that the welders looked down rather than up at the joint to be sealed. A total of 747 vessels were launched during the war at that first Richmond shipyard alone. If Kaiser had not quite reproduced the mass production capacity of a Ford plant, he had revolutionized shipbuilding by borrowing heavily from that model.

The new construction techniques pioneered by Kaiser in shipbuilding extended also to the cities he had to construct adjacent to them for housing shipyard workers. Army cantonments had been rapidly built in World War I, and again in World War II, but cities like Kaiser's Vanport City outside Portland, Oregon were privately built for civilian workers. Because of the very low vacancy rate for housing in the Portland area, the Maritime Commission authorized Kaiser to build a city of 6,000 units along the Columbia River. Land clearing began three days later and within four months the first 700 buildings were ready for occupancy. Nine months after construction began, Vanport contained 19,000 people and at least 40,000 were anticipated. The construction work went fast, but the social innovations overshadowed any technological ones. With a large proportion of women, many without partners, as residents, free bus service, child care, community kitchens where hot meals could be picked up and taken home, and similar amenities provided planned accommodation to the needs of the shipyard workers.

The building of large number of homes, very quickly, using innovative "manufacturing" techniques was made famous by William Levitt in the years after the war. In breathless prose, the July 3, 1950 issue of *Time* magazine described the transformation of 1,200 acres of potato fields on Long Island into Levittown, a city of 40,000 souls occupying 10,600 homes. It was not only their rapid building but the means that excited *Time*. They described trucks arriving with pallets of lumber, pipes, bricks, shingles, and copper tubing, dropped every 100 feet. Ditching machines with toothed buckets on an endless chain digging a 4-foot trench around a 25 ft×32 ft rectangle every 13 minutes. All this was followed by building crews of specialists, completing a house somewhere in the development every 15 minutes. Levitt and Sons was becoming, according to *Time*, "the General Motors" of housing (*Time* quoted in Rome, p. 16).

The analogy to mass production was obvious. Of those specialized crew of workers, each was responsible for one of the 26 tasks into which the building had been divided. Since they typically dealt with prefabricated subassemblies many traditional carpenter skills were not needed, and because the workers were nonunion they could be equipped with labor-saving tools like spray-paint guns. And Levitt went further. Like Ford, he undertook vertical integration, operating his own lumber mill and nail-making plant.

Across the United States, other developers were building ever more extensive suburban cities using production methods suggested by both the auto industry and the wartime shipyards. In 1949 three developers bought 3,500 acres of farmland between Los Angeles and Long Beach, and between 1950 and 1952, a hundred houses each workday, five hundred in a week, were put up. Construction crews were made up of 35-man teams, each team subdivided by task. In 1951 more than 4,000 workers were hired, mostly veterans unskilled in the building trades. Prewar subdivisions typically had five houses per acre; this one had eight. It took 15 minutes to dig a foundation and in just one hundred-day period crews poured concrete into 2,113 of them. And so it went down the line: one crew finishing its work, to be replaced immediately (or as soon as the cement, plaster or paint dried) by another. The workers may have moved from one unit to the next rather than standing in a line for the work to come to them, but it was an assembly line nonetheless.

Neither the shipyard cities nor the large suburban developments like Levittown and Lakewood, whatever novel building techniques were used in their construction, were thought of as being "manufactured." That term was reserved for "mobile homes," essentially self-contained trailers which made up a full quarter of the homes outside of cities built during the 1970s.

The postwar years were, by any account, glory days for Detroit. The massive contracts of World War II were followed by a huge pent-up demand from Americans for cars. The first models after the end of war production tended to be very like their last prewar counterparts, but soon led by General Motors, where former Hollywood designer Earl Harley revolutionized auto styling, the cars became flamboyant symbols of the 1950s. The 1946 Cadillac was the first in a long line of cars to sport tail fins which, like the "spoilers" of later decades, defined their era. Cars were bigger, heavier, more powerful, more flagrantly "styled" than ever before. By 1970 three of the biggest corporations in the country were automobile manufacturers (including General Motors at number one), and three others were petroleum companies which, to a large degree, relied upon and also made them viable.

It had been a great many years since Detroit had deserved any reputation for technological innovation. Since the adoption of mass production, the auto industry had excelled mainly in corporate management and product design rather than improvements in the technology either of automobiles or their production. In 1946, however, D.S. Harder, Vice President of Manufacturing for the Ford Motor Company coined the word "automation" to describe the method of fabrication in its new engine production plant in Cleveland, Ohio. The November 1946 issue of *Fortune* carried a story on the "Automatic Factory" and in 1948 the term was picked up by the magazine *American Machinist*, which defined it as "the art of applying mechanical devices to manipulate work pieces into and out of equipment, turn parts between operations, remove scrap, and to perform these tasks in timed sequence with the production equipment so that the line can be put wholly or partially under pushbutton control at strategic stations" (October, 1948).

The three components of automation were first, automatic machines to perform the production, second, devices to pass the work pieces from one automatic machine to another, and third, some sort of control mechanism (with feedback capacities) to control the whole series of operations. Of these, automatic machines went back at least as far as Oliver Evans' flour mill and transfer machines had been used by the Waltham Watch Co. as early as 1888. Even control devices with feedback were not new, as with the case of James Watt's steam engine governor. What made this new "automation" so powerful was the recent availability of computers to control the process. In 1955 the first computer to be used in production was installed in a chemical plant to control distillation, an experiment sponsored by the Air Force. In 1957–8 several electric power plants and oil refineries installed computers to keep track of and regulate production. By 1966 some 15–20,000 computers were in use by private industry, perhaps most for data processing of one kind or another but increasingly for production as well.

One dramatic episode has been chronicled by the historian David F. Noble. In this case, GE engineers developed "record-playback" machine tools, with which a master machinist would cut a work piece to specifications while his movement were recorded on punched tape. That tape could then be played back in another machine tool producing an identical part. This process was soon rejected in favor of another process called "numerical control" or N/C. In this, the blueprint was translated directly into mathematical instructions which were then stored on the tape, the machine tool thus being programmed without the need for the master machinist at all. GE, the Massachusetts Institute of Technology (MIT), and the Air Force all worked on this project which was driven, as Noble (1984) convincingly argues, not so much by technical superiority as the desire to replace labor, and especially expensive, activist, unionized labor, as much as possible.

N/C machine tools became standard in manufacturing and the "automatic factory," with its dream of eliminating workers completely, became a popular sensation. The 1946 Ford engine plant had actually employed 4,500 workers, but the question remained, what would the world look like if the dreams of engineers and corporate managers actually came true? One answer was given by Kurt Vonnegut, Jr, who was a copywriter at GE at the time of its "record-playback" experiments. His novel, *Player Piano*, was published in 1952, describing a United States where the government and the corporation were indistinguishable, the important decisions were made by a giant computer, and except for a cadre of elite engineers, no one had real work to do.

Such grim (though in this case also darkly comic) scenarios enjoyed a vogue for a few years, but then largely died out. The most powerful labor unions, like the auto workers and the West Coast longshoremen, quickly negotiated contracts which guaranteed them "a piece of the machine." In other industries, payrolls did not so much shrink as fail to expand as quickly as business would have otherwise warranted. And finally, industry spokespersons argued, apparently convincingly, that automation was, after all, only the latest form of a long-term process of technological improvement and need not be feared as something new and fatal to employment.

Closely related to automation, robots also began to appear in American factories. The popular images of the robot, and even the word itself, came from the Czech play *R.U.R.* by The Brothers Capek first staged in the 1920s. These stage robots were originally designed to be factory workers, but by the time of the action they could also be purchased for office work and be used as soldiers. Although cunningly designed to look like people, they were simply production machines. One of the managers of Rossum's Universal Robots asks the visiting Helena Glory "What sort of worker do you think is the best from a practical point of view?" In her naiveté Helena answers, "The best? Perhaps the one who is most honest and hard-working." It is of course the wrong answer: "No," replies Domaine, the General Manager, "the cheapest. The one whose needs are the smallest" (Capek 1961, p. 9).

The actual robots that began to appear on factory floors by 1970 did not look like human beings, but were designed and programmed to duplicate human dexterity in certain productive processes using sensors, servo-mechanisms, and computer chips. In that year General Motors bought over 60 "one-arm, hydraulically and pneumatically operated robots for assembly line chores" (*Santa Barbara News-Press*, 17 February 1970). Ford and Chrysler had also invested in such machines, which were used initially mostly for spot welding. By the mid-1970s an estimated 6,000 robots were at work doing such other jobs as heavy lifting, welding, die-casting, and paint-spraying. Union opposition was muted, at least in part, according to business leaders because robots took over only dangerous, dirty jobs which allowed workers to move up into "more rewarding jobs rather than putting them out on the street." At the same time, sellers reminded buyers that "the robot never gets a cold, doesn't mind heat and dust, seldom experiences an inefficient Blue Monday and never lifts its arm to carry a picket sign."

All of these innovations in production technology worked to modify the particulars of the mass production regime, but did little to reform its general nature. The greatest challenge, it turned out, came from Japanese automakers. In 1950 Eiji Toyoda, a young engineer and member of one of Japan's leading manufacturing families, visited Ford's River Rouge plant just as his uncle had done in 1929. The family had been making cars since 1937 but between then and 1950 had produced only 2,685, compared with the Rouge's normal production of 7,000 a day at mid-century. Toyoda returned to Japan convinced that he could not only copy but improve upon Ford's classic mass production. His new plan was called the Toyota Productive System, or more familiarly, "lean production."

Virtually every aspect of mass production was modified. Cars, for example, were made from many pieces of sheet metal, stamped into shape over dies in great presses, then welded together. Unless one had a different press for each part, dies had to be changed, a difficult and time-consuming process undertaken in American plants as seldom as possible and then only using specialized workers. Toyoda, using rollers to move the heavy dies and simple adjusting mechanisms, was able to use regular production workers to change dies every few hours. Each change took three minutes, as compared with a day in an American plant. The frequent changing of dies cut the need for large inventories and revealed any mistakes quickly before they were embodied in thousands of cars.

Workers were trained to be both flexible and responsible. In an American plant, for example, "moving the metal" was the highest goal with the result that defects were reproduced by the thousands requiring some plants to devote 20 percent of their floor space and a quarter of their workers to "rework," that is, fixing the mistakes. At Toyota each worker on the line had the ability and responsibility to stop production when a defect was found so that the cause could be immediately corrected. Other innovations involved a closer cooperation with makers of subassemblies and the famous "just in time" delivery of parts (called *kanban*) so as to reduce inventories. Also consumer preferences are closely monitored and car models stay in production for only 4 years, as compared with ten in the US.

Some of the aspects of lean production were already in use in the United States, especially in such batch industries as the furniture, and others seemed so intertwined with Japanese culture that a transfer to this country appeared unthinkable. Yet, as the production of cars became globalized, Japanese plants were built in the United States and some American firms entered into partnership with Japanese manufacturers to produce cars here. The Saturn was introduced and manufactured at a plant far from Detroit where at least some elements of lean production could be undertaken. The greatest impact, however, was perhaps in quality. Before World War II, Japanese manufactured goods had a reputation in America for being cheap and shoddy. By the end of the twentieth century, at least in the areas of electronics and automobiles, Japanese products were seen as the best. Japanese cars scored much higher in quality and reliability than their Detroit counterparts. The shortcomings of mass production, from worker alienation to defective products, were displayed for all to see.

By the early twenty-first century the health and prognosis for American manufacturing was uncertain. A generation before there had been Utopian talk of entering a "postindustrial" age, but the ideal of an emphasis on consumption rather than production tended to ignore the need for someone, somewhere, to actually make the things to be consumed. Talk of a "service economy" conjured up the old saw that no society could get rich giving each other haircuts. The disappearance of manufacturing jobs became a significant political scandal, 2.8 million manufacturing jobs were lost between early 2001 and the Spring of 2004, but the role of technology in their loss was not at all clear. It seemed reasonable to assume that after almost two centuries of "labor-saving" devices some labor must have been "saved." On the other hand, jobs exported to Mexico or Southeast Asia used machines, many of them quite traditional, like sewing machines. The appointment, in April 2004, of a "manufacturing czar" to help stem the tide of job losses, will, one would hope, lead to a closer look at how, not just where, things get made.

BIBLIOGRAPHY

Bix, Amy Sue. *Inventing Ourselves Out of Jobs: America's Debate Over Technological Unemployment, 1929–1981* (Baltimore: Johns Hopkins University Press, 2000).

Capek, The Brothers, *R.U.R. and The Insect Play* (London: Oxford University Press, 1961).

Dinerstein, Joel. *Swinging the Machine: Modernity, Technology, and African American Culture between the Wars* (Amherst: University of Massachusetts Press, 2003).

Foster, Mark S. *Henry J. Kaiser: Builder in the Modern American West* (Austin: University of Texas Press, 1989).

Holland, Max. *When the Machine Stopped: A Cautionary Tale from Industrial America* (Boston: Harvard Business School Press, 1989).

Hounshell, David A. *From the American System to Mass Production: The Development of Manufacturing Technology in the United States* (Baltimore: Johns Hopkins University Press, 1984).

Hughes, Thomas P. *American Genesis: A Century of Invention and Technological Enthusiasm, 1870–1970* (New York: Viking, 1989).

Juravich, Tom. *Chaos on the Shop Floor: A Worker's View of Quality, Productivity, and Management* (Philadelphia: Temple University Press, 1985).

Licht, Walter. *Industrializing America: The Nineteenth Century* (Baltimore: Johns Hopkins University Press, 1995).

Neushul, Peter. *Science, Technology and the Arsenal of Democracy: Production Research and Development During World War II.* Unpublished doctoral dissertation (History) (Santa Barbara: University of California, 1993).

Noble, David F. *Forces of Production: A Social History of Industrial Automation* (New York: Alfred A. Knopf, 1984).

Pursell, Carroll. *The Machine in the Garden: A Social History of Technology* (Baltimore: Johns Hopkins University Press, 1995).

Rosenberg, Nathan. "Technological change in the machine tool industry, 1840–1910," *Journal of Economic History*, 23 (1962): 414–43.

Scranton, Philip. "Diversity in diversity: flexible production and American industrialization, 1880–1930," *Business History Review*, 65 (Spring 1991): 27–90.

Scranton, Philip. "The politics of production: technology, markets, and the two cultures of American industry," *Science in Context*, 8 (1995): 369–95.

Smith, Merritt Roe. *Harper's Ferry Armory and the New Technology: The Challenge of Change* (Ithaca: Cornell University Press, 1977).

Smith, Merritt Roe. ed. "Army ordnance and the 'American system' of manufacturing, 1815–1861," *Military Enterprise and Technological Change: Perspectives on the American Experience* (Cambridge: MIT Press, 1985): 39–86.

Tulin, Roger. *A Machinist's Semi-Automated Life* (San Pedro: Singlejack Books, 1984).

US Commissioner of Labor. *Thirteenth Annual Report of the Commissioner of Labor, 1898: Hand and Machine Labor*, I. (Washington: GPO, 1899).

Waldie, D.J. *Holy Land: A Suburban Memoir* (New York: St Martin's Press, 1996).

Womack, James P., Daniel T. Jones and Daniel Roos. *The Machine That Changed the World* (New York: Rawson Associates, 1990).

CHAPTER FOUR

Technology and Agriculture in Twentieth-Century America

DEBORAH FITZGERALD

It is a paradox of American agriculture that it has come to represent both a set of homespun values that champion hard work, thrift, honesty, and modesty that many urbanites believe characterize rural life, as well as an extractive, arrogant, at times brutal exploitation of the land for the purpose of short-term production and wealth. On the one hand, for many people, the words "agriculture" and "rural" continue to elicit images characteristic of a pre-industrial landscape, of wholesome farm families, tidy farmhouses nestled among fields of grain and pastures dotted with livestock. For others, however, the realities of livestock confinement systems, farmhouses abandoned by bankrupt farm families, highly processed foods, and the vertical integration of growing and processing seems a more apt picture of what agriculture has become. The numbers tell a remarkable story. In 1940, 23 percent of Americans lived on farms; in 1970, less that 5 percent lived on farms. In 1940, 53 percent of rural people lived on farms, but in 1970 only 18 percent did. In 1945, an average farm was worth $60.51 per acre; in 1990, that price had risen to $850. Between 1945 and 1970, the average farm doubled in size from 195 to 373 acres. And whereas in 1950 one farmer fed 10 people, by the late 1980s a farmer could feed 90. There is simply no question but that agriculture and rural life have been fundamentally transformed, changing everything from how farmers operate to what we eat. Historians and other social scientists are now beginning to piece together not only what happened over the last 100 years, but why changes took the shape that they did (Danbom 1995).

It is also true that, despite the fact that the great bulk of historical writings about twentieth-century agriculture deals with political and economic issues, the most important frame of reference for these changes has been technological and scientific innovation. The arduous work that farm families perform, their isolation from the larger urban culture, and the very thin margin of their prosperity, have combined to make both farmers and agricultural entrepreneurs highly sensitive to any means of decreasing costs or increasing profits. And there has been no shortage of people eager to sell farm families up-to-date things. Hybrid seeds and pedigreed livestock, chemical concoctions such as pesticides, fertilizers, herbicides, and livestock feeds, equipment such as tractors and cultivators, automatic milkers and computers, better roads and silos, larger acreages and drainage systems, electrified fences and houses, indoor plumbing and automobiles – all such things have not only smoothed farm life but also brought farm families deeper into the complex web of modernity, with all the costs and benefits that it entails. Agriculture today is a direct product of the dramatic institutional innovations of the late nineteenth century, and of the continued expansion of scientific, social scientific, and technological research and development through the twentieth century.

To better appreciate the depth and breadth of this transformation, and its essentially scientific and technological character, one must recognize the systematic nature of agricultural technologies. When we think of these technologies, we tend to think of the *things* one finds on farms, such as combines, electric motors, milking machines, tractors, irrigation pivots, and hay balers. However, a farmer with a tractor but no gas, or no credit system for buying the tractor in the first place, does not really have a functioning technology. He has an artifact that he cannot use. Thinking of agricultural technologies as things farm families have is thus a woefully inadequate approach. Instead, we need to focus on what Thomas P. Hughes calls *technological systems*, that is, networks of things, people, regulations, landscapes, forms of expertise and practice, financial arrangements, and so forth, that enable each farm to function within the larger state and national context. In agriculture, important agricultural systems include paved roads, railroads and shipping, electrical grids, plumbing and sewage systems, credit systems, marketing and processing agreements, and so forth. These are the connective tissues of the agricultural body, making it possible and in some cases necessary for farm families to produce certain crops, under certain cropping arrangements, at certain times. The increasing prevalence of these technological systems in twentieth-century agriculture have made the farm both a more pleasant place to work and more vulnerable to financial failure. We will return to this paradox later (Hughes 1983).

Particularly since the farm crisis of the mid-1980s, many historians trying to document and analyze what has happened over the last 100 years have relied upon cultural and social, in addition to economic, analytical styles. The result has been an invigorating expansion of our knowledge of rural and agricultural history, and one can see the beginnings of a robust appreciation for technology and science in those stories. Several new themes have emerged from this. One has centered on the role of the federal government in creating the agricultural research, development, and regulatory system. Another has focused directly upon technological and scientific innovations themselves, not only in the field but in the home and marketplace as well. Here one sees especially clearly the difficulty of separating "things" from "systems"; scholars have found it nearly impossible, and nonsensical, to try and isolate agricultural materials from their larger contexts. Yet another theme centers on what has happened on twentieth-century farms: how has farm work changed, and how have these changes affected family and community relations? New attention has been given to the role of women in the farm economy, and the ways in which modernization has affected women and men differently in the countryside. In the rest of this essay I will elaborate on the issues suggested in these three themes.

To understand why American agriculture looks like it does, and why it became so dominated by a technological and scientific ethos in the twentieth century, one must first look at the historical role of the state. With the Basic Land Ordinance of 1785, and the Homestead Act of 1862, the federal government sought to both raise revenues and encourage farmers to move west and establish farms. Although deeply flawed, these federal acts established the federal government as both the most important patron and client of agriculture. It also created problems. The land was mapped in a highly regular, grid-like format, a system that ignored natural landforms as well as crucial resources. And in its eagerness to raise money, the government sold a great deal of the best land to the railroads, which campaigned aggressively and not entirely honestly to persuade new immigrants to farm in the middle and arid west. But it was the programs and principles established by the federal government in the nineteenth century that were key to the rationalization of agriculture, more so than even private enterprise, which simply built upon an ideology created by the state in the first place. The Jeffersonian idea that farmers represented the highest virtue and nobility among Americans, and that American success would stem from a strong and plentiful agriculture, set the groundwork for generous federal support. The government, from the beginning, championed a commitment to abundant productivity and rational management of the agricultural enterprise, a stance that has trumped all other measures of success for both farmers and the country. Agriculture was one of the first productive activities to acquire departmental status in the federal government in 1862, and from the beginning received lavish funding. The bureaucratic system that resulted from this federal mandate has been crucial in shaping everything farmers do, because the system comprises an agricultural college in all 50 states, plus research centers in key states, and the funding and regulatory ability to make it all work. While there were no academically-trained agricultural engineers or economists when the institution-building really took off in the 1880s, by the early 1920s most colleges were offering advanced degrees in these subjects. Academic specialties such as agricultural chemistry, home economics, agricultural engineering, veterinary medicine, and agricultural economics were established, and research programs in these fields linked projects in the states with those in the federal government. Eventually these partnerships would include the private sector, which funded special research projects of regional importance. The graduates from these programs fanned out to do research in the federal government, teach in colleges and high schools, design farm machines in implement companies, breed grains for cereal makers, and so forth, spreading the gospel of scientific and technical agriculture. By 1930, the research that was conducted and the lessons that were taught in agriculture were sophisticated, quantitative, and geared to problems easily remedied by scientific agriculture and engineering expertise. The primary effort was "making two blades of grass grow where one grew before," but other practices also supported this goal. The breeding of fruits and vegetables to conform to standard shapes and sizes for easier packing and marketing, the creation of grades and standards for inspection and regulation of farm and orchard products, and the branding of fruits and vege-tables such as Sun Kist and Del Monte to link with an emerging and highly com-petitive consumer market, are but a few ways in which scientific and technological capabilities blended seamlessly with a capitalist economy of abundance (Rosenberg 1976; Busch and Lacy 1983; Danbom 1995).

To a certain extent, this dedication to a scientific and technological point of view was perfectly in keeping with more general state-building activities during this period. As James Scott argues, science and technology offer the state tools for keeping track of citizens as well as all they produce, trade, purchase, and sell. Keeping track of agriculturalists was part of the state's managerial campaign as well, an elaborate system of offices, agents, and regulations that ensured the transparent development of an agricultural economy. But the state was not the only one intent upon "seeing" what farmers were doing, and trying to direct them towards serving an expanding industrial base. In the 1910s and 1920s, urban businessmen, social leaders, journalists, and others involved in the Country Life movement studied farm families and tried to persuade them to adopt more modern and "efficient" practices in the home and in the fields, primarily so that urbanites could enjoy a plentiful and cheap food supply. In practical terms, this is what happened, as the outbreak of World War I created huge markets for American farm products. Here was born the idea that farmers should produce as much as possible, and with it farmers' own belief that larger profits could only be achieved through larger yields. But it would not be until the 1920s that this enthusiasm for technologies of abundance began to bear fruit (Cochrane 1993; Danbom 1995; Scott 1998).

Perhaps nowhere has the imprint of the state in agricultural contexts been more apparent than in the West, where the arid climate created challenges for farmers and growers accustomed to the rich soils and moderate rainfall of the Midwestern states. Although warned by its own scouts that speculators would make sensible use of this land nearly impossible, the federal government plotted land there without regard to its particular circumstances, and speculators did indeed operate with an extractive mindset in designing get-rich-quick agricultural schemes. But it was the government itself that supplied the engineering and economic muscle for redesigning this territory with dams and irrigation systems, capturing water in the mountains and aquifers and re-routing it to supply cities, large-scale farms, and later suburban and recreational sites that would not have existed without hydraulic engineering. The USDA (United States Department of Agriculture) was not the only federal agency involved in setting and implementing agricultural policy; the Interior Department (1849) and Bureau of Reclamation (1902), especially in the western states, were equally busy in creating the conditions under which land and water were available to farmers, fishermen, and others seeking to make a living from nature. Similarly, the great dam-building boom of the 1930s had long-lasting consequences not only for irrigation farmers, but for those who fished, hunted, and cut timber. In many places, dams were the foundational agricultural technology (Pisani 1984; Worster 1985; Fiege 1999).

Once the complicated gridwork of state support was in place, agricultural innovations appeared frequently and often with significant consequences. The central goal for virtually all innovations was to take the surprise out of agriculture. If mastery over productive circumstances is a hallmark of business enterprise, at least in corporations and boardrooms, then figuring out a way to control the unpredictabilities of farm production was a central concern of those seeking to modernize agriculture. This control took many forms, including redesigning plants and animals, developing machines to replace the labor of humans and animals, integrating farm production with processing and marketing, and of course designing foods and food-selling venues that could guarantee the disposal of excessive farm products. One powerful way to achieve such control, at least theoretically, was introduced with Mendelian genetics around 1900. At first blush, Mendelism seemed to offer scientists the ability to increase good and remove bad characteristics from plants and animals, but it soon became clear that genetics was more complicated than that. Nonetheless, breeders were soon working hard on one of the major farm commodities, maize, breeding it to meet particular criteria, and by the early 1930s it was advertised in such terms. Corn that had deeper roots than average turned out to be wind-resistant; corn that had high protein made good hog feed; plants that grew large ears were higher-yielding. By the early 1940s, most seed companies no longer sold traditional corn seed. This early biotechnology had several consequences. First, agricultural scientists enjoyed being on the cutting edge, and were eager to put their training to work either for the public interest in land-grant colleges, or for profit and quick results in the private sector. Henry A. Wallace, editor of the popular *Wallaces' Farmer* and grandson of the Secretary of Agriculture, not only promoted hybrids in his publication, but started the Hy-Bred Seed Company, later known as Pioneer Hybrids. Second, farmers discovered the promise and danger of innovation. While hybrid corn promised much higher yields than before, this would be more than offset by the dropping prices farmers received when the market was glutted with the stuff. Fancy corn seed also carried a fancy price, at least three times what farmers had paid in the past. It would become a pattern of agricultural innovation that nearly every technical advance brought with it a social or economic slippage. Cochrane calls it the "agricultural treadmill": farmers must run faster, buy more sophisticated "inputs," expand their farms, just to keep up with other farmers, all of whom are trying to stay afloat (Kloppenburg 1988; Fitzgerald 1990).

A stunning example of the power of genetics to transform plants is the case of the tomato. Inspired by the threat of a shortage of laborers to harvest tomatoes, researchers at the University of California began working on developing a machine to replace migrant laborers. They discovered, however, that the tomatoes then in production would not withstand the rough machine handling, and plant breeders were called in to develop a tougher skinned tomato that would be amenable to this new process. The innovation, then, was both a new kind of tomato and a new kind of machine, and in the mid-1960s this combination was adopted by tomato growers who could afford a dramatically more expensive style of farming. Within a few years, 85 percent of the farmers raising tomatoes were forced out of tomatoes or, in some cases, out of agriculture entirely. Tens of thousands of migrant laborers were also put out of work. Some critics suggest that the state, in this case the University of California, should not be supporting technological changes that undermined the livelihoods of small farmers, and in the case of tomatoes, a lengthy lawsuit failed to settle the question of how to balance the claims of small farmers against the claims of industry. But with large-scale processors such as Del Monte and Campbell's willing to pay for such innovations, the rapid mechanization and vertical integration of tomatoes was assured (Friedland and Barton 1975; Kramer 1977; Hightower 1978).

In recent decades, livestock have also been redesigned in response to apparent market benefits, and usually this research has been sponsored by both federal and private interests. The discovery that growth hormones could be artificially produced led to the commercial production of bovine growth hormone, which caused cows to produce much more milk, in the 1970s. Despite the fact that there was a long-term market glut of fresh milk and other dairy products, many farmers felt they would be forced out of business by those farmers who adopted the new technology. Those who adopted it found that their veterinary bills were much higher as cattle required injections and often developed infections and other ailments as a consequence of increased milk production. Hogs and cattle have been specially bred to be leaner, in deference to increased consumer concerns with health, and these farmers too find that animals without fat demand additional attention and, often, more technology. Chickens have been bred to be larger-breasted, again ostensibly in deference to consumers, and here as well the top-heavy chickens bring new problems to poultry farmers. In an effort to reduce processing costs, breeders have also developed a feather-less chicken which, much like the fat-less hog, requires special attention particularly with respect to temperature control. Hens have been bred to lay more eggs, more frequently, although the confinement system of achieving this has generated its own set of new problems. Confined and crowded birds tend to peck each other to death (scientists are working on changes to the beak), and are more vulnerable to disease and stress-related illness and death (Goodman and Watts 1997).

In other ways, too, technology has transformed agriculture. The fruit industry, developed largely by growers and investors rather than traditional farmers, early on turned its attention from simply growing fruit to the thornier problems of marketing and processing. The success of the California fruit, nut, and vegetable growers, organized into producer co-operatives, depended upon a clear mimicking of more traditional industries, in which machinery, vertical integration, favorable regulation, and advertising would help guarantee stable and predictable markets. Some historians have suggested that citrus was barely agricultural by the 1930s, so systematic and industrialized had its production become through organizations such as Sunkist. Others argue that, from the growers, perspective, the fruit and nut business was meant to be more pastoral, based on horticultural knowledge, small communities, and hard work, an image that businesses such as Diamond Walnuts strive to maintain. Whatever the intention, however, the character of the Western produce business rewarded those who were most business-like, market-savvy, and who aggressively pursued the latest expertise and technology in meeting marketing goals. Sometimes it was technology in the form of new harvesting machines that made this possible, and sometimes it was an ideology of mass production and processing. In either case, it was hard for California growers to avoid becoming industrial, so embedded were they in national systems of transportation, storage, and marketing (Tobey and Weatherell 1995; Stoll 1998; Vaught 1999).

Closely related to this was the creation of an interlocking system of production, processing, distribution, and consumption that was virtually unparalleled in history. Before World War I, this was a fairly rudimentary system. Farmers grew as much as they could, hoping to sell it to a familiar buyer at a high price. Agricultural experts at the colleges might try to persuade farmers to grow something new, or start raising livestock, or enlarge the farm size, but most farmers looked to their own experience and that of their neighbors to make such decisions. The war alerted farmers to the power of markets as never before, and the farm papers such as *Wallaces' Farmer* and *Country Gentleman* educated farmers on world markets, pending legislation related to farming, historic patterns of prices and costs, and reported on what farmers all over the world were doing. A severe farm depression following the war made communication between farmers and farm advisors all the more crucial, although it was unable to stem the tide of farm foreclosures and bankruptcies that characterized the early 1920s. It was in this climate of financial and rural crisis that the federal Bureau of Agricultural Economics was established in 1922, and it quickly became the largest and most powerful unit in the USDA. It attempted to consolidate research and extension efforts on a national scale and to put farming on a rational, businesslike basis (Fitzgerald 2003).

In the meantime, farmers, engineers, and equipment dealers continued their quest to make farm life and work less arduous, both inside the home and out in the field, although the federal government left most of this work to the private sector. The field was the first to get attention. In the 1830s, Cyrus McCormick developed the first practical harvester, a machine that helped reduce the number of hours required to plow an acre of wheat from 35 in 1840 to 20 in 1880. Nineteenth-century manufacturers such as J.I. Case and Allis-Chalmers realized that their skill and success in designing steam engines for factories and other industrial sites could be applied to agricultural work as well. They focused on wheat harvesting, developing stationary steam engines that could be used in the field. These gargantuan threshing machines, and the huge crews that operated them, traveled from farm to farm and threshed wheat and other small grains on a contract basis. A great deal of skill was involved in threshing and, like skilled workers in the trades, threshing workers took pride in their expertise and experience. Threshing was also a marvel of engineering, giving many rural people their first glimpse of machine power and promise. These things made threshing a deeply symbolic cultural event as well, an annual ritual in which the community came together to bring in their crops, follow the thresher from farm to farm, work together cooking for dozens of people, and finally produce and enjoy a harvest feast. By the early 1920s, smaller-scale harvesting machines were developed, and by the late 1920s the combined harvester-thresher, or combine, replaced the old steam engines for good. One of the ironic consequences of this shift from large-scale to smaller-scale mechanization was that farmers no longer depended upon each other for help and community at harvest. They gained more individual flexibility and control, but lost the annual coming together to work (Rikoon 1988; Isern 1990).

Machines were developed for many other field and barn operations as well, and each one seemed to both solve old problems and create new ones. Most notable was the tractor, a small machine designed to replace mules and horses in the task of dragging tools like cultivators, harrows, and seeders across the fields. The first tractors, interestingly, were large, heavy, steam-powered machines designed for the big fields of California, Canada, Argentina, and other places with flat, spacious landscapes. Some implement dealers were skeptical that American farmers would buy scaled-down tractors, but companies like John Deere believed that the market would follow a good machine. Before the late 1920s, tractors were generally very poorly made, often without standardized parts, and often sold to farmers lacking any knowledge of internal combustion engines. Companies would set up to build a line of tractors, but go out of business very quickly. Henry Ford developed a small, light-weight tractor that hit the market in 1917, and he controlled 71 percent of the tractor market before stopping production just 11 years later. By the late 1920s, there were a variety of reputable tractor manufacturers in business, and even reluctant farmers began replacing their horses (Williams 1987).

Engineers and others tried to mechanize farm operations for one of two reasons. One reason was that there was a perceived or real problem with farm labor, and the other reason was that farmers wanted to operate on an entirely different and expanded scale in which it was unrealistic to hire field hands. Most often these two reasons worked in tandem. Problems between farm owners and farm laborers certainly did not originate in twentieth-century America. With some crops, such as cotton and tobacco, a plentiful supply of inexpensive African-American workers discouraged mechanization. When the workers left the area, however, as they did in the South in the 1920s, research on mechanizing the harvest began in earnest. Some crops, like cotton and tomatoes, were difficult to mechanize because of their particular ripening characteristics; machines had neither the visual discriminating ability nor the gentle touch that most fruits and vegetables required. But even cotton harvesters that did not yet work at the harvest could "work" in other ways: in Texas, some growers parked their non-functional machines next to the fields, a reminder to human cotton pickers that their jobs were less than secure. It was not until just after World War II that the Rust brothers and International Harvester perfected a cotton picking machine. Other kinds of harvesting, like milking cows, were accomplished relatively early, pushed forward by an aggressive regulatory apparatus that was concerned with health and safety (McMurray 1995; Foley 1997; Harper 2001).

Farmers in the plains in the 1920s were interested in machinery because it would enable them to farm much more land than with horses alone. The enthusiasm for large-scale farming, especially among wheat growers and speculators, encouraged manufacturers to develop reliable and mass-produced harvesting machinery. These farmers, and many college agriculturalists, argued that a family could not support itself growing wheat on the standard homestead of 160 acres, but required at least 600 acres to make a living. But because the wheat harvest was very time-sensitive, farmers could not realistically plan on getting such large crops in on time with horses. Although combines were first used in the Pacific Northwest as early as the 1880s, it was not until the 1920s that good machines became available and farmers were willing to scale up their production. When manufacturers demonstrated their new combines, farmers were ready. In Montana, for instance, the number of farmers using a combine jumped from 10 in 1923 to 264 in 1926. In Minnesota, 11 farmers used a combine in 1927, but it was up to 110 just 2 years later. As with other technologies, combines carried consequences. At a cost of anywhere from $1,000 to $3,000, the combine was the biggest purchase most farmers had ever made, and the debt load they incurred tied them inexorably to producing as much of the crop as possible. The resulting reduction in the number of farms, and increase in the size of farms, especially in the high plains states, led to the increased isolation of farm families, the loss of many rural schools and churches, and a heightened level of risk for these families. The dominance of this large and mechanized style of farming also had severe environmental consequences, and seems to have been at least partly responsible for the Dust Bowl of the 1930s (Worster 1979; Fitzgerald 2003).

By the post World War II era, agriculturalists and, more importantly, business people, became increasingly interested in the integration and consolidation of agricultural processes, a trend that gained momentum in the 1970s and 1980s. Although little historical work has yet been done on this, the trend was quite apparent. One example was the confinement system of farming used in poultry- and hog-raising. As late as the 1960s, both chickens and pigs were raised within a pen or coop, and had free access to an open yard. The job for the farmer was feeding and watering, cleaning out the pens, and supervising veterinary visits. This system was radically transformed in the late 1970s with the consolidation of the poultry industry and the demands of large processors; poultry farmers were required to scale up or get out of the business. Scaling up, however, meant increasing flock size to an industrial scale, investing in automated equipment, and accepting the supervision and financing of the large processors. Hog farmers faced much the same choice. Large processors consolidated and transformed the industry, turning farmers into contractors to the industry. In the confinement system, up to 2,000 animals are kept in tightly confined quarters, fed and watered automatically, in a climate and light controlled building. This type of contract farming also shifted financial control of farming from farmers to processors, and often farmers retained little decision-making power or authority over their own land. The large scale of operations has led, not only to farmers leaving the business, but serious environmental issues regarding waste disposal (Goodman and Watts 1997).

The process by which farm products were turned into food, fibers, and commercial byproducts demonstrates not only the transformative power of technology but also the creation of a middle ground between city and country, factory and farm. It is a space in which cows become steak, chickens become breasts, cotton becomes sheeting, corn cobs become fiberboard, soybeans become filler in dried, prepared foods. It is also a place of dangerous labor for recent immigrants and those who are undereducated and geographically stranded. Workers in pork- and beef-packing plants are poorly paid, and they are frequently injured by the slaughtering and processing machinery. Although the plant is in a rural place, there is little agrarian about it. Here, the distinction between urban and rural loses its meaning. In the swirl of bones, blood, grains, chaff, juices, seeds, and skins, what is "natural" and what is "technological" is blurred beyond telling. William Cronon's story of the relationship between the city and the country by way of wheat, lumber, and meat vividly captures the transformation of "nature's bounty" into the fuel of urban growth, a process that over time seems to alienate both farmers and urban consumers from the source of their food and material goods (Cronon 1991).

The traffic from farm to table raises many questions about the nature of the food supply, and here the story of twentieth-century consumption patterns reflects a tremendous imprint of technology and science. One of the most striking things about recent food consumption is just how vertically integrated it has become. Particularly in looking at the creation and success of the fast-food industry, one is impressed with the exacting control food entrepreneurs have exerted over every aspect of the enterprise. Studies of the fast-food industry find a powerful single-mindedness, a dedication to making the perfect potato, steer, and chicken into a standardized French fry, hamburger, or bucket of wings no matter the cost. The transformation of plants and animals into food units has never been so highly managed and controlled over time and space, and this is a story of not only business acumen and cultural domination, but also of farming in the service of mass consumption of standardized foods. None of this would be possible were it not for the agricultural scientists creating crops and livestock with very specific characteristics amenable to the demands of the fast-food industry, and the agricultural engineers fashioning both the machines and the transportation and assembly processes upon which fast-food establishments depend (Schlosser 2001; Belasco and Scranton 2002).

The response of rural families to the introduction of both domestic and farm technologies was variable over geographic regions, income levels, and time period, and many writers have tried to capture both the deep sense of tradition and persistence among farm families with the emerging demands and opportunities presented by modern technologies and consumer goods. By exploring the rhythms of farm work and community life through the twentieth century, scholars have documented both what the pre-industrial farm encompassed and how modern home and production practices have reshaped the lives of rural people. One thing that has become clear is that farm families have long been subjected to the promises of technology for higher productivity, lightened work load, and more money in the farmers pocket; innovations small and large have been the rule rather than the exception in rural life over the last 100 years.

Still, the traditional patterns of work and socializing in the countryside formed a solid bedrock against which innovations were measured. Farm families were embedded in a network of local kin and friends, helped each other with farm chores as well as raising children and caring for elders, discussed the virtues and problems of new ideas and innovations, supported or ignored agitation by politicians and businessmen, tried to combine the reliable traditions with the onslaught of modernity. Large national phenomena such as the world wars, the introduction of automobiles and paved roads, and the farm credit programs of the New Deal, rearranged farm families commitments and aspirations. The mechanization and scaling up of farms frequently led to the decline of farms themselves, and families reshuffled their work to accommodate changed circumstances. As the number of dairy farms declined, for example, the number of cows per farm increased, in a pattern characteristic of industrializing agriculture. The shift from local to national and international markets for orchard crops like peaches, dairy products like cream, or the eggs from farmyard chickens, which all, incidentally, were typically the purview of women, pushed many into off-farm work after World War II. Similarly, the increasingly business-oriented and technologically sophisticated style of farming of the 1930s and 1940s also reshaped gender and community relations in rural America. The standards of social reciprocity and work-sharing among farm families were challenged when machines replaced human labor, and when rural populations declined. But families did not passively accept modernizing technologies and consumer goods, instead taking their time evaluating which ones would support their work styles and which were too disruptive or expensive (Adams 1994; Neth 1995).

This "accommodation and resistance" to modernity is apparent not only in the adoption of technologies such as the telephone and home electrification, but also with innovations that would seem unproblematic. The introduction of paved roads, for instance, was strongly opposed by many New England farmers, who saw it as a way for urbanites to arrange for fast driving on quiet country roads, something that was difficult on rutted dirt roads. Similarly, mail-order catalogues threatened to undermine the very fabric of rural communities, not only taking essential business away from small general stores, but also introducing urban styles and, some feared, consumer desires into previously contented families. The Amish represent the most striking example of rural people who rejected on principle nearly all new technologies. Virtually any innovation held the potential to upset the delicate balance of family and community obligations and expectations, and each one was weighed and considered carefully before adoption or rejection. Many families struggled to decide which part of the farm needed new technology more, the home or the barn, a debate usually won by the barn. Often rural communities refashioned technologies to suit themselves. The telephone, for instance, was one technology many isolated farmers were eager to obtain, but their desires were hindered by the lack of infrastructure in the countryside when telephone companies refused to string lines across the underpopulated landscape. Clever farmers came up with ways to capture the radio waves without the phone company, however, fashioning phones out of materials on their farms, such as barbed wire fences! Similarly, farm families often set up their own rural electrification organizations in response to what they saw as unreasonable or unnecessary terms offered by the telephone company. Again and again, they found ways to make technology work for them, rather than simply accepting the technology that was offered (Adams 1994; Neth 1995; Kline 2000; Harper 2001).

The farm crisis in the mid-1980s, during which many farm families suffered bankruptcy, occasioned some soul-searching among both agriculturalists and scholars. Some looked back over the last few decades, examining how farmers changed the way they farmed to take advantage of technological promises as well as their banker's none-too-subtle pushes for modernization. Since World War II, the scale of most farms had grown considerably and so had their debt load. New machinery, larger fields, higher veterinary bills, more specialized feed and seed, all were supported by both the agricultural college experts and the banking and credit community, who urged farmers to grow and expand as foreign demands for American farm products seemed to increase. Caught in a credit crunch when markets fell apart, many farmers found that corporate and bank consolidations had changed the rules of the game. Familiar loan officers were replaced by those from the city, and traditional credit terms were changed to reflect a strictly business-like approach. A farmer's history and capability over the long term seemed not to matter so much anymore. The cost of industrializing the farm in the 1980s was much as it had been in the 1920s. While many families survived this period, it became clear that continuing to farm would be difficult. Adopting the latest technology, and following the latest advice from experts, was no longer sufficient to succeed; indeed, it might lead to failure (Barlett 1993; Dudley 2000).

The difficult farm economy has had secondary consequences as well, and these too grow out of the fundamentally technological and global nature of modern agriculture. As more farm families leave the farms, abandoned houses and dilapidated barns dot the landscape, and the main streets of small towns lose barbers, coffee shops, and grocery stores. Those left in the countryside are harder pressed to make a living in farming or commerce and, like miners or fishermen, find themselves stranded in a land that no longer supports them. Ironically, new people do move into these towns, but they are most often recent immigrants hired to work at the processing plants or to follow the harvest. Their agricultural future is no brighter than that of traditional farmers in most areas.

The history of twentieth-century technology and agriculture is thus a complicated and ambiguous tale, not so unlike the contradictory visions that opened this essay. Historians still have much to learn about the precise relations between technology and the rural economy and culture of America, but critics of the contemporary scene have been more vocal than supporters. There is no question that America has available an abundance of cheap and healthy food, but the costs of this circumstance – economic, political, social – are not yet clear.

BIBLIOGRAPHY

Adams, Jane. *The Transformation of Rural Life: Southern Illinois, 1890–1990* (Chapel Hill: University of North Carolina Press, 1994).
Barlett, Peggy F. *American Dreams, Rural Realities: Family Farms in Crisis* (Chapel Hill: University of North Carolina Press, 1993).
Belasco, Warren and Philip Scranton. *Food Nations: Selling Taste in Consumer Societies* (New York: Routledge, 2002).
Busch, Lawrence and William B. Lacy. *Science, Agriculture, and the Politics of Research* (Boulder: Westview, 1983).
Cochrane, Willard W. *The Development of American Agriculture: A Historical Analysis* (Minneapolis: University of Minnesota Press, 1993).
Cronon, William. *Nature's Metropolis: Chicago and the Great West* (New York: W.W. Norton, 1991).

Danbom, David B. *Born in the Country: A History of Rural America* (Baltimore: Johns Hopkins University Press, 1995).

Danbom, David B. *The Resisted Revolution: Urban America and the Industrialization of Agriculture, 1900–1930* (Ames: Iowa State University Press, 1979).

Dudley, Kathryn Marie. *Debt and Dispossession: Farm Loss in America's Heartland* (Chicago: University of Chicago Press, 2000).

Fiege, Mark. *Irrigated Eden: The Making of an Agricultural Landscape in the American West* (Seattle: University of Washington Press, 1999).

Fitzgerald, Deborah. *The Business of Breeding: Hybrid Corn in Illinois, 1890–1940* (Ithaca: Cornell University Press, 1990).

Fitzgerald, Deborah. *"Every Farm a Factory": The Industrial Ideal in American Agriculture* (New Haven: Yale University Press, 2003).

Foley, Neil. *The White Scourge: Mexicans, Blacks, and Poor Whites in Texas Cotton Culture* (Berkeley: University of California Press, 1997).

Friedland, William H. and Amy Barton. "Tomato Technology." *Society*, no. 13 September/October (1975): 34–42.

Goodman, David and Michael J. Watts, eds. *Globalising Food: Agrarian Questions and Global Restructuring* (London: Routledge, 1997).

Harper, Douglas. *Changing Works: Visions of a Lost Agriculture* (Chicago: University of Chicago Press, 2001).

Hightower, Jim. *Hard Tomatoes, Hard Times: A Report of the Agribusiness Accountability Project on the Failure of America's Land Grant College Complex* (Rochester, Vermont: Schenkman, 1978).

Hughes, Thomas P. *Networks of Power: Electrification in Western Society, 1880–1930* (Baltimore: Johns Hopkins University Press, 1983).

Isern, Thomas D. *Bull Threshers and Bindlestiffs: Harvesting and Threshing on the North American Plains* (Lawrence: University Press of Kansas, 1990).

Kline, Ronald R. *Consumers in the Country: Technology and Social Change in Rural America* (Baltimore: Johns Hopkins University Press, 2000).

Kloppenburg, Jr, Jack. *First the Seed: The Political Economy of Plant Biotechnology, 1492–2000* (Cambridge: Cambridge University Press, 1988).

Kramer, Mark. *Three Farms: Making Milk, Meat and Money From the American Soil* (Boston: Little, Brown, 1977).

McMurray, Sally. *Transforming Rural Life: Dairying Families and Agricultural Change, 1820–1885* (Baltimore: Johns Hopkins University Press, 1995).

Neth, Mary. *Preserving the Family Farm: Women, Community, and the Foundations of Agribusiness in the Midwest, 1900–1940* (Baltimore: Johns Hopkins University Press, 1995).

Pisani, Donald J. *From the Family Farm to Agribusiness: The Irrigation Crusade in California and the West, 1850–1931* (Berkeley: University of California Press, 1984).

Rikoon, Sanford J. *Threshing in the Midwest, 1820–1940: A Study of Traditional Culture and Technological Change* (Bloomington: Indiana University Press, 1988).

Rosenberg, Charles E. *No Other Gods: On Science and American Social Thought* (Baltimore: Johns Hopkins University Press, 1976).

Schlosser, Eric. *Fast Food Nation: The Dark Side of the All-American Meal* (Boston: Houghton Mifflin, 2001).

Scott, James C. *Seeing Like a State: How Certain Schemes to Improve the Human Condition Have Failed* (New Haven: Yale University Press, 1998).

Stoll, Steven. *The Fruits of Natural Advantage: Making the Industrial Countryside in California* (Berkeley: University of California Press, 1998).

Tobey, Ronald, and Charles Weatherell. "The Citrus Industry and the Revolution of Corporate Capitalism in Southern California, 1887–1944", *California History*, 1995, **74**: 74–86.

Vaught, David. *Cultivating California: Growers, Specialty Crops, and Labor, 1875–1920* (Baltimore: Johns Hopkins University Press, 1999).

Worster, Donald. *Dust Bowl: The Southern Plains in the 1930s* (New York: Oxford University Press, 1979).

Worster, Donald. *Rivers of Empire: Water, Aridity, and the Growth of the American West* (New York: Oxford University Press, 1985).

Williams, Robert C., *Farmall, Fordson and Poppin Johnny: A History of the Farm Tractor and it's Impact on America* (Urbana: University of Illinois Press, 1987).

CHAPTER FIVE

House and Home

GAIL COOPER

Introduction

To casual observers, the house has a dual character. One face of the house is the building itself – four walls and a roof define the minimum of shelter, but these essentials come fashioned in innumerable architectural styles. A second consists of the gadgets, machines, and systems of service crammed within the basic box. While one seems to be the home's historic identity and the other its modern self, in the estimation of many, those two halves have now become an integral whole. Indeed, the history of the twentieth-century house and home is the melding of its new services and established character. At the end of the American Revolution it was still possible for a group of disaffected Tories to disassemble their wood frame houses, ship them to the Penobscot River, and reassemble their homes on the northern side of the river in what they expected to be British Canada, only to discover, upon the promulgation of the Treaty of Paris, that they were actually within the boundaries of Maine. In contrast, by the end of the twentieth century, American homes were rooted in place by sewer pipes and water mains, and tied to the land by electric power lines; to move the architectural shell of the modern house would be to leave behind more than half its value and function.

Yet it would be a mistake to assume that the historic house was untouched by technology or technological change. Architectural features provided systems of heating, cooling and ventilation before machinery replaced them, and innovations in construction constantly changed such factors as who owned, built, and designed houses. In a country where land was cheap and plentiful, the expense of the house itself drew constant scrutiny. Many technical innovations worked to lessen the costs of construction and to broaden the demographics of home ownership. In the nineteenth century, the balloon frame house, constructed with light-weight timber framing, reduced the time, the cost of materials, and the skills necessary for putting up a new home. In the twentieth century, similar savings were made by displacing craft traditions with industrial practices. That industrial model included the incorporation of modular parts and standardized industrial products; pre-fabrication; and on-site mass production. Such a blending of the democratic ideals of home ownership with an enthusiasm for industrial efficiency might itself stand as a sketch of twentieth-century America.

So, if technology and the *house* is one half of this story, then technology and the *home* is the other. Modern technology is more obviously on view within the walls of the house, but which technology is deemed essential or appropriate to the home is as changeable as the conception of the American family. In the twentieth century, the power revolution finally came to the home with electrification, and a vast range of choices appeared which were both technological and cultural in character. In contemplating whether the home should be technologically self-sufficient or part of a commercial network, we asked: Does every home need the scaled-down technology of the commercial laundry or the public restaurant? In surveying the labor force at home, we asked: Should kitchens be equipped for labor-saving efficiency or for a full range of sophisticated services? The communications revolution has been similarly provocative. Where once the home was considered a retreat from the world of work and business, the technologies of sociability and entertainment which crowd the modern home are only faintly separated from those providing business communication and information. Swept up within the networks of power and technology, the twentieth-century home could no longer claim to be a retreat from the modern and the commercial.

The House

The American house has been profoundly shaped by democratic ideals of home ownership. Today, roughly 68 percent of Americans own their own home. Such high rates reflect more than individual success in an open economy, however; affordable home ownership became the goal of private institutions and government alike for the myriad social benefits that it brought with it. Ownership of property has long been associated with social stability, and Thomas Jefferson expected that the economic independence of the yeoman farmer would sustain his political independence. By the 1920s, employers were less concerned with workers' independence than they were with labor radicalism, but, in those years, the general conviction that property holding created social stability reappeared as a paean to home ownership in particular. Herbert Hoover noted that the home owner "works harder outside his home; he spends his leisure more profitably, and he and his family live a finer life and enjoy more of the comforts and cultivating influences of our modern civilization" (Rome 2001, p. 20). Corporate welfare programs in the 1920s included schemes to promote home ownership among working-class families. We might say that American workers in the early decades were enjoined literally to "buy in" to the American system. However, the expense of a home remained beyond the reach of many working-class families, and at least a third of the nation lived in substandard housing in the 1920s.

If there is an evolving technology of American residential construction, a great deal of it has centered on the reduction of costs. In order to accomplish that, social critics urged that the construction industry adopt the methods of industrial production to reap the cost savings in volume production, standardized parts and designs, and simplified tasks. Residential housing needed to escape the restrictions of local resources and skilled labor. Some cost reductions would be achieved through new materials, but the advantages of many new materials was their potential for reducing the expenses of skilled labor.

At the beginning of the century, the application of industrial methods to construction was limited largely to exceptional cases, where building lay beyond the bounds of the traditional construction trades. Company housing may have been one of the first examples of mass production techniques applied to residential building. Engineering firms such as Lockwood Greene designed both factory and worker housing in remote mining and lumbering towns. The firm's use of standardized designs and economies of scale successfully reduced costs for such large buyers, but more importantly solved the problem of creating a town where none had existed before. In a similar attempt to address problems of access, large department and catalog stores like Sears, Montgomery Ward, and Eatons, sold prefabricated homes, many of them erected in remote mountain and lake locations beyond the reach of local building trades. Prefabrication took residential construction even closer to the industrial model by shifting the bulk of construction from the building site to the factory.

In the first decades of the twentieth century then, mass production methods constituted the exception to residential construction rather than the rule. Their impact can best be seen not in the practice of building itself but rather in uniform industrial products incorporated into traditional building practice. In industrial products, America embraced uniformity without reservation. Beginning in 1929, that popular enthusiasm was both shaped and reflected in *Fortune Magazine*'s photo essays by Margaret Bourke White, who made the repetitive shapes of industrial mass production an expression of the modern aesthetic, and the outpouring of the factory appear as a latter-day cornucopia. Closely allied to industrial uniformity was the movement for standardization of products across the range of manufacturers. Such mundane but necessary building materials as screws, nails, pipes, toilets, doors, windows, lumber, and innumerable other items increasingly came in standard weights, lengths, and measurements. Business used standardization to tame the endless variety of products, and to reduce capital intensive inventories.

Industrial uniformity and *business standardization* were joined by a third element, *engineering efficiency*. The national craze for efficiency was centered in the engineering community but spread widely. In 1911 engineer Frederick Winslow Taylor published *The Principles of Scientific Management*. Taylor's notion of efficiency in the workplace was largely aimed at challenging traditional work practices such as the *stint*, in which workers jointly agreed on an appropriate work pace for all in the shop thereby capping production for the day. Taylor argued for the general principle that management should exert greater control over the factory by splitting all work into planning and execution, and that workers should concern themselves only with the physical labor of production. Taylor's ideas on efficiency were soon applied to a vast range of technical and social problems. In those contexts, efficiency took on a wide array of meanings, but in many of its applications, it was used to assault the traditional prerogatives of labor.

The impact of the national enthusiasm for uniformity, standardization, and efficiency on construction is clearly illustrated in the development of plywood. Wood is remarkably varied in its characteristics, and its use as a building material rested on a foundation of craftsmanship. Carpenters, for example, might employ as many as fifteen different kinds of wood in a single chair, carefully matching the demands of the application to the characteristics of each type of wood. However, its great variety between types and its lack of uniformity between samples of the same kind, made it less predictable without that expert eye. The development of plywood, thin sheets of veneer bonded together with adhesive, gave wood uniform building characteristics. In addition, it was marketed in standard four by eight foot panels and standard thicknesses. Plywood represented the industrialization of this craft material. Many of the new building materials carried the patina of modern scientific values. At the same time, as Slaton (2001) points out in her history of reinforced concrete, they radically shifted established patterns of labor and business. In the 1920s, the United States Gypsum Company marketed a pressed-plaster wall board under the brand name Sheetrock that eliminated the traditional steps used by carpenters and plasterers to create smooth wall surfaces (Goldstein 1998, p. 23).

Government Efforts

In the early decades of the century, the government became increasingly concerned about the quality of American housing and its affordability. Herbert Hoover extolled the social benefits of home ownership. It was, he said, "the foundation of a sound economy and social system" (Rome 2001, p. 19). However, the private marketplace did not seem to be providing a solution to the problem of adequate housing. In 1920, an estimated one-third of citizens lived in inadequate housing, and home ownership rates in the non-farm population ran a mere 41 percent (Rome 2001, p. 20). Buyers had the option of buying a starter house and upgrading it as their finances improved, but this piecemeal strategy was inadequate to the modern house which already incorporated a range of services, like electricity and plumbing, that were most economically built in from the start. Under the auspices of the Federation of American Engineering Societies, Hoover organized a major investigation of waste in industry. The final report urged industry to employ a greater scale in building construction as the path to efficiency and cost reduction. In 1921, Hoover was appointed Secretary of Commerce, and the next year he created a division of building and housing within the Department of Commerce.

As President of the United States, Hoover returned to the issue of housing. In 1931, he sponsored the President's Conference on Home Building and Home Ownership, and unsurprisingly it looked at "mass production" as a solution to the problem of affordable housing. However, between 1921 and 1931, conditions had changed substantially. By the early Depression years, many believed that home construction could become an important economic stimulus for the sagging economy. While solving a problem for individual families, home construction might also cure the nation's ills. However, critics pointed out that it could also undermine consumer spending, as financially strapped, working-class families might pay for a new home by economizing on all of the rest of their purchases.

The federal government responded not just with a technical solution but with a financial one as well, by making federal monies available for new home purchases.

Begun under Hoover's auspices, the program flourished under Franklin Delano Roosevelt's administration. In 1934, the passage of the National Housing Act created the Federal Housing Administration (FHA) that offered federally guaranteed loans and mortgages. A long-term amortized mortgage made purchase easier for new home buyers who needed only the 20 percent down payment to move into their own home. Just as significantly, the FHA provided small loans of up to $2,000 to existing homeowners for home repair and modernization. *Better Homes and Gardens* magazine publicized their availability, and roughly one in eight homeowners took advantage of these home improvement loans (Goldstein 1998, p. 28). That might mean something as simple as a new coat of exterior paint, or as basic as a new roof. However, "modernization" opened up the issue of the extent to which basic starter homes and older housing stock were able to accommodate the new domestic technologies – vacuum cleaners, stoves, washing machines, refrigerators. The crux of the problem for many was electrical service.

Electrification

The idea that the starter home was a basic shell that buyers could retrofit with amenities and appliances as their circumstances improved, meant that few houses were constructed with full electrical service. Ronald Tobey points out that most houses were built with electrical wiring that was adequate for lighting and not much else. Overhead light fixtures often incorporated an outlet for small appliances like an iron, but neither the typical electrical service nor the outlet was designed to sustain water heaters, refrigerators, vacuum cleaners or washing machines. In 1922, 80 percent of houses either had no electricity or were wired for lighting only. The difference between illumination wiring and full domestic service was substantial. Only 10–20 percent of domestic consumers were likely to install full service in 1928 (Tobey 1996, p. 36). Along with guaranteed loans, the FHA issued standards for electrical wiring that mandated two circuits (one for power, another for lights) and multiple wall outlets (Tobey 1996, p. 113).

The expense of rewiring for electrical modernization was only one of the barriers to adopting a modern electrical house. The power companies believed that there was little potential in marketing to residential consumers and their policies had a self-fulfilling character. Most utilities assumed that domestic consumers would never consume a sufficient quantity of power to make it profitable to the provider and they grudgingly provided service to domestic customers because of government mandates. Indeed, while industrial customers were billed on a sliding scale that reduced the per unit price as consumption increased, domestic consumers paid the same rate per energy unit regardless of their usage and receive no benefit from increased consumption. Thus the utilities' expectations about residential customers led to a rate structure that reinforced their assumptions. Only the most prosperous 20 percent of residential customers, those who could afford to install full electrical service, were likely to consume enough energy to provide the utilities with a profit.

These assumptions by power companies about domestic electrical usage, that only a small number of households at the top could be considered profitable electrical consumers, had a profound impact on the electrical appliance industry. Without a mass market, the volume of appliances sold in the US remained small and prices remained high. Appliance manufacturers designed, built, and priced their products for the elite. In 1929, the average price for electric refrigerators was $268; for ranges, $111; for washing machines, $116. This price structure too was self-fulfilling; through the 1920s, most consumers chose to spend their consumer credit on automobiles (31 percent) rather than household appliances (8 percent) (Tobey 1996, p. 66).

A substantial reconsideration of the consumer market for electricity and household appliances came with the Depression. The loss of industrial markets made domestic households the most promising consumers around. What demonstrated the potential for an expanded residential electrical usage was the Tennessee Valley Authority (TVA) in 1933. TVA set out to address the problems of the rural community where electrical access of any kind was the critical problem. If residences in small towns lacked full electrical service, many country houses lacked even electrical illumination. The 1930 Census revealed that while 85 percent of non-farm families had electrical service only 13 percent of farm families did. Instead, farm families used gasoline engines, gas-mantle lamps, and oil stoves rather than their electrical equivalents (Kline 2000, p. 5). As the new technologies created a substantial difference between rural and urban lifestyles, observers worried it would lead to rural depopulation. Commercial companies often balked at the expense of running electric lines for long distances between rural neighbors, and experts questioned whether rates of household consumption would ever repay such an investment. The concern for rural electrification prompted the federal government to sponsor rural cooperatives under the Rural Electrification Administration in 1935 that focused on both financing electric distribution systems and promoting consumption.

These government programs demonstrated that domestic consumption of electricity would rise in volume if rates were sufficiently low. Once domestic consumers were recognized as a profitable market for power, then electrical modernization, and household appliances followed in a shifting of the market around new models of consumption and economies of mass production.

Post World War II

It is on-site mass production that seems so emblematic of the twentieth-century enthusiasm for the spread of the industrial model. The most famous mass-produced housing was Levittown, built by Abraham Levitt and Sons, on Long Island from 1947 to 1951. Levitt developed his techniques building wartime housing, and simply pursued them on a larger scale when building restrictions eased after the war. His tract development of more than 17,000 homes allowed him to employ economies of scale, standardized designs, pre-cut lumber, a more complete utilization of power tools, and an organization of labor that some have called the inverted assembly line, where houses remained fixed while crews moved from site to site.

While these techniques did prove economical, the spread of home ownership in the post-war years was sustained in large part by the expansion of the FHA program for guaranteed mortgages. The Servicemen's Readjustment Act of 1944 authorized veterans' loans. By 1961, 5.6 million veterans loans had been taken up by veterans from World War II and the Korean War (Goldstein 1998, p. 35). These loans were the flowering of the amortized mortgage, introduced in the 1920s to spread the cost of purchase over a longer time-period. In many ways, Levitt's tract houses were starter homes with lots of opportunities for expansion and improvement, but starter homes after the war were profoundly different from their prewar predecessors. Increasingly, banks offered "package mortgages," agreeing to include in the home loan the cost of major appliances like stoves, refrigerators, dishwashers, washers, and dryers, which effectively spread the purchase price of these items over the thirty-year life of the loan. Thus full electrical service was a given and many homes included an astonishing array of household appliances as well. By mid-century then, the construction industry had made an important statement about the integral character of the house and its technical services.

Such integration is illustrated by the rapid spread of air conditioning in new home construction. While the most affordable and popular option for cooling in existing buildings was the window air conditioner, new construction offered an economical opportunity for building central air conditioning systems into even modest homes. A survey by the National Association of Home Builders reported that 40 percent of the 255 leading builders were planning to market air-conditioned houses in 1953 in homes priced at $15,000 or less. When included in house design from the start, air conditioning ducting was dramatically reduced in cost. By 1957, one California bank required the roughing-in for air conditioning in any home costing more than $20,000. Roughing-in included large insulated ducts, adequate space for the equipment, and a return line for homes with slab floors. These additions cost only $250–$300. However, speculative builders believed that air-conditioned homes would attract buyers only if they could make sufficient savings to offset the cost of this luxury item. Air conditioning advocates argued that the new mechanical system replaced the need for conventional window ventilation; in an effort to make the whole house absorb the cost of the air conditioning system, builders were urged to eliminate attic fans, screens, storm windows, and cross ventilation. The resultant redesign of the house around the air conditioning system not only built in the possibility of mechanical cooling and ventilation, but in some cases the necessity for it as well, since the modern house had few of the architectural features of passive cooling and little insulation within its walls (Cooper 1998, p. 154).

While technological services were increasingly built in from the start, postwar homeowners embraced the concept of "sweat equity." For a small cash down payment, buyers secured a basic house and increased its value by investing their own labor in home improvement projects. These addressed both style and function, individualizing standard designs, and upgrading the amenities of the house.

Landscaping, paint, and trim were within skills of most homeowners, while better quality finish and built-in furniture required more elaborate knowledge and tools. Forty years later, it was difficult to find a Levittown home that had not been substantially altered.

As Carolyn Goldstein illustrates, the do-it-yourself phenomenon was fed by a growing industry for home improvement products. Small power tools, such as Black & Decker's quarter-inch power drill, proved to be a commercial success. By 1952, Business Week reported about a hundred such products (Goldstein 1998, p. 49). Many new products reduced the level of skill required of do-it-yourselfers; latex paints replaced oil-based paints; paint rollers replaced brushes; PVC piping replaced copper tubing; wallpaper came pre-cut and pre-pasted. In addition, these products came to the homeowner through new kinds of outlets that replaced full service hardware stores with self-service home improvement centers. Rationalized as the improvement of home value, Goldstein points out, however, that "the appeal of do-it-yourself transcended cost-benefit analysis" (Goldstein 1998, p. 37). Like many activities within the domestic sphere, it was never clear whether home improvement projects were to be considered work or creative play.

Suburbanization

Institutional preferences for new home construction rather than urban renewal has left a profound impression on the housing stock. While the historic preservation movement increased national interest and support for the preservation of older and historic domestic structures in the postwar era under the guidance of the National Trust for Historic Preservation, a private, non-profit organization established in 1949, the bulk of the nation's housing needs has been filled by new construction. And the majority of those new homes have been built in suburban, tract developments. The adaptation of mass production techniques greatly intensified the environmental impact of home building. Cited on landscapes with little regard for their environmental impact, subdivisions were often followed closely by such ills as flooding, erosion, wildlife displacement, and septic-tank failures. Adam Rome argues that the transformation of environments at the city's edge was highly visible and their loss was influential in raising general environmental awareness. However, municipal governments typically used zoning to uphold property values and promote economic development rather than to protect sensitive environments. To add to the problem, the boundaries of city or county government seldom incorporated entire eco-systems even if they had been inclined to enact protective legislation.

The Home

Ironically, while the twentieth-century house seemed inevitably destined to be swept up into the industrial mass production enthusiasm – standardized, uniform, and efficient – the American home represented as its antithesis. To many the home was tied to leisure, domesticity, and a retreat from the bustle of the outside world.

However, despite such idyllic definitions, the home was always a workplace that produced everyday necessities for the family. Such conceptions profoundly shaped the technologies considered appropriate for those domestic spaces, but rather than choosing between these competing ideals, the spaces and services of the American house were designed to accommodate both.

The Home as Workplace

When you consider the home as woman's workplace, the most significant technical development was the widespread provision of basic services such as water and electricity. While begun in the nineteenth century, the twentieth century witnessed the spread of these fundamentals across urban and rural areas alike.

The provision of domestic water and sewers was an especially acute urban problem. The dense population of the cities bred recurrent waves of epidemic illness. Stagnant water and blocked sewers contributed to Philadelphia's yellow fever epidemic in 1793, and a concern for civic cleanliness lead to the nation's first municipal water system in Philadelphia in 1801 at Centre Square, followed by an improved pumping station at the Fairmont Waterworks in 1815. Under these conditions, private sanitary habits could well become a matter for public policy. Ogle (1996) points out that as early as 1840 there was a flurry of patenting activity centered on improved sanitary fixtures, and individual households adopted private waste disposal systems. By the 1870s, cities had begun to think of plumbing as most appropriately connected to a larger external sanitation system, and the principle of interconnection was established along with government oversight in the 1880s. By the turn of the century, new understandings in bacteriology reinforced the importance of municipal rather than individual solutions.

Increasingly, however, the impetus for many urban water systems came as much from the demands of industry as from its growing population. In Chicago, it was primarily the impact of the city's large meat packing houses on waste disposal and sanitation that prompted the city to undertake its massive engineering project to reverse the flow of the Chicago River. By drawing drinking water from Lake Michigan and disposing of sewage in the Chicago River, city engineers provided a sanitary water supply for the city. Indeed, water service to domestic households was sometimes subordinated to industrial needs and schedules. In Pittsburgh, for example, housewives in the city's working-class neighborhoods discovered that water pressure in the municipal system was often insufficient to provide residential customers with water during the hours that nearby factories were operating.

Piped water had a profound impact on women's work. Water is fundamental to cooking and cleaning, and the job of hauling water was one of housekeeping's most physically demanding tasks. Piped water greatly decreased the physicality of housework, and sewer drains provided nearly as much relief. Whether the chore was performed by husbands, wives, or children, families not only shouldered the burden of carrying clean water inside the house but also faced the necessity of hauling dirty water outside for disposal. Dumping water in the yard or the streets often created mud just beyond the doorways which foot traffic quickly brought back into the house. Abundant water and efficient disposal made an enormous difference in housework.

A third essential service that transformed housework was electricity, for it marked a genuine power revolution in the home. One sharp contrast between industrial and domestic work was the length of time that household labor was performed without the aid of a mechanical power source after the steam engine transformed the industrial world. When power came, it came first to the cities and belatedly to the farms. At the turn of the century, the National Grange worried that heavy work and long hours were ruining women's health (Kline 2000, pp. 11–12).

Nothing better demonstrates the transformative power of water, sewers, and electricity than laundry. The traditional laundry day was called "Blue Monday,"and laundry was the first household task that housewives hired out if they could afford it. The washing of white clothes often involved hauling water for at least four separate wash tubs to accommodate washing, rinsing, bluing, and starching, and, the labor of the subsequent disposal of each. Hung up to dry on one day, the housewife returned to the chore of ironing the next. Ironing clothes with a succession of sad irons, heated on the kitchen stove, made this an especially hot and tedious chore in the summertime, when a hot stove heated the entire house for the rest of the day. The first washing machines saved the housewife the disagreeable task of rubbing clothes on a washboard, but as the machines were not plumbed, they still involved hand filling and draining. It was often municipal services – the combination of water, sewers, and electricity – that did more than commercial products to relieve the burden of household laundry.

The technological evolution of the house in parallel with industrial progress was not an obvious development. Rather than equip the household with the latest technical advances, some imagined that commercial services and industrial products would provide an alternative to traditional household production. Indeed, for the first few decades of the century, commercial steam laundries provided a competitive alternative to individual household washing machines. In the same vein of taking housework out of the house, in the nineteenth century, social critic Charlotte Perkins Gilman argued for the benefits of the kitchenless apartment house, where families would rely upon communal dining halls for their meals. She advocated the professionalization and commercialization of all housework, arguing that employing specialized machinery, economies of scale, and well-trained experts in centralized establishments would provide better products and services; secure a place in the commercial economy for women workers; and free the individual housewife to pursue work suited to her own interests and talents.

Re-imagining household work within the larger perspective of an industrializing economy became an even more pressing exercise by the 1920s, when the numbers of young women willing to accept jobs as domestic servants declined dramatically. This change in the available labor pool was concurrent with the power revolution in the home. Rather than embrace a radical change in the character of housework and home life, however, critics argued that the use of new technologies and efficient organization would maintain the housewife at the center of the domestic household by bringing housework within the scope of a single worker. The electrification of the home brought "electrical servants," such as vacuum cleaners.

For those who wanted to improve the home rather than revolutionize it, the goal was to apply industrial models of efficiency in the home rather than replace household production. In 1919, writer Christine Frederick urged housewives to borrow the basic concepts of scientific management from industry and to adapt them to the home by applying rational planning to the workday. However, it was engineer and psychologist Lillian Gilbreth whose own brand of scientific management proved to be most influential in shaping the way that modern kitchens were designed. With her husband, Frank, Gilbreth applied management techniques in industry that centered on the reduction of worker fatigue through the analysis of basic movements called "therbligs" ("Gilbreth" spelled backwards). After her husband's death in 1924, Gilbreth began to apply such motion studies in the home. She advised housewives to arrange their new appliances – stove, sink, and refrigerator – in a triangular design that minimized the number of steps between work areas. To further reduce fatigue, she advocated all work surfaces, such as tables and counters, be set at one convenient height to eliminate the need to stoop or strain, and that storage of pots and pans be within easy reach.

The kitchen was one of the first rooms in the twentieth-century house to be standardized, due in large part to the collaboration between Gilbreth and appliance manufacturers. A utility company hired her to design model kitchens to illustrate the application of her ideas. Manufacturers of appliances were anxious to find a bridge between their products and female consumers, and Gilbreth was just one of a number of experts and home economists who brought engineering, science and commerce to bear on the problems of the home. As Graham (1998) points out, in some cases, Gilbreth's ideas were imperfectly realized. For example, she urged consumers to achieve a uniform counter height by cutting the wooden feet of their tables and appliances to a height that was best for each individual woman. Manufacturers heeded her call for a uniform counter height but achieved that by adopting one standardized height for kitchen cabinets and appliances. Standardization rather than individualization was an easier goal to attain in the commercial realm. Yet when Richard Nixon stood in a model kitchen in Moscow to debate the merits of the capitalist system with Soviet Premier Nikita Kruschev, that kitchen became a symbol of American prosperity, and it largely reflected Gilbreth's ideas – base cabinets with easy storage, counters and appliances of uniform height, and a step-saving arrangement of appliances.

Domestic technology has certainly lightened the physical demands of housework, yet to characterize it simply as "labor saving" is to miss an important trend. Across the century, studies show that the number of hours women devoted to housework remained surprisingly unchanged. Instead, as Cowan (1983) illustrates, housewives repeatedly used the benefits of domestic technology to increase the standards of living for their family rather than reduce the number of hours spent in housework. For example, vacuum cleaners replaced such physically demanding chores as the need to beat rugs and sweep floors. However, the apparent ease of vacuum cleaning, opened the way to the adoption of wall-to-wall carpeting. Washing machines enabled more frequent cleaning of clothes and bed linens. Air conditioning made possible hot meals in the summertime. Housewives used new technology to raise the standards of cleanliness, nutrition, and comfort for their families. Such patterns illustrate that the home was more than women's workplace.

Sociability at Home

Modern technologies which were adopted in the home were in part a reflection of what tasks and what tools seemed appropriate for the housewife. And that in turn was shaped by attitudes about household production vis à vis the commercial economy: Should we buy or make? Not all household technology is concerned with the production of products, however. Many gadgets in American homes are there for the creation of more ephemeral things like sociability, leisure, and entertainment.

For example, the telephone was originally conceived as a technology that would aid business communication, yet customers showed a surprising willingness to adapt it to sociability. As Claude Fischer reminds us, telephone communications were quickly understood as private not public, and intimate not commercial (Fischer 1992, p. 76). Telephones were especially valued by farm families who faced rural isolation. With the development of rural cooperatives to provide service, as many as 70 percent of farm households had a phone by the turn of the century (Kline 2000, p. 27). Such high rates of telephone service did not spread through the general population until after 1950 (Fischer 1992, p. 70).

While American households may have been slow to purchase refrigerators and other household appliances, the response to the radio was immediate and enthusiastic. Commercial broadcasts began in 1920, and by 1925 at least ten manufacturers produced a radio that could be plugged into a household outlet. Indeed, in 1925, families spent as much for radio as they did for electricity itself (Tobey 1996, pp. 22–3). Radio allowed Americans to enjoy the benefits of entertainment at home, and provided a form of family recreation at a time when men and women were more likely to socialize separately in gender specific activities such as women's sewing circles, or men's sporting teams. Equipping the home for entertainment blossomed in the postwar era with the rapid spread of television. At a time when parents worried about rising rates of juvenile delinquency, keeping the children home under adult supervision enhanced the appeal of home entertainment technology. Video cassette recorders, by duplicating the programming that is shown in theaters, erased one of the last distinctions between home entertainment and its public equivalent.

The technologies of house and home, outside and inside, are in constant tension with those of the industrial and commercial world. We continue to draw a distinction between our private and our public lives, and to use new technologies to enhance our abilities to retreat into the sanctuary of the home. Yet the two have never been wholly separate. Our embrace of mass production as the key to prosperity means that the industrial model has increasingly been applied to the construction industry, and the values of efficiency and uniformity have been imported into our homes and kitchens. The acceptance of technical services and household appliances as part of our most basic starter homes means that the integration of the architectural house with its technical services is one of the important stories of the twentieth-century house and home.

BIBLIOGRAPHY

Ackermann, Marsha E. *Cool Comfort: America's Romance with Air-conditioning* (Washington, DC: Smithsonian Institution Press, 2002).

Banham, Reyner. *The Architecture of the Well-tempered Environment* (London: Architectural Press, 1969).

Condit, Carl W. *American Building: Materials and Techniques from the First Colonial Settlements to the Present*. 2nd edn (Chicago: University of Chicago Press, 1982).

Cooper, Gail. *Air-Conditioning America: Engineers and the Controlled Environment, 1900–1960* (Baltimore: Johns Hopkins University Press, 1998).

Cowan, Ruth Schwartz. *More Work for Mother: The Ironies of Household Technology from the Open Hearth to the Microwave* (New York: Basic Books, 1983).

Duncan, Susan Kirsch. *Levittown: the Way We Were* (Huntington, NY: Maple Hill Press, 1999).

Fischer, Claude S. *America Calling: A Social History of the Telephone to 1940* (Berkeley: University of California Press, 1992).

Goldstein, Carolyn M. *Do it Yourself: Home Improvement in 20th-Century America* (New York: Princeton Architectural Press, 1998).

Graham, Laurel. *Managing on Her Own: Dr. Lillian Gilbreth and Women's Work in the Interwar Era* (Norcross, Ga.: Engineering & Management Press, 1998).

Hardyment, Christina. *From Mangle to Microwave: The Mechanization of Household Work* (New York: Basil Blackwell, 1988).

Hayden, Dolores. *The Grand Domestic Revolution: A History of Feminist Designs for American Homes, Neighborhoods, and Cities* (Cambridge, Mass.: MIT Press, 1981).

Horowitz, Roger and Arwen Mohun eds. *His and Hers: Gender, Consumption, and Technology* (Charlottesville: University Press of Virginia, 1998).

Kline, Ronald R. *Consumers in the Country: Technology and Social Change in Rural America* (Baltimore: Johns Hopkins University Press, 2000).

Lerman, Nina E., Ruth Oldenziel, and Arwen Mohun eds. *Gender and Technology: A Reader* (Baltimore: Johns Hopkins University Press, 2003).

Melosi, Martin V. *The Sanitary City: Urban Infrastructure in America from Colonial Times to the Present* (Baltimore: Johns Hopkins University Press, 2000).

Mohun, Arwen. *Steam Laundries: Gender, Technology, and Work in the United States and Great Britain, 1880–1940* (Baltimore: Johns Hopkins University Press, 1999).

Motz, Marilyn Ferris and Pat Browne eds. *Making the American Home: Middle-class Women & Domestic Material Culture, 1840–1940* (Bowling Green, Ohio: Bowling Green State University Popular Press, 1988).

Ogle, Maureen. *All the Modern Conveniences: American Household Plumbing, 1840–1890* (Baltimore: Johns Hopkins University Press, 1996).

Parr, Joy. *Domestic Goods: the Material, the Moral, and the Economic in the Postwar Years* (Toronto: University of Toronto Press, 1999).

Rome, Adam Ward. *The Bulldozer in the Countryside: Suburban Sprawl and the Rise of American Environmentalism* (New York: Cambridge University Press, 2001).

Slaton, Amy E. *Reinforced Concrete and the Modernization of American Building, 1900–1930* (Baltimore: Johns Hopkins University Press, 2001).

Smulyan, Susan. *Selling Radio: The Commercialization of American Broadcasting, 1920–1934* (Washington: Smithsonian Institution Press, 1994).

Stage, Sarah and Virginia B. Vincenti eds. *Rethinking Home Economics: Women and the History of a Profession* (Ithaca: Cornell University Press, 1997).

Strasser, Susan. *Never Done: A History of American Housework* (New York: Pantheon Books, 1982).

Tarr, Joel A. *The Search for the Ultimate Sink: Urban Pollution in Historical Perspective* (Akron, Ohio: University of Akron Press, 1996).

Tobey, Ronald C. *Technology as Freedom: the New Deal and the Electrical Modernization of the American Home* (Berkeley: University of California Press, 1996).

Williams, James C. *Energy and the Making of Modern California* (Akron, Ohio: University of Akron Press, 1997).

Wright, Gwendolyn. *Moralism and the Model Home: Domestic Architecture and Cultural Conflict in Chicago, 1873–1913* (Chicago: University of Chicago Press, 1980).

Wright, Gwendolyn. *Building the Dream: A Social History of Housing in America* (New York: Pantheon Books, 1981).

CHAPTER SIX

The City and Technology

JOEL A. TARR

Historically, cities are a product of the interaction of technology and society, as a complex of tools and skills produced an economic surplus that permitted humans to live in non-agricultural settlements. Today, technology provides what might be called the "sinews" of the city: road, bridge and transit networks; water and sewer lines and waste disposal facilities; and power and communications systems. Other technologies, such as the streetcar, the subway, the motor truck and the automobile have provided mobility (and sometimes immobility) within the city and its region. Additional technologies have shaped the character of the built environment and the character of the cityscape. These technological systems made it possible for large numbers of residents to live in cities and also to increasingly separate work and residence. Technology facilitated city growth and diversification; over the course of two centuries it has caused profound changes in the patterns of urbanization in the United States and in the organization of urban society (Tarr and Dupuy 1988).

Technology, however, is not autonomous, and public and private decisions structured the manner in which it was allocated throughout the city and its region. To a large extent, urban technologies, because they often utilized the city streets both above and below ground, depended upon governmental action such as the granting of a franchise, a variance, or some sort of permission, for their operations. Usually, municipal action was involved, but upper levels of government, such as the county and the state, also came into play, frequently leading to conflict with the municipality over control. During the nineteenth century, municipal services were usually allocated on the principle that the abutter pays, leading to an urban "landscape of inequality" (Einhorn 1991, pp. 104–43).

Municipal government, particularly during the period of great city building during the late nineteenth and early twentieth centuries, tended to be vulnerable to private interests seeking to secure city franchises. Rampant corruption, involving political machines and corrupt city councils, often resulted from the quest for governmental privilege. During the Progressive Period in the first decades of the twentieth century, the concept of protecting the public good and insuring equality of service delivery gained powerful adherents and municipal services became more equally distributed. Still, for the remainder of the century, decisions about the provision of infrastructure often rested on the outcome of struggles between public and private interests. Driving governmental support for construction of technological systems were concerns about the public order, public safety and the public health (i.e., preventing the spread of epidemic disease). The actors who reflected this set of views included a number of commercial elites, professionals, and sanitarians (Gluck and Meister 1979).

This chapter is divided into three time periods: 1790–1870; 1870–1920; and 1920 to the present day. The period from 1790–1870 can be characterized as that of the walking or pedestrian city; the five decades between 1870 and 1920 as the networked or wired, piped, and tracked city; and the years since 1920 as the period when the automobile and motor truck, accompanied by energy and communications technologies, have been predominant. These periods, however, are malleable, and there is considerable overlap between them, as will be noted in the various sections. Certain elements of the built environment were quick to change in response to innovation and potential profit, while others have persisted over long periods of time.

A further comment on terminology involves the use of the terms technology, infrastructure, and public works. While they are often used interchangeably in this essay, they can have specific meanings, as will be made clear. Infrastructure and public works are largely urban terms and usually refer to various technological systems. Infrastructure can be either public or private, and sometimes both, while government constructs public works. Who should construct and operate urban technological systems, however, has often been a matter of dispute and control has shifted back and forth over time, as will be seen, between the public and the private sectors (Jacobson and Tarr 1996).

The Walking City, 1790–1870

During the period 1790–1870, the urban population grew from approximately 202,000 to over 15 million. In 1790, there was no city with a population over 50,000; in 1870, there were 25 that exceeded that figure, with three over 300,000 and one close to a million. Cities were originally very compact and dense and, while they grew extensively in these years, with the exception of a few major cities such as New York, Chicago, Philadelphia and St Louis, those in 1870 were still largely compact rather than spread. Often they were clustered around an ocean, lake or river port, with a commercial orientation. Although the larger cities had factory districts as part of their economic mix, the smaller ones presented a jumble of small businesses and workshops with an occasional factory. Limited separation existed, if at all, between work and residence (Tarr and Konvitz 1987, pp. 96–203).

Urbanites of all classes generally walked to work. Given the limited transportation and communications facilities available, clustering made the most sense in order to expedite communications. Governments on many levels, federal, state, county and city, as well as private/public partnerships, financed public works projects throughout these years, with transportation systems the most critical. The end purpose of these public works projects was to spur economic development as well as to populate the continent (Lively 1955).

During these years cities began to construct some of the technological systems that today we take for granted. After about 1830, transportation innovations began to provide alternatives, especially for members of the elite and the middle classes. The first public transport innovation was the omnibus or horse-drawn bus, based on a French model, and used in New York City, Philadelphia, and Boston in the 1830s. The commuter steam railroad came next, also in the 1830s, followed by the horse or mule powered streetcar in 1851. All systems were privately owned. These transportation innovations created a "mobility revolution," and stimulated the development of a series of peripheral communities or suburbs, connected to the central city. In addition to being a facilitator of suburbanization, the railroad was also a vast generator of economic growth, spurring economic development by penetrating the hinterland and linking cities to rich natural resources and to an urban network (Binford 1985, pp. 83–152).

In these same decades, urban government began increasingly to supply various services. Government saw its role as aiding the private economy (especially downtown business interests) and real estate developers. In the 1840s and 1850s, a group of urban professional politicians, who viewed public works as a means to cater to the voters, took power and tried to win the support of various interest groups, and to channel public funds into their own pockets and the party coffers (Bridges 1984). Another important interest group in these decades and through the end of the century were sanitarians and physicians concerned with the public health, who lobbied for construction of improved water supply and sewer systems.

The provision of water supplies through centralized systems was probably the most important technological and infrastructure development of the walking city period. Ample water supplies were required for domestic and industrial uses, street cleaning, and to fight the disastrous conflagrations that often plagued antebellum cities. Until well into the second half of the nineteenth century, most American urbanites depended on local sources for water – they dug their own wells and built cisterns to catch rainwater, used public wells, drew water from neighborhood ponds, streams and springs, and even purchased water from vendors peddling it on the streets. Usually there was a mix of private and public wells. In Philadelphia, for instance, in the early eighteenth century, entrepreneurs dug wells on public property for a rental fee and sold water to the public. Later in the century, the city purchased private pumps and assessed residents for their use. In New York City, in the late 1780s and 1790s, the municipality tried to increase the supply of water by subsidizing well construction and providing funds for repair, cleaning and construction from a statewide tax.

Local supplies, in spite of municipal involvement, were inadequate to provide for the needs of growing cities. Wells and ponds became visibly polluted and groundwater receded. Epidemics of yellow fever and cholera swept through the cities and firemen often lacked water to fight fires. In 1798, in response to a yellow fever epidemic, Philadelphia constructed the first American municipal water supply system. Others cities gradually followed, although the provision of improved water supplies frequently encountered obstacles over questions of the best source of water and opposition from vested interests in existing privately owned systems (Blake 1956).

Eventually, in city after city, a coalition of physicians and sanitarians, industrialists, and fire insurance companies compelled action: Cincinnati and Pittsburgh installed water systems in the 1820s, New York opened the Croton Reservoir in 1841, and Boston the Cochituate system in 1848. By 1860 the nation's sixteen largest cities had waterworks, with a total of 136 systems (57 public; 79 private). The larger cities were more likely to have publicly owned waterworks and the smaller cities privately owned. Public ownership was necessitated not only by the large capital requirements of the systems but also by the inadequacies of the private companies. Cities that began with private water supply companies, such as New York and Chicago, shifted to public ownership because of the refusal of the private companies to provide adequate water for civic purposes such as street flushing and fire hydrants or to eliminate pollution, to enlarge their works in anticipation of population growth, or to service distant districts (Melosi 2000, pp. 73–89).

During the period up to 1870, water works diffused among the urban network, with large cities adopting them first and smaller cities moving more slowly because of the large capital expenditure required. In most cities, water supplies were unevenly distributed, with affluent residential districts and the central business district receiving piped-in water first while poor districts were supplied by corner hydrants or continued to rely on wells and springs (Jacobson and Tarr 1996).

The provision of water works only solved part of the city's metabolic functioning, since used water and human wastes had to be disposed of. Ideally, they should have been removed from the settled area of the city but in most locales in this period householders deposited human wastes and wastewater in cesspools and privy vaults located close by residences or even in cellars. By the 1820s and 1830s, most large cities had instituted periodic emptying of vaults by private scavengers under city contract or by city employees, but the experience was unsatisfactory whether the service was performed by municipal employees or private contractors.

Construction of a sewerage system to remove these wastes was the logical answer but building such a system was a massive capital undertaking. Many householders, especially in smaller cities and towns, improvised with various plumbing systems to provide water and dispose of wastewater (Ogle 1998). While both private and public underground sewers existed in larger cities such as New York and Boston, they were intended mainly for storm water, to prevent flooding and accumulation of "miasma" breeding puddles of stagnant water. The majority of nineteenth-century cities had no underground sewers at all but rather relied on street gutters for storm water removal (Melosi 2000, pp. 17–42).

As cities became larger and denser, however, existing methods of waste removal became increasingly inadequate. Household adoption of new water-using appliances increased the stress placed by population growth on the cesspool/privy system. The water closet (WC), installed by affluent families to take advantage of its cleanliness and convenience caused the most serious problems. The flow of contaminated water from these appliances rapidly overran cesspool capacity, flooding yards and alleys with fecally polluted wastewater and raising fears of dangers to the public health (Tarr 1996, pp. 114–17).

After extensive debates over alternative technologies and their relation to different disease hypotheses, sanitarians and engineers largely agreed that the water carriage system of waste removal was the preferred solution. Their conclusions were largely based upon the experience of British, German and French cities. Water carriage solved the problem of collection and transportation simultaneously and offered the most public health protection. In the 1850s, Brooklyn, Chicago, and Jersey City constructed the first planned and centralized municipal systems and other cities began to emulate them (Melosi 2000, pp. 90–102).

Civil engineers such as John B. Jervis, the chief engineer of New York's Croton and Boston's Cochituate Aqueducts, and Ellis S. Chesbrough, builder of the Chicago sewers, supervised construction of these urban systems. Neither Jervis nor Chesbrough had a university education and secured their training on major public works projects such as the Erie Canal. They typified the practically trained civil engineers who helped develop municipal water and sewer systems in the middle of the nineteenth century (Koeppel 2000, pp. 185–275). Technology transfer was also vital to the construction of the nineteenth century urban infrastructure, with much borrowing from European countries.

While the technologies of transport, water supply and wastewater removal were the most significant innovations made in the walking city, there were also a number of other important developments that effected both the built environment and the quality of urban life. Major innovations in building and construction methods and materials – the balloon frame and cast iron framing – simplified the provision of housing for expanding populations and growing business need for space. New bridge technologies, especially the use of iron truss bridges for railroads and wire cables for suspension bridges facilitated and improved bridge construction (Roberts and Steadman 1999, pp. 93–137). And, the use of manufactured gas, made from organic materials like coal and rosen and distributed over piped networks, made cities safer at night through improved street lighting and improved home illumination for households that could afford it (Tarr 1999).

As the compact urban city began to spread, better communications became a necessity. The telegraph (1844) had its widest application in connecting cities over space, but it was also adapted to urban businesses, municipal service delivery systems and private service delivery (district telegraph companies). Telegraph appliances such as the printing telegraph, the gold stock printer and the private – line networks greatly increased the speed of the transmission of prices and other business information. In 1851, Boston installed the first fire alarm telegraph (it was modeled on the concept of the human nervous system), and by 1870 thirteen other large cities had followed its example. Some cities also installed telegraphic police signal systems although they were not as prevalent as the fire alarm systems (Tarr, Finholt and Goodman 1987).

The period of the Walking City witnessed a number of significant urban technological developments that led to its reconfiguration. Private entrepreneurs established horse-powered streetcar systems throughout the cities, increasing the separation of work and residence. Municipalities built water and sewerage systems, installed telegraphic fire and police alarm systems, and furnished or contracted for improved street lighting. The last decades of the Walking City period witnessed the gradual transformation from a "piecemeal, decentralized approach" to city-building towards one involving more centralized and networked technologies (Peterson 1979). Many of these urban technological systems would become increasingly commonplace across the urban network in the next period.

The Emergence of the Networked City, 1870–1920

The period between 1870 and 1920 was one of intense urbanization. The number of persons living in cities increased from about 15,000,000 in 1870 to 25,000,000 in 1900, and to 54,000,000 in 1920. By 1920, there were 43 cities with between 100,000 and 250,000 population, thirteen with 250,000–500,000, nine with between 500,000 and 1,000,000, and three with over a million. These increases stemmed from three sources: natural increase, farm to city movement, and foreign immigration. Not only did the urban population and the number of cities increase dramatically, but the urban network, which had been entirely east of the Mississippi in 1860, now extended from coast to coast. In response to population increases, the spatial area of cities grew.

In this period, the compact and congested walking cities expanded over larger areas and their central cores experienced residential decline. Members of the elite and of the middle class, many of whom had earlier lived in the core, moved to the city's outlying areas and suburbs, seeking rural amenities, cheaper land, and escape from the city's noise and congestion. Improved transportation enabled the rise of streetcar suburbs. While the omnibus and the commuter railroad served only a limited and relatively affluent population, the cheaper streetcars carried many more passengers. The first streetcar systems – the horsecar lines – increased mobility although their restricted speed (5–6 mph), limited their impact. Inventors continually sought alternatives to the horse as a source of power, resulting in innovations such as the steam "dummy," cable cars, and various type of electric locomotives. Frank Sprague's electric streetcar, with an overhead trolley and spring pole, first demonstrated in Richmond, Virginia in 1888, was the critical innovation. In the 1890s the electrically powered streetcar (or "trolley") rapidly replaced the horse car and the cable car (McShane 1994, pp. 1–80).

Electric streetcars traveled at approximately 10–20 mph, greatly expanding the areas within commuting distance of the downtown core. From 1890 to 1902, track mileage increased from 5,783 to 22,577, almost all of it operated by electricity, while rides per urban inhabitant jumped from 111 to 181. Five years later, in 1907, track mileage had advanced 53.5 percent to 34,404 and rides per inhabitant to 250, as the use of public transit far out-distanced urban population increase. Other forms of transportation innovation and rapid transit included elevated railroads and subways. Private companies holding municipal franchises permitting them to use the city streets usually owned the streetcar systems; in return for the franchise, they assumed financial and other obligations such as street paving (Roberts and Steadman 1999, pp. 28–42).

As population spread spatially, entrepreneurs and city builders transformed the downtown areas into districts devoted almost entirely to business and commercial uses with a concentration of office buildings, banks, specialized retail outlets, and department stores. The twice-daily flow of commuters riding streetcars into and out of the downtown for purposes of work and shopping became a regular phenomena. Other urbanites, especially women, used the streetcar at off peak hours to venture into the downtown to shop and browse at the new consumer palaces known as department stores. The flood of downtown commuters and the resulting congestion created demands for improved transit, bridges, and tunnels as well as improved streets and traffic circulation (Fogelson 2001).

In the 1870s, the development of the skyscraper began a radical transformation of the cityscape. Skyscrapers were made possible by a number of technological developments, including steel framing, fireproofing, the safety elevator, communications improvements such as the telegraph and telephone, and heating, ventilation, plumbing and lighting systems. These, in turn, depended for their operation on infrastructure systems such as water supply and sewers. Before the skyscraper appeared, downtown office structures were largely constructed of masonry and were usually no higher than six stories. In the 1870s and 1880s, New York and Chicago pioneered with buildings like the ten-storey 230-foot Western Union Building (1875) and the ten-storey Home Insurance Building (1885). By the early twentieth century New York City possessed structures as tall as the 302-foot Flatiron Building (1902) and the 792-foot Woolworth Building (1913). Other large cities such as Pittsburgh also constructed a number of skyscrapers, although others, like Philadelphia, maintained height restrictions. The motivation for building tall buildings was not only a desire to avoid space constraints but also to provide a cultural statement of symbolic value and capitalistic visibility (Landau and Condit 1996).

While the Central Business District (CBD) was being transformed, the areas adjacent to it, often known as the zone of transition, became extremely dense, as they absorbed displaced core populations as well as new entries into the city seeking jobs in the CBD or in the many small workshops that characterized these areas. Thus, the improved transportation systems had effects of both deconcentration and concentration – permitting affluent urbanites to separate work and residence with suburban residences but also forcing the concentration of working class people with limited residential choice in dense districts near their jobs (Jackson 1985, pp. 20–115).

Much of the urban infrastructure built during this expansionist period owed its impetus to professional politicians, downtown city boosters, and real estate speculators. Trained engineers, produced by a host of new engineering colleges (85 by 1880) helped design most urban technological systems to serve urban needs efficiently. Municipalities employed a growing number of civil engineers as city and consulting engineers. Because city engineers appeared to represent the values of economy, efficiency and professionalism that reformers desired, municipalities drew heavily on them to serve as city managers in the Progressive Period (c. 1900–14) and after (Schiesl 1977).

Numerous urban reform groups, many of them women's clubs, developed in the late nineteenth and early twentieth centuries in opposition to control of the city building process by political machines and poor urban environmental conditions, especially in urban slums. They pushed vigorously for improvements in the functioning of urban technological systems and environmental and public health improvements. Thus, they agitated for institutional changes such as the creation of local and state boards of health and for municipal housekeeping improvements such as clean water supplies, the building of sewers, efficient garbage collection, control of smoke pollution, clean streets, cheaper transportation, and improvements in housing (Schultz 1989, pp. 111–82).

As cities grew in the late nineteenth and early twentieth centuries, demand and supply interacted to diffuse urban technologies throughout the system. The number of water works for instance, increased from 1,878 in 1890 to 3,196 in 1897 while miles of sewers increased from 6,005 in 1890 (cities >25,000 population) to 24,972 in 1909 (cities >30,000 population), about three-quarters combined sewers and the remainder mainly sanitary sewers. Improved public works technologies also spread to regions such as the South where urbanization and improvement had lagged, and to smaller cities not yet equipped with such networks.

As urban technologies diffused throughout the urban network, they created unanticipated problems. The pollution of municipal water supplies by upstream cities who discharged raw sewage into the streams that downstream cities utilized for water supply was most severe. The belief that running water purified itself and the absence of any authority powerful enough to constrain one city from contaminating the metabolic systems of others caused the problem. Science and technology ultimately remedied the situation by clarifying the nature of water borne disease and developing biologically based water filtration technology. Engineers and chemists also developed efficient methods of sewage treatment but diffusion of sewage treatment plants was much slower than that of water filtration systems because they primarily benefited downstream cities rather than the cities that paid for construction (Tarr 1996, pp. 179–218).

While municipal authorities usually operated water and sewer systems in this period, controversies over the private or public ownership of other urban technological systems preoccupied many cities. During the late nineteenth century electric light and power, gas and transit became integrated into the urban fabric and were perceived to be nearly as important to urban functioning as water supplies. Just as piped-in water had earlier shifted from a luxury to a necessity, so now other technology-based utility services began the same transformation. Since the majority of water works were publicly owned (70 percent in 1920), this suggested to some that the same course should be followed for the other utilities. Heated political battles took place over the question of utility regulation or municipal ownership. In some cities, such as New York, public-private partnerships evolved, while in some smaller cities, municipal ownership resulted (Jacobson and Tarr 1998).

The period between approximately 1870 and 1920 was a critical stage with regard to the impact of technology on the city. In these years, the basic patterns of water, sewer and transit systems were laid down. In addition, other communications and energy-related technologies such as the telegraph and telephone, and manufactured gas and electricity, extended their distribution lines throughout the city. The rate of expansion of the supply of infrastructure was especially rapid from 1890–1915, when the number of waterworks increased from 1,878 to 9,850, the population served by filtered water from 310,000 to 17,291,000 (1890–1914), and the miles of sewers increased from about 16,000,000 to over 47,500,000. In addition, by 1920, approximately half of urban households were served by electricity while 35 percent had telephones (Rose 1995).

The Domination of the Automobile, the Development of the Spread City, and the Rise of Telematics, 1920–2000

During the period from 1920 to 2000, the US urban population increased from 54,000,000 to over 226,000,000 million. The suburban share of the total has grown steadily, with over 50 percent of the nation's population living in suburbs by 2000; suburban population increased by 14 percent from 1990 to 2000 alone. Change, however, was not seamless, and a convenient breaking point for this period is 1945, after the experiences of the Great Depression and World War II.

The 1920s were a period of rapid urban expansion and suburbanization, but the Great Depression (1930s) and World War II produced significant slowdowns. Suburbanization, however, exploded again in the late 1940s and continued during successive decades. Two other demographic trends developed in the postwar period: a regional shift in the distribution of large cities and urbanized population towards the so-called Sun Belt, a move taking place primarily after 1950, and the development of the outer city or Edge City at the periphery of many metropolitan regions, beginning mainly in the 1970s.

The primary technology facilitating the suburban trend continued to be the automobile (and the motor truck). Infrastructures such as highways, and especially the Interstate Highway System (1956), played a critical supporting role (Rose 1990). Other technologies such as the airplane, electrical power, the telephone, and pre-fabricated housing also contributed to suburbanization, but without the automobile the process would have been slower and different in location and design (Jackson 1985, pp. 157–89) Government on all levels, especially on the federal level, continued to play a critical role, shaping the impact of technology on cities and metropolitan growth processes in various significant ways.

Increases in automobile ownership in the last 80 years of the twentieth century were continuous, except for a dip during the interruptions of the depression and World War II. While initially automobile ownership was heaviest in rural areas, automobiles, motor buses, and trucks were soon largely concentrated in cities (McShane 1994). In some ways the decade of the 1920s was the most impressive because of the phenomenal increase in the rate of ownership. In the 20 years from 1910 to 1930, the number of auto registrations in the country grew from 458,377 to 22,972,745 at a time when population was increasing from 91,972,266 to 122,775,046 or from 1 car to every 201 persons to 1 to every 5.3.

The automobile both accelerated the process of urban growth and suburbanization set in motion by the streetcar and altered its form and location. It enlarged and extended metropolitan areas, multiplied the flow of commuter traffic between the downtown and outlying residential areas, and greatly increased street congestion in the downtown cores. Urban growth along the lines of streetcar tracks had often left large undeveloped areas, but the automobile, with its flexibility, was able not only to extend the urban boundary but also to stimulate a filling in-process of housing development (Monkkonen 1988, pp. 182–205).

The decade of the 1920s witnessed the emergence of the modern automobile-dependent residential suburb, with many middle-class homes equipped with a range of electrical appliances such as the vacuum cleaner and washing machine. While these appliances may have shifted more household tasks to women, they also undoubtedly lightened onerous domestic loads (Strasser 1982, pp. 202–81). Because, however, of the failure of electrical utilities to reduce rates or to standardize fixtures, electrical appliance ownership was largely confined to the urban middle and upper classes, replicating the earlier experience with water and sewers (Tobey 1996).

As automobile usage surged in the 1920s, traffic problems within the core of cities greatly increased. In Pittsburgh, for instance from 1917 to 1929, the number of automobiles in the CBD increased 587 percent, the number of motor trucks 251 percent, and the numbers of streetcars 81 percent (Tarr 1978, pp. 25–8). Downtown business interests throughout the nation called for planning to alleviate traffic congestion and new road networks to both facilitate entry into downtown and to permit the bypass of through traffic. These same groups often also called for new rapid transit construction to facilitate the transport of people in and out of the core. In many locations, however, automobile usage had begun to eat into transit ridership and pose a threat to their financial stability (Barrett 1983, pp. 129–218).

Planners and members of the new engineering field of traffic engineering, developed primarily in response to the automobile, viewed downtown congestion as an engineering problem, requiring both planning and public works construction. The CBD infrastructure accommodations to the automobile included the widening and double-decking of streets, the elimination of grade crossings, and the development of a variety of traffic controls. In addition, street surfacing with smooth pavements (mostly asphalt) took place throughout the urban areas. Hundreds of bridges and tunnels were also built by cities and counties to facilitate cross river transportation, while Chicago, New York, Pittsburgh, and Los Angeles built limited access roadways and parkways into downtown before World War II (McShane 1994, pp. 203–28).

The needs of the automobile and the motor truck for improved roads and highways, bridges, and tunnels, expressed by automobile clubs, business organizations and engineering associations, resulted in extensive construction. The mileage of well-surfaced roads greatly increased and innovative limited access roads were built in some states, such as New York's parkways pioneered by Robert Moses. Some federal funding from the Bureau of Public Roads and massive state funding provided partial financing, but most significant was Oregon's initiation of the gasoline tax in 1919. By 1929, all states had enacted the tax, which became the principal source of highway revenues (Foster 1981).

The rate of increase of automobile ownership in the 1920s was matched by the growth in telephone usage, simulated by improvements in operating technology such as central switching and dialing. The telephone, like the automobile, appears to have had both centralizing and decentralizing effects. While permitting the separation of central offices from production facilities and the out movement of factories to the periphery of cities, it also encouraged the clustering of office activities in the central urban core (de Sola Pool 1977).

Water and sewage works and improvements in the 1920s continued to be important, with a tripling of the amount of public monies committed to them, leading to a doubling of the populations served by treated water and sewage. No longer did suburbs seek annexation or consolidation with the central cities because of a desire for superior municipal services, and many of the larger suburban municipalities developed their own services. In addition to water and sewage, other public services, such as fire and police departments, now became commonplace in the suburbs (Teaford 1979).

While the federal government had only a limited involvement in the provision of technological infrastructure before the 1930s, this shifted sharply in the depression decade. The New Deal evolved as a governmental response to the economic hardships caused by the Great Depression and the construction of urban infrastructure became a major way to "prime the pump." The increased federal involvement was largely directed by various relief agencies such as the Works Progress Administration (WPA) and the Public Works Administration (PWA). The Federal government was involved in a huge range of infrastructure and technology-related projects, including roads, sewers, waterworks, multiple purpose dams, bridges, parks, docks, and wharves; and airports, hospitals, and other public buildings (Gelfand 1975).

Not as visible as these infrastructures, but still extremely significant for the modernization of the home, was the New Deal's restructuring of the market for appliances and subsidization of refrigerator purchase. As Ronald C. Tobey notes, "the federal government diffused the material benefits of modern technology to the mass of white households as a matter" – in FDR's (Franklin D. Roosevelt) words – "of right" (Tobey 1996, p. 177). Here we have an example of government supporting technology diffusion in the home as well as in the public sector.

In the decades after World War II, suburbanization increased at a rapid rate as veterans returned from overseas, created families, and sought improved living conditions. Government policies such as the Veterans Bill and the tax deductibility of mortgage interest both facilitated and accelerated this process. The mechanization of housing construction, most strikingly displayed in Levittown outside of Philadelphia and in Long Island, resulted in massive suburban developments in many metropolitan areas (Kelly 1993). By 1960, suburban population had equaled central city population and by 1980, it had surpassed it. Simultaneously, central cities in the north and mid-west experienced population decline and changed demographic composition.

The needs of the growing suburban areas combined with the pent-up demands of central cities to produce a vigorous period of infrastructure growth. Most of this increase came in the areas of sewer and water works, road and highway construction, and school building, reflecting the impacts of suburbanization, the automobile, and the baby boom. Most dramatic and far reaching of the network changes was highway expansion, particularly as a result of the Interstate Highway Act of 1956. Throughout the 1950s truckers, automobile clubs, highway contractors, the automobile industry, engineering associations, and businessmen's groups applied pressure on Congress to provide Federal funding of new highway construction. The need for defense was also cited as a rationale. The legislation that emerged provided something for everyone, with urban interests perhaps receiving the most. The Federal government agreed to distribute its 90 percent payment of interstate expenses according to local needs, with the cost of freeway construction in congested urban areas being the greatest (Rose 1990).

Automobile use exploded in these decades. Between 1945 and 1970, automobile registrations increased from 25,796,000 to 89,280,000, and from 1980 to 1998, from 121,601,000 to 131,839,000. In 1950, 52 percent of households owned an automobile and 7 percent owned two or more; by 1995, the number of vehicles per household was 1.78, or almost an average of two vehicles per household. Even though highway mileage expanded, automobile use and hence congestion outdistanced it. In many metropolitan areas journey-to-work patterns shifted, with a diminution of traffic flows from periphery to core, counter flows from core to employment centers in the suburbs, and an increase in trips to destinations on the periphery (Roberts and Steadman 1999, pp. 208–17).

As automobile proliferation accelerated, urban public transit lost ridership and private companies went bankrupt. Because many cities regarded transit as a public good, they increasingly took over its provision. By 1965, more than half the urban transit system had become publicly owned. In the 1970s, Federal funds began to be supplied to localities for urban transit. Transit ridership, however, barely grew from 1985 to 1998, and public subsidies have continually increased. The main transit type to experience growth was light rail vehicles, but these were confined to a relatively small number of cities; buses carried the largest number of transit riders by far (Cervero 1998, pp. 415–45). Although urban and regional planners have strongly advocated increased transit service, the American public remains committed to the automobile.

Major shifts in regional growth accompanied the massive suburbanization. The new regions whose populations exploded were in the so-called Sun Belt, including the states of Florida, North and South Carolina, Georgia, Texas, Oklahoma, New Mexico, Arizona, and California. In 1990, for instance, five cities – Houston, San Diego, Dallas, Phoenix, and San Antonio – became part of the nation's top 10 although none had been in that cohort in 1950. In 1920, eight of the nation's 10 largest cities were in the north and in 1950 seven of the nation's largest cities were still in that region; by 1990, however, the number had shrunk to four, with three in the south and three in the west. Even more significantly, by 1990, 40 of the nation's hundred largest cities were in the south, and only 30 in the north (Abbott 1987).

The air conditioner was the primary technology making it possible to live in hot and humid climates comfortably all year round. The first application of air conditioning was in industry, followed by motion picture theatres and large auditoriums in the 1920s. The postwar period witnessed a great expansion of domestic air conditioning. Window room air conditioners were used to retrofit existing structures while suburban tract developers often offered centralized air conditioning. Air conditioning, of course, depended upon the extension of electric systems and the provision of cheap electricity, and its extensive adoption severely strained the electrical utilities in the 1960s and 1970s. As urban populations shifted to the Sun Belt states, the nation became increasingly dependent on air conditioning technology and its high energy demands (Cooper 1998).

The period from the 1970s through the 1990s also experienced another geographic phenomena, not necessarily confined to any one region but entirely automobile dependent. This is the so-called outer city or Edge City, as described by the journalist Joel Garreau (Garreau 1991). In these peripheral but ever-spreading areas of the metropolis, a mass of urban activities that were formerly the monopoly of the central city have developed. Most prominent in the outer city are the new multiple-purpose centers (or "mini-cities") which provide concentrations of retailing, entertainment, offices and other consumer-oriented and employment activities. These are located on or close to the beltways and freeways constructed since the Interstate Highway Act of 1956 and are surrounded by residential areas. They represent, according to one study, "the liquefaction of the urban structure" and the growth of "polycentric, intensively...networked urban regions" (Graham and Marvin 2001, p. 115). In short, in many metropolitan regions, the distinction between city and suburb and centralization and decentralization, have all but disappeared (Teaford 1995).

Any discussion of the city and technology during this period requires a comment about environmental improvements. Well into the second half of the century, American cities suffered from a number of pollution problems, including smoke filled skies and sewage and industrial waste polluted rivers (Tarr 1996). Municipal and state action accomplished some improvements, as did the movement from coal to natural gas and petroleum as fuels and railroad substitution of the diesel-electric for the steam locomotive. The development of the Environmental Movement in the 1960s and the passage of federal legislation in the 1970s improved environmental quality in cities even further. Under the various acts passed, especially the Federal Water Pollution Control Act of 1972 (the "Clean Streams Act"), and the Clean Water Act, Federal dollars poured into sewer and sewage treatment projects. Other acts that produced urban environmental improvements included the Clean Air Acts (the ending of lead additives to gasoline) and the Super Fund Acts of the 1980s. Some of these Acts included specific technology-forcing provisions, reflecting the conviction that only incentives would push some firms to install innovative and environmentally beneficial technologies (Hays 1987).

The most significant technologies aside from the automobile that are reconfiguring cities and city life are telecommunications or so-called telematics. Telematics refers to "services and infrastructures which link computer and digital media equipment over telecommunications links" (Graham and Marvin 1996, pp. 2–3). They provide the technological foundations for computer networking and data, voice, image and video communications. Cities have always had communications functions but now telematics has increased this role, and especially for so-called global cities with major financial and trade links over large areas of the world. Cellular phones, broadband cable networks, microwave systems, and satellites are transforming economic and social life, as well as the spatial arrangements of cities. Whether the use of these technologies will lead to the dissolution of the city as we have known it or whether it will lead to a strengthening of urban life and urban forms is still uncertain (Graham and Marvin 1996).

Conclusions

This chapter has discussed technology and the city in the context of the city building process over time. Transportation has been viewed as the primary shaping technology because it determines the city's spatial organization. Thus, the chapter is organized into discussions of the walking city, the networked city, and the automobile city. These periods, of course, overlapped along many dimensions and various technologies assumed importance at different times. Some elements of the built environment changed very rapidly, while others changed very slowly. For instance, different urban networked technologies, especially those that are underground, are many years old. Communications technologies, however, have changed extremely rapidly, especially in the last decade.

From a spatial perspective, cities have experienced patterns of concentration and deconcentration over time, with major changes in the last three decades. These more recent changes have involved regional shifts in urban location, increases in suburbanization, and development of the outer city. The technologies most responsible are the automobile, air conditioning and the development of many forms of telematics or communications technologies.

Today we face major questions regarding the survival of the traditional city and its forms. Technology has been the force facilitating and extending these changes, but ultimately humans decide what type habitats they want to reside in and under what conditions. Technology made possible the creation of the city as a center for human habitat thousands of years ago and perhaps now it will result in its demise. On the other hand, it may also facilitate the emergence of new forms of the city providing a more sustainable habitat for urban dwellers (Graham and Marvin 2001).

BIBLIOGRAPHY

Abbott, Carl. *The New Urban America: Growth and Politics in Sunbelt Cities* (Chapel Hill: University of North Carolina Press, 1987).
Barrett, Paul. *The Automobile and Urban Transit: The Formation of Public Policy in Chicago, 1900–1930* (Philadelphia: Temple University Press, 1983).
Binford, Henry C. *The First Suburbs: Residential Communities on The Boston Periphery 1815–1860* (Chicago: University of Chicago Press, 1985).

Blake, Nelson M. *Water for the Cities: A History of the Urban Water Supply Problem in the United States* (Syracuse: Syracuse University Press, 1956).

Bridges, Amy. *A City in the Republic: Antebellum New York and the Origins of Machine Politics* (Ithaca: Cornell University Press, 1984).

Cervero, Robert. *The Transit Metropolis: A Global Inquiry* (Washington, DC: Island Press, 1998).

Cooper, Gail. *Air-conditioning America: Engineers and the Controlled Environment, 1900–1960* (Baltimore: Johns Hopkins University Press, 1998).

de Sola Pool, Ithiel ed. *The Social Impact of the Telephone* (Boston: MIT Press, 1977).

Einhorn, Robin L. *Property Rules: Political Economy in Chicago, 1833–1872* (Chicago: University of Chicago Press, 1991).

Fogelson, Robert M. *Downtown: Its Rise and Fall, 1880–1950* (New Haven: Yale University Press, 2001).

Foster, Mark S. *From Streetcar to Superhighway: American City Planners and Urban Transportation, 1900–1940* (Philadelphia: Temple University Press, 1981).

Garreau, Joel. *Edge City: Life on the New Frontier* (New York: Doubleday, 1991).

Gelfand, Mark I. *A Nation of Cities: The Federal Government and Urban America 1933–1965* (New York: Oxford University Press, 1975).

Gluck, Peter R. and Meister, Richard J. *Cities in Transition: Social Changes and Institutional Responses in Urban Development* (New York: New Viewpoints, 1979).

Graham, Stephen and Marvin, Simon. *Telecommunications and the City: Electronic Spaces, Urban Places* (London: Routledge, 1996).

Graham, Stephen and Marvin, Simon. *Splintering Urbanism: Networked Infrastructure, Technological Mobilities and the Urban Condition* (London: Routledge, 2001).

Hays, Samuel P. *Environmental Politics in the United States, 1955–1985* (New York: Cambridge University Press, 1987).

Jackson, Kenneth T. *The Crabgrass Frontier: The Suburbanization of the United States* (New York: Oxford University Press, 1985).

Jacobson, Charles D. and Tarr, Joel A. "No single path: ownership and financing of infrastructure in the 19th and 20th centuries," in Ashoka Mody, ed., *Infrastructure Delivery: Private Initiative and the Public Good* (Washington, DC: The World Bank, 1996).

Kelly, Barbara M. *Expanding the American Dream: Building and Rebuilding Levittown* (Albany: State University of New York Press, 1993).

Koeppel, Gerard T. *Water For Gotham: A History* (Princeton: Princeton University Press, 2000).

Landau, Sarah Bradford, and Condit, Carl W. *Rise of the New York Skyscraper 1865–1913* (New Haven: Yale University Press, 1996).

Lively, Robert A. "The American system: a review article," *Business History Review* 24 (Summer 1955): 81–95.

McShane, Clay. *Down the Asphalt Path: The Automobile and the American City* (New York: Columbia University Press, 1994).

Melosi, Martin V. *The Sanitary City: Urban Infrastructure in America from Colonial Times to the Present* (Baltimore: Johns Hopkins University Press, 2000).

Monkkonen, Eric H. *America Becomes Urban: the Development of U.S. Cities and Towns 1780–1980* (Berkeley: University of California Press, 1988).

Ogle, Maureen. *All the Modern Conveniences: American Household Plumbing, 1840–1890* (Baltimore: Johns Hopkins University Press, 1998).

Peterson, Jon. "The impact of sanitary reform upon American urban planning, 1840–1890," *Journal of Social History* 13 (Fall 1979): 83–104.

Roberts, Gerrylynn K. and Steadman, Philip. *American Cities & Technology: Wilderness to Wired City* (London: Routledge, 1999).

Rose, Mark. *Interstate: Express Highway Politics, 1939–1989* (Memphis: University of Tennessee Press, 1990, 2nd edn).

Rose, Mark. *Cities of Light and Heat: Domesticating Gas and Electricity in Urban America* (State College: Pennsylvania State University Press, 1995).

Schiesl, Martin J. *The Politics of Efficiency: Municipal Administration and Reform in America: 1880–1920* (Berkeley: University of California Press, 1977).

Schultz, Stanley K. *Constructing Urban Culture: American Cities and City Planning, 1800–1920* (Philadelphia: Temple University Press, 1989).

Strasser, Susan. *Never Done: A History of American Housework* (New York: Pantheon, 1982).

Tarr, Joel A. *Transportation Innovation and Spatial Change in Pittsburgh, 1850–1934* (Chicago: Public Works Historical Society, 1978).

Tarr, Joel A. *Searching for the Ultimate Sink: Urban Pollution in Historical Perspective* (Akron: University of Akron Press, 1996).

Tarr, Joel A. "Transforming an energy system: the evolution of the manufactured gas industry and the transition to natural gas in the United States (1807–1954)," in Olivier Coutard, ed., *The Governance of Large Technical Systems* (London: Routledge, 1999).

Tarr, Joel A., Finholt, Thomas, and Goodman, David: "The city and the telegraph: urban telecommunications in the pre-telephone era," *Journal of Urban History* 14 (November, 1987): 38–80.

Tarr, Joel A. and Dupuy, Gabriel, eds. *Technology and the Rise of the Networked City in Europe and America* (Philadelphia: Temple University Press, 1988).

Tarr, Joel A. and Konvitz, Josef W. "Patterns in the development of the urban infrastructure," in Howard Gillettte, Jr and Zane L. Miller, ed., *American Urbanism: A Historiographical Review* (New York: Greenwood Press, 1987), pp. 194–226.

Teaford, John C. *City and Suburb: The Political Fragmentation of Metropolitan America, 1850–1970* (Baltimore: Johns Hopkins University Press, 1979).

Teaford, John C. *Post-Suburbia: Government and Politics in the Edge Cities* (Baltimore: Johns Hopkins University Press, 1995).

Tobey, Ronald C. *Technology as Freedom: the New Deal and the Electrical Modernization of the American Home* (Berkeley: University of California Press, 1996).

CHAPTER SEVEN

Technology and the Environment

BETSY MENDELSOHN

Regardless of our intellect and clever tools, people are basically organisms that interact with the environment physiologically through eating, respiration, contact, and our senses. We might imagine an ideal primitive person who experiences direct contact with the environment, but today we perceive the environment as a bit farther off than the surface of our skin or lungs because we have placed a complex of tools and technological systems between it and ourselves. Our conception of "the environment" may even break it down into constituent parts, such as wild nature, air quality in the streets of our city, or water quality in our reservoirs. Do we really think of ourselves, however, as organisms immersed in environments, taking them in, influencing them, and adapting to their qualities? As the human species, do we acknowledge that our biological, genetic agenda is to create a better fit with environments that increasingly blend technology into nature? In the twentieth century, we learned that some of our chemical technologies improve our lives but also create diseases like cancer that kill some of our cohort before we reproduce. In the twenty-first century we may learn that only some of us thrive in technological environments that provide too much food and require too little physical work. The rapid pace at which people blend technology into the environment shapes us as individuals and as a species.

As Americans, we celebrate the environmental origins of our national story. Europeans fled or adventured to this country on an errand into the wilderness to build a new society in a savage land. Manifest Destiny spread that errand into a vast and varied continent, displacing and transforming the Native Americans who dwelled here. In 1893, Frederick Jackson Turner's interpretation of territorial expansion characterized the frontier experience as the mechanism that absorbed many different peoples and transformed them into Americans. The factors of this experience included immersion in wide open spaces, struggling against nature, repeatedly creating community, and from these struggles developing a political culture based on individualism and self-reliance. How, Turner asked, will this process of Americanization continue among the floods of people then immigrating not to the wild frontier but to the artificial environment of the city? One can imagine him in a testy conversation with Emma Lazarus, whose poem on the Statue of Liberty described southern and eastern European immigration to this country: "huddled masses" yearning to "breathe free" not in nature, but in America's cities.

Americans have sought advantages by developing technology that uses the environment effectively and by developing science that makes this use efficient. From the agricultural improvement societies of the early nineteenth century to the National Nanotechnology Initiative of the early twenty-first century, science and technology have grown to dominate our interpretation of and interaction with our environments. Some technologies enable us to use existing environments better and others enable us to transform them. It is misleadingly simple, however, to say that "in the beginning" pre-scientific understandings of nature generated only insignificant technologies and that our modern scientific models permit us to create powerful technological systems that dominate the environment. Native Americans used a simple tool, fire, to shape the ecosystems of the continent. Even our most powerful technologies, conversely, cannot shift the environmental parameters we require as a species; at most, we interpose technology between difficult environments and ourselves or we apply technologies toward healing the harms that difficult environments cause. Our human genome fits itself better with our modern technological environment through evolutionary process, and speedier DNA sequencing and the recently completed map of the genome will help scientists to understand this process.

American technology today consists of many tools and systems. People tend to see the elements of this system much better than the whole, perhaps because the systems are so reliable that we notice them only in rare times of crisis when they break down. This can occur when the larger environment challenges the normal parameters within which technological systems operate. For example, persistent summer heat waves kill people who do not drink a lot of water when blackouts make their air conditioners inoperable. This simple remedy, drinking water, is no longer common sense because air conditioning and the electricity that makes it possible have become naturalized into the built environments in which most Americans live. After the California electricity crisis of 2001, public inquiry revealed that electric utilities colluded to under-provide electricity over the preceding years. The high electricity prices and rolling blackouts during that hot summer showed the public that crises arise not only out of technological limitations but also out of cavalier planning by people (California 2003). The people who write the software for technological systems or who make policy for influential business organizations are extremely distant from the majority of the public who rely on them. Governmental and business organizations responsible for technological systems, in turn, require experts in "systems engineering" to adjust the internal dynamics of their work habits. Most Americans today rely on systems that fulfill the basic needs of food, water, shelter and security, including gasoline, electricity, food distribution, municipal water supply, and emergency response systems. Most Americans are not able to provide these items and services for themselves, so that our reliance on technological systems requires us to depend on people we do not know who create technology we do not understand.

In addition to these factors in our relationship with the environment – our basic identity as organisms, our collective identity as a democratic nation forged in nature, our increasing reliance on science to create our technologies, and the dependence that arises from our increasing reliance on systems technologies – society has a relationship with "the environment" as perhaps most people conceive of it, with landscapes, animals, water and air. Whereas we can generalize that through 1900 we knew that the environment was more powerful than our technology and in the twentieth century we sought to make technology more powerful than the environment, over the last 30 years we have created technology that harnesses environmental characteristics and shapes them more subtly to our purposes. Environmental sustainability has become an ideal that Americans value highly, though we argue about whether we should achieve it through public policy or private action. Most Americans believe that technology supports the human project of living on earth for a long time, though a persistent minority tradition, as diverse as Thoreau, the Amish and EarthFirst!'s Dave Foreman, prefer to live in environments that incorporate less technology. On the international stage, the United States exports modern technological systems and landscape stewardship plans overseas to less developed countries. Economists in the late 1980s drew on world fact books to establish that nations act to preserve environmental quality – by passing environmental laws and creating environmentally oriented government agencies – only after their economies have surpassed a threshold per capita income. At an international environmental conference in the 1990s, many nations argued that poverty is the greatest cause of environmental degradation because it forces the poor to farm new lands. It seems that economic growth and environmental quality come together because prosperity permits both the satisfaction of life needs and the surplus to buy environmentally friendly technologies. Others argue that affluent societies consume vastly greater amounts of resources: we may use, create and consume things – such as cars, food, and houses – which individually impact the environment far less than in poorer nations, but we consume much, much more of them so that the absolute impact is far greater. Because we are affluent, Americans can pay to distance ourselves from the environmental impacts of our lifestyles, which may include buying inexpensive teak patio furniture from Indonesia, consumer electronics made in the environmentally degraded border area of Mexico, or cheap oil from the polluted estuaries of Nigeria.

Settlement and Land Transformation

Hundreds of years before the great economic surpluses of today, the material culture of Native Americans and European colonists revealed much about their environments. They processed natural resources to fulfill basic needs and to create emblems that expressed cultural, political, and spiritual meaning. Their buildings, tools, clothing, food, and totems seem one step from nature, perhaps altered by fire, mechanical shaping, and other physical processes implemented by hand. Behind this simplicity expressed in artifacts, however, lies a systemic, complex knowledge about the suitability of environmental materials for particular ends and the ways to acquire and transform these materials.

Technology consists most obviously of tools, but also of the knowledge to use them and the patterns or social expectations of their use. For example, European colonists set foot on a continent already shaped by 15,000 years of Native American technology. It is easy to imagine the artifacts of this technology that we have seen in natural history museums, wood spear throwers, stone points, sinew lashing, bone awls, fired pottery, snares, and dugout canoes. Dioramas capture the community knowledge that embedded their use, women grubbing in messy, polycropped fields and men repairing weapons. These models, however, recreate a static depiction of using tools that does not show the transfer of knowledge about their use or fabrication. It is impossible to capture in concrete artifacts and representations, for example, the Natives' use of fire to create the landscapes that maintained their environments over time (Pyne 1997). Lost are the habits of knowing when to burn, where to avoid the fire and where to fan it, how to advise neighbors, when to return to a burned place, or gauging burns according to weather and animal and plant populations as they shifted through time. Seasonal burning, used for thousands of years, was a type of technological system with which the entire ecosystem evolved. Small field studies can only suggest its impact on ecosystems, including its effect on plant and insect species that today are pests. Colonists from Massachusetts to Virginia described their encounter with the tall trees and open floor of the Eastern seaboard forests (Whitney 1994). The great Western fires at the turn of the twenty-first century demonstrate the cost of 100 years of fire suppression: an abundance of detritus and undergrowth enabled destructive infernos that cost millions of dollars in helicopters, chemical suppressants, back-burning, firebreaks, pumped water, hours of labor, incinerated structures, and many lives (Holloway 2000). The Natives' annual singed landscape of long ago has become a modern tinderbox in the West and a haven for Lyme Disease in the suburbanized East.

Agriculture sustained many Native American peoples and all of the colonists. As an activity, it displaced natural ecosystems with plots of reduced species composition, at times fertilized, weeded and watered to boost their productivity. In addition to cropland, colonists cut native grasses in estuarine and fresh water marshes, relying on seasonal water highs to fertilize these fields. Both peoples shared resources in uncultivated areas such as wood, fruit, animals, birds, and brush. During seasonal migrations of birds or fish, communities collaborated in the harvest and colonists used a variety of preservation techniques to save food for the early spring, or annual starving time. Both hunted wild animals, but colonists added to the mix of creatures in the woods by letting their pigs run wild. In the eighteenth century, two colonial technologies transformed the use of common resources: fencing and milldams. Each tool embodied an emergent, underlying right to use geographic areas of the environment exclusively and each interrupted the flow of wild and feral animal resources on which communities relied. As fencing and milldams proliferated, people turned to markets to provide substitutes for fish and game and oriented their agricultural practices toward the production of market crops that sold for money (Cronon 1983; Merchant 1989; Judd 1997).

Agricultural landscape transformation not only created cultivated fields, but also displaced systemic negative impacts from those who experienced the benefits. For example, the simplest European cultivation technique of plowing fields increased dirt-laden runoff during storms and the spring melt. Hundreds of farmers in a watershed plowed their fields, but the river that drained their valley deposited the humus of the hillsides in the concentrated marshy fringe of the stream. The deforestation that preceded cultivation reduced the amount of thirsty roots in the soil to such a degree that the hills absorbed less rain. Farmers suffered over the long run from losing their topsoil, even though they benefited from harvesting their fields and using or selling their trees. Streams flowed high during storms and the dry hills yielded little moisture during the summer. Displaced negative effects from deforestation and cultivation included reduced fish populations as they lost their marshy spawning habitat. Erratic streamflow also harmed navigation. The sedimentation of downstream riverbeds exacerbated floods in the more densely populated coastal areas. This pattern of displaced impacts illustrates a characteristic of environments, that a discrete action has remote and easily unforeseen effects, especially when many people throughout a landscape perform that action.

The "age of wood" extended to the middle of the nineteenth century, when iron and steel began to compose more than the edges of wooden tools. This transition misleads, however, for the forests fell magnificently to charcoal burners who fueled the smelting of iron ore and facilitated the industrial revolution. Forests also fell to the sprawling cities and the settlement of the prairies, as mortise-and-tenon buildings yielded to balloon frames that used measured lengths of lumber and nails. Wood, nails, sod, tarpaper, a stove, and straw sticks created the houses that protected late nineteenth-century settlers from the prairie winters of the Dakotas. Mineral resources crept into American material culture as iron and steel components of tools and as the mineral fuel to refine and fabricate these metals. Buildings became heated, especially in urban markets, by furnaces and stoves fueled by coal. Manufacturing plants adopted coal-fired steam boilers to provide horsepower by any canal or railroad track that could supply the heavy fuel, rather than at a particular location on a falling stream. Cities like Chicago could rise around their industries in a flat prairie landscape because they were fueled by wood and dirty soft coal carried to the city by boat, and later by the railroad. The switch from waterpower meant that steam engines, which burned large quantities of wood and coal, could be located in the heart of cities where people worked and breathed. In the countryside, the switch from waterpower factories meant that coal mining and timbering served metropolitan centers. Cities received air pollution from the switch to steam engines and mineral fuels, but the countryside received mine tailings and deforested landscapes.

Throughout a national hinterland of resources, the General Land Office imposed a survey of potential property lines in a mile-square grid, from the 1810s through re-surveys at the end of the nineteenth century. City directories reveal that lawyers and surveyors numbered prominently among early inhabitants as they brought the knowledge of surveying and property law into new regions of the country. As early as the 1860s, John Wesley Powell noted that this system of surveying boded ill for the arid West beyond the 100th Meridian because the mile-square unit arose from late eighteenth-century expectations for a viable farm in the East (Powell 1878). The impact of the survey on organizing landscapes is visible from an airplane, whose perspective shows a crazy quilt of land uses occupying contiguous squares. As a technological system, the land survey succeeded only partially in its political goal of transferring property to individuals and generally failed to transfer property in ways that were sustainable. The federal government tinkered with the process of selling off the public domain, but never altered it more fundamentally because that would have challenged the strong popular association of the neutral grid with the promise of democracy embedded in property ownership. As Powell noted, yeoman farmers could not benefit from small landholdings in the arid west; to prosper they required either centrally planned and highly capitalized irrigation or large landholdings for ranches.

Of all regions of the country, the flat, moist Midwest seems best suited to fulfill the agricultural ideals of the land survey. Rather than choosing flat, treeless land that looked most like fields, however, Midwestern settlers favored timbered areas because they associated forests with fertile soil, so they claimed forested land along the many sloughs and streams that drained the prairie (McManis 1964). In the 1850s, about the time that the balloon frame house permitted standardized construction, settlers claimed land on the prairies, wet and dry, that composed the bulk of the Midwest. Agricultural societies promoted techniques for enhancing drainage and tools for cutting through the prairie, which was not grass but rather a carpet of tough perennials whose roots interlaced and descended up to twenty feet. Rain and snowmelt characteristically puddled on this flat prairie landscape, seeping into the clay and draining only slowly to streams with a defined bed. Artificial systems that hastened drainage included ditching and drainage tiles, perforated cylinders interred in a graded network several feet below the surface of the ground. Sometimes farmers put several miles of tiles in one quarter-section field. The productivity of today's Midwestern agriculture is predicated in large part on 150 years of drainage technology.

The negative consequences of drainage include those associated with plowing and deforestation, the reduced fish populations, increased flood highs, and greater unpredictability of navigation. Drainage also added another impact, injury to neighbors who received the water drained from one farmer's fields. In the 1860s, the legal system played a key role in legitimizing the new drainage technology by naturalizing it as a perfection of the environment. Whereas before a certain time, neighbors held each other accountable for flooding each others' fields with drainage water, after a few cases it became standard for the draining neighbor to be relieved of compensating neighbors for any injury. Far from being a scientific rationale, courts such as the Illinois Supreme Court stated that "nature has ordained such drainage," whatever the injury to downslope neighbors (Gormley v. Sanford 1869). This single court case, and the adoption of its reasoning by neighboring courts, reduced the unpredictable costs of drainage and hastened the spread of this land improvement system across the landscape.

Urbanization

To create cities, Americans devised many technological systems that permitted dense concentrations of people to live together safely. The areas of streams, forests and highways shared in rural areas expanded in cities to include a diversity of environmental characteristics. For example, rivers, roads, alleys, and sidewalks were common areas in cities, in which the public had an easement that trumped their private use by abutting landowners. Dense concentrations of people relied on local government to coordinate their shared use of these public ways because they facilitated commerce. Cities also created networked systems to enhance or compensate for environmental quality in neighborhoods. Key among urban fears were epidemic disease and market irregularity. The antebellum city developed systems of inspection for health, safety, market honesty, and nuisance, and even enforced intangible qualities such as beauty and quiet. By the end of the nineteenth century, cities had constructed networked systems of parks, sewerage, gas, electricity, drainage, water purification and delivery, garbage pickup and processing, and public transportation. By 1910, most immigrants to the USA lived in the artificial, urban environments that Turner suspected to be incapable of forging Americans. Increased administrative capacity, supported by a mix of property and sales tax financing, arose to serve the sophisticated infrastructure that carried the metabolism of the modern city (Teaford 1984; Novak 1996; Tarr 1996; Melosi 2000).

Cities thrive in a flux of environmental phenomena. Water comes from rain and snowmelt and sewers empty into natural water bodies like rivers or the ocean. The air itself dilutes and blows away the accumulated pollution of a city's crowded residents. Cities rely on these natural environmental behaviors and they place great demands on them. The rapid drainage caused by aspects of rural development like deforestation and drainage occurs much more effectively in paved urban areas. Cities also represent a concentrated human hunger for food and other resources and a great elimination of trash and biological wastes (Cronon 1991). People shared the nineteenth-century city with tens of thousands of horses, dairy cows and free-range pigs, feral dogs and cats, and a population of pigeons, sparrows, rats, roaches, and human disease micro-organisms, each of which had its own food and elimination habits (Hartog 1985; McShane and Tarr 1997). Modern cities control these fellow-residents closely with merely extensions of nineteenth-century techniques: prohibitions, licensing laws, building codes, police enforcement, and poison. The technological systems that continue to keep this urban ecology in order include tools, knowledge, and habit.

In addition to internal urban ecology, cities also carry on a constant commerce with an interstate market that supplies food, lumber, raw materials, and fuel from a broad hinterland (Cronon 1991). Closer to home, nineteenth-century suburbs supplied fresh market produce, fired bricks from local claypits, gravel for roads and grit for concrete, and ornamental plants for parks. However broadly cities obtained their resources, they tended to eliminate their wastes in concentrated streams. Suburbs also received urban trash as fill for marshy areas or for the very pits that provided clay, grit and gravel (Colten 1994). Air pollution emerged from thousands of minor activities in the street, but most dramatically from the smokestacks of coal-fired factories, trains, boats, and buildings. The appearance of smoke indicated activity and implied prosperity in nineteenth-century birdseye views and added atmosphere to photographs. Water pollution emerged as storm runoff and as effluent from sewerage. Almost all cities that developed sewerage in the nineteenth century combined domestic, industrial and storm sewage into one networked system of pipes. While this effectively removed industrial waste from decentralized outflows throughout cities, it also concentrated all wastes into a few, massive sources of effluent. Cities purified their wastes by depending on wild bacteria living in oxygenated streams to decompose it, but sewage concentrations exhausted the oxygen in the water and killed the beneficial bacteria, thereby permitting the dangerous microorganisms in effluent to persist and spread. Only in the twentieth century, when cities became so large as to overwhelm the purifying power of wild bacteria, did cities create centralized sewage treatment plants which artificially aerated sewage concentrations, thereby making a perfect work environment for beneficial bacteria. Twentieth-century cities reduced the risk of water-borne epidemics even more by purifying their drinking water with chlorine (Tarr 1996).

Studying the Nineteenth-Century Environment

Nineteenth-century engineers created technologies that compensated for what they perceived as environmental inadequacies, basing them on a few measurements of environmental characteristics. Military engineers who planned harbors and civil engineers who planned canals, for example, measured the dimensions of rivers such as depth and width using surveying instruments and rate of flow using floats and a clock. They also read the landscape qualitatively and spoke with local residents, seeking vegetation changes and eroded banks that indicated the behavior of water during floods. Surveys occurred over a few days, but landscape and memory held clues to watery behavior over time. Only as the frontier was settled and volunteers recorded weather characteristics did residents begin to fit the snapshots of surveys into the long-term characteristics of their new abiding places.

The flux of natural resources that move through rural and urban areas travel within patterns of larger earth systems, the most obvious of which is the weather. This includes rainfall, temperature, storms, and seasons, all of which were phenomena of unknown cause and scantily known pattern. In the eighteenth century savants like Benjamin Franklin studied weather and farmers predicted basic agricultural events like last frost, early frost and tomorrow's weather; mariners, likewise, used instruments to anticipate the power of wind and wave that they harnessed for travel or that they fled. The instruments for measuring weather-related environmental phenomena included weather vanes, thermometers and barometers. Only in the early nineteenth century did statisticians devise methods for interpreting a large number of regularly recorded observations made by these instruments. Other students of weather interpreted these data, retrospectively, by mapping them over geographic territories and in relation to time. By the 1860s, the telegraph system communicated these data speedily, which permitted a statistician to synthesize and interpret the meaning of measurements made near-simultaneously across a broad region. After the telegraph, meteorologists began to model relationships among space, time, barometric pressure, temperature, and precipitation, and from this emerged patterns for the origin, perpetuation and decay of weather systems (Porter 1986; Fleming 1990; National Weather Service 1995).

In addition to America's environmental political origins, it has been "nature's nation," in which entrepreneurs and states described the wealth of nature in order to benefit from its natural surplus (Opie 1998). The clergy, surveyors, boosters and naturalists who studied these resources reveal that Americans hold two independent, overlapping conceptions of their environment. Clergy and naturalists found in natural history an activity to witness the divine in a holistic book of nature, for example William Wigglesworth's jubilee landscape, William Bartram's literary swamps, John Muir's spiritual storms, Aldo Leopold's wise mountains, and Julia Butterfly Hill's recent years in a Redwood called Luna (Leopold 1949; Miller 1956; Vileisis 1997; Hill 2000). These inspirational conceptions of nature, however, do not shape daily environmental policy as much as the various scientific disciplines which emerged at the end of the nineteenth century. In the post-bellum period, state and federal governments established public schools and administrative agencies that catalogued the inner workings of nature in order to use resources more effectively. Whereas in the early nineteenth century several Eastern states sponsored naturalists to catalogue the mineral, animal and plant wealth of their states, after the Civil War governments took on this task in earnest. By 1900, state and federal governments had assumed the contours of present-day bureaucracy for hands-on management of the resources that once they had only studied. The transition occurred because it was a short step from creating environmental information and writing environmental legislation, to assuming ownership and stewardship of environmental resources. In some cases, courts referred to a state's study and promotion of fish conservation as a rationale for permitting its expropriation of lakes from private to public ownership (Fuller v. Shedd 1896).

These studies of natural history coincided with the widespread adoption of lithography for maps and book illustration, which communicated popularly through images. As these books proliferated, their illustrations followed an old tradition of showing objects in isolation from their environments. Only around 1900 did scientists, artists, and museum educators reintegrate species with their environments in their investigations, depictions and dioramas. In the physical sciences, notably geology, field geologists, and artists created new ways of measuring and delineating landscapes to convey geological processes over time and area. The great Western surveys of the 1860s and 1870s by King, Hayden, Powell, and Wheeler generated remarkable illustrated reports, notably Hayden's report on Yellowstone with chromolithographs after paintings by Thomas Moran. The success of Moran's images insured that artists and photographers would be included in subsequent federal surveys. Art became a powerful ally for state-sponsored environmental goals, such as the initial landscape conservation movement that dedicated Yellowstone to federal stewardship, because published art captivated the popular imagination.

In the private sector, popular illustrated books fueled the nature study movement of the Progressive Era, especially the bird books promoted by members of the many state Audubon Societies. The movement was catalyzed by shame and grief at the extinction of wild populations of the buffalo and passenger pigeon, the wholesale slaughter of migrating birds for market, the destructive impact of collection-based natural history by boys, and the callous use of bird breeding plumage to decorate women's hats. The movement's pedagogy availed itself of many emergent technologies, including books, dioramas, photographs, lantern slides, and museums (Doughty 1975). It promoted both conceptions of environment, the divine and the scientific, to establish conservation habits among children. For example, it drew on inquiries by scientists at federal agencies to explain what hawks ate in order to distinguish good from bad birds. This combination of the scientific and the moral continues in ecological education today with modern labels, for example in the landscape restoration movement that distinguishes native from alien species. Environmental movements reveal how communication technologies shape the message, and that mixed moral and scientific message is the same whether communicated by the written word, in a museum diorama, on TV, or via the Internet.

Science and Environmental Models

Key to a scientific understanding of environments is our ability to model them theoretically and to measure their characteristics to test those models. Sedimentary geologists in the Midwest, for example, examined the deposition of gravel, sand and clay around Lake Michigan to theorize that the lake had shrunk for 5,000 years. Although they examined this landscape scientifically as late as the 1890s, they found undeveloped expanses around Chicago and in Indiana that showed how the modern lake and drainage patterns created features that the ancient, larger lake had created farther from the receding shore. They drew on knowledge created by hydraulic engineers to understand the sorting and deposition of gravels and sediments of different weights in water flows of different speeds. In the same decade topography, a technique of using surveying instruments to measure and map elevation, revealed for Chicago's flat lake plain as much as for the dramatic landscapes of the West, that the most minor changes in grade determine water drainage. This scientific environmental knowledge arose after 60 years of activities fitting a dense human population into a flat, wet landscape. Residents had already improved the land for settlement, agriculture, navigation, clean water and sanitary infrastructure, bridges, roads, railroads, and industry. They had done so with varying degrees of success in anticipating strange events due to the high water table, and they had done so intuitively, using rudimentary measurements and qualitative observations to plan their systems.

The scientific era of managing this watery landscape was built on a legacy of development that had shaped social expectations and property institutions to a great degree. Progressive Era engineers had difficulty convincing a population that their proposed huge, expensive drainage projects would correct sanitary and flooding problems effectively and equitably. Residents throughout the city did not believe that systems of drainage tunnels interred five miles away would make the water in their taps clean, so they resisted paying taxes to fund these projects by going to court. Indeed, in the 1970s Chicago's growing population produced so much effluent and lake levels had risen so much, that engineers proposed a vast, networked underground storage reservoir, the Deep Tunnel, to inter storm drainage during peak flows so that it could be treated and released safely to the environment over time. So critical had

Chicago's flooding and dirty water management become, that the federal government has paid for 75 percent of this $3 billion project (Metropolitan 1999). Engineers now use this method in many other cities.

Today, we use sophisticated and varied instruments to monitor our environments. Most of us continue to understand the eighteenth-century instruments of thermometer, barometer, and wind vane, but how many of us rely on the measurements given in weather reports rather than looking out the window or even going outside to figure out what to wear? Even in a scientific era of environmental measurement, we also trust subjective, qualitative information, the information provided by our senses. However, the most compelling new information about environmental systems, including whole-earth systems, is beyond our human powers of sense. Obviously, the instruments we send aloft by balloon, plane and satellite, operate in environments hostile to human activity and acquire data about radiation, gas composition, and other things that we cannot. This new information not only helps solve environmental problems, but also illuminates fundamental tensions among us about science, complexity and risk, three hallmarks of modernity.

In the nineteenth and twentieth centuries, scientific disciplines and the instruments they relied upon proliferated. The computer and electronic revolution of the mid-twentieth century permitted smaller devices to record more observations faster and in remote locations. Whereas in the early twentieth century, scientists used aerial photos to capture images of forests that implied its health, in the late twentieth century, data generated by satellites could be analyzed to reveal the health of the trees' respiration. Behind the often-colorful maps of satellite data lie equations that correlate several data sets, the logic of these correlations flowing from models of environmental behavior. For example, remotely sensed data about carbon dioxide concentrations reveals the amount of tree respiration only when plugged into a complex equation whose variables represent a forest measured on the ground. Working through an equation certainly seems like a more precise way to determine forest health than looking at a photograph.

Our brains make up causal stories to connect the dots of our observations, and by this process we learn through experience to react to some things and ignore others. Instruments do not make up stories, but the software that collects and interprets their data uses assumptions based on environmental models to highlight anomalous measurements. The story people tell about the discovery of the ozone hole that forms seasonally over Antarctica has become a morality tale of modern science. The version that has become urban legend, however, erroneously asserts that the National Aeronautics and Space Administration (NASA) satellites disregarded abnormal data about the hole as false. This moral, that people should not follow technology without question, should be replaced by the moral of the real story. In 1978, NASA launched a satellite to measure atmospheric ozone that flagged measurements under a threshold of 180 DU (Dobson Units) as possibly false readings caused by encoding or transmission errors. In July 1984, NASA interpreted the satellite data from the previous October and compared a wave of flagged, very low measurements to those taken on the ground at a research station in Antarctica. However, because the ground-based instruments had erroneously collected data on the wrong wavelength, NASA scientists could not use them to check their satellite data. A year later, NASA scientists Bhartia, Heath, and Fleig confirmed very low readings by comparing them with ground-collected data and published their findings at a specialists' meeting. Unfortunately for those who believe that American science and satellites embody the best remote sensing, non-NASA scientists Farman, Gardiner, and Shanklin had published a prior article in a more accessible journal, *Nature*. Scientists took 19 months to confirm the "ozone hole" because they knew its grave, global implications would jolt public fears about skin cancer and that this social impact required them to be very confident in their findings (Pukelsheim 1990). The moral of this story is much less sinister and more like the familiar Murphy's Law, that if it is possible to collect your check data incorrectly, people will do so. The story also reveals how dependent we have become on expertise, scientific data, and complex models to create believable models of the environment.

Within a few years, many nations endorsed the Montreal Protocol that phased out the production and use of CFCs. These chlorine compounds, commonly used as refrigerants and aerosol propellants, migrate up through the atmosphere and thin the layer of atmospheric ozone which reflects a portion of the sun's ultraviolet rays away from the earth. Chemist Thomas Midgely (1889–1944) worked on a team of General Motors researchers who developed CFCs. Midgley also worked on a team of researchers who developed tetraethyl lead as a gasoline additive that permitted engines with high compression ratios and therefore more power (Sloan 1964). When the atmospheric impact of 40 years of CFC use came to light in 1985, the United States had already begun its phase-out of lead as a gasoline additive.

Whereas lead's toxicity was common knowledge in the 1920s, the impact of CFCs had been theorized in the mid-1970s and established only in 1985. The stories of these synthetic chemicals and their environmental problems are similar for two reasons in addition to their common inventor. For one, laboratory testing did not anticipate the effects of millions of people using these chemicals. Just as flooding becomes more severe when forests are cut down, drainage tiles are interred, or cities and suburbs are paved over, the impacts of something's introduction into the environment must be expanded to include its introduction by many people, hundreds of millions in today's populous world. For another, the impact of these two chemicals' introduction into the environment was not anticipated before consumers and manufacturers adopted them for the huge benefits they brought to the immediate user. Our enthusiasm for the latest invention may reduce our wariness, or aversion to risk, and may desensitize us to anticipating remote impacts. Only in the last 30 years have manufacturers and consumers considered the fate of objects after they no longer perform their marketed purpose, and environmental impacts have appeared in the criteria for good production published by the International Standards Organization (International 2002). Refrigerator and auto manufacturers may have recovered CFCs handily at manufacturing facilities, but over the decades tens of thousands of refrigerator and auto repair shops released CFCs when technicians bled systems before recharging them. Our legal system has been late to consider and regulate the pollution effects of the millions of items that Americans own, use and discard, many of which contain small amounts of dangerous substances, such as the minuscule amount of radioactive compounds on a watch face or the tiny batteries in a child's blinking sneaker. Collected together in landfills or incinerated, however, these tiny amounts concentrate and in their water-borne or air-borne forms may endanger people. A characteristic of technology and environment interactions is that we underestimate the aggregated impact of all of our small behaviors.

Agriculture

Americans have created technological environments for the animals and plants that form our food. In particular, cows, pigs, and chickens have traveled a long distance from pastures and barnyards to feedpens and battery cages. To create a fourfold increase in feed efficiency between 1935 and 1995, producers removed chickens from the outside environment of farms and placed them in controlled indoor environments. Beginning in the 1910s, efficiency experts had drawn on the disciplines of epidemiology and nutrition to create productive environments. These came at some cost, as robust viruses and treatment-resistant bacteria continue to break out in dense populations of chickens and are contained only by destroying millions of birds. Four-fifths of the nation's poultry derives from Southern facilities, where manure leachate pollutes local waters to the extent of killing fish and endangering human health. The constant administration of antibiotics to control endemic diseases creates the physiological conditions for further epidemics, at least one of which has leapt the species boundary between chickens and people (Boyd 2001). Industrialized meat production, therefore, relates to environment in several ways: the changing landscape of farms, the changing environment of animals, the concentration of animal production in particular regions that suffer pollution, and the contamination of meat supplies with pathogens that could injure people.

Crops also thrive in artificial environments, but the resistance of their weed and insect pests to chemical controllers has prompted some to adopt organic agriculture as a means of using beneficial insects and integrated pest management to sustain yields. The limited technologies condoned by organic farmers animated policy discussions in the late 1990s as the Department of Agriculture required a diversity of state laws to yield to federal rules that define organic farming practices and food labeling. In addition to the economic interests of farmers desiring to use fewer herbicides and pesticides, the organic farming movement reacts to a demand by consumers for food they perceive to be healthy and natural. Consumers pay premium prices to eat food that has not been genetically modified, that does not harbor antibiotic-resistant bacteria, whose animals did not receive synthetic growth hormones, and that does not carry pesticide and herbicide residues. Other consumers desire meat from animals that lived more natural lives, eggs whose hens lived outside of battery cages, cows which grazed grass instead of living in feedlots, pigs which likewise saw the sun at some point. The environmental reasons for producing food with less technology cross categories from economic to humane to scientific.

Agricultural technology impacts the land directly to create a controlled environment, albeit out-of-doors, that produces greater amounts of superior crops. Corn is the

most intensively studied of these crops because it comprises livestock feed and the
corn syrup that appears almost universally in the processed foods characteristic of the
last 30 years. Since the 1990s, corn also provides the ethanol that appears as a 10 percent
additive to gasoline sold in the Midwest, especially in urban areas seeking to meet
federal Clean Air Act standards. In 1996, the federal government approved corn with
DNA that had been engineered to include a gene from the bacterium *Bacillus
thuringiensis* (Bt) which creates an insecticide within the corn tissue. Bt-corn kills
borers when they nibble the stalk and because farmers apply less pesticide to Bt-corn,
other insects suffer less harm from broadcast pesticides (Bessin 1996). Because Americans
have genetically engineered Bt-corn, residents of many other countries reject it
out of fear.

Two processes central to agriculture have impacted the landscape broadly: the control
of water and the creation and maintenance of fields and pastures. Farm drainage
brought millions of acres into crop production by the muddy expedient of ditching
and interring networks of tile drains. Twentieth-century federal projects for flood
control and irrigation permitted crops and livestock to flourish in areas that posed
risk either because they were floodplains or because they received little rainfall.
Deforestation also prepared landscapes for crops. Agricultural societies and state and
federal agencies promoted tilling practices meant to increase yields and conserve soil,
the latter notably after the combination of deep plowing and dry weather created the
dust storms of the 1890s and 1930s. Because we embed our artificial systems of food
production within large, very complex environmental processes, our activities will
always provoke unanticipated responses.

Information Technology and Environmental Models

The greatest impact that technology has made on the relationship of people with the
environment has been on our knowledge of that environment and on our conception
of our individual and species place in relation to it. As Perry Miller and others have
shown, ideas of nature, derived from religious writers and other authorities, shaped
the interaction of the first settlers with the New World. These may have indicated the
spiritual and political realities of nature and place of people, but technology has
provided fragments of evidence that support or challenge conceptions of this
relationship. As this chapter has shown, Americans increasingly have sought evidence,
facts, things that are measured by instruments, to authorize their notions of the
relationship of people and the earth. Technology, therefore, has become more important
to human endeavor because it is the means by which people learn about their
environment.

Books began to broadcast knowledge of cosmology, maps of earth systems, and
natural history in the fifteenth century, and eventually woodcuts and engravings yielded
to high-quality photographic images. The learned library of yesterday, however, has
leapt off paper and into organized patterns of light that travel near-instantaneously
across the earth. A harried teacher on the East Coast can illustrate a lecture about
old growth forest by noodling through the Web and downloading images into

presentation software. The gatekeepers of the book world, editors, publishers and the market, are replaced on the Web by millions of voluntary contributors, openly available indexes, and curious armchair travelers. Because contributors and users make it together through shared infrastructure, the Web embodies some aspects of the *noosphere* conceived of by Teilhard de Chardin in 1925, though lacking the ultimate element of consciousness. Teilhard imagined "a human sphere, a sphere of reflection, of conscious invention, of conscious souls" which hovers above the animal world; his neologism used the Greek root "noos" for mind (Cunningham 1997). Science fiction author David Brin wrote his novel *Earth* in 1990 to imagine the creation of such a web-based, planetary-scale consciousness that mediates between human desires and environmental realities. A mere technological system has no consciousness, but millions of Americans interact with virtual communities and would feel bereft without them. The web has made possible verbal, and now aural and visual, contact with like-minded people we have never met in person, contact that seems immediate and intimate. It has democratized access to information and data about the environment, images of our neighborhoods from remote satellites, and communication with our elected representatives. Since 1993 when the first browsers were released popularly, the web has been linking people across the world.

The advances in science which measure environmental phenomena require literate, enumerate people to understand them. All people make decisions based on experience and knowledge, but some are better informed, with experience more relevant to a particular environmental dilemma. As science models environmental qualities more precisely, people with a non-scientific worldview become marginalized from influencing environmental policy. Social scientists have devised systems of quantifying qualitative values such as beauty and tradition; while they incorporate fuzzy feelings into a policymaking process, these techniques also reduce the complexity of environmental preferences to a great degree. In the current climate of awe for science and quantitative methods, these techniques can give the impression of conveying judgments about policy that are more truthful or accurate than those obtained by qualitative methods.

In 1969, photographs take by the Apollo astronauts permitted Americans to see a beautiful earth, alone, against the background of an empty universe. In tandem with archeology and gene sequencing inquiries, the "blue marble" view popularized ecology, or the earth's household economy, as a frame for the endeavors of its intra-related human family. Through educational systems, recent generations of children have grown up with basic knowledge about ecology, earth systems, and the genetic relatedness of all people. Television has been the tool of this environmental education to such an extent that modern Americans get a better view of nature on TV than by taking a walk in the woods. Remote sensing cameras on satellites permit us a unique perspective of our one, whole earth, and television broadcasts footage of remote corners of the earth, such as sulfur-metabolizing ecologies on the ocean floor and stone-age peoples in Borneo. Many Americans have seen Charles and Ray Eames' 1977 film, "Powers of Ten," in which nine minutes of photographs and clever animation place a picnicker in New York City in the context of the universe (10^{25}) and of his constitutive atoms (10^{-18}) (Eames Office 2002). Image-based communications technologies have rendered abstract environmental conceptions into compelling narratives that are accessible by all. They have democratized knowledge by bringing the earth's variety and complexity within view of anyone.

The rise of mass communications media is perhaps responsible for the trend in American society that leads some to spend wealth on preserving natural areas that they never will visit. In the late 1980s, sociologists and economists created survey instruments that could capture not only people's "willingness to pay" to obtain better air quality, but also to improve environmental qualities somewhere else, that they would never experience directly. In the 1990s, non-profit organizations "sold" the cost of preserving hectares of Amazon rainforest, issuing certificates of thanks to people who donated money. The "existence value" of beautiful animals, plants, and landscapes seems to motivate an increasing number of people either to change the way they use technology or to facilitate the creation of nature preserves which exclude technology, and sometimes even exclude people. As a sign of this vicarious consumption of nature, Discovery Channel offers much of the science, history, technology, and environment programming on Cable television and their website offers viewers an opportunity to be a virtual shark for a few minutes.

The modern technologies that enable people to work powerfully also permit us to earn a living without using our bodies. Thousands of years of evolved muscles lie fallow for many Americans unless we go out of our way to exercise them. In association with the low cost of food, especially of meat and dairy products, an inactive lifestyle creates conditions across our population that let 50 percent of us suffer a heart attack or stroke. The leading cause of these life-threatening events is a high level of cholesterol in our bloodstreams, the product of genetic disposition in some people, but of a slothful lack of activity in the rest of us. The arthritis that afflicted our ancestors in their 40s because of hard labor in the fields has become transformed, by technology, into the heart disease that a lifetime of rich food and little activity visits upon us in our older age.

The environment in which we spend the most time is the home, but most of us spend much of our waking life in a separate workplace. The work environment has changed dramatically in response to technology, and the human animal has responded to these shifts. Americans have shifted toward more sedentary and repetitious work, though many lower wage jobs in custodial services, food processing, and agriculture require constant activity. Agriculture remains the most dangerous occupation, especially for children. The "American system of production" innovated in the nineteenth century reduced craftsmen to laborers who repeated tasks and eventually tended machines that performed the bulk of the work. As factories grew larger and more efficient, employees were aggregated into a single input to production called labor, and any injuries or deaths they suffered were perceived as costs of production. Production lines as innovated by Henry Ford came to be epitomized by the movement efficiency studies of Federick W. Taylor. In the twentieth century, the ever-larger business corporation represented a classic workplace, with people working indoors at defined tasks for 8 hour days, commuting by public transportation from distant residential neighborhoods. When manufacturing jobs fled this country for cheaper labor overseas in the 1960s through 1980s, we transitioned to a service economy epitomized by the cubicles of Scott Adams' cartoon character, Dilbert. The modern work environment does not seem to be designed for the animal part of people, with its fixed work stations and long days of sitting still, staring at a fixed point, little sunlight, and indoor air heavily polluted from off-gassing carpet, paint, and laminated furniture. In tandem with a heavy diet, a job in the service industry seems to require a health club membership.

If we have excellent visual reproductions of natural environments, will we be less willing to preserve the real thing? Television has familiarized millions of Americans with nature and earth sciences, broadcasting awareness of the environment and also shaping that awareness. In the early 1970s, the life insurance company Mutual of Omaha broadcast the weekly show "Wild Kingdom," which consisted of predators bringing prey to their inevitable, messy end. Has this greater understanding fostered us to steer an environmentally sustainable course in our lives (or to buy life insurance)? Our home environments recede as we experience the sights and sounds of wilderness from our living room couches: we may be more comfortable learning about the rainforest virtually than experientially. Will familiarity and knowledge create an awareness of the importance of carbon and hydrologic cycles or the vulnerability of people to toxins? Or, will impersonating a wolf by linking to MIT's Media Lab remove our environments, conceptually, a fraction more from the surface of our skin, our lungs and our stomachs. Will a fantasy environment based on clever software and speedy digital processors ever substitute for the real world? Will we genetically engineer ourselves so that we benefit from our changes to earth systems but do not suffer from our errors, such as the cancer-causing ozone hole? If so, then the technology that we already have embedded in our environments will complement the technology that we blend into our bodies.

BIBLIOGRAPHY

Bessin, Ric. "Bt-corn." (May 1996) Accessed February 28, 2003, at http://www.uky.edu/Agriculture/Entomology/entfacts/fldcrops/ef118.htm.
Boyd, William. "Making meat: science, technology and American poultry production," *Technology and Culture* 42 (2001), 631–64.
Brin, David. *Earth* (New York: Bantam Books, 1990).
California Public Utilities Commission. "FERC releases documents relating to evidence of energy market manipulation in California." March 27, 2003. Accessed May 13, 2003 at http://www.cpuc.ca.gov/.
Colten, Craig E. "Chicago's waste lands: refuse disposal and urban growth, 1840–1990," *Journal of Historical Geography* 20 (1994), 124–42.
Cronon, William. *Changes in the Land: Indians, Colonists, and the Ecology of New England* (New York: Hill and Wang, 1983).
Cronon, William. *Nature's Metropolis: Chicago and the Great West* (New York: W.W. Norton, 1991).
Cunningham, Phillip J. "Pierre Teilhard de Chardin and Noogenesis," *CMC Magazine* (March 1997). Accessed on February 21, 2003 at http://www.december.com/cmc/mag/1997/mar/cunnref.html.

Doughty, Robin W. *Feather Fashions and Bird Preservation: a Study in Nature Protection* (Berkeley: University of California Press, 1975).

Eames Office. "Eames films," 2002. Accessed February 21, 2003 at http://www.eamesoffice.com/filmsintro.html.

Fleming, James Rodgers. *Meteorology in America, 1800–1870* (Baltimore, Md.: Johns Hopkins University Press, 1990).

Fuller v. Shedd, 161 Ill. 462 (1896), at 489.

Gormley v. Sanford, 52 Ill. 158 (1869), at 162.

Hartog, Hendrik. "Pigs and positivism," *Wisconsin Law Review* (1985), 899–935.

Hill, Julia Butterfly. *The Legacy of Luna: the Story of a Tree, a Woman, and the Struggle to Save the Redwoods* (San Francisco, Ca.: Harper San Francisco, 2000).

Holloway, Marguerite. "The Los Alamos blaze exposes the missing science of forest management," *Scientific American* (August 2000). Accessed May 8, 2003 at http://www.sciam.com.

International Standards Organization. "ISO and the environment," (Geneva, Switzerland: ISO Central Secretariat, 2002). Accessed May 12, 2003 at http://www.iso.ch/iso/en/iso9000–14000/tour/isoanden.html.

Judd, Richard. *Common Lands, Common People: the Origins of Conservation in Northern New England* (Cambridge, Mass.: Harvard University Press, 1997).

Leopold, Aldo. *A Sand County Almanac, and Sketches Here and There* (New York: Oxford University Press, 1949).

McManis, Douglas R. *The Initial Evaluation and Utilization of the Illinois Prairies, 1815–1840*; University of Chicago Department of Geography Research Paper, no. 94 (Chicago: University of Chicago Press, 1964).

McShane, Clay and Tarr, Joel A. "The centrality of the horse in the nineteenth-century American City," in Raymond A. Mohl, ed. *The Making of Urban America* (Wilmingon, Del.: Scholarly Resources, 1997), pp. 105–30.

Melosi, Martin V. *The Sanitary City: Urban Infrastructure in America from Colonial Times to the Present* (Baltimore, Md.: Johns Hopkins University Press, 2000).

Merchant, Carolyn. *Ecological Revolutions: Nature, Gender, and Science in New England* (Chapel Hill, NC: University of North Carolina Press, 1989).

Metropolitan Water Reclamation District of Greater Chicago. "Tunnel and reservoir plan." August 8, 1999. Accessed May 10, 2003 at http://mwrdgc.dst.il.us.

Miller, Perry. *The American Puritans, Their Prose and Poetry* (Garden City, NY: Doubleday, 1956).

National Weather Service. "National weather service history." December 15, 1995. Accessed May 10, 2003 at http://www.erh.noaa.gov/er/gyx/history.html.

Novak, Wiliam J. *The People's Welfare: Law and Regulation in Nineteenth-century America* (Chapel Hill, NC: University of North Carolina Press, 1996).

Opie, John. *Nature's Nation: an Environmental History of the United States* (Fort Worth, Tex.: Harcourt Brace College Publishers, 1998).

Porter, Theodore M. *The Rise of Statistical Thinking, 1820–1900* (Princeton, NJ: Princeton University Press, 1986).

Powell, John Wesley. *Report on the Lands of the Arid Region of the United States* (Washington, DC: Government Printing Office, 1878).

Pukelsheim, F. "Robustness of statistical gossip and the Antarctic ozone hole." *Institute of Mathematical Sciences Bulletin* 19 (1990): 540–2. Accessed March 6, 2003 at http://www.statsci.org/data/general/ozonehol.html.

Pyne, Stephen J. *America's Fires: Management on Wildlands and Forests* (Durham, NC: Forest History Society, 1997).

Sloan, Alfred P. *My Years at General Motors* (New York: Doubleday, 1964).

Tarr, Joel A. *The Search for the Ultimate Sink: Urban Pollution in America* (Akron, Oh.: University of Akron Press, 1996).

Teaford, Jon C. *The Unheralded Triumph: City Government in America, 1870–1900* (Baltimore, Md.: Johns Hopkins University Press, 1984).

Vileisis, Ann. *Discovering the Unknown Landscape: a History of America's Wetlands* (Washington, DC: Island Press, 1997).

Whitney, Gordon Graham. *From Coastal Wilderness to Fruited Plain: a History of Environmental Change in Temperate North America, 1500 to the Present* (Cambridge; New York: Cambridge University Press, 1994).

CHAPTER EIGHT

Government and Technology

CARROLL PURSELL

In the year 2000, the National Academy of Engineering drew up a list of the twenty "Greatest Engineering Achievements of the 20th Century." From number one, "Electrification," to number 20, "High-performance Materials," virtually every one of these achievements was initiated or facilitated through the efforts of the federal government. Computers (8), Highways (11), Internet (13) and Nuclear Technologies (19) are obvious examples of the technologies which government encouragement, in any of a number of forms, have made possible.

For the last quarter century, high government officials have been telling the American people that the government is the Problem, not the Solution. A generation of very young dot-com entrepreneurs, possibly confusing the putative "Nanny State" with their own experience with parental restraints, have turned to some form of libertarian thinking to insist that they "can do it on their own." Without minimizing the role of individual inventors, private corporations, or the consuming public, it is important to realize the critical role of governments, not only the federal but also those at state and local levels, in creating and maintaining our technological environment. This role was an early and deliberate function of the new American Republic and has continued, unabated, to the present.

The active role of the government in promoting technology in general, and specific tools and machines in particular, included numerous ways to create a demand, provide the rules of play and level the playing field, referee activities, subsidize in one way or another the research, development, marketing and use of devices and systems, train people in how to design, build, operate, repair and shop for technologies, as well as designing, building, and maintaining the engineering infrastructure that provides transportation and communication, brings in fresh water and carries away waste, provides energy and food, and so on and so on. It is not too much to say that without the very visible hand of an activist government, our technology would be very different in shape, distribution, and availability. In providing for both national defense and the common welfare, the government has taken an active role in fostering our technological environment.

The several colonial governments, as well as the British Parliament, acted to encourage or discourage particular technologies in North America, and the federal government of the United States, from its inception, redoubled those efforts. Subsidies were offered to entrepreneurs who planned canals and turnpikes, manufacturers who started new industries, and ingenious mechanics who sought to introduce new tools and machines. The Constitution made provision for a Patent Office, and one was established in 1792. A new patent law in 1836 established what has been called the world's first modern system, under which inventions were vetted for novelty and usefulness before the issuance of a patent. Over the years, literally millions of patents have been issued, although the efficacy of the system has never been without its skeptics. The prevailing assumption has been that, as President Lincoln once wrote, "the patent system . . . added the fuel of interest to the fire of genius in the discovery and production of new and useful things." Over the years, there was an endemic impression that the system needed improvement but, since no one could demonstrate with certainty what it did, no one could feel certain of what changes it might accomplish.

One particularly important site of early American technological innovation was the string of federal armories established by the Congress to supply the military with small arms. It was in these, and particularly at that situated at Harper's Ferry, that the so-called American System of Manufacture was developed in the antebellum period. Also called "armory practice," this famously consisted of the production of standard (if not always precisely identical) parts by use of special-purpose automatic machines. From these, arsenals mechanics, familiar with the process, fanned out into a number of other key industries, spreading the idea of interchangeability. As Merritt Roe Smith has shown, this innovation was driven by a military which dreamed of interchangeability of weapon parts and willingly spent the considerable sums of money to achieve that result. The deep-pockets of the government were at least as significant as the vision of interchangeability on the battlefield.

In 1802, a military academy was established at West Point to train engineers and artillerists for the army, and until the Civil War this was a major source for the civil engineers who designed and built the new nation's transportation network. At first employed as consultants to lay out the best routes for canals and roads, then railroads, they were also needed to draw up specifications and contracts, choose materials, and finally, in the case of the railroads, to develop operating procedures. The military, as it turned out, was the closest analogy to the developing large corporations which operated over great distances and encompassed numerous functional divisions from personnel to maintenance. As importantly, the Corps of Engineers did exploration and mapping and was responsible for making and keeping the great inlands waterways of the Mississippi basin open to navigation.

What the US Army Corps of Engineers, and other agencies like the Coast & Geodetic Survey, did for the nation's transportation and commerce, the land-grant schools and United States Department of Agriculture (USDA) did for the agricultural system of the country. The year 1862 saw the Congress pass the Morrell Land Grant Act, the Pacific Railroad Act, and set up a Department of Agriculture. The strict-constructionist southern members of Congress who had been trying to limit the role of the federal government had withdrawn at the outbreak of the Civil War, and the nation's farmers were the object of a burst of federal activism that gave them new institutions to serve them. The new department undertook scientific studies to improve agricultural practices, and the land-grant colleges (at least one in each state and territory) undertook to provide a tertiary education for the sons and daughters of farmers and mechanics.

In the years after the Civil War, no national purpose was as enthusiastically pursued as the exploration and exploitation of the trans-Mississippi West. To help discover, categorize and exploit the natural resources of the West, the Congress in 1879 established a Geological Survey (USGS). Studies by USGS scientists did much to explain to the miners the new conditions they were finding in the Rocky Mountains where, for example, ores of the newly discovered gold and silver fields proved difficult to work with older and more traditional technologies and inherited knowledge. The Survey is perhaps best known today for the detailed maps it produces of the United States.

By the turn of the twentieth century, engineering and science were developing so rapidly that the nation's industrial, agricultural, and natural resource sectors were all feeling both the promise and perils of rapid innovation. The social interventionist nature of Progressivism generally extended to include a realization that the federal government would have to deploy research and development to understand and effectively regulate such widespread industrial activities as the production of food and drugs, the exploitation of natural resources such as forests, grazing land and western waters, the dumping of industrial wastes into navigable waters, and the emerging radio and aviation industries. The years from just before 1900 through the 1920s saw the birth of a new wave of government bureaus set up around an industry to engage in research, education and regulation based on the best science and engineering available.

The extension of homesteading laws to the arid West, that is the lands west of the 100th meridian, created a classic mismatch of theory and practice. Based on the desire to preserve the country as a nation of yeoman farmers, the 160-acre allotments were adequate to support a family on fertile lands with adequate rainfall. In much of the West, however, small farms without access to water for irrigation purposes were next to useless. In 1902, a federal Bureau of Reclamation was set up to locate and construct irrigation works, not only large dams but also artesian wells.

By 1919, the Bureau had undertaken 26 projects which were in various stages of completion. Among these, 100 large dams had been built and about 11,000 miles of canals dug to carry water away to farms. Three million acres were planned to be served by the projects at a cost, so far, of $125 million. The dream of making the desert "bloom like a rose" had its successes, but also its problems. It proved easier to legislate a democratic distribution of the water than to actually deliver it equitably. And ironically, while the Bureau was hailed at its inception as a part of President Theodore Roosevelt's Conservation Movement, well before the end of the century it had won the enmity of environmentalists who counted the loss of natural rivers, wild fish stocks, and a general unbalancing of ecological stability. In this it joined its federal rival, the Army Corps of Engineers.

By the opening of the twentieth century, all the leading industrial nations had established some sort of government agency to establish standards not only of length and weight, but of the myriad other quantities that research was bringing forward.

The founding generation had provided for "weights and measures," but had not foreseen the need to standardize the ohm and watt, let alone the curie, a unit of atomic decay. In 1901, the US joined these other nations by setting up the Bureau of Standards and its organic act laid out its duties: "the custody of the standards; the comparison of the standards used in scientific investigations, engineering, manufacturing, commerce, and educational institutions with the standards adopted or recognized by the government; the construction, when necessary, of standards, their multiples and subdivisions; the testing and calibration of standard measuring apparatus; the solution of problems which arise in connection with standards; the determination of physical constants and the properties of materials, when such data are of great importance to scientific or manufacturing interests..." These are all activities basic to any efficient industrial society, and best done by the federal government.

A Bureau of Mines was established in 1910 to aid the eastern coal and western hard-rock mining industries. Although expressly forbidden to do much in the way of regulation of the industry, the appalling number of deaths among working miners provided one of the first research and educational focuses. Under the mandate to increase mining efficiency, the Bureau undertook a number of studies such as an investigation of the use of electricity in operations. Over the years, the Bureau has carried on a program of useful, if not dramatic, research on behalf of the industry. When the Organization of Petroleum Exporting Countries (OPEC) oil embargo was instigated in 1973, for example, it proved to be one of the few centers able to undertake work on alternative types of coal production, transportation and use.

Another acknowledgement of the growing importance of industrial research was an attempt, launched in 1916, to set up federally authorized and financed engineering experiment stations in each of the states. Thought of as an explicit analog to the agricultural experiment stations authorized by the Hatch Act in 1888, these new stations were to help bridge the gap between the lab and the workplace, helping to bring into industrial practices new improvements springing from scientific and engineering research. The legislation had strong support from corporate sponsors of industrial research and from the land-grant colleges which were to become the sites of the new stations, but strong opposition from state colleges and universities which were not a part of the land-grant system slowed it down enough that it became lost in the general rush to pass preparedness legislation in the face of the continuing European war. Although some stations were established, they never received federal authorization and regular financial support.

Even though in 1903 Wilbur and Orville Wright were the first to get a heavier-then-air craft into the air and sustain flight for any length of time, so close were others to doing the same thing that improved airplanes quickly followed from a number of quarters. By the outbreak of the European War in 1914 combatants were able to make use of this new weapon, first for observation and then for dropping bombs and shooting down the enemy's planes. So quickly were airplanes developed that the United States found itself outclassed and rushed in 1915 to establish a National Advisory Committee on Aeronautics (NACA). An independent agency, the NACA moved quickly to get research and development started by using grants and contracts, for example with the aeronautical laboratory at MIT (Massachusetts Institute of Technology). This method of supporting work by industrial and university engineers and scientists became a model for other agencies, especially during and after World War II.

In the modern nation state, only the central government has legitimate and efficient access to the technology of violence. From the early nineteenth century, the federal arsenals had not only manufactured weapons but also made enormous contributions to their technical advancement. As during the Civil War, in World War I, the government moved quickly to improve the quality of its armaments. The setting up of the NACA in 1915 was one example. Another was the appointment of the Naval Consulting Board in that same year; chaired by none other than Thomas Edison himself, the Board included such other significant figures as Elmer Sperry, inventor of the gyroscope, and Willis R. Whitney, one of the most important researchers at General Electric's laboratories. The following year President Woodrow Wilson, at the request of the astrophysicist George Ellery Hale, created the National Research Council under the umbrella of the National Academy of Sciences, itself a creation of the Civil War years.

It has been said of World War I, as of World War II, that victory came more from the manufacture and deployment of massive amounts of industrial products than from any newly invented weapons. Nevertheless, the formation of a Chemical Warfare Service underscored the way in which new technologies, some of them science-based, were being called upon by the military forces. The popular image of poison gas use hung over the war and American chemists, some of whom donned uniforms and moved to government laboratories, struggled to produce new gases and protections against them. Gas masks, for example the one patented by Garrett Morgan, the Cleveland, Ohio African-American inventor, had been largely the interest of miners but now became a research and production priority. By and large Americans started so late, and were in the war for such a short time, that the cycle of research–development–production–procurement–training had little chance for completion. One new product, which came to be called tear gas, did find a postwar domestic market with police departments which wanted to control crowd of strikers and political demonstrations.

At the time of the outbreak of the European War in 1914, many of the chemicals used in the United States, from aspirin to super-phosphates, were the product of the German chemical industry, protected by patents taken out in this country. During the war these patents were confiscated by the government as alien property and made available at a very low cost to the American chemical industry through a quasi-private entity known as the Chemical Foundation. The Foundation, governed by representatives from the largest American companies such as E.I. du Pont, then licensed the German patents to American producers. The giveaway was unsuccessfully challenged in court, and marked the beginning of the large-scale production of other than basic chemicals in the country.

Roads in the country had always been primarily local affairs, with the great National Road, extended westward from Maryland beginning in 1808 being a notable exception. Then in 1894 an Office of Road Inquiry (later the Bureau of Public

Roads) was set up, first to make an inventory of rural roads with an eye toward the improvement of farm life and efficiency. In 1916 for the first time, partly in response to the Good Roads Movement that was sparked first by the bicycle craze and then by early automobile enthusiasts, and partly as a wartime matter, the Bureau began to try to rationalize the nation's roads. Federal funds were made available to those states which agreed to inventory and categorize their roads, improve them, and coordinate main arteries with adjacent states. By 1925 governments throughout the country were spending a bit over $1 billion a year on road improvement and construction. The Bureau of Public Roads continued to do engineering research on road construction techniques and materials throughout the period.

As is suggested by the need for more and better roads, the 1920s was a period of unprecedented access to new and exciting consumer durables. Cars, household appliances, phonographs and radios supplemented other consumer technologies such as air travel and motion pictures to produce a heady sense of material progress that seemed to sum up all that modernity had to offer. Largely invisible, though inevitable, many of these technologies required a governmental involvement to function with any kind of satisfactory outcome.

In 1920 station KDKA made the first radio broadcast, sending news of President Warren G. Harding's presidential victory to 2,000 listeners. Eight years later the number of stations broadcasting had reached 700 and 40 million Americans were tuning in. Since there is only so much room on the broadcast bands it was clear that some agency was needed to sort out who should be licensed to broadcast on what wavelength and at what power. Congress made several false starts at addressing the problem but finally, in 1927, passed legislation establishing the Federal Radio Commission. This commission was to issue licenses during the first year, after which it became an appellate body and the licensing was done by the Secretary of Commerce. In addition to making regulations to prevent interference and so forth, it had the power to regulate the technologies to be used with an eye toward maintaining the quality of the signal sent out. It was a prime example of the way in which the federal government had to step in to regulate the ways in which a new technology was applied, not only to protect the interests of all citizens but also the business environment itself.

The first successful heavier-than-air flight made by the Wright brothers at Kitty Hawk in 1903 had given America a brief lead in airplane design, but that was gone by World War I. The military had given some aid to the inventors by buying a few of their machines, but it was the war itself which ignited an aviation industry in the country. After the Armistice, surplus airplanes were flown about the country by barnstormers who entertained local crowds with stunts and rides. The government again intervened and after having the Army fly mail between New York City and Washington, granted air mail contracts to those hearty enough to take up flying for a living. The first transcontinental deliveries began in 1924 and by 1929 four domestic airlines were in business.

As commercial aviation gained momentum, the airplane, like the radio, needed to be wrapped in a web of regulations and facilities which would both encourage business and protect the public. Airfields and beacons had to be established, routes distributed, safety standards set and enforced, and aircraft themselves had to be licensed and inspected. In 1926 the Air Commerce Act set up an Aeronautics Branch in the Department of Commerce to oversee this new technology and its application.

While most attention from historians has been directed towards the activities of the federal government, state and local governments were also being propelled by the twin forces of industrialization and modernization to come up with new initiatives and new ways of dealing with old problems. No better example can be given than that of the City Manager movement that swept mid-sized cities between the wars. Engineers had been employed by cities either to see to specific infrastructure projects or to supervise all the construction and maintenance work that was needed. Now, they were put in charge.

As the primary scholar of this phenomenon put it, "Governmental problems have become intricate and even more insistent. They call for solution with the aid of science, not with the wisdom of a ward politician." Technically trained managers (by 1927, 398 of the nation's 863 managers were engineers), it was hoped, would substitute science for prejudice, and professional ethics for partisan politics. As it turned out, the city manager form of urban government had its greatest success in middle-sized, middle-class communities where opposition to the development plans of business interests had the most difficulty in expressing itself. Over the years also, urban managers became a separate profession with its own educational and career path, and engineers were less often drafted to fill the role.

Herbert Hoover, though his degree from Stanford University was in geology, had had a successful career as a mining engineer and came to the presidency in 1928 with a better grasp of technology that any other president. Early in his tenure he assembled a blue ribbon team of social scientists and put them to work studying the effects of what they called "recent social trends." As it turned out, many of these were thought to have been triggered by new technologies and their findings, published after Hoover had left office under the title of *Recent Social Trends*, attempted to document the many ways in which new technology had "impacted" American society. The conclusions were disparate and sometimes contradictory, but as a pioneer study of the subject it indicated to its authors that technology was a powerful shaper of society and that technical change was inevitable.

Later studies by government bodies during the 1930s, such as *Technological Trends and National Policy, Including the Social Implications of New Inventions* (1937) issued by the National Resources Committee, and *Technology on the Farm* (1940) issued by the Department of Agriculture, took the optimistic view that technology would inevitably evolve, its evolution would create on balance more good than harm, and that it was the business of the federal government to create programs to protect the most vulnerable sectors of the population, as for example with unemployment insurance and job retraining.

The coming of the Great Depression in 1929 laid bare the flaws in the American economic system and the lack of a safety net to provide for those the system victimized. Throughout the 1920s scientists and engineers had proclaimed a new Machine

Age, one that freed workers from drudgery and provided a cornucopia of new and exciting consumer goods: cars, home appliances, entertainment media, and all the rest. With the coming of mass unemployment, however, the heralded labor-saving machines seemed more like labor-displacing devices, and the new consumer goods were beyond the reach of those who could no longer pay for them. Once again it appeared to be up to the government, in this case Franklin D. Roosevelt's New Deal administration, to appeal from technology drunk to technology sober. As it worked out, the federal government proved itself more willing to pick up the pieces after the capitalist train-wreck than to throw the policy switches to prevent it in the first place.

Several of the large-scale technological projects of the Depression years were actually already underway when Roosevelt took office. A World War I era chemical plant on the Tennessee River had been the object of a drawn-out political battle between those who wanted it turned over to private interests and others who wanted it maintained as a public service. At last the latter side won out and a Tennessee Valley Authority (TVA) was established to bring economic development to a badly depressed part of the rural South through the damming and regulation of the rivers of the Tennessee Valley. It was a comprehensive effort involving a string of dams to provide flood control and irrigation water, as well as the reclamation of land long abused and eroded by inappropriate farming methods. People were moved from land to be flooded and resettled in model villages. It was to be a model for other regional basin developments throughout the country: an example of what the federal government could do to make life better through the mobilization and deployment of technology.

The most striking and controversial aspect of the TVA was its generation of electric power for the region. Private power interests, while reluctant to provide service in areas they considered unprofitable, reacted strongly against the "socialist" plan to provide public power at cost. The public power forces won and for many years the TVA was the proud evidence that the Enlightenment Project was alive and well – the rational application of technology could indeed lead to social improvement. Ironically, in the years after World War II the TVA began to seem more and more like any publicly owned utility. It was an enthusiastic advocate of nuclear power plants. The "clean" electricity of its hydro plants was one of the reasons TVA was hailed as an environmentally sound operation, but to supplement that power the administration now turned to coal-fired plants, with fuel coming from strip-mines. The ideal lived on, inspiring President Lyndon B. Johnson in the 1960s to propose a Mekong Delta Authority for southeast Asia as an alternative to war, but TVA's moral account had by then been heavily overdrawn.

Not only the Tennessee but the entire Mississippi River basin had repeated and worsening problems with flooding as eroded farms, logged over mountains and paved over urban areas sped water from over half the continent down to New Orleans. As the government film *The River* put it in 1938, there was no such thing in nature as a perfect river and through the '20s and '30s the Corps of Engineers worked to build locks and levies which would keep the Mississippi and its tributaries within their banks at flood time. The twin goals of flood control and navigation dictated, for the

Corps, that the whole basin should be brought under engineering control. Water was notoriously rationed out to the Missouri River by a committee which met each morning to decide how much was needed for navigation. The Corps' massive Atchafalaya Basin project in Louisiana pitted engineering against ecological logic and used vast amounts of concrete to keep the Mississippi from taking its natural course, one which would have devastating consequences for New Orleans.

The electrification of American homes and workplaces had been one of the triumphs of the previous generation, but the New Deal found that many homes in urban areas were wired only for light and not for appliances, while only 10 percent of farms got electricity from central power stations. In the first case, a large proportion of Americans rented their homes and landlords were often reluctant to take on the expense of upgrading wiring. In the second, private power companies were reluctant to run lines miles into the countryside to serve a handful of farms which might not use much electricity in any case. The government's answer to the first problem was to write wiring standards into the rules for FHA (Federal Housing Authority) mortgage loans. The second problem was attacked through the REA (Rural Electrification Administration) which was set up in 1936.

The REA operated by guaranteeing bank loans to farmer-owned electrical cooperatives. The co-ops would use their loans to bring wires into their territory and then distribute electrical power bought from private utilities. Again advocates had to counter the claim that this was somehow "socialistic" but the co-ops spread rapidly and by the war rural America was essentially electrified. It was a necessary precondition for the postwar push to create "factories on the farm" in rural America.

One of the fears of private power companies was that farmers would use too little power to justify the construction of lines. To counter this possibility a REA "circus" traveled the countryside displaying an array of household appliances and farm machinery which could be driven by electricity. Encouraged to use as much electricity as possible, both to make life and work easier and to capture economies of scale, farm families responded with a full-scale electrification of farm life. After the war a federal agency similar to the REA was established to bring the telephone to farms, and it too was rapidly successful.

One thread that ran through much of thinking about government and technology during the Great Depression was the need for what was sometimes called a Technology Czar. It was an analog of the often-reiterated claim that science should be elevated to Cabinet prominence with a Secretary to look after and coordinate the many scientific initiatives and activities of the federal government. A Technology Czar would do the same, making sure that overlooked technologies were brought to the fore and that agency efforts were coordinated. Both the Soviet Union and Nazi Germany, it was assumed, had such a command and control function, and if democracies were to survive they too needed to take charge of the process, not leaving it to the vagaries of individual genius and corporate self-interest.

During the 1930s these calls were turned aside, but with the outbreak of war once again in Europe, what had seemed somewhat un-American in peacetime took on a more urgent logic. Vannevar Bush – inventor of the integral computer, electrical engineer, Vice President of MIT, President of the Carnegie Institution of Washington, and most significantly at the moment Secretary of NACA – was aware in 1940 that there was no single federal agency to develop what he called "instrumentalities of war." He was instrumental in getting Roosevelt to establish the National Defense Research Committee (NDRC) in that year, and the following, in having created the Office of Scientific Research and Development (OSRD) which absorbed the NDRC and the Committee on Medical Research.

In the manner of the NACA in World War I, Bush had the OSRD move quickly to give grants and contracts to civilian scientists and engineers working in university, industrial and foundation laboratories to invent and improve new weapons. He quickly spun off the research effort to develop an atomic bomb, and busily worked toward creating what Hunter Dupree has called an electronic environment for war. Critics of the OSRD charged it with being elitist and only partial – enlisting primarily technical people at the best schools and biggest corporations, and concentrating on physicists and electrical engineers to the neglect of such other disciplines as geology and biology. Bush fought off efforts by Congress, especially Sen. Harley Kilgore of West Virginia, to intensify the mobilization of science and technology. Just as Roosevelt had said that he had dismissed Dr New Deal and called in Dr Win the War, so Bush sought to mobilize the nation's technical resources with as little disruption of the status quo as possible. It was a decision which left the rich very rich indeed.

In the years before the war, a group of European scientists had been working toward the theoretical possibility of harnessing the energy locked inside the nucleus of the atom. As Hitler locked down Europe, a number of these fled to America where the most famous of them, Albert Einstein himself, wrote to President Roosevelt suggesting that the Nazi might be working on plans to build an atomic bomb and urging that America enter into a race to beat him to it. Bush chaired a committee to look into the matter and, deciding that it had sufficient merit to pursue, recommended that a project be started. The US Army Corps of Engineers, experienced in large-scale construction and the management of complex projects, was chosen to organize and direct what was code-named the Manhattan Project.

Operating out of university laboratories, but mainly from large and secret facilities at Los Alamos, Oak Ridge, and Hanford, Washington, the Manhattan District engineers and scientists built a test bomb which was finally set off at Alamagordo, New Mexico, in July, 1945. The bombs had been made for use over Japan and were dropped on Hiroshima on August 6, 1945 and on Nagasaki three days later. The massive mobilization of trained personnel and funds became a model for the notion that when it put its mind to it, the federal government could accomplish almost anything of a technical nature. The project became the model for placing an astronaut on the Moon, deciphering the human genome, developing an artificial heart, finding a cure for cancer, and any number of other large-scale and expensive technical initiatives. They did not all work as well.

As World War II began to wind down, Bush turned his attention to the future. The nation's research scientists and engineers had enjoyed an unprecedented amount of funding and prestige and the results were impressive, even without the public's knowledge of the atomic program. It seemed wise to plan for continued technical support for the services, and some young Navy officers were already laying plans for what would become the Office of Naval Research (ONR). It also seemed likely that a similar level of attention and resources could significantly enhance the nation's health and promote economic growth. A large number of research reports, obviously classified during wartime, could be made public for the benefit of a wide range of businesses.

Bush's report, titled *Science the Endless Frontier* played to the hopes and fears of a generation which could almost remember when the 1890 federal census had discovered that there was no longer a frontier line in the West, and the historian Frederick Jackson Turner had declared that this would have grave consequences for a nation that had been reborn both politically and economically each generation by moving west. Science, Bush promised, would provide that renewal with a space of the imagination into which succeeding generations of the nation's best and brightest could move to extract value for the country as a whole.

Basically a political conservative and no great friend of large, activist government, Bush suggested the establishment of a national research foundation through which a self-perpetuating body of the country's technical elite could distribute funds to civilian researchers strictly on the basis of technical merit. The Director of the Bureau of the Budget termed the report "Science the Endless Expenditure," triggering Bush's ire but pointing to a political problem the author had not addressed: if science was good, true, and beautiful, how much support could ever be enough?

It took 5 years before something like the report's recommended agency was founded. President Truman was not comfortable with several of the enabling legislation's provisions. For one thing, he believed that patents taken out on government-funded research results should be freely available to the public that paid for them. For another, he wanted to see the social sciences supported along with the natural, biological and engineering. He also wanted to see the research funds geographically spread across the country on something like a traditional per capita basis, rather than being concentrated in the hands of elite researchers in elite schools. And finally, he insisted that the agency be politically responsible in the sense that its board should be appointed by the president rather than being self-perpetuating. These attempts to democratize federally funded science flew in the face of Bush's belief that scientists should be left free to do what they thought best.

When a National Science Foundation (NSF) was finally established in 1950 it was the result of a compromise: patents were to remain proprietary, social science support was permitted but not mandated, funds were to be distributed on the basis of merit as assessed by panels of peers, and the governing Board was appointed by the President with advice from the foundation. One very significant victory for the Bush forces was that the NSF would concentrate on basic research, leaving technological applications to others, presumably private corporations.

Equally significant for the future was that during the 5 years of debate, most of the technologically important responsibilities the NSF might have had had already been distributed. A fledgling National Institutes of Health took over responsibility for health and medical technologies. The Atomic Energy Commission had been set up to regulate that important technology and NACA divided responsibility for missiles with the armed services – which, of course, each had their own competing and overlapping research and development efforts.

The overwhelming concentration on what Bush called the "instrumentalities of war" had virtually cut off the wartime manufacture of civilian technologies and this, with the pent-up spending power of war workers, including significantly new numbers of women and African-Americans, created a heavy demand for consumer technologies after the war. The first cars and other consumer durables to be produced from 1945 onward were, or course, basically older models of prewar designs but the large backlog of research and development for war purposes promised a quick upgrading of older technologies and the introduction of new ones. Some, like television for the home and cotton-picking machines for the farm, were technologies that had become available just before the war and were now made widely available. As historian Lizabeth Cohen has suggested, America became a "consumers' republic" in which buying things became reinterpreted as a political act and, in fact, eventually took the place of older forms such as voting and debate.

Not only was there a growing market for new and better technologies, there were more technologists to design and maintain them. An uncounted number of service men and women had been trained in some sort of technological expertise during the war, whether in radio, radar, auto, or airplane mechanics, as pilots and in construction work. These came back to a civilian society in which many of these skills could be put directly to use or modified for other purposes. Veterans who aspired for higher education could use the so-called G.I. Bill to attend college to study engineering or any other subject at government expense.

During the war, many thousands more had worked in industrial plants, turning out the ships, airplanes, tanks, munitions, and all the other requirements of a massive military effort. Most famous among these were perhaps the women recruited out of their homes, domestic service (especially for African-American women) or clerical positions to learn to operate machine tools, weld, or in the case of the celebrated Rosie, to rivet. At the renowned Liberty shipyards of Henry Kaiser in California and Oregon, not only were ships virtually mass-produced using innovative techniques of subassembly, but the workers themselves, especially women and African-Americans, were themselves mass-produced – quickly trained to do the heavy and exacting work of shipbuilding.

For those who were too young to have been in the war, ROTC or NROTC (Reserve Officer Training Corps or Naval Reserve Officers Training Corps) membership in college provided funds for education in exchange for a fixed period of service. In David Beer's memoir *Blue Sky Dreams* (1996) we learn of his father who studied engineering at Auburn University on an NROTC scholarship, then served his time as a Navy pilot, then went to work for Lockheed in Sunnyvale, California, as an aeronautical engineer working on secret "black budget" projects in aerospace technology. It was an almost archetypical technical career in the Military-Industrial Complex of the Cold War era.

The 14 million returning service men and women, and those a bit later like David Beer's father, typically married and wanted to move back into civilian life in their own homes. These were provided in massive numbers by developers like William Levitt on the East Coast and those who built Lakewood in the Los Angeles area. Beginning in the late 1940s in a potato field on Long Island, he began to mass-produce the kinds of houses that defined the postwar suburbs. Scraping the land clear and level, streets and lots were laid out (mostly with septic tanks, not sewer systems) and houses built by the thousands one step at a time – foundations were laid in long rows, then pre-assembled wall sections were added, and so on until they were finished. It was very like a Ford assembly line except the workers moved rather than the product. Housing starts in 1950 were 1.9 million, twice the prewar record.

Governments at all levels facilitated this work. Local jurisdictions changed zoning restrictions so that development could take place, then provided the engineering infrastructure of roads and school buildings. The federal government provided G.I. loans ("no money down") for mortgages and federal FHA regulations, as well as local government building codes, facilitated adequate electrical wiring and therefore encouraged the sale of appliances.

Since 1916 the federal government had been providing some funds and technical advice for roads, but their construction and maintenance was still largely a state and local matter. Even before the war, however, there had been talk of a far-flung federal highway system to serve like the limited-access toll-roads which states were beginning to build, like the famous Pennsylvania Turnpike begun just before the war and the New Jersey Turnpike, opened in 1952. During the war, partly out of concern for possible postwar unemployment, a proposed system was laid out and at last, in 1954, President Dwight D. Eisenhower gave the go-ahead for a National Defense Highway System, popularly known as the Interstate Highway System, now 42,795 miles in length. The roadways were laid out on an ample scale, to allow for additional lanes, and the roadbeds were more substantial than those of ordinary highways. Changing patterns of federal subsidy helped shift massive amounts of even trans-continental freight movement from trains to 18-wheel trucks and numerous on- and off-ramps became the sites of countless newly franchised motels and fast-food restaurants. The whole system was, of course, subsidized by low gasoline and diesel prices and financed, in part, by federal and state fuel taxes.

The elaboration of the freeway system, even in California, could of course not go on forever. In 1993 what was called Los Angeles' "final freeway" was opened. Running eight lanes wide for 17.3 miles through nine cities, it cost $2.2 billion. One of its interchanges, that with the San Diego Freeway, was composed of five levels, seven miles of ramps, 11 bridges and 2 miles of tunnels. It covered 100 acres and stood seven stories high. It was the apotheosis of the American love of the highway.

The utter destruction of the economies of both Germany and Japan presented a dilemma for American policymakers after the war. On the one hand, strong economies in both countries had allowed them to undertake military adventures which had cost America dearly, and other countries, like the Soviet Union, even more. On the other hand, it made good sense to try to get them back on their feet as a functioning part of a capitalist world market economy. On June 5, 1947, Secretary of State George Marshall announced the scheme which became known as the Marshall Plan. Some 20–25 percent of Germany's industrial plant had been destroyed during the war and all sorts of machinery for manufacturing, mining and transportation was needed, as well as coal and food. The American commitment to rebuild the German economy was a major part of the $22.5 billion that the country spent on foreign aid between 1945 and 1949.

Japan faced a similar problem, and a host of American experts, many of them engineers and other technologists, traveled to the occupied country to help get it back on its feet. Because of old and worn-out machinery and antique techniques, in 1947 the average Japanese steel workers produced only one-eighteenth as much as their American counterpart. American engineers from the steel industry visited and evaluated the plants, teams of Japanese engineers were brought to the US to tour mills, and the US government bought Japanese steel during the Korean war to provide a market for change. Most famously, statistical quality control was introduced by W. Edwards Deming and other American experts. This became one of the major contributors to the ascendance of the Japanese automobile industry.

World War II not only brought the defeat of Germany and Japan, but it hastened the collapse of those far-flung empires which European nations had been accumulating for over a century, particularly in Asia and Africa. The new nations, such as India, which were set up out of the wreckage of empire had been systematically looted of the resources and kept in a state of dependent under-development over the years and were now keen to modernize and join the family of nations. They had before them two strategies for that development: one, the command and control economy and one-party rule of the Soviet Union, and the other a relatively free-market, democratic pattern of the United States. Between these two worlds, the Third World was eagerly courted by both superpowers, which very much wanted the new nations in their own orbit of influence.

Part of the postwar American plan for developing nations was the transmission of technical aid to help with their modernization. In January, 1949, President Harry S. Truman announced his Point Four program for such aid, which was to include both the "technical, scientific, and managerial knowledge necessary to economic development," and "production goods – machinery and equipment – and financial assistance." The resulting Act for International Development (1950) provided the plan for using American technological know-how to kick-start the development of what were called developing countries. One major project, proposed by President Lyndon B. Johnson in 1965, was the Lower Mekong Basic Project which he envisioned as a kind of Tennessee Valley Authority for Southeast Asia.

Another way in which the federal government furthered development around the globe was through the support of the activities of such giant international construction firms as Brown & Root (later a part of Haliburton) and Bechtel. Such companies were busy around the world developing mines and oil fields, building harbors and airports, nuclear power plants, and hydroelectric projects. Intensely political in their connections and operations, Brown & Root had been closely associated with Johnson for his whole career and won many contracts for building government-sponsored projects, including much of the American infrastructure in wartime Vietnam. After it was absorbed by Haliburton, its close association with Vice President Richard Cheney was noted when that company won the prime contract for rebuilding Iraq after the 2003 war. Bechtel, in turn, was closely associated with President Richard M. Nixon and had excellent success in winning contracts for foreign projects financed through the World Bank and similar international funding agencies as well as from the federal government itself. It too became deeply involved in rebuilding infrastructure in Iraq.

On October 4, 1957, the Soviet Union launched Sputnik, the world's first artificial satellite. The consternation, not to say panic, was palpable – the despised enemy had produced a technological spectacle which amounted to a worldwide public relations coup of major proportions. *Sputnik* showed what a government could accomplish when it set out to, and Washington responded with a menu of scientific and engineering initiatives to counter its effect. The National Defense Education Act (NDEA) poured money into university fellowships for science and engineering students and educational curricula at all levels was reformed to beef up training in science and mathematics.

One of the most far-reaching reforms was the creation, in 1958, of NASA, the National Aeronautics and Space Administration, into which was folded the old NACA. A crash program was undertaken to catch up to the Russians in space, an important part of which was the Army's missile program under the former German rocket expert Werner von Braun at Huntsville, Alabama. Rivalries between the armed services were adjudicated (they all wanted their own missiles) and NASA began to pioneer the large-scale project management techniques for which it became famous.

John F. Kennedy charged the outgoing Eisenhower administration (falsely as it turned out) with allowing a "missile gap" to develop and on May 25, 1961, announced that America would land astronauts on the Moon within the decade, an expensive bit of international showmanship which was accomplished on July 20, 1969. More importantly, the successive generation of satellites photographed the earth's surface in aid of mineral exploration, gathered military intelligence, transmitted television transmissions, and helped stranded motorists position themselves.

The Cold War which emerged so soon after the end of World War II provoked what was widely considered to be an arms race with the Soviet Union. The logic was persuasive: offense and defense were always in an unstable balance and each side had to think ahead to not only what they wanted to do, but what the other side might be planning to do. The disappointingly short duration of America's nuclear monopoly after the war (the Russians tested their atomic bomb in August 1949) seemed to indicate that despite popular and official prejudices to the contrary, the Soviets were perfectly capable of very competitive research and development when it came to armaments. Therefore, if they had atomic bombs, we needed more and larger ones, and even a hydrogen bomb. If they made intercontinental ballistic missiles (ICBMs), then we need to be able to know how to bring them down. If they had a vast land army, we needed tactical nuclear weapons, perhaps even some capable of being delivered by battle tanks at the front.

But as the longtime government science advisor Herbert York realized, there was also a sense in which America was in a race with itself. We knew what we were doing, we could assume that eventually they would find out and invent a way to counter that, so we had to begin thinking now about how to override their counter measures. It was a self-perpetuating feedback system fed by vast amounts of federal funds. Monies poured into private defense and aerospace industries, the nation's universities, and of course was spent by government agencies themselves. There was no typical year, but from 1961 to 1967, for example, Lockheed Aircraft, the top defense contractor, got $10,619 million in contracts. In 1964 alone, MIT, the top academic recipient of defense funding, received $46,819,000. And among government agencies the Department of Defense spent, on military functions, $7,762 million. The Atomic Energy Commission spent another $1.5 billion, much of which was for the nuclear arsenal.

This vast treasure may or may not have made America safer, but it certainly tended to starve civilian technologies of the money and trained personnel to push innovation faster and farther. It has been noted that both Germany and Japan, discouraged from maintaining their own defense forces during these years, were able to stage a significant challenge to the United States in terms of civilian technologies such as electronics, automobiles, cameras, and similar consumer goods.

The technology to harness the atom had been driven of course, by the perceived need to build up a nuclear arsenal that would either deter or win an all-out war with the Soviet Union. Neither scientists nor politicians, however, were completely comfortable with the idea that the "sweet" science of nuclear physics was good only to wage an apocalyptic war. The dream of "energy too cheap to meter" provided a parallel and much more comforting goal. At first however, the policy of government monopoly on nuclear fuel and the entire shroud of secrecy in which the whole subject of atomic matters was cloaked made any such program problematic.

Then in 1953 the new President, Dwight D. Eisenhower, unveiled an "Atoms for Peace" program which would carefully share nuclear technology with allies to use for civilian purposes. That same year a full-scale nuclear-powered electrical plant was authorized for a site at Shippingport, Pennsylvania, and the next year legislation was passed to allow the private ownership of reactors (thought the fuel itself was still owned by the government). The Shippingport plant came on-line in 1957 and two more started operations in 1960. By the '90s there were 58 commercial reactors in the country generating 9 percent of the nation's electricity. The sharing of American technology with other nations had helped spread it even more widely abroad: twenty other nations had a total of 100 plants in operation.

The 1979 nuclear accident at the Three Mile Island plant in Pennsylvania marked a serious setback for the nuclear power industry. It focused safety concerns which had been consistently downplayed by the Atomic Energy Commission but had always been in the background, even when one plant was seriously proposed for construction in New York City. But other problems persisted as well. Electrical power produced by the atom never became as cheap as the dream had anticipated, and its economic desirability was always tied to the price of alternative fuels, mainly coal and natural gas. And finally, persistent environmental concerns both about the plants and about the fate of the waste fuel rods remained unresolved. By the end of the century no new plants had been built for many years and none were planned for the near future.

No technology of the late twentieth century seemed to have a greater impact than the computer. The first examples, Mark I at Harvard and Electronic Numerical Integration and Computer (ENIAC) at the University of Pennsylvania, were built with government funds for war work. Work at MIT after the war on hardware for the Strategic Air Ground Environment (SAGE) led to the conversion from analog to digital computing, as well as computing in real time. As it turned out, it was a prime example of the way in which some projects fail at their military missions but nevertheless have wide and significant civilian applications.

Most of the early "mainframes" were very large indeed; the Mark I being 51-feet long, 8-feet high, and 3-feet wide, weighing 5 tons and containing 2,200 counter wheels and 3,300 relay components as well as 530 miles of wire. The device which broke out of this mould was the IBM 650 which was introduced in 1954 and became the first standard machine for business, rather than scientific and military, use. Software did not keep up with hardware, and languages such as FORTRAN, COBOL, and ALGOL had to be learned by serious users.

The invention of the transistor, by a Bell Laboratories team led by William Shockley, led the replacement of unreliable vacuum tubes in all sorts of electronic devices. The microprocessor was first marketed by Intel in 1971, one of the new and growing electronics firms to settle in California's Silicon Valley just south of San Francisco. It was there in 1975 that a group of enthusiasts formed the Homebrew Club, apparently stimulated by the announcement in January of that year of the Altair 8,800, a computer in a kit that sold for only $400. The most famous of the members of the club, as it turned out, would be Stephen Wozniak and Steve Jobs who formed Apple Computers in 1976. Already assembled and programmed, their Apple proved to be the catalyst for the spread of a true "home" computer. The government as a source of research and development funds, as well as a market for equipment, had made it a major force in the development of the computer. This was clearly shown in the evolution of what came to be called the Internet.

The Internet had its origin in the worries by the military that a nuclear attack would wipe out normal lines of communication in the country. Concerned with what they called 3C – Command, Control, and Communication, the Advanced Research Projects Agency (ARPA) undertook efforts in 1966 to put together a network of time-sharing computers distributed around the country in 17 computer centers. The notion of "packet switching," which would allow "packets" of information to seek out their own best routes through the telephone system, was to be critical to this network. In October 1972 ARPANET, as it was called, was unveiled as a medium strictly for the exchange of scientific information between scientists and engineers working on military topics. By the end of 1973 however, over three-quarters of the traffic was in the form of email and a group of researchers with a shared love of science fiction had started a chat group. In 1983 the Department of Defense gave up and established MILNET for military research exchange and 3 years later the National Science Foundation set up NSFNET for scientists working on civilian projects. ARPANET was finally shut down in 1990, by which time the World Wide Web and powerful search engines had carried the Internet in directions and scope far beyond what the government had initially intended.

Given the widespread agreement that technological change was usually seen as flowing from research and development, governments at all levels thought it wise to undertake their own efforts along these lines. At the city level, Santa Barbara, California, enjoyed the free advice of the local Engineers Club in 1965 which helped them develop arguments to counter the state's Department of Transportation plans to build an elevated freeway along the beach. In New York City the liberal Republican mayor, John Lindsey, appointed a Scientific and Technical Advisory Council for the city, also in 1965, which counted as members such luminaries as T. Keith Glennan, first administrator of NASA, Detlev Bronk, president of Rockefeller University, and executives from Consolidated Edison and Socony Mobile Oil among others.

A survey conducted in 1967 discovered that five of the 50 largest cities had some such advisory setup, but also that 22 state and territorial governments had such bodies. The oldest of these was set up in New York State in 1959 but most had come about since 1963. California announced its own Governor's Science Advisory Committee in 1966, a group which was chaired by a distinguished physicist at the University of California, Los Angeles, contained two Nobel laureates, and also city and county politicians and representatives from labor, agriculture and industry.

Since the war, the country had poured a tremendous amount of treasure and technical talent into competition with the Soviet Union, both in the form of the arm's race and the space race. With the advent of nuclear arms treaties and apparently more reasonable leadership in the Kremlin, it looked very much like, as the phrase of the day had it, "peace might break out." That possibility not only raised the specter of unemployment in the aerospace and other arms industries, but also raised the possibility of converting a generation of engineers and scientists from the arts of war to those of peace. No state was more dependent upon federal Cold War spending than was California, and the possibility of post-arms race recession there prompted to Governor Edmund G. (Pat) Brown to use some of his discretionary funds to make contracts with the involved industry designed to see whether or not their talent and experience with war research could be brought to bear upon such civilian issues as pollution and transportation. The aerospace firms undertaking the studies came up with predictably high-tech solutions but before anything could come from them, defense and aerospace funding ramped up again and the matter was dropped.

Several states undertook to encourage that celebrated but fickle national characteristic, Yankee ingenuity. The belief that every garage or basement might harbor the next Thomas Edison led to the institution of Inventors' Fairs around the country in the 1960s. In North Carolina an Inventors Congress and Technology Utilization Symposium was held in May, 1965, which featured exhibits by not only the inventors themselves, but also by NASA, the Small Business Administration, the Department of Defense, the National Bureau of Standards, the US Patent Office, and various businesses. The three-day congress had presentations, speeches, and panel discussions in abundance, but the highlight was the presentation of awards on the last afternoon. "Part-time" inventors attended from 28 states and two foreign countries, but the first place in the tools category went to a man who had invented a "finger level" and first place in the crop division went to a new green pea-sheller. The results suggested that the "lone" inventor was perhaps not in the best position to produce the kind of economic growth stimulated by technological change that was sought by all states as well as the federal government.

Out of a concern for the unlooked-for effects of government-sponsored technologies, and also to strengthen the hand of congress when dealing with technological initiatives from the executive branch, an Office of Technology Assessment (OTA) was proposed in 1967. Over the next 5 years the matter was studied from many angles and by different bodies, most significantly perhaps by the National Academy of Sciences. Importantly, the Academy made four assumptions that tended to shape what was to come. First, it assumed that the choice was between thoughtful and thoughtless technological change, discounting the possibility of resisting change at all. Second, they confessed to a belief that over time, the benefits of technological change had "vastly" outweighed any negative effect. Third, it believed that "human behavior and institutions" were the real problem, not technology itself. And finally, it asserted that such an office must act like a "partner" of business, not a "policeman". As President Nixon was reported to have warned, technology assessment should not be allowed to become technology harassment. When the office was finally established in 1972, that partnership meant that the small staff of the OTA did indeed make assessments based on data provided by business, rather than generated independently. Nevertheless, so long as it lasted it provided the congress with a useful source of technological advice independent of the White House and when different political parties dominated those two branches, its partisan potential was always suspected. The office was finally abolished early in the administration of Ronald Reagan.

These same years saw a concerted effort to perfect the institutions of science and technology policy within the federal government and to frankly increase the support of technologies directly, rather than at one remove through the support of science. Ever since the advent of *Sputnik* it had been thought necessary for each new president to announce a new "science policy" and appoint a new science advisor to see it forward. When Richard Nixon came to the White House in 1969, however, his relationship with the science establishment seemed especially difficult.

For one thing, there had been a small but highly visible group of "Scientists and Engineers for Johnson" working against him and he perceived the Vietnam War, especially, as an issue which divided him from the science community. This divide was dramatically highlighted on March 4, 1969, when a well-publicized "strike" of scientists and engineers took place at the Massachusetts Institute of Technology, a school which had contributed more than its share of scientific advisors to Washington and received more than its share of federal funding.

In October 1969 President Nixon appointed a Task Force on Science Policy to look into the possibility of institutionalizing some better means for establishing and articulating a clear science policy for the nation. The Task Force enthusiastically endorsed the notion and recommended in 1970 that President's Scientific Advisory Council (PSAC) and other executive science advisory agencies be strengthened and given responsibility for such a policy. Stung by the opposition of these very groups to the Vietnam War and his plans to press forward with an anti-ballistic missile (ABM) program, Nixon rejected the report's advice.

Then in 1971 Congress cut funding for the supersonic transport (the SST) project which was enthusiastically supported by Nixon as well as by NASA, the Pentagon, the Federal Aviation Agency, and the aerospace industry. Although Great Britain and France went ahead to produce the *Concord*, American scientists and environmentalists questioned its mission, its economics, and especially the effect upon the environment of massive sonic booms and pollution affecting the ozone layer. It has been suggested (Stine p. 65) that this opposition was a significant factor in Nixon's decision to abolish the PSAC and the White House Office of Science and Technology, agencies that had evolved since the Eisenhower years.

The scientific community, which had for so long succeeded in having the nation's technology policy subsumed under the presumably broader and more fundamental heading of science policy, was jolted when the Nixon administration called upon the elite NSF, the very bosom of basic research, to spend more time and money on applied research. In 1971 the NSF responded by initiating a program titled RANN, an acronym for Research Applied to National Needs. The President had hoped that by targeting funds on specific technological goals, the nation's sagging economy would be boosted by new products and processes. The alarm of the scientific community, firmly wedded, at least publicly, to the notion that new technology only grows out of basic research, was only somewhat allayed by the fact that almost 40 percent of even RANN's funds were earmarked for scientific research. The pressure remained, however, and in 1981, at the beginning of the first administration of Ronald Reagan, the NSF was forced to establish a separate engineering directorate.

When President Gerald Ford replaced the disgraced Nixon, he bowed to congressional pressure moving forward to re-establish the White House machinery for science policy and signed into law the National Science and Technology Policy, Organization, and Priorities Act (1976). The next years, however, continued to see a flurry of congressional hearings and proposals to somehow find the right policy for optimizing technological change. In 1979 a congressional bill, called the National Science and Technology Innovation Act was put forward and an Office of Industrial Technology was suggested for the Department of Commerce. It was passed and the office was established the following year. Also in 1980, a National Technology Foundation was proposed and in 1982 the Small Business Innovation Development Act was passed to increase the flow of federal R&D funds into small firms. In 1983 legislation was introduced to establish an Advanced Technology Foundation. Some of these larger gestures died in the Congress, but during these years a host of smaller efforts to increase innovation bore fertile witness to the all but unanimous belief that whatever the best means might be, it was the responsibility of the federal government to aggressively promote technological advances which would work to improve the health, welfare, economic advantage, and military security of the American people.

The administrations of both President Ronald Reagan and George Bush resisted the pressure from Congress to do something to stimulate industrial technology. Conservative Republicans, they preferred to leave that to private enterprise: specifically, any aid from the government threatened to differentially benefit smaller industries at the expense of the very large ones which already had not only market share but their own research and development facilities. The standoff was a classic one – how to use the government to stimulate new technologies (and therefore presumably the national economy) without threatening established, one might say entrenched, special interests. Every president wanted to have a "technology policy," every Congress – indeed perhaps every member of Congress – had her or his own pet projects or powerful constituents to placate. At heart, technology proved to be tenaciously political.

One promising new direction for technical development had grown in part out of the Point 4 experience with foreign technical aid, and in part out of the environmental movement which had been presaged by Rachel Carson's best selling book *Silent Spring* (1962) and inaugurated with the first Earth Day in 1970. The idea that Third World under-development was matched by American *over-development* was one which had both a political and an ideological appeal for many in the counter culture and the environmental movement. Advocates were inspired especially by two books: E.F. Schumacher's *Small Is Beautiful* (1973) and Amory Lovins, *Soft Energy Paths* (1977). Advocating what he called Buddhist economics, or "economics as if people mattered," Schumacher advocated small-scale development, depending upon local resources, labor and markets. Lovins rejected "hard" energy systems, such as nuclear and centrally produced electricity, as both wasteful and uneconomical, advocating instead a combination of conservation and locally produced energy from alternative systems such as wind and solar.

Individuals and small groups undertook appropriate technology projects on their own, ranging from organic gardening to composting toilets, but other projects such as light rail or bicycle paths clearly needed government support. Under Governor Jerry Brown (1974–82) California established an Office of Appropriate Technology and undertook to construct "green" state office buildings, run state vehicles on natural gas or methane, and provide subsidies to utilities and individuals who undertook to install alternative energy sources. In 1977 the federal government established the National Center for Alternative Technologies in Missoula, Montana, and President Jimmy Carter gave some support to the movement, even installing solar collectors on the roof of the White House. They were taken down by the next President, Ronald Reagan, however, and both in Washington and in California new Republican administrations rolled back support for appropriate technologies.

One of the ways in which appropriate technologies were marginalized by those who had a stake in a different set of machines and institutions was to feminize them: real men did not ride bicycles, they drove muscle cars (and later SUVs). Rambo and the Terminator were the masculine heroes, not organic farmers or those who installed solar water heaters. The high-tech weapons of adventure movies are only a small part of the way in which the boundaries between the media and the military have been blurred. A war room in Washington was designed by a Walt Disney "imagineer" and is called the *Enterprise*. Training for the troops takes place, in part, on computer screens where the distinction between video games and war games has less to do with the technology than with the purpose. Troops in the field can be linked with troops at home by computer links which allow the integration of real time simulations with the actual movement of troops and equipment. And the television news is brought to us by reporters with videophones connected by satellite with 24-hour cable news channels skilled in entertainment values. In the war with Iraq, daily reports from information officers behind the lines were literally staged in a venue designed to look like that of a television anchor.

As for the weapons themselves – the reconnaissance drones, smart bombs, bunker-busters, laser guided missiles and the rest – the direct outgrowth of the old canard that life is cheap in the Orient, and that Asiatic hoards can only be met by superior weapons which protect American lives even as they destroy those of the enemy. Out of the war in Vietnam and perfected through military actions against a dozen small and underdeveloped countries, an arsenal of computer-controlled weapons of devastating power has made the country used to short wars and few (American) casualties.

Weapons of mass destruction deliverable anywhere in the world on very short notice by the last of the superpowers were only one example of the globalization of technology at the end of the twentieth century. Another was the Y2K scare, which imagined that airplanes might fall from the skies over Europe because American software programmers, eager to save expensive storage space in computers and believing that their work would soon be superceded, had taken the short-cut of using only two digits to designate years in writing dates.

Globalization may be a new concern but it represents an old tendency – one harking back at least to the Enlightenment. The extensive European empire of the nineteenth century, especially the British beginning even in the eighteenth, were formal and deliberate attempts at globalization. The very core of modernity was the collapsing of time and space, so that the railroad and the telegraph, the steamship and the major stock and commodity markets, were linked globally. American farmers, for example, came into direct competition with wheat growers in Russia, Argentina, and Australia when news of their crops and prices on the world market were telegraphed to Chicago and formed the basis of what was paid domestically.

By the end of the twentieth century the technologies of exchange had advanced to the point where a withdrawal of cash from an Automated Teller Machine (ATM) anywhere in the world made an instantaneous debit in one's account anywhere else in the world. American cars were made in Canada and Japanese cars in the United States. American television changed the language and expectations of people all over the world and the French government fought a rearguard action against American language, in 2003 banning the word Internet from official documents in favor of one sounding more authentically Gaelic.

The penetration of American technology and other forms of culture into the rest of the world, especially after World War II, was a result devoutly desired by the federal government and actively pursued by scores of governors and mayors who led trade delegations overseas. The World Bank and the International Monetary Fund, for example, heavily subsidized by the United States, loaned money to foreign nations to hire American engineering firms and buy American technologies. Free trade policies, and treaties such as NAFTA (North American Free Trade Agreement) were designed to open up other economies to American goods. As the British had discovered in the nineteenth century when they invented the idea, "Free Trade" greatly benefits the developed at the expense of the underdeveloped.

Technology has always moved with comparative ease across international boundaries, regardless of official national policies. Attempts by the British in the eighteenth century to prevent the export of the new textile machinery and the expatriation of textile mechanics utterly failed to keep the United States from establishing the industry in America with British technology. In the late twentieth century the US was more successful in exporting its technology than in limiting its use abroad, and that technology became both an important vector and object of globalization.

BIBLIOGRAPHY

American Public Works Association. *History of Public Works in the United States, 1776–1976* (Chicago: APWA, 1976).

Boffey, Philip M. *The Brain Bank of America: An Inquiry into the Politics of Science* (New York: McGraw-Hill, 1975).

Cohen, Lizabeth. *A Consumers' Republic: The Politics of Mass Consumption in Postwar America* (New York: Alfred A. Knopf, 2003).

Dickson, David. *The New Politics of Science* (New York: Pantheon Books, 1984).

Dupree, A. Hunter. *Science in the Federal Government: A History of Policies and Activities to 1940* (Cambridge: Harvard University Press, 1957).

Edwards, Paul N. *The Closed World: Computers and the Politics of Discourse in Cold War America* (Cambridge: MIT Press, 1996).

Horwitch, Mel. *Clipped Wings: The American SST Conflict* (Cambridge: MIT Press, 1982).

Hughes, Thomas P. *American Genesis: A Century of Invention and Technological Enthusiasm, 1870–1970* (New York: Viking, 1989).

Hughes, Thomas P. *Rescuing Prometheus* (New York: Pantheon Books, 1998).

Kevles, Daniel J. "Federal legislation for engineering experiment stations: the episode of World War I," *Technology and Culture*, 12 (April 1971): 182–9.

Lakoff, Sanford and Herbert F. York. *A Shield in Space? Technology, Politics, and the Strategic Defense Initiative* (Berkeley: University of California Press, 1989).

Lambright, W. Henry. *Presidential Management of Science and Technology: The Johnson Presidency* (Austin: University of Texas Press, 1985).

McDougall, Walter A.... *The Heavens and the Earth: A Political History of the Space Age* (New York: Basic Books, 1985).

Pursell, Carroll W., Jr. "Government and technology in the great depression," *Technology and Culture*, 20 (January 1979): 162–74.

Pursell, Carroll W., Jr. *The Machine in America: A Social History of Technology* (Baltimore: Johns Hopkins University Press, 1995).

Pursell, Carroll W., Jr. ed., *Technology in America: A History of Individuals and Ideas.* 2nd edn (Cambridge: MIT Press, 1990).

Pursell, Carroll W., Jr. *White Heat: People and Technology* (Berkeley: University of California Press, 1994).

Rae, John B. *The Road and Car in American Life* (Cambridge: MIT Press, 1971).

Riordan, Michael and Lillian Hoddeson. *Crystal Fire: The Birth of the Information Age* (New York: W.W. Norton & Co., 1997).

Roland, Alex, *Model Research: The National Advisory Committee for Aeronautics, 1915–1958*, 2 vols (Washington: NASA, 1985).

Rose, Mark H. *Interstate: Express Highway Politics, 1941–1956* (Lawrence: Regents Press of Kansas, 1979).

Sapolsky, Harvey M. "Science advice for state and local government," *Science*, 160 (April 19, 1968): 280–4.

Seely, Bruce. *Building the American Highway System: Engineers As Policy Makers* (Philadelphia: Temple University Press, 1987).

Smith, Merritt Roe, ed. *Military Enterprise and Technological Change: Perspectives on the American Experience* (Cambridge: MIT Press, 1985).

Stine, Jeffrey K. *A History of Science Policy in the United States, 1940–1985.* Science Policy Study Background Report No. 1, Task Force on Science Policy, Committee on Science and Technology, House of Representatives, 99th Cong., 2 sess. (September 1986).

Ronald C. Tobey. *Technology as Freedom: The New Deal and the Electrical Modernization of the American Home* (Berkeley: University of California Press, 1996).

White, Leonard D. *The City Manager* (Chicago: University of Chicago Press, 1927).

York, Herbert F. *Making Weapons, Talking Peace: A Physicist's Odyssey from Hiroshima to Geneva* (New York: Basic Books, 1987).

Chapter Nine

Medicine and Technology

James M. Edmonson

Technology is often blamed for what seems wrong with American medicine today: it is too expensive, too fragmenting, too impersonal. And yet, technology is at the heart of modern medical miracles. We place our greatest hopes in technology for the relief of suffering and illness. Technology has become, moreover, a hallmark of American medical practice. Comprehending technology's role in our medical past is therefore essential to understanding the very character of American medicine. According to many commentators and historians, American medicine has long possessed a "can do" attitude, and a corresponding impatience with inactivity. In America, doing "something" was far preferable to patient watchfulness. And technological solutions to complex medical problems seem to hold a great appeal to Americans, favorably disposing them to welcome and even prefer a "mechanical fix" over preventive medicine. These generalizations do not always emerge unscathed following closer historical scrutiny, but it nevertheless still stands that American medicine has embraced technology, and displayed a marked penchant for new devices and instrumentation.

Definitions of "medical technology" abound. Recent definitions can be so all-encompassing as to become almost meaningless. For example, Nobel laureate Frederick C. Robbins, writing on technology assessment, offered the following definition: "Health technology is used here in a broad sense to include the techniques, drugs, biologicals, equipment, and procedures used by health care professionals in providing health care and in operating the systems within which care is provided. Thus a drug, vaccine, or surgical operation would fall within this definition, as would the computerized data system of a hospital or a computed tomography scanner" (Robbins 1979, p. 176). Throughout this essay, there is an emphasis upon the instrumentation and machines that became part of medical practice, which reflects the influence of the most important works to date in this field (Reiser 1978; Davis 1981). Recent studies emphasizing the social construction of medical technology prompt a broad interpretation of the term "technology", as articulated by Keith Wailoo: "I define *technology* broadly as 'knowledge producing tools,' and therefore consider not only instruments but the vastly expanding number of new drugs, surgical techniques, clinical facilities, and formalized research protocols, such as randomized clinical trials, as technologies. Perhaps the term *technological system* might be more appropriate to describe such an assemblage" (Wailoo 1997, p. 13). The reader is encouraged to consult the appended bibliography for the growing body of literature concerning the social construction of medical technology (Pickstone 1992; Baker 1996; Wailoo 1997; Aronowitz 1998; Sandelowski 2000; Stanton 2002).

Technology and American Medicine at the turn of the Twentieth Century

Whether by natural inclination or by force of circumstance, doctors in the late nineteenth century assumed a role defined by their ability to act, to care for patients surgically as well as medically, and hence technology – in the form of instrumentation – comprised an important part of their professional identity. Possessing tools is one thing; being eager to use them is yet another. Commentators have observed a distinct aggressiveness typifying American medicine (Payer 1988). This has often been attributed to the effect of the vast frontier upon the people who came to settle in it. Newcomers had to fight and subdue nature, so the argument goes, and in this struggle they developed an aggressive character. An alternative explanation resides in the challenge posed by sectarian medicine in nineteenth-century America. Orthodox "allopathic" doctors fell back upon bloodletting and "heroic" drug therapy to distinguish themselves from homeopaths, botanical, eclectics, and other rivals. The American approach to disease consisted of diagnosing it aggressively, and then to rooting it out vigorously. In the process, the imperative to intervene became a critical aspect of the physicians' identity in America (Warner 1986). This was reinforced by the dominant role played by business in American society. Physicians acted as independent businessmen, competing for patients in an ostensibly open market. But at the same time, American doctors wanted to be seen as belonging to a liberal profession, with its own code of ethics and conduct, that would not be subverted by commerce. Assuming the mantle of science and its associated technologies became central to resolving these tensions within the ranks of American medicine at the close of the nineteenth century.

Physicians' embrace of technology was stimulated by the advent of new instrumental ways of identifying and explaining illness that became central to the physician's task and his identity. Diagnosis consisted of locating the site of origin of a patient's symptoms, and instruments played an important part in this process. One of the first such methods was auscultation, or listening to sounds within the body to detect disease. Auscultation assumed a new, instrumental form with the development of the stethoscope. Originally devised to reveal heart sounds, doctors employed the instrument to analyze sounds of respiration and associated diseases, including pneumonia, pulmonary edema, pulmonary phthisis, and emphysema. With the advent of this central instrument, technology would henceforth be inextricably linked to the practice of medicine. Indeed, the stethoscope itself became emblematic of medicine (Reiser 1978; Davis 1981).

The impact of the stethoscope and other diagnostic instruments upon the physician–patient relationship proved somewhat ambiguous. Few would contest its diagnostic advantage, of facilitating a non-invasive dissection of the body, revealing pathologies and lesions. The stethoscope furnished information that the patient could not yield (nor themselves even hear), and did so with a greater degree of precision. At the same time, however, sole reliance upon diagnostic information supplied by the stethoscope could lead physicians to discount patients' experience and opinions. The same could be said of instruments that enabled the physician to see within the body – specula, endoscopes, ophthalmoscopes, and the like. Why listen to their subjective and biased testimony when one could listen to the objective evidence of the stethoscope? The value placed upon dialogue with the patient subsided in direct relation to the new esteem for instrumentally produced diagnostic information. Additionally, there arose the inclination to see patients solely as diseased parts, and not the whole of a person (Reiser 1978).

The changes wrought by the stethoscope were pushed still further with a fundamental redefinition of medicine's scientific basis beginning in the 1860s. With the advent of the germ theory, the conception and treatment of disease was placed upon a new footing. Doctors increasingly turned to instruments to identify and quantify disease; respiration, blood circulation, and body temperature could be gauged by instruments that measured physiological functions in numbers or depicted them on graphs (Keele 1963). Partisans of the new instrumentation argued that clinical medicine needed to be reformed by assimilating the tools of experimental clinical science. Physiology, for example, lent instruments for pulse measurement (sphygmograph) and blood pressure determination (sphygmomanometer). That instrumentation yielded reproducible readings that could be studied, shared, and discussed. Other instruments originating in the laboratory included thermometers (to measure body temperature), spirometers (to measure lung function), and dynamometers (to gauge muscular force) (Davis 1990). In time, a scientific consensus would emerge to define what readings constituted normalcy and health, and this diagnostic measure in turn would provide a guide to more effective and rational therapeutics. Such information could immediately affect the care of patients in acute situations, as for example the monitoring of blood pressure during surgery in the first decade of the twentieth century by Harvey Cushing and George W. Crile. Instrument-generated information also had a much broader beneficial impact upon society as a whole, by revealing endemic but as yet unseen and undiagnosed conditions, like hypertension. Results of this magnitude served to accelerate the acceptance of instrumentation as an integral part of modern medicine.

Medical Technology and the Hospital

Medical technology found an important new venue in the waning years of the nineteenth century: the hospital. Before the twentieth century, medicine remained a home-centered activity and most Americans viewed the hospital as a medically marginal welfare institution. Indeed, hospitals originated in the incidental medical facilities provided for inmates of almshouses, jails, or military posts. Most hospitals functioned as either charitable institutions managed by lay trustees, or as municipal agencies of social control not yet controlled by physicians. Such places were little more than dormitories for the destitute sick, scarcely better than the dreaded "pest houses" of the past; technology played little or no role in their care of patients. Hospitals catered chiefly to persons who could not afford the cost of treatment and convalescence in their homes. Self-respecting persons preferred care at home, and few doctors kept regular office hours, preferring instead to make house-calls on their patients. In contrast to this norm, going to a hospital therefore implied that one had failed in the world, and carried a not inconsiderable social taint, not to mention the specter of communicable disease (Starr 1982).

In the quarter century before 1900, the character and role of hospitals changed dramatically and technology was at the heart of this transformation. The innovations of antiseptic and aseptic surgery could be implemented most successfully in the controlled environment of the hospital, and medical practice consequently shifted progressively from home to hospital. As aseptic principles, instrumentation, and sterilizing equipment came into wider use in hospitals across America, surgery increased dramatically in the 1890s. By the turn of the century, tonsillectomies and adenoidectomies (reflecting the popularity of the theory of focal infection), gynecological surgery, and most significantly, appendectomies predominated, soon followed by gastric, urologic, and neurologic surgical operations.

Growth in hospital size, complexity, and staffing to support these new functions fostered a dramatic increase in operating expenses, and ultimately brought hospitals in America to modify if not abandon their role as charitable institutions. To meet rising costs, lay trustees began welcoming pay patients and conceded greater control to the physicians, and especially surgeons, who brought their much-needed fees. In this situation, lay trustees often found themselves at odds with physicians and surgeons who demanded more autonomy, and who clearly wished to transform the hospital from a charitable to a medical institution (Vogel 1980; Rosenberg 1987). In their bid for greater professional autonomy, doctors invoked the virtues of progress and prosperity through science (and by implication, technology), although it would be some time before science could yield many tangible results (Shortt 1983).

By 1900, the hospital thus became the chief venue for the delivery of modern, technologically bound medical care in the mind of the American public. Importantly, hospitals increasingly accommodated and catered to a new audience: the middle class. In the United States, this process proceeded further than elsewhere due to the prevalence of private over public responsibility for hospitals. In the absence of government funding and control, hospitals openly vied for patients with only market forces to serve as a check upon growth. This is indeed borne out by the remarkable expansion of hospitals in America between the Civil War and World War I. In 1870, barely 200 hospitals existed in the United States, and one third of this number consisted of mental institutions. By the eve of World War I, the United States counted close to 4,500 hospitals of various size and description. A once marginal institution, now stood at the very center of medicine and it was a technologically complex venue analogous to the industrial factory.

While technology certainly played a pivotal role in this change, it would be misleading to depict it solely as a technologically driven sequence of events. Indeed, recent work on the American hospital in the period from 1880 to 1930 reveals that the adoption of new machine-embodied medical technologies, particularly the x-ray and the ECG, did not proceed as rapidly as one might have believed from glowing press reports (Blume 1992; Howell 1995). Patient records tell a more complicated story, and do not document an uncritical embrace of the new technologies. The routine use of these new diagnostic modalities necessitated structural changes in the receiving environment of the hospital. Physicians and technicians had to acquire new skills in operating such equipment, and were compelled to devise new ways of recording and organizing patient information, which now often came in the graphic and numerical language of the machine. By the close of World War I, medical technologies had profoundly transformed the hospital. Hospitals henceforth assumed the role of diagnostic center, outfitted with complex machines for that purpose, and their organization and administration changed accordingly. More important, perhaps, physicians' professional identity was increasingly linked to the new technologies.

The linkages between the hospital and technology are seen perhaps most dramatically in the medicalization of birth in the opening decades of the twentieth century. In 1900, less than 5 percent of women gave birth in a hospital; by 1940, half of all women, and 75 percent of all urban women had their children in a hospital. Women were initially drawn to the hospital by improved anesthetics, to lessen their suffering, and the antiseptic environment, which in principle promised to vanquish puerperal fever and other infections associated with childbirth. In making this move, however, women conceded control over the birth process to physicians. The most visible proponent of this change was the obstetrician Joseph B. De Lee, who saw birth as a potentially pathological condition that should be averted through instrumental intervention. He advocated "prophylactic forceps delivery" and episiotomy (surgical opening of perineum). To this was added the prospect of Caesarean section and induction of labor. Birth thus became a surgical event, controlled by physicians who wielded the technology, and decision-making passed out of the hands of the prospective mother. Postpartum care of infants at the hospital also involved machines for the first time, in the form of the incubator. A simple warming device became a complex life-support system designed to create a complete artificial environment for the premature infant. The shift to hospital birth was further promoted by federal funding of medically aided maternity care in the 1920s and 1930s (Leavitt 1989; Baker 1996).

Discussion of hospitals and medical technology remains incomplete without mention of the role nurses played in the melding of the two. Much of the instrumentation and many of the machines lay in their hands and thus played a role in defining the professional identity of nursing. And yet that identity was fraught with ambivalence about technology. In one view, nurses functioned as the hand maidens of technology, extending physicians' reach while remaining in an essentially subservient role. In yet another, nursing represented the antithesis of technology, by embracing an ethos of care and nurture. Intriguingly, while physicians derived cultural authority by virtue of their association with technology, nurses found the converse to be true; even while their work grew more bound to technology, nurses' cultural authority became more centrally grounded in their gender. These relations deserve sympathetic study, but their analysis has until recently been hampered by nursing's invisibility upon the stage of medical history (Sandelowski 2000).

Science and Specialization

At the turn of the twentieth century, medicine was being transformed by a combination of scientific and technical advances that together amounted to a revolution in thought and practice. American physicians avidly followed developments in bacteriology in Europe and a generation of medical students flocked to German universities in pursuit of advanced training. The leaders amongst them, like William H. Welch of Johns Hopkins, made the bacteriological sciences a fundamental part of the curriculum in the better American medical schools. In a landmark 1910 report commissioned by the Carnegie Foundation, "Medical Education in the United States and Canada," the educator Abraham Flexner cited Johns Hopkins as coming closest to the ideal that he proposed. Flexner advocated placing medical education within the structure of American universities, away from the self-interested control of practitioners who ran proprietary medical schools. In addition to a grounding in the basic medical sciences and laboratory instruction, Flexner recognized the importance of clinical teaching in close proximity. These recommendations, when followed, cemented the newly emergent relationship of hospitals and medical schools in the opening years of the twentieth century (Ludmerer 1985).

On a practical level, in terms of new therapeutic means, bacteriology had an impact, beginning in the early 1890s and accelerating after 1900. Across the United States municipalities created bacteriological laboratories to monitor and safeguard the general health of urban populations, and contain epidemic disease where possible. Beginning in 1894, city and state public health departments began the production of diphtheria antitoxin, the first medication (specifically, a biological therapeutic) to target a specific disease, in this case the most feared of childhood illnesses. Private industry entered the fray the following year when H.K. Mulford of Philadelphia commenced manufacture of the antitoxin. Medicine and business soon forged a new relationship. As pharmaceutical companies assumed a new biomedical research function, they necessarily entered into a collaborative venture with academic medical centers. World War I hastened this process, as the American pharmaceutical industry responded to the sudden loss of access to the products of the more advanced German industry. In the 1920s and 1930s, American companies created in-house research programs, attracting academic scientists, and supported university-based research. During this period, the pharmaceutical industry laid the foundation for the subsequent successes of the antibiotic era (Liebenau 1987; Swann 1988).

Technology was transforming American medical practice in other unanticipated ways. The emergence of medical and surgical specialties, particularly those wed to instrumentation, comprised a central feature of this development. Board certification comprised the culmination of this process. First instituted in the United States for ophthalmology in 1916, board certification constituted an alternative to licensure or advanced university degrees. It entailed examination and certification by established specialists, drawn chiefly from medical school faculties, and receipt upon passing the exam of a diploma that could be hung on the office wall for public scrutiny. This was reinforced by the spread of specialty residencies, which began at Johns Hopkins in the 1890s and Mayo Clinic around 1912, but remained rare outside of national medical centers until 1920. The number of specialist fields recognized by the American Medical Association (AMA) in 1923 was twenty-three and growing; by 1940 some thirteen fields had board certification (Stevens 1971).

Not all doctors welcomed the intrusion of instruments into medicine and the fracturing of the profession into myriad specialties. Some medical practitioners decried the decline of the "art and mysteries" of clinical medicine, and too great a reliance upon instruments exerted a demeaning effect upon the profession (Evans 1993; Lawrence 1994). Traditionally, being a physician meant also having a cultured background, carrying one's self in a gentlemanly way, and possessing a broad understanding of medicine derived from wisdom and experience acquired over a lifetime. While American physicians increasingly invoked the rhetoric of science to bolster claims to professional autonomy, they feared that too close a reliance upon technology – instruments – threatened to reduce bedside practice to a mere trade that anyone with the requisite technical training might pursue. Some members of the medical profession resented the advance of specialization, which implied an unacceptable narrowing of a practitioner's professional domain. Many in the ranks of the AMA feared that too strong an emphasis upon "commercialism" was invading medicine, and that this insidious influence appeared most in the ranks of specialists. The AMA criticized specialists for implying that the general practitioner, who constituted over 90 percent of physicians at the beginning of the twentieth century, was incompetent to properly treat certain diseases or conditions. Despite these reservations, American medicine was wed to technology by the eve of World War I.

Impact of World War I on Medicine and Medical Technology

World War I had a profound and lasting impact upon American medicine. Certain technologies and practices received a boost, notably x-ray technology and blood transfusion, and these filtered into civilian medical life once the war was over. The war also fostered the growth of group clinic practice created by physicians and surgeons inspired by the efficiency of military medical units bringing together specialists.

Blood transfusion remained a problematic and risky therapy until the discovery in 1901 of blood groups (and the importance of matching blood types) by Karl Landsteiner, and the adaptation by George Crile of cannula to connect blood vessels of donor to recipient (1907). These issues were still in the process of being resolved on the eve of the war; the practice of transfusion was gaining ground in the United States, but was as yet not universally accepted. The theater of war created a vast experimental laboratory in which to test established methods, sort out problems, and develop new instruments and procedures. Direct artery to vein anastomosis, a surgical procedure in itself, was supplanted by indirect transfusion using syringes and transfer tubes. More important, wartime experience affirmed the superiority of human blood over saline and other solutions, but also clarified the danger of blood-type incompatibility and revealed the ominous possibility of transmitting blood-born disease to recipients. Resolving these issues would subsequently become part of medicine's peacetime research agenda, leading to bloodbanking in the 1930s (Schneider 1997).

No medical technology was more impacted by the war than the x-ray. American medical units serving abroad increasingly incorporated radiologic examinations among routine diagnostic procedures, particularly since so many of the patients they saw suffered from projectile wounds and fractures. In the process, an important cadre of personnel received training in the medical use of the x-ray and would carry this over to the workplace at major university hospitals. The technology itself – film, x-ray tubes, power units – underwent refinement, particularly to make it more portable and reliable, thus improving the results subsequently attained. Many physicians gaining wartime experience opted for a career re-direction upon return to civilian life, choosing to specialize in radiology. Hospital radiology departments flourished in the postwar period, becoming an important element in transforming the hospital into an important diagnostic center (Howell 1995).

Reorganization of hospital services and the rise of the group clinic was a less dramatic, but important and lasting legacy of World War I. The group practice clinic had been inaugurated by the Mayos in Rochester, Minnesota in 1892, but did not really come into its own until after 1901. The success of the Mayo Clinic, combined with lessons learned during the conflict, resulted in a proliferation of group clinics after World War I, the most successful being the Cleveland Clinic founded by George Crile in 1921. Even before America entered into the war, Crile visited clinics and performed surgery in wartime France. In the summer of 1915, Surgeon General W.C. Gorgas asked Crile to outline a plan for organizing and equipping a base hospital unit, complete with doctors, nurses, and support personnel, to staff military base hospitals in Europe and Britain, should the United States enter the war. Crile's plan became the model for the Lakeside Unit, as well as those sponsored by medical centers at Harvard, University of Pennsylvania, Chicago, and other universities. It emphasized the concept of medical teamwork, based upon a division of labor amongst specialists in different fields. Upon returning to civilian life Crile and others, borrowing from their military experience, created group clinics that featured specialists from every branch of medicine and surgery worked in close concert; by 1930 there were about 150 such group practice clinics in the United States. From the military, physicians also borrowed the principle of triage, using advanced diagnostic capabilities to ascertain which patients would benefit from the array of services available at their clinic. Patients with chronic (rather than acute) conditions not susceptible to the quick fix of surgery would be deferred elsewhere, typically to a municipal hospital. In so doing, the Cleveland Clinic and similarly constituted group practice clinics could boast an enviable record of success for the patients they admitted for care.

The Golden Age of Medicine

About 1920, American medicine entered a period that has been characterized as its "Golden Age," which lasted for approximately the next half century. During this "Golden Age" medicine seemed capable of fulfilling the promise of forever conquering illness, rising from one success to the next. Medical scientists had in the nineteenth century identified the microbes that caused infectious disease and developed effective therapeutic means in the laboratory, with technology playing a vital role. After the turn of the twentieth century, university laboratories and pharmaceutical companies developed new chemical remedies – chemotherapy – that vanquished disease when vaccines could not. In 1910 the German immunologist Paul Ehrlich introduced Salvarsan, an arsenic compound (also known as 606, the six hundred and sixth substance tried empirically by the scientist) that destroyed the syphilis-causing microorganism. This was the first "magic bullet," a drug that actually cured a life-threatening disease. It was in turn followed by sulfa drugs in the 1930s, which proved fairly effective against streptococcal and other bacterial infections. But penicillin, discovered by Alexander Fleming in 1928, emerged as by far the most dramatic of the "magic bullets," a true miracle drug effective against pneumonia, syphilis, and many other bacterial sources of infection. Building upon the basic penicillin research of British scientists H.W. Flory and E.B. Chain, American laboratories began the industrial production of the drug during World War II. In the late 1940s, the era of oral antibiotics dawned, with the introduction of streptomycin, para-aminosalicylic acid, and isoniazid, effective against tuberculosis. Taken together, these achievements constituted ample proof of the existence of a "Golden Age" (Burnham 1982; Brandt and Gerdner 2000).

Alongside pharmaceutical developments stood new instruments and machine technologies that supported public expectations that medicine could stave off disease and make our lives better and longer. The phenomenal growth of medical technologies in the mid-twentieth century has been attributed in part to the rise of third party payers, in the guise of private health insurance and, later, public insurance programs (Medicare and Medicaid). While third party payers in 1950 covered 40–50 percent of hospital costs, this rose to 90 percent by the 1970s. The prevailing philosophy regarding health care in America was that no one should have to forego medical care, particularly life-saving measures, because they could not pay. Under this regime health care providers, namely doctors and hospitals, behaved as if there were no limitation, since insurers would fully reimburse them. Much as the natural wealth and abundance of America undergirded political democracy (a la David Potter, *People of Plenty*), the seeming unlimited financial resources available to medicine stimulated the rampant use of technology in health care (Rothman 1997).

The origins of this situation date to the 1930s, with the advent of Blue Cross programs across the country. Blue Cross was a prepaid private insurance program expressly created to come to the aid of voluntary not-for-profit hospitals hit hard by the Depression. Its viability depended upon a successful campaign to convince middle-class Americans that it was their responsibility, not the government's, to pay for health care. Blue Cross also had to convince potential subscribers that the hospital could provide valuable services, preventive as well as curative. A masterful media campaign in the late 1930s and early 1940s did just this, placing marvelous new medical technologies at the heart of hospitals' mission. Advanced technologies and surgery, epitomizing the best of modern medicine, thus became the chief selling points in the hands of J. Walter Thompson and other premier advertising firms employed by Blue

Cross. Their media campaigns also juxtaposed municipal and voluntary hospitals, identifying the latter as the technologically superior choice. Partisans of Blue Cross asserted that its services obviated the need for a compulsory national health insurance program, which they painted as un-American. As a health care program, however, Blue Cross was by design and intent exclusionary. The moderately affluent middle class was its target audience, while the poor, elderly, and infirm could not afford its fees (Rothman 1997).

When medical costs began to rise after World War II, Blue Cross made an even stronger connection between leading-edge, machine-embodied medicine and first class quality of health care. Medical breakthroughs, so the argument went, were essential to the kind of care middle-class Americans expected and demanded. Such breakthroughs did not come cheaply, however, so cost increases comprised an unavoidable facet of modern medical care in America. Medicare, passed in 1965 after considerable debate and wrangling, helped middle-class Americans cope with the rising cost of health care without violating the sanctity of private health insurance. Medicare categorized the elderly as an exception, deserving of government support, and thereby provided a buffer against rising health care costs that became a feature of aging. High-tech medicine thus evaded – for a time, at least – the cost constraints of the marketplace and flourished (Rothman 1997).

Dilemmas of Medical Technologies: the Iron Lung and Artificial Kidney

Advanced medical technologies, regardless of their costs, sometimes embodied compromises that had to be balanced against the relief they promised. The most conflicted of such technologies was the "iron lung," a total body or tank-type respirator developed by Philip Drinker and Louis Shaw in the late 1920s for sustaining those whose lung function was impaired by poliomyelitis. Power companies, in their search for remedies to electric shock, carbon monoxide poisoning, and drowning, funded its initial development. In times of polio epidemic, which rose dramatically in the late 1940s and early 1950s, the "iron lung" became a life-saving device seen at hospitals around the country, chiefly in pediatric facilities. Contrary to popular perception, comparatively few persons were doomed to live out their lives confined in an "iron lung"; of the more than 175,000 persons who contracted polio, only 500 became chronically dependent upon mechanical ventilation in the "iron lung." Nevertheless, it became a poignant symbol for the diminished quality of life that could accompany certain life-saving mechanical technologies (Maxwell 1986).

Lewis Thomas, president of the Memorial Sloan-Kettering Cancer Center, in particular disparaged the "iron lung," calling it a "halfway technology" that offered only palliative relief of disease, but did nothing to change the underlying cause (Thomas 1974). He praised instead the "real high technology of medicine," attained only through basic research in biologic science that yields a clear understanding of disease mechanisms, and cited for proof the dramatic successes attained through immunization, antibiotics, and chemotherapy. The policy implications of this stance were clear to Lewis: "real high technology" was in the long run far more cost effective than "halfway technology," and therefore society's resources should be allocated to basic research, which Lewes was certain would lead to definitive, conclusive and rational kinds of therapy. Apparent vindication of this view came with the development of polio vaccines, by Jonas Salk (1952) and Albert Sabin (1960), that eliminated poliomyelitis as a public health problem (Thomas 1986).

Another machine that epitomized the dilemmas of medical technology was the artificial kidney, making life-saving dialysis possible for people with end-stage renal disease. Originally developed by Willem Kolff in the Netherlands in the late 1930s, the dialysis machine filtered blood impurities using a permeable cellophane membrane. By the late 1940s, his design was technically viable but not produced commercially at that time. In 1950, Kolff came to work at the Cleveland Clinic in the United States and he subsequently collaborated with Baxter Travenol Co., a producer of intravenous and saline solutions, to market the artificial kidney in 1956. (Kolff tried to keep costs down by using a Maytag washing machine as the tank of the artificial kidney, but the manufacturer, fearing litigation, later forbade this use of their product.) It was initially thought to be most appropriate for acute cases (drug intoxication, third degree burns, and mismatched transfusions) that held the promise of restored renal function, in contrast to patients suffering from chronic and irreversible end stage renal disease. Over time, however, it became more widely used for chronic cases, even including terminally ill patients who could not reasonably hope to be "saved" by this "wonder machine" (Van Noordwujk 2001).

By the early 1960s, long-term dialysis by machine won acceptance, thanks to improved cannulas and shunts, more effective use of anticoagulants, and the rise of for-profit dialysis centers. At the same time, kidney transplant became a reality, made practical, thanks to immunosuppressants and antibiotics. Despite these advances, the therapies were expensive and often in short supply. Selection committees composed chiefly of physicians arose to allocate scarce, costly resources, and therefore had to address new ethical and moral quandaries, including the painful debate over who should receive dialysis. In principle, patients with the best medical prognosis for dialysis received the nod, but the medical criteria and counter indications were still being formulated, leading committees to consider not only matters of age and pre-existing disease, but intangibles like "net social worth" and "state of mind" as well (Fox 1979).

This unsatisfactory situation came to an end only in 1972, when federal legislation (Public Law 92–603) mandated Medicare coverage of the costs of end-stage renal disease treatment for those who could not afford it. Many soon feared that the expense of this program would spin out of control, bankrupting Medicare. This did not happen, but the impact was not insignificant: in the first decade the end-stage renal disease accounted for 3 percent of Medicare expenditures. This, in turn, stimulated the development of medical technology assessment programs, and the search for cost containment measures that could be applied to all medical technologies, not just dialysis.

Technology assessment originated out of a desire to better understand and control the negative environmental impact of technology, and out of concern over Congress's inability to evaluate complex scientific and technical issues. The Office of Technology Assessment came into being in 1972 and lasted until 1995. During that time technology assessment came to include medicine, because after 1965 the federal government functioned as a third party payer, and it was therefore anxious to determine the viability and efficacy of therapies and diagnostic testing that it would be asked to pay for. This concern was heightened in the early 1970s by the notable failure of medical technologies, including the Dalkon shield intrauterine device and defective cardiac pacemakers. In response, the Food and Drug Administration (FDA) received authority, under the Medical Device Amendment of 1976, to regulate the marketing of new medical devices, much as it already did for drugs. But the FDA's responsibility was limited to product safety and efficacy, not the assessment of the social, ethical, or economic impact of medical technologies. Therefore the Office of Technology Assessment created a Health Program in 1975 and Congress instituted the National Center for Health Care Technology to address these concerns. Despite efforts to analyze the pace and direction of technical innovation in medicine, new devices and instrumentation proliferated in the 1970s and 1980s (Foote 1992).

Patterns of Diffusion of New Technologies: Ultrasound, Endoscopy, Computed Tomography, and Cardiac Pacing

In the waning years of medicine's "Golden Age," before the advent of managed care, hospitals and group practices seized upon new technologies and integrated them into patient care with abandon. Continued spread of advanced medical technology was further promoted by the emergence of a "medical-academic-industrial complex" supported by government funding of research and development. Precedent went back to penicillin production in World War II, when government and university collaboration achieved the industrial production of antibiotics (Parascandola 1980). Technologies and technological capabilities developed during the conflict found new application in medicine in the years following the war. The American health care system, because it was based chiefly upon free enterprise and third party payment, rather than a government-run national health care program, could absorb the associated costs, further fueling the diffusion of technology in medicine. These developments are illustrated by the advent and spread of four post World War II technologies: ultrasound, endoscopy, computed tomography (the CT scanner), and cardiac pacing.

The beginnings of ultrasound date to the early years of the twentieth century, originating in the search for means to locate icebergs (of ample interest following the *Titanic* disaster) and submarines in World War I. Following the war, ultrasound also found industrial applications, particularly for detecting unseen flaws in materials. The diagnostic application of ultrasound took place in 1937 when the Austrian neurologist Karl Dussik and his brother, a physicist, created a two dimensional image of the brain. This work was not successfully pursued until after World War II, when physicians, engineers, and physicists collaborated to develop clinically practical ultrasound devices. Significantly, many of those involved had acquired expertise in sonar and radar during the war, and now sought to transfer their knowledge to the civilian sphere. In addition to bringing technical expertise, many of the researchers employed war surplus ultrasound equipment for their early work. John Wild, a surgeon at the

University of Minnesota, borrowed a radar training machine from the nearby naval air station to measure different densities of benign and malignant tissue (including breast exams done in 1951) and collaborated with Honeywell, a major military contractor. Similar relationships existed with corporations involved in sonar research and development, notably Radio Corporation of America (RCA) and Raytheon. Wild's research, like that of many others in this field at university medical centers, was funded by the National Institutes of Health, which before that time supported basic, not applied (or clinical) research (Yoxen 1987; Koch 1993).

The pattern of diffusion of ultrasound within medicine departed from the model set by radiology. Rather than remain in the control of one new specialty claiming domain over ultrasound, this new technology was assimilated into a variety of specialties. Obstetrics, neurology, ophthalmology, and cardiology acquired their own distinct variants of ultrasound, each the product of their respective research agendas and clinical concerns. For example, in obstetrics and gynecology, ultrasound originated as a diagnostic modality to detect suspected pathological conditions, like uterine cysts or ovarian tumors. With improvements in contact compound scanner design in 1958, the procedure became simpler, and soon routine. Ultrasound was gradually assimilated into research programs, including the periodic monitoring and documentation of fetal development. By the late 1970s, it became customary for pregnant women in the United States to receive an ultrasonogram of her fetus as tangible proof of its well-being. An unanticipated consequence of multiple or parallel lines of development in respective specialties was that the market for ultrasound equipment became quite broad, as each subsection of the market demanded hardware tailored to its particular needs (Blume 1992).

Endoscopy provides further example of new patterns of innovation in medical technology, illustrating the importance of interdisciplinary research and development. Endoscopy dates to the introduction of the lichtleiter by Bozzini in 1805, but remained a diagnostic tool of little use until the development of the semi-flexible gastroscope by Rudolf Schindler in the 1930s. Even with Schindler's improvements, endoscopy remained a harrowing ordeal, not unlike sword-swallowing. This changed with the advent of fiberoptic endoscopy, which dawned in February 1957 when Basil Hirschowitz, in Ann Arbor, Michigan, passed a gastroscope down his throat and, a few days later, down that of a patient. This innovation involved interdisciplinary cross-pollination, as research in physics informed and enriched the development of new instrumentation in medicine. Hirschowitz had read papers on transmission of optical image via a glass fiber and visited the authors Hopkins and Kapany, who had suggested using fibers in an endoscope instead of conventional lenses. Working with his physicist colleagues Peters, Curtis, and Pollard at Michigan, Hirschowitz produced coated optical glass fibers and fashioned an endoscope with a bundle of fibers. In so doing, they had resolved important technical problems in an academic medical setting, which were subsequently transferred to the manufacturing sector. Persuaded of the instrument's potential, American Cystoscopic Manufacturers, Inc. (ACMI) agreed to produce a clinical model, but only if Curtis, Peters, and Hirschowitz served as consultants in the manufacture of the fiberoptic bundles. With their help, the firm introduced the ACMI 4990 Hirschowitz fiberoptic gastroduodenoscope in October 1960 (Rosenberg, Annetine, and Dawkins 1995).

Initial hesitance by clinicians gave way to enthusiasm as endoscopes evolved and proved capable of a greater variety of tasks. Refinements of the late 1960s and early 1970s included addition of channels for biopsy forceps and controlled tip deflection. Fiberoptic technology spread from gastroscopy to colonoscopy, bronchoscopy, and other endoscopic domains, and enhanced the therapeutic potential of each. The fiberoptic colonoscope was modified in 1971 to perform polypectomies using a wire loop snare. Therapeutic gastrointestinal endoscopy that followed included cannulation of the pancreatic duct, removal of biliary stone, and placement of feeding tubes by gastrostomy. What had begun as a diagnostic instrument thus acquired remarkable new therapeutic modalities (Edmonson 1991).

Endoscopists in the late 1970s contended that their instrumentation had reached a final developmental plateau. This complacency ended with the advent of video endoscopy in 1982, when Michael Sivak at the Cleveland Clinic began clinical trials of a Welch-Allyn, Inc. gastroscope featuring a computer-chip television camera (charge-coupled device, or CCD) at the distal end (dispensing with the eyepiece, lens system, and fiberoptic image bundle). The image captured by the CCD was processed by computer and viewed on a television screen. Coupling the computer and endoscope also transformed the management and manipulation of endoscopic images, offering unique advantages for documentation, review of findings, objective comparison of repeated examinations, and teaching. It has been speculated that computers will enhance endoscopy still further by facilitating three-dimensional imaging, robotics, and computer simulation of procedures.

Minimally invasive surgery made practicable by video endoscopy, found great reinforcement by the regime of cost containment that emerged in the mid-1980s. Thanks to the new technology, the diameter of instrument shafts could be reduced to a mere 2.8 mm, rendering video endoscopes far less cumbersome than fiberoptic models. Compared to conventional surgery, endoscopic surgery reduced the need for anesthesia, could be achieved through a smaller incision, and was often performed as an outpatient procedure, reducing patient "turn around time." Arthroscopy, laparoscopy, and other endoscopic surgery beyond the domain of gastroenterology burgeoned with advent of video, and continues to displace conventional, invasive surgery.

The computed tomography, or CT, scanner epitomizes high-tech medicine. As one of the first computer-controlled medical technologies, its development required a major research and development commitment from its producers, and taxed heavily the financial resilience of both equipment producers and health care consumers. The CT scanner diffused through American hospitals, notably academic medical centers, more rapidly than any other modern medical technology. In so doing, it exposed some of the peculiarities and weaknesses of the American health care system, prompting the search for cost containment measures that presaged the constraints imposed in the present era of managed health care.

The CT scanner originated in attempts by Godfrey Hounsfield, an electronics engineer at EMI (Electric & Musical Industries, Inc.) with wartime radar experience, to use the computer for pattern recognition, employing machines to recognize and classify data. He brought together x-ray equipment, a cathode ray tube, and a computer to create radiologic cross sections of the human body; its chief advantage over conventional radiology resided in the greater precision and sensitivity of the image it produced. Initial research and development in Britain resulted from the partnership of EMI and the Department of Health and Social Security (DHSS), an unusual pairing at the time. The first machine was ready in 1969, and DHSS was committed to purchase several more. Entry into the American health care market loomed as a key to commercial success, however. There, the market was broad and expenses paid for by third party coverage, and physicians were bound to their patients by a "social contract" that guaranteed the best possible health care, regardless of cost (Süsskind 1981; Blume 2000).

The first two production model CT scanners were acquired by the Mayo Clinic and Massachusetts General Hospital in 1973. Orders came quickly, far in excess of original anticipated numbers, after the debut of new scanners at international meetings of radiologists. Within 5 years, almost five hundred scanners were being installed in American hospitals each year, and its diffusion in the medical marketplace was more rapid than that of any modern medical technology. Radiologists readily accepted the new technology, assimilating it into their specialty and favorably influencing hospitals' decision to purchase a scanner. Almost continual technical development sustained the demand, as new and improved models appeared frequently. As R&D costs grew, smaller firms were edged out by larger players like GE, a traditional manufacturer of radiology equipment, that could muster far greater resources. This boom subsided by 1980, but not before giving rise to concern over alarming escalation of "machine-embodied" health care costs. The CT scanners were themselves expensive: head scanners cost over $350,000 in 1975 and later body scanners could reach $1 million, and their operation required specially trained radiological technicians. For the patient, a scan could cost several hundred dollars, and averaged about $150 (Banta 1984; Blume 2000).

To contain rampant spread of expensive technologies, in 1974 the federal government instituted Certificates of Need, in which hospitals had to justify capital expenditures. In a very short term, this measure in fact prompted more growth, as purchasers scrambled to acquire new technology before the legislation took effect, and in the long run, hospital administrators found ways around this roadblock. A far more effective measure was the institution in 1983 of rate regulations in the form of DRGs (Diagnosis Related Groups). Under this program, the government established limits on how much it would reimburse Medicare health care providers for different categories of illness. Hospital economics changed overnight, creating a newfound concern for efficiency and cost containment. Private insurers, particularly health maintenance organizations (HMOs), could also influence the diffusion and expense of technologies by rationing services under their control and introducing disincentives that discourage "excessive" usage. Cost containment of medical technology raised new ethical issues for physicians, and threatened the integrity of the "social contract" binding physician and patient. Some commentators felt that cost containment measures placed the burden of deciding where to allocate resources upon physicians' shoulders, and thus potentially forced physicians to make decisions contrary to their patients' well-being. This directly undermined the physician's role as the patient's advocate, creating a fundamental ethical dilemma for the medical profession (Mechanic 1986).

Like ultrasound, cardiac pacing initially depended upon military spin-off technology brought into the civilian sector following World War II. Physicians seeking to implant the first pacemakers, for example, employed mercury-zinc batteries developed first for the armed forces. At this phase of pacing, cardiothoracic and cardiovascular surgeons dominated the field, working in tandem with engineers, most often in academic medical centers. Interdisciplinary collaboration bore fruit by 1960, when the Buffalo surgeon William Chardack successfully implanted a battery-powered pacemaker designed with the help of Wilson Greatbatch, an engineer. The next decade saw gradual evolution toward a smaller, longer lasting, and more reliable pacemaker. In the ensuing decade, pacemakers became much more complex devices, incorporating microprocessors and managing a greater range of cardiac functions. Meanwhile, the number of pacemakers soared, reaching approximately 500,000 by 1980. In the process, the locus of pacemaker innovation shifted to manufacturers, with unforeseen consequences (Jeffrey 2001).

Medicine and industry comprised separate cultures with different values and motivations. Doctors, for example, saw themselves as members of a liberal profession that benefited from transparency and thus freely shared information. Businesses, in contrast, valued secrecy to preserve a competitive edge. In consequence, industry wrested more control over innovation, if only to safeguard its research and development efforts. In a period of rapidly evolving technology, like the 1970s, manufacturers rushed new pacemakers to the market, sometimes too hastily. Reports of deaths and injuries resulting from faulty pacemakers contributed to a growing public perception that new technologies needed to be more carefully monitored, a responsibility conferred upon the FDA by passage in 1976 of the Medical Device Amendment. Pacemaker manufacturers, including industry leader Earl Bakken of Medictronic, rankled under FDA review of their products, which threatened to stifle innovation. The industry continued to thrive, however, basing much of its success upon effectively marketing the pacemaker to physicians. Company representatives, like the traditional drug "detail man," made the rounds and schooled doctors in new indications that would dictate pacemaker applications and taught internists and cardiologists how to implant the devices. A scandal involving Medicare fraud and kickbacks to promote pacemaker use brought down two firms in 1984, leading to closer scrutiny of the industry for the safety and benefit of individual patients. To the surprise of some, the pacemaker industry thrived even in the era of cost containment in the 1990s and beyond. Product development and diversification to address a greater variety of indications and a growth in the patient population (the aged) combined to sustain the industry's growth (Jeffrey 2001).

Malaise and Accommodations

By the late 1970s, American medicine was beset by a growing public malaise, a sense that the luster of the Golden Age was tarnished by spiraling costs and ethical conundrums.

To this was added a new and profound philosophical questioning of medicine's promise to continue delivering "magic bullets." The most credible critique came from Thomas McKeown, who questioned whether medical science and technology were indeed responsible for the increases in longevity and diminished morbidity that Western society had experienced over the preceding century or so. McKeown looked at tuberculosis, long the scourge of humankind, and traced its diminution to public health measures, better nutrition, and rising standards of living. His epidemiological and demographic analyses showed improvements in population health and longevity *before* the advent of medical therapeutic advances. In the place of infectious disease, new illnesses of lifestyle (i.e. cardiovascular disease, cancer) posed threats to well-being against which the interventionist approach of biomedicine proved ineffectual. The implicit faith in medicine was further shaken in the 1980s by the AIDS pandemic, which initially seemed intractable and beyond medicine's means.

While McKeown challenged the medical profession's assertion that it deserved credit for improving health generally, other critics contended that medical profession had in fact wrought harm in the form of iatrogenic (physician-caused) medical disasters. They pointed to the tragedies of thalidomide, Diethylstillbestrol (DES), etc. that wrought great human suffering. Illich's *Medical Nemesis: The Expropriation of Health* (1976) accused organized medicine of fabricating evidence for improving health and misrepresenting the success of its efforts, characterizing their claims as "reminiscent of General Westmorland's proclamations from Vietnam" (p. 24). Illich (1976) contended that medicine was bent on making people ill to induce a doctor-dependence, in collusion with pharmaceutical companies, lawyers, and health insurance providers. Assertions of medical mysogeny also joined the chorus of discontent, most vocally articulated by Barker-Benfield's *Horrors of the Half-Known Life* (1976).

Further loss of medicine's authority accompanied the advent of managed care, as physicians ceded a significant measure of control to third party payers, insurance companies, and managed care organizations. Under the new regime of managed care, cost containment through prospective payment (DRGs), lower prices, and more restrictive use of services and facilities have become the driving force in a competitive environment. The debacle of the Clinton administration's failed health care reform of 1993–4 accelerated the move from traditional fee-for-service to managed care, and assured that the marketplace, not government, would control access to medical technologies. In this environment, technologies are judged not simply upon clinical viability, but upon cost effectiveness, as well. Physicians under managed care have been placed in the position of gatekeepers, effectively restricting access to specialists and high-tech procedures. Managed care has had other unforeseen consequences for the medical profession, notably a constriction of time allotted for each "patient encounter," and this in turn has had ramifying effects ranging from the quality of that encounter to the training of the next generation of physicians. There has been a recent middle-class consumer backlash against the rationing of managed care, however, since high technology medicine is equated with high-quality medicine. Therefore striking a balance between rampant unbridled growth and uncompassionate, parsimonious constraint of medical technology will lay at the heart of health care politics of the twenty-first century (Burnham 1982; Rothman 1997; Ludmerer 1999; Brandt 2000).

BIBLIOGRAPHY

Arney, William R. *Power and the Profession of Obstetrics* (Chicago: University of Chicago Press, 1982).

Aronowitz, Robert A. *Making Sense of Illness: Science, Society, and Disease* (Cambridge, U.K.: Cambridge University Press, 1998).

Baker, Jeffrey P. *The Machine in the Nursery: Incubator Technology and the Origins of Newborn Intensive Care* (Baltimore: Johns Hopkins University Press, 1996).

Banta, H. David, Behney, Clyde J. and Willems, Jane Sisk. *Toward Rational Technology in Medicine* (New York: Springer Publishing Company, 1981).

Banta, H. David. "Embracing or rejecting innovations: clinical diffusion of health care technology," in Reiser, Stanley Joel and Anbar, Michael, eds, *The Machine at the Bedside: Strategies for Using Technology in Patient Care* (Cambridge; New York: Cambridge University Press, 1984).

Banta, H. David. *An Approach to the Social Control of Hospital Technologies* (Geneva, Switzerland: Division of Strengthening of Health Services, World Health Organization, 1995).

Barker-Benfield, G.J. *The Horrors of the Half-Known Life: Male Attitudes Toward Women and Sexuality in Nineteenth-Century America* (New York: Harper & Row, 1976; 2nd edn in 2000).

Blume, Stuart S. *Insight and Industry: on the Dynamics of Technological Change in Medicine* (Cambridge, Mass.: MIT Press, 1992).

Blume, Stuart S. "Medicine, technology, and industry," in Cooter, Roger, and John Pickstone, eds, *Medicine in the Twentieth Century* (Amsterdam: Harwood Academic Publishers, 2000): pp. 171–85.

Brandt, Allan M. and Gerdner, Martha. "The golden age of medicine," in Cooter, Roger, and John Pickstone, eds, *Medicine in the Twentieth Century* (Amsterdam: Harwood Academic Publishers, 2000): pp. 21–37.

Bud, Robert, Finn, Bernard, and Trischler, Helmuth, eds *Manifesting Medicine: Bodies and Machines* (Amsterdam: Harwood Academic Publishers, 1999).

Burnham, John C. "American medicine's Golden Age: what happened to it?" *Science* 215 (1982): 1474–79.

Caspar, Monica and Berg, Marc. "Constructivist perspective on medical work: medical practices and science and technology studies," *Science, Technology, and Human Values* 20 (1995): 395–407.

Davis, Audrey B. "Medical technology," in Trevor I Williams, ed., *A history of technology*, (Oxford: Clarendon Press, 1978) vol. VII: The Twentieth Century c. 1900 to c. 1950 Part II; 1317–62.

Davis, Audrey B. *Medicine and Its Technology: an Introduction to the History of Medical Instrumentation* (Westport, Conn.: Greenwood Press, 1981).

Davis, Audrey B. "American medicine in the gilded age: the first technological era." *Annals of Science* 47 (1990): 111–25.

Duffin, Jacalyn. *To See with a Better Eye: a Life of R.T.H. Laennec* (Princeton: Princeton University Press, 1998).

Dutton, Diana Barbara. *Worse than the Disease: Pitfalls of Medical Progress* (Cambridge, UK: Cambridge University Press, 1988).

Edmonson, James M. "History of instruments for gastrointestinal endoscopy," *Gastrointestinal Endoscopy* 37 (1991): Supplement, 27–56.

Edmonson, James M. *American Surgical Instruments: An Illustrated History* (San Francisco: Norman Publishing, 1997).

Evans, Hughes. "Losing touch: the controversy over the introduction of blood pressure instruments into medicine," *Technology & Culture* 34 (1993): 784–807.

Foote, Susan Bartlett. *Managing the Medical Arms Race: Public Policy and Medical Device Innovation* (Berkeley: University of California Press, 1992).

Fox, Renee. "The medical profession's changing outlook on hemodialysis (1950–1976)," in Renee Fox, *Essays in Medical Sociology: Journeys into the Field* (New York: Wiley, c. 1979): pp. 122–45.

Howell, Joel D., ed. *Technology and American Medical Practice, 1880–1930: an Anthology of Sources* (New York: Garland Publishing, 1988).

Howell, Joel D. *Technology in the Hospital: Transforming Patient Care in the Early Twentieth Century* (Baltimore: Johns Hopkins University Press, 1995).

Illich, Ivan. *Medical Nemesis: The Expropriation of Health* (New York: Pantheon Books, 1976).

Jacobson, Nora. *Cleavage: Technology, Controversy, and the Ironies of the Man-Made Breast* (New Brunswick, NJ: Rutgers University Press, 2000).

Jeffrey, Kirk. *Machines in Our Hearts: the Cardiac Pacemaker, the Implantable Defibrillator, and American Health Care* (Baltimore: Johns Hopkins University Press, 2001).

Kaufman, Sharon. *The Healer's Tale: Transforming Medicine and Culture* (Madison: University of Wisconsin Press, 1993).

Keele, Kenneth D. *The Evolution of Clinical Methods in Medicine* (Springfield, Il.: Charles C. Thomas Publisher, 1963).

Koch, Ellen B. "In the image of science? Negotiating the development of diagnostic ultrasound in the cultures of surgery and radiology," *Technology and Culture* 34 (1993): 858–93.

Lawrence, Ghislaine, ed. *Technologies of Modern Medicine* (London: Science Museum, 1994).

Leavitt, Judith Walzer. *Brought to Bed: Childbearing in America 1750–1950* (Oxford and New York: Oxford University Press, 1986).

Leavitt, Judith Walzer. "The medicalization of childbirth in the twentieth century," *Transactions & Studies of the College of Physicians of Philadelphia* (ser. 5) 11 (1989): 299–319.

Liebenau, Jonathon. "Medicine and technology," *Perspective in Biology and Medicine* 27 (1983): 76–92.

Liebenau, Jonathon. *Medical Science and Medical Industry: the Formation of the American Pharmaceutical Industry* (Baltimore: Johns Hopkins University Press, c. 1987).

Ludmerer, Kenneth M. *Learning to Heal: the Development of American Medical Education* (New York: Basic Books, 1985).

Ludmerer, Kenneth M. *Time to Heal: American Medical Education from the Turn of the Century to the Era of Managed Care* (Oxford: Oxford University Press, 1999).

Maines, Rachel P. *The Technology of Orgasm: "Hysteria," the Vibrator, and Women's Sexual Satisfaction* (Baltimore: Johns Hopkins University Press, 1999).

Marks, Harry M. "Medical technologies: social contexts and consequences," in W.F. Bynum and Roy Porter, eds, *Companion Encyclopedia of the History of Medicine* (New York: Routledge, 1993), vol. 2: pp. 1592–618.

Marks, Harry M. *The Progress of Experiment: Science and Therapeutic Reform in the United States, 1900–1990* (Cambridge, U.K.: Cambridge University Press, 1997).

Maxwell, James H. "The iron lung: halfway technology or necessary step?" *Milbank Quarterly* 64 (1986): 3–29.

McKeown, Thomas. *The Role of Medicine: Dream, Mirage or Nemesis?* (London: Nuffield Provincial Hospitals Trust, 1976).

Mechanic, David. *From Advocacy to Allocation: the Evolving American Health Care System* (New York: The Free Press, 1986).

National Research Council (US). Committee on Technology and Health Care: Medical Technology and the Health Care System; a Study of the Diffusion of Equipment-Embodied Technology; a Report (Washington: National Academy of Sciences, 1979).

Ott, Katherine. *Fevered Lives: Tuberculosis in American Culture Since 1870* (Cambridge, Mass.: Harvard University Press, 1996).

Ott, Katherine, David Serlin, and Stephen Mihm, eds. *Artificial Parts, Practical Lives: Modern Histories of Prosthetics* (New York: New York University Press, 2002).

Parascandola, John, ed. *The History of Antibiotics: A Symposium* (Madison, Wis.: American Institute of the History of Pharmacy, 1980).

Payer, Lynn. *Medicine and Culture: Varieties of Treatment in the United States, England, West Germany, and France* (New York: Henry Holt and Co., 1988).

Pickstone, John V. *Medical Innovations in Historical Perspective* (New York: St Martin's Press, 1992).

Reiser, Stanley Joel. *Medicine and Reign of Technology* (Cambridge, U.K.: Cambridge University Press, 1978).

Robbins, Frederick C. "Assessing the consequences of biomedical research," in National Research Council (US). Committee on Technology and Health Care: Medical Technology and the Health Care System; a Study of the Diffusion of Equipment-Embodied Technology; a Report (Washington, National Academy of Sciences, 1979): pp. 166–77.

Rosen, George. *The Specialization of Medicine with Particular Reference to Ophthalmology* (New York: Arno Press and the New York Times, 1972).

Rosen, George. *The Structure of American Medical Practice, 1875–1941* (Philadelphia: University of Pennsylvania Press, 1983).

Rosenberg, Charles E. *The Care of Strangers: the Rise of America's Hospital* (New York: Basic Books, 1987).

Rosenberg, Nathan, Annetine C. Gelijns, and Holly Dawkins, eds. Sources of Medical Technology: Universities and Industry [Committee on Technological Innovation in Medicine; Medical Innovation at the Crossroads, vol. 5] (Washington, DC: National Academy Press, 1995).

Rothman, David J. *Beginnings Count: the Technological Imperative in American Health Care* (New York: Oxford University Press, 1997).

Sandelowski, Margarete. *Pain, Pleasure, and American Childbirth: from the Twilight Sleep to the Read Method, 1914–1960* (Westport, Conn.: Greenwood Press, 1984).

Sandelowski, Margarete. *Devices & Desires: Gender, Technology, and American Nursing* (Chapel Hill: University of North Carolina Press, 2000).

Schneider, William H. "Blood transfusion in peace and war, 1900–1918," *Social History of Medicine* 10 (1997): 105–26.

Shortt, S.E.D. "Physicians, science, and status: issue in the professionalization of Anglo-American medicine in the nineteenth century," *Medical History* 27 (1983): 51–68.

Stanton, Jennifer, ed. *Innovations in Health and Medicine: Diffusion and Resistance in the Twentieth Century* (London: Routledge, 2002).

Starr, Paul. *The Social Transformation of American Medicine* (New York: Basic Books, 1982).

Stevens, Rosemary. *American Medicine and the Public Interest* (New Haven: Yale University Press, 1971).

Stevens, Rosemary. *In Sickness and in Wealth: American Hospitals in the Twentieth Century* (New York: Basic Books, 1989).

Süsskind, Charles. "The invention of computed tomography," *History of Technology* 6 (1981): 39–80.

Swann, John Patrick. *Academic Scientists and the Pharmaceutical Industry: Cooperative Research in Twentieth-Century America* (Baltimore: Johns Hopkins University Press, 1988).

Thomas, Lewis. *The Lives of a Cell: Notes of a Biology Watcher* (New York: Viking, 1974).

Thomas, Lewis. "The technology of medicine," in *Lives of a Cell: Notes of a Biology Watcher* (New York: Viking, 1975): pp. 35–42.

Thomas, Lewis. "Response to James H. Maxwell's essay, 'The iron lung'," *Milbank Quarterly* 64 (1986): 30–33.

van Noordwijk, Jacob. *Dialysing for Life: the Development of the Artificial Kidney* (Dordrecht; Boston: Kluwer Academic Publishers, 2001).

Vogel, Morris J. *The Invention of the Modern Hospital: Boston, 1870–1930* (Chicago: University of Chicago Press, 1980).

Warner, John Harley. *The Therapeutic Perspective: Medical Practice, Knowledge, and Identity in America, 1820–1885* (Cambridge, Mass.: Harvard University Press, 1986).

Wailoo, Keith. *Drawing Blood: Technology and Disease Identity in Twentieth-Century America* (Baltimore: Johns Hopkins University Press, 1997).

Yoxen, Edward. "Seeing with sound: a study of the development of medical images," in Bijker, Wiebe E., Thomas P. Hughes, and Trevor Pinch, eds, *The Social Construction of Technological Systems: New Directions in the Sociology and History of Technology* (Cambridge, Mass.: MIT Press, 1987): pp. 281–303.

PART III

SITES OF CONTEST

CHAPTER TEN

The North American "Body–Machine" Complex

CHRIS HABLES GRAY

It might be argued that nothing typifies the American sense of identity more than the love of nature (nature's nation) except perhaps its love of technology (made in America). It is this double discourse of the natural and the technological that…makes up the American "Body–Machine" complex.

(Seltzer 1990, p. 141)

The Nature–Technology Synthesis

It should be no surprise that one of the main sites of technological innovation in America has been the human body. Tools to make us work better, medical interventions to make us live better, cosmetics and clothes to make us look better, vehicles to make us move better, foods and drugs to make us feel better, and weapons so we can kill better. Our "natural" body served by "unnatural" technology is a very American compromise, perhaps eventually a synthesis. It is at the heart of the America of the twenty-first century but it has always been a part of our history, of who we are. Technology may well define what is most unique about humans but it is not more important than our very bodies. The nexus of the two is in many ways definitive of any culture.

Conceptions of the human body have continually changed over time and through cultures they have always been a crucial part of identity. But they go beyond that. Our ideas about our bodies are a key aspect of our social life.

Our bodies and our perception of them constitute an important part of our socio-cultural heritage. They are not simply objects which we inherit at birth, but are socialized (enculturated) throughout life and this process of collectively sanctioned bodily modification may serve as an important instrument for our socialization (enculturation) in a more general sense. That is, in learning to have a body, we also begin to learn about our "social body" – our society. (Polhemus 1978, p. 21)

Technology is a particularly important part of this body dynamic. In North America this is demonstrably so. Technology has been, and still is, a central force in the way the body is conceived and constructed in the US and Canada. The love of nature and the love of technology that Mark Seltzer referred to when he described the "American 'Body–Machine' complex" are only part of the dynamic that has shaped it. It is more than a dialectic between nature (body) and culture (technology), or between the body as pain (Puritanism) and pleasure (freedom). It is systems and systems of systems combining ideas and facts and artifacts and bodies. It happens throughout society. In particular, we can look at the individualized citizen, who as the fundamental political unit in the body politic, is part of many systems but always in the end is based on a specific body or bodies. Human rights (habeas corpus, the Bill of Rights) and obligations (jury duty, military service) are almost always embodied.

The body-technology dynamic of the First Peoples, the many tribes that inhabited North America before European exploration and colonialization, is beyond the scope of this essay. Suffice it to say that there was no single Native American culture, a wide range of cultures coexisted with many different technologies and ideas about the body. And these many different influences did not disappear with the advent of European cultures; there was resistance, rejection, acceptance, integration, compromise, and loss as the indigenous cultures added important elements to the emerging American culture. But it is fair to say that the highly technologized view of nature and the body, which is so American today, was not a predominant part of human culture on this continent 100 years ago, let alone 500.

Although it was present in military drill and other scattered sites (such as the culture and technology of bathing), the American "Body–Machine" complex did not emerge clearly until the rise of industrialism and the spread of the idea of the human motor. In particular, the work of efficiency engineers such as Frederick Taylor and the Gilbreths institutionalized its more mechanistic aspects. Science-Fiction, that most American of literary genres, began imagining robots and androids and engineered humans at the beginning of the twentieth century in literature and, soon after in film. Technoscience was not far behind in instantiating many of the wilder fantasies.

This very North American dance between nature, technological innovation, and individualized liberty has not only spawned an economy of unprecedented fecundity, but also produced a number of innovations like feminism (whose second wave is often credited in part to the birth control pill), environmentalism (today a strange hybrid of high science and the love of nature with management practices dependent on systems theories), gay liberation (growing out of the embodied politics of feminism as feminism sprang from the embodied arguments and actions of the Civil Rights movement), and now transgender liberation (which relies in large part on intense medical interventions).

The result of all this is our current cyborg society. The "cyborg," a term coined by an immigrant American for a NASA conference, is the perfect expression of the "Body–Machine" complex, natural and artificial in homeostatic harmony. The continuing importance of technology in shaping the role of the body in our society can be seen in such contemporary technological issues as military policy (women in combat, minimizing casualties, obsession over dead bodies), medicine (cloning, abortion, reproductive technologies, living cadavers, the body as commodity), and human rights (surveillance, privacy). Our very idea of the citizen today, in terms of both obligations and rights, has been shaped by technology. Future forms of citizenship will certainly be based, in large part, on the technologies that are forming and defining our bodies today. But to really understand where we are and where we might go in the future, we need a richer understanding of the history of the American body–technology relationship.

Origins of the American Body–Machine Complex

Colonial America was not any one culture. There were the thriving Native American tribes still as different one from another as the many European and African ethnicities and religions that were scattered along the coasts. Correspondingly, there were many different attitudes toward the body and technology, but certain patterns seem clear to some historians. Professor Chaplin of Harvard University is a leading expert on this period, especially in terms of the British. She argues that,

> Three sets of ideas were especially relevant for colonizers – hypothesis about the physical nature of new territories, information about technology appropriate to the resources of new places, and assessments of the human bodies suited to these places. (Chaplin 2001, p. 14)

Already, according to Chaplin, nature, technology, and bodies were key epistemological priorities for colonists. This had practical implications she points out. These were the categories of European success. "Demystifying nature, displaying bodily strength, and using technology all became measures of colonial power" (p. 15).

The Roussean admiration for the "natural" Indians of the explorers evolved into a disdain that was widespread among the colonists, although certainly not a uni versally held opinion. But for the majority of colonists, often living in fear of native attack and just as often desiring tribal lands, it was a natural point of view. Colonial ideas of power started with the body and ended with the dispossession of the Indians. "Indians' lack of technology to develop nature, and their resulting lack of true property, were thus results of corporeal weakness, not of cultural difference" (p. 15).

The crime was not having a white body. Superior technology, resistance to disease, and their fruits all came from that.

> Subjection of matter and subjection of bodies – both topics framed the idea of English conquest of America, and both revealed the serious consequences of grounding empire in nature. (p. 15)

In practice, much of this was worked out in military terms, quite appropriate for the US, sometimes called a country made of war. Chaplin points out that,

> It was within the context of war that the English especially reexamined their ideas about Indian bodies and further developed their criticisms of native technologies. (p. 244)

Again, as with the general issue of relations, "The body was the springboard from which the English then launched arguments about Indians' technical inferiority" (p. 322) which lead logically to the conclusion that,

> That is the asserted English place in America rested on the foundational claim that English bodies were better suited to the new world than were Indian bodies. (p. 323)

But at the same time, many of the colonists were influenced by the deep ambivalence of Puritanism, and indeed, Christianity in general, expressed toward the body. The body, especially the female body, was the locus of sin, it was a corrupt version of the perfect celestial body of God. Still, as influential as religion was during this period, European pride remained more important, linking the superior body with superior technology, and the colonists added their own emphasis, the efficient body based on will. The self-made man, the self-improver. This is one of the central ideas of that great man, perhaps the first "American," Benjamin Franklin. But such ideas were not his alone. Many of the rebel militias were called "Minute men" because they could turn out so efficiently. Even as rebels, Americans were surprisingly well organized; as time went on, the culture developed a system that not only conquered most of North America, but also went on to dominate the world. Perhaps this started with Benjamin Franklin, perhaps much earlier, but a key transition was the professionalization of the rebel army by formal European-based drilling. In any event, through this process and others, according to the great historian of technology, Thomas Hughes, the American people,

> had acquired traits that have become characteristically American. A nation of machine makers and system builders, they became imbued with a drive for order, system, and control. (Hughes, *American Genesis*, 1989, p. 1)

This "characteristically American" approach can be seen in all aspects of the culture, but let us consider two particularly interesting ones – race and gender.

Chinn (2000), a professor of English, shows in her work *Technology and the Logic of American Racism*, that racism, while not scientific, has always relied on technology and pseudo-science to justify itself. In this process, the body is the main form of evidence, but how that evidence is interpreted is a social-cultural decision. In terms of race, it almost always seems to start with skin color, but Chinn shows that in the US the discourse of race went on to use fingerprints, phrenology, blood chemistry, and finally DNA in its quest to validate racism. Chinn finds this particularly amusing in the case of DNA testing, to see whether or not the descendants of the slave Sally Hemmings were also descendants of President Jefferson.

> Perhaps the greatest irony of DNA research is that a tool that has placed unprecedented numbers of African Americans behind bars over the decade since its development is now invoked as the proof that those incarcerated bodies are barely differentiated from the bodies of those who turn the key. Indeed, they could very well be related. (2000, p. 167)

Gender is another intensely contested category in North American history and the construction of different ideas of gender has always depended, in part, on technologies among other factors.

> The possibilities for moves toward more self-conscious gender identity were affected by a variety of historical developments. In the United States, the end of the Civil War

meant the reassessment of gender roles. Industrialization, the rise of a professional class, a pattern of economic depression, and the growth of urban centers all caused realignments in gender stereotypes. Historians have noted the "feminization" of American culture during this period. (Blanchard 1995, p. 39)

Of course, such "feminizations" are very debatable, as anyone who looks at the savage arguments about gender identity, sissies, longhairs, wimps, queers, lesbos, and so on that started in the 1960s and has not let up since. Such passionate contestation centers around womanhood, manhood, and the desire to show that the relationship of technology and identity is very complex. For example, despite political equalization there is strong evidence that women's self-definitions, even self-worth, are more linked to their bodies than ever. Through the technologies of "mirrors, movies, and marketing" young women's self-consciousness today is more about their appearance than their substance. Joan Jacobs Brumberg (1997) gives a fine history of this in *The Body Project*. The technologies that have shaped the female consumerist mass consciousness, which besides the mirror, movies, and marketing (certainly a very important technology in its own right) include sanitation napkins, tampons, douches, body deodorizers, and cosmetics of many types. Beyond that, of course, there are clothes, accessories, and everything a woman might own, actually.

It is not that there is not an ideal male consumer as well, it is just that his desires are commodified in a somewhat different form, the car as penile prosthesis, for example. Still, it is striking that the male and female images seem to be overlapping in more and more ways. More muscles on women, more plastic surgery for men. The ideal for both sexes is thin, young, symmetrical, wealthy, and arrogant.

You can go so far as to say that the system that generates gender identities is not just full of technologies, but that it is a technology in itself, and that gender, both embodied and disembodied, is a technology as well. The same could be said of the human body itself, especially when it is modeled as a living, electrical system.

"I Sing to the Body Electric American Nervousness"

It seems no accident that tales of electricity are intertwined with the story of the American Revolution through the protean figure of Benjamin Franklin. Ralph Waldo Emerson rhapsodized about the soul as a dynamo and Walter Whitman sung to the "body electric" (Armstrong 1998, p. 19). It was a spiritual thing, and not. For many Americans, the spirit was close to hard work (good works), and so the electric body was an economic concern. "Electricity also implied a bodily economy." In the 1870s growing fears of the pace of modern life led to theories about nervous exhaustion, or "neurasthenia" as Dr George M. Beard called it. From his view, it was a specifically "American Nervousness" (Armstrong 1998, p. 17).

Americans, working hard as machines, seemed to these doctors to be on the edge of burning out. According to Dr Beard and his close collaborator Dr A.D. Rockwell "The American constitution is more susceptible to electricity than the English or German" (quoted in Armstrong 1998, p. 31).

As electricity spread throughout the culture, a bizarre locus for the electrification of American culture was the battle between AC and DC currents over who would power the electrocution chair. Each alliance wanted the other to have that honor, thus associating their opponent's current with death. This is part of the famous "Battle of the Systems" between Thomas Edison's DC (direct current) and Nikolai Tesla's AC (alternating current), each with various corporate giants as allies. The Edison forces actually organized the smuggling of Westinghouse (of the eventually victorious AC alliance) equipment from Brazil to be used in an electric chair. Thus leading to the famous advertising slogan "Do you want the executioner's current in your home?" (quoted in Armstrong 1998, p. 34).

In a more positive vein the spread of telegraph and later telephone and power networks across the country shaped America's self-image as one body politic with electrical nerves.

> From the late 1840s onward, the feeling of unity created by telegraph lines inspired both scientific and lay writers to compare technological and organic communications systems. With little effort, they incorporated telegraph lines into the long-standing metaphorical system describing society as a living body. Because organic webs – not just spiders' webs but the webs of living tissue – resembled telegraph networks physically as well as functionally, they became the perfect metaphorical vehicle for these new communications systems. (Otis 2001, p. 121)

Electricity flows over networks, carrying energy and information, networks of power. These technologies had a profound impact on American culture in the nineteenth century, as Laura Otis amply documents in *Networking: Communicating With Bodies and Machines in the Nineteenth century.*

The body politic is real enough in its way. But so too is the living individual body and the tale of technology and bodies in America is fundamentally about specific bodies and how they are transformed. As the body is changed through technologies, the pressure to commodify it inevitably increases.

The American Body for Sale

The strange continuum from selling the idea of the body (advertising) to the actual trade in body parts reflects the tremendous importance of economic factors in the American body–technology relationship.

Carroll Pursell, a historian of American technology, has written about how American attitudes on bathing were driven in part by marketing and in part by fear of illness. It made for a potent combination. And, according to Pursell, the religious injunction by John Wesley that "Cleanliness is next to godliness" had less impact than the general idea that one should not "stink above ground," as Wesley also said (1994, p. 179). Achieving "gentility" seems to have also been important, but the spread of bathing was driven most of all, it seems, by new and improved technologies for providing water, for heating it, and for presenting it in a nice surrounding, such as a deep, white, porcelain, claw-footed tub.

While the "technology of bathing" appeared in the eighteenth century, even in 1829 there were only 401 baths in Philadelphia. But by 1860, there were 4,000 in Boston and the spread continued. In 1923, 4,800,000 were installed nationwide (p. 180). Within a hundred years, Americans had become serious bathers.

Production produced baths and therefore bathers, but it is workers who produce production. And it produces them. Armstrong (1998), lecturer in English at Royal Halloway, University of London, stresses that "Production subsumes the body, rendering it a breakable tool" (p. 98). Armstrong also talks of the impact of capitalism on the American body, and how writers as diverse as Poe, Twain, and Nathaniel West have explored this system of the "fractured" and "dismantled," body (p. 98). By the early 1900s the country was primed to respond to this anxiety, so with the advent of mass advertising succoring the plight of the American body became a major theme in North American consumer culture.

Armstrong concludes that in many important ways . . .

> commodity capitalism is *dependent* upon – as well as producing – a fragmentation of bodily integrity . . . Advertising posits a body-in-crisis, a zone of deficits in terms of attributes (strength, skill, nutrition), behaviors (sleep, defecation, etc.), with matching remedies. (p. 98, original emphasis)

As examples he gives Fleishmann's Yeast and the danger of "intestinal fatigue," of Listerine and the scourge of halitosis, and Kotex. These were followed by products, and campaigns, around "crows feet, bromodosis (smelly feet), comedones (blackheads), sour stomach, office hips, perspiration . . ." (p. 99). The claims became almost hysterical. According to the ads, technological solutions to the most horrible problems were just a simple purchase away. Toilet paper could prevent surgery (Scott Tissue ad 1931), jaw atrophy was warded off by chewing gum (Dentyne 1934), and amputations were avoided by better bandages (Johnson & Johnson 1936, p. 99).

So modifying the body is hardly a new theme. But in the twenty-first century all indications are that many of the modifications will be much more basic then anything yet tried. Scientists can change us now "at the source," at the genetic level. But genetic engineering is not without its dangers. Our ability to manipulate genes lags behind our understanding of what they do and how they do it. To help bridge this gap the US government launched the Human Genome Project. This multimillion dollar initiative cataloged all of the human genome with the goal of perfecting gene sequencing technology and the bioinformatic (computerization of biological information) apparatus. While the sequence of human DNA is inherently useful knowledge, the truly important information is knowing which part of the DNA does what, and that is beyond the scope of the project. Meanwhile private companies attained the same goal, claiming their newer technology beat the Human Genome Project to a full catalog of human DNA. Besides, they wanted to own it.

Kimbrell (1993) has written a frightening book called *The Human Body Shop: The Engineering and Marketing of Life*. He shows just how far this commodification of the human body has progressed though a long history that includes slavery. But even while slavery survives as indentured servitude and in the horrible ancient tradition of "trafficking" in women, the human body is being redefined as just another source of saleable commodities, and therefore profits.

It began with blood, the first body product that developed a real market. British economist Richard Titmuss proved this when he brilliantly analyzed how blood is collected and he found that blood banks received more and better quality blood from volunteers than from those who were paid for their blood. Britain collects almost all blood voluntarily. In the US, despite strong donation programs, much of the blood is bought from poor people. The bloodstocks in the UK far surpass that of the US in both quantity and quality. Still, many people assume that a commodity only has value if it has a price. In the US there has been a long legal struggle over whether or not blood is a commodity. Early court cases found that it was not and they allowed the medical community to regulate blood and blood products, but over time, especially as blood has become worth more, it has become increasingly commodified. Kimbrell reports that by the middle of the 1980s the US was the leading exporter of blood, then a $2 billion market; so dominant is the US in the production of blood products (60 percent of the world's total) that it has been dubbed "the OPEC of blood." The US processes its blood for the rare factors that are particularly valuable. The Red Cross also sells millions of liters of plasma that they collect for free and over 400 commercial blood centers buy and sell blood from the poor.

The market for rare blood factors led to another major step in the commodification of blood. Margaret Green has a rare type of AB negative blood. In her tax returns, she claimed as business expenses her trips to Serologicals, Inc. to sell her plasma and the cost of her special diet and medications. Eventually the tax court agreed and granted her the status of a "container" so that she could claim a full deduction for her travel. However, they did deny her claim for the depletion of her minerals, ruling that her body was not a "geological mineral resource."

The relentless spread of this "body for sale" culture includes the commercialization of reproduction as well as the culture of transplants, as seen in earlier chapters. Genetics has taken this process the furthest with the actual patenting of natural processes.

Kimbrell traces this strange legal story carefully. In 1971 a microbiologist who worked for General Electric applied, with GE, for a US patent on an oil-eating microbe. The Patent and Trademark Office (PTO) rejected the application, but the Court of Customs and Patent Appeals overruled this, stating that it was "without legal significance" that the patented object was alive. In 1980 the US Supreme Court upheld that ruling.

In 1988, the PTO granted Patent No.4,736,866 to Harvard University on a living animal, a transgenic mouse which possessed genes from chickens and humans. They had made the mouse susceptible to cancer so they named it "Oncomouse." The rights to the patent were bought by DuPont, who had financed the research. Oncomouse was modified at the germ line level, which means that the modifications will be reproduced when the mouse is mated or cloned (somatic alterations are genetic engineering interventions that are not passed on). The PTO mistakenly accepted a great deal of language that the Harvard and DuPont lawyers had included as wishful thinking. The patent actually grants Harvard and DuPont the rights to any "transgenic nonhuman mammal" whose cells have been altered to make it susceptible to cancer.

Four years later, in 1992, three more genetically engineered mice were patented, including a second one from Harvard which will suffer, through all its generations, from an enlarged prostrate gland.

When the Supreme Court allowed the patenting of the oil-eating microbe, they specified that humans could not be patented because the Thirteenth Amendment of the Constitution outlaws slavery, but they failed to mention "genetically engineered human tissues, cells, and genes." Kimbrell notes that an engineered kidney, arm, or other body part might legally be patentable. This certainly applies to genes, as the sad case of John Moore illustrates. His genes were patented by someone else.

A leukemia sufferer, Moore had his spleen removed in 1976 at the University of California at Los Angeles (UCLA). His doctor and a researcher, David Golde and Shirley Quan, used part of his spleen to breed Moore's white blood cells. Moore recovered and it turned out that his white blood cells produced strong anti-cancer and anti-bacteria biochemicals. In 1981, Golde, Quan, and UCLA applied for a patent on the genetic information in Moore's cells. Over the next few years, they licensed Moore's genes to a number of corporations.

Moore found this out and, as a good American, he sued. The California Supreme Court found that while Moore did not own his own cell line and had no property rights to "the tissues of his own body," he was due some money since his signed consent form did not give UCLA or his doctors the right to profit from his body. Several other such cases have confirmed that an individual cannot patent part of his body but an institution such as the University of California can. It gets worse.

Patent No.5,061,620 means that the genetic information in your stem cells, the cells in your bone marrow that produce blood, belong to Systemix, Inc., of Palo Alto, California. The patent should have only covered the way Systemix extracts these cells, a very difficult process, but the PTO, for some inexplicable reason, granted a patent that "covers the stem cells themselves."

In 1991, a National Institutes of Health (NIH) researcher filed for a patent on 2,337 brain genes and the next year he started his own company with $70 million in venture capital. The European Patent Office has received applications from Baylor Medical School to patent genetically altered human mammary glands. Numerous other people have attempted to patent genes, but as of this writing none have been approved. Looking at the recent history, one cannot be optimistic about future attempts.

More than other cyborg technosciences, genetics foregrounds the issue of human vs. post-human. Genetics offers the most likely, and certainly the most effective, way of using artificial evolution to produce intelligent non-human creatures. We have to ask, who is monitoring the dangers of such eugenic engineering or other potential disasters? But genetics isn't the only important site for technological transformations of the body, there is an older case of the technologized body, and just as important. The body as a machine.

From Human Motors to Mechanical Humans

Many thinkers have argued that the human body is just a machine, perhaps one with a soul as René Descartes claimed. But it took many years of rethinking and re-conceptualizing the body to make this idea seem obvious. And it is not just about the body as part of the factory or as part of the army, as important as those instances are. The body is also regimented in daily life outside of work and war. It can be as simple as, "sit up straight!"

The story of "The Rise and Fall of American Posture," as one article is called, shows how technology changed the very stance of the human body in the nineteenth and twentieth centuries, first for tighter posture, then there was a widespread relaxation of standards, and then a counter-reformation of sorts was staged, before eventually rigid posture as a widespread value and a sign of good character, was abandoned. Yosifon and Stearns (1998) point to a redefinition of "middle-class etiquette" in the mid-1700s for a shift from the languid posture of the nobility to a more rigid form. In particular, they note that "new military codes" (p. 1059) played an important role in this transition, after all there is a direct link between technology and military formations and many have argued that historically the army was the first real machine back when civilization was young.

It took a while for these European shifts in posture to reach the Americas. One of the first signs that rigidity had arrived was John Adams berating himself for distorting his body and "other failures of self control" (p. 1059). Adams was a self-improving man, counting on his will more than anything, but technology can often reinforce social norms. In the late 1800s, Yosifon and Stearns note that

> Family pictures, both visual and literary, emphasized children who could stand and sit straight, and of course, the available photographic technology required holding still. (p. 1060)

In another example,

> Clothing provided one vital support. Women's fashions, in the main, concealed the legs while constraining the lower back, particularly if corsetry was involved. Certain potential defects like bowed legs might thus be ignored, while the basic insistence on holding oneself erect was facilitated by the stiff, laced bodice and the supportive stays of ordinary dress. Men's tight vests would not prevent a determined slouch but they, too, helped remind the wearer of good carriage at least from the waist up, particularly when sitting. Parlor furniture encouraged careful posture as well. (pp. 1060–1)

When the social pressure for rigid posture waned it was across the board. Softer furniture, especially in theatres... "After World War I, the spread of radio listening promoted informal sitting" (p. 1063). With clothes it was the same. Elaborate woman's undergarments disappeared and after a 1910 controversy, corseting declined significantly (p. 1064).

The attempt to reintroduce "good posture" also depended on technology. In particular, the use of posture charts and photography and "a host of scales and assessment procedures" was significant. The Iowa Posture test is a good example of this (p. 1075).

> The concern with posture suggests a reassessment of the body itself, male and female alike. Posture discussions from the 1890s onward frequently had a sexual element, if only because bodies were best portrayed nude...Did posture discipline help some people adjust to more overt sexuality in real life, providing standards that would compensate for new indulgence? (p. 1083)

Widespread availability of full length mirrors from 1897, because of the development of a continuous process of pulling annealed glass, made body image a more powerful psychodynamic. "People saw their own bodies more often, and the posture standards may have played a role in the assimilation of this experience" (p. 1084). And it wasn't just mirrors, the rest of the house furnishings played a role. "Furniture after World War II moved to new levels of informality, with reclining lounging chairs and suburban lawn gear. Clothing on the whole, became still looser, accommodating a variety of stances" (p. 1091).

Body styles, like fashion, seemed to go back and forth. But since the last shift to "looseness" there has been no swing back.

> The end of extensive struggle over posture coincided with a revealing development in bedding. By the 1960s and particularly the 1970s, mattresses, for the first time, began to be advertised in terms of their implications for posture maintenance and back support.... The use of bedding to sustain the back, rather than personal discipline or any conscious effort, signaled the end of an era. (pp. 1090–1)

This ebb and flow shows the complex relationship between technology, culture, and the body. In many instances, it is the idea of the machine that shapes our bodies. This was particularly true during the industrial revolution. Labor truly became another element in the industrial process, and so every effort was made to control workers, prevent them from organizing themselves, to force them into rigid and limited roles. The worker was a "human motor" to many of the managers of this era. And they were aided by a new breed of manager-engineer, the efficiency expert.

The rise of industrial capitalism has witnessed the first "scientific" attempts to convert workers into just another element of production. One of the driving metaphors for this was "the human motor," as the historian of technology Rabinbach (1990) explains in his book of the same name. He traces the history of the disciplining of the worker-body from early Christian appeals against idleness, through punitive control, to today's focus on internal discipline.

> Consequently, the ideal of a worker guided by either spiritual authority or direct control and surveillance gave way to the image of a body directed by its own internal mechanisms, a human 'motor.'

At the beginning of the industrial revolution former peasants and freeholders, accustomed to the cyclical work patterns of agriculture, resisted the relentless production of industrialism in what their employers considered a moral failing. But physicians and engineers re-conceptualized it as "fatigue" to focus on possible "treatments" that would produce higher productivity. Rabinbach shows the underlying force behind this "invention" of the problem was "the daydream of the late nineteenth-century middle classes – a body without fatigue."

Starting in the mid-1800s, intellectuals in Europe and North America began scientifically analyzing the working body specifically and work in general. Etienne-Jules Marey, a French physician, focused on medical measurement, as well as hydraulics and time-motion photography, one of the first "engineer(s) of life." These engineers tried to make real the claims of René Descartes (the most famous proponent of the body=machine metaphor) and Julien Offrayde La Mettrie (who wrote *L'Homme machine* in 1748), that we are simply *La Machine animale*, as one of Marey's works is called.

Studies such as Marey's and those of other physicians, such as Paul Bert, who analyzed the diet of prisoners at the same time in *La Machine humaine*, gave substance to the old Cartesian metaphor. In Europe, a widespread movement to study the "science of work" developed, within which different currents argued for either more supervision of the worker or, influenced by Marxism, their empowerment. Other leftist currents, such as anarchists and Christian socialists, rejected the very metaphor of man-machines.

The next step for the scientists, Marxist or capitalist, was to analyze this "human machine" as it worked with a focus on its "scientific management." This simplification was the great contribution of the American efficiency expert Frederick Taylor and his many disciples.

> Taylor's fundamental concept and guiding principle was to design a system of production involving both men and machines that would be as efficient as a well-designed, well-oiled machine. (Hughes 1989, p. 188)

It was a popular idea with those it served, and it spread worldwide.

> Europeans and Russians adopted "Taylorism" as the catchword for the much-admired and imitated American system of industrial management and mass production. (Hughes 1989, p. 188)

Resistance to the European and Taylorist forms of work rationalization based on vitalist, romantic, and individualistic points-of-view was fragmented on the left by Marxism's scientific claims – it is no accident that Lenin fervently embraced Taylorism when the Bolshiviks came to power. But the deciding factor in the struggle over the conception of work was war. As far back as Marey, the Prussians' defeat of the French was a major issue. In the US, the strong labor resistance to Taylorism was brushed aside with the US entry into World War I and the militarization of the economy.

The history of industrialism is indistinguishable from the rise and perfection of modern war. Industrialized destruction needs industrial production. The development of managed bureaucracies is as important to large-standing armies and navies as it is to industries benefiting from economies of scale. From the use of interchangeable parts to the perfection of the assembly line, military thinking and its hunger for material goods were behind the creation of what has been called the American system of manufacture.

After the triumph of the idea of the "human motor" came its fall. Workers did not behave as machines, which should have been predicted when soldiers at the end of World War I failed to kill and die with machine-like precision, and instead mutinied. So the metaphors and programs aimed at mechanizing – or at least rationalizing – work shifted. In some cases they took on a decidedly fascist cast, as with the German approach called psychotechnicism which attempted to bring "the tempo of the machine...into harmony with the rhythm of the blood." Other industrialists started dreaming of wholly replacing workers with machines.

It was during this period that two Czech brothers, the Capeks, coined the term "robot" from the Czech and Polish word for indentured worker, robotnik. Karl Capek's play, R.U.R., about the invention and triumph of Rossum's Universal Robots, swept the world in the 1920s. The play's success marks the popular under-standing of industrialism's long attempt to make the worker a producing machine. While production processes and the integrating system have shifted over time, the basic desire has never wavered.

Robot research is taking off in the twenty-first century, but despite some optimistic predictions robots as intelligent as mice, let alone humans, seem distant. But what is here now are cyborgs, and that is certainly strange enough.

Cyborg Society Made in America

At the center of the American "Body–Machine" complex "is the notion *that bodies and persons are things that can be made.*" Today, North Americans labor at remaking themselves at an incredible rate. Grim yuppies imbibe wheat germ soaked in vegetable juice between bouts on weight machines or lift dead iron to re-sculpt their bodies (over $1 billion is spent on exercise machines yearly in the US). Meanwhile, techno-punks pierce themselves for sexual display and pleasure and everyone (or at least one-third of North Americans) diet.

But things have progressed beyond such crude interventions. Bodies can now be (re)made technologically, not just morally or willfully through the self-discipline of abstinence and exercise. Today, metaphorically and physically, the discipline of tech-noscience is incorporated into the body as information and it is surgically added, prosthetically, as bionics and interfaces. North American cyborgs are probably the most prolific in number and kind.

The term "cyborg" was coined to describe the possibilities of intimate and liberating technologies. As Manfred Clynes and Nathan Kline explain,

> For the exogenously extended organizational complex functioning as an integrated hemostatic system unconsciously, we propose the term "Cyborg." The cyborg deliberately

incorporates exogenous components extending the self-regulatory control function of the organism in order to adapt it to new environments. If man is in space, in addition to flying his vehicle, he must continuously be checking on things and making adjustments merely in order to keep himself alive, he becomes slave to the machine. The purpose of the Cyborg . . . is to provide an organizational system in which such robot-like problems are taken care of automatically and unconsciously, leaving man free to explore, to create, to think, and to feel. (Clynes and Kline 1960, p. 27)

"Cyborg" is derived from the term "cybernetics," which was coined by the American mathematician Norbert Wiener to mean the study of systems of all kinds. Wiener argued that all systems, whether living or not, were governed by the same sets of rules and relationships. In 1960, the eclectic genius Manfred Clynes created the term "cyborg" from "cybernetic organism" to refer to that class of things that were self-regulating systems that included both living and artificial subsystems. His first example was a white rat with an osmotic pump attached that would automatically inject some drug into the rat's system when certain levels were reached. His initial point was that humans could eventually be modified in various ways (drugs, prosthetics, genetics) so we could survive in space without a space suit but it soon became clear that such modifications were already taking place in many venues.

The term "cyborg" has been widely adopted in popular culture and in political debates yet is not much used in science and engineering. Still, the reality is that such hybrid systems, combining the living and the dead, the artificial and the natural, the evolved and the invented, are proliferating at an incredible rate in our culture. From genetic engineering to the man-machine weapon system of the military to medical bio-implants, cyborgian technosciences and perspectives are everywhere. The central and most interesting case is the ongoing modification of humans. Even when we are not directly cyborged, through vaccinations that reprogram our immune system or implanted chips to monitor our hearts or blood sugar levels, we are accelerating our integration with machines. Most of us in the West and in the urban areas of the Third World live lives that are almost completely mediated by machines. They deliver our music and entertainment, they deliver us to work and play, they analyze our productivity and our health, and they are, more and more, being implanted into our bodies to perform these and other functions more efficiently.

The effective integration of humans and machines is crucial for space exploration, high technology industrial production, today's medicine, mass media, and war. The US invasion of Afghanistan has demonstrated how effective the high-tech version of this is, as the 9/11 hijackers who used knives to turn themselves into powerful cyborg suicide weapon systems have shown that there is a "low-tech" version of cyborg soldiers as well. But this is just the tip of the iceberg. The incredible growth of technoscience is behind these developments, as it is behind the invention of weapons of mass destruction, the destruction or monoculturalization of much of nature, and many other trends that actually threaten the human future, including the engineering of our own replacements.

Within decades, some humans will be genetically modified to an extent that, in terms of their DNA, they will be different species: post-humans. Clynes, in his 1960 article (co-authored with Nathan Kline) that named cyborg, also wrote about how cyborg marked the beginning of "participatory evolution." The issue is not whether or not we're going to be cyborgs or even post-humans. We are already cyborged and post-humans are inevitable. The question is, what kinds of cyborgs, what kinds of post-humans, and who will decide?

Convicted murderer Joseph Jernigan transformed from Dead Man Walking to Dead Man Digitalized when he donated his body to science. In 1993, the Texas convict became the Visible Man, now on total display in books, on CD-Roms, and through the World Wide Web. Jernigan has been immortalized as 15 gigabytes of data not for his life of crime, which culminated in the murder of a 75-year-old man who interrupted one of his burglaries, but because he was a fit 39-year-old killed neatly with chemicals (Wheeler 1996). As Cartwright describes,

> ...prison workers attached an IV catheter to Jernigan's left hand and administered a drug that effectively suppressed the brain functions which regulate breathing...the catheter...functioned as a kind of prosthetic disciplinary hand of the state of Texas...(Cartwright 1997, p. 130)

After his execution, his body was quickly flown to the Center for Human Simulation in Colorado where it was frozen in a block of gel at −70 °C (−160 °F). He was chosen as the best corpse from a number of candidates, then was quartered, an old medieval punishment but in this case just a stage in his immortalization. The four blocks were shaved into 1,871 thin slices that were filmed, digitalized, and entered into a sophisticated database that allows 3-D reconstructions of his body so accurate that viewers can admire the dragon tattoo on his chest. This murderer is the archetypical human, anatomically speaking.

The Visible Woman was not a murderer but a 59-year-old Maryland housewife. When she died, she was treated the same, except that technological advances allowed her body to be sliced into 5,000 sections. The Visible Man and the Visible Woman are prime examples of the ongoing digitalization of the body. Every aspect of the human is being converted into computer information, whether it is blood gas compositions, heart rates, brain waves, or the genetic code itself.

Contemporary medicine depends on this mathematization of the human body, and this process will only increase as scientists perfect real-time scanning instruments and delve deeper and deeper into the nano processes that vitalize our flesh, power our feelings, and make our thoughts possible. All high-tech medicine is cyborg medicine, for it involves this digitalization.

Modifying ourselves through medicine is also becoming more and more common. Every year millions of interventions are performed to suck out or insert fat, carve better facial features, modify the immune system, or otherwise "improve" the natural body. All these procedures raise important political issues, from the nature of informed consent to the wisdom of using medical resources to improve someone's buttocks while others die for lack of basic care. Another set of key cyborg political issues are linked to the ancient cycle of reproduction, decline, and death (see Gray 2001 for the full cyborg life cycle). Thanks to medical advances such as penile prosthesis, the vibrator, and transsexual surgery, sex has also become a cyborg issue. But let us first look at one of the fastest growing aspects of cyborg medicine – the increasing use of drugs to modify behavior and bodily processes on a massive scale.

The explosion of psychotropic and other drug use stems from three breakthroughs. First, there is the intimate understanding of body chemistry as a balancing act of hormones and other chemicals. The mathematical modeling of the biochemistry of consciousness, for example, means that not only can drugs be designed to produce specific mental effects, but that their production in the body can be controlled efficiently. The second breakthrough is innovations in monitoring the brain and the body in action. Real time three-dimensional brain scans are now possible and that means the testing of drugs can be improved and accelerated, even if the scientists do not yet fully understand what they see. Finally, society's supposed hatred of "bad" illegal drugs is matched by its love of officially sanctioned "good" drugs. It has become socially acceptable to medicate oneself not just for bone loss or incontinence or headaches, but also to achieve sanity or even just happiness.

Since before there was institutional medicine, when there was just placating the spirits and healing, drugs have been used to modify human consciousness and the body. Medicine, with its ability to reprogram the immune system and many other pharmacological interventions, has built on this history with a vast array of drugs that block pain, kill invading viruses and bacteria, and modify bodily processes. Some of these interventions have very dangerous ramifications that could have been avoided if the complex and permeable cybernetic relations between human bodies and other organisms were better understood. Antibiotics are a case in point, as their overuse in treating humans and animals has produced microenvironments that effectively evolve new resistant strains of the very organisms we have tried to kill.

New understandings are leading to whole new generations of active drugs. Prozac and Viagra are good examples. Viagra, the hit of 1998, is just one of a new wave of "baby boom" drugs that are supposed to make life longer and better. These boomer drugs include Propecia (baldness), Lipitor (cholesterol), Evista (bone density), Detrol (bladder control), and Onata (sleep disorders). Their extreme marketability stems from the common human desire for immortality, the ubiquitous cult of youth, and capitalism's relentless pursuit of profit.

Pharmaceuticals are big money. Over $20 billion for research alone was spent in 1998 just by US companies; Pfizer realized $2.2 billion in profits in 1997 *before* Viagra (Handy 1998). Pharmaceutical profits are growing at an incredible rate. The relationship between drug production and profitability is not always obvious. For instance, the big companies withdrew from research into new antibiotics because they assumed that there was not going to be a market for such drugs. Since common bacteria are developing resistance to the most powerful antibiotics, largely because drug companies have supported the massive over-prescription of the antibiotics they already produce, this assumption has already proven incorrect. But there are no new antibiotics ready. What may turn out to be a major health crisis of the early twenty-first century will have resulted directly from the imperative to maximize profits. Economics are always political, especially when medical policy is determined by profits, even if the causal chain is complicated by bacterial evolution and other exotic factors.

Many drug-related political issues are more predictable. Some Health Maintenance Organizations (HMOs) refused funding for Viagra and were immediately attacked. This is an issue that legislators – overwhelmingly male and aging – have great enthusiasm for, yet it is no surprise that they have not found the same energy for forcing HMOs to supply birth control and other reproductive services to women. Medications are not free and so their distribution involves class issues as well, especially when it comes to government health policy. As more cyborgian technologies become available, who will have access to them? Only the rich and well-insured?

The new class of psychotropic (mind-effecting) drugs also has a number of surprising political ramifications. What can the drug wars possibly mean in the context of a whole raft of mood-elevating drugs such as Prozac? What is the line between treating depression and getting high? If mild depression can be treated chemically should it be classed as a mental illness? Is there such a thing as cosmetic personality surgery for mild behavioral quirks? The vast increases in our understanding of the biochemistry of the body mean that the range of possible interventions increases apace. The temptation to medicalize everything from grumpiness to aging will be very powerful indeed. Already, when one looks at the extraordinary range of direct cyborgian interventions, it is clear that the whole body is open for modification.

Haraway (1985) first raised the politics of cyborgization in her brilliant "Manifesto for Cyborgs" where she urged the left, especially feminists, not to demonize technology but rather to take responsibility for it. Instead of being naive about many of the militaristic and capitalistic origins of much cyborgization, Haraway was actually among the very first to point them out. But she argued that it doesn't mean that technology in general, or cyborgization in particular, is wholly evil. It has many origins and it has many implications that are not necessarily authoritarian, most particularly in medicine. She also pointed out that as socially constructed creatures, cyborgs implicitly reject simplistic notions of naturalized gender and all other such givens such as race. It is no coincidence that it is cyborgian medicine that has allowed for transsexuality and transgender communities to exist, for example. But the implications are broader, we are entering the age of cyborg citizens.

Cyborg Citizens

More and more analysts are warning us that technological changes require political responses (Gray 2001; Fukuyama 2002). This is especially true in light of the fear and perhaps loathing that rapid technological changes can produce. Two Canadian theorists, Arthur and Louise Kroker, perform this tension in their work. For example, they have written at length about how technological change is inducing "panic" in North American culture.

> Panic sex in America is the body in the postmodern condition as a filter for all the viral agents in the aleatory apparatus of the dead scene of the social, and where, if the body is

marked, most of all, by the breakdown of the immunological order, this also indicates, however, that there is a desperate search underway for technologies for the body immune from *panic fashion* (the "New Look" in the Paris fashion scene) and *panic science* (the deep relationship between AIDS and Star Wars research) to *panic policy* (the urinal politics of contemporary America) and *panic eating* (the double occurrence in America today of a schizoid regime of dietary practices, the explosion of eating disorders, from bulimia to anorexia, on the one hand; and, on the other, and intense fascination with the recuperation of the healthy mouth), culminating with the recent High Fashion edict that the slightly robust woman's body is back as a counter-aesthetic in the age of AIDS and disappearing bodies. (Krokers, p. 15, original italics)

They go on to declare that this can lead to a type of "Body McCarthyism" (p. 10), where certain kinds of bodies are labeled subversive just for existing. This is a real danger. As technologies modify us, and allow for much more intrusive interventions into our bodies, even our thoughts, we need a stronger democracy to preserve our freedom. In a world where soon tiny (nanotech) cameras might be everywhere, where 100 percent accurate lie detector tests exist, where a body can be surveilled from afar, even to tell whether or not someone has used drugs in the last year, our traditional political technologies seem somewhat weak. That is why I've proposed a Cyborg Bill of Rights (Gray 2001), for example. To allow people to choose how they want their body modified, when they want to die, how they want to impact their consciousness, the right to information held on them by large bureaucracies, whether they are corporate or governmental. Human or post-human, democracy needs citizens and institutions that can protect our rights. Otherwise, American democracy will become technologically obsolescent.

It begins with understanding the incredible technological transition our bodies are going through. It is unlike any time in human history before, even though historians don't like to admit this. America, with its special mix of nature and technology is the culture where these problems will be addressed first. As Hughes (1989) concludes

> If the nation, then, has been essentially a technological one characterized by a creative spirit manifesting itself in the building of a human-made world patterned by machines, megamachine, and systems, Americans need to fathom the depths of the technological society, to identify currents running more deeply than those conventionally associated with politics and economics. (1989, pp. 3–4)

Made in America. Americans are makers and doers; remaking our bodies is part of it. And the future will be what we make of it and ourselves.

BIBLIOGRAPHY

Armstrong, Tim. *Modernism, Technology and the Body: A Cultural Study* (Cambridge: Cambridge University press, 1998).

Benthall, Jonathan. *The Body Electric Patterns of Western Industrial Culture* (Plymouth Latimer Trend & Company, 1976).

Blanchard, Mary W. "Boundaries and the Victorian body aesthetic fashion in gilded age America," *American Historical Review*, vol. 100, no. 1 (February 1995): pp. 21–50.

Brumberg, Joan Jacobs. *The Body Project: An Intimate History of American Girls* (Vintage, 1997).

Califia, Pat. *Sex Changes: The Politics of Transgenderism* (San Francisco: Clies Press, 1997).

Cartwright, Lisa. "The visible man" in Jennifer Terry and Melodie Calvert, eds, *Processed Lives* (Routledge, 1997): pp. 123–38.

Chaplin E. Joyce. *Subject Matter Technology, the Body, and Science on the Anglo-American Frontier, 1500–1676* (Cambridge: MA Harvard University Press, 2001).

Clynes, Manfred and Kline, Nathan. "Cyborgs in space," *Astronautics* (September 1960): 26–7, 74–5.

Crary, Jonathan, and Sanford Kwinter, eds, *Incorporations* (Zone 1992).

Chinn, Sarah E. *Technology and the Logic of American Racism: A Cultural History of the Body as Evidence* (Continuum, 2000).

David, Kathy. *Reshaping the Female Body: The Dilemma of Cosmetic Surgery* (Routledge, 1995).

Fausto-Sterling, Anne. *Myths of Gender* (Basic Books, 1997).

Favazza, Armando R. *Bodies Under Siege Self-mutilation and Body Modification in Culture and Psychiatry*, 2nd edn (Baltimore: Johns Hopkins, Press, 1987, 1996).

Fukuyama, Francis. *Our Posthuman Future Consequences of the Biotechnology Revolution* (Farrar Straus and Giroux, 2002).

Gray, Chris. "The culture of war cyborgs technoscience, gender, and postmodern war," in Joan Rothschild, ed., *Research in Philosophy & Technology*, special issue on technology and feminism, vol. 13 (1993): pp. 141–63.

Gray, Chris. "Medical cyborgs artificial organs and the quest for the posthuman," in C.H. Gray, ed., *Technohistory Using the History of American Technology in Interdisciplinary Research* (Melbourne Fl.: Krieger Publishing Co., 1996) pp. 140–78.

Gray, Chris. *Postmodern War: The New Politics of Conflict* (New York Guilford; London: Routledge, 1997).

Gray, Chris. *Cyborg Citizen* (New York/London: Routledge, 2001).

Gray, Chris, Steven Mentor and Heidi Figueroa-Sarriera. "Cyborgology" in Gray, Mentor, Figueroa-Sarriera, eds. *The Cyborg Handbook* (New York: Routledge, 1995): pp. 1–16.

Handy, Bruce. "The viagra craze," *Time*, May 4, 1998, pp. 50–7.

Haraway, Donna. "A cyborg manifesto science, technology, and socialist feminism in the 1980s" originally published in *Socialist Review*, 1985.

Hughes, Thomas P. *American Genesis: A Century of Invention and Technological Enthusiasm 1870–1970* (Penguin, 1989).

Kimbrell, Andrew. *The Human Body Shop* (San Francisco: Harper San Francisco, 1993).

Kroker, Arthur and Marilouise Kroker, eds, *Body Invaders: Panic Sex in America* (St. Martin's Press, 1987).

Laqueur, Thomas. *Making Sex Body and Gender from the Greeks to Freud* (Cambridge: MA Harvard University Press, 1990).

Maines, Rachel. "Socially camouflaged technologies," *IEEE Technology and Society Magazine*, vol. 8, no. 2 (June 1989): pp. 3–11.

Marvin, Carolyn. *When Old Technologies Were New Thinking About Electric Communication in the Late Nineteenth Century* (New York: Oxford University Press, 1988).

Otis, Laura. *Networking: Communicating With Bodies and Machines in the Nineteenth Century* (Ann Arbor University of Michigan Press, 2001).

Polhemus, Ted, ed. *The Body Reader Social Aspects of the Human Body* (Pantheon, 1978).

Pursell, Carroll. *White Heat People and Technology* (Berkeley: University of California Press, 1994).

Rabinbach, Anson. *The Human Motor* (Basic Books, 1990).

Rashaw, Domeena. "Inflatable penile prosthesis," *Journal of the American Medical Association*, vol. 241, no. 24, 1979.

Sandoval, Chela. "New sciences cyborg feminism and the methodology of the oppressed" in Gray, Mentor, Figueroa-Sarriera, eds, *The Cyborg Handbook* (New York: Routledge, 1995): pp. 407–22.

Seltzer, Mark. "The love master" in Joseph A. Boone and Michael Cadden, eds, *Engendering Men: The Question of Male Feminist Criticism* (New York: Routledge, 1990): pp. 141–9.

Tiefer, Lenore, Beth Pederson, and Arnold Melman. "Psychological follow-up of penile prosthesis implant patients and partners," *Journal of Sex and Marriage Therapy*, vol. 14, no. 3 (Fall 1988): pp. 184–201.

Tiefer, Lenore, Steven Moss, and Arnold Melman. "Follow-up of Penile Prosthesis Implant Patients and Partners," *Journal of Sex and Marriage Therapy*, vol. 14, no. 3 (Fall 1991): p. 124.

Vlahos, Olivia. *Body: The Ultimate Symbol Meanings of the Human Body Through Time and Place* (J.B. Lippincott 1979).

Wheeler, David. "Creating a body of knowledge," *Chronicle of Higher Education*, February 2, A6, A7, A14.

Yosifon, David and Peer N. Stearns. "The rise and fall of American posture," *The American Historical Review*, vol. 103, no. 4 (October 1998): pp. 1057–95.

CHAPTER ELEVEN

Gender and Technology

REBECCA HERZIG

Broadly conceived, both gender and technology shape our daily experiences of the world at the most concrete, mundane levels: how we eat, sleep, and work, how we think, love, and grieve. Consider, for instance, the influence of gender and technology evident in the contemporary public toilet, as found in restaurants, bus stations, movie theaters, shopping malls, and factories across the United States. Clearly labeled for Men or Women, Boys or Girls, the sex segregation of these facilities is familiar to anyone who has tried to accompany a small child of a different sex into the "wrong" restroom. The partition of contemporary public toilets does not end with separately labeled entries, but often extends into each aspect of the interior space – from urinals, sinks, and stall dividers to amenities such as diaper-changing tables, tampon dispensers, and sanitary waste disposal bins. No fixed distinction between the bodily needs of ladies and gentlemen (or "females" and "males") forces these design specifications. The briefest recollection of Jim Crow legal restrictions indicates that the segregation of public facilities is not determined by natural differences between classed, raced, and sexed bodies (Higginbotham 1992, p. 254). The contemporary public toilet could just as easily – and pragmatically – be segmented by parenting status or by age, or could be left undivided altogether. The material and spatial form of the contemporary public toilet reveals neither the influence of nature nor the intrinsic superiority of certain technical specifications, but instead a shifting set of cultural precepts: the expectation that women should sit rather than stand to urinate, for example, or that men have no real use for a diaper-changing table.

Just as norms of gender mold the material form of the modern public toilet, the intransigent physicality of the built environment also molds the gender of the individuals who enter it. Each person who uses a sex-segregated public toilet is compelled to either assume the behaviors appropriate to that space, or to suffer the consequences of serious social transgression. In Texas, for example, a woman was jailed and prosecuted after long lines at one toilet drove her into the facility designated for "men"; in New York, transgendered activists were arrested, stripped, and physically probed after using sex-segregated toilets at Grand Central Station. Given the tremendous energy expended to maintain the dimorphic character of the American public toilet, we might properly consider it "a technology of gender enforcement" (Halberstam 1997, p. 186).

In the case of the toilet, gender and technology appear thoroughly intertwined. Thus to fully understand the influence of either gender or technology on daily life, we must attend to the ways in which gender and technology reciprocally shape one another. As the editors of one recent collection summarize, "[i]t is as impossible to understand gender without technology as to understand technology without gender" (Lerman *et al.* 1997, p. 30). A generation of historical scholarship supports this conclusion, demonstrating how norms of manhood and womanhood transform the design, development, distribution, and use of particular technologies, even as particular artifacts and technological systems transform the lived experience of gender (Wajcman 1991; Berg and Lie 1995).

Although self-identified feminists have been at the forefront of historical research on relations between gender and technology, the concept of gender did not originate in feminism. The term itself emerged within linguistics, where "gender" is used to denote the categories of nouns found in different languages (such as the feminine *la porte* vs. the masculine *le tableau* in French). Although linguists have long debated to what extent the gendering of nouns affects our apprehension of the world around us (Cook 2002), most have assumed that gender holds no necessary relationship to the intrinsic attributes of the things named. (It would be difficult to argue, for instance, that a door is somehow more feminine than a table.) Social theorists recognized the utility of distinguishing between words and things in this fashion, and adopted the term "gender" to emphasize the apparent disjunction between physical attributes and social *conceptions* of those attributes. The coining of the term "gender identity" in 1963 gave the disjunction between the corporeal and the social new practical implications, as clinicians devoted increasing scrutiny to discrepancies between physiological characteristics (such as testes) and characteristics acquired through socialization (such as habits of speech). Interestingly, this new clinical terminology emerged alongside the development of techniques of human hormonal manipulation, chromosomal assessment, and reconstructive surgery. Throughout its history as an analytical tool, in other words, *gender* has been part and parcel of shifting technological practice (Hausman 1995; Balsamo 1996).

The concept of gender thus acquired currency among Anglophone theorists as a way to refer to historically specific – and, feminists hoped, alterable – social relations. *Sex*, as scholars began to use the term, named all given somatic differences between the females and males of a species; *gender* named all those differences and hierarchies which have been created and maintained through habit, custom, and law. In an influential 1972 book, sociologist Ann Oakley summarized the distinction as one between "biological differences between male and female: the visible difference in genitalia, the relative difference in procreative function" and "culture…the social classification into 'masculine' and 'feminine'" (p. 16). Today, common parlance frequently conflates the two, as when hospital birth certificates check one box (M or F) to note the "gender" of a newborn. Like all words, *gender* continues to hold multiple, even contradictory meanings, and it does not translate well across time and place. Speakers of German, for instance, make no similar distinction between "sex" and "gender" (Scott 1988; Haraway 1991).

While the advent of gender as a category of analysis has enabled greater attention to the contingency of particular historical practices, specifying the point of contact between gender and actual bodies within these formations remains a difficult matter. Since claims about "biological differences" are often used to bolster existing social hierarchies, feminists have been understandably eager to protect the analytical concept of gender from the sticky residue of biological sex (Haraway 1991). Yet the physicality of bodies is not easy to ignore, particularly for historians studying issues such as sexual violence, sterilization abuse, or disease transmission. The *matter* of sexual difference therefore remains a topic of persistent historiographical debate.

For example, historians have long critiqued the ways in which tools such as callipers, cephalometers, craniometers, and parietal goniometers were used to substantiate alleged differences between racialized, sexed bodies in the nineteenth century (Stepan 1996; Herndl 1999; Briggs 2000). Readers of these accounts readily acknowledge the absurdity of period obstetrical accounts of enslaved women's "imperviousness" to the pain of birth, and identify the historical contingency of such claims about woman's nature. Yet no equally ready dismissal appears with respect to our own, contemporary techniques for assessing and measuring physical difference, such as magnetic resonance imaging or androgen screening (Kessler 1998; Fausto-Sterling 2000). For some historians, the use of gender as a category of analysis actually presupposes a self-evident, timeless division between male and female bodies. As one historian stated firmly: "Women menstruate, parturate and lactate; men do not" (Cowan 1979, p. 30). Some claims about sexual difference (such as imperviousness to pain) are placed in historical context; others are not. In short, relations between "sex" and the mutable, contradictory practices of "gender" remain as contentious in current historiography as in feminist philosophy.

In its controversial relationship to physicality, the concept of gender raises tensions similar to those evident in debates over "social construction" in the history of technology. Just as historians of gender continue to grapple with the problem of embodiment, so, too, historians of technology continuously engage the concrete materiality of the artifacts they study. Unlike many other intellectual or social historians, historians of technology display a serious regard for physicality, for the relevance of "thingness or tangibility" (Marx and Smith 1994, p. xi). And, as for historians of gender, the elastic word *technology* (which might refer at once to artifacts, activities, processes, and "know-how") generates analytical slippage among its historians (Bijker *et al.* 1987, p. 4; MacKenzie and Wajcman 1999). At times, "technology" refers to obdurate material objects; at other times, it refers to symbolic representations of those objects. Interestingly, even this slippage reflects the complicated entanglement of gender and technology. In one recent article, sociologist Stefan Hirschauer suggests that the concept of gender has been "semantically spoiled as mere 'software' in the construction of the two sexes" (1998, p. 25). As this comment reveals, technology and its metaphors ("hardware" vs. "software") continue to inform our understandings of human difference, even as our notions of sexual difference affect the design and use of new technologies.

Given the multiple points of connection between technology and gender, it is perhaps not surprising that historians of gender and historians of technology both tend to emphasize the methodological importance of "intersectionality," of the analysis of mutually constitutive relationships. Recent studies of technology, for instance, stress the importance of a "systems approach" to technological change, arguing that individual artifacts (such as automobiles) cannot be properly understood outside an interlocking web of materials, people, institutions, and environments: roadways, legal regulations, oil companies, marketing firms, ozone layers, and so on (Hughes 1987; Law and Hassard 1999). While thinking in terms of interdependent networks marked a major development within mainstream history of technology (a development no doubt influenced by the rise of cybernetic thinking after WWII), it is useful to recall that systemic analysis is rooted in the very term *gender*. As originally employed in linguistics, "gender" holds significance only as a relational category of difference: the markers *la* and *le*, for example, have no content when extracted from a specific pattern of language. So, too, as a category of historical analysis, gender emerges only through reciprocally formative relationships. Gender cannot be reduced to an attribute held by a single "man" or "woman," any more than gendered articles (*la* or *le*) make sense outside of an encompassing semantic web. Gender necessarily refers not to the stagnant property of an individual, but to an ongoing, inherently incomplete process of differentiation.

Considering gender as a relational process would appear to demand attention to men as well as women. This attention, however, has not always been present in studies of technology. As historian Judith McGaw notes, non-feminist historians "have customarily studied female actors as women and male actors as people" (McGaw 1989, p. 173). Some feminist historians, in turn, have ignored the contingency and variability of masculine power, erroneously assuming that men always possess a clear, stable sense of their gender interests (Baron 1991, p. 29). In neither event does a focus on men and manliness necessarily address patterns of gender *relations*; as a result, inattentive studies of masculinity can quickly become simply one more way to erase women from histories of technology. And erasure abounds: of the 1,300 entries in a recent biographical dictionary of the history of technology, for example, Stanley has found that fewer than a dozen of the included entries address women inventors or engineers (Stanley 2000, p. 431; for contrast, see Stanley 1993). In the context of such blatant oversight, many historians of technology continue the painstaking work of retrieving women's contributions from the dustbin of history. Focusing on what Gerda Lerner has termed "compensatory" research, these historians endeavor to recuperate the forgotten (or systemically neglected) technical contributions of women and girls (Lerner 1975).

The most illuminating studies of masculinity and technology thus approach manhood and boyhood as part of a larger web of historical formations. In a study of the shift from letter-press printing to computerized photo-composition in the newspaper industry, Cynthia Cockburn once noted that men were positioned as "strong, manually able and technologically endowed" in relation to women's positioning as "physically and technically incompetent" (Cockburn 1983, p. 203). Other studies show that, on occasion, "technical competence" is treated as the special domain of *women*. Nelly Oudshoorn, for instance, demonstrates the stereotypes of male technical "unreliability" or disinterest that have permeated debates over oral hormonal contraceptives for men (Oudshoorn 2000). In a study of different institutions in mid-nineteenth-century Philadelphia, historian Nina Lerman describes how gendered hierarchies of "technical skill" were further arranged and divided along the shifting lines of class and race (Lerman 1997). Whether men or women are positioned as technically incompetent, the mutual shaping of manhood, womanhood, and technology again appears paramount.

A thoroughgoing consideration of gender and technology thus does not merely add a few more stories of individual inventors or artifacts to stable firmament of historical knowledge. Rather, it entirely transforms understandings of the past. As Joan Rothschild, Carroll Pursell, and numerous others have noted, central historical questions are re-framed once gender is rigorously incorporated as a category of analysis (Rothschild 1983; Pursell 1993). Moving beyond assumptions of fixed differences between males and females to examine unstable and contradictory processes not only opens new approaches to the most familiar topics in the history of American technology, but also allows us to rethink the historical formation of "fixed differences" themselves.

Consider, for example, the central topic of early industrialization. At least one historian has argued that the mechanization of textile production – a central event in the rise of the domestic manufactures – arose from a lack of male workers. Early mills were forced to rely on the labor of women, "a work force of limited physical strength relative to the one made up of men." The "fact" of women's physical limitations, it is suggested, in turn "inspired greater reliance on inanimate power," thereby driving the turn toward water-powered machines (Steinberg 1991, p. 42; for a divergent perspective, see Jeremy 1981, p. 202). Citing no evidence attesting to women's bodily weakness (or even evidence suggesting period *beliefs* about women's weakness), women's purported limitations are given a primary role in directing the course of technological development. That women in New England had long been performing carding, spinning, warping, and weaving without the assistance of water-powered machinery goes unmentioned. So, too, does the fact that men's bodies as well as women's might be assisted by devices reliant on inanimate power (such as water-powered sawmills and gristmills typically operated by men). Sexual divisions of labor are instead presumed to be based on timeless somatic distinctions, and are thus taken as a cause, rather than a consequence, of historical developments.

In contrast, historians sensitive to the import of gender have demonstrated the significance of ideas about womanhood in the industrialization of New England. The employment of unmarried, native-born white women in early textile mills was central to the rise of the factory system at Lowell and elsewhere: a populace skeptical about large-scale domestic manufactures and repulsed by the specter of Britain's polluted, polluting mills was put at ease by images of well-disciplined, chaste farmgirls tending the gleaming machines of the young republic. Racialized attitudes about the purity and independence of these "daughters of freemen" not only assuaged fears of the contamination of industrial capitalism, but also shaped the first collective protests organized by workers (Dublin 1979). Other studies of industrialization – such as

McGaw's superb history of Berkshire paper-making – have suggested that newly potent sexual divisions of labor are themselves one of industrialization's most powerful legacies (McGaw 1987, p. 377; Baron 1991, p. 18).

The study of conflicting beliefs about the intrinsic physical or moral capacities of women (and men) also transforms other familiar subjects in the history of American technology, such as the practices of engineering. Some writers have explained the long-standing over-representation of men in American engineering professions (approximately 96 percent in 1980) through recourse to women's unsuitable personal and/or intellectual abilities (Zimmerman 1983, p. 3). Citing boys' higher scores on standardized Advanced Placement tests in physics, for example, psychologist Julian Stanley argues that "females" clearly face a "serious handicap in fields such as electrical engineering and mechanics," an innate mental limitation which renders it "inadvisable to assert that there *should* be as many female as male electrical engineers" (Stanley, cited in Fausto-Sterling 2000, p. 118). This sentiment has been echoed in professional newsletters, electronic discussion lists, and policy roundtables.

In contrast to explanations based on personal taste or ability, other writers chart the practices of social exclusion and privilege that encourage or discourage work in engineering (Hacker 1983). These practices include not only outright prohibition from certain schools, professional societies, or industrial workplaces, but also local, daily forms of humiliation. The engineering classmates of white suffragette Nora Stanton Blatch (1883–1971) once deliberately scheduled a date for the young woman so that she would not appear in a collective photograph (Oldenziel 2000, p. 21). Jennie R. Patrick battled constant psychological and physical violence in the newly integrated public schools of Gadsen, Alabama en route to becoming the first African-American woman to obtain a PhD in chemical engineering in the United States (Patrick 1989). Foreign-born women and men with experience in computer programming or electrical engineering entering the US under the H-1B visa program (a temporary employment visa for professionals) are continually subject to the vagaries of US immigration policy, policy which produces an uncommonly vulnerable (hence uncommonly compliant) labor force (Kumar 2001; Martín 2001). Awareness of the historical variability of gendered experience allows for new perspectives on practices of engineering in the United States.

Attention to gender not only transforms histories of familiar subjects like industrialization or engineering, but also expands our very sense of what – and who – constitutes "technology." As Ruth Oldenziel has noted, the very concept of *technology* bears the marks of its emergence amidst nineteenth-century racial, economic, and sexual hierarchies. Even today, Cheris Kramarae has suggested, the term typically refers to "the devices, machinery and processes which men are interested in" (Kramarae 1988, p. 4; Oldenziel 1999). So narrow has been this traditional association that historians tend to overlook even women's most public, visible involvement with metal and machines. To begin, we might remember that women, too, have always earned wages operating, maintaining, and repairing factory machinery: from the massive looms of the early nineteenth-century textile factory to the electronics assembly lines of today's *maquiladoras* and Free-Trade Zones (Peña 1997; Ong 1997). We might also note that women have been routinely employed as highly skilled technical laborers: from the command of telephone switchboards operators to the computation of ballistic trajectories (Lipartito 1994; Light 1999). Furthermore, we might note that the relevant "technology" in a workplace is not necessarily a computer, an assembly line, or even a piece of machinery. When asked why tasks at a McDonald's franchise tend to be sorted by gender, for instance, one worker's reply focused on the relevance of the arrangement of space and the heat of cooking surfaces. "[More women than men work window] because women are afraid of getting burned [on the grill], and men are afraid of getting aggravated and going over the counter and smacking someone" (quoted in Leidner 1993, p. 198). In other circumstances, cooking might be considered a feminine activity and public presentation might be considered a masculine activity; here gender works differently. Once again, particular technologies (a hamburger grill or cash register) become invested with the physical or emotional capacities of particular bodies, bodies which, in turn, become associated with particular types of wage labor.

Contemplation of the gendering of grill-work and counter-work begins to query relationships between mechanized (often masculinized) and unmechanized (often feminized) work – queries which provoke further transformation of our view of technological history. For instance, the "unmechanized" household, long treated by historians as an atavistic vestige of America's pre-industrial past, turns out to be completely enmeshed in the story of metal and machinery usually recounted in mainstream histories of technology. As McGaw suggests, "to explain the growth of cotton manufacture, meat packing, flour milling, and sugar refining, we will ultimately need to explain women's increasing conversion of cloth, meat, flour, and sugar into household linen, clothing, and a radically different family diet" (McGaw 1989, pp. 179–80). By foregrounding women's oft-ignored household labor, feminist historians have revealed the mutually constitutive relationships between household and factory, production and consumption, paid and unpaid work. Households appear not as exceptions to larger technological orders, but as their necessary site of enactment (Strasser 1982; Cowan 1983; Horowitz and Mohun 1998).

A consideration of unpaid, routine, privatized household labor also shifts attention to new artifacts. As Cowan astutely noted in 1979,

> The crib, the playpen, the teething ring and the cradle are as much a part of our culture and our sense of ourselves as harvesting machines and power looms, yet we know almost nothing of their history. (p. 32)

The very ubiquity of such objects, their constant presence in everyday life, eliminated them out of the purview of conventional history. Feminist research reveals the technical sophistication and social relevance of these forgotten objects, further extending the definition of "technology" beyond steam engines, telegraphs, and the racialized manhood associated with them. This research provides historical accounts of objects like model cars, dolls, cupboards, and refrigerators and their larger systems of use (Pursell 1979; Cowan 1987; Rand 1995; Horowitz 2001; Ulrich 2001).

Awareness of the significance of everyday objects and the significance of routine, unpaid labor has also extends a consideration of technological practice beyond the factory or household to the human body itself. As feminist theorist Gayle Rubin has noted, "men and women are closer to each other than either is to anything else – for instance, mountains, kangaroos, or coconut palms. Far from being an expression of natural differences, exclusive gender identity is the suppression of natural similarities" (Rubin 1975, p. 179). How "natural similarities" become intransigent differences is the focus of much recent scholarship on gender. In accounts of penile enlargement techniques, breast augmentation and reduction, or eyelid surgeries, the "separate spheres" of public/private, production/consumption, and mechanic/organic begin to collapse altogether (Kaw 1989; Haiken 1997; Zita 1998; Jacobson 2000; Friedman 2001). For example, Lisa Jones (1994) traces the rise of a lucrative transatlantic trade in human hair since the 1970s, and describes the global economic politics invested in the creation of this highly technologized, disposable commodity. The hair in this trade, usually grown on the heads of women in Asia or the former Soviet republics and processed by urban workers in New York, is not simply a product of human bodies. It eventually becomes part of the visceral experience of fashion seekers, burn victims, leukemia patients, alopecia sufferer, and other users. Embodied gender appears at once the cause and effect of particular technologies.

Nowhere have the relations between embodiment and larger social processes been subject to more sustained critical inquiry than in women's roles as reproducers, as "bearers and rearers of children" (McGaw 1982, p. 821). Popular discussions of reproductive technologies tend to focus on cloning, in vitro fertilization, or other highly visible devices, drugs, and techniques developed in the past 30 years (often referred to as "new reproductive technologies" or NRTs). Historians, however, have discussed a much broader range of tools, including abortifacient and emmenagogic supplements (from RU486/prostaglandin to herbal remedies such as pennyroyal or savin), fetal diagnostic and surveillance technologies (such as ultrasound, fetal monitors, amniocentesis, or pre-natal genetic screening), birthing intervention technologies (forceps, anesthetics, surgical vacuums), contraceptive and fertility enhancement technologies (intrauterine devices, pessaries, condoms, ovulation indicators), and so on. The invention of such technologies, historians have long noted, does not necessarily lead to their implementation, nor does implementation necessarily determine patterns of use. Indeed, studies of reproductive technology amplify the complexity of causality and agency. In the case of reproductive technology, even defining relevant subjects who might "cause" or "act" becomes a difficult analytical task. Consider the technology of sonography. Who, Saetnan asks, might we consider the "user" in the case of the sonograph?

> Is the physician who refers a patient for sonography and receives the lab results the user? Or is it the state, which sanctioned routine sonograms and pays their cost? What of the physician in charge of the sonography laboratory? Or the operator who conducts the examination? Or is the user the pregnant woman carrying the fetus being examined? Or her partner, who comes along to view the images? Or perhaps the fetus itself? (2000, pp. 15–16)

The status of users and user agency is further muddled by the complexity of the social processes which permeate sonography. We need only contemplate the place of the sonograph in the creation of fetal protection statutes, practices of selective abortion, or the transformation of the experience of pregnancy into an act of consumption to recognize the myriad dimensions of state, corporate, and cultural influence (Hubbard 1997; Roberts 1997; Taylor 2000).

Reproductive technologies such as sonographs and birth control pills also return historians to the ever-troubling matter of sexed bodies (Barad 1998). At first glance, of course, the development of new reproductive technologies seems a perfect argument against the contingency of sexual difference, a convincing demonstration of the irreducible, universal division between "male" and "female" underlying social practices of gender (e.g., "women menstruate, parturate and lactate; men do not"). The contraceptive efficacy of standardized dosages of hormones, for instance, seems to provide clear evidence of some transcultural, transhistorical womanliness. Seen in another light, however, the oral contraceptive pill appears to highlight the thoroughly historical – and technological – nature of bodies.

The pill was designed to mimic a "normal" 28-day menses, complete with a few "blank" pills at the end of each cycle to shutdown the hormonal supply. The resulting drop in hormonal levels produces a regular shedding of the uterine lining, a fabricated periodicity referred to as "letdown bleeds" or "hormone withdrawal bleeds" to distinguish it from "true menses" (Oudshoorn 1994; Potter 2001, p. 142). In this sense, ideas about female regularity and periodicity were built into the form and function of the pill. As we have learned, however, the politics of an artifact's design never determine outcome in a simple, linear way. Even in the drug's earliest trials, pill users appropriated the technology in their own ways and to their own ends, actively skipping or doubling pills (Marks 2000, p. 164). Increasing numbers of women and girls avoid monthly bleeding altogether by simply skipping the "blank" pills – raising the prospect of the technological "obsolescence" of women's menstruation (Coutinho and Segal 1999).

The prospect of the planned obsolescence of "the female curse" made possible by women's active appropriation of a sophisticated technology thus crystallizes lingering questions about relations between bodies and history, materiality and sociality, sex and gender. The lesson of the birth control pill is not that sexual differences are false or non-existent, but that sexual differences are constituted through specific technological activities. Like the subtle systems of governance embedded in the contemporary public toilet (how are water pipes metered for cost assessment and billing? What range of control does the thermostat allow, and to whom?), so, too, the pill embodies and regulates certain modes of being. Appreciating the density of relationships between gender and technology sharpens our understanding of both, and allows us to move beyond simplistic determinist claims about a technology's social "impact."

Yet appreciating the interconnections between gender and technology begins to beg a new question: if gender and technology are so thoroughly intertwined, can we reasonably continue to distinguish the two categories? Given the preponderance of psychopharmaceuticals, artificial limbs, pacemakers, and genetically modified foods, is there any reasonable line of demarcation between *gender* and *technology*? Despite much careful scholarship identifying the increasingly blurry boundaries between the organic and the mechanic and between male and female, embodied experience presents recurrent – even brutal – reminders that there are, at least for the time being, still crucial distinctions between the obduracy of artifacts and the mortality of human beings. Equally crucially, different forms of embodiment still engender context-specific, disproportionate vulnerabilities. We have already seen some of the consequences facing individuals found in the "wrong" public facility; far more deadly cases of gender enforcement are all too easy to list. In 1989, to take but one example, a 25-year-old man, armed with a Sturm Ruger Mini-14 semi-automatic rifle and bandoliers of ammunition, entered the University of Montréal School of Engineering and began systematically shooting all the women he could identify. By the end of his rampage, fourteen women were dead, and another thirteen people were wounded (Malette and Chalouh 1991). Distinctions between women and men – forged, maintained, and bolstered through mundane, repetitive technological activity – continue to come to rest in flesh, blood, and bone.

BIBLIOGRAPHY

Balsamo, Anne. *Technologies of the Gendered Body: Reading Cyborg Women* (Durham: Duke University Press, 1996).

Barad, Karen. "Getting real: technoscientific practices and the materialization of reality," *Differences* 10:2 (1998): 87–128.

Baron, Ava, ed. *Work Engendered: Toward a New History of American Labor* (Ithaca: Cornell University Press, 1991).

Berg, Anne-Jorunn and Merete Lie. "Feminism and constructivism: do artifacts have gender?" *Science, Technology, and Human Values* 20:3 (1995): 332–51.

Bijker, Wiebe, Thomas P. Hughes and Trevor Pinch, eds. *The Social Construction of Technological Systems* (Cambridge: MIT Press, 1987).

Briggs, Laura. "The race of hysteria: 'overcivilization' and the 'savage' woman in late nineteenth-century obstetrics and gynecology," *American Quarterly* 52:2 (June 2000): 246–73.

Cockburn, Cynthia. *Brothers: Male Dominance and Technical Change* (London: Pluto Press, 1983).

Cook, Gareth. "Debate opens anew on language and its effect on cognition," *The Boston Globe* (Thursday, February 14, 2002): A10.

Coutinho, Elsimar M. and Sheldon J. Segal. *Is Menstruation Obsolete?* (New York: Oxford University Press, 1999).

Cowan, Ruth Schwartz. "From Virginia Dare to Virginia slims: women and technology in American life," in Martha Moore Trescott, ed., *Dynamos and Virgins Revisited: Women and Technological Change in History* (Metuchen, NJ: Scarecrow Press, 1979): pp. 30–44.

Cowan, Ruth Schwartz. *More Work for Mother: The Ironies of Household Technology from the Open Hearth to the Microwave* (New York: Basic Books, 1983).

Cowan, Ruth Schwartz. "The consumption junction: a proposal for research strategies in the sociology of technology," in Wiebe E. Bijker, Thomas P. Hughes, and Trevor Pinch, eds, *The Social Construction of Technological Systems* (Cambridge: MIT Press, 1987): pp. 261–80.

Dublin, Thomas. *Women at Work: The Transformation of Work and Community in Lowell, Massachusetts, 1826–1860* (New York: Columbia University Press, 1979).

Fausto-Sterling, Anne. *Sexing the Body: Gender Politics and the Construction of Sexuality* (New York: Basic Books, 2000).

Friedman, David M. *A Mind of its Own: A Cultural History of the Penis* (New York: The Free Press, 2001).

Hacker, Sally L. "Mathematization of engineering: limits on women and the field," in Rothschild, Joan, ed. *Machina ex Dea: Feminist Perspectives on Technology* (New York: Pergamon Press, 1983): pp. 38–58.

Halberstam, Judith. "Techno-homo: on bathrooms, butches, and sex with furniture," in Jennifer Terry and Melodie Calvert, eds, *Processed Lives: Gender and Technology in Everyday Life* (New York: Routledge, 1997): pp. 183–93.

Haiken, Elizabeth. *Venus Envy: A History of Cosmetic Surgery* (Baltimore: Johns Hopkins University Press, 1997).

Haraway, Donna. *Simians, Cyborgs, and Women: The Reinvention of Nature* (New York: Routledge, 1991).

Hausman, Bernice L. *Changing Sex: Transsexualism, Technology, and the Idea of Gender* (Durham: Duke University Press, 1995).

Herndl, Diane Price. "The invisible (invalid) woman: African-American women, illness, and nineteenth-century narrative," in Judith Walker Leavitt, ed. *Women and Health in America*, 2nd edn (Madison: University of Wisconsin Press, 1999): pp. 131–45.

Higginbotham, Evelyn Brooks. "African-American women's history and the metalanguage of race," *Signs* 17:2 (Winter 1992): 251–74.

Hirschauer, Stefan. "Performing sexes and genders in medical practices," in Marc Berg and Annemarie Mol, eds. *Differences in Medicine: Unraveling Practices, Techniques, and Bodies* (Durham: Duke University Press, 1998): pp. 13–27.

Horowitz, Roger, ed. *Boys and Their Toys? Masculinity, Class, and Technology in America* (New York: Routledge, 2001).

Horowitz, Roger and Arwen Mohun, eds. *His and Hers: Gender, Consumption, and Technology* (Charlottesville: University Press of Virginia, 1998).

Hubbard, Ruth. "Abortion and disability," in Lennard J. Davis ed., *The Disability Studies Reader* (New York: Routledge, 1997): pp. 187–200.

Hughes, Thomas P. "The evolution of large technological systems," in Wiebe Bijker, Thomas P. Hughes, and Trevor Pinch, eds, *The Social Construction of Technological Systems* (Cambridge: MIT Press, 1987): pp. 51–82.

Jacobson, Nora. *Cleavage: Technology, Controversy, and the Ironies of the Man-Made Breast* (New Brunswick: Rutgers University Press, 2000).

Jeremy, David J. *Transatlantic Industrial Revolution: The Diffusion of Textile Technologies Between Britain and America, 1790–1830s* (Cambridge: MIT Press, 1981).

Jones, Lisa, "The hair trade," in *Bulletproof Diva: Tales of Race, Sex, and Hair* (New York: Doubleday, 1994): 278–97.

Kaw, Eugenia. "Medicalization of racial features: Asian American women and cosmetic surgery," *Medical Anthropology Quarterly* 7:1 (1989): 74–89.

Kessler, Suzanne. *Lessons from the Intersexed* (New Brunswick: Rutgers University Press, 1998).

Kramarae, Cheris. *Technology and Women's Voices: Keeping in Touch* (London: Routledge & Kegan Paul, 1988).

Kumar, Amitava. "Temporary access: the Indian H-1B worker in the United States," in Alondra Nelson and Thuy Linh N. Tu, with Alicia Headlam Hines, eds, *Technicolor: Race, Technology, and Everyday Life* (New York: New York University Press, 2001): pp. 76–87.

Law, John and John Hassard, eds. *Actor Network Theory and After* (Oxford: Blackwell, 1999).

Leidner, Robin. *Fast Food, Fast Talk: Service Work and the Routinization of Everyday Life* (Berkeley: University of California Press, 1993).

Lerner, Gerda. "Placing women in history: definitions and challenges," *Feminist Studies* 3 (Fall 1975): 5–14.

Lerman, Nina E. " 'Preparing for the duties and practical business of life': technical knowledge and social structure in mid-nineteenth-century Philadelphia," *Technology and Culture* 38 (January 1997).

Lerman, Nina E., Arwen Palmer Mohun, and Ruth Oldenziel. "The shoulders we stand on and the view from here: historiography and directions for research," *Technology and Culture* 38:1 (January 1997): 9–30.

Light, Jennifer. "When computers were women," *Technology and Culture* 40:3 (July 1999): 455–83.

Lipartito, Kenneth. "When women were switches: technology, work, and gender in the telephone industry, 1890–1920," *American Historical Review* 99:4 (October 1994): 1074–111.

MacKenzie, Donald and Judy Wajcman. "Introductory essay: the social shaping of technology," in *The Social Shaping of Technology* (Buckingham: Open University Press, 1999): pp. 3–27.

Malette, Louise and Marie Chalouh, eds. *The Montreal Massacre*, trans. Marlene Wildeman (Charlottetown, PEI: Gynergy Books, 1991).

Marks, Lara. "Parenting the pill: early testing of the contraceptive pill," in Ann Rudinow Saetnan, Nelly Oudshoorn, and Marta Kirejczyk, eds, *Bodies of Technology: Women's Involvement in Reproductive Medicine* (Columbus: Ohio State University Press, 2000): pp. 146–76.

Martín, Carlos E. "Mechanization and 'Mexicanization': racializing California's agricultural technology," *Science as Culture* 10:3 (2001): 301–26.

Marx, Leo and Merritt Roe Smith. "Introduction," in Merritt Roe Smith and Leo Marx, eds, *Does Technology Drive History? The Dilemma of Technological Determinism* (Cambridge: MIT Press, 1994).

McGaw, Judith A. "Women and the history of American technology," *Signs* 7:4 (1982): 798–828.

McGaw, Judith A. "No passive victims, no separate spheres: a feminist perspective on technology's history," in Stephen H. Cutcliffe and Robert C. Post, eds, *In Context: History and the History of Technology* (Bethlehem: Lehigh University Press, 1989): pp. 172–91.

McGaw, Judith A. *Most Wonderful Machine: Mechanization and Social Change in Berkshire Paper Making, 1801–1885* (Princeton: Princeton University Press, 1992 [1987]).

Oakley, Ann. *Sex, Gender, and Society* (New York: Harper & Row, 1972).

Oldenziel, Ruth. *Making Technology Masculine: Men, Women, and Modern Machines in America, 1870–1945* (Amsterdam: Amsterdam University Press, 1999).

Oldenziel, Ruth. "Multiple-entry visas: gender and engineering in the US, 1870–1945," in Annie Canel, Ruth Oldenziel and Karin Zachmann, eds, *Crossing Boundaries, Building Bridges: Comparing the History of Women Engineers, 1870s–1990s* (Amsterdam: Harwood Academic, 2000): pp. 11–49.

Ong, Aihwa. "The gender and labor politics of postmodernity," in Lisa Lowe and David Lloyd, eds, *Politics of Culture in the Shadow of Capital* (Durham: Duke University Press, 1997): pp. 61–97.

Oudshoorn, Nelly. *Beyond the Natural Body: An Archaeology of Sex Hormones* (London: Routledge, 1994).

Oudshoorn, Nelly. "Imagined Men: representations of masculinities in discourses on male contraceptive technology," in Ann Rudinow Saetnan, Nelly Oudshoorn, and Marta Kirejczyk, eds, *Bodies of Technology: Women's Involvement in Reproductive Medicine* (Columbus: Ohio State University Press, 2000): pp. 123–45.

Patrick, Jennie R. "Trials, tribulations, triumphs," *Sage* 6:2 (Fall 1989): 51–3.

Peña, Devon G. *The Terror of the Machine: Technology, Work, Gender, and Ecology on the U.S.-Mexico Border* (Austin: Center for Mexican American Studies, 1997): 177–212.

Potter, Linda S. "Menstrual Regulation and the Pill," in Etienne van de Walle and Elisha P. Renne, eds, *Regulating Menstruation: Beliefs, Practices, Interpretations* (Chicago: University of Chicago Press, 2001): pp. 141–54.

Pursell, Carroll W. "Toys, technology, and sex roles in America, 1920–1940," in Martha Moore Trescott, ed, *Dynamos and Virgins Revisited: Women and Technological Change in History* (Metuchen, NJ: Scarecrow Press, 1979): pp. 252–67.

Pursell, Carroll W. "The construction of masculinity and technology," *Polhem* 11 (1993): 206–19.

Rand, Erica. *Barbie's Queer Accessories* (Durham: Duke University Press, 1995).

Roberts, Dorothy. *Killing the Black Body: Race, Reproduction, and the Meaning of Liberty* (New York: Pantheon Books, 1997).

Rothschild, Joan, ed. *Machina ex Dea: Feminist Perspectives on Technology* (New York: Pergamon Press, 1983).

Rubin, Gayle. "The traffic in women: notes on the political economy of sex," in Rayna Reiter, ed., *Toward an Anthropology of Women* (New York: Monthly Review Press, 1975).

Saetnan, Ann Rudinow. "Women's involvement with reproductive medicine: introducing shared concepts," in Ann Rudinow Saetnan, Nelly Oudshoorn, and Marta Kirejczyk, eds, *Bodies of Technology: Women's Involvement with Reproductive Medicine* (Columbus: Ohio State University Press, 2000): pp. 1–30.

Scott, Joan Wallach. "Gender: a useful category of historical analysis," *Gender and the Politics of History* (New York: Columbia University Press, 1988): 28–50.

Stanley, Autumn. *Mothers and Daughters of Invention: Notes for a Revised History of Technology* (Metuchen, NJ: Scarecrow Press, 1993).

Stanley, Autumn. Review of Lance Day and Ian McNeil, eds, *Biographical Dictionary of the History of Technology, Isis* 91:2 (2000): 431–2.

Steinberg, Theodore. *Nature Incorporated: Industrialization and the Waters of New England* (Cambridge: Cambridge University Press, 1991).

Stepan, Nancy. "Race and gender: the role of analogy in science," in Evelyn Fox Keller and Helen E. Longino, eds, *Feminism and Science* (New York: Oxford University Press, 1996): pp. 121–36.

Strasser, Susan. *Never Done: A History of American Housework* (New York: Pantheon Books, 1982).

Taylor, Janelle S. "Of sonograms and baby prams: prenatal diagnosis, pregnancy, and consumption," *Feminist Studies* 26:2 (Summer 2000): 391–418.

Ulrich, Laurel Thatcher. *The Age of Homespun: Objects and Stories in the Creation of an American Myth* (New York: Alfred A. Knopf, 2001).

Wajcman, Judy. *Feminism Confronts Technology* (University Park, PA: Pennsylvania State University Press, 1991).

Zimmerman, Jan, ed. *The Technological Woman: Interfacing with Tomorrow* (New York: Praeger, 1983).

Zita, Jacquelyn N. *Body Talk: Philosophical Reflections on Sex and Gender* (New York: Columbia University Press, 1998).

CHAPTER TWELVE

Labor and Technology

ARWEN P. MOHUN

How does technological change affect the way work gets done? How do social and cultural factors shape the organization of work and the design of workplace technologies? What does it mean to be "skilled" or "unskilled"? Historians of technology have been most attracted to questions about labor concerning the physical process of work itself (rather than issues such as the formation of unions or labor politics). In opening up the technological "black boxes" of tools, machines, and workprocess, they endeavor to understand how the material and social aspects of labor are intertwined, each shaping the other. In the past, topics of broader interest in the field, including the history of engineering (especially Taylorism) and innovation in industrial manufacturing processes, helped guide the development of scholarship. More recently, the field has also given attention to the relationships between paid and unpaid work, and production and consumption. Scholars have also focused on the definition and proliferation of technological knowledge and the role of gender in shaping work and technology.

An Overview of Themes

In 1932, at the height of the Great Depression, Edsel Ford (1893–1943) commissioned the Mexican muralist, Diego Rivera (1886–1957), to create a series of frescoes illustrating the theme "Detroit Industry" in the central courtyard of the Detroit Institute of the Arts (DIA). Rivera was a Marxist, deeply critical of the class relations of monopoly capitalism. But he was also a technophile, a believer in technological progress and an enthusiast about many of the material products of industrialization (Downs 1999). The images he created for the DIA express his ambivalent and complex understanding of the costs and benefits of industrialization. They simultaneously celebrate the technological ingenuity of Detroit's industrialists and the sublimity of large machines, while condemning the dehumanizing qualities of work within these "master machines," in ways that continue to capture the imaginations of historians.

Rivera interpreted the theme of "Detroit industry" broadly. The mural's twenty-seven panels depict a variety of topics from the origins of agriculture to the production of poison bombs. However, the largest and most central panels depict the assembly line and foundry at Ford Motor Company Rouge automobile assembly plant. "The Rouge," as it was widely known, was the ambitious creation of Edsel's father Henry

Ford (1886–1957). It was, at the time it opened, one of the largest factories in the world. In the interwar era, its fame spread throughout the industrializing world as a model for the systematization of mass production; considered so paradigmatic, in fact, that the term "Fordism" was widely used, even outside the United States to describe this strategy of production (Hughes 1989).

In both panels, the gray, metal body of the assembly line snakes like a living thing back and forth across the huge expanse of the mural. Workers bend and twist in rhythm with this mechanical beast. Like the crazed factory worker in Charlie Chaplin's 1936 film, *Modern Times*, one can imagine them unable to shake off its cadence even outside the factory gates. What Rivera's images do not make apparent is that these mechanized men have also entered into one of the great Faustian bargains of modernity. In exchange for submitting to the dictates of mechanization, they received the then extraordinary wage of $5 a day, enabling them to purchase bountiful, low priced, mass-produced consumer goods that such technological innovation made possible. Along with millions of other Americans, they might, in fact, someday purchase an automobile. But for assembly line workers, the price was more than simply $500 at the dealer's. Killing speed, mind-numbing repetition, subjugation to the dehumanizing logic of the assembly line constituted the trade-off for participation in the market economy.

Workers' enslavement to the rhythm of the assembly line and the dictates of monopoly capitalism is certainly an essential and distinctive characteristic of this particular work/technology relationship. But it is a vision that severely limits workers' own agency. Historians have shown that even on the assembly line, men and women carved out space for themselves and defined the meaning of their work in ways that defied their bosses and the logic of the machine (Meyer 2001). It is also clear that there were real limits even to Ford's ingenuity in the application of mechanization techniques. In the nooks and crannies of the Rouge (and the background of Rivera's mural), women still sewed upholstery piece by piece while machinists and other craftsmen made the machines that made the cars.

And were we to follow the automobiles as they jerked off the chain and moved out past the gates of the factory, the full complexity of the relationship between technology and wage labor would become even more apparent. Even in the twentieth century, not all work or perhaps even most work fit the mass-production paradigm. New technologies brought with them new needs for workers that were not tied to the mechanics of production and old ways of making and doing things persisted because it was neither economically nor technically possible to mechanize them. Much as capitalists (and sometimes consumers) might wish for total control, all the historical evidence suggests that mechanization was and is an uneven and unpredictable process.

"The mechanic will gyp you," automobile owners have been warning each other since the dawn of automobility. Their warning carried with it not only the bitter taste of experience but also a middle-class anxiety about being dependent upon the technical knowledge of working-class men to keep their machines on the road. If some mechanics might take advantage of their customers, others could use that knowledge to improvise solutions to mechanical problems unimagined by the automobile's designers and producers. If computer diagnostics and modular parts now threaten to undermine the mechanic's autonomy, for the first one hundred years of this technology's existence, a screwdriver, wrench set, and a good ear could suffice to put many machines back on the road. Occasionally, as in the work of the rural New York mechanic described by Douglas Harper, such mechanics might even improve upon the ideas of the original designers (Harper 1987).

"Automobile mechanic" was a new job in the twentieth century that evolved alongside America's dependence upon a complex machine that needed regular main-tenance and frequent repairs. Henry Ford might have been able to create the means to produce an inexpensive automobile, but he could not have designed one that could be used without the intervention of this other group of workers. Nor would he necessarily have considered that to be essential. After all, early twentieth-century America was full of machines that required maintenance and repair (Borg 1999). A host of other workers also used automobiles and automobility to earn a daily wage in ways that increased rather than lessened their independence. Teamsters, ubiquitous in urbanizing America, gradually found themselves liberated from the challenges of maintaining and managing horses. Like chauffeurs, taxi, and bus drivers, they parlayed the skill of driving into a myriad of other livelihoods. In the same way, the introduction of other new technologies, most recently computers, has resulted in many different kinds of work, not all of which involved mindless, repetitive enslavement to machines and their capitalist owners.

If we were to follow the workers rather than their products off the floor of the Rouge, we might discover something else. Workers are also consumers and consumption is a means through which people in industrialized societies decide how work will be done, who will do the work, and what it will be worth in the market place. For instance, the hard-earned dollars of the assembly line worker might be used to purchase a washing machine or it might be used to pay someone else to do the laundry. The consequences of these technological choices rippled out across the American landscape, transforming how and where work was done for everyone from housewives to farmers to line workers at the Rouge.

It is important to recognize, however, that while industrialization may have changed how all kinds of work were done, wage laborers' relationship to technological change differed from that of housewives and farmers in some very fundamental ways. First of all, the primary purpose of most production technologies (such as looms or stamping presses or assembly lines) is to create wealth for capitalists by adding value to the labor of workers. Tools and machines are prostheses that make workers stronger, faster, and more accurate than they would be working with their bare hands. Or, more chillingly, the worker becomes prosthesis of the machine, a "hand" facilitating its work. Ultimately, the process is what matters, not the needs or desires of the individual worker who conducts it.

While all users of technology make choices about how it will be used, in the process of reshaping the technology itself, workers' choices are often circumscribed by the power relationships of wage labor. Workers may exercise some choice about the type of employment sought, but once in a job, most can make only minor changes to the technologies they use. This is particularly true of the machine operatives and assembly line workers. In the former case, because they do not own the machines they use but must adapt themselves to the machine. In the latter case, it is because they control only a tiny part of a process which is severely circumscribed in time and space by the rhythm and organization of a larger process. This lack of control is, of course, less true about workers who use tools and those who engage in processes outside the regimes of mass production.

Workers' relative powerlessness in shaping the technologies they use has had profound historical consequences. Mindless and powerful, the new machines that became more and more a part of workers' lives with industrialization, tore the unsuspecting limb from limb or more slowly twisted and crippled bodies forced to adapt to their imperatives. In linking productive technologies into a system, assembly lines forced workers into a kind of time-and-physical discipline that defied nature. The alienation produced by such lock-step discipline surpassed even the familiar tedium of stepping behind a plow or hemming sheets and tablecloths. Mechanization not only requires workers to work *with* machines that are not always of their choosing, but also to work *like* a machine.

Technological knowledge also takes on distinctive characteristics in the context of wage labor. In this setting, it is almost always equated with "skill." Skill implies not only abstract knowledge about a particular technology or process, but also the ability to manipulate or use it successfully. For instance, the knowledge base of a skilled automobile mechanic is different than that of an automotive engineer because the engineer primarily needs a theoretical knowledge of how cars work. On the other hand, theoretical knowledge does the mechanic no good if he or she cannot fix a specific car. Skilled workers tend to be difficult to replace because substitutes cannot be rapidly trained. Both formal training and tacit knowledge – a "knack" with technology – constitute skill. Historians have noted that in American history, workers' claims about who has skill and how it is acquired is often defined by divisions within the working class based on race, ethnicity, and gender (Milkman 1987). White men in relatively unmechanized trades have often claimed a monopoly. It also turns out that when historians have looked at the actual content of work, the claim to be skilled is only partly based in workers' technological knowledge. Skill, to a certain extent, is in the eyes of the beholder (Mohun 1996).

Mechanization and Nineteenth-Century Industrialization

The assembly line at River Rouge is the progeny of a long lineage of industrial workplaces. It shares with them characteristics going back to the first years of the Industrial Revolution. Even the earliest eighteenth-century textile mills gathered workers in one place, divided up work processes between increasingly specialized machines and workers, and used mechanization to replace traditional skills and animal power (Landes 1969). In the majority of these workplaces, more and more workers became machine operatives – "hands" – whose relationship with technology involved tending automated looms and spinning machines, filling in gaps where machine-makers could not find the mechanical means to tie together broken threads, load fresh bobbins, or adjust for differences in organic materials.

Without doubt, even these tasks required a certain kind of skill – the knack of setting up a machine, of listening for a sound that meant something was not working correctly – but this was not the kind of skill that took years of practice to acquire. Nor was it the kind of skill that craft guilds felt compelled to protect. For these reasons, machine operatives often came from the social groups with the least access to the lengthy training process of apprenticeships and with the least power to command high wages: women, recent immigrants, and, in the twentieth century, African-Americans. In the United States, manufacturers were particularly drawn to women because they would work for lower wages and seemed, at least initially, to be only transient members of proletanized labor. They also rationalized their choices by arguing that women were naturally more tolerant of the tedious repetition that characterized such jobs and incapable of the kind of independent decision-making that characterized more skilled (and highly paid) forms of work.

Conventions of assuming some industrial jobs would always be done by men and others by women ("sexual division of labor") both derived from and contradicted the patterns established in household and pre-industrial labor. Technological knowledge acquired by women in the home such as sewing or ironing could help provide a pathway to industrial employment. But other jobs were regendered in the process of being industrialized. In textile mills, women tended looms but men operated the mules – machines that drew out thread. This is despite the fact that in cottage industry, men had often been the weavers and women the spinners. Machine manufacturers even built these newly developed social conventions into the size and shape of devices workers would operate. Most women, for example, were not tall enough to comfortably operate the mules because machine-builders assumed a male worker.

Throughout much of the nineteenth century, only a minority of industrial wage-workers shared the operative's relationship to technology. And even where mechanization was utilized, it extended just to discrete parts of a process that could be done by a single individual on a stationary machine. Factory floors swarmed with workers carrying raw materials, tools and parts, and finished goods from machine to machine, storeroom to workroom. Crafty mechanics and manufacturers gradually figured out ways to make the parts of complicated devices like sewing machines and bicycles so that they could be fitted together with a minimum of adjustment from randomly chosen parts. But the actual assembly process still took place on something very much like the workman's bench under the guidance of a generalist who understood how the entire object should fit together.

Outside the brick walls of factory buildings, more and more people also found themselves drawn into wage labor. Their interactions with technology, new and old, varied widely. In the lofts and tenement rooms of Boston, New York, and Philadelphia, women took the sewing skills learned at their mothers' knees and earned a living stitching together sailors' shifts and men's shirts with a needle and thread. This kind of work bridged the pre-industrial with the industrial, unpaid domestic "women's work" with the market economy. After the introduction of the sewing machine in the 1840s, some saved their pennies and bought a machine to speed the process while many others moved to the lofts of small-time jobbers. Even while the home gradually ceased to be a site of productive labor for the middle and upper classes, working-class people churned out an extraordinary variety of goods for the consumer market, using little more than their fingers and a few simple tools. Artificial flowers, boxes, matches, fur and feather pulling were among the many activities that went on in the cramped quarters of their tenement rooms.

Other workers interacted with the newest and most sophisticated technologies of their age but in fundamentally different ways than their brothers, sisters, and cousins who toiled in factories. Railroads, for instance, provided employment to more than 400,000 Americans in 1880 (Licht 1983, p. 33). While the backbreaking labor of loading cars and laying track must have seemed utterly familiar to tired men with long histories as day laborers, the technology of railroads provided a strikingly new kind of work environment for other employees. The work of engineers, firemen, brakeman, and car-couplers brought them into daily contact with the most powerful machines that most nineteenth-century Americans would see in their lifetimes. Unlike the steam engines that drove more and more factories, they operated in public for all to see, tearing violently across the landscape. It is no wonder that little boys of that era dreamed of growing up to be engineers and grown-ups shuddered at the potential destructive power of the same technology.

Railroad work also differed from other kinds of wage labor because it involved a technological system that operated across time in space in an era in which most technology was specific and local. Workers had to learn to think in a new way about how their actions: a switch thrown incorrectly, a locomotive repaired badly, could affect strangers hundreds or even thousands of miles away. By 1877, they had learned the lessons of time-space transcending technologies well enough to create the first national strike, spread along the rail lines from its origins in West Virginia.

As machines became larger, more powerful, and more often the locus of work, accidents also became more frequent and more severe. The grim toll of railroad fatalities is particularly illustrative of callousness with which many nineteenth-century capitalists made choices about the design and deployment of workplace technology. Worker fatalities on railroads averaged 3.14 per thousand workers (Aldrich 1997, p. 15). Since railroad employment included relatively low-risk jobs such as taking tickets and cleaning cars, the percentages within the most dangerous job categories were substantially higher. Such numbers did not even take into account non-fatal injuries.

Railroad company executives resisted adopting technologies like air brakes, auto-matic coupling, and engine stoking despite the widespread concurrence that these devices that would make railroad labor safer and easier for workers. They reasoned that it was cheaper to pay an occasional death benefit to the widow of a worker crushed between cars than to expend large amounts of capital to renovate the tens of thousands of railroad cars already in use. This began to change substantially only with the intervention of the Federal Government through the passage of the Safety Appliance Act in 1893 (Aldrich 1997, p. 172). As a consequence of this peculiar form of technological conservativism, bystanders observing the passage of this quintessentially modern machine through the landscape might still catch sight of brakemen skittering along the tops of cars and struggling to turn the manual brakes up into that decade (or even later on some freight lines). Other trainmen displayed their profession's stigmata of missing fingers, hands and feet – some of the lesser consequence of standing between two railroad cars in order to couple them together. The loss of limbs was so common among railroad workers in the nineteenth century that worker magazines ran advertisements for prostheses and employers looked to hire workers who had already lost fingers with the idea that they would be more careful than their undamaged fellows.

This kind of involvement with large, dangerous, charismatic technologies – particularly work involving large objects or processes involving iron and steel – was a masculine domain. The work itself might be dirty, repetitious, and bone-breaking but it was also a source of fierce pride for the workers who participated in it. Association with such technologies was a source of cultural power. Male workers did their utmost to gender these technologies and the processes involved in making and using them male. In many occupations, they not only excluded women, but also defended their territory against the incursion of African-American men and men who belonged to ethnic groups, that seemed, in the ever-changing schema of American racial categories, to be less than white – Italians, Irish, Eastern European Jews. They made their claim by utilizing and creating a set of cultural ideas about the gendered meaning of work and gendered technological competence that remain powerfully embedded in American culture. No woman drove a locomotive for an American railroad until 1969, more than 25 years after the introduction of diesel engines put an end to any last claims about the significance of physical strength for such a job. A half-century earlier, the identification between masculinity and railroading was so powerful that the Pennsylvania Railroad, then America's largest railroad company, employed men even in the kinds of clerical positions that were gendered female in most other businesses.

Nowhere was the identification between gender, race, technology, and prestige more obvious than in the culture of machine shops. Machinists controlled a techno-logical skill key to the process of industrialization: they knew how to construct machinery with the control and precision that made it possible to mechanize production. Carefully measuring and setting their machines, they peeled away layers of metal to make everything from mechanized looms to the huge steam engines that drove the workings of an increasing number of factories. Any error and pistons would stick, gears fail to mesh, and the worker's knowledge built into the machine would manifest itself as an ill-wrought piece of goods. It is little wonder that these men considered themselves the aristocracy of labor, that they held their heads up high as they headed to work in their ties and bowler hats, that they commanded high wages and defied their employer's efforts to control their pace of work or shop-floor culture.

Scale, Scope, and Systematization, 1880–1920

The late nineteenth century marked another watershed in the changing relationship between workers and technology in the workplace. Jobs like machinist, locomotive engineer, and artificial flower maker survived virtually unchanged well into the twentieth century, but became less and less the norm in industrial production. In part, the change came through the continually mounting pace of mechanization. A growing number of inventors and innovators bent their minds to creating machines to do everything from folding cardboard boxes to stirring molten steel. Increasing scale also played a role. Larger factories led to more and more minute divisions of labor. Economies of scale demanded the adoption of enormous, complex machines.

This technological culture also gave rise to a self-created group of systematizers who self-consciously applied themselves to the process of "rationalizing" the workplace. Like their predecessors, part of their aim was explicitly economic: to lower the price of finished goods by reducing labor costs and making production more efficient. But rationalization also equated with shifting more control over work processes from workers into the domain of managers. By the 1910s and 1920s, this set of ideas and practices had evolved into something resembling an ideology, sometimes referred to as the "gospel of efficiency." It brought a kind of factory-logic out from behind factory walls and into all kinds of work, paid and unpaid.

The efficiency movement is often identified with Frederick Winslow Taylor (1856–1915) and his followers, proselytizers of a mixed bag of rationalizing techniques they called "scientific management." But the origins of this wave of rationalization and its eventual manifestation in technologies like the assembly line are more widespread. Historians have found their roots not in *productive* industries like textile manufacture, but in *processing* industries like steel manufacturing and meat processing (Biggs 1996). They point out that these two types of industries provide different kinds of challenges to rationalizers. In productive industries, each step of the processes must be carried out correctly or the results will show in the end product. Production involves many more types of skilled workers than processing. In processing, much of the work involved simply moving materials through each step of the process. In nineteenth century iron-and-steel manufacturing, for instance, the most skilled workers were the puddlers who judged the quality and readiness of molten metal in the smelter. Experience and careful judgment was also required in preparing the beds for casting and in a few other tasks, but the vast majority of steel workers provided the strength of their backs and the flexibility of human arms and legs. It was these less-skilled workers who were the first target of factory rationalizers.

The great innovation of this first generation of systematizers was to use mechanical means to move work from place to place – conveyor belts, chain drives, etc. Without question, such innovations saved a great deal of backbreaking labor. But in the meat-packing industry, the other implications for workers became immediately apparent. Where once individual butchers had considered each animal carcass as distinctive, shaped by nature in ways that required individual consideration in the process of dismemberment, meatpacking workers now focused only on a single part of the animal.

Eight or more hours a day they repeatedly removed the same leg, stripped out the same viscera, sectioned virtually the same portion of meat. On the chain drive, the carcass then passed onward as another one rapidly took its place. Division of labor eliminated the lengthy training traditional butchers underwent to understand the complex anatomy of cattle, making it possible to hire cheaper, more replaceable workers. Bringing the carcasses to workers mechanically eliminated some of the hard physical labor of moving large pieces of meat around. This "disassembly line" historians have argued, is the direct predecessor of Henry Ford's production assembly line (Hounshell 1984).

Taylor's role in the process of rethinking industrial labor was as much cultural as material. He and his followers turned a set of practical techniques for improving manufacturing into an ideology, a set of beliefs about how all of society could and should be organized. Taylor claimed that any process could be analyzed and system-atized using his techniques. The "human factor" as it later came to be called would be treated analytically as part of a mechanical system. In a particularly telling statement he asserted, "In the past, the man must be first; in the future, the system will be first" (Kanigel 1997).

Taylor's system was complex, involving a variety of often-sensible changes to the disorganized, ad hoc organization of workplaces. But he is best remembered and was most controversial in his own time for the introduction of "time motion study." This technique purportedly allowed experts with stopwatches to analyze the movements of workers carrying out a particular process. This information was used to establish the "one best way" to do a job and a standard pace at which the job should be carried out. Once the method and pace had been established, workers could be retrained to work more quickly and penalized if they did not through the use of piece rates. Trying to get management control over the pace of work was nothing new in American industry, but Taylor also made a radical claim: this system would benefit both employers and workers. Workers would learn how to work more efficiently and would therefore earn more money. Production would increase, resulting in bigger profits for employers (Kanigel 1997).

Significantly, Taylor's claims about the origins of his system did not begin with watching workers on a factory floor assembling consumer goods. In his own telling, it began with observing a manual laborer employed to load pigs of iron onto a railroad car in a Philadelphia area steel mill. "Schmidt," as he was called in Taylor's accounts, had somehow found the means to lift and carry the pigs more easily than his fellow workers. Taylor broke down and analyzed each of Schmidt's simple movements and then improved upon them. He offered Schmidt a financial incentive to carry out his work according to Taylor's instructions and had soon increased his pace. Schmidt was soon toting 47 *tons* of iron each day under Taylor's tutelage and careful scrutiny.

After Taylor set up shop as a consultant to industry in 1893, time-motion study became a new locus of conflict between workers and employers. Workers resented the incursion of outsiders who claimed to be able to understand the essential character of their work with only cursory examination. They also recognized that, in practice, the piece rates set on the basis of such studies were set in such a way that the profits from added productivity would largely go into the pockets of employers. And they recognized that such close scrutiny gave foremen and forewomen the power to stop practices such as soldiering, taking unauthorized breaks, and making informal agreements about the pace of work.

Initially, capitalists' efforts to use time-motion study to improve efficiency and gain shop-floor control took place quietly, behind the gates of individual factories. But in 1910, a strike at the US Government's Watertown Arsenal led to a Congressional hearing, which put the labor implications of Taylorism on trial. Molders in the arsenal's foundry had walked out in protest of the presence of an efficiency expert trying to establish appropriate times and therefore piece rates for their work. They claimed that the expert lacked enough specific knowledge to be able to fairly say how long any given job would take. In 1916, two of the Taylorists' most distinctive tools, time-motion studies and their particular methods of setting wage rates, were banned from government contractors' workplaces for the next 33 years (Aiken 1985 [1960], pp. 234–5).

Ford's assembly line combined these two ways of thinking about rationalizing production (bring the work to worker, treat the worker as a machine, as part of a system). Without doubt, these techniques made it much cheaper to manufacture many kinds of goods. But assembly line work also offered employers unprecedented control over the pace and character of work. Previously, employers had largely relied on surveillance, piece rates, and the tyranny of the factory clock to keep workers churning out goods. The assembly line much more effectively imprisoned workers in time and space. Like the meatpacking industry's disassembly line that had partly inspired it, the chain drive and its subsidiary conveyors and belts brought the work to the worker. No more getting up to get materials or to sharpen tools or to take finished products away. No more soldiering because the line set the pace of work. In some cases, the "hand" did not even seem to need his or her legs anymore except to clock in at the beginning of the shift. Nor did he or she have any sense of the complete logic of the object being assembled.

It should be pointed out that neither the technology of the assembly line nor the efforts to rationalize work was inherently anti-worker. Systematizers often claimed that greater efficiency would ultimately benefit everyone by leading to greater production, higher profits, and the elimination of unnecessary work. Workers themselves also recognized that many nineteenth-century workplaces were badly organized and frustratingly inefficient. They also resented the sometimes-capricious judgment of all-powerful foremen. They welcomed efforts to improve production and to eliminate unnecessary work. Industrialization had, in fact, involved a long history of workers themselves contributing to the improvement of machines and processes, but in practice, new production and management techniques were mostly put in place by employers to control workers and increase profits.

Henry Ford became a hero in his own age for the innovations he oversaw. But capitalists in a wide variety of other industries could only dream about intensive mechanization and systematization. It was not possible to simply wave a magic wand and create a machine to replace proud, expensive craft workers. For others, the dream was futile despite the existence of viable technology. For instance, batch producers in small shops turning out small amounts of goods found new machinery uneconomical and cumbersome. It was cheaper, if more exasperating, to stay with simpler tools and more expensive, independent workers (Scranton 1997).

Other products simply did not lend themselves to mechanization or assembly line techniques. Ford's efforts to apply mass-production methods to make ships for World War I proved an expensive failure. The size and complexity of large vessels simply did not lend itself to his methods. In a completely different way, commercial laundry owners found ironing machines and other devices could help them increase the scale of their factories and eliminate the most expensive workers. But progress came with a cost. Their "raw materials" – shirts, tablecloths, and undergarments – could not be standardized. All machine processing involves a certain amount of destruction and waste, particularly if some materials are more delicate than others. This kind of waste was not acceptable to customers who wanted their heirloom napkins and favorite shirtwaists back, clean and intact (Mohun 1999).

As capitalist enterprises had grown in size and complexity, more and more workers found themselves employed not to piece together a material product, but rather to help operate the information technologies that coordinated companies employing hundreds of thousands of employees often spread over great distances. Others, particularly women, took on the growing number of clerical jobs in businesses that primarily dealt in information such as banks and insurance companies.

Historians have pointed out that as early as the 1840s, railroad companies used paperwork to control far-flung employees such as stationmasters who collected money for the company. But the so-called great merger movement of the late 1890s is a watershed in the establishment of a large number of truly huge, bureaucratized corporations. Some of the largest of these companies were banks and insurance companies. They did not produce a material product at all. Instead, they dealt in information. Early twentieth-century statistics from the Metropolitan Life Insurance Company provide a dizzying testament to the amount of human labor needed to manage information in the age before computers. The filing system alone took up two floors of the company's New York headquarters. Sixty-one employees spent their days keeping track of twenty-million insurance applications, 700,000 accounting books, and half-a-million death certificates. In the same building, women, organized into huge typing pools, bent over rows of typewriters churning out the endless reams of correspondence and paperwork needed to coordinate this massive enterprise. In 1915, one writer estimated that 1,170 typewriters were in use in the Metropolitan building (Zunz 1990, pp. 114–15).

In an earlier period, a small number of male clerks had toiled to keep the ledgers of manufacturers and financial institutions. This job was widely seen as a steppingstone to a management position, a way to "learn the company." As companies grew larger and the need for paperwork increased far beyond the capacity of the company to promote clerks, clerical work became feminized. Mid-nineteenth-century male clerks had conducted their work using technologies that pre-dated industrialization: bound ledger books and quill pens. The ability to write a "fine hand" was a marketable skill that ambitious young men worked hard to acquire. Feminization of clerical work coincided with the introduction of a variety of office machines that, like their industrial counterparts, were intended to speed up and systematize the passage of information through offices (Davis 1982). The introduction of the typewriter was particularly significant. One of the clerk's jobs was to write letters and create documents on behalf of his employer. However, the personal character of handwriting and the interpretation inherent in creating that correspondence meant that he was a visible intermediary in the process. Letters churned out by a typing pool lacked any such personal dimension. Secretaries could even compose letters or documents for their employers and then have their intellectual labor rendered completely invisible once the letter was typed up and signed by someone else.

The feminization of office work was clearly driven by the economics of female labor. Women also sought out these jobs because they were cleaner and carried more status in the marriage market than factory work, while men avoided them because they did not pay well and offered little hope of promotion. Despite the obvious economics of sexual division of labor, employers and manufacturers of office machinery went to great lengths to justify the technological dimensions of these jobs on gendered grounds. Using the typewriter, they argued, is very much like playing the piano (an activity that was also gendered female in Victorian America). Other office technologies also helped employers re-gender office work. The adding machine and time clock contributed to the development of a new, largely female office job – the comptometer – an employee who not only added up hours worked for a payroll office, but also compiled statistics on work hours and productivity for efficiency experts (Strom 1992).

Consumption, Work, and Urbanization

The changing spatial character of work in late nineteenth-century America also had profound consequences in workers' relationship to technology. Early factories had often been situated in rural settings, in villages perched on the banks of fast-running streams and rivers. The first generations of industrial workers slipped easily back and forth between wage labor and subsistence agriculture. Late nineteenth-century wage labor was increasingly based in cities or in situations in which workers were utterly dependent on the market for the necessities of everyday life. Moreover, the technologies they used at work and in their homes bore less and less resemblance to each other.

This distancing between home and work and growing dependence on the marketplace was part of a larger historical phenomenon. Historians have pointed out that the rapid expansion of the industrialization of production in the late-nineteenth century coincided with widespread changes in habits of consumption. In effect, this marked an extraordinary transformation in where and how work was done. Almost all Americans increasingly bought what they once would have made. While the wealthier classes had always paid other people to do things for them, industrialization physically and economically separated producers and consumers. Early nineteenth-century housewives had often worked alongside their servants or "helps" preparing food or making clothes or other household goods. Servants remained a fact of middle- and upper-class life until World War II but industrialization changed their roles and the roles of their employers. As more and more people purchased the shoes, shirts, bread, and soap their grandparent had fashioned at home, the household became a center of consumption rather than production. Middle-class women gradually became household managers. Servants (except, perhaps the cook) filled non-productive roles such as household cleaning and maintenance, nursing and child-minding, running errands and making household purchases. And men's unpaid household labor almost completely disappeared from urban and suburban households until the emergence of a mid-twentieth century emergence of the culture of male home improvement hobbies.

The great labor conflicts of the late nineteenth and first half of the twentieth centuries were partly fueled by this emergence of a new kind of consumer culture and the growing distance between producers and consumers. Higher wages were central to workers' demands, commensurate with what was termed an "American Standard of Living." In these discussions, workers defined themselves as citizen consumers. They argued that society owed them more than bare subsistence – a Malthusian existence. Meat as well as bread, houses, automobiles, and eventually washing machines were their due (Glickman 1997). This set of rights also imagined a division between male work and female consumption and unpaid household labor. Men would be paid a "living wage" so that their wives and daughters could stay out of the labor market. Demands for shorter work hours also accompanied the commodification of leisure and the disappearance (particularly of men's) productive labor out of the household. Coney Island, the corner saloon, and sales floor of an urban department store all beckoned on a Saturday afternoon. Most employers were slow to realize that their workers could also be their customers, that higher wages might result in greater sales. For producers of raw materials like steel, the connection did indeed seem tenuous, but for producers of consumer goods, like Henry Ford, an employee parking lot full of Model T's was testament to the hidden economic logic of the five-dollar day.

In turn, the distancing of production from consumption meant the middle and upper classes also had less and less of a sense of personal responsibility towards the invisible legions that sewed their clothing, packaged their crackers and candy, and assembled their automobiles. By the early twentieth century, progressive reformers had begun trying to rekindle that connection, sometimes by using the objects themselves to evoke the lives of invisible workers. Middle-class members of the Consumers' League, for example, led a series of efforts to convince female consumers to buy only products made under conditions beneficial to workers. A 1928 campaign, for example, called attention to the unsanitary and unpleasant conditions in which women workers hand-dipped chocolates. It is a testament to the distance between these workers and consumers, that candy purchasers responded not by demanding better conditions for workers, but by switching to machine-made confections presumably made in more sanitary conditions (Cooper 1998).

An older, pre-industrial technological regime offered few options in doing the most basic kinds of day-to-day work. For instance, in the preparation of food, one could cook a meal one's self or pay someone else to do it, using ingredients very close to their natural state. The rapid technological transformation of both paid and unpaid work provided consumers with a wide range of choices in how such work might be done and by whom. The late twentieth-century consumer can make a meal from the same kinds of raw materials as his or her eighteenth-century predecessor or microwave a prepared dinner or open and heat a can or buy already prepared food that might or might not be delivered to the home. Each choice involves different technologies and different kinds of labor, for instance, different modes of farming (factory or organic? local or international?), workers to prepare and deliver it (who makes frozen entrees and how?). In effect, consumption becomes an act of deciding how, where, and by whom work will be done.

Historically, these choices have been driven by a wide variety of factors. Some forms of work, performed domestically, carry powerful emotional meanings. They are, particularly for women in the roles of housewife and mother, labors of love and therefore worth keeping within the home. Until very recently, food preparation seemed to fall into this category (Cowan 1983). Other tasks have moved in and out of the home depending upon the technologies available both commercially and domestically. For instance, with the introduction of paper dress patterns in the late nineteenth century, many women who had paid dressmakers to make their clothes began to do the work themselves. The introduction of looser fitting styles, more amenable to mass production, and standardized sizes in the interwar years shifted the balance towards factory-made garments (Gamber 1997).

Most historians have focused their attention on middle-class consumers. But workers are also consumers. They also make choices about where work will be done. For instance, early twentieth-century reformers lamented the tendency of working-class women to buy baked goods and deli food rather than preparing inexpensive stews and breads at home. Their assumption that homemade was better ignored the domestic technologies and time constraints with which workers struggled. Tiny stoves in hot tenement rooms fueled by expensive fuel made the prospect of hours of cooking very unattractive. Cooking techniques and knowledge of ingredients gained in rural areas often oceans away from American neighborhoods also did not necessarily translate well, leaving women with a deficit of skills with which to cope with this new urban environment. It is no wonder they chose to pay someone else to do the work.

Science-based Technologies, Transportation and Communication

As America entered the twentieth century, work was also transformed by two other factors: the proliferation of science-based technologies and the role of new transportation and communications technologies in delocalizing the connection between production and consumption. Eighteenth- and nineteenth-century factory production largely focused on making familiar objects and substances using new methods: cloth, steel, gunpowder, etc. Novelties tended to be mechanical devices, cherry pitters, bicycles, steam engines, that were understandable from visual inspection. Beginning in the late nineteenth century, more and more workers found themselves not only using novel technologies as tools in their jobs but making or maintaining or operating technologies that had never before existed anywhere in the world. Many of these technologies had originally been created by scientists or other technical specialists in research and development laboratories of large corporations. They were often based on new discoveries in electricity and chemistry and were difficult to compre-hend and reproduce by those without technical training. For workers, who first spun nylon or assembled computers, technology also becomes black-boxed in a whole new way.

If twentieth-century industrialization and technological change created a variety of jobs that had never before existed in the world, it also transformed some of the most ancient and seemingly immutable kinds of work. For instance, nursing had long been a job associated with the most basic activities of feeding and caring for persons too sick to care for themselves. It became more and more a profession of managing complex medical technologies in the context of hospitals. Nurses traditionally came to know the bodies and needs of their patients through conversation, physical touching, and observation. As nursing began to professionalize after the American Civil War, this distinction was formalized into a set of protocols that distinguished the labor of doctors and nurses. Nurses were enjoined from using tools or invasive techniques to observe or treat patients. However, the introduction of a succession of new medical technologies: more and more injectable medications, intravenous feeding, and a variety of monitoring technologies, challenged those protocols. Doctors wanted patients treated and observed using these technologies but did not want to be present every time a needle was inserted or a reading taken. The history of nursing in the twentieth century, therefore, has been characterized by a constant set of negotiations over who will use which technologies and what that usage will mean in terms of prestige, professionalization, and relationships with patients (Sandelowski 2000).

To take a very different example, agriculture is one of the oldest of all human technology-intensive forms of work. In the last four centuries, agriculture has undergone a whole series of technological transformations, each of which required different types of workers and different kinds of knowledge. However, twentieth-century changes have perhaps been the most profound because they originated in the science laboratories of universities and in corporate boardrooms.

The industrialization of farm work followed some of the same patterns already described in this essay. The use of a growing variety of gas-powered machinery from Fordson tractors to combines made it possible to carry out farming on a larger and larger scale. Agricultural scientists in land grant universities also tackled the two most labor intensive parts of growing crops: weed and pest control and harvesting. The introduction of a broad range of new chemicals, including DDT and 2-4-D after World War II enabled farmers to spray rather than sending large numbers of workers through fields to pick off insects and hoe weeds (Daniel 2000). Scientists also treated plants themselves as technologies, designing square tomatoes that could be harvested mechanically and hybrid corn that could not be manipulated genetically by farmers themselves (Fitzgerald 1990). Consequentially, farmers found themselves deskilled and farm workers found themselves displaced by machinery.

In the same way that late nineteenth-century industrialization changed the landscape and with it social and economic relationships by concentrating production in large cities, twentieth-century changes in agriculture have changed the land and social relations upon it. In the 1950s, the adoption of chemicals and machines gradually put an end to the racially based system of sharecropping and tenant farming that had characterized Southern agriculture since the end of the Civil War. Large landowners no longer needed the labor system that had replaced slavery to work their land (Daniel 2000). In the Midwest, chemically based agriculture and sophisticated harvesting machinery had virtually eliminated the system of itinerant labor and huge work crews that once characterized farm life. Raising wheat is now largely a solitary endeavor carried out in the air-conditioned cab of a combine.

Fears of Automation

Beginning in the 1930s, mechanization and industrialization led to a widespread public debate about not only the dehumanizing of work, but also the possibility that too much technological ingenuity could lead to widespread unemployment. Are we "inventing ourselves out of jobs?" commentators asked (Bix 2000). The impact of the Great Depression had called into question the assertion by Ford, Taylor, and other systematizers that more efficient production would lead to cheaper products which would lead to more consumption and, in turn, more jobs to make those products.

The so-called manpower shortages of World War II temporarily silenced such worries, but they reappeared in the postwar era along with the first ripples of what would later be called de-industrialization. Kurt Vonnegut's dark 1952 novel *Player Piano* imagined a world in which engineers had automated industry to the point that no workers were needed at all. IQ and aptitude tests determined whether young people would be trained as engineers or work in the army or the "reeks and wrecks" – public works crews. Automation was justified in Taylorist terms: human workers were lazy, incompetent, and prone to error. In Vonnegut's fictional world, engineers had bypassed the necessity of figuring out ways to make a human being act like a machine. They had simply eliminated the human beings (Vonnegut 1952).

Vonnegut's distopian vision was based in part on his own experience working at General Electric in Schenectady, New York, during a period in which the company was working on techniques for automating machine tools (Noble 1984, p. 166). As suggested earlier, the job of machinist had long stood as the quintessential exemplar of skilled, male labor. Postwar engineers hoped to turn the process of cutting complex parts out of metal into something that could be done with the push of a button by collecting the machinist's knowledge on a tape and later a computer program (Noble 1984).

Not just novelists worried about automation and unemployment. A 1955 Congressional Hearing on "automation and technological change" featured a parade of witnesses testifying about the costs and benefits of new technologies. Advocates claimed that the lower cost of goods and the creation of new kinds of jobs maintaining and supporting the new machinery more than made up for job losses. Others were not so sure. Labor leader Walter Reuther expressed his concern about the fate of older and more specialized workers. By the early 1960s, technological unemployment had become a fact of life for more and more workers and a hot political issue. President Kennedy went so far as to ask the Department of Labor to create an Office of Automation and Manpower to track statistics and set up programs to retrain displaced workers. Critics could point to Detroit where a 12 percent unemployment rate coexisted with enormous gains in automobile production. In 1958, for example, General Motors had announced that they planned to increase production 25 percent but hired only 5 percent more workers (Bix 2000, pp. 247–50, 254, 256).

In historical perspective, postwar fixations on automation represent a partial misunderstanding of the impact of technological change on wage labor in America. Such discussions still assumed that automation was the primary solution to the rising cost of American labor. They had not counted on the power of new communications and transportation technologies to make it feasible to carry on manufacturing without substantial automation in the developing world where labor costs were much lower. Capitalists who went abroad found workers who were not only willing to work for less but who also had skills acquired from other parts of their lives that had largely disappeared from American culture because of the impact of consumer culture. Women in Korea, Thailand, and Mexico were already skilled sewers because they made their families' clothes rather than purchasing them.

Conclusion

Productive labor has not disappeared out of the United States. Across the country, workers still assemble cars and package food and make a thousand variations on the ubiquitous consumer products we take for granted. And other workers still engage in work that could be characterized as pre-industrial (although it would be difficult to find an example of work that has not been changed technologically by industrialization). As summer approaches, road crews set out their orange cones and stand, shovels in hand, by the side of the highways, ready to shovel the dirt that cannot be moved by machines. In workshops and studios, potters, luthiers, cabinetmakers, and other craftspeople turn out handmade objects one at a time.

In the last few decades, much has been made of the impact of one particular technology, the computer, on work. A little bit of historical perspective may in fact be useful in shedding light on this phenomenon. As with the automobile, with which this essay began, there is no single kind of computer work. Forms of labor related to this technology are extraordinarily diverse. Like automobiles, computers are mass-produced objects made for a consumer marketplace. In factories across the world, impoverished women assemble microprocessors. Like their predecessors who dipped chocolates (or made hats or assembled televisions), many cannot afford to buy what they make. Unlike the candy makers, many also would not know how use the product they help put together. Computers are a very twentieth-century kind of technology in this sense. Elsewhere, very different kinds of workers write code, repair computers, or enter data (replacing the file clerks that once climbed ladders to file and retrieve information).

Perhaps more striking is the way computers have redefined the physical nature of work. More and more American workers, like their counterparts in other industrialized countries, use a computer keyboard or a touch screen as prosthesis between their own bodies and the thing they are making or doing. Even in the Rouge, still standing, but a shadow of its former grandeur, many autoworkers do not make direct physical contact with the cars they are building. Were Diego Rivera to portray the same spaces now, they would be relatively empty of people. The sinewy rhythm of men's bodies bending to their tools is more and more being replaced by workers standing at the side of the line, monitoring a series of robots. Nineteenth-century utopians such as Edward Bellamy imagined a future in which technology would free workers from toil, giving them leisure time to improve their minds and enjoy pleasure outside the workplace. Mid-century critics of automation worried about the spread of technological employment. As it turns out, the number of hours worked by the average American has increased over the last decade and unemployment levels have hovered at record lows. Technological change has not resulted in less *time* spent working. Instead, wage labor has ceased to be synonymous with hard physical work. Even many industrial workers no longer expect to wear out their bodies in the course of doing their jobs. If technology is indeed socially constructed, this is the striking choice to have been made, undoubtedly with unforeseen consequences.

BIBLIOGRAPHY

Aiken, H.G.J. *Scientific Management in Action: Taylorism at Watertown Arsenal, 1908–1915* (Princeton: Princeton University Press, 1985 [1960]).

Aldrich, M. *Safety First: Technology, Labor, and Business in the Building of American Work Safety, 1870–1939* (Baltimore: Johns Hopkins University Press, 1997).

Biggs, L. *The Rational Factory: Architecture, Technology, and Work in America's Age of Mass Production* (Baltimore: Johns Hopkins University Press, 1996).

Bix, A.S. *Inventing Ourselves Out of Jobs? America's Debate over Technological Unemployment, 1921–1981* (Baltimore: Johns Hopkins University Press, 2000).

Borg, K. "The 'Chauffeur Problem' in the early auto era: structuration theory and the users of technology," *Technology and Culture* 40 (October 1999): 797–832.

Cooper, G. "Love, war, and chocolate: gender and the American candy industry, 1890–1930," in Roger Horowitz and Arwen Mohun eds, *His and Hers: Gender, Consumption and Technology* (Charlottesville: University of Virginia Press, 1998): pp. 67–94.

Cowan, R.S. *More Work for Mother: The Ironies of Household Technology from the Open Hearth to the Microwave* (New York: Basic Books, 1983).

Daniel, P. *Lost Revolutions: The South in the 1950s* (Chapel Hill: University of North Carolina Press, 2000).

Davis, M. *A Woman's Place is at the Typewriter: Office Work and Office Workers, 1890–1940* (Philadelphia: Temple University Press, 1982).

Downs, L.B. *Diego Rivera: The Detroit Industry Murals* (Detroit: Detroit Institute of the Arts, 1999).

Fitzgerald, D. *The Business of Breeding: Hybrid Corn in Illinois, 1890–1940* (Ithaca: Cornell University Press, 1990).

Gamber, W. *The Female Economy: The Millinery and Dressmaking Trades, 1860–1930* (Urbana: University of Illinois, 1997).

Glickman, L.B. *A Living Wage: American Workers and the Making of Consumer Society* (Ithaca: Cornell University Press, 1997).

Harper, D. *Working Knowledge: Skill and Community in a Small Shop* (Chicago: University of Chicago Press, 1987).

Hounshell, D. *From American System to Mass Production: The Development of Manufacturing Technology in the United States* (Baltimore: Johns Hopkins University Press, 1984).

Hughes, T.P. *American Genesis: A Century of Invention and Technological Enthusiasm* (New York: Viking, 1989).

Kanigel, R. *The One Best Way: Frederick Winslow Taylor and the Enigma of Efficiency* (New York: Viking, 1997).

Landes, D.S. *The Unbound Prometheus: Technological Change and Industrial Development in Western Europe from 1750 to the Present* (Cambridge: Cambridge University Press, 1969).

Licht, W. *Working for the Railroad: The Organization of Work in the Nineteenth Century* (Princeton: Princeton University Press, 1983).

Meyer, S. "Work, play, and power: masculine culture on the automotive shop floor, 1930–1960," in Roger Horowitz, ed., *Boys and their Toys? Masculinity, Class, and Technology in America* (New York: Routledge, 2001): pp. 13–32.

Milkman, R. *Gender at Work: The Dynamics of Job Segregation by Sex during World War II* (Urbana: University of Illinois, 1987).

Mohun, A.P. "Why Mrs. Harrison never learned to iron: gender skill, and mechanization in the American steam laundry industry," *Gender and History* 8 (August 1996): 231–51.

Mohun, A.P. *Steam Laundries: Gender, Technology, and Work in the United States and Great Britain, 1880–1940* (Baltimore: Johns Hopkins University Press, 1999).

Noble, D. *Forces of Production: A Social History of Industrial Automation* (New York and Oxford: Oxford University Press, 1984).

Sandelowski, M. *Devices and Desires: Gender, Technology, and American Nursing* (Chapel Hill: University of North Carolina Press, 2000).

Scranton, P. *Endless Novelty: Specialty Production and American Industrialization, 1865–1925* (Princeton: Princeton University Press, 1997).

Strom, S.H. *Beyond the Typewriter: Gender, Class, and the Origins of Modern American Office Work, 1900–1930* (Urbana: University of Illinois Press, 1992).

Vonnegut, K. *Player Piano* (New York: Dell, 1952).

Zunz, O. *Making America Corporate, 1870–1920* (Chicago: University of Chicago Press, 1990).

PART IV

TECHNOLOGICAL SYSTEMS

CHAPTER THIRTEEN

The Automotive Transportation System: Cars and Highways in Twentieth-Century America

BRUCE E. SEELY

Transportation was a paramount issue for nineteenth-century Americans pursuing the experiment of developing a democratic nation on a continental scale. From the beginning, then, transport technologies were more than the means of moving people and goods. As railroads stitched the states together, they also called into being an industrial economy while steam locomotives became an icon of American technical capabilities. Trains also introduced a fascination with speed, despite Henry David Thoreau's plaintive question about what people might do after reaching their destination more quickly. During the twentieth century, an automotive transportation system composed of highways, motor vehicles, and much more assumed all of these roles. The linkage of roads and cars was not automatic; highways have developed in cultures without vehicles. But Americans combined automobiles and improved highway into a system of enormous technological, economic, political, and social significance. As had often been the case, initial technical explorations occurred in Europe but residents of the United States transformed roads and autos into the first "car culture," creating perhaps the most important socio-technical system in the modern world.

Pioneering Highways and Automobiles, 1880–1910

Few observers of nineteenth-century American life could have predicted that personal vehicles would eventually dominate American transportation, the economy, and American life. Early experiments with turnpikes and plank roads after 1790 quickly exposed the limited range of horse-drawn road transport. Moreover, after extended political wrangling surrounded construction of the National Road to Cumberland, Wheeling, and westward to Illinois, constitutional limitations ended federal participation in road-building. Canals, and then the telegraph/railroad combination provided superior long-distance transportation. As train tracks crossed the continent, the power of steam locomotives stood in marked contrast to wagons on rutted, sometimes impassable roads.

Yet by the 1880s, railroads were a hated institution in rural America, resented for their domination in transport and resulting political power. At that same time, many middle-class citizens discovered the safety bicycle which, unlike the high-wheeled ordinary, did not require risking one's neck. In a short time, millions of bicycles appeared on city streets and country roads and riders discovered the terrible condition of most roads. These experiments with personal transportation inspired the first demands for better roads. Bicycle manufacturers such as Alfred Pope, joined a vocal chorus of complaints led by the bicycle club, the League of American Wheelmen. A few farmers also wanted better farm-to-market roads, although most opposed the higher property taxes that accompanied road improvement. Railroad corporations quickly became the largest corporate supporters of this Good Roads Movement, since better rural roads allowed the rail system to connect isolated farms to emerging national markets. Bicyclists, farmers, and railroad corporations all stood to benefit from road improvements.

Following serious lobbying efforts, Congress formed the Office of Road Improvement in the Agriculture Department in 1893 to gather and disseminate information on better materials and improved construction techniques. A cadre of engineers committed to Progressive-era goals of efficiency through technical expertise soon published booklets, conducted demonstration projects, and undertook research and testing. Renamed the Office of Public Roads in 1905, and later the Bureau of Public Roads, the organization guided federal highway activities until the creation of the Department of Transportation in 1967.

At first, the competence of American highway engineers lagged far behind their European counterparts. The French, thanks to the École des Ponts et Chausés founded in the mid-seventeenth century, possessed the best roads in the world. The British also developed improved roads for privately constructed turnpikes in the mid-1700s, and Thomas Macadam introduced a technique for building a durable, stone-surfaced road. Americans knew little about the crucial European finding that it was vital to keep moisture out of road foundations. Roads here had begun as unimproved dirt tracks with location determined more by the first travelers than by engineering surveys. Surface treatments were rare, for even gravel was expensive to move. Few cities boasted paved streets until after the Civil War. The basic problem was the limited funding and even more limited knowledge possessed by the local officials responsible for maintaining American roads. Rather than pay taxes, local residents usually joined their neighbors twice a year to fill the worst mudholes and grade the ruts. In the South, convict labor performed this work, but nowhere were professional engineers involved. By the time federal engineers completed the first road census in 1904, Americans had more than two million miles of roads, but only 154,000 miles were improved.

Congress at first refused to provide federal construction funds, for everyone saw roads as a local responsibility. In 1893 and 1894, state governments in Massachusetts and New Jersey hesitantly created the first highway departments. A new factor spurred this decision beyond a general desire to improve rural life – rural free mail delivery. But federal highway engineers in the Office of Public Roads played crucial roles in shaping these agencies, even without the power of the purse. These engineers typified Progressive reform efforts that sought to shift authority from politics to more efficient, apolitical experts. After 1900, they drafted and promoted model highway department legislation that placed highway departments under engineering control to eliminate graft and waste. The model bill was widely adopted, as first eastern and then midwestern and Pacific Coast states created highway departments. Only southern and mountain states lagged behind.

Once in place, federal engineers also helped guide the activities of these new departments. They trained state and local engineers and launched an extensive program to demonstrate construction techniques to local officials. They showed how to build durable surfaces with local materials, such as oyster shells or mixtures of sand and clay, and how to use oil to reduce dust. Federal engineers also studied paving materials, including brick, gravel, concrete, and asphalt, for all-weather roads. By 1910, the nation's road system still showed enormous variation from county to county and state to state, but the basic structure of expert authority over American road improvement efforts was in place.

Road improvement programs overlapped with early experiments with self-propelled vehicles. Again, inspiration came from Europeans, such as Belgian Etienne Lenoir, who built early internal combustion engines (1860), and German engine builder Nicholas Otto (1878), whose four-stroke engine was widely adopted. Other Germans, including Gottlieb Daimler and Carl Benz, constructed self-propelled vehicles by 1885 and reliable machines after 1890. American inventors read about European experiments in technical periodicals and soon built their own machines. Machinist Ransom Olds tried a steam vehicle in 1887, and others drove electric cars in Chicago and Philadelphia in the early 1890s. Charles and Frank Duryea of Springfield, Massachusetts, were tinkering by 1890 after reading about Benz in *Scientific American*. The event that captured American imaginations was the widely reported Paris-Bordeaux-Paris race of 1895. In its wake, Americans filed 500 patent applications, launched two trade journals (*Horseless Age* and *Motorcycle*), and imported the first European vehicles. That year, Henry Ford built a car and the Pope Manufacturing Company added electric vehicles to its line of bicycles. American promoters also sponsored a race in Chicago at Thanksgiving, in which the Duryea brothers outran a Benz in a snowstorm. The Duryeas sold twelve cars the following year, and were not alone in capitalizing on favorable publicity. Hiram Maxim (1937) (inventor of the machine gun) launched a car company, while the Stanley brothers began making steam cars in 1898 and Ransom Olds started selling a light-weight gas-powered runabout. By 1899, at least 40 companies had built about 2,500 cars.

These early efforts had several common traits. Even while most entrepreneurs drew inspiration from European activities, early American car builders also drew guidance from the bicycle industry. Maxim commented that bicycles "had directed men's mind to the possibilities of long-distance travel over the ordinary highway." Until then, he wrote, "We thought the railroad was good enough" (Rae 1965, p. 6). Clearly the popularity of bicycles demonstrated a public interest in personal transportation. As important, car builders borrowed from bicycle makers a variety of tools, techniques, and experiences – electric resistance welding, pressed steel parts, painting and finishing. Bicycle makers fine-tuned mass production using interchangeable parts, and taught vehicle builders about managing the flow of machining, finishing, and assembly of parts, about precision, and about early quality controls. The first automobile producers, including Pope and the Duryeas, also borrowed design features such as tubular frames, sprocket and chain drives, and pneumatic tires.

The other key trait of early cars was the lack of uniformity and range of technical options. The configuration of the basic elements – engine, drive train, passenger seating, and so forth – were much contested. Some early designers used a tricycle configuration, others employed four wheels. Bodies for most early cars were borrowed from carriages, and steering options included tillers as well as wheels. Drivers sometimes were behind the passengers. Automotive pioneers had substantial latitude as they pondered design options, including the choice of power plant. Electric cars initially dominated, if taxis are counted. Indeed, Pope Manufacturing built about 500 electric cabs and only 40 gasoline vehicles in 1898. Steam also had adherents, and Stanley Steamers with flash boilers started almost as fast as other cars and held speed records. Kirsch (2000) argued that the gasoline-powered vehicles ultimately dominated not through inherent technical superiority and virtue, but because of choices and actions, including poor management and business strategies by electric vehicle producers. Kirsch also observed that gasoline vehicles proved most successful after electric accessories such as lights had created a gasoline-electric hybrid. The point is that the "best" answer was not obvious in the 1890s.

Producing Automobiles, 1900–30

Design choices narrowed during the first decade of the twentieth century, as the car sales jumped from 4,000 in 1900 to 187,000 in 1910 and registrations increased from 8,000 to 496,000. Cars flourished in the American environment for several reasons. The absence of tariff barriers helped, as did a larger market and more consumers with higher per capita incomes (i.e., a larger middle class), extensive experience in quantity production of consumer goods, and substantial enthusiasm for technology. The American atmosphere rewarded many who played with this emerging technology.

Evidence of enthusiasm can be found in the range of inventions that became standard components on most automobiles. These included steering wheels (1901), porcelain insulation on spark plugs (1902), running boards and force-feed engine lubrication (1903), shock absorbers, canopy tops with glass windows, Prest-O-Lite acetylene lamps (1904), bumpers (1906), brakes on the wheels (ca. 1906, with asbestos pads in 1907–08). Water-cooled engines were introduced on Locomobiles in 1902 and became standard by 1910. Increasingly, the tinkers and inventors chose gasoline engines. One response to the explosion of creativity was the formation of the Society of Automotive Engineers in 1905, whose founders decided to establish standards for thousands of parts, ranging from spark plugs and screws to wheel rims and headlight brackets.

These technical developments made automobiles more reliable, but that alone does not explain their rapid adoption. During these same years, a variety of institutional, structural, and social adjustments proved equally pivotal in fostering widespread public acceptance of automobiles. One of many legal issues sorted out concerned automobile registration. At first strictly a local matter, states eventually registered vehicles and worked out reciprocity agreements with neighboring governments. New York began this in 1901, and by 1910 thirty-five states required registration; all had accepted the idea by 1915. Licenses were another contested issue, for early motorists resisted restrictions. But cities, led by Chicago in 1899, began to require operator's licenses. After 1906, the states again entered the picture, with Massachusetts imposing the first road test. Most states were less demanding, and in 1909 only a dozen eastern states required licenses and some allowed mail-order requests. Speed limits brought more motorist complaints, but public opinion in cities proved more insistent. Limits settled in the range of 15–20 miles per hour by 1906, and then crept higher. Speeding never went away, despite Wilmington, Delaware's attempt to shame speeders by driving them through the streets in the back of a barred truck.

Other institutional difficulties had to be overcome before mass ownership of automobiles was feasible. Insurance was important in litigious America, but only four companies wrote auto policies in 1902 and they lacked the knowledge needed to set rates. Moreover, collisions were frequent from the outset – apparently two of the six cars in Chicago collided in the mid-1890s. Thus initial insurance rates were four times higher for cars than horse-drawn wagons. Parking also vexed early motorists. Auto clubs sometimes provided parking for members, while public garages were associated with dealerships or, in New York, with large department stores. Breakdowns and access to gasoline (or battery recharging facilities for electric cars) created other headaches for early motorists. Gasoline might be found in livery stables, general stores, or apothecaries, but all drivers doubled as mechanics. Greater mechanical reliability helped, but service stations, first developed by auto clubs and expanded by the petroleum industry after 1913, were an important development. Indeed, the automotive transport system could not grow until these arrangements were in place.

One factor not to be dismissed in the acceptance of automobiles was a high degree of public enthusiasm. This outlook showed clearly in public interest in racing, but it also shaped the efforts of auto makers as well. Few men founded car companies because of rational calculations of profit, according to historian Davis (1988). He showed that 239 car companies appeared in Detroit between 1897 and 1933, despite a very high failure rate. Their founders had been bitten by the bug, with Davis reporting that most owners viewed their involvement as more than a business investment; that they built cars for motorists, not money. Very early, automobiles were viewed as a measure of one's social status and position. Thus Walter Chrysler paid more than $4,000 for his first car (a Locomobile) at a time when he earned $350 a year as a railway mechanic. Davis found such desire for prestige also influenced the choices of manufacturers, and led most Detroit auto makers, including Cadillac, Pierce Arrow, Packard, and Hudson, to build technically excellent luxury cars for drivers of high social position.

Despite many virtues, these automobile companies rarely provided models for success. Much more influential were the efforts of a handful of car makers who disconnected dreams of social position from manufacturing decisions. These men adopted a radically different outlook to car making. Every bit as enthusiastic about building automobiles, they designed affordable, flexible machines for average drivers. Ransom Olds, for example, focused on a low-cost machine, building a light vehicle that looked like a buggy with a gasoline engine. He sold perhaps 5,000 curved-dash Olds runabouts a year between 1901 and 1904. As late as 1909, 50 companies sold such vehicles at prices ranging from $250 to $600. But American terrain, poor roads, and weather quickly proved too much for lightly built and cheaply engineered cars. Henry Leland, founder of Cadillac, on the other hand, drew upon his experience at precision toolmaker Brown & Sharpe and introduced micrometers to achieve manufacturing precision. He demonstrated the result in 1908, by shipping three cars and spare parts to Britain, disassembling the cars, and randomly replacing 90 parts from the spares. His mechanics rebuilt the cars and drove them for 500 miles. Such attention to detail proved expensive, although Leland did not hand-build his cars, and in 1908 he sold 2,380 Cadillacs.

Several manufacturers sought to link low price and careful construction. William C. Durant, for example, shifted from making carriages in Flint, Michigan, to running the Buick Motor Car Company in the early 1900s. By 1908, when Buick produced 8,847 cars at a price of $1,000 to $1,200, the company was one of the largest assemblers. Yet the man whose name is most associated with the American car – Henry Ford – soon overshadowed Durant's successes.

Ford's tinkering began with a small gasoline-engine runabout in 1895. His first two companies failed, largely because Ford seemed more interested in racing or in asserting total control over his enterprise. He established the Ford Motor Company in 1903, having decided "The way to make automobiles is to make one automobile like another automobile, to make them all alike, to make them come from the factory alike – just like one pin is like another pin." He also combined volume-production and precision-manufacturing, working with several young production engineers with few preconceptions about building cars. These men came from New England factories using mass-production techniques to assemble firearms, sewing machines, or bicycles. Ford introduced three models in 1904–05 before the Model N (1906) caught on at a price of $600; it sold almost 6,000 units in 1908. Then came the Model T, a car suited for American conditions with high ground clearance, heat-treated vanadium steel, an 20-horsepower four-cylinder engine, better springs, and a simple two-speed transmission. Even before Ford introduced it in October 1908 at a price of $825, the company had 15,000 orders in hand.

Most car makers assembled autos from parts machined by others, but Ford wanted more control and built his own factory. The Highland Park plant, designed by Albert Kahn and opened in January 1910, provided space for an array of specially designed machine tools. Ford's premise was that if each part was right, the car would work. Moreover, by paying attention to the flow of parts and work, Ford's engineering team increased production from 24,000 in 1910 to 170,000 in 1912. Pushing the static assembly process further than that proved difficult, however. To expand annual output to 200,000 cars meant dealing with a million lamps, 800,000 wheels and tires, 90,000 tons of steel, 400,000 cowhides, 6 million pounds of hair for seats, and two million square feet of glass. This challenge shaped the experiments at Highland Park that in 1913 led to moving assembly lines. Charles Sorenson, project leader, first installed a conveyor to carry engine molds in the foundry. He next turned to magnetos, which each worker assembled alone in 18 minutes. Sorenson placed 29 workers at one long bench and let each worker perform a few steps. Assembly time dropped to 13 minutes, and after more tinkering, to five. With a moving belt added in 1914, fourteen workers could assemble 1,355 magnetos each 8-hour shift. Sorenson's team applied this idea to all subassemblies, even upholstered seats, and started a chassis assembly line in August 1913. The team developed slides and other materials-carrying systems to deliver parts into position. Historian Hounshell (1984) observed that Ford's strategy differed from efficiency expert Frederick W. Taylor's. Instead of making each worker move efficiently, Ford created an efficient process by shifting control of the pace and process from workers to managers. By 1914, production at Highland Park had increased to about 300,000 cars; a year later, output exceeded 500,000.

Ford's team invented very little of this. Moving belts had been developed for "disassembly lines" in meat packing plants, while precision machine tools and gauges to achieve correct fits had appeared in American factories during the nineteenth century. But Ford's engineers put all of the pieces together and created the most significant American contribution to manufacturing. And the ramifications of the assembly line and mass production appeared quickly. Ford quickly discovered that he could not retain his workers, as the new pace caused many craftsmen to flee the factory. Indeed, critics from Aldous Huxley, in his dystopian 1932 novel *Brave New World*, to Charlie Chaplin, in his 1936 movie "Modern Times," assailed the consequences of an assembly line world. Ford solved some problems with the $5 daily wage – denounced by other employers, yet not available to all his employees. He discovered the basic bargain of American labor relations, by which workers ceded workplace control in return for higher wages. An unintended consequence was the ability of his workers to buy Model Ts, especially as scale economies steadily lowered the price to $290 in 1924. By that time, Ford annually assembled two million cars and half the cars in the world were Fords.

To achieve this record, Fordism limited design changes, so expensive special-purpose machine tools produced millions of identical parts. Ford extended this capital-intensive approach in 1916, breaking ground for the largest factory complex in the world. Completed in the mid-1920s, his River Rouge plant employed 75,000 workers and included a steel mill, glass factory, more than 45,000 machine tools, and 90 miles of railroad track. He also acquired forests in Michigan's Upper Peninsula, a railroad, iron mines, and ore boats. While Lenin considered Ford the epitome of modern capitalism, Ford simply carried vertical integration to a new pinnacle.

Ford's domination of the auto industry also altered its basic shape. The massive capital investment required for mass-production restricted entry by new firms; indeed, the number of car makers shrank from 108 in 1920 to 44 in 1929. The post-Ford auto industry was an oligopoly in which only a handful of smaller firms survived in the luxury niche (Packard, Cord, Duesenberg). By 1930, Ford had only two serious competitors – Chrysler and General Motors. Both had made the transition to large-scale mass production. Chrysler took shape in the mid-1920s, formed by Walter Chrysler from the wreckage of struggling car makers Maxwell, Chalmers, and Dodge. The acquisition of Dodge in 1928 was pivotal, for this firm gave Chrysler a dealer network and production capacity sufficient to introduce the Plymouth, a low-priced, mass-produced vehicle designed to compete with Ford. Chrysler struggled at times, but the Plymouth enjoyed enough success make Chrysler a member of the Big Three.

General Motors rounded out this exclusive club. William Durant, the carriage-maker turned car producer, was its initial organizer. He dreamed of becoming America's largest auto maker, but embraced a different strategy than Ford – growth by acquisition. Incorporating GM in 1908 as a holding company, he began buying parts-makers, car and truck builders, and production facilities. To his base at Buick, Durant added Cadillac, Olds, Oakland, Cartercar, Elmore, Champion Ignition (spark plugs), and others. Unfortunately, Durant never tried to manage the growing empire and in 1910 his bankers brought in Walter Chrysler and Charles Nash for sound management. Durant remained a big stockholder, however, even as he began expanding another car maker – Chevrolet. In 1915, Durant regained control of GM, through the financial backing of the Dupont family, which acquired a significant holding of General Motors stock. Durant resumed shopping, adding parts-producers Dayton Engineering Laboratory Company (DELCO), Hyatt Roller Bearing, Fisher Body, Samson Tractor, and Frigidaire – arguing that cars and refrigerators were boxes with an engine. Again, Durant made no effort to rationalize these holdings; companies were not even required to purchase parts from suppliers within the corporation. By 1920, financial and organizational chaos again reigned as the economy slowed after World War I, and this time the Dupont family forced Durant out of General Motors for good.

The chairman of GM's board, Pierre Dupont, assigned the task of restoring order to Alfred Sloan of Hyatt Roller Bearing. Sloan, like Dupont, had earned an engineering degree at MIT and both men embraced a rational engineering approach. In taming General Motors, Sloan earned the nickname "the Organization Man." First he gained control of the decentralized operating units with comprehensive financial and statistical reporting. By 1925, Sloan's staff produced an annual economic forecast, against which he tracked production units through 10-day and monthly reports. Recognizing that the automobile market was saturated, he introduced central marketing activities, with the key strategy being a corporate structure that differentiated production divisions by price. Thus Chevrolet, the low-priced line, competed with Ford but not with other GM divisions, whose cars were priced in rising increments. GM offered "a car for every purse and purpose," creating a marketing mechanism that followed from the well-established principle that cars conveyed social status. Thus Chevrolet owners were urged to step up to Oakland or Pontiac, while even Buick owners aspired to own Cadillacs.

Sloan recognized mass consumption as a necessary corollary of mass production, and offered motorists excuses to buy new cars. He also sought to differentiate GM's car divisions. A central element here was a research center headed by Charles Kettering, whose company (DELCO) Durant purchased in order to acquire Kettering's crucial invention, the electric self-starter. After 1920, Kettering's staff tackled problems ranging from development of an air-cooled engine and automatic transmissions to engine knock and colorful paints. Improvements appeared first in Cadillacs and slowly worked their way down through the divisions. Deliberately seeking to highlight these novelties and differences between old and new, GM also introduced the annual model change. But the key step was the hiring of Harley Earl, a Southern California designer, to style GM's cars. Cosmetic changes distinguished the new from the old, especially after the Duco lacquer paints developed by Kettering's lab allowed bright new colors each year. Finally, Sloan embraced credit purchases through the General Motors Acceptance Corporation (founded by Durant in 1919) to expand the market. He also allowed dealers to take a loss on trade-ins.

GM's approach to the car business contrasted sharply with Ford's, but it worked. Ford opposed credit purchases until 1928, and made few adjustments to the Model T as competitors introduced closed cabs, more power, and better features. More importantly, despite pressure from his son Edsel, Ford refused to consider any organizational adjustments. Ford saw no reason to change, as the company built 15,007,003 Model Ts. He finally stopped production in 1927 only after his market share had plummeted to 15 percent. But the difficult transition to the new Model A exposed the last crucial difference between GM and Ford. The last Model T rolled off the line in late May 1927; the first Model A appeared in November but full production came several months later. Ford's reliance on specialized, one-of-a-kind machine tools made re-tooling expensive and slow and the change-over cost Ford as much as $250 million. GM, on the other hand, had developed a "flexible" style of mass production. William Knudsen, hired by Sloan to run Chevrolet in 1922, installed general-purpose tools that could be changed easily. During annual model changes, GM engineers rearranged and retooled assembly and subassembly lines in a matter of weeks. As historian Hounshell observed, "the Model T dictum of maximum production at minimum cost gave way to planning for change" (1984, p. 264).

This approach gave GM a huge advantage over Ford by the late 1920s. In 1929, GM claimed 32.3 percent of the car market to Ford's 31.3 percent. But the value of Sloan's managerial developments became fully apparent during the Depression. With its planning, forecasting, and reporting capabilities, GM made money every year, while Ford reported profits twice. More shockingly, Chrysler passed Ford in 1937, taking 25.4 percent of the market to Ford's 21.4 percent. By 1940, Ford held less than 19 percent of the American automobile market. Clearly, successful mass production required organization and structure.

Highways as Complex Systems, 1920–40

During the 1920s, cars became a necessity to many Americans. Total annual production reached 2 million in 1920 and 5.5 million in 1929, bringing registrations from 9.2 million to 26.5 million. By 1930, the US boasted 85 percent of the world's auto production capacity. But this increase in numbers depended upon changes in other parts of the automotive transportation system, especially roads. After 1910, demands for improved roads grew as motorists and auto makers added their voices to those demanding road improvements. While state highway departments slowly developed roads systems (with significant variation from state to state), engineers in the Office of Public Roads focused on promoted federal legislation to fund road improvements. In 1912, the Congress authorized a pilot program for rural post roads, and in 1916 passed the Federal-Aid Highway Act to begin the process of building a national road system jointly with the states. Initially limited to rural post roads, in 1921, the Congress, again at the urging of the federal highway engineers, shifted attention to the main routes connecting cities. Federal funds increased from $5 million in 1916 and $25 million in 1921 to about $75 million a year in the 1920s, while surfaced road mileage rose from 387,000 miles in 1921 to 694,000 in 1929, including most roads on state systems.

This road network was not simply the product of lobbying by powerful automobile manufacturers, as suggested by economist St Clair (1986). American highway policy was driven by federal highway engineers who initially stressed that roads existed to improve the quality of rural life, not to service motor cars. Priorities changed after 1920, but federal and state highway engineers remained key figures in the legislative and policy arenas, trusted by Congressmen, presidents, and the public. Other supporters of cars and highways generally followed the lead of the engineers who shaped the administrative structure of highway departments as engineering bureaucracies, proposed funding mechanisms (no tolls), and placed priority on building main roads between, but not into, cities. After 1920, engineers installed an economic and technical calculus for highway planning that emphasized vehicle movement and travel time saved, leaving little room for land-use or aesthetic criteria. Federal engineers in the Bureau of Public Roads cooperatively created university curricula, shaped a highway research program, and developed construction standards and materials specifications. They insured that the top priority was the federal-aid highway system, 7 percent of each state's road mileage outside of cities. The architect of this expert-driven highway policy was Thomas MacDonald (1924), Chief of the Bureau of Public Roads under six presidents from 1919 to 1953.

Yet there was more to a national road system than funding and organizational structures. Better roads were a complex system of many parts that included, for example, new construction techniques. In 1900, hand-labor and horses built roads by moving as little earth as possible. Steam shovels, steam rollers and stone crushers found occasional use, but horse-drawn scrapers moved the dirt. After 1920, however, the internal-combustion engine mechanized road construction, led by the crawler tractor that emerged from the farm fields of California's Imperial valley. After 1925 the Caterpillar Tractor Company and, its equipment painted "HiWay Yellow," dominated the industry with innovations such as self-propelled motor graders (1931). At the same time, Robert LeTourneau, who originally supplied plows and dozer blades to Caterpillar, designed a powered scraper. By the late 1930s, he had designed a tractor with huge pneumatic tires that pulled scrapers at higher speeds; these "earthmovers" facilitated huge excavation projects. Similar steps mechanized asphalt and concrete paving operations. Mixing plants grew larger as powered spreaders, levelers, and finishing machines laid long sections of hard road surface. By 1946 the mileage of paved and dirt roads were equal – 1.5 million miles each. Long before that, automobile companies ceased designing cars with high clearances for bad roads.

Paved roads only highlighted other shortcomings in the highway system, notably safety. By the 1920s the annual highway death toll exceeded 25,000. In 1924, Commerce Secretary Herbert Hoover convened the first national conference on highway safety, yet fatalities climbed to 37,000 in the late 1930s. Initially, the assumptions of the American workplace prevailed on highways, as driver behavior was blamed for accidents. Only much later was attention given to designing safe highway/vehicle environments, with fewer metal posts and unprotected bridge abutments and with recessed knobs, padded dash boards, and seat belts. Still, halting steps toward safety were taken in the 1920s and 1930s. Signs, for example, eliminated uncertainty about routes. Wisconsin's highway department developed a numbering system for its 500-mile state system in 1918, while Minnesota introduced the first state shield in 1921. By 1925, the main national routes were numbered, with US 1 running north-south on the east coast and US 2 paralleling the Canadian border. Federal and state highway engineers also developed uniform traffic signs in 1927, using yellow for warning signs and white for directional signs. Red stop signs came later, after the development of durable red pigments. Round signs marked railroad crossings, stop signs were octagonal, warning signs were diamonds, and information was on rectangles. Through shape or color, drivers could recognize warnings but actually seeing signs at night was difficult until the introduction of luminous materials. Initially "cat's eyes" lenses that focused light on a mirror were the only reflectors. But in the 1920s and early 1930s, inexpensive plastic reflectors and paint with tiny glass spheres appeared, while Minnesota Mining and Manufacturing (3M) introduced "Scotchlite," a plastic reflective sheeting.

Pavement markings also made roads safer. In the nineteenth century, several cities marked safety zones and crosswalks, but Wayne County, Michigan, near Detroit, claimed the first centerline in 1911 and painted its road system by 1922. California began striping state highways in 1924. But to see better at night, Michigan engineers introduced a "reflectorized highway" in 1938, installing 6,900 plastic reflectors on poles at 100-foot intervals along seventy miles of road between Detroit and Lansing. That same year, glass spheres mixed in paint produced reflective highway lines, and by 1965 state, city, and county highway department used 21.5 million gallons of traffic paint and 107 million pounds of reflector beads.

Lighting was the most important safety development. In 1937, 20 percent of traffic moved at night but 60 percent of the 39,700 fatalities on the nation's highways occurred after dark. In the 1920s, gas and arc lights, or incandescent bulbs with tungsten filaments lit city streets. Gas-filled incandescent bulbs, introduced in 1930, mercury vapor and sodium vapor lamps in 1934, and aluminum reflectors (luminaires) allowed lights to be mounted twice as high (25–30 feet), reducing the number of poles and allowing regular roads to be lit. This mattered because vehicle headlights penetrated no further than about 150 feet in 1917. When travelling at 55 miles per hour (81 feet per second), drivers had less than two seconds of sight. The new streetlights extended visibility to between 700 and 1200 feet.

Another element of the highway system concerned finances, for property taxes could not support local and state road-building efforts. One source of revenue was license and registration fees, which provided $100 million for the states in 1921 and $259 million in 1928, with another $50 million going to local road builders. Since total construction costs averaged about $1 billion a year, highway agencies also relied upon bond financing. In 1921, about 27 percent of state funds and 43 percent of local highway funds came from bond sales. But in 1919, Oregon pioneered the most important revenue source – the gasoline tax. These levies generated $3.2 million, or 0.8 percent of the states' road construction funds, in 1921, but $254 million, 27.6 percent of the total, in 1928. Petroleum producers did not approve, but historian Burnham (1961) called this the only popular tax in American history. The only source of state revenue that did not diminish during the Depression, highway builders and automobile supporters united by 1935 to promote state constitutional amendments earmarking gasoline tax revenues for road construction.

Automotive Transportation and American Life, 1900–40

When the complex technological systems of roads and cars were combined, the result was an even more complicated socio-technical system. Auto executive and politician George Romney noted in his introduction to John Rae's history of automobile makers that the automobile is " 'deeply intertwined in the nation's social and economic fabric…' " (Rae 1959, p. v). The interaction of society and the automotive transportation system appeared in the way Americans worked and lived, as well as in their goals and expectations. Few technological systems have had such wide-ranging effects.

One of the clearest effects of automotive transportation was on the railroads, once the largest supporter of road improvements. Surprisingly early, motor vehicles were taking business from rail carriers. The Union Pacific, for example, reported hints in 1911 and clear evidence by 1914 that motor vehicles damaged their short-haul freight and passenger businesses. By 1916, automobiles delivered 19 billion more passenger-miles (54 billion) than railroads, and during the 1920s railroad passenger revenue fell 32 percent. While this loss came from private autos, freight began to be moved by trucks. Less-than-carload lots shipped short distances on railroads declined from 50 to 75 percent during the 1920s. The morning "milk run" from the countryside into large cities was another victim of truck transportation. Such changes hit rail carriers hard, for such traffic was lucrative. In response to the competition, by 1925 large rail carriers investigated replacing local trains with buses and trucks. The managers of the Pennsylvania Railroad envisioned becoming an integrated transportation company employing various transportation technologies. Indeed, during the late 1920s executives from the Pennsylvania and other leading railroads helped bring into existence the first transcontinental bus line, Greyhound. But limited profits, the onset of the Depression, the inertia of railroad managements, and regulatory restrictions combined to prevent the realization of that vision. After 1920 transportation in America increasingly meant motor vehicles at the expense of rail carriers.

Other economic consequences of the automotive transport system were equally significant. Between 1900 and 1910, the value of automotive production jumped from 150th to 21st on the list of American industries, and the motor car pulled other industries with it. Before 1900, gasoline accounted for 10 percent of refinery output, but cars expanded the market for petroleum products exponentially. It was not clear, however, that the industry could supply enough fuel, until a new catalytic cracking process (1913) increased the fraction of oil refined into gasoline. At the same time, new oil fields in East Texas and California supplied the flood of fuel for millions of mass-produced cars. The rubber industry faced similar challenges in developing better ways of mounting more durable tires. Stronger tire fabrics eventually allowed use of pneumatic tires on the heaviest vehicles. Steel and glass producers also benefited from the motor car, although both had to develop new production techniques. By the 1920s, automobiles consumed 90 percent of the petroleum, 80 percent of the rubber, 75 percent of the plate glass, 20 percent of the steel, and 25 percent of the machine tools produced in the US. About 400,000 workers earned a living assembling cars and at least three times that many worked in industries dependent upon the motor car. Automobiles drove the American economy.

We must not, however, assume that the automobile *determined* the shape of the American economy. The automobile/highway system certainly had social and economic implications for Americans, but the changes sprang from the broader society. Critics blamed automobiles for changing public morality after 1920, connecting cars to dating in rural areas, new women's fashions, and women's use of cosmetics, alcohol, and cigarettes. Cartoons, social critics and small-town preachers highlighted how young people used cars to escape protective or prying eyes. To be sure, automobiles (and radios) ended the isolation of rural Americans and connected them to the more varied experiences of towns and cities. In the process, the technologies helped create national consumption patterns, and at best facilitated the changes in customs and lifestyle that so concerned older and more fundamentally religious Americans. The electric starter, for example, that allowed women – and other drivers – to start a gasoline engine effortlessly also allowed them to participate easily in the liberating experience of driving. But despite the entertaining images on the covers of *LIFE* magazine, cars were less responsible for change than the novel wartime experiences young people enjoyed in the US and Europe.

In fact, many motorists shaped automotive technology to fit their needs, not the other way around. Ironically, rural residents, who were worried about automobiles, and youngsters turned automobiles into tools they controlled. Historians Wik (1972) and Kline (2000), among others, have shown that vehicle owners used cars in ways never envisioned by their builders. Henry Ford, who had rural roots, was attuned to these possibilities and soon produced tractors as well as cars. But even he did not imagine every use of the Model T. Farmers, for example, used them to drive threshing engines and saw mills. Others developed and sold special attachments and accessories, including large tires and plows a Model T could pull. Nor were farmers alone in remolding the Model T. Enterprising motorists added extra seats to create motor buses, or removed the seats completely to carry produce to nearby cities. Kits and accessories turned Model Ts into campers, so that vacations, once an upper class activity, were within the reach of those whose cars served as mobile hotel rooms. Camping grounds sprang up across the country, while less adventurous travelers stayed at new tourist courts or motels (that term was coined in 1925). Roadside restaurants appeared to serve hungry travelers. The economic consequences of tourism soon became apparent in areas possessing natural beauty or cultural or historical landmarks. The growing national and state park networks were indicators of changing patterns of travel and leisure time.

Automobiles alone could not cause such changes. To be sure, the freedom to travel by car made vacations feasible, but an important prerequisite for both car ownership and vacations were rising income levels for families in the middle and working classes. In addition, these and other activities were abetted by public policy choices at all levels of government. Automobiles required significant accommodations, especially in cities. By the 1920s officials in almost every city were struggling to manage the swarm of cars. City councils adopted streetlights and signals, parking bans, one-way streets, and other traffic restrictions. Detroit and Los Angeles adopted integrated plans for wide automobile boulevards and expanded transit systems, although the transit plans soon disappeared. Street railway franchises appeared undemocratic and old-fashioned, burdened by unsavory histories of corruption that compared unfavorably with the modern, personal freedom of automobiles. Historian Barrett (1983) has demonstrated that Chicago tightly restricted streetcar franchises for these reasons, refusing fare increases even as city officials spent significant sums to satisfy motorists. Urban street railways were not victims of a conspiracy led by GM and Firestone to buy trolley systems to install buses, as some have argued. More damaging were unfavorable public perceptions and policy decisions that favored cars and handicapped transit franchises.

The issue was largely decided by 1930, even as public officials were discovering that traffic control ordinances were inadequate for coping with growing congestion. A few places explored more radical solutions. Robert Moses used Long Island's state park authorities to construct the first motor parkways, an option available to no other city. Money, in fact, was always the limiting factor, for Congress did not authorize even limited funds for urban highway construction until 1938. A few other cities experimented with arterial roads such as Jersey City's elevated causeway over the Meadowlands, Chicago's Lake Shore Drive, and the Arroyo Seco expressway in Los Angeles. In the late 1930s, Detroit constructed a sunken, multi-lane highway with intersecting streets carried on overpasses, but costs limited the project to one mile. Robert Moses built parkways with federal work-relief funds during the Depression. Indeed, road work was the largest single unemployment activity of the federal government during the 1930s, further emphasizing the growing federal role in road work. But because Congress and FDR opposed expanding the federal government's role in this expensive arena, cities received little state or federal funding for roads at this time.

This effort to fit automobiles into cities was not the only evidence of American fascination with cars during the 1930s and 1940s. To be sure, the Depression was hard on auto makers, as production dropped below two million cars in 1932 and 1933. But most Americans had decided cars were a necessity, not a luxury, and the last possession many people gave up during the Depression was their car. In Hollywood's version of John Steinbeck's *Grapes of Wrath*, the Joad's truck was a symbol as important as the heroic family members. And when the nation went to war in 1941, the army did so on wheels. Germany pioneered blitzkrieg warfare, but American armies relied so completely on motorized transport that the Allies built a gasoline pipeline from Britain after D-Day. British military historian Keegan grew up in the 1940s with an enduring memory that "Americans traveled in magnificent, gleaming, olive-green, pressed-steel, four-wheel-drive juggernauts, decked with what car sales-men would call option extras…There were towering GMC six-by-sixes and compact and powerful Dodge four-by-fours. Pilot fishing the rest or buzzing nimbly about the lanes on independent errands were tiny and entrancing jeeps" (Keegan 1982, p. 88). Car makers produced much of the dizzying array of equipment and weapons, ranging from machine guns and aircraft, to tanks, ships, and artillery. While civilian cars disappeared from dealer show rooms, the assembly lines of the auto industry largely explained the Allied victory.

Automotive Transportation in the Postwar World

At war's end, Americans quickly resumed their love affair with the automobile. Everyone it seemed, wanted a new car and automobile production soared. Only 69,000 cars had rolled off assembly lines in 1945, but output rose to 2.1 million in 1946, 3.6 million in 1947, and 5.1 million in 1949. Pent-up demand allowed car makers to sell everything they made, leading to a dangerously arrogant mindset within the industry. As Keats (1958) showed in *Insolent Chariots*, car makers began ignoring consumers as they adopted instead high-pressure sales techniques and lost interest in quality or the pursuit of technical innovations. One of the few changes were high-compression V-8 engines, which allowed car makers to introduce heavier vehicles loaded with accessories – the basic car of the 1950s. In this environment, GM's Harley Earl and other designers literally shaped the industry. Fascinated by the twin-tailed P-38 Lightning aircraft, Earl introduced the fins and chrome ornament that Plymouth and others carried to excess in the late 1950s. The resulting behemoths grew longer, weighed more, and boasted larger engines with more horse-power and lower fuel economy.

The monsters of the 1950s reflected affluent postwar America and mirrored the firms that produced them. GM had become the largest industrial firm in the world, but Sloan's control and reporting system turned into a sluggish, multi-layered bureaucracy that complicated decision-making. Ford finally developed a modern business structure after almost expiring during the war. Robert McNamara and other operations research engineers from the Pentagon (the "Whiz Kids") installed accounting and reporting mechanisms while Earnest Breech taught Henry Ford II to run a car company. In both firms, financial managers displaced engineers as the key corporate decision-makers. Few executives at the Big Three resembled Edward Cole, president of Chevrolet in the 1950s who designed V-8 engines, brought out the 1955 Chevy, and bore responsibility for both the Corvette and the Corvair.

In this environment, the last small auto companies expired. Two celebrated postwar start-ups, Kaiser-Frazer and Tucker, failed, while the surviving independents foundered after riding an initial wave of consumer demand. Studebaker and Packard merged only to fail in 1963. Hudson and Nash combined to form American Motors in 1954 and for a time beat the odds under George Romney. His key insight was that Americans would buy a smaller, less expensive car than the Big Three offered. He bet American Motors future on the Rambler, and was vindicated as sales passed 100,000 in 1958 and reached half a million by 1960.

This success contrasted markedly with the fate of Ford's chrome-laden Edsel, whose disastrous debut in 1958 hinted at a consumer backlash against Detroit. The growing popularity of foreign cars carried a similar meaning. Imported European cars (Hillman, Austin, Fiat) were an oddity in the early 1950s, with sales of 12,000 in 1949 and 57,000 in 1955. Then the situation changed, thanks largely to Volkswagen's Beetle, which offered a reliable, sturdy, low-priced yet quirky car. It defied the norms of conspicuous consumption promoted by the Big Three, yet VW imports rose from 1,000 in 1953 to 120,000 in 1959, the first-year imports accounted for 10 percent of American sales (more than 600,000). Detroit car makers argued they could respond if they wished. Under McNamara's guidance, Ford brought out the Falcon, while Chrysler introduced the Dart and GM the Corvair – a rear-engine car obviously patterned on the Beetle. But large cars produced more profit, leading American auto makers to treat compact cars as a distraction. The history of the Mustang is instructive, for the small, sporty car introduced by Lee Iaccoco in 1965 sold a record 418,000 units its first year. But by 1972 Iaccoco himself labelled the ever-larger accessory laden car a pig that had left its audience behind.

Not surprisingly, the sales of imports continued to grow. American sales of the Beetle climbed to 383,000 in 1963, accounting for two-thirds of all imports. Overall imports sales jumped from the half-million mark to over 900,000 in 1966 and first surpassed a million in 1967; imports held 15 percent of the market by 1970. The surge was driven by the arrival of Japanese cars. Led by Datsun, Japanese companies explored the US market in the early 1960s, selling 7,500 units in 1963 and 82,000 in 1967. Then imports doubled in 1968, and by 1975 both Toyota and Datsun passed VW, with Japanese firms controlling 18 percent of the American market. The energy crisis strengthened their position, for only imports were positioned to meet the demand for smaller fuel-efficient cars. Japanese firms shipped 1.37 million cars to the US in 1976, 2.4 million in 1980. By that time, Toyota and Honda had earned reputations for high-quality products and consumer satisfaction (symbolized by the cup holder) as well as fuel efficiency. These and other Japanese companies began opening assembly plants in the US to deal with rising protectionist sentiment. By 1986, importers held 25 percent of the American car market, a figure that rose to 28 percent in 1990.

Detroit answered this challenge ineptly at first. American designs were uninspired in comparison with the Honda Accord or Civic or the Toyota Corolla. They fell far short of Japanese standards for quality – even though American engineers had pioneered the statistical quality control techniques used in Japan. Labor relations in American assembly plants were abysmal, symbolized by a wildcat strike at Chevrolet's Lordstown plant in 1972, in which workers ignored both corporate and union officials. Moreover, American manufacturers struggled to meet new government rules regarding emissions. The link between automobile pollution and smog was established in the

Los Angeles basin after 1950, and California mandated emissions control equipment for the 1966 models. Federal legislation in 1965 set less restrictive federal guidelines for 1968, but the Federal Clean Air Act of 1970 tightened pollution standards. Detroit car makers needed an extension to 1977–8 in order to meet the new law, while Honda's CVCC engine, Mazda rotary engine, and Mercedes Benz diesels met the standards on time. American companies also struggled to meet fuel economy standards. And they also had to cope with safety requirements under the National Traffic and Motor Vehicle Safety Act of 1966, which created the National Highway Traffic Safety Administration. That agency imposed numerous safety standards, including seat belts, impact-absorbing steering columns, and air bags, and also could order the recall of defective cars. In all of these areas – quality, engineering, performance, and design – imports outperformed American cars. The postwar honeymoon enjoyed by American car makers had dissolved and the Big Three seemed to have lost their way.

The Interstate Era

A similar story of initial promise and dashed expectations describes highway development after 1945. The postwar wave of new cars posed enormous challenges for engineers developing the nation's road system. Federal funding jumped to $500 million annually, but many states could not match their share. Moreover, first, rising wage levels and later material shortages caused by the Korean conflict hampered road-building programs. Finally, disputes about construction priorities prevented the Congress from adjusting the existing highway policy and priorities. Federal and state engineers had hoped to emphasize a new system of high-speed interregional roads linking the nation's cities. The idea had surfaced during the 1930s, and dominated a Bureau of Public Roads document prepared for Franklin Roosevelt in 1939, "Toll Roads and Free Roads." Congress authorized such a 40,000-mile system in 1944, in part to provide jobs if demobilization brought back the Depression. But the conflicting desires of other road users in urban and rural areas deadlocked highway policy reforms through the early 1950s.

Toll financing offered one way to pay for the expensive express roads between cities. The Pennsylvania Turnpike, completed in 1940 with federal work-relief funds, provides a model adopted in eastern and Midwestern states. By 1953, states had completed 762 miles of toll road, with 1,100 miles under construction; in 1963 the toll road total reached 3,500 miles. But this financial mechanism had limited application, and did little to help many states match federal-aid appropriations for the US-numbered system (primary roads), urban arterials, and important secondary roads. From 1950 through 1956, the Congress struggled to forge an acceptable plan. President Eisenhower even asked wartime colleague Lucius Clay to broker a solution, to no avail. In 1955, however, a financial plan appeared that provided more funds for all roads, in part by creating a highway trust fund to receive all taxes on gas and new excise levies on tires and other auto-related purchases. To help the states, the federal government agreed to provide 90 percent of the cost of the proposed Interstate system of 41,000 (later 42,500) miles at an estimated cost of $25 billion. By earmarking gas and vehicle taxes, Congress had solved a major political headache, for legislators needed only to authorize expenditures from the fund every 2 years, not find the money. The great postwar road-building boom was launched.

Despite overwhelming public support for their efforts, state and federal engineers began encountering loud complaints in less than 10 years. First, construction on the Interstate roads started slow and took longer than expected. Highly publicized corruption trials of a few state officials and Congressional hearings cast doubt upon the expertise of highway builders – their claim to political legitimacy and authority. Worse, as Interstate highways poked into urban areas, they displaced tens of thousands of residents. Highway agencies, convinced these roads were desperately wanted by the public, occasionally acted high-handedly and quickly aroused the century's first widespread opposition to roads. Robert Moses' style of displacing thousands while building the Cross-Bronx Expressway (Interstate 95) in New York City epitomized engineering arrogance. Mumford (1963) criticized urban express highways on aesthetic and democratic grounds, as Kelley's *The Pavers and the Paved* (1971) and Leavitt's *Superhighway – Superhoax* (1970) attacked the lack of accountability of road-building agencies. The shared power structure of federal-aid allowed state and federal engineers to pass the buck on citizen complaints. Highway engineers, on the other hand, were totally unprepared for this "Freeway Revolt." In the end, public protests halted road projects in Boston, New Orleans, San Francisco, Washington, Philadelphia, San Antonio, and many other cities. Neighborhood groups, sometimes joined by civil rights organizers, complained about inadequate compensation for condemned property, lack of public notice, and the linkage of expressways to urban renewal, which located Interstates in poor minority communities. In some instances, environmental issues halted road projects, especially after the Environmental Policy Act (1969) required the mandatory filing of environmental impact statements. As a result of the protests, road construction practices were significantly overhauled after 1970 to allow for public participation earlier in the planning process. This was a sea change of major proportions, ending six decades of engineering control of American road building as politicians reasserted control of state highway departments.

The "Freeway Revolt" actually stopped very little construction. By 1980, drivers used more than 40,000 miles of Interstate highway and often took them for granted. These highways differed significantly from even the best roads built before 1950. Designed for speed, highway engineers also attempted after 1963 to build them safer by creating a "forgiving roadside." Pressure for improved safety grew from increased awareness of problems in vehicles, such as those highlighted in Nader's expose on the Corvair, *Unsafe at Any Speed* (1965). Highway engineers responded by placing bridge abutments away from the pavement and burying guardrail ends to prevent impaling cars that ran off the road. Breakaway signposts and later collapsible light standards came into issue. The Jersey barrier, a concrete divider with a tapered base that redirects a car's wheel, appeared on the New Jersey turnpike in the mid-1950s, and slowly spread as a means of preventing head-on crashes. High-mast light poles, introduced in the late 1960s, made highway intersections as bright as day yet required only a few light poles. Studies of signs led to colors and lettering more visible to motorists moving at high speeds. Raised pavement markers – reflectors attached directly to the road to supplement painted lines – were proposed in the late 1920s but only adopted in southern states before the 1960s. They spread further north with the introduction of better adhesives and snow plow blades with neoprene edges that rode over the markers. Taken together, these adjustments reduced the carnage on highways from an all-time high of 56,278 in 1972 to about 42,000 per year in the early 1990s. Finally, in many urban areas, sound barriers and landscaping typified attempts to limit the impact of Interstate roads on surrounding housing divisions. None of these changes were cheap. Urban roads could cost tens of millions of dollars per mile after property purchases were included. When the last leg of the original system was completed in the mid-1990s, the estimated total construction cost topped $329 billion (in 1996 dollars, which works out to $58.5 billion in 1957 dollars).

Despite the substantial controversy that surrounded the postwar road-building program, roads and the automotive transportation system, of which they were a part, increased in significance for the American economy and for the lives of individual Americans. Indeed, patterns and trends evident in the 1920s and 1930s continued unabated. Personal fascination with cars remained as strong as ever, as seen in Robert Post's history of drag racing and in the phenomenal public following of NASCAR and stock car racing. Similarly, many Americans built their lives around cars. Vacations and leisure travel were firmly ensconced as a core activity of the American family during the 1950s – an even more affluent era than the 1920s. The appearance of Holiday Inn motels in 1952, followed by the first motel attached to a Howard Johnson restaurant a year later, marked the emergence of national lodging chains. McDonald's restaurants began growing into an international icon after Ray Kroc started selling franchises in 1954; by 1960 there were 200 restaurants and the era of fast-food restaurants, offering everything from chicken and donuts to ice cream and tacos, had begun.

The automobile influenced more than personal travel. After 1950, an entire lifestyle took shape in suburbs because of automotive transportation. Suburbs had first appeared outside on urban peripheries as street railways extended their lines in the 1890s, but the postwar version consisted of single-family tract homes connected to the rest of the world by cars and Interstate highways. The growing subdivisions outside cities pulled retail establishments away from downtown department stores and shops, accelerating one of the most unanticipated consequences of Interstate highways into cities – the decline of central business districts. City officials who backed expressway construction watched helplessly as residents used them to flee to the suburbs, as stores closed, and as property values declined. Even in 1953, 1,800 shopping centers had sprung up, and that number had swollen to 45,721 in 2002. They provided almost 5.7 billion square feet of retail space and accounted for 50 percent of all retail sales in the US – $1.18 billion annually. Left behind in cities, however, were those who could not afford to move, and they watched as highway departments targeted their neighborhoods for freeway locations because it was far easier – politically and financially – to link roads for urban renewal. Mumford's critique of roads and cities seemed ever more cogent.

As this evidence suggested, the economic consequences of the automotive transport system continued to increase. Another pivotal postwar shift was the continued replacement of trains by motor vehicles. Passenger trains disappeared steadily until the federal government created AMTRAK, while many consumer goods were moved almost exclusively by truck. The Interstate system, which constituted one percent of the road mileage, carried 20 percent of the traffic. By the 1970s, long-haul truckers were celebrated on Top 40 radio as an American symbol of rugged independence and freedom. And in the wake of these changes came entirely new land-use patterns as trucking warehouses grew up near Interstate exist ramps, replacing railroad freight yards in importance. By the late 1990s, several studies reported that the success of Amazon and e-retailers depended substantially upon rapid trucking and delivery services via the Interstate highway network.

Thus the "car culture" remains the central fact of modern American life. Indeed, during the last decade of the century, the gloomy picture surrounding automotive manufacturing in the United States lightened. Highway engineers explored "smart highways" in pursuit of the dream of automatic vehicle control, while American auto makers recovered market share and technical leadership. Imports dropped to less than 20 percent by 1995, as the most important vehicles of the decade were distinctly American – the minivan (first developed by Chrysler), sports utility vehicles (SUVs), and pick-up trucks. Indeed truck production nearly doubled during the 1990s. GM struggled to find its way, but Chrysler recovered from near-bankruptcy under Lee Iaccoco, while Ford moved back to the top of the Big Three. Some models were afflicted by the American tendencies of creeping size and weight increases (witness the HUMMER phenomenon), but auto makers also embraced the microelectronics revolution in many components. These changes, in combination with economic prosperity in the US (including low gasoline prices), and economic difficulties in Japan, allowed American car companies to recover some ground lost in the 1970s and 1980s.

American car makers do not dominate the economy as completely as during the 1950s, but GM president Charles E. Wilson's 1953 comment that "What's good for the country is good for General Motors and what's good for General Motors is good for the country," retains a measure of validity. The dot-com boom captured headlines in the 1990s, but revival of American auto firms was certainly significant. Yet in a final irony, this revival came as national identifications diminished in an auto industry composed of multinational manufacturers. Partnerships and mergers abounded, as Ford acquired ownership stakes in Volvo, Jaguar, and Mazda, while GM is linked to Vauxhall, Saab, Hummer, and several Japanese producers, including Isuzu and Suzuki. Some Japanese models actually have more American-made components than cars from the Big Three. Yet in this increasingly global industry, the American market remains the most important, as the epitome of the car culture.

BIBLIOGRAPHY

Barrett, Paul. *The Automobile and Urban Transit: The Formation of Public Policy in Chicago, 1900–1930* (Philadelphia: Temple University Press, 1983).
Belasco, Warren J. *Americans on the Road: From Autocamp to Motel, 1910–1945* (Cambridge: MA: MIT Press, 1979).

Berger, Michael. *The Devil Wagon in God's Country: The Automobile and Social Change in Rural America, 1893–1929* (Hamden, CT: Archon Books, 1979).

Brodsly, David. *L.A. Freeway: An Appreciative Essay* (Berkeley: University of California Press, 1981).

Burnham, John Chynoweth. "The gasoline tax and the automobile revolution." *Mississippi Valley Historical Review* 48 (December 1961): 435–59.

Caro, Robert. *The Power Broker: Robert Moses and the Fall of New York* (New York: Knopf, 1974).

Chaiken, Bernard. "Traffic marking materials – summary of research and development," *Public Roads* 35 (December 1969): 251–6.

Cray, ed. *Chrome Colossus: General Motors and Its Times* (New York: McGraw-Hill, 1980).

Davis, Donald Finlay. *Conspicuous Production: Automobiles and Elites in Detroit, 1899–1933* (Philadelphia, PA: Temple University Press, 1988).

Flink, James J. *The Automobile Age* (Cambridge, MA: MIT Press, 1988).

Halberstamm, David. *The Reckoning* (New York: Morrow, 1986).

Haycraft, William R. *Yellow Steel: The Story of the Earthmoving Equipment Industry* (Urbana: University of Illinois Press, 2000).

Hine, Thomas. *Populuxe* (New York: Knopf, 1986).

Hounshell, David. *From the American System to Mass Production: The Development of Manufacturing Technology in the United States, 1900–1912* (Baltimore: Johns Hopkins University Press, 1984).

Jakle, John A. and Keith A Sculle. *The Gas Station in America* (Baltimore: Johns Hopkins University Press, 1994).

Jakle, John A. *The Motel in America* (Baltimore: Johns Hopkins University Press, 1996).

Jakle, John A. *Fast Food: Roadside Restaurants in the Automobile Age* (Baltimore: Johns Hopkins University Press, 1999).

Keats, John. *The Insolent Chariots* (Philadelphia: Lippincott, 1958).

Keegan, John. "Suddenly, there were the Americans," *American Heritage* (June 1982): 86–9.

Kelley, Ben. *The Pavers and the Paved* (New York: D.W. Brown, 1971).

Kirsch, David A. *The Electric Vehicle and the Burden of History* (New Brunswick, NJ: Rutgers University Press, 2000).

Kline, Ronald. R. *Consumers in the Country: Technology and Social Change in Rural America* (Baltimore, MD: Johns Hopkins University Press, 2000).

Labattut, Jean and Wheaton J. Lane, eds. *Highways in Our National Life: A Symposium* (Princeton: Princeton University Press, 1950).

Leavitt, Helen. *Superhighway – Superhoax* (Garden City, NY: Doubleday, 1970).

Liebs, Chester H. *Main Street to Miracle Mile: American Roadside Architecture* (Boston: Little, Brown, 1985).

Lewis, David L. and Laurence Goldstein, eds. *The Automobile and American Culture* (Ann Arbor: University of Michigan Press, 1983).

MacDonald, Thomas H. "The financing of highways," *Annals of the American Academy of Political and Social Science* 116 (November 1924): 160–8.

Maxim, Hiram Percy. *Horseless Carriage Days* (New York: Harper & Brothers, 1937).

Meyer, Stephen. *The Five Dollar Day: Labor Management and Social Control in the Ford Motor Company, 1908–1921* (Albany: State University of New York Press, 1981).

Mohl, Raymond. *Urban Planning and the African American Community: In the Shadows* (Thousand Oaks: Sage Publications, 1997).

Mumford, Lewis. *The Highway and the City* (New York: Harcourt, Brace & World, 1963).

Nader, Ralph. *Unsafe at Any Speed: The Designed-in Dangers of the American Automobile* (New York: Grossman, 1965).

Nelson, Walter Henry. *Small Wonder: The Amazing Story of the Volkswagen* (Boston: Little, Brown, 1965).

Nevins, Allan. *Ford*, 3 vols (New York, Scribner: 1954–63).

Post, Robert C. *High Performance: The Culture and Technology of Drag Racing, 1950–2000*, 2nd. rev. edn (Baltimore: Johns Hopkins University Press, 2001).

Preston, Howard L. *Automobile Age Atlanta: The Making of a Southern Metropolis, 1900–1935* (Athens: University of Georgia Press, 1979).

Rae, John B. *American Automobile Manufacturers: The First Forty Years* (Philadelphia: The Chilton Company, 1959).

Rae, John B. *The American Automobile: A Brief History* (Chicago: University of Chicago Press, 1965).

Rice, Edward M. "Lighting and the modern highway," *Roads and Streets* 81 (March 1938): 45–6.

Rose, Mark H. *Interstate: Express Highway Politics, 1941–1956*, 2nd. rev. edn (Knoxville: University of Tennessee Press, 1989).

Rose, Mark and Bruce E. Seely. "Getting the Interstate system built: road engineers and the implementation of public policy, 1955–1985," *Journal of Policy History* 2 (Winter 1990): 23–56.

The Rouge: The Image of Industry in the Art of Charles Sheeler and Diego Rivera (Detroit: Detroit Institute of Arts, 1978).

"Saga of highway striping in black and white," *Public Works 102* (August 1971): 72–3.

St Clair, David James. *The Motorization of American Cities* (New York: Praeger, 1986).

Seely, Bruce E. *Building the American Highway System: Engineers as Policy Makers* (Philadelphia: Temple University Press, 1987).

Wik, Reynold M. *Henry Ford and Grass Roots America* (Ann Arbor: University of Michigan Press, 1972).

Yates, Brock W. *The Decline and Fall of the American Automobile Industry* (New York: Empire Books, 1983).

CHAPTER FOURTEEN

Airplanes

ROGER E. BILSTEIN

Early Aeronautics

In 1903, when the Wright brothers became airborne in a powered, heavier-than-air flying machine, their feat represented the climax of over a century's activities in the realm of human flight. In Paris, France, a hot air balloon crafted by the Montgolfier brothers carried passengers aloft in 1783; in the 1850s, the British scientist Sir George Cayley (1774–1857) fashioned a series of experimental gliders with rudimentary tail surfaces; Otto Lilienthal (1848–96), a German engineer, carried out over 2,000 glider flights and codified considerable details about construction and materials before dying in a crash. Moreover, during the 1860s, the formation of aeronautical organizations in Britain and France meant that their respective journals provided enthusiasts with the means to circulate ideas and information. Using domestic and foreign sources, Americans could take advantage of a growing number of aeronautical legacies. Samuel Pierpont Langley (1834–1906), distinguished astronomer and head of the Smithsonian Institution in Washington, DC, built an "Aerodrome" to achieve the first powered flight in a winged airplane, but failed twice late in 1903. Just nine days after Langley's second failure, the unheralded Wright brothers flew into history near Kitty Hawk, North Carolina.

Wilbur (1867–1912) and Orville (1871–1948) Wright, sons of a mid-western religious leader, grew up in a comfortable family environment that encouraged reading and learning. The Wright family eventually settled in Dayton, Ohio. Inveterate tinkerers, Wilbur and Orville established a local newspaper and enjoyed financial success as builders of high-quality bicycles. Both became fascinated by the goal of human flight, and addressed the problem with determined, step-by-step thoroughness they had acquired from building and racing their bicycles. They also wrote to the Smithsonian for the latest information on flying machines. Although much of the information they received turned out to be inaccurate, the process of building on extant data and correcting problems as they proceeded proved to be an important element in achieving eventual success. The brothers built their own wind tunnel and accumulated essential tables for lift and drag with various wing shapes. They demonstrated an ingeniously intuitive ability to translate their wind tunnel data into full-scale designs, then working out fabrication problems in the process of constructing full-size wings. Next, they put together large gliders and looked for a site with robust head winds to test them, choosing a section of the Atlantic coastline near Kitty

Hawk, North Carolina. By train, horse-drawn wagon, and boat, they made their way to the remote, sparsely populated region known as the Outer Banks. Between 1900 and 1903, periodic expeditions to the sand dunes of Kill Devil Hills led to effective techniques for control of roll, pitch, and yaw with their aircraft. In the process, they both became proficient glider pilots, a skill that differentiated them from other aspiring aeronauts of the era. At home in Dayton, further aeronautical research led to effective propeller design and the construction of a 12-horsepower gasoline engine. Then, in the winter of 1903, they returned to Kill Devil Hills for the ultimate test of their powered, heavier-than-air, piloted flying machine.

After flipping a coin, Wilbur's initial attempt resulted in a stall and a damaged rudder. Following repairs, it became Orville's turn. On December 17, 1903, he piloted the plane over a distance of 120 feet in 12 seconds. They made three more flights, including Wilbur's one-minute journey of 852 feet. They sent their father a telegram that succinctly reported their success, packed up their airplane, and boarded the train for home.

Because Langley and many other would-be fliers had come to grief, most people did not believe subsequent reports of the little-known Wright brothers. For the next 5 years, the Wrights – inherently shy and also leery of possible patent infringements – quietly continued their flight trials at Huffman Prairie, not far from their hometown of Dayton. Meanwhile, European aviation proceeded at a vigorous pace. Eventually, Alberto Santos-Dumont (a Brazilian expatriate living in France) made a powered flight in 1906. Most Europeans hailed him as the first person in history to accomplish the feat of sustained flight in a true airplane. Other entrepreneurs repeated Santos-Dumont's feat, including Louis Bleriot's monoplane in 1907, machines built by Voisin, and others.

Back in the United States, Glenn Curtiss and his associates flew a successful aircraft in 1908, followed by some highly publicized distance flights. That summer, the Wrights finally emerged from relative obscurity to validate their claim as the first to fly. At Fort Myer, Virginia, near Washington, DC, Orville awed spectators during public trials for a military contract. Wilbur boarded a transatlantic ocean liner with a second machine and took Europe by storm. In the following years, the Wrights signed a contract with the US Army and organized the Wright Company. Curtiss also organized a manufacturing firm. Aerial exhibitions on both sides of the Atlantic subsequently made aviation into a fascinating phenomenon of the new twentieth century, and numerous builders optimistically took a flyer in the aeronautics business (Crouch 1989; Jakab 1990).

The frail aircraft of the pre-World War I era possessed neither the range or carrying capacity to support commercial applications, although demonstrations of aerial express and mail delivery occurred. Still, most civil aviation seemed to revolve around headline events that featured races and air show antics. A number of women became active fliers. Some, like Katherine Stinson, survived their experience on the exhibition circuit; others, like Harriet Quimby did not. A rash of wrecks and a growing death roll of inexperienced pilots created a negative image of flight in the minds of many Americans. Proponents of aviation spoke optimistically about the benefits of rapid transportation and the joys of flight, but the rhetoric fell far short of the reality.

In 1914, following the outbreak of World War I, the direction of aviation technology took a dramatic new turn. Early in the conflict, the warring powers realized the wealth of information available from aerial surveillance and photographic images of enemy activity along the combat zone. The combatants poured funding into aeronautical research and development as the airplane rapidly evolved from a relatively sedate flying machine to the status of a deadly combat weapon. Journalists filed lurid stories about knights of the air. Pilots themselves – engaged in bitter duels thousands of feet above the trenches – knew this to be a myth as they struggled with the psychological strains of combat fatigue and the alarming fatality rate among their comrades. Germany sent huge dirigibles on bombing missions to British cities across the Channel, bringing death and destruction to civilians in workplaces and homes far from the combat zone. Both sides soon equipped themselves with long range, multi-engine bombers to bomb strategic targets, inevitably situated in urban areas whose inhabitants had thought they would be insulated from the carnage of frontline trenches. Total war became a grim reality.

Into this cauldron of rapidly evolving modern combat, the United States arrived in April 1917 as a comparatively naïve partner of its cohorts at war with the Central Powers. The United States had little time to train military airmen and ramp up airplane production before the Armistice in November 1918. Although some builders, like Glenn Curtiss, and some suppliers had exported planes and accessories to the allied powers earlier in the war, the country had no wartime manufacturing capability that came anywhere close to its compatriots. Nonetheless, in a country where mass production had already been taken for granted, its citizens and its Congress expected to see thousands of American planes and pilots at the European front. Most aviation companies had close ties with the automobile industry, whose executives confidently predicted thousands of planes and engines. Despite grandiose forecasts, the industry failed to make good on its promises. Consequently, the majority of American fliers in Europe piloted aircraft built in Britain, France, or Italy. The only American combat planes to reach the combat zone were de Haviland DH-4 scout bombers (with Americanized spelling) copied from a British design. As for America's failure to meet production goals, a sordid trail of graft and corruption could be found. The major factors, however, involved the specialized, time-consuming aspects of building wooden-framed, fabric-covered airplanes – requiring legions of skilled craft workers – as opposed to automotive assembly lines where steel frames and metal bodies could be assembled by less skilled personnel.

There were some bright spots. One group of automotive executives put together a team of engineers who designed the rugged Liberty engine, with production versions coming off the line in about six weeks. The engine equipped hundreds of DH-4 planes and military surplus made it an economical, workable choice to power a variety of postwar designs. The wartime contracts also created a broader aeronautical infrastructure of suppliers who made aircraft instruments, specialized engine components, and other aviation accessories in the postwar era. Also, there were significant developments within the military services involving centers for research and engineering. The process of training a future nucleus of young aircraft designers and engineers took a step forward as universities inaugurated wartime courses within existing engineering departments (Kennett 1991; Bilstein 2001a).

Evolution of an Industry

One of the most significant legacies of the wartime era involved the origin of the National Advisory Committee for Aeronautics (NACA). Following the outbreak of World War I, Americans realized that European aviation had not only been ahead of the United States but that progress overseas was accelerating even more rapidly under the pressure of combat. Congress finally took action, establishing the NACA in 1915 "to supervise and direct the scientific study of the problems of flight, with a view to their practical solutions." This phraseology, along with other concepts, was drawn directly from the British Advisory Committee for Aeronautics, used as a model for the American counterpart. The original NACA had advisory powers only, relying on other government agencies or university laboratories to pursue its recommended aeronautical investigations on a shoestring budget. Recognizing the need for dedicated research facilities, Congress appropriated funds to establish a center located at an Army air base near Langley, Virginia. By the end of the 1930s, "Langley" had become the catchword for one of the world's leading organizations in aeronautical research.

The NACA's rise to prominence represented a mixture of shrewd management, technological panache, and unusually dedicated personnel who enjoyed the thrill of operating on the leading edge of an exciting new technology. The young agency also rode the crest of an expanding national economy that made aviation a growth industry, yielding plenty of opportunities for the NACA to contribute. Continued connections with European expertise also yielded considerable benefit. America's acknowledged shallowness in theoretical aerodynamics led to the recruitment of Dr Max Munk, a student of Dr Ludwig Prandtl at the renowned German research university in Gottingen. At Langley, Munk supervised the design and construction of a state-of-the-art high-density wind tunnel, which contributed to several important aerodynamic advances. By the late 1920s, a huge tunnel for testing full-sized aircraft spurred advances in the efficiency of wing-mounted engines, validated the use of retractable landing gear, and aided the general design of numerous aircraft types. The NACA design for a cowling to encircle the cylinders of radial engines, with a radical reduction of drag, constituted a major contribution in the design of high performance military planes and for production of economical airliners. Throughout the stressful years of the depression of the 1930s, notable progress continued to characterize NACA research, including significant advances in anti-icing technology. High speed aircraft designs especially benefited from studies involving laminar flow wings, based partially on theories acquired from European sources (Hansen 1987; Roland 1985).

A remarkable series of programs funded by the Daniel Guggenheim Fund for the Promotion of Aeronautics also resulted in fundamental contributions to the progress of aviation in the United States. In 1928, for example, one project led to successful techniques and practical instrumentation for "blind flying" at night and in bad weather. Other initiatives led to basic research in meteorology for more accurate weather forecasting, an indispensable tool for maintaining airline schedules and for military operations. Funding from the Guggenheim program accelerated the organization of schools of aeronautical engineering, graduating dozens of skilled professionals who designed and supervised the manufacture of increasingly sophisticated aircraft designs. The Guggenheim fund also recruited Dr Theodore von Karman from Europe. Joining the faculty of the California Institute of Technology, the brilliant and tireless von Karman not only energized research and development on the West Coast and elsewhere, but also mentored a cadre of gifted students in advanced studies and also took the initiative in organizing early research into rocketry (Hallion 1977; Gorn 1992).

In the meantime, a series of flying achievements kept aviation in the headlines, building enthusiasm for aviation programs to come. During 1919, planes crossed the Atlantic for the first time; during the 1920s, fliers circumnavigated the world and completed historic polar flights. In the spring of 1927 (20–21 May), Charles Lindbergh captured world press attention with his non-stop flight from New York to Paris in 33 hours and 39 minutes. Lindbergh's achievement loomed large because he flew solo in a single-engine plane and completed a direct route between two of the world's premier cities. The decades between the wars witnessed dozens of other outstanding flights that demonstrated the growing capability of aircraft to reduce travel time, not only within nations but also between continents.

The MacRobertson race in 1934 featured an intercontinental route that leaped from Great Britain through the Middle East and Asia to end in Australia. Over 20 international contestants signed on for the event. Britain entered the de Havilland DH.88 Comet, a highly streamlined, twin-engine, compact two-seater designed specifically to win the race. Eventually it did (20–23 October), but not by the large margin that had been expected. Nipping at its heels the entire way was a Dutch crew in a KLM airliner – an American DC-2. The DC-2 commercial airliner, also carrying a cargo of mail, turned in a startling display of reliability and a performance that not only closely matched that of the sleek DH.88 racer but also could exceed that of front-line British military planes of the era. As the British periodical, *Saturday Review*, reported, the DC-2's overall record "was almost incredible but it is true." The American airline transport symbolized a revolution that had rapidly occurred by the late 1930s, when fabric-covered biplanes were dramatically eclipsed by modern, all-metal monoplanes with retractable landing gear and a powerful family of radial engines (Gwynn-Jones 1991).

The new generation of aircraft represented a combination of research carried out by organizations like the NACA, advances in aircraft engines and fuels, metallurgy, and advanced engineering such as stressed skin construction. Like many techniques successfully applied by engineers in America, stressed skin construction possessed strong links with advanced European technology. American designers became especially attracted to the idea, which promised to reduce the structural weight of the aircraft, increase the payload, and enhance speed. At about the same time, NACA testing demonstrated the considerable advantages of retractable landing gear as other engineers and manufacturers introduced engines that developed greater horsepower in relation to their weight, variable pitch propellers, and better methods of coping with problems of aerodynamic drag (including flush riveting of metal aircraft skin), all of which contributed to improved aircraft performance.

Design improvements like these led to outstanding new civil aircraft like the Boeing 247, the Douglas DC-2 and DC-3. The Boeing plane entered service first, in 1933. Its design unfolded as a result of close collaboration of engine manufacturers (Pratt & Whitney), an airline (National Air Transport), and the manufacturer, all with careful attention to airline economics. Moreover, the Boeing included passenger amenities such as a lavatory, heating and cooling vents for individual passengers in the cabin, and attention to plans for seating and cabin insulation that reduced omnipresent noise. Boeing also made use of certain state-of-the-art fabrication techniques that had been worked out in the design of an advanced bomber design of the era, the B-9. Regrettably, in order to achieve performance, designers of the 247 decided on a comparatively small cabin that seated only ten passengers, and its design did not commend itself to the second-generation enlargements that seemed to become standard for subsequent airline designs. In contrast, the original DC-2 (1934) could seat 14 passengers, and the DC-3 that quickly followed in 1936 seated 21 passengers. With a cruising of about 185 mph, about the same as a Boeing 247, the DC-3 had a range of 1,500 miles – nearly twice that of the Boeing – with double the passenger load. The Douglas transports also came equipped with de-icing equipment and variable pitch propellers, enhancing their performance and reliability across a wide range of operating regimes. By 1938, DC-3 transports carried 95 percent of all United States airline traffic. The plane became an export success, operating with over 30 foreign airlines; in 1939, roughly 90 percent of airline traffic in the world traveled aboard the Douglas transport. The remarkable success of the DC-3 accounted for its widespread use in World War II and helped explain why American builders of airline transports dominated the world market for years after the war (Miller and Sawers 1970; van der Linden 1991).

In parallel with progress in technology, aviation also made its mark in the day-to-day activities of the modern world, particularly in the case of air mail and passenger service. The air mail saga began in 1918, when the United States Post Office Department organized the first aerial schedules. Relying on sturdy DH-4 planes from war surplus, the Post Office originally based its network in the eastern section of the United States. By 1925, the Post Office had installed a string of flashing beacons that guided day and night flights that extended from the Atlantic to the Pacific Coast. This transcontinental service averaged 32 hours, offering mail delivery three days ahead of train schedules. The US Air Mail service became recognized as one of the era's outstanding achievements. In 1925, the Air Mail Act turned over the service to private operators, who carried mail under contract to the Post Office. Over the years, these early routes formed the basis for major airlines, including United, American, Eastern, TWA, Northwest, Delta, and others. The private operators went shopping for better, faster aircraft so as to compete more effectively in winning the new mail contracts. Fortunately, the Air Commerce Act of 1926 worked to their advantage. The legislation established the Bureau of Air Commerce, which took charge of licensing pilots as well as builders of airframes, engines, and the maintenance personnel who kept them in operational shape. Other activities included improved procedures for airway navigation and airfield facilities. The licensing protocols, in particular, encouraged insurance companies to offer reasonable rates for new planes that began to appear; the insurance provisions encouraged bankers to become more inclined to extend loans for the construction of new planes, and the pace of aviation development in the United States accelerated. These elements of an essential infrastructure were in place well before Lindbergh made his epic journey from New York to Paris, which certainly gave a welcome boost to the aviation community. By itself, however, the so-called Lindbergh boom could not have triggered the pace of development that followed his flight (Bilstein 1983).

The customer base for airline services expanded rapidly during the 1920s. Among the earliest users of airmail services, banks relied heavily on rapid delivery of checks, interest-bearing securities, and similar documents whose timely delivery meant saving money. Aside from banking, many businesses relied on airmail service to speed up the delivery of advertising copy, bills of lading for commodities being shipped by train and steamship, and innumerable items of other business correspondence. A variety of businesses saved money by reducing their normal inventories, relying on air express to take care of sudden requirements. Air express also evolved as a routine service for companies that suddenly required an emergency part, for shipping perishable commodities like fresh-cut flowers, and for delivering pharmaceuticals.

Eventually, the government deliberately legislated changes in the formula for carrying mail so as to encourage aircraft manufacturers to produce larger, more efficient planes that could also carry passengers. At the same time, the prospects of saving time in the course of out-of-town business trips began to attract growing numbers of adventurous airline patrons. Moreover, the trend towards decentralization of business activities during the 1920s and 1930s meant that more factories and subsidiary activities began to locate in smaller cities all over America. Consequently, the number of intercity air travelers continued to increase. Although many potential airline passengers continued to view airplanes as inherently unsafe contraptions, the airline industry and organizations like the Bureau of Air Commerce and the NACA continued to improve safety and reliability. The airlines also sponsored public relations campaigns to convince travelers of the enhanced safety of flying, even though insurance companies continued to charge an additional premium for travelers who boarded airplanes. In 1940, the industry reached a notable level of maturity when major insurers like Equitable Life acknowledged convincing levels of airline safety and announced insurance rates for airline travel that cost no more than the rates for rail travel. For use on long flights over water, designers in the United States took the lead in developing large, structurally efficient, multi-engine flying boats. During the 1920s, a Russian émigré, Igor Sikorsky, won contracts from Pan American Airways to build several such aircraft for the airline's mail and passenger routes from the United States to numerous destinations in the Caribbean region. In the 1930s, Pan Am's expanding route structure led to new four-engine flying boats from Sikorsky as well as bigger planes supplied by the Glenn Martin company and by Boeing. The latter's Model 314 Clipper began flying in 1938, supporting Pan Am's routes across the Pacific, and also carrying mail and passengers across the Atlantic in 1939. High fares on these transoceanic flights clearly limited the clientele to the very rich, assorted corporate nabobs, and high-level government personnel. But the overall statistics for airline travelers (including traffic on overseas routes) confirmed the growing popularity of air travel. American airlines carried 475,000 people in 1932, and reported a record 4 million air travelers in 1941 (Solberg 1979; Smith 1983; Bilstein 2001b).

In the two decades between the wars, another aviation phenomenon began to take shape. The builders of smaller, single-engine aircraft with one to four seats became known as the "light plane" industry, even though some of their products mounted twin engines and seated more passengers. Their planes populated a segment eventually designated as "general aviation," a term that encompassed all activities outside the realm of scheduled airlines and military aviation. General aviation activities ran the gamut, from crop dusting, to aerial surveying, to forest fire patrol. Many postwar operators relied on cheap war surplus airplanes that they modified to suit the task at hand. As the usable backlog of such aircraft dwindled, numerous smaller manufacturers designed and produced planes to do the job. By the mid-1920s, with business de-centralization increasing, a number of builders began to offer enclosed-cabin aircraft suitable for business flying. By the end of the decade, the number of general aviation planes numbered into the hundreds, ranging from three-place biplanes (pilot in back with two passenger seats up front) having open cockpits to Stinson designs with an enclosed cabin seating a pilot and three passengers. Large corporations occasionally acquired transport-sized planes like the Ford tri-motor, which were refurbished with padded wicker seats, Dictaphones, and miniature bars for offering "bootleg" alcoholic drinks during the Prohibition era.

Although the Depression of the 1930s disabled many corporations, the survivors realized that corporate planes could often enhance their chances of responding rapidly to business opportunities. As a result, a few light plane manufacturers managed to weather the Depression decade and to produce outstanding designs. Piper, Cessna, and Beechcraft, all survived, prospered during World War II, and became leaders in the postwar era. Piper's fortunes rested on the diminutive but versatile J-3 Cub, with engines of 45 to 65 horsepower. The Cub proved to be an efficient instructional plane as well as an adaptable design for countless utilitarian tasks. Cessna's products focused on comfortable cabin aircraft suitable for business people to fly by themselves or with two or three associates at 120 mph. Beechcraft also produced corporate air-craft, but designed high performance planes with retractable landing gear. In 1937, Beechcraft introduced the classic Model 18 – a sleek twin-engine design that looked like a small airliner and could fly at 190 mph. The six-passenger "Twin Beech" required a pilot and co-pilot, so that corporate operators usually needed to spend additional funds to develop their own flight department. But Beechcraft sold several dozen before the war, including deliveries to 23 foreign countries (Rowe and Miner 1994; Bilstein 2001a).

Military aviation between the wars struggled with the low budgets that characterized funding for the US Army and US Navy. Still, army and naval aviation units managed to acquire some first-line equipment and to conduct maneuvers that led to increasing appreciation of the potential of military aircraft. Sometimes, aggressive officers sabotaged their careers in the process of challenging a moss-backed establishment. In 1921, US Army brigadier general William (Billy) Mitchell shattered myths about the invulnerability of large warships to aerial attack by successfully bombing and sinking several major vessels (ex-German navy ships) including a captured German battleship. Mitchell adamantly championed an independent air force and endorsed a series of trials to demonstrate the vulnerability of cities to long-range air attacks. In 1926, after several years of jousting with superior officers and launching stinging attacks against what he perceived as official malfeasance, the outspoken Mitchell was court-martialed for "insubordination and conduct unbecoming to an officer."

Ironically, provisions within the Air Corps Act of 1926 inaugurated the position of Assistant Secretary of War for Aeronautics and gave the former Army Air Service its new name – Army Air Corps. Not the independent air force that Mitchell fought for, but a notable step forward. The new organization never received funds for enough planes, but was able to contract for a number of up-to-date types, allowing for advanced planning that obsolete equipment would have discouraged. Moreover, the Air Corps activated new tactical schools that encouraged young officers to consider the strategies and logistics of new approaches involving aerial warfare. Monoplane fighters like the Boeing P-26 replaced biplanes during the 1920s, and a series of large bombers pointed the way towards a formidable new weapon.

The Air Corps moved fitfully but determinedly towards the evolution of a strategy for long-range bombers. Many of the technological advances of the decades between the wars – flaps, variable pitch propellers, stressed skin construction, high octane fuels, and muscular new engines – contributed to the appearance of bold new designs. During the 1930s, a coterie of imaginative young officers continued to buck entrenched bureaucracy and pursue equally imaginative means to fund the construction of remarkable pre-war experimental bombers that pointed the way to the future. One was the huge Douglas XB-19, with a wing span of 212 feet and equipped with the first tricycle landing gear fitted to a large bomber. Its size and complexity pointed to later designs for large aircraft. Meanwhile, the Air Corps evinced more interest in a smaller bomber with a wing span of 103 feet, designated XB-17, which promised lower costs and producibility; prototype models joined air force squadrons as early as 1937. Until it was joined by the Consolidated B-24 Liberator later in the war, the B-17 Flying Fortress bore the brunt of early strategic bombing raids over occupied Europe in World War II.

While the United States Army Air Corps felt its way towards the awesome weapon it eventually became, the United States Navy also found itself searching for the most promising directions in developing naval air power. In some ways, the changes that occurred within American naval aviation were more dramatic. After a series of discouraging experiences with large, rigid airships for long-range patrols over the open ocean, the navy turned to smaller, non-rigid airships (blimps) that proved so effective during World War II. The navy also funded a series of long-range flying boats that proved invaluable in wartime service. The twin-engine Consolidated PBY Catalina series became redoubtable workhorses for American, British, and allied units around the world.

The most significant trend involved the evolution of aircraft carriers, the specialized planes to operate from them, and the emergence of a new dimension of naval warfare. The architecture of aircraft carriers evolved from British types that appeared towards the end of World War I. Following Billy Mitchell's bombing trials in 1921, American interest intensified, spurred by younger officers who contended that naval fleets would clearly need protection from land-based air attack. In the Pacific region, with vast open seas and numerous islands that could harbor enemy air bases, American ships would be vulnerable unless accompanied by carrier-based aviation for their defense. The first US Navy carriers emerged as comparatively speedy vessels, built from the keels and general specifications originally laid down for cruisers, and they set the pattern of subsequent American preference for "fast carriers." Because aviation operations at sea placed a premium on engine designs that stressed reliability and ease of maintenance within the confines of an aircraft carrier's limited space, the US Navy specified relatively uncomplicated radial engines for its planes rather than liquid-cooled engines often used in army designs. Working with the NACA and engine manufacturers, the navy's influence markedly improved radial engine types up through World War II.

By the late 1930s, the American naval aviation had worked out significantly advanced strategy and tactics for carrier-based aviation and had begun to acquire modern aircraft that won control of the air over the Pacific theater of operations. Originally, naval doctrine called for aircraft carriers to deploy planes as scouts and to protect the main fleet from enemy attack – a defensive, rather than offensive posture. During fleet exercises conducted during the late 1920s and early 1930s, the idea of using carriers and their torpedo bombers for offensive operations took shape. The use of carrier task forces during World War II symbolized a fundamental change in naval air doctrine (Goldberg 1957; Reynolds 1968; Copp 1980; Vander Meulen 1991).

Air Power in World War II

In September 1939, German armed forces poured across the Polish border, marking the start of World War II in Europe. Despite early political commitments to non-intervention and neutrality, the United States inevitably drifted closer to involvement as the result of diplomatic moves in the interest of national security and in the process of producing military goods for Great Britain and France (until the latter's collapse in the spring of 1940). Air power became increasingly significant early in the war, especially in the late summer of 1940 during the Battle of Britain. As an increasingly visible partner of the United Kingdom, the United States supplied high octane fuel that enhanced the performance of Royal Air Force (RAF) Hurricanes and Spitfires. As victors in the Battle, the RAF blunted the myth of the German Air Force's invincibility. The survival of Britain assured the Anglo-American allies of production centers, transportation facilities, and air bases crucial to the campaign against Germany and the eventual liberation of the European continent.

The scope of the war widened in December 1941, when Japanese aircraft carriers launched their aircraft to attack US Navy shipping and other military targets at Pearl Harbor in Hawaii. A state of war between America and the "Axis Powers" (Germany, Italy, and Japan) ensued. Luckily, the American aircraft carriers based at Hawaii escaped destruction, and their survival played a key role in turning back Japanese thrusts in the Pacific. While holding the line in the Far East, the Allies decided to concentrate first on the defeat of Hitler in Europe, where Britain and Russia were heavily engaged, before forcing the surrender of Japan.

The Air Corps had received a new designation in June 1941, and went to war as the United States Army Air Force (conventionally shortened to USAF). During campaigns in northern Africa and in the Mediterranean theaters during 1942–3, air power played a growing role, both strategically and tactically. Military aviation also played a key role in the Battle of the Atlantic, where patrol aircraft kept German submarines off balance, thus ensuring the safety of convoys carrying crucial troops, supplies, and equipment through dangerous seas. At the same time, American and British bomber offensives against occupied Europe became more intense. Operating from bases in Britain, medium bombers struck at military targets across the English Channel. Heavy bombers like the Boeing B-17 and Consolidated B-24 pounded strategic objectives all across occupied Europe, where they faced determined opposition from German pilots in fighter planes like the Messerschmitt Bf-109 and the Focke-Wulf 190. As USAF bomber losses mounted, the Allies managed to increase the range of fighter escorts by adding droppable fuel tanks to aircraft such as the Republic P-47 Thunderbolt and the newer North American P-51 Mustang. Following the invasion of France in June 1944, fighters not only continued to protect bomber formations from enemy air attacks, but also provided close tactical air support for ground troops, hitting enemy formations with heavy machine guns, rockets, and light bombs. By the end of the war, bombers as well as specialized fighters like the Northrop P-69 Black Widow carried radar units to help pinpoint enemy targets at night. Pressed by Soviet armies from the east and advancing Allied forces from the west, Germany finally surrendered in May 1945.

Meanwhile, the tempo of the air war in the Pacific continued to escalate. In the spring of 1942, as a result of US Navy victories in the Battle of the Coral Sea and the Battle of Midway, fighters like Grumman's F3F Wildcat and F4F Hellcat won control of the air from the Japanese "Zero" fighters. Both were historic air battles, with the outcome determined entirely in the skies by carrier planes from both sides. These engagements, in which Japan lost valuable aircraft carriers as well as their planes and pilots, shifted the momentum to US forces in the Pacific theater. Although costly, the capture of Japanese-held islands reduced its crucial geographic assets, giving the US Air Force and US Marine fighter squadrons additional air bases to support further offensives and to send bombers against distant Japanese targets. The B-29 bombing campaign against the Japanese home islands proved particularly destructive, capped by atomic bombs dropped on Hiroshima and Nagasaki in August 1945. After these aerial blows, Japan finally surrendered.

One of the most significant American contributions to the Allied cause revolved around its prodigious production capabilities. In the case of American air power assets, the process of gearing up had actually begun during the late 1930s – a direct result of orders from overseas. Against the background of Nazi aggression in Europe, both Britain and France signed contracts with US aircraft manufacturers that totaled several hundred million dollars. Following the fall of France in 1940, Britain picked up French orders, and by that autumn, the RAF held contracts for 14,000 American planes and 25,000 engines worth $1.5 billion. During official postwar assessments, US Air Force planners concluded that these overseas orders had effectively accelerated its program for wartime aircraft production by a full year. At war's end, the United States had produced over 812,000 engines and a record 324,750 aircraft; about 231,000 went to the USAF with the rest delivered to the US Navy and to Allied units (Goldberg 1957; Morison 1963; Copp 1980; Sherry 1987).

Additionally, the government and its contractors conducted several outstanding development and production feats such as the Boeing B-29. Although B-17 and B-24 heavy bombers carried out the majority of heavy raids in various theaters of the conflict, the Air Force forged ahead with an even more ambitious weapon. The order for the XB-29 went out in August 1940, a prescient move for a country not yet at war. The big new plane weighed twice as much as the B-17, had twice the range, and carried 10,000 pounds of bombs, compared to the 6,000 pounds for the Flying Fortress. With big new engines and advanced aerodynamics, the Boeing Superfortress looked so good on paper that well before the plane's first flight occurred in September 1942, the Air Force negotiated contracts for more that 1,500 units of the bomber. In addition to pressurized fuselage sections for the crew, the plane featured remote-controlled machine guns. The plane's size and complexity meant that it had a maze of ancillary control systems and requisite instrumentation. Government and contractor officials faced a daunting task of constructing cavernous new assembly buildings, acquiring innumerable machine tools, and coordinating the production of thousands of parts fabricated in diverse locations from coast to coast. The myriad elements of manufacturing for the B-29 required advanced management techniques that presaged systems engineering techniques of the postwar era. Large subassemblies of the B-29 were designed to be put together by thousands of relatively unskilled workers, including women. Special effort went into the production of training films to instruct assembly line workers as well as military maintenance personnel. In addition, there was a basic 2,000-page maintenance manual, plus dozens of separate publications for specific systems. All this spawned a small production and printing industry devoted expressly to the care and grooming of the Superfortress fleet (Vander Meulen 1995; Bilstein 2001a).

Controversy over the impact of air power soon developed even before the war had ended, especially when the USAF initiated discussions to become a separate armed force. Clearly, air superiority assisted Allied offensives when strategic bombing deprived the enemy of crucial fuel supplies, disrupted transport networks, and created severe shortages of war material in general. The impact of close air support in tactical engagements became an unquestioned asset in every theater of operations. Many critics argued against strategic bombing on moral and ethical grounds. Others argued that bombing – including the atomic bomb – may have actually prevented the war from dragging on, adding to already frightfully high casualty lists (Goldberg 1957; Sherry 1987).

In any case, wartime experiences gave rise to the phrase, "Air Age World," especially in terms of travel. With America and its Allies remaining heavily engaged around the world, the necessity for rapid transportation of key personnel, medical supplies, and urgently needed cargo received a high priority. By 1942, various operations within the American armed forces coalesced into the Air Transport Command (ATC), as well as a specialized service operated by the US Navy. Equipment for the ATC ran the gamut, from single-engine light planes to converted bombers, but the remarkable DC-3, re-designated C-47, became the backbone of the ATC around the world. The C-47 carried dangerously heavy loads and functioned in demanding combat environments never intended for its design as a civilian airliner. Larger doors enabled it to operate as a paratroop plane and air-borne ambulance as well as all-purpose aerial hauler for ammunition, volatile fuel, howitzers, jeeps, and anything else that troops could wedge into its fuselage. In the China-Burma-India theater, the C-47 and other planes struggled over the towering Himalayas – the fabled "Hump" – to carry essential supplies to beleaguered soldiers in China, where they pinned down thousands of Japanese troops that might have been sent elsewhere. The ATC built airfields on every continent, organized radio services along its far-flung routes, accumulated invaluable meteorological and navigational data around the world, and generated a pool of skilled airway professionals. By the end of the war, acquisition of four-engine, long-range transport like the Douglas C-54 (the civilian DC-4) gave new momentum to long-distance routes, especially across the Atlantic.

The ATC's activities changed intercontinental air travel from a state of high-risk adventure to a matter of daily routine. At its peak of operations, the ATC dispatched aircraft across the Atlantic Ocean at an average rate of one plane every thirteen minutes. In the process, the time required to travel between distant continents dramatically decreased from a matter of weeks to a matter of days, or, within a military theater of operations, to a matter of hours. Often unheralded as a wartime phenomenon, the Air Transport Command's technological legacy to postwar international travel constituted an invaluable bequest (Military Airlift Command 1991).

Postwar Aviation

The pattern of general aviation development in the postwar era often reflected trends established in the prewar years such as agricultural activities, photography, surveying, and other utilitarian activities. With so many inexpensive war surplus trainers available after 1945, operators quickly converted them into agricultural planes for spraying and dusting. But these re-treads did not always offer optimum safety during the abrupt maneuvers required of "ag planes" at grass-top levels with a full load of chemicals, and they did not offer the pilot much protection in case of a crack-up. Specialized designs eventually made their appearance, although debates about spreading herbicides and pesticides from the air, creating potential environmental hazards, continued to dog the agricultural aviation community. In addition to airplanes, agricultural aviation also began to use helicopters designed with a main lifting/propulsion rotor and a smaller rotor to counteract torque, a type successfully developed by Igor Sikorsky in 1939. Helicopters soon became ubiquitous eyes in the sky for traffic observers hired by local radio stations. Similarly, given the helicopter's unique abilities to maneuver and land in very restrictive areas, they proved especially useful for law enforcement agencies, emergency rescue, and transportation to isolated work sites such as off-shore drilling rigs (Boyne and Lopez 1984; Bilstein 2001b).

The most rapidly expanding sector of general aviation involved business aviation. Again, the availability of war-surplus light planes – their service as trainers and liaison duties at an end – helped feed an early postwar enthusiasm for private flying. Soon, a new generation of postwar designs, with better soundproofing, and more efficient engines made their appearance. Although numerous aspiring builders hoped to cash in on the anticipated postwar boom in private flying, Piper, Cessna, and Beechcraft continued to pace the general aviation industry. For one thing, the boom never attained its anticipated strength. For another, the trio of industry leaders held a big advantage in terms of their networks of established dealerships and service centers. Piper's designs continued to feature metal framework covered with fabric, but the company's stable of two-place Cubs and four-place Cruisers made it a profitable operation. Cessna also offered two and four-place types, but featured all-metal designs and more powerful engines that offered better performance. The four-place 170 series of the late 1940s typically mounted a 145 horsepower engine and cruised at over 130 mph. Subsequent improvements increased its performance and kept it in production for decades. Beechcraft advertised even better performance with its rakish-looking Bonanza, a roomy four-place plane with a distinctive V-shaped tail that became an enduring trademark. Moreover, the Bonanza came with a retractable, tricycle landing gear, a feature that definitely placed its design in the realm of postwar modernity. Beechcraft introduced a new postwar corporate twin-engine aircraft with modern tricycle gear – the Queen Air – eventually followed by the larger, faster, Beech King Air.

These and other planes found a receptive clientele. Many individual business people, along with a growing number of corporations, found that business flying held distinctive advantages in terms of maximizing travel time in an increasingly diverse commercial world. The trend towards business decentralization dating from the prewar decades became a major phenomenon as companies decided to build new facilities in smaller cities where property taxes were lower, labor was cheaper, and where they might be located closer to sources of raw materials or promising new markets. The Interstate Highway System, implemented during the 1950s, also promoted business diversification, since many new business operations could be located with convenient access to an efficient, high-speed highway network. All of this led to subsequent expansion of travel destinations for commercial activities involving finance, insurance, construction, sales, and ancillary activities that accompanied the physical dispersion of corporate business. Harried executives often found that the only way to quickly and conveniently travel to increasingly remote locales required a personal or corporate aircraft. Business-flying became more reliable with the availability of improved radio and navigation equipment. In the case of corporate travel, in planes like the Beech King Air, passengers could relax in pressurized comfort, appreciate the luxury of an on-board lavatory compartment, use folding tables and airborne communications for business conferences en route, and unwind on the way home with their favorite snacks and beverages. Given its improved convenience, reliability, and amenities, business flying became a fixture of American commerce. In the field of general aviation, manufacturers tended to view proposals for corporate jets as too problematic. Finally, a maverick entrepreneur named Bill Lear designed and built a compact, speedy plane, the LearJet, introduced in 1964. Believing that time-pressed executives would pay relatively higher prices for faster planes, Lear's gamble succeeded. Other builders quickly followed suit and executive jets soon numbered in the tens of thousands (Bilstein 2001a).

Similarly, the commercial airline business took off after 1945. In terms of airline equipment, an important momentum accrued from the introduction of two out-standing four-engine types during the war – the unpressurized Douglas DC-4 and the pressurized Lockheed Constellation. Early postwar versions of these transports, including the DC-4's pressurized successor, the DC-6, set new standards for trans-continental service and links between major cities in the United States, attracting a rising number of airline passengers. They also pioneered popular routes across the Atlantic, the Pacific, and into Latin America. For several years, airlines proceeded to follow prewar standards of first-class service, since their primary clientele came from well-paid business executives and other well-to-do travelers. As the economic efficiency of the airliners continued to improve and transports increased in size, the airlines began to offer family and excursion fares. By 1951, airlines in the United States carried more passengers than Pullman services on railroads; by 1957, airline travelers exceeded all train travelers and bus passengers combined. Moreover, the availability of affordable coach-class fares and rapid travel times on round trips to Europe and other parts of the world brought an increasing democratization to both domestic and international air travel. Building on the pre-eminence established by the DC-3 in pre-war service with foreign carriers, the superior designs offered by American manu-facturers in the postwar era made them the airliners of choice for the majority of the world's long-range airline fleets. Their popularity began a long tradition of favorable export balances for American airline transports, engines, and equipment.

Although the jet-propelled combat planes built by Germany and Britain appeared during World War II, jet engines for civil designs lagged until the British introduced the deHavilland Comet into service in 1952. Within 2 years, structural problems grounded the Comet until 1958. In the meantime, Boeing parlayed design work on a jet tanker into the 707 airliner, taking advantage of better engines and a swept design to propel the United States into the lead in the competitive field of jet passenger transports. Douglas jet airliners eventually captured a secure spot as the world's number two supplier. In 1969, Boeing once more achieved a coup with the introduction of the 747 jumbo jet, a plane that set new standards for civil airlines. After years of futile efforts to challenge the American giants, Europe organized a consortium, Airbus Industrie, in 1970, and launched a series of progressively larger jet transports that eventually surpassed Douglas (by now McDonnell Douglas) as the number two builder and challenged Boeing for world leadership in the production of commercial jet airliners (Brooks 1982; Newhouse 1983; Irving 1993).

In the postwar diplomatic environment, acknowledgement of Cold War antagonisms between the Union of Soviet Socialist Republics (USSR) and the democratic west kept military progress at a high pitch. For one thing, in 1947, the United States Army Air Force emerged as an independent service – the United States Air Force (USAF). It functioned within a new, cabinet-level Department of Defense that included an Assistant Secretary of the Air Force on an equal footing with counterparts for the army and navy. To a considerable degree, this new aeronautical visibility resulted from the awesome demonstration of strategic air power in World War II. In a further testimony to this wartime legacy, the Strategic Air Command became a major bureaucracy, with air bases sited around the globe and equipped with many squadrons of expensive new bombers. The Department of Defense also presided over a growing network of expensive radar networks to detect potential Soviet air attacks. Life in what was called the "Air Age World" after 1945 proved to have a high worry factor.

Piston-engine equipment constituted early American long-range bombers like the lumbering, six-engine Convair B-36, designed for round-trip intercontinental missions to deliver increasingly lethal nuclear weapons. But a new generation of jet bombers soon appeared, including Boeing B-47 Stratojet medium-range aircraft and the huge Boeing B-52 Stratofortress, designed to strike targets around the globe. Depending on the bomb load and length of the mission, in-flight refueling required the development of fleets of aerial tankers to support bombers as well as a phalanx of speedy new jet fighters. High-speed flight beyond the speed of sound (Mach 1) had been a goal of aerodynamicists for several years and was first achieved in 1947 by a rocket-propelled aircraft, the Bell X-1, developed by the Air Force and the NACA. But the dramatic increase in performance during the Cold War derived from a new family of jet (gas turbine) engines.

The technology for jets originated in work accomplished in the 1930s by Frank Whittle in Britain and by Hans von Ohain in Germany. During the war, the British shared their success with the United States, sending detailed plans, an engine, and eventually Whittle himself to jump-start American work in this field. Direct descendants of this engine powered the first American combat jets like the Lockheed F-80 Shooting Star and Grumman F9F Panther, stalwarts for the United States during the war in Korea (1950–53). A second generation of jet fighters had also emerged, adding more powerful axial flow engines derived from advanced German wartime development. Moreover, the new American fighters appeared with swept wings, another legacy from German aerodynamic research. These features became the hallmarks of 600 mph fighters like the North American F-86 Sabre, which became the dominant air combat fighter in the Korean conflict. Subsequent designs stressed the goal of air superiority in the event of engagements with Soviet fighters. Within the aerospace industry, growing export market often offset the high costs of these complex aircraft. When American fighters became involved during the Vietnam War in the 1960s and 1970s, speeds typically exceeded Mach 2, and guided, air-to-air missiles became standard weapons. Although fighters continued to fly ground attack missions, the need for slower aircraft in close ground support roles became clear, resulting in wider dependence on specialized helicopters equipped with a mix of rapid-firing guns and lethal missiles. Utilization of large helicopters for carrying troops and supplies also proliferated.

The term "aerospace" dated to the 1950s, when aviation companies became involved with missiles, rocketry, and the advanced electronic and guidance systems that characterized them. During the 1960s, the drive for weight-saving components with high strength led to wider use of exotic alloys and composite structures using synthetic materials. Additionally, the major aerospace companies reflected a move towards internationalization of many programs, a trend of the industry since the 1960s. Components for Boeing airliners, Lockheed fighters, General Electric engines, and subcontracted products often arrived from foreign nations, just as American manufacturers supplied many components for various models of Airbus transports and Rolls-Royce engines built in Europe.

In subsequent decades, aerodynamic sophistication and multiple roles for combat planes vastly expanded the installation of complex electronic suites aboard every aircraft. The US Navy's twin-engine Grumman F-14 Tomcat carried a pilot as well as a back-seat electronics officer. Variable-geometry wings (either swept forward or back) enhanced its combat capabilities and provided the big plane with requisite slow-speed characteristics necessary for takeoff and landing operations from the decks of aircraft carriers. Its sophisticated complement of avionics allowed its crew to perform long-range interception duties which might require tracking and attacking several different targets with long range missiles, all at the same time. Procurement costs for "high-tech" planes spiraled sharply. During the 1970s, the Air Force decided it needed a simpler, dedicated air-to-air fighter like the Lockheed Martin F-16. Originally designed and built by General Dynamics, single-engine, single-seat F-16 still had such a high price tag that the Department of Defense agreed to arrangements with several NATO countries, who also wanted the plane, to share the costs of development and production. The F-16 became a phenomenally successful program, with several dozen air forces around the globe eventually acquiring the plane. Inevitably, the design accumulated additional electronic systems to perform close air-support missions in addition to its fighter/interceptor role (Bright 1978; Boyne and Lopez 1979; Hallion 1992; Hayward 1994; Isby 1997).

The success of remotely controlled Unmanned Aerial Vehicles (UAVs) during operations in Desert Storm (1990–91), the Balkans (mid-1990s), and in Afghanistan (2001–02) focused more popular attention on these fascinating aircraft. The technology actually dated to the World War I era; improved radio control systems led to target "drones" during World War II. By the 1980s, they had reached a new plateau in terms of reconnaissance capabilities, quiet engines, and construction to enhance their "stealth" qualities. During deployment in Afghanistan, remotely controlled UAV operations reported a number of successful missions, including a UAV armed with rockets that successfully attacked a column of enemy vehicles. Military experts continued to see UAV technology as an increasingly valuable asset in gathering intelligence for tactical operations as well as in long-range, strategic duties using satellite-based navigational techniques. In 2001, an RQ4 Global Hawk, capable of jet-propelled speeds of 390 mph, completed an epic trans-Pacific journey that took it all the way to Australia.

Dramatic variations in designs for manned aircraft also became operational during the 1990s. On the one hand, the Northrop F-117 stealth aircraft, designed to attack military installations as well as industrial sites, incorporated special construction techniques and surface coatings to minimize its radar signature to the point where it was nearly undetectable. It was not intended for air-to-air engagements. The Northrop B-2 stealth bomber – designed in the form of a giant flying wing – carried larger weapon loads on intercontinental missions. These aircraft, as well as other American combat planes, could deliver an awesome array of "smart weapons" guided by lasers, global positioning systems, and other electronic technologies to achieve unparalleled accuracy. Other notable aeronautical advances led to the unique Bell V-22 Osprey, a cargo aircraft designed with two engines – mounted at the end of either wing tip – that swung huge rotors to achieve lift-off like a helicopter. At the appropriate altitude, the engines and rotors transitioned from the vertical to the horizontal, giving the aircraft forward speeds that exceeded conventional helicopters.

One forthcoming combat plane, the Lockheed Martin F-35 Joint Strike Fighter boasted stealth characteristics along with advanced gadgetry to attack a variety of ground targets as well as carry out air-fighting. Its cost (estimated at $30–$35 million apiece) made it necessary to plan for its use by all three United States military services – army, navy, and marines. The Royal Air Force also contributed to the plane's research and development costs since they and the US Marines intended to use a variant that featured vertical lift capability similar to the British-designed Harrier types.

Joint programs like this, including international involvement, underscored the need for collaborative arrangements in order to cover the extremely high prices of new civil and military aircraft. The soaring costs of R&D and the dwindling number of different types ordered by the armed services were part of the reasons for a remarkable era of mergers in the 1990s, when events leading to the demise of the Cold War also led to a radically shrinking number of major aerospace contractors. The outstanding success of Airbus Industrie also contributed to pressures on American competitors. One of the most dramatic events took place in 1997, when its long-time rival, Boeing, absorbed McDonnell Douglas (Bilstein 2001a).

As a technological phenomenon, aeronautical symbolism became a hallmark of the twentieth century. In terms of popular culture, cartoon adventures like *Terry and the*

Pirates appeared in hundreds of newspapers from the 1930s into the postwar era; films and novels with aeronautical themes abounded. Automobile companies became one of the most persistent enterprises that used symbols of flight to imply speed, rigorous engineering standards, and efficient design. In myriad ways, the aviation phenomenon became an icon of modern technology (Bilstein 2001b).

BIBLIOGRAPHY

Bilstein, Roger. *The Enterprise of Flight: The American Aviation and Aerospace Industry* (Washington, DC: Smithsonian Institution Press, 2001a).

Bilstein, Roger. *Flight in America: From the Wrights to the Astronauts*, 3rd edn (Washington, DC: Smithsonian Institution Press, 2001b).

Bilstein, Roger. *Flight Patterns: Trends of Aeronautical Development in the United States, 1918–1929* (Athens: University of Georgia Press, 1983).

Boyne, Walter and Lopez S. Donald, eds. *The Jet Age: Fifty Years of Jet Aviation* (Washington, DC: Smithsonian Institution Press, 1979).

Boyne, Walter and Lopez S. Donald. *Vertical Flight: The Age of the Helicopter* (Washington, DC: Smithsonian Institution Press, 1984).

Bright, Charles. *The Jet Makers: The Aerospace Industry from 1945 to 1972* (Lawrence, Kans.: Regents Press, 1978).

Brooks W. Peter. *The Modern Airliner: Its Origins and Development*, rev. edn (Manhattan, Kans.: Sunflower University Press, 1982).

Copp S. DeWitt. *A Few Great Captains: The Men and Events that Shaped the Development of U.S. Airpower* (Garden City, NY: Doubleday, 1980).

Crouch, Tom. *The Bishop's Boys: A Life of Wilbur and Orville Wright* (New York: W.W. Norton, 1989).

Goldberg A. Alfred. ed. *A History of the United States Air Force, 1907–1957* (Princeton: Van Nostrand, 1957).

Gorn H. Michael. *The Universal Man: Theodore von Karman's Life in Aeronautics* (Washington, DC: Smithsonian Institution Press, 1992).

Gwynn-Jones, Terry. *Farther and Faster: The Adventuring Years, 1909–39* (Washington, DC: Smithsonian Institution Press, 1991).

Hallion, Richard. *Legacy of Flight: The Guggenheim Contribution to American Aviation* (Seattle: University of Washington Press, 1977).

Hallion, Richard. *Storm Over Iraq: Air Power and the Gulf War* (Washington, DC: Smithsonian Institution Press, 1992).

Hansen R. James. *Engineer in Charge: A History of the Langley Aeronautical Laboratory, 1917–1958* (Washington, DC: U.S. Government Printing Office, 1987).

Hayward, Keith. *The World Aerospace Industry: Collaboration and Competition* (London: Duckworth, 1994).

Irving, Clive. *Wide Body: The Triumph of the 747* (New York: Morrow, 1993).

Isby C. David. *Fighter Combat in the Jet Age* (London: HarperCollins Publishers, 1997).

Jakab, Peter. *Visions of a Flying Machine: The Wright Brothers and the Process of Invention* (Washington, DC: Smithsonian Institution Press, 1990).

Kennett, Lee. *The First Air War, 1914–1918* (New York: Macmillan/The Free Press, 1991).

Military Airlift Command, Office of MAC History. *Anything, Anywhere, Anytime: An Illustrated History of the Military Airlift Command, 1941–1991* (Scott Air Force Base, Ill.: Headquarters MAC, 1991).

Miller, Ronald and Sawers, David. *The Technical Development of Modern Aviation* (New York: Praeger, 1970).

Morison, Samuel Eliot. *The Two-Ocean War: A Short History of the United States Navy in the Second World War* (New York: Atlantic Monthly Press, 1963).

Newhouse, John. *The Sporty Game: The High-Risk Competitive Business of Making and Selling Commercial Airliners* (New York: Knopf, 1983).

Reynolds G. Clarke. *The Fast Carriers: The Forging of an Air Navy* (New York: McGraw-Hill, 1968).

Roland, Alex. *Model Research: The National Advisory Committee for Aeronautics, 1915–1958*, 2 vols (Washington, DC: U.S. Government Printing Office, 1985).

Rowe K. Frank and Miner, Craig. *Borne on the South Wind: A Century of Kansas Aviation* (Wichita, Kans.: Wichita Eagle and Beacon Publishing Co., 1994).

Sherry S. Michael. *The Rise of American Airpower: The Creation of Armageddon* (New Haven: Yale University Press, 1987).

Smith K. Richard. "The intercontinental airliner and the essence of airplane performance," *Technology and Culture* 24 (July 1983): 428–49.

Solberg, Carl. *Conquest of the Skies: A History of Commercial Aviation in America* (Boston: Little, Brown, 1979).

van der Linden F. Robert. *The Boeing 247: The First Modern Airliner* (Seattle: University of Washington Press, 1991).

Vander Meulen, Jacob. *Building the B-29* (Washington, DC: Smithsonian Institution Press, 1995).

Vander Meulen, Jacob. *The Politics of Aircraft: Building an American Military Industry* (Lawrence: University Press of Kansas, 1991).

CHAPTER FIFTEEN

Technology in Space

ROGER D. LAUNIUS

Space technology in the United States emerged largely from questions of international rivalry and world prestige that dominated the Cold War with the Soviet Union, and international relations have remained a powerful shaper of the effort ever since. At first there was the Moon race, intensely competitive, in which the two superpowers locked in Cold War struggle sought to outdo each other. No cost seemed too high, no opportunity to "best" the other seemed too slight. Using a unique set of costly technologies, the astronauts planted the US flag on the surface of the Moon when the great moment came in 1969, not unlike the Spanish flag planted by Columbus in America. The irony of planting that flag, coupled with the statement that "we came in peace for all mankind," was not lost on the leaders of the Soviet Union who realized that they were not considered in this context a part of the "all mankind" mentioned. With the lessening of Cold War tensions since the 1960s, and the demise of the Soviet Union in 1991, international cooperative efforts have dominated the development and use of space technology. From a myriad of bilateral space science missions to the hugely complex International Space Station being built by sixteen nations, relations among cultures have dominated the effort to explore the region beyond the atmosphere.

Rocketry and the Rise of Spaceflight, 1900–40

The first four decades of the twentieth century witnessed a rise in the belief that spaceflight was both possible and practicable, and a corresponding effort to advance into space. Fueled by such modern science fiction writers as Jules Verne (1828–1905) and H.G. Wells (1866–1946) – who based their work on the latest scientific discoveries about the universe – many scientists and engineers grew excited by the possibility of spaceflight and sought to make it a reality (Gunn 1975; Ash 1977). The linkage of advances in rocket technology to spaceflight interests at the beginning of the twentieth century, however, made possible the modern space age. Led by a trio of pioneers – Konstantin Eduardovich Tsiolkovskiy (1857–1935) in Russia, Hermann Oberth (1894–1989) in Germany, and Robert H. Goddard (1882–1945) in the United States – research into rocket technology exploded in this era (Walters 1962; Lehman 1963; Kosmodemyansky 1985; Logsdon 1995; Launius 1998).

Goddard especially engaged in sophisticated rocket research during this period, launching the first liquid-fueled rocket on March 16, 1926, near Auburn, Massachusetts. Although inauspiciously rising only 43 feet in 2.5 seconds, this event heralded the modern age of rocketry. Goddard continued to experiment with rockets and fuels for the next several years. A spectacular launch took place on July 17, 1929, when he flew the first instrumented payload – an aneroid barometer, a thermometer, and a camera – to record the readings. Between 1930 and 1941 Goddard carried out ever more ambitious tests of rocket components in the relative isolation of New Mexico. This effort culminated in a successful rocket launch to an altitude of 9,000 feet in 1941. With US entry into World War II, Goddard spent the remainder of his life working on rocket technology for the US Navy, some of which led to the development of the throttlable Curtis-Wright XLR25-CW-1 liquid rocket engine that later powered the Bell X-1 past the supersonic barrier in 1947 (Lehman 1963, pp. 140–4, 156–62; Braun and Ordway 1986, pp. 46–53; Winter 1990, pp. 33–4).

Concomitant with Goddard's research into liquid fuel rockets, and perhaps more immediately significant because the results were more widely disseminated, were the activities of various rocket societies. The largest and most significant was the German organization, the "Verein fur Raumschiffahrt" Society for Spaceship Travel, or VfR. Although spaceflight aficionados and technicians had organized at other times and in other places, the VfR emerged soon after its founding on July 5, 1927, as the leading space travel group. It succeeded in building a base of support in Germany, publishing a magazine and scholarly studies, and in constructing and launching small rockets. One of its strengths from the beginning, however, was the VfR's ability to publicize both its activities and the dream of spaceflight. Wernher von Braun (1912–77), then a neophyte learning the principles of rocketry, was both enthralled and impressed with the VfR's activities. Other similar organizations soon formed in other nations, most importantly the British Interplanetary Society and the American Rocket Society (Winter 1983).

The Rocket and Modern War, 1940–57

World War II truly altered the course of rocket development. Prior to that conflict, technological progress in rocketry had been erratic. The war forced nations to focus attention on the activity and to fund research and development. Such research and development was oriented, however, toward the advancement of rocket-borne weapons rather than rockets for space exploration and other peaceful purposes. This would also remain the case during the Cold War era that followed, as competing nations perceived and supported advances in space technology because of their military potential and the national prestige associated with them.

During World War II virtually every belligerent was involved in developing some type of rocket technology, but the most spectacular early successes in developing an operational rocket capability took place in Nazi Germany where the charismatic and politically astute Wernher von Braun oversaw the V-2 ballistic missile program. The brainchild of von Braun's rocket team operating at a secret laboratory at Peenemünde on the Baltic Coast, this rocket was the immediate antecedent of those used in the US space program. A liquid propellant missile extending some 46 feet in length and weighing 27,000 pounds, the V-2 flew at speeds more than 3,500 miles per hour and delivered a 2,200 pound warhead. First flown in October 1942, it was employed against targets in Europe beginning in September 1944, and by the end of the war 1,155 had been fired against Britain and another 1,675 had been launched against Antwerp and other continental targets. The guidance system for these missiles was imperfect and many did not reach their targets, but they struck without warning and there was no defense against them. As a result the V-2s had a terror factor far beyond their capabilities (Neufeld 1995).

The V-2 was assembled using forced labor from the Dora concentration camp at a factory called Mittelwerk. In the process of assembling the V-2, more than 20,000 prisoners died, many more people than died in the V-2 raids aimed at the Allies. This single act, more than anything else, has led many to question the morals of von Braun and his rocket team. Rip Bulkeley has christened the defenders of von Braun in World War II the "Huntsville School," so named for where it originated (Bulkeley 1991). First, and most important, this school of historiography casts von Braun and the German rocketeers who built the V-2 and then came to America at the end of World War II, as far-sighted visionaries with an integrated space exploration plan that would foster a future of great discovery in the "final frontier."

At the same time, the "Huntsville School" minimized the wartime cooperation of von Braun and his "rocket team" with the Nazi regime in Germany, while maximizing the team's role in the development of American rocketry and space exploration. Both were conscious distortions of the historical record promulgated for specific personal and political reasons. Even today, few Americans realize that von Braun had been a member of the Nazi party and an officer in the SS and that the V-2 was constructed using slave labor from concentration camps. They also do not understand that the United States had developed a very capable rocket technology in such places as the Jet Propulsion Laboratory, in the US Air Force, and at several private corporations. The result has been both a whitewashing of the less savory aspects of the careers of the German rocketeers and an overemphasis on their influence in American rocketry (Launius 2000; Neufeld 2002).

A characterization of von Braun offered by humorist Tom Lehrer in the 1960s, as the United States was involved in a race with the Soviet Union to see who could land a human on the Moon first, may ultimately be the closest to reality. He condemned von Braun's pragmatic approach to serving whomsoever would let him build rockets regardless of their purpose. "Don't say that he's hypocritical, say rather that he's apolitical," Lehrer wrote. " 'Once the rockets are up, who cares where they come down? That's not my department,' says Wernher von Braun." Lehrer's biting satire captured well the ambivalence of von Braun's attitude on moral questions associated with the use of rocket technology (Lehrer 1965).

As World War II ended, US military forces brought captured V-2s back to the United States for examination. Clearly, the technology employed in this weapon was worthy of study and its secrets were a top priority for military intelligence officials sifting through what remained of the impressive array of German military technology. Along with them – as part of a secret military operation called Project Paperclip – came many of the scientists and engineers who had developed these weapons (McGovern 1964;

Lasby 1971; Hunt 1991). Von Braun intentionally surrendered to the United States
in hopes that he could continue his rocketry experiments under US sponsorship,
coolly calculating that his work would be better funded in the United States. The
German rocket team was installed at Fort Bliss in El Paso, Texas, and launch facilities
for the V-2 test program were set up at the nearby White Sands Proving Ground in
New Mexico. Later, in 1950, von Braun's team of over 150 people was moved to the
Redstone Arsenal near Huntsville, Alabama, to concentrate on the development of
a new missile for the US Army. Between 1946 and 1951, 67 captured V-2s were test-
launched on non-orbital flights. These technological "war reparations," as some
historians termed them, sparked a significant expansion of US knowledge of rocketry
(Ordway and Sharpe 1979; Koppes 1982; DeVorkin 1992; Ash and Söllner 1996;
Judt and Ciesla 1996).

Beginning soon after the war, each of the armed services worked toward the fielding
of intercontinental ballistic missiles (ICBM) that could deliver warheads to targets
half a world away. Competition was keen among the services for a mission in the new
"high ground" of space, whose military importance was not lost on the leaders of the
world. In April 1946, the US Army Air Forces gave Consolidated Vultee Aircraft
(Convair) Division a study contract for an ICBM. This led directly to the development of the Atlas ICBM in the 1950s. At first, many engineers believed Atlas to be
a high-risk proposition. To limit its weight, Convair Corporation engineers, under the
direction of Karel J. Bossart, a pre-World War II emigrant from Belgium, designed
the booster with a thin, internally pressurized fuselage instead of massive struts and
a thick metal skin. The "steel balloon," as it was sometimes called, employed engineering techniques that ran counter to the conservative engineering approach used by
Wernher von Braun and his "Rocket Team" at Huntsville, Alabama. Von Braun,
according to Bossart, needlessly designed his boosters like "bridges," to withstand
any possible shock. For his part, von Braun thought the Atlas was too flimsy to hold
up during launch. The reservations began to melt away, however, when Bossart's team
pressurized one of the boosters and dared one of von Braun's engineers to knock
a hole in it with a sledge hammer. The blow left the booster unharmed, but the recoil
from the hammer nearly clubbed the engineer (Sloop 1978, pp. 173–7).

The Titan ICBM program emerged not long thereafter, and proved to be an enormously important ICBM program and later a civil and military space launch asset
(Stumpf 2000). To consolidate efforts, Secretary of Defense Charles E. Wilson
(1886–1972) issued a decision on November 26, 1956, that effectively took the
army out of the ICBM business and assigned responsibility for land-based systems to
the air force and sea-launched missiles to the navy. The navy immediately stepped up
work for the development of the submarine-launched Polaris ICBM, which first
successfully operated in January 1960 (Sapolsky 1972; Launius and Jenkins 2002).

The Air Force did the same with land-based ICBMs, and its efforts were already
well-developed at the time of the 1956 decision. The Atlas received high priority
from the White House and hard-driving management from Brigadier General Bernard
A. Schriever, a flamboyant and intense air force leader. The first Atlas rocket was test-
fired on June 11, 1955, and a later generation rocket became operational in 1959.

The Titan ICBM and the Thor intermediate-range ballistic missile followed these systems in quick succession. By the latter 1950s, therefore, rocket technology had developed sufficiently for the creation of a viable ballistic missile capability. This was a revolutionary development that gave humanity, for the first time in its history, the ability to attack one continent from another. It effectively shrank the size of the globe, and the United States – which had always before been protected from outside attack by two massive oceans – could no longer rely on natural defensive boundaries or distance from its enemies (Emme 1964).

During the early 1950s, many air force officers had become convinced that the United States also needed a shorter-range missile, an intermediate range ballistic missile (IRBM) that could be deployed to Europe. Both the army and the air force wanted their own IRBM programs, however, and rather than proceed with one effort the Joint Chiefs of Staff compromised by advocating that the air force develop the Thor, while the army and the navy worked jointly on the Jupiter IRBM (Neufeld 1990, pp. 146–7). Thor had the goal of achieving flight within the shortest possible time; gaining approval in November 1955 and completing its first launch pad test in January 1957 and a flight test the next September. On February 28, 1959, a Thor missile, combined with an Agena second-stage, launched the first air force satellite, Discoverer I, into orbit. Under NASA's control during the 1960s, the system evolved into the highly successful Delta launch vehicle, one of the standard vehicles still used to launch many payloads into orbit (Schwiebert 1965; Armacost 1969).

The army's Jupiter IRBM was also highly successful. Developed in two versions by Wernher von Braun's rocket team at Huntsville, Alabama, used as a basis an earlier Redstone rocket. Jupiter A was an IRBM designed to carry a warhead and was deployed by NATO forces in Europe until 1963, when it was removed as part of the settlement to the Cuban Missile Crisis. Jupiter C was a research vehicle. On August 8, 1957, the army launched the first Jupiter C to an altitude of 600 miles and was recovered 1,200 miles down-range, from the Atlantic by US Navy teams. This launch proved that this vehicle would have been capable of reaching orbit before the Soviet launch of Sputnik 1 on October 4, 1957. Had it done so, the history of the space age might have unfolded remarkably differently (Emme 1964, pp. 109–14; Nash 1997).

All of the military's ballistic missile programs achieved their objectives relatively quickly. Within a decade of their beginning, the first and second generation of launchers had been successfully fielded. This achievement was, above all else, a question of management of large-scale technology (Johnson 2002). Historian Robert Perry noted, "The *management* of technology became the pacing element in the Air Force ballistic missile program. Moreover – as had not been true of any earlier missile program – technology involved not merely the creation of a single high-performance engine and related components in a single airframe, but the development of a family of compatible engines, guidance subsystems, test and launch site facilities, airframes, and a multitude of associated devices" (Quoted from Emme 1964, p. 150).

But this success came at a very high price. Spurred by the Cold War with the Soviet Union, public officials invested an enormous sum in launch technology. In the summer of 1957, for instance, President Dwight Eisenhower met with the National Security

Council to review the guided missile program and learned that since the beginning of his term in January 1953 through fiscal year 1957 the nation had spent $11.8 billion on space technology. "The cost of continuing these programs from FY 1957 through FY 1963," he found, "would amount to approximately $36.1 billion, for a grand total of $47 billion" (Launius 1996, p. 130). This is the initial investment, enormous by even the standard of the 1950s but an astronomical $326 billion in current dollars that gave America its first generation of space launchers. It developed the Delta, Atlas, and Titan boosters, as well as the solid rocket technology that is ubiquitous for space access.

The Pursuit of Satellite Reconnaissance

At the same time that these activities were underway, to combat the Soviet Union President Dwight D. Eisenhower supported the development of reconnaissance satellites as a means of learning about potentially aggressive actions. The safety from surprise attack promised by reconnaissance satellites was an especially attractive feature for Eisenhower and leaders of his generation because they remembered well the Japanese attack at Pearl Harbor on December 7, 1941, and were committed to never falling for such a sucker punch again. At a meeting of key scientific advisors on March 27, 1954, to discuss the use of space for military purposes, Eisenhower warned that "Modern weapons had made it easier for a hostile nation with a closed society to plan an attack in secrecy and thus gain an advantage denied to the nation with an open society." Reconnaissance satellites were a counter to this threat. Issues of national security, therefore, prompted most of the Eisenhower Administration's interest in the space program during the 1950s (Coolbaugh 1988).

After Sputnik, this program shifted into high gear. The Department of Defense developed two types of satellites, the first of which was named Samos which never proved reliable. More significant was the Central Intelligence Agency's (CIA) CORONA program, the first successful mission of which was in August 1960. More than 120 CORONA satellites were launched until the early 1970s, when the system was replaced by a much more massive satellite commonly referred to as the "Big Bird," but actually named the KH-9 HEXAGON (Peebles 1997; Day, Logsdon, and Latell 1998).

Thereafter, the United States operated much bigger and better versions of its reconnaissance satellites. In the late 1960s, the US Air Force began operating a communications intelligence satellite named CANYON that intercepted Soviet telephone transmissions. Follow-on versions of this satellite, named VORTEX and MERCURY, continued to operate into the twenty-first century. In the early 1970s, the CIA deployed a satellite named AQUACADE for intercepting the faint radio signals from Soviet missile tests, using a giant mesh dish for detecting the electronic whispers. Modern versions named MERCURY and ORION were launched in the 1980s, and even more upgraded versions were launched in the 1990s. These satellites are believed to have truly massive antennas that unfurl in geosynchronous orbit. Additionally, in December 1976, the NRO launched the KH-11 KENNAN. The KH-11 allowed images to reach an intelligence expert, or the desk of the president of the United States, within minutes. It revolutionized intelligence collection and versions of the KH-11 equipped with some infrared capability (later called CRYSTAL and now called by some highly-secret code name) continue to operate today and their images are vital to US military operations (Richelson 1990).

The International Geophysical Year and the Sputnik Crisis

A combination of technological and scientific advances, political competition with the Soviet Union, and changes in popular opinion about spaceflight came together in a very specific way in the 1950s to affect public policy in favor of an aggressive space program. This found tangible expression in 1952 when the International Council of Scientific Unions (ICSU) started planning for an International Polar Year, the third in a series of scientific activities designed to study geophysical phenomena in remote reaches of the planet. The Council agreed that July 1, 1957, to December 31, 1958, would be the period of emphasis in polar research, in part because of a predicted expansion of solar activity; the previous polar years had taken place in 1882–3 and 1932–3. Late in 1952 the ICSU expanded the scope of the scientific research effort, to include studies that would be conducted using rockets with instrument packages in the upper atmosphere and changed the name to the International Geophysical Year (IGY) to reflect the larger scientific objectives. In October 1954 at a meeting in Rome, Italy, the Council adopted another resolution calling for the launch of artificial satellites during the IGY to help map the Earth's surface. The Soviet Union immediately announced plans to orbit an IGY satellite, virtually assuring that the United States would respond, and this, coupled with the military satellite program, set both the agenda and the stage for most space efforts through 1958. The next year the United States announced Project Vanguard, its own IGY scientific satellite program (Green and Lomask 1970; Bulkeley 1991, pp. 89–122).

By the end of 1956, less than a year before the launch of Sputnik, the United States was involved in two modest space programs that were moving ahead slowly and staying within strict budgetary constraints. One was a highly visible scientific program as part of the IGY, and the other was a highly classified program to orbit a military reconnaissance satellite. They shared two attributes. They each were separate from the ballistic missile program underway in the Department of Defense, but they shared in the fruits of its research and adapted some of its launch vehicles. They also were oriented toward satisfying a national goal of establishing "freedom of space" for all orbiting satellites. The IGY scientific effort could help establish the precedent of access to space, while a military satellite might excite other nations to press for limiting such access. Because of this goal a military satellite, in which the Eisenhower administration was most interested, could not under any circumstances precede scientific satellites into orbit. The IGY satellite program, therefore, was a means of securing the larger goal of open access to space. Before it could do so, on October 4, 1957, the Soviet Union launched *Sputnik 1* and began the space age in a way that had not been anticipated by the leaders of the United States.

A full-scale crisis resulted on October 4, 1957, when the Soviets launched *Sputnik 1*, the world's first artificial satellite as its IGY entry. This had a "Pearl Harbor" effect on American public opinion, creating an illusion of a technological gap and provided the impetus for increased spending on aerospace endeavors, technical and scientific educational programs, and the chartering of new federal agencies to manage air and space research and development. This was all the more important because of a long-standing belief that the United States would be the first spacefaring nation (Ordway and Liebermann 1992; McCurdy 1997).

Sputnik led directly to several critical efforts aimed at "catching up" with the Soviet Union's space achievements. Among these:

- A full-scale review of the civil and military space programs of the United States, including scientific satellite efforts and ballistic missile development (Inaugurated November 8, 1957).
- Establishment of a Presidential Science Advisor in the White House who had the responsibility of overseeing the activities of the Federal government in science and technology (Established November 22, 1957).
- Creation of the Advanced Research Projects Agency in the Department of Defense, and the consolidation of several space activities under centralized management (Created February 7, 1958).
- Establishment of the National Aeronautics and Space Administration to manage civil space operations for the benefit "of all mankind" by means of the National Aeronautics and Space Act of 1958 (Signed into law on July 29, 1958).
- Passage of the National Defense Education Act of 1958 to provide Federal funding for education in scientific and technical disciplines (Passed by Congress on September 3, 1958).

A direct result of this crisis, NASA began operations on October 1, 1958, absorbing into it the earlier National Advisory Committee for Aeronautics intact; its 8,000 employees, an annual budget of $100 million, three major research laboratories – Langley Aeronautical Laboratory, Ames Aeronautical Laboratory, and Lewis Flight Propulsion Laboratory – and two smaller test facilities. It quickly incorporated other organizations into the new agency, notably the space science group of the Naval Research Laboratory in Maryland, the Jet Propulsion Laboratory managed by the California Institute of Technology for the Army, and the Army Ballistic Missile Agency in Huntsville, Alabama, where Wernher von Braun's team of engineers were engaged in the development of large rockets. Eventually NASA created several other centers, and today has ten located around the country.

NASA began to conduct space missions within months of its creation, and during its first 20 years NASA conducted several major programs:

- Human space flight initiatives – Mercury's single astronaut program (flights during 1961–3) to ascertain if a human could survive in space; Project Gemini (flights during 1965–6) with two astronauts to practice space operations, especially rendezvous and docking of spacecraft and extravehicular activity (EVA); and Project Apollo (flights during 1968–72) to explore the Moon.

- Robotic missions to the Moon (Ranger, Surveyor, and Lunar Orbiter), Venus (*Pioneer Venus*), Mars (*Mariner 4*, *Viking 1* and *2*), and the outer planets (*Pioneer 10* and *11*, *Voyager 1* and *2*).
- Aeronautics research to enhance air transport safety, reliability, efficiency, and speed (X-15 hypersonic flight, lifting body flight research, avionics and electronics studies, propulsion technologies, structures research, aerodynamics investigations).
- Remote-sensing Earth-satellites for information gathering (Landsat satellites for environmental monitoring).
- Applications satellites for communications (*Echo 1*, *TIROS*, and *Telstar*) and weather monitoring.
- An orbital workshop for astronauts, *Skylab*.
- A reusable spacecraft for traveling to and from Earth orbit, the Space Shuttle.

The figure of Dwight D. Eisenhower has dominated recent study of the Sputnik crisis and the origins of the space age, and he has emerged as a much more effective leader than thought at the time. Rather than a smiling, do-nothing, golf-playing president, Eisenhower's leadership handling the Soviet Union in space now increasingly appears far-sighted and rationale. To ensure against Soviet aggression, Eisenhower supported the development of ICBM-deterrent capabilities and reconnaissance satellites as a means of learning about potentially aggressive actions (Burrows 1987; Richelson 1990; McDonald 1997; Peebles 1997; Day, Logsdon and Latell 1998).

The historiography of space technology came of age with the publication of Walter L. McDougall's (1985) Pulitzer Prize-winning book on the origins and conduct of the space race. This book analyzes the Cold War rivalry in race with the preparations for and launch of *Sputnik 1* on October 4, 1957, through the race to the Moon in the 1960s. The author argues that the mandate to complete Apollo on President John F. Kennedy's schedule of "before this decade is out" prompted the space program to become identified almost exclusively with high-profile, expensive, human spaceflight projects. This was because Apollo became a race against the Soviet Union for recognition as the world leader in science and technology and by extension in other fields as well. McDougall juxtaposes the American effort of Apollo with the Soviet space program and the dreams of such designers as Sergei P. Korolev to land a Soviet cosmonaut on the Moon. The author recognizes Apollo as a significant engineering achievement but concludes that it was also enormously costly both in terms of resources and the direction to be taken in state support of science and technology. In the end, NASA had to stress engineering over science, competition over cooperation, civilian over military management, and international prestige over practical applications. Not all agree with all of McDougall's arguments, but since the publication of... *the Heavens and the Earth* historians have been striving to equal its scintillating analysis, stellar writing, and scope of discussion.

One of the issues that McDougall tackles is the fear of a "missile gap" between the capability of the Soviet Union and the United States, with the Soviets having superiority. This supposed gap, which later proved a chimera, motivated considerable space policy debate in the latter 1950s and early 1960s. It proved especially significant in the aftermath of Soviet successes in spaceflight technology in 1957–8, as shown in the work of Peter J. Roman. Roman (1995) details how the Eisenhower administration dealt with a myth put forward by Congressional Democrats that the United States was falling behind the Soviet Union in terms of military might. He also explores how the White House came up with what became the basic defense policy of the United States, reducing the size of traditional forces and relying more on nuclear missiles, "The New Look."

The Lunar Landing Program

The "missile gap" spilled over into Kennedy's decision in 1961 to make a commitment to land Americans on the Moon by the end of the decade as a means of demonstrating US superiority in space activities. A unique confluence of political necessity, personal commitment and activism, scientific and technological ability, economic prosperity, and public mood made possible the May 25, 1961, announcement by President John F. Kennedy to carry out a lunar landing program before the end of the decade as a means of demonstrating the United States' technological virtuosity. This decision has been analyzed in a classic publication by John Logsdon (1970), which argues that the lunar decision was a rational choice by the president, designed to meet a series of political challenges. The rational choice argument begins with Logsdon's assertion that space was a political tool that Kennedy chose to use to win one battle of the Cold War, that of international prestige. According to this model, the battle for prestige was political and although the Apollo program indirectly produced technological advances it was of little direct value in terms of the military balance of power.

In the context of international rivalry with the Soviet Union, furthermore, John Logsdon and Alain Dupas (1994) assess how much of a race the Moon landing decision created between the two cold-warring nations. They find that both nations expended tremendous resources in rivalry over the Moon. Using recently available Soviet documents, they find that the Soviets made several secret attempts to develop hardware for a lunar landing that would beat the United States to the Moon. That they were unsuccessful in doing so resulted from "personal rivalries, shifting political alliances and bureaucratic inefficiencies." These "bred failure and delays within the Soviet lunar-landing program." The Americans were successful, on the other hand, because they enjoyed "consistently strong political and public support."

Without question, the human landings on the Moon represented the singular achievement of NASA during its formative years. For 11 years after Kennedy's 1961 decision, NASA was consumed with carrying out Project Apollo. This effort required significant expenditures, costing $25.4 billion over the life of the program, to make it a reality. Only the building of the Panama Canal rivaled the Apollo program's size as the largest non-military technological endeavor ever undertaken by the United States; only the Manhattan Project was comparable in a wartime setting (Brooks, Grimwood, and Swenson 1979; Bilstein 1980; Murray and Cox 1989).

After the tragic fire that killed three astronauts – Gus Grissom, Ed White, and Roger Chaffee – during a ground test on January 27, 1967 sent NASA back to the design tables to make the spacecraft more reliable, the first Apollo mission to capture public significance was the flight of *Apollo 8*. On December 21, 1968, it took off atop a *Saturn V* booster from the Kennedy Space Center in Florida. Three astronauts were aboard – Frank Borman, James A. Lovell Jr., and William A. Anders – for a historic mission to orbit the Moon. After *Apollo 8* made one-and-a-half Earth orbits, its third stage began a burn to put the spacecraft on a lunar trajectory. It orbited the Moon on December 24–5 and then fired the boosters for a return flight. It "splashed down" in the Pacific Ocean on December 27 (Zimmerman 1998). Two more Apollo missions occurred before the climax of the program, but they did little more than confirm that the time had come for a lunar landing.

That landing came during the flight of *Apollo 11*, which lifted off on July 16, 1969, and, after confirmation that the hardware was working well, began the three-day trip to the Moon. Then, on July 20, 1969, the Lunar Module – with astronauts Neil A. Armstrong and Edwin E. "Buzz" Aldrin aboard – landed on the lunar surface while Michael Collins orbited overhead in the Apollo command module. After checkout, Armstrong set foot on the surface, telling millions who saw and heard him on Earth that it was "one small step for [a] man – one giant leap for mankind." Aldrin soon followed him out and the two explored their surroundings, planted an American flag but omitted claiming the land for the US as had been routinely done during European exploration of the Americas, collected soil and rock samples, and set up scientific experiments. The next day they rendezvoused with the Apollo capsule orbiting overhead and began the return trip to Earth, splashing down in the Pacific on July 24.

Five more landing missions followed at approximately six-month intervals through December 1972, each of them increasing the time spent on the Moon. The scientific experiments placed on the Moon and the lunar soil samples returned have provided grist for scientists' investigations ever since. The scientific return was significant, but the program did not answer conclusively the age-old questions of lunar origins and evolution. Three of the latter Apollo missions also used a lunar rover vehicle to travel in the vicinity of the landing site, but despite their significant scientific return none equaled the public excitement of *Apollo 11* (Chaikin 1994).

Not long after the first lunar landing in July 1969, Richard Nixon told an assembled audience that the flight of *Apollo 11* represented the most significant week in the history of Earth since the creation. Clearly, at least at that time, the president viewed the endeavor as pathbreaking and permanent, a legacy of accomplishment that future generations would reflect on as they plied intergalactic space and colonized planets throughout the galaxy. Hans Mark, director of NASA's Ames Research Center during the 1960s, recently voiced a less positive result for Apollo. "President Kennedy's objective was duly accomplished, but we paid a price," he wrote in 1987, "the Apollo program had no logical legacy." Mark suggested that the result of Apollo was essentially a technological dead end for the space program. It did not, in his view, foster an orderly development of spaceflight capabilities beyond the lunar missions (Mark 1987, p. 36).

Nixon's statement was political hyperbole made at the time of the dramatic lunar landing. Both he and the nation as a whole soon largely forgot about Apollo and the space program. Mark's later and more reflective statement revealed the skepticism of a leader in the techno-scientific establishment who was disappointed by the direction of later efforts in space. Somewhere between these two extremes probably lies a responsible set of conclusions about the Apollo program and its achievements, failures, and effect on later activities.

There are several important legacies (or conclusions) about Project Apollo that need to be remembered about the *Apollo 11* landing. First, and probably most important, the Apollo program was successful in accomplishing the political goals for which it had been created. Kennedy had been dealing with a Cold War crisis in 1961 brought on by several separate factors – the Soviet orbiting of Yuri Gagarin (1934–68) and the disastrous Bay of Pigs invasion of Cuba were only two of them – that Apollo was designed to combat. At the time of the *Apollo 11* landing, Mission Control in Houston flashed the words of President Kennedy announcing the Apollo commitment on its big screen. Those phrases were followed with these: "TASK ACCOMPLISHED, July 1969." No greater understatement could probably have been made. Any assessment of Apollo that does not recognize the accomplishment of landing an American on the Moon and safely returning before the end of the 1960s is incomplete and inaccurate, for that was the primary goal of the undertaking.

Second, Project Apollo was a triumph of management in meeting the enormously difficult systems engineering and technological integration requirements. James E. Webb, the NASA administrator at the height of the program between 1961 and 1968, always contended that Apollo was much more a management exercise than anything else, and that the technological challenge, while sophisticated and impressive, was also within grasp. More difficult was ensuring that those technological skills were properly managed and used. Webb's contention was confirmed in spades by the success of Apollo. NASA leaders had to acquire and organize unprecedented resources to accomplish the task at hand. From both a political and technological perspective, management was critical (Webb 1969; Lambright 1995). For 7 years after Kennedy's Apollo decision, through October 1968, James Webb politicked, coaxed, cajoled, and maneuvered for NASA in Washington. In the process, he acquired for the agency sufficient resources to meet its Apollo requirements.

More to the point, NASA personnel employed a "program management" concept that centralized authority over design, engineering, procurement, testing, construction, manufacturing, spare parts, logistics, training, and operations. The management of the program was recognized as critical to Apollo's success in November 1968, when *Science* magazine, the publication of the American Association for the Advancement of Science, observed:

> In terms of numbers of dollars or of men, NASA has not been our largest national undertaking, but in terms of complexity, rate of growth, and technological sophistication it has been unique ... It may turn out that [the space program's] most valuable spin-off of all will be human rather than technological: better knowledge of how to plan, coordinate, and monitor the multitudinous and varied activities of the organizations required to accomplish great social undertakings.

Understanding the management of complex structures for the successful completion of a multifarious task was a critical outgrowth of the Apollo effort.

This was a task not without difficulties. The scientific and engineering communities within NASA were far from monolithic, and differences among them thrived. Add to them representatives from industry, universities, and research facilities, and competition on all levels to further their own scientific and technical areas was the result. The NASA leadership generally viewed this pluralism as a positive force within the space program, for it ensured that all sides aired their views and emphasized the honing of positions to a fine edge. Competition, most people concluded, made for a more precise and viable space exploration effort. There were winners and losers in this strife, however, and sometimes ill will was harbored for years. Moreover, if the conflict became too great and spilled into areas where it was misunderstood, it could be devastating to the conduct of the lunar program. The head of the Apollo program worked hard to keep these factors balanced and to promote order so that NASA could accomplish the landing within the time constraints of the president's directive (McCurdy 1993).

Third, Project Apollo forced the people of the world to view the planet Earth in a new way. *Apollo 8* was critical to this sea change, for on its outward voyage, the crew focused a portable television camera on Earth and for the first time humans saw their home from afar, a tiny, lovely, and fragile "blue marble" hanging in the blackness of space. When the *Apollo 8* spacecraft arrived at the Moon on Christmas Eve of 1968, the image of Earth was even more strongly reinforced when the crew sent images of the planet back while reading the first part of the Bible – "God created the heavens and the Earth, and the Earth was without form and void" – before sending holiday greetings to humanity. Writer Archibald MacLeish summed up the feelings of many people when he wrote at the time of Apollo that "To see the Earth as it truly is, small and blue and beautiful in that eternal silence where it floats, is to see ourselves as riders on the Earth together, brothers on that bright loveliness in the eternal cold – brothers who know now that they are truly brothers" (Quoted in Nicks 1970). The modern environmental movement was galvanized in part by this new perception of the planet and the need to protect it and the life that it supports.

Finally, the Apollo program, while an enormous achievement, left a divided legacy for NASA and the aerospace community. The perceived "golden age" of Apollo created for the agency an expectation that the direction of any major space goal from the president would always bring NASA a broad consensus of support and provide it with the resources and license to dispense them as it saw fit. Something most NASA officials did not understand at the time of the Moon landing in 1969, however, was that Apollo had not been a normal situation and would not be repeated. The Apollo decision was, therefore, an anomaly in the national decision-making process. The dilemma of the "golden age" of Apollo has been difficult to overcome, but moving beyond the Apollo program to embrace future opportunities has been an important goal of the agency's leadership in the recent past. Exploration of the Solar System and the universe remains as enticing a goal and as important an objective for humanity as it ever has been. Project Apollo was an important early step in that ongoing process of exploration (Launius and McCurdy 1997).

The Space Shuttle Era

The US civil space program went into something of a holding pattern after the completion of Project Apollo in December 1972. The major program of NASA for the decade was the development of a reusable Space Shuttle that was supposed to be able to travel back and forth between Earth and space more routinely and economically than had ever been the case before. NASA leaders worked between the fall of 1969 and early 1972 to convince President Richard Nixon that this shuttle was an appropriate follow-on project to Apollo. They were successful in January 1972. The shuttle became the largest, most expensive, and highly visible project undertaken by NASA after its first decade, and it continued as a central component in the US space program through the end of the twentieth century (Heppenheimer 1999; Jenkins 2001).

The Space Shuttle that emerged in the early 1970s consisted of three primary elements: a delta-winged orbiter spacecraft with a large crew compartment, a 15 by 60-feet cargo bay, and three main engines; two Solid Rocket Boosters (SRB); and an external fuel tank housing the liquid hydrogen and oxidizer burned in the main engines. The orbiter and the two solid rocket boosters were reusable. The Shuttle was designed to transport approximately 45,000 tons of cargo into near-Earth orbit, 100 to 217 nautical miles (115–250 statute miles) above the Earth. It could also accommodate a flight crew of up to ten persons, although a crew of seven would be more common, for a basic space mission of seven days. During a return to Earth, the orbiter was designed so that it had a cross-range maneuvering capability of 1,100 nautical miles (1,265 statute miles) to meet requirements for liftoff and landing at the same location after only one orbit. This capability satisfied the Department of Defense's need for the Shuttle to place in orbit and retrieve reconnaissance satellites (Heppenheimer 2002).

NASA began developing the shuttle soon after the decision, with the goal of flying in space by 1978, but because of budgetary pressure and technological problems the first orbital flight was delayed until 1981. There was tremendous excitement when *Columbia*, the first operational orbiter, took off from Cape Canaveral, Florida, on April 12, 1981, 6 years after the last American astronaut had returned from space following the Apollo-Soyuz Test Project in 1975. After two days in space, where the crew tested *Columbia*, excitement permeated the nation once again as it landed like an aircraft at Edwards Air Force Base, California. The first flight had been a success, and both NASA and the media ballyhooed the beginning of a new age in spaceflight, one in which there would be inexpensive and routine access to space for many people and payloads. Speculations abounded that within a few years Shuttle flights would take off and land as predictably as airplanes and that commercial tickets would be sold for regularly scheduled "spaceline" flights (Jenkins 2001).

In spite of the high hopes that had attended the first flight of *Columbia*, the shuttle program provided neither inexpensive nor routine access to space. By January 1986, there had been only twenty-four Shuttle flights, although, in the 1970s, NASA had projected more flights than that for every year. While the system was reusable, its complexity, coupled with the ever-present rigors of flying in an aerospace environment, meant that the turnaround time between flights was several months instead of several days. In addition, missions were delayed for all manner of problems associated with ensuring the safety and performance of such a complex system. Since the flight schedule did not meet expectations, and since it took thousands of work hours and expensive parts to keep the system performing satisfactorily, observers began to criticize NASA for failing to meet the cost-effectiveness expectations that had been used to gain the approval of the shuttle program 10 years earlier. Critical analyses agreed that the Shuttle had proven to be neither cheap nor reliable, both primary selling points, and that NASA should never have used those arguments in building a political consensus for the program. In some respects, therefore, there was some agreement by 1985 that the effort had been both a triumph and a tragedy. The program had been an engagingly ambitious program that had developed an exceptionally sophisticated vehicle, one that no other nation on Earth could have built at the time. As such it had been an enormously successful program. At the same time, the shuttle was essentially a continuation of space spectaculars, à la Apollo, and its much-touted capabilities had not been realized. It made far fewer flights and conducted far fewer scientific experiments than NASA had publicly predicted.

All of these criticisms reached crescendo proportions following the tragic loss of *Challenger* during a launch on January 28, 1986. Although it was not the entire reason, the pressure to get the shuttle schedule more in line with earlier projections throughout 1985 prompted NASA workers to accept operational procedures that fostered short cuts and increased the opportunity for disaster. It came 73 seconds into the flight, about 11:40 a.m. EST, as a result of a leak in one of two SRBs that detonated the main liquid fuel tank. Seven astronauts – Francis R. Scobee, Michael J. Smith, Judith A. Resnik, Ronald E. McNair, Ellison S. Onizuka, Gregory B. Jarvis, and Christa McAuliffe – died in this accident, the worst in the history of spaceflight. The accident, traumatic for the American people even under the best of situations, was made that much worse because *Challenger's* crewmembers represented a cross-section of the American population in terms of race, gender, geography, background, and religion. The explosion became one of the most significant events of the 1980s, as billions around the world saw the accident on television and empathized with any one or more of the crewmembers killed (Corrigan 1993).

Several investigations followed the accident, the most important being the presidentially mandated blue ribbon commission chaired by William P. Rogers. It found that the *Challenger* accident resulted from a poor engineering decision, an O-ring used to seal joints in the SRBs that was susceptible to failure at low temperatures, introduced innocently enough years earlier. Rogers kept the commission's analysis on that technical level, and documented the problems in exceptional detail. The commission did a credible if not unimpeachable job of grappling with the technologically difficult issues associated with the *Challenger* accident (Vaughan 1996).

With the *Challenger* accident, the shuttle program went into a two-year hiatus while NASA worked to redesign the SRBs and revamp its management structure. James C. Fletcher, the NASA Administrator between 1971 and 1977, was brought back to head the space agency a second time with the specific task of overhauling it.

NASA reinvested heavily in its safety and reliability programs, made organizational changes to improve efficiency, and restructured its management system. Most important, NASA engineers completely reworked the components of the shuttle to enhance its safety and added an egress method for the astronauts. A critical decision resulting from the accident and its aftermath – during which the nation experienced a reduction in capability to launch satellites – was to expand greatly the use of expendable launch vehicles. The Space Shuttle finally returned to flight without further incident on September 29, 1988, without any major accidents thereafter. Through all of these activities, a good deal of realism about what the shuttle could and could not do began to emerge in the latter 1980s (Mack 1998).

Two books also stand out as exposés of the *Challenger* accident. The first, by Malcolm McConnell (1987), investigated the immediate causes of the accident and roundly criticized NASA management. McConnell highlighted the pressures to launch, the objections of engineers, and the internal debates on the subject, and argued that NASA leaders caused the disaster by pressing operations officials to launch when they did so that the president could mention it in that evening's State of the Union Address. Perhaps a more important book was by Joseph J. Trento and Susan B. Trento (1987), a sweeping denunciation of NASA management in the post-*Challenger* era that emphasized the agency's putative "fall from grace" after Apollo. They argued that the giants of the 1960s, the people who had successfully managed the lunar program, were gone and had been replaced with government bureaucrats who played the political game and sold the Shuttle as an inexpensive program, in the process sowing the seeds of disaster. The Trentos blamed the Nixon administration for politicizing and militarizing the space program. Every NASA administrator since that time, they said, has had to play hard, but against bigger opponents, in both arenas. They argued that the failure was not caused by the space vehicle's O-rings that allowed the explosion of the Space Shuttle, but by the political system that produced them. Neither these works, nor other discussions of the subject, have satisfactorily explained this accident. While these criticisms require reasoned consideration in the study of space exploration's history, they abandon one of the most cherished principles of historical scholarship, the "shibboleth of objectivity." Called "that noble dream" by Charles Beard and others, the quest for objectivity has motivated historians above all else for most of the twentieth century.

Robotic Exploration of the Solar System

In addition to the shuttle, the US space program began a succession of spectacular science missions in the 1970s. For example, Project Viking was the culmination of a series of missions to explore Mars that had begun in 1964. Two identical spacecraft, each consisting of a lander and an orbiter, were built. Launched on August 20, 1975, *Viking 1* landed on July 20, 1976, on the Chryse Planitia (Golden Plains). *Viking 2* was launched on September 9, 1975, and landed on September 3, 1976. One of the important scientific activities of this project was the attempt to determine whether there was life on Mars, but the Viking landers provided no clear evidence for the presence of living microorganisms in soil near the landing sites (Ezell and Ezell 1984).

Once every 176 years Earth and all the giant planets of the Solar System gather on one side of the Sun. This geometric line-up made possible close-up observation of all the planets in the outer solar system (with the exception of Pluto) in a single flight, the "Grand Tour." The flyby of each planet would bend the spacecraft's flight path and increase its velocity enough to deliver it to the next destination. This would occur through a complicated process known as "gravity assist," something like a slingshot effect, whereby the flight time to Neptune could be reduced from 30 to 12 years. Two Voyager spacecraft were launched from Kennedy Space Center in 1977 to image Jupiter and Saturn. As the mission progressed, with the successful achievement of all its objectives at Jupiter and Saturn in December 1980, additional flybys of the two outermost giant planets, Uranus and Neptune, proved possible – and irresistible – to mission scientists. Eventually, between them, *Voyager 1* and *Voyager 2* explored all the giant outer planets, 48 of their moons, and the unique systems of rings and magnetic fields those planets possess (Schorn 1998; Dethloff and Schorn 2003).

A space science project much in the news in the 1990s, both for positive and negative reasons, was the $2 billion Hubble Space Telescope that had been launched from the Space Shuttle in April 1990. A key component of it was a precision-ground 94-inch primary mirror shaped to within microinches of perfection from ultra-low expansion titanium silicate glass with an aluminum-magnesium fluoride coating. The first photos provided bright, crisp images against the black background of space, much clearer than pictures of the same target taken by ground-based telescopes. Controllers then began moving the telescope's mirrors to better focus images. Although the focus sharpened slightly, the best image still had a pinpoint of light encircled by a hazy ring or "halo." NASA technicians concluded that the telescope had a "spherical aberration," a mirror defect only 1/25th the width of a human hair, that prevented Hubble from focusing all light to a single point.

At first many believed that the spherical aberration would cripple the 43-foot-long telescope, and NASA received considerable negative publicity, but soon scientists found a way to work around the abnormality with computer enhancement. Because of the difficulties with the mirror, in December 1993, NASA launched the shuttle *Endeavour* on a repair mission to insert corrective lenses into the telescope and to service other instruments. During a weeklong mission, *Endeavour's* astronauts conducted a record five spacewalks and successfully completed all programmed repairs to the spacecraft. The first reports from the Hubble spacecraft indicated that the images being returned were afterward more than an order of magnitude greater than those obtained before (Smith 1994; Mack 1998).

A more intriguing but less well-developed aspect of this history is the way the two programs played off of each other and perhaps served as two sides of the same coin. Eric Chaisson (1994) makes the case that some of the technology of the Hubble Space Telescope was developed initially for the satellite reconnaissance programs of the Department of Defense (DOD) and that the problems with the space telescope could have been minimized had the DOD been more forthright in assisting NASA. This is an intensely suggestive possibility that requires additional investigation.

In the late 1980s, a new generation of planetary exploration began. Numerous projects came to fruition during the period. For example, the highly successful *Magellan* mission to Venus by 1993 had provided significant scientific data about the planet. Another such project was the troubled *Galileo* mission to Jupiter, which even before reaching its destination had become a source of great concern for both NASA and public officials because not all of its systems were working properly, but it did return useful scientific data. Finally the ill-fated *Mars_Observer* was launched and reached its destination in 1993 but was lost as a result of an on-board explosion.

The Dream of a Space Station

In 1984, as part of its interest in reinvigorating the space program, the Ronald Reagan administration called for the development of a permanently occupied space station. Congress made a down payment of $150 million for Space Station *Freedom* in the fiscal year 1985 NASA budget. From the outset, both the Reagan administration and NASA intended Space Station *Freedom* to be an international program. The inclusion of international partners, many now with their own rapidly developing spaceflight capabilities, could enhance the effort. As a result, NASA leaders pressed forward with international agreements among thirteen nations to take part in the Space Station *Freedom* program (McCurdy 1990; Launius 2003).

Almost from the outset, the Space Station *Freedom* program proved controversial. Most of the debate centered on its costs versus its benefits. At first projected to cost $8 billion, for many reasons, some of them associated with tough Washington politics, within 5 years the projected costs had more than tripled and the station had become too expensive to fund fully in an environment in which the national debt had exploded in the 1980s. NASA pared away at the station budget, and in the end the project was satisfactory to almost no one. In the latter 1980s and early 1990s a parade of space station managers and NASA administrators, each of them honest in their attempts to rescue the program, wrestled with *Freedom* and lost.

In 1993, the international situation allowed NASA to negotiate a landmark decision to include Russia in the building of an International Space Station (ISS). On November 7, 1993, the United States and Russia announced they would work together with the other international partners to build a space station for the benefit of all. Even so the ISS remained a difficult issue through the 1990s as policymakers wrestled with competing political agendas without consensus. With the first crew's arrival on-orbit at the ISS in 2000 the program entered a new era, for it signaled a permanent human presence in space.

It also fulfilled one of the primary goals of spaceflight, a space station floating above Earth. Sometimes this goal has been envisioned in art and literature and film as an extravagant way station to the planets – as in many science fiction films ranging from *2001: A Space Odyssey* to the *Star Trek* series to *Mission to Mars* – and at other times more realistically as spare research outposts with teams of scientists deciphering information about our universe. No matter the depiction, the space station has been a central goal of the spacefaring community of the United States. It was promulgated as a necessity for exploration of the Solar System, for once a rocket overcomes Earth's gravity and reaches orbit travelers are "halfway to anywhere" they might want to go. At that halfway point, space stations serve as the transit point for vehicles traveling back and forth to Earth and those that would fly to the Moon and the planets. The ISS is envisioned as an anchor tenant for a research park in space, contributing critical knowledge necessary to make life on Earth more rewarding and to aid humanity's movement beyond this planet. Like the base camp at the foot of Mount Everest, the ISS is intended as the "jumping off" point for exploration beyond Earth orbit.

Humans Versus Machines in Space

One of the unique surprises of the space age that opened with Sputnik in 1957 has been the rapid advance in electronics and robotics that has made possible large-scale spaceflight technology without humans not only practicable but also desirable. This has led to a central debate in the field over the role of humans in spaceflight. Perhaps more can be accomplished without human presence. Clearly, if scientific understanding or space-based applications or military purposes are driving spaceflight as a whole, then humans flying aboard spacecraft have little appeal. Their presence makes the effort much more expensive because once a person is placed aboard a spacecraft the primary purpose of that spacecraft is no longer a mission other than bringing the person home safely. But if the goal is human colonization of the Solar System then there are important reasons to foster human spaceflight technology.

This debate has raged for decades without resolution. It is reaching crescendo proportions in the first decade of the twenty-first century as the ISS is coming online and discussions of future efforts beyond the station emerge. Scientist Paul Spudis observed: "Judicious use of robots and unmanned spacecraft can reduce the risk and increase the effectiveness of planetary exploration. But robots will never be replacements for people. Some scientists believe that artificial intelligence software may enhance the capabilities of unmanned probes, but so far those capabilities fall far short of what is required for even the most rudimentary forms of field study." Spudis finds that both will be necessary. "The strengths of each partner make up for the other's weaknesses," he writes. "To use only one technique is to deprive ourselves of the best of both worlds: the intelligence and flexibility of human participation and the beneficial use of robotic assistance" (Spudis 1999, p. 31).

Conclusion

Spaceflight has represented the unique creation and operation of technological systems that accounted for the perceptions of the United States as a people who master machines. Americans are a technological and an organizational people, and the structures created to carry out space exploration are not just the so-called hardware of the system, but also the management structure, the organizations, the processes and procedures of operation, the people assigned, and the transportation and information networks that interconnect everything. In NASA this technological system included not just the spacecraft, but also the organizations, people, communications, manufacturing components, and even the political structure. It is the task of the modern makers of systems to direct the values of order, system, and control that are embedded in the machines of modern technology.

BIBLIOGRAPHY

Michael H. Armacost. *The Politics of Weapons Innovation: The Thor-Jupiter Controversy* (New York: Columbia University Press, 1969).

Brian Ash ed. *The Visual Encyclopedia of Science Fiction* (New York: Harmony Books, 1977).

Mitchell G. Ash and Alfons Söllner, eds. *Forced Migration and Scientific Change: Émigré German-Speaking Scientists and Scholars after 1933* (New York: Cambridge University Press, 1996).

Edmund Beard. *Developing the ICBM: A Study in Bureaucratic Politics* (New York: Columbia University Press, 1976).

Roger E. Bilstein. *Stages to Saturn: A Technological History of the Apollo/Saturn Launch Vehicles* (Washington, DC: NASA Special Publication-4206, 1980).

Edgar M. Bottome. *The Missile Gap: A Study of the Formulation of Military and Political Policy* (Rutherford, NJ: Farleigh Dickenson University Press, 1971).

Wernher von Braun and Frederick I Ordway III. *History of Rocketry and Space Travel* (New York: Çrowell Co., 1986 edn).

Courtney G. Brooks, James M. Grimwood, and Loyd S. Swenson Jr. *Chariots for Apollo: A History of Manned Lunar Spacecraft* (Washington: NASA Special Publication-4205, 1979).

Rip Bulkeley. *The Sputniks Crisis and Early United States Space Policy: A Critique of the Historiography of Space* (Bloomington: Indiana University Press, 1991).

William E. Burrows. *Deep Black: Space Espionage and National Security* (New York: Random House, 1987).

Andrew Chaikin. *A Man on the Moon: The Voyages of the Apollo Astronauts* (New York: Viking, 1994).

Eric J. Chaisson. *The Hubble Wars: Astrophysics Meets Astropolitics in the Two-Billion-Dollar Struggle over the Hubble Space Telescope* (New York: HarperCollins, 1994).

James S. Coolbaugh. "Genesis of the USAF's first satellite programme," *Journal of the British Interplanetary Society* 51 (August 1998): 283–300.

Grace Corrigan. *A Journal for Christa: Christa McAuliffe, Teacher in Space* (Lincoln: University of Nebraska Press, 1993).

Dwayne A. Day, John M. Logsdon, and Brian Latell eds. *Eye in the Sky: The Story of the Corona Spy Satellite* (Washington, DC: Smithsonian Institution Press, 1998).

Henry W. Dethloff and Ronald A. Schorn. *Grand Tour: A History of Project Voyager* (Washington, DC: Smithsonian Institution Press, 2003).

David H. DeVorkin. *Science with a Vengeance: How the Military Created the U.S. Space Sciences after World War II* (New York: Springer-Verlag, 1992).

Eugene M. Emme, ed. *The History of Rocket Technology: Essays on Research, Development, and Utility* (Detroit: Wayne State University Press, 1964).

Edward Clinton Ezell and Linda Neuman Ezell. *On Mars: Exploration of the Red Planet, 1958–1978* (Washington, DC: NASA SP-4212, 1984).

Constance McL Green and Milton Lomask. *Vanguard: A History* (Washington, DC: NASA Special Publication-4202, 1970; rep. edn Smithsonian Institution Press, 1971).

James Gunn. *Alternate Worlds: The Illustrated History of Science Fiction* (Englewood Cliffs, NJ: Prentice-Hall, 1975).

T.A. Heppenheimer. *The Space Shuttle Decision: NASA's Quest for a Reusable Space Vehicle* (Washington, DC: NASA SP-4221, 1999).

T.A. Heppenheimer. *Development of the Space Shuttle, 1972–1981 (History of the Space Shuttle, Volume 2)* (Washington, DC: Smithsonian Institution Press, 2002).

Linda Hunt. *Secret Agenda: The United States Government, Nazi Scientists, and Project Paperclip, 1945 to 1990* (New York: St Martin's Press, 1991).

Dennis R. Jenkins. *Space Shuttle: The History of the National Space Transportation System, the First 100 Missions* (Cape Canaveral, FL: Dennis R. Jenkins, 2001, 4th edn).

Stephen B. Johnson. *The Secret of Apollo: Systems Management in American and European Space Programs* (Baltimore, MD: Johns Hopkins University Press, 2002).

Matthias Judt and Burghard Ciesla. *Technology Transfer Out of Germany after 1945* (New York: Harwood Academic Publishers, 1996).

Clayton R. Koppes. *JPL and the American Space Program: A History of the Jet Propulsion Laboratory* (New Haven, CT: Yale University Press, 1982).

Arkady Kosmodemyansky. *Konstantin Tsiolkovskiy* (Moscow, USSR: Nauka, 1985).

Henry Lambright, W. *Powering Apollo: James E. Webb of NASA* (Baltimore, MD: Johns Hopkins University Press, 1995).

Clarence Lasby. *Project Paperclip: Germans Scientists and the Cold War* (New York: Atheneum, 1971).

Roger D. Launius. *NASA: History of the U.S. Civil Space Program* (Malabar, FL: Krieger Publishing Co., 1994).

Roger D. Launius. "Eisenhower, sputnik, and the creation of NASA: technological elites and the public policy agenda," *Prologue: Quarterly of the National Archives and Records Administration* 28 (Summer 1996): 127–43.

Roger D. Launius. *Frontiers of Space Exploration* (Westport, CT: Greenwood Press, 1998).

Roger D. Launius. "The historical dimension of space exploration: reflections and possibilities," *Space Policy* 16 (2000): 23–38.

Roger D. Launius. *Base Camp to the Stars: The Space Station in American Thought and Culture* (Washington, DC: Smithsonian Institution Press, 2003).

Roger D. Launius and Dennis R. Jenkins, eds. *To Reach the High Frontier: A History of U.S. Launch Vehicles* (Lexington: University Press of Kentucky, 2002).

Roger D. Launius and Howard E. McCurdy, eds. *Spaceflight and the Myth of Presidential Leadership* (Urbana: University of Illinois Press, 1997).

Tom Lehrer. "Wernher von Braun," on the record album *That was the Year That Was* (1965).

Milton Lehman. *This High Man* (New York: Farrar, Straus, 1963).

John M. Logsdon. *The Decision to Go to the Moon: Project Apollo and the National Interest.* Cambridge, MA: The MIT Press, 1970.

John M. Logsdon. gen. ed. *Exploring the Unknown: Selected Documents in the History of the U.S. Civil Space Program*, vols 1–5 (Washington, DC: NASA SP-4407, 1995–2001).

John M. Logsdon and Alain Dupas. "Was the race to the moon real?" *Scientific American* 270 (June 1994): 36–43.

Malcolm McConnell. *Challenger: A Major Malfunction* (Garden City, NY: Doubleday and Co., 1987).

Howard E. McCurdy. *The Space Station Decision: Incremental Politics and Technological Choice* (Baltimore, MD: Johns Hopkins University Press, 1990).

Howard E. McCurdy. *Inside NASA: High Technology and Organizational Change in the U.S. Space Program* (Baltimore, MD: Johns Hopkins University Press, 1993).

Howard E. McCurdy. *Space and the American Imagination* (Washington, DC: Smithsonian Institution Press, 1997).

Robert A. McDonald. *Corona Between the Sun and the Earth: The First NRO Reconnaissance Eye in Space* (Bethesda, MD: ASPRS Publications, 1997).

Walter A. McDougall... *The Heavens and the Earth: A Political History of the Space Age* (New York: Basic Books, 1985, rep. edn, Baltimore, MD: Johns Hopkins University Press, 1997).

James McGovern. *Crossbow and Overcast* (New York: William Morrow, 1964).

Pamela E. Mack, ed. *From Engineering Science to Big Science: The NACA and NASA Collier Trophy Research Project Winners* (Washington, DC: NASA SP-4219, 1998).

Hans Mark. *The Space Station: A Personal Journey* (Durham, NC: Duke University Press, 1987).

Charles A. Murray and Catherine Bly Cox. *Apollo: The Race to the Moon* (New York: Simon & Schuster, 1989).

Philip Nash. *The Other Missiles of October: Eisenhower, Kennedy, and the Jupiters, 1957–1963* (Chapel Hill: University of North Carolina Press, 1997).

Jacob Neufeld. *Ballistic Missiles in the United States Air Force, 1945–1960* (Washington, DC: Office of Air Force History, 1990).

Michael J. Neufeld. *The Rocket and the Reich: Peenemünde and the Coming of the Ballistic Missile Era* (New York: The Free Press, 1995).

Michael J. Neufeld. "Wernher von Braun, the SS, and concentration camp labor: questions of moral, political, and criminal responsibility," *German Studies Review* 25/1 (2002): 57–78.

Oran W. Nicks. *This Island Earth* (Washington, DC: NASA Special Publication-250, 1970).

Frederick I. Ordway III and Randy Liebermann, eds. *Blueprint for Space: From Science Fiction to Science Fact* (Washington, DC: Smithsonian Institution Press, 1992).

Frederick I. Ordway III and Mitchell R. Sharpe. *The Rocket Team* (New York: Crowell, 1979).

Curtis Peebles. *The Corona Project: America's First Spy Satellites* (Annapolis, MD: Naval Institute Press, 1997).

Jeffrey T. Richelson. *America's Secret Eyes in Space: The U.S. Keyhole Spy Satellite Program* (New York: Harper & Row, 1990).

Peter J. Roman. *Eisenhower and the Missile Gap* (Ithaca, NY: Cornell University Press, 1995).

Harvey M. Sapolsky. *The Polaris System Development: Bureaucratic and Programmatic Success in Government* (Cambridge, MA: MIT Press, 1972).

Ronald A. Schorn. *Planetary Astronomy: From Ancient Times to the Third Millennium* (College Station: Texas A&M University Press, 1998).

Ernest G. Schwiebert. *A History of U.S. Air Force Ballistic Missiles* (New York: Frederick A. Praeger, 1965).

John L. Sloop. *Liquid Hydrogen as a Propulsion Fuel, 1945–1959* (Washington, DC: NASA, SP-4404, 1978).

Robert W. Smith. *The Space Telescope: A Study of NASA, Science, Technology, and Politics* (New York: Cambridge University Press, 1989, rev. edn 1994).

David L. Snead. *The Gaither Committee, Eisenhower, and the Cold War* (Columbus: Ohio State University Press, 1999).

Paul D. Spudis. "Robots vs. humans: who should explore space," *Scientific American* 10 (Spring 1999): 25, 30–31.

David K. Stumpf. *Titan II: A History of a Cold War Missile Program* (Fayetteville: University of Arkansas Press, 2000).

Joseph J. Trento and Susan B. Trento. *Prescription for Disaster: From the Glory of Apollo to the Betrayal of the Shuttle* (New York: Crown Publishers, 1987).

Diane Vaughan. *The Challenger Launch Decision: Risky Technology, Culture, and Deviance at NASA* (Chicago: University of Chicago Press, 1996).

H.B. Walters. *Hermann Oberth: Father of Space Travel* (New York: Macmillan, 1962).

James E. Webb. *Space Age Management: The Large-Scale Approach* (New York: McGraw-Hill, 1969).

Frank H. Winter. *Prelude to the Space Age: The Rocket Societies, 1924–1940* (Washington, DC: Smithsonian Institution Press, 1983).

Frank H. Winter. *Rockets into Space* (Cambridge, MA: Harvard University Press, 1990).

Robert Zimmerman. *Genesis: The Story of Apollo 8* (New York: Four Walls Eight Windows, 1998).

CHAPTER SIXTEEN

Nuclear Technology

M. JOSHUA SILVERMAN

Introduction

For the historian, the study of nuclear technologies is a study of contrasts. On the one hand, nuclear technologies represent some of most impressive scientific and technical achievements of the modern age. They have embodied humanity's greatest aspirations, including world peace, improved health care, and unlimited energy. On the other hand, nuclear technologies have aroused seemingly intractable conflict and social turmoil, giving tangible form to some of humanity's greatest fears, including nuclear annihilation, genetic mutations, and environmental disaster.

Similar contrasts emerge from the application or use of nuclear technologies. While some nuclear technologies have been at the center of vibrant political and technological controversies over the past 50 years, others have permeated modern life in ways both mundane and fantastic. Debates about nuclear weapons, nuclear power, and nuclear waste have commanded attention from the ivy-covered walls of the world's leading universities to the marble halls of official government power. Governments spend billions of dollars each year to clean up nuclear weapons production facilities, handle radioactive waste, and care for workers and citizens sickened from exposure to radiation. At the same time, nuclear technologies are used on a daily basis for medical imaging and treatment, detection systems, and measuring devices in hospitals, businesses, and research institutions. The mundane acceptance of these nuclear technologies stands in sharp contrast to the controversies surrounding their more high-profile cousins.

The phrase "nuclear technology" refers to devices or techniques that make use of ionizing radiation. In its broadest sense, "radiation" is the transmission of energy from any source; light, heat, radio waves, and microwaves are all types of radiation. Ionizing radiation is distinct in its tendency to add or strip electrons from an atom, creating charged particles or "ions."

Ionizing radiation causes atoms to behave differently by changing their physical properties. Most atoms are stable in their normal state, meaning that they exist in their current form indefinitely. Lead is lead and gold is gold, and despite the efforts of alchemists, turning one into the other is not something nature permits. Some atoms, however, are unstable in their current form. Unstable atoms undergo a process of radioactive decay, in which they change their physical structure and release excess energy until they achieve a stable form.

Most nuclear technologies are based on the predictability of the process of radio-active decay, or the fact that, under regular physical and chemical conditions, elements generate distinct types and quantities of energy. Nuclear technologies take advantage of this predictability by harnessing or tracking the energy released by decaying atoms to accomplish tasks such as power generation, measurement, and detection.

The energies released by unstable atoms can have significant impacts on living organisms. The history of nuclear technology therefore includes environmental and medical impacts as well as scientific and technical developments. This legacy, which has contributed to the controversies surrounding many nuclear technologies, is an integral part of its history.

The Development of Nuclear Technology, 1895–1939

Key Scientific Advances

Nuclear technologies originated alongside the discovery and control of radiation in the 1890s. Experimental physicists had observed that some elements, in the proper physical or chemical states, would emit unseen energies. In 1895, the German physicist Wilhelm Roentgen noted that a cathode ray tube stimulated by an electrical current could expose photographic film. Investigating this phenomenon, Roentgen found that he could develop a skeletal image of his hand by placing it between the film and the cathode ray tube, and under certain conditions he could even see the bones of his hand when he placed it next to the tube. He recognized that the tube produced an unseen energy, which he dubbed "x-rays," that passed easily through flesh but were largely blocked by bone and metal. When Roentgen published his findings, along with a skeletal image of his wife's hand, he created an immediate sensation. Numerous researchers quickly replicated his findings, and several began to market techniques for the controlled production of "x-rays" from what they called "Roentgen ray machines."

In 1896, the French physicist Henri Becquerel discovered that uranium salts gave off energy sufficient to expose film. Unlike Roentgen's cathode ray tube, which generated x-rays only when stimulated by an electrical current, the uranium salts produced the effect without any external charge. Becquerel thus identified uranium as a substance that emitted energy in its natural state, drawing attention to this relatively obscure element.

Pierre and Marie Curie coined the term "radioactivity." In 1898, the Curies announced that they had measured more energy from a sample of uranium than could be accounted for by the uranium itself. They speculated that the sample contained additional elements that also demonstrated the phenomenon they termed "radio-activity." The Curies ultimately identified two additional radioactive elements, radium and polonium, in their research on the properties of radiation.

Early Nuclear Technologies

Although Roentgen sought neither patents nor financial benefits, his 1895 discovery nonetheless sparked the rapid development of the x-ray machine, the first signific-ant nuclear technology. Roentgen had used a commonly used device in physics experimentation, the cathode ray tube, consisting of an evacuated glass tube capped with metal plates, or electrodes, at either end. (The two electrodes are known as a cathode and an anode, hence the name cathode ray tube.) Running an electric current across the tube caused it to glow, a phenomenon initially attributed to "cathode rays" and now known to be produced by electrons.

The Roentgen Ray Machine quickly spread throughout the medical communities of Europe and the United States. Physicians in every major city in the US and Europe were using x-ray machines within a year after the product was introduced. Military doctors saw value for the machine near the battlefield, as it could locate metal fragments in wounded soldiers, and attorneys began to employ x-ray evidence in medical malpractice and criminal cases.

Radium found an even wider range of applications, thanks both to its generation of heat and light as well as to the Curies active promotion of the material's industrial value. Medical practitioners were interested in radium's "warming" ability, believing it held therapeutic value for a wide variety of ailments. Indeed, during the first decades of the twentieth century many physicians and resort spas touted the medicinal value of radium-infused medicines or "radioactive" waters. Doctors of both high and low reputations marketed elixirs, balms, bathing salts, and inhalants that contained, or purported to contain, radium for ailments ranging from tuberculosis to arthritis.

Clock and instrument manufacturers found radium's luminosity to be especially useful. Companies used radium-bearing paints to mark the numbers on dials and faces so that the display would glow in the dark. Glowing timepieces were quickly adopted as a military necessity, offering a tactical advantage by allowing soldiers to read instruments and gauges at night without the use of lights that would reveal their position. Luminous dials also became a public success, a commercial application of science in a rapidly developing mass marketplace for consumer goods.

Health Effects

Although the medical community showed great enthusiasm for the diagnostic and therapeutic use of radioactivity, both physicians and technicians who operated x-ray machines quickly noted that the energies could be damaging. The initial effects of prolonged exposure to x-rays – skin burns and hair loss – were obvious and immediate, and most users of the Roentgen Machines sought to prevent either from happening unless they considered it necessary for treatment. Both x-ray technicians and some patients developed cancers from over-exposure to the rays.

The health effects of radiation exposure affected the manner in which nuclear technologies developed. For example, Thomas Edison abandoned his promising experiments with x-ray equipment after one of his laboratory assistants, Clarence Dally, suffered hair loss and skin lesions from over-exposure. Dally, along with many early x-ray machine manufacturers, would die of radiation-induced cancer a few years later. Successive generations of equipment promised better control over the intensity and direction of the rays, allowing for reduced exposures for patients and practitioners.

Scientific researchers also received large radiation doses in their laboratories and workshops. Like the x-ray workers, many scientists working with radioactive materials became ill as a result of their extensive exposure to radioactive elements. Marie Curie, for example, died from leukemia, the disease likely caused by her prolonged exposure to radium and other radioactive materials.

The practice of painting watch dials with radium provided the most significant radiation-related health consequences. Radium is chemically similar to calcium, which the human body tends to concentrate in bones and teeth. At a New Jersey factory where the work was done, young women used small brushes to apply the radium-based paints. The women would use their mouths to keep a fine point on the brushes, and in so doing swallowed significant quantities of radium over time. Several of the dial painters began to develop unusual cancers and ailments, often concentrated in the jaw and throat. Health investigators linked these illnesses to the workplace, observing that the practice of "tipping" the brushes with the lips caused the dial painters to receive a major radiation dose in the course of doing their jobs.

The plight of the radium dial painters marked the first major industrial hygiene concern about occupational exposure to radioactive materials. Like most such disputes, the issue was not resolved without a legal battle. Although investigators and labor leaders believed they had clear and convincing evidence that radium was the cause of the dial painters' problems, the employer denied any responsibility for the illnesses. The company's position benefited from the popularity of radium treatments in professional medicine. Many well-respected doctors used radium extensively for therapeutic applications, and they doubted that the substance could cause such diseases in people who worked with it.

The dial painters episode established the political dynamics of radiation-related health and environmental controversy. The cast of characters and positions – the company (later the government) denying a link between workplace exposure and disease, an advocacy group using a health and safety issue for political leverage, and a medical community apparently influenced by the political goals of its financial benefactors – would repeat itself in future decades in disputes over worker safety, public health, and environmental protection.

Professionalization, Industrial Development, and Ongoing Research

Even before the dial painters episode, some radiation professionals had sought to develop standards and set limits for occupational exposure. Researchers and scientists in radiation-related fields wanted better information about the health effects of exposure as reports of fatal cancers continued. Similarly, many physicians were interested in a better understanding of the positive and negative consequences of radiation.

Public awareness of shoddy radiation-related medicines also grew in the 1920s. Radium's perceived medicinal value declined as evidence of its harmful consequences mounted. As the safety of radium came into question, professional radiation users sought to distinguish legitimate applications from quackery. These users recognized that the viability of radiation-based industrial and medical practice depended, at least in part, on the widespread belief that the technology was safe and would be used responsibly.

In the latter 1920s, medical and industrial radiation users formed the International Committee on Radiation Protection (ICRP) and an American affiliate, the National Committee on Radiation Protection (NCRP). These organizations set voluntary standards for occupational radiation exposure and industrial hygiene, which industrial and medical practitioners employed on a common-sense basis. These organizations have continued to be involved in radiation health and safety issues, with specific roles, functions, and agency structures developing along with scientific and political changes.

Research in atomic physics during the first decades of the twentieth century represents one of the most fertile areas of research and investigation in modern scientific history. Scientists developed new experimental techniques to help them learn more about the structure of the atom and the nature of the forces that bind it together. Perhaps the most significant experimental device was the cyclotron, invented in 1929 by University of California physicist Ernest Lawrence.

Like other contemporary physicists, Lawrence was interested in the effects of atomic collisions. Researchers used particle accelerators to fire atomic particles at experimental media in an effort to improve understanding of atomic structures and properties. Lawrence found he could increase the speed of particles by cycling them around two electromagnetic poles, building momentum and velocity until released. The collisions of these very high-speed particles with target elements produced a greater range of effects than traditional linear accelerators, including the discovery of unusual isotopes of known elements as well as the formation of completely new, man-made elements, such as plutonium.

As with many nuclear technologies, the cyclotron was quickly used for medical applications. Working with his brother John, a physician, Lawrence identified a number of short-lived isotopes that could be used for diagnosis or treatment and helped to develop methods to employ them. The Lawrence brothers investigated treatments for cancer as well as methods for imaging and detection.

Nuclear Technology and Nuclear Weapons

World War II stands as the single most important event in the development of nuclear technology. Prior to the war, scientists and industries used small quantities of radioactive material in specialized applications. During the war, however, the United States, Great Britain, and Canada employed unprecedented quantities of radioactive materials for a task that had only been the stuff of science fiction: the production of nuclear weapons.

Nuclear weapons were the product of a highly complex technological system created specifically for that task. Nuclear weapons were not – indeed, could not have been – created by an inventor tinkering in a workshop. Instead, the process of nuclear weapons production linked government, academic, and corporate actors in dynamic political, technological, and economic relationships. Producing nuclear weapons required the development of an entire industrial infrastructure, including raw material supply, chemical and metal processing, nuclear engineering, and weapons design and development. The success of the Manhattan Project, and subsequent development of other nuclear technologies, is thus rooted in the development of a sophisticated system of production, the military-industrial complex.

The Decision(s) to Build the Bomb

The Allied effort to construct an atomic bomb was sparked by fears that Germany had begun its own atomic weapons program. In 1938, two German physicists, Otto Hahn and Fritz Strassman, reported that they had successfully achieved fission, the splitting of an atom, under controlled conditions. Although earlier researchers had observed fission, Hahn and Strassman's announcement led many scientists to recognize the possibility of harnessing a fission reaction into a new, incredibly powerful weapon – and left them alarmed by the prospect of such a device in Hitler's hands.

A tremendous gulf typically separates a scientific or technical insight – the recognition that something is possible – and its transformation into a technological artifact. To get from idea to design to functional object usually requires a series of difficult conceptual and mechanical steps, for ideas tend to be more fluid on the blackboard than objects are in physical form.

The gulf separating Hahn and Strassman's work and the development of an atomic weapon was extraordinarily wide. A number of complicating factors stood in the way. First, military planners did not see value in pursuing atomic weapons given the difficulties involved in their development and the uncertainty of success. In addition, there was no scientific or industrial infrastructure capable of supporting the necessary research and development work, nor was there a design to model such a project after. Last, but certainly not least, even modest cost estimates exceeded the capacity of any institution other than a large national government. In other words, the development of atomic weapons faced political, scientific, technical, and economic hurdles.

The project faced an additional hurdle in the United States. The scientists who initially proposed nuclear weapons research and development were émigrés from eastern and southern Europe, areas controlled by fascist regimes. These foreign scientists were not trusted with American state secrets, and were excluded from the military's highest-priority scientific and industrial projects, such as the development of radar. As a result, they had more time to spare on the atomic bomb effort than their American counterparts.

Although their loyalty to America was questioned by some decision-makers, their expertise and their opposition to fascism and Hitler was not. Leo Szilard, Enrico Fermi, Edward Teller, and Eugene Wigner (to name a few key figures of the Manhattan Project) had all emigrated to the United States during the previous decade to escape anti-semitic, fascist regimes in Germany and Italy. All were Jewish except Fermi, who had a Jewish wife. Alarmed by the prospect of a Nazi-controlled atomic weapon, these scientists played a critical role in prompting the American government to undertake what became the Manhattan Project and a leading role in its success.

The official effort began with an appeal to President Franklin Roosevelt in 1939. Leo Szilard convinced Albert Einstein (another Jewish émigré) to sign a letter to the

President explaining the possible consequences of Hahn and Strassman's work in Germany. Carried by Roosevelt's advisor Alexander Sachs, the Einstein-Szilard letter reached the President, who grasped its basic message – that Germany might be developing a new way to destroy its enemies. Passing the letter to his chief military advisor, Roosevelt wrote, "this requires action."

Although the President's expression of interest soon led to the formation of a high-level "Uranium Committee," very little action took place over the next 2 years. American military strategists, focused on near-term needs, saw little value in the theoretical insights of the physicists. The US did not commit significant resources until 1941, after a British scientific committee concluded that an atomic weapon was feasible.

This commitment meant moving control of the project away from the moribund Uranium Committee and to the Office of Scientific Research and Development (OSRD), headed by American engineer Vannevar Bush. Bush had read the British report and agreed that uranium research and military development needed to be a high priority. While OSRD could coordinate the scientific work, Bush realized that only a military organization could make an actual weapon. By mid-1942, he had persuaded Roosevelt to assign that task to the US Army Corps of Engineers.

Giving the project to the Army was a gamble. On one hand, a weapons development project of this magnitude clearly required a substantial organizational infrastructure and a military orientation, both of which the Corps of Engineers possessed. On the other hand, the Corps had never undertaken a project of this type before, and most of its leadership shared the normal military view that there was no reason to expend resources during a war on a scientific concept that might not produce an actual weapon.

General Leslie Groves, however, was not a traditional military man. Groves had recently directed the construction of the Pentagon, at the time the largest construction project ever undertaken in the US Gruff and impatient, he was hard on subordinates and intolerant of the academic nature of scientists. Groves had enough scientific training to grasp the implications of the project, however, and once he was given control of what became the Manhattan Project, he became fully committed to moving it forward.

The Manhattan Project: Building the Atomic Bomb

The name "Manhattan Project" refers to the atomic bomb development program of the Manhattan Engineer District (MED) of the US Army Corps of Engineers. Directed by Groves, the Manhattan Project became an enormous industrial and scientific undertaking, quickly surpassing the Pentagon in cost to become the most expensive construction project in American history.

Building an atomic weapon, however, required more than willingness to spend money. The Manhattan Project had to overcome major scientific, engineering, and managerial hurdles in a very limited amount of time. The project faced difficulties in resolving numerous scientific and technical unknowns facing production and design elements, developing realistic budgets and timelines, coordinating multiple production activities scattered across the country, and managing the project's disparate professional cultures. Indeed, while each scientific and technical step involved in the process was significant in itself, the most formidable challenge facing the Manhattan Project was the integration of academic scientists and industrial engineers into a military organization.

The science was suggestive but not definitive. Although Hahn and Strassman had demonstrated that fission could be achieved in a controlled setting, nobody was certain that the process could actually create destructive force. Even if an explosive chain reaction was possible, there were no blueprints or precedents for the many new devices and production steps necessary to design and construct a workable weapon. And even if the science and the engineering were possible, no organization had ever successfully coordinated such a multidimensional scientific and technical undertaking under any condition, let alone under the stresses of a major war.

The forces that bind an atom together are the most powerful on the planet. An atom that fissions, or splits, releases a large amount of energy relative to its size. A large number of fissioning atoms would release an enormous quantity of energy. A "chain reaction" would be necessary for such a release to be possible, such that the energy released by one atom would cause additional atoms to fission, which in turn would cause more atoms to fission, and so on until the supply of fissionable atoms was spent.

A chain reaction could only occur with a large quantity of suitably unstable atoms brought together in a configuration that harnessed the energy released by the splitting atoms to cause additional fission reactions. Such occurrences do not often happen in nature (except in stars), for they result in nuclear explosions or other "criticality" events that release an enormous quantity of radiation and destructive force.

Scientists recognized that while uranium was unstable enough to undergo fission, it only did so when bombarded with "fast," or high-energy, neutrons. Natural uranium can absorb "slow," or lower energy, neutrons without fissioning. Since many of the neutrons released during fission are slow neutrons, a chain reaction in natural uranium would require a relatively large quantity of energy to sustain itself. Many scientists in 1941 were not convinced that natural uranium could support a chain reaction by itself, and were certain that it would not be suitable for a weapon.

Two other elements – uranium-235 and plutonium – appeared more capable of sustaining a chain reaction. Uranium-235, a naturally occurring isotope of uranium, is more unstable – and therefore more fissionable – than normal uranium-238. The trick was to isolate a sufficient quantity of this isotope, which constitutes about 0.7 percent of all natural uranium, to support an explosive chain reaction.

Plutonium is a man-made element, discovered by Glenn Seaborg, a chemist at the University of California, Berkeley, in February 1941. Plutonium is produced by fissioning uranium atoms, and Seaborg identified the new element and developed a method for chemically separating the plutonium from the uranium in the laboratory. Additional research confirmed that the element's physical structure made it highly susceptible to fissioning, and therefore a good candidate for sustaining a chain reaction.

The OSRD had tasked the University of Chicago's Metallurgical Laboratory, or Met Lab, with much of the initial scientific coordination for the project. Among the Met Lab's first tasks was determining whether a chain reaction was possible with natural uranium. A team of researchers, directed by the Italian physicist Enrico Fermi, constructed a uranium and graphite reactor that Fermi had designed, in a squash court under the school's football field. This group achieved the world's first self-sustaining nuclear chain reaction on December 2, 1942. Fermi had established that natural uranium could be used to fuel a nuclear reactor – and therefore for plutonium production.

Groves focused the Manhattan Project's efforts in three major efforts at three separate locations. First was the effort to separate the different isotopes of uranium and create "highly enriched" uranium suitable for a weapon, centered at the MED's headquarters facility in Oak Ridge, Tennessee. Second was the plutonium production effort at Hanford, in eastern Washington state. The third location, at Los Alamos, New Mexico, housed the project's scientific research and weapons development teams. Today, Oak Ridge, Hanford, and Los Alamos are cardinal points on the map of nuclear technology. Equally important, but far less well-known, were dozens of industrial facilities that processed and shaped uranium metal. Private companies, working under wartime contracts, provided the MED with uranium compounds and other strategic metals to feed into the secret facilities.

Groves preferred to build the major facilities in remote locations to help ensure both safety and secrecy. Given the hazards of building and operating nuclear reactors – meltdowns and explosions – Groves recognized that reactor development work could not continue in the heart of Chicago. He also believed that decentralization and compartmentalization would enhance security; the loss of one facility would not necessarily cripple the project, and it would be harder for a spy to gather all of the data required to make the project work. The emphasis on secrecy and the compartmentalized nature of the project frustrated many of its key scientists, who were used to an open exchange of ideas as a means of testing theories and advancing knowledge.

Although scientific insights sparked the Manhattan Project, building an actual atomic device required sophisticated engineering approaches. The MED hired corporate contractors, such as the Du Pont Company, to play a major role in the development effort. The engineers did more than operationalize science; they pioneered new knowledge and new practice in ways that scientists could not have anticipated.

For Manhattan Project planners, time was of the essence. Managers were always looking to reduce the time necessary to get the system up and running. The assumption that Germany had previously begun a similar project led to tremendous pressure to begin constructing facilities before resolving major scientific principles and design questions.

This approach posed management challenges and exacerbated tensions between scientists and engineers, especially at Hanford. The Met Lab scientists advocated constructing a scaled-up version of Fermi's squash-court reactor to produce the necessary plutonium quickly. Du Pont, by contrast, wanted to flesh out system design as much as possible before starting construction, on the belief that blueprints are easier to change than poured concrete and welded steel. The scientists accused Du Pont of slowing down the project; the company in turn objected to the reckless approach of the physicists. Events at Hanford ultimately vindicated Du Pont's approach, as the extra safety margins the company included in the reactor design (over the objections of the scientists) proved necessary to maintain a chain reaction.

Similar cultural tensions were at work at Los Alamos, where the people with the skills required to calculate the proper design of a weapon often clashed with the people who possessed the skill to actually build it. As with Hanford, the history of Los Alamos demonstrates the key role played by "translators" such as University of California physicist Robert Oppenheimer and Navy Captain William "Deak" Parsons, who were able to work with the laboratory's scientific and technical cultures, facilitating relations and communications between them.

Although the Manhattan Project is most closely identified with science and technology in popular memory, the successful operation of a technical system requires managers. Management decisions – in the form of planning, forecasting, budgeting, and decision-making in conditions of uncertainty – were at least as important as the scientific and engineering knowledge required to accomplish the mission. The Manhattan Project coordinated the construction and operation of three major production facilities, contracted with dozens of manufacturing plants across the country to provide raw materials, chemical processing, and metal fabrication, and generally kept the project's diverse participants working together. The marriage of governmental management with applied science and technology supplied by universities and corporations became an enduring feature in the continued development of nuclear technology.

Success – but at what cost?

Although the MED was ultimately successful in developing atomic weapons, the project raised problems in a variety of areas. The Manhattan Project's production efforts, followed by the use of two atomic weapons against Japan, generated a large quantity of wastes, left a legacy of health effects, and sparked a series of intractable social, political, and cultural controversies.

The Manhattan Project was successful on its own terms. It developed two different types of atomic weapons, one using highly enriched uranium and the other using plutonium. It tested the plutonium design at Alamogordo, New Mexico, in July 1945, and provided the bombs used against Japan the following month. Hiroshima was destroyed by the uranium bomb on August 6, and Nagasaki by the plutonium bomb on August 9. The attacks caused massive damage, causing over 200,000 deaths in the two cities. Japan surrendered on August 15, bringing World War II to a close.

Nuclear weapons had political impacts even before being used against Japan. President Harry Truman learned of the successful Alamogordo test while at the Postdam Conference with Stalin and Churchill, and he used the knowledge to position the US in opposition to its wartime ally, the Soviet Union. After the war, "the bomb" played a central role in the emerging Cold War between the US and the Soviets. As a result, with the exception of a brief postwar lull, the American nuclear weapons production effort never abated. The production system continued to operate at its full capacity well into the 1960s, fueling a nuclear arms race between the two superpowers.

The creation and use of nuclear weapons also had significant and multifaceted cultural effects. The impact of "the bomb" was felt in the arts, commerce, and education, as well as in domestic and international politics. Citizens around the globe sought to comprehend the awesome power and awesome responsibility that unleashing atomic forces entailed. Science fiction provided the most accessible examples, such as Godzilla, the prehistoric creature raised from the deep by nuclear tests. So too did comic books, creating heroes such as Spider-Man and the Incredible Hulk, normal humans transformed by radiation exposure into super-beings.

The Manhattan Project also left a significant environmental and health legacy. The effects of the bombings of Hiroshima and Nagasaki – especially the lingering effects of radiation exposure on human health and genetic mutation – posed unprecedented challenges for the medical world. In addition, the MED's production activities generated an enormous quantity of wastes that neither the engineers nor the scientists knew how to dispose of safely. During the war, waste management was a low priority, an issue that could be deferred until later. After the war, the rapid rise in Cold War tensions led to the continuing deferral of the problems in both the United States and the Soviet Union. System managers failed to address many difficult technical issues regarding waste management, leaving a dangerous and more complex set of problems as a result.

The Atomic Energy Commission: Nuclear Weapons and Atoms for Peace

During World War II, nuclear technology became intertwined with political and military objectives in the United States. After the war, the nation's leaders debated whether a military or civilian agency should control atomic weapons. In 1946, Congress established the Atomic Energy Commission (AEC) to maintain and develop the nation's nuclear capabilities. Although the AEC was a civilian agency, military requirements dominated its agenda. Nonetheless, the agency significantly affected the development of civilian applications from nuclear medicine to commercial nuclear power.

Expanding the Production System

The AEC officially assumed control over the MED production system on January 1, 1947. The agency's first mission was to expand the capacity of the nuclear weapons complex, both by adding onto existing facilities and by constructing several additional plants. During its first decade, the AEC expanded the facilities at Oak Ridge, Los Alamos, and Hanford while building more than a dozen new facilities for research and weapons production. These plants were spread across the country, and were run by a variety of corporate and university contractors.

Throughout the 1950s, the AEC strove to produce as much plutonium, enriched uranium, and nuclear weapons as possible, increasing capacity and pushing the system to its limits. As a result, the US arsenal grew from the equivalent of one remaining atomic bomb at the end of World War II to several dozen by 1949. The 1950s and

1960s saw huge increases in production; by the late 1980s, the US had produced over 80,000 nuclear warheads, many of which had a destructive capacity literally hundreds of times greater than those used against Japan in 1945.

Although much of the technology of nuclear weapons production was revolutionary in its initial design, the ongoing development of the productions system tended to follow the initial paths developed during the war. During its construction boom of 1949–56, the AEC generally employed modified versions of uranium processing, gaseous diffusion, production reactors, chemical separation, and component assembly developed under the MED. The production system stabilized after this expansion period, operating without major upgrades or changes through the end of the Cold War.

Nuclear Medicine and Atoms for Peace

In addition to expanding the nuclear weapons production complex, the AEC also sought to encourage peaceful, commercial uses of nuclear technology. The most widespread use of nuclear technology in the civilian sector after World War II was the most widespread use before the war – medicine. The AEC focused much of its attention on the development and spread of nuclear medicine techniques, especially the use of radioactive isotopes for diagnosis and treatment.

Isotopes are different configurations of the same element, containing the same number of protons and electrons but different numbers of neutrons. Many isotopes are unstable, and so release energy as they decay. Isotopes of an element all have identical chemical properties, so bodies and mechanical systems do not distinguish between them. A doctor or researcher can therefore use a radioactive isotope as a "tracer" by measuring the energy the isotope releases. For example, a doctor may introduce a radioactive isotope of oxygen into a patient's body to evaluate the functioning of the body's pulmonary and circulatory systems.

Other isotopes are used for treatment of disease, such as radioactive iodine for hyperthyroidism. In such applications, as with the focused use of radiation therapy, radiation is used to destroy tumors or other unwanted tissues. Thanks in large part to sponsorship by government agencies, nuclear medicine is firmly in the medical mainstream in the developed world, with over ten million nuclear medicine procedures being performed annually in the United States alone.

Nuclear medicine received a significant boost from the American-led "Atoms for Peace" program. In a December 1953 speech to the United Nations General Assembly, President Dwight Eisenhower committed the United States to applying atomic science to the benefit of all of humanity. The Atoms for Peace program included a sizable research and development effort and was accompanied by a substantial promotional campaign.

Eisenhower's speech was designed primarily to boost the US in international public opinion, further illustrating the political role of nuclear technology. The initial "Atoms for Peace" proposal consisted of an internationally controlled pool of fissionable materials, donated by nuclear-capable countries, which would be used for research and peaceful applications worldwide. Eisenhower did not expect the Soviets to be willing to release any of their fissionable material – the US had a much larger production capacity and stockpile at the time – and had no specific plans for how the materials might be used.

The "Atoms for Peace" program did help the international spread of nuclear technology, providing quantities of fissionable materials and isotopes for medical and research purposes. Researchers from around the world participated in the programs, developing expertise that enabled the use of nuclear medicine techniques, and later nuclear power plants, in dozens of nations.

Submarine Propulsion and Space Applications

Physicists and engineers had long been attracted to the idea of generating power from a controlled atomic reaction, and the Atomic Energy Commission actively supported research and development of such applications. The production reactors at Hanford (and later at Savannah River) did generate power, in the form of heat, as a by-product of the fission process. These reactors were designed for plutonium production, so the heat was a waste product and was not captured for productive use.

Despite the interest in commercial electrical generation, the first large-scale application of nuclear power was in naval propulsion. By the 1940s, the Navy had become dependent on submarines. The strategic value of submarines, however, was limited by the capacity of their diesel engines. Diesel submarines needed to surface regularly to take in air and vent exhaust, and the length of their missions was limited to the amount of fuel they could carry. The Navy looked to nuclear propulsion as a way to generate power without the need to surface, and as a system whose running time would not be limited by the longevity of the fuel supply.

Having seen the Army direct the Manhattan Project, the Navy developed an internal "crash course" of its own, in cooperation with the AEC, under the direction of Admiral Hyman Rickover. Rickover spent time at Oak Ridge immediately after World War II, learning aspects of nuclear science and engineering, and took over the joint Navy-AEC effort in 1948. Like Groves, Rickover was driven, committed to his project, and hard on subordinates. Like Groves, he directed a project that many in his organization did not think was possible, integrated multiple sites spread across the country, and involved numerous industrial contractors, military personnel, and government bureaucrats (though unlike Groves, Rickover did not have to contend with academic scientists). The Navy successfully tested its first prototype in 1952, and launched the first nuclear-powered submarine, the Nautilus, in 1954.

The basic science behind the Nautilus had been largely developed by the MED and AEC. As with the Manhattan Project, however, a tremendous amount of engineering and design work was needed to turn the reactor concept into a viable submarine propulsion system. With strict discipline and tremendous central authority, Rickover created not only a new submarine but also a new culture within the Navy. This culture emphasized safety, regimentation, and control; there is little room for error when dependent on the performance of a nuclear reactor under thousands of feet of water.

With the success of the Nautilus submarine, the US Navy adapted the propulsion system for use on aircraft carriers. Nuclear-powered carriers and submarines continue to play a major role in naval operations. The Soviet Union developed nuclear-powered submarines as well, and competition between the two superpowers in this area fueled some of the most sophisticated research and development activities of the Cold War.

The AEC also experimented with using nuclear propulsion outside the water. During the 1950s, the agency supported the development of a nuclear-powered airplane, which would allow the craft to remain airborne indefinitely, just as the nuclear-powered submarine allowed the craft to remain underwater. Although the AEC pursued the nuclear aircraft concept for over a decade, it ultimately abandoned the project when engineers concluded that the weight of the lead shielding needed to protect the pilot from the engine's radiation comprised the aerodynamics of the plane – in essence, it would be too heavy to fly. Smaller-scale projects investigated the possibility of atomic trains, which also raised safety concerns for operators and the public, and nuclear rockets, which proved feasible but were abandoned because no missions were identified for them.

Although nuclear-powered rockets have not been deployed, the National Aeronautics and Space Administration (NASA) does use nuclear power in its unmanned space vehicles. The agency uses radioisotope thermoelectric generators (RTGs) to power instruments and command-and-control systems, although not for propulsion. RTGs use the heat generated by a long-lived radiation source, typically plutonium, to provide a steady power supply to on-board equipment. RTGs have no moving parts, using a thermocouple to transform the heat produced by the decaying plutonium into electrical power. NASA's use of plutonium in the Cassini space vehicle sparked significant public controversy in 1997 because of fears that an explosion in the atmosphere (similar to the Challenger disaster) would spread radioactivity widely. NASA continues to use nuclear technologies for space exploration and travel, relying on the Department of Energy's nuclear weapons laboratories and facilities for research and production work.

Nuclear Power

Electricity-generating nuclear power plants are perhaps the best-known application of nuclear technology. Thermal generation plants produce electricity by using an energy source to boil water and produce steam. The steam is used to turn turbines, which generate electricity. Unlike traditional thermal generation plants, which burn fossil fuels such as coal, nuclear power plants produce heat by maintaining a controlled fission reaction in a nuclear reactor.

Nuclear power plants contain inherent advantages as compared to other forms of electrical generation. The primary advantage is that nuclear fuel sources contain far more units of energy than fossil fuel sources; uranium is, from an engineering perspective, a more efficient energy source than coal, oil, or natural gas. A typical uranium rod used in a modern nuclear reactor can produce as much power as several tons of coal. A fission reaction also has advantages over burning fossil fuels in that the reactor does not release greenhouse gases. In this regard, the actual operation of a nuclear reactor is cleaner than the operation of a coal-fired plant.

Nuclear power plants also contain some inherent disadvantages as compared to other forms of electrical generation. A nuclear reactor is a highly engineered system, far more complex in design and operation than a typical coal-fired plant. Nuclear plants are thus far more expensive to build, maintain, and operate than other forms of electrical generation. Safety concerns further complicate the design and operation of nuclear power plants. The consequences of a nuclear accident are much more severe than those of an accident at a fossil-fuel plant; there is no comparable fear of "meltdowns" at a coal-burning facility. Finally, although it does not generate greenhouse gases, nuclear power creates extremely hazardous, long-lasting radioactive wastes.

Developing Nuclear Power

Scientists and planners had long envisioned that nuclear technology would benefit mankind through the development of a virtually unlimited supply of electrical power. Speaking to a group of science journalists in 1954, AEC Chairman Lewis Strauss famously opined that electricity from nuclear reactors would be "too cheap to meter." Like most things that sound too good to be true, nuclear power has not lived up to its grand expectations.

Although the AEC publicly committed to generating electrical power from nuclear fission early in its history, the agency faced both technical and economic difficulties in developing a safe, reliable, and cost-effective reactor. Although politically desirable, systems capable of generating electricity needed extensive design and engineering development, and technically workable designs proved costly. Despite the lure of cheap electricity, the embedded costs in a nuclear reactor are steeper than those in fossil-fuel plants, due to the increase in complexity of design, construction, operations, maintenance, decommissioning, and waste disposal. As a result, the price per unit of power from nuclear reactors was not competitive with existing fossil-fuel generation systems despite the inherent efficiency of nuclear fuel.

The AEC was able to circumvent, but not fully resolve, the technical and economic problems through subsidies and political fixes that facilitated the development of a nuclear-power industry. On the technical side, the AEC supported much of the research and development work necessary to develop working power-reactors. The agency conducted extensive research at its national laboratories and provided financial support for external programs to bolster the fledgling nuclear industry.

The submarine propulsion program also provided substantial direct and indirect support, and research and development for nuclear generation of electricity proceeded in parallel with the submarine propulsion program through the mid-1950s. The first electrical generation from a nuclear reaction took place at an AEC facility in Idaho in 1951, where Rickover's naval propulsion program was constructing the Nautilus reactor. The first working commercial reactor, outside of Pittsburgh, Pennsylvania, debuted in 1957. When President Dwight Eisenhower officially flipped the switch with the wave of an atomic wand, he started up a modified submarine reactor at a facility built and operated by Westinghouse, a major AEC contractor in the submarine program, under the direction of the agency's naval nuclear propulsion division.

The AEC also assumed responsibility for the final disposal of spent fuel, the primary waste product of nuclear power plants. The agency knew that waste management was a troubling issue in the nuclear weapons complex and recognized that safely managing radioactive wastes from commercial nuclear power was important to the viability of the industry. By assuming responsibility for spent fuel, the agency sought to relieve the plant owners of the technical and political problems associated with the waste.

A key financial problem hindering the development of nuclear power involved liability. No insurance company was willing to write a policy; the possible costs of a large-scale nuclear accident would bankrupt the insurer. A 1957 AEC study concluded that a serious accident at a reactor near Detroit would result in over $7 billion in property damage and cause thousands of deaths and tens of thousands of injuries. Congress addressed this problem in 1957 with the Price-Anderson Act, which capped the liability of a nuclear accident at $560 million – a fraction of the possible costs.

Encouraged by federal subsidies and incentives, American electric utility companies began to invest in nuclear power plants in the early 1960s. The industry boomed as the cost of fossil fuels skyrocketed in response to the Arab Oil Embargo of 1973, and by the latter 1970s nearly one hundred nuclear plants were operating or under construction in the United States. As of 2000, the United States had 104 operating nuclear power plants, the most of any country. These plants supply approximately 20 percent of the nation's electricity.

Other nations moved to adopt nuclear power, typically gaining assistance from either the United States or the Soviet Union in developing expertise and fissionable materials. France has built a large nuclear industry; its 59 nuclear plants supply more than 76 percent of the nation's electricity. Japan also embraced nuclear power, with 53 nuclear plants that supply more than 33 percent of its electricity.

The international spread of nuclear power raises fears of the international spread of nuclear weapons, as many nuclear reactor types can be modified to generate weapons-grade fissionable materials. Nuclear-capable nations have taken political steps to prevent weapons proliferation by creating international bodies such as the International Atomic Energy Agency (IAEA) to oversee activities at the nearly 500 nuclear power plants operating worldwide. The IAEA establishes standards for reactor operations, tracks nuclear materials, and conducts inspections of nuclear plants to determine if facilities or supplies are being diverted to weapons uses.

Nuclear Controversies

Opposition to Nuclear Power

Although nuclear power benefited from strong support from official sources, the industry has also faced significant public opposition. Opponents have cited cost, safety, waste management, and weapons proliferation as causes for concern about the use and spread of nuclear power. This opposition, like the official support, has shaped the ongoing development of the industry and the technology.

The earliest concerns about nuclear power were rooted in location. In the early 1960s, utilities proposed building several plants in California along the Pacific Coast, in areas subject to earthquakes. Opponents challenged the plans, arguing that the geologic instability of the area made it inappropriate for nuclear reactors. Throughout the 1960s and 1970s, opponents to nuclear power seized on different aspects of nuclear power, from waste disposal to safety hazards to nuclear weapons proliferation, to argue against building additional nuclear power plants or siting them in particular locations.

The AEC and electric utility industry responded on several fronts. Numerous experts and studies, produced by the agency and by the industry, demonstrated the great care taken with planning and designing systems capable of providing safe, reliable power. The AEC also played a regulatory role, emphasizing that it would police the industry to assure that the public was properly protected from possible nuclear accidents.

The AEC thus assumed two incompatible roles – as promoter of nuclear technology and as regulator of the nuclear power industry. Facing increased public opposition to nuclear power, Congress split the agency in 1974. The Nuclear Regulatory Commission assumed the oversight role, responsible for licensing and regulating the commercial nuclear industry. The nuclear weapons production system moved to the newly created Energy Research and Development Authority, which in 1976 was merged into the newly created Department of Energy (DOE). DOE retains control over the nuclear weapons complex and national laboratories.

Nuclear power suffered a major setback in 1979, when a malfunction at one of the reactors at the Three Mile Island nuclear facility (TMI) galvanized public concerns about the dangers of nuclear power. For several tense days, the nation watched as this reactor, just outside of Harrisburg, PA, stood at the edge of an apparent disaster. In the end, the TMI reactor suffered a partial core meltdown and released a small quantity of radioactivity into the environment. Although well short of a disaster, the incident nonetheless undermined official arguments about the safety of nuclear power.

The American commercial nuclear power industry was already on the defensive in the late 1970s, suffering from public protests about the safety of nuclear power as well as cost overruns at plants already under construction. Despite its lack of injuries and limited release of radioactivity, the TMI accident effectively crippled the industry in the United States. While over one hundred nuclear power plants continue to operate in the US, no new plants have been ordered since 1979, and many plants already under construction at the time of the TMI accident were never completed.

The nuclear industry suffered another major setback in 1986, when a Soviet nuclear reactor at Chernobyl suffered a full-scale meltdown, causing 30 immediate deaths, leading to over 110,000 evacuations, and spreading an enormous quantity of radio-activity over large portions of Europe. The health and environmental effects of the incident are still being assessed, and the damage will continue to mount over time in increased rates of cancer and birth defects. Chernobyl further undermined arguments about the safety of nuclear power, even in parts of the world where the particular design (which contributed to the incident and the volume of radiation released) was not used.

Opposition to Nuclear Weapons Production and Testing

Movements protesting the existence and use of nuclear weapons emerged almost simultaneously with the bomb itself. Many of the scientists involved in the Manhattan Project began to question the wisdom of developing atomic weapons as their work neared fruition. Initially motivated by fear of a Nazi super-weapon, many of the same scientists who pushed for the project saw little need for an atomic bomb once Hitler was defeated and Japan was sure to follow.

This feeling only escalated after the war. Many scientists believed that, having developed these weapons, they had the responsibility to assure that they were used for the benefit of humanity instead of its destruction. The scientists did trust the military with control over nuclear weapons or the ongoing development of nuclear technology. This "scientists movement" advocated international control over nuclear weapons, arguing that if individual nations retained ownership, no other nation could ever feel safe.

The scientists movement did not succeed in creating a new international entity to control nuclear technology. The argument failed on political grounds, unable to establish a consensus – even among scientists – for an international body of unprecedented authority and uncertain mandate. American political leaders proved reluctant to relinquish a nuclear monopoly that could be employed to the nation's strategic advantage.

The American nuclear monopoly ended in August 1949, when the Soviet Union tested its first nuclear weapon. Both nations had already laid the groundwork for a nuclear arms race in policies and technological systems; still, the Soviet detonation surprised most American leaders, who did not expect their adversary to develop nuclear capability so quickly.

Radioactive fallout provided the galvanizing issue for the anti-nuclear movement in the 1950s. Nuclear weapons testing reaffirmed the axiom that "what goes up must come down." Large quantities of radioactive material are often drawn up into the atmosphere by the atomic fireball. As it cools, this material settles to the ground as "fallout" over great distances from the test site itself.

Although the AEC assured the American public that it would not face any risk from radioactive fallout when it began testing nuclear weapons at a remote site in Nevada in 1951, actual testing practice quickly proved otherwise. In May 1953, for example, a significant quantity of radioactive fallout from test shot "Harry" blanketed the southern Utah town of St George.

The most serious single episode took place the following year, in the Marshall Islands in the southern Pacific Ocean. The "Castle-Bravo" test featured a thermonuclear device of unexpectedly high explosive yield, which subsequently created an unexpectedly large quantity of fallout that hit populations in several areas presumed to be safe. Marshallese Islanders and American servicemen on other islands were subject to several hours of fallout and had to be evacuated; dozens of people required medical attention. A Japanese fishing boat, also outside the restricted area, was blanketed with the radioactive dust. By the time it returned home, all of its crew members were sick from radiation exposure. One sailor soon died, sparking an international incident and focusing worldwide public opinion on the dangers of the nuclear age.

Faced with ongoing pressure to limit atmospheric fallout because of possible health and genetic damage, the US and Soviet Union agreed to abandon atmospheric testing in 1962. That same year saw the Cuban Missile Crisis, in which the two superpowers came literally to the brink of nuclear war. Having come so close to the abyss – and having decided not to engage in the awful conflict – tensions between the two nations began to ease.

The 1962 Test Ban Treaty moved nuclear weapons testing underground, and effectively dampened the movements that protested nuclear weapons. Widespread public opposition to nuclear weapons proliferation, like the tensions between the two superpowers, remained at a fairly low level through the 1970s. In the early 1980s, however, President Ronald Reagan increased nuclear weapons production activities as well as other American military activities, re-igniting Cold War tensions with the Soviet Union. During the 1980s, increased nuclear weapons production and deployment again sparked public concern, especially in Europe.

With the fall of the Berlin Wall in 1989 and the collapse of the Soviet Union in 1991, the Cold War and the nuclear arms race came to an abrupt end. Radioactive materials have a longer half-life than political ideologies, however, and the weapons-grade material for tens of thousands of nuclear warheads, as well as thousands of warheads themselves, continue to pose international security problems. At the dawn of the twenty-first century, fears of a major nuclear war between the two superpowers have faded, but the possibilities an attack from a rogue state or terrorist organization, or a limited nuclear war between India and Pakistan, have emerged in its place.

Radioactive Waste

Waste is a by-product of any production activity, and processes involving nuclear technologies are no exception. Radioactive wastes pose especially difficult technical, political, and cultural issues because of their longevity; wastes from nuclear power and nuclear weapons production remain highly radioactive for tens of thousands of years. Radioactive waste disposal thus raises questions that have to be answered for several millennia, an unprecedented timescale for human planning.

The nuclear weapons production complex has generated a tremendous quantity of highly toxic and radioactive wastes in both the US and former Soviet Union. Engineers for the Du Pont company identified waste management as an important unresolved problem from the time they began design work at Hanford and Oak Ridge in the early 1940s. Given the pressures of wartime, dealing with waste was simply not a high priority.

Waste management continued to be a secondary consideration even after the war. The rapid transition from World War II to Cold War meant that production remained paramount. There was no extended postwar shutdown of the wartime production network, no time to develop new approaches to production and waste management.

The problems have become more difficult over time. Congress and the American public finally "discovered" the environmental legacy of nuclear weapons production as the Cold War came to a close in the latter 1980s. Decades of secrecy about production and environmental management activities gave way to external investigations and reforms within DOE in an effort to turn the agency into a more responsible environmental actor. The task of cleaning up after the nuclear weapons production complex promises to be as challenging, expensive, and long-lasting as the Cold War itself.

Wastes generated by commercial nuclear power plants are also a great source of controversy and debate. The Nuclear Regulatory Commission requires spent fuel from nuclear plants to be secured for ten thousand years, which is the approximate length of the history of human civilization. Ten thousand years ago, humans were first establishing settled communities; ten thousand years from now the wastes will still be deadly. Plutonium-239, one of the most toxic substances on the planet, has a half-life of 24,000 years. Assuming that any human institution or engineered structure will prove suitable for radioactive waste disposal therefore requires technological and cultural leaps of faith.

The United States government had promised, from the earliest days of nuclear power, to handle the disposal of the spent nuclear fuel. Controversy has flared since 1970, when the AEC announced its first disposal site, in rural Kansas. Intense local opposition, along with evidence of flawed geologic data, caused the agency to abandon the idea before the facility was developed. In the 1980s, seeing little progress on the development of a solution, Congress dictated that one site, Nevada's Yucca Mountain, be studied as the repository. However, Congress made this decision before substantial characterization of the site had been completed, in effect selecting it "site unseen." Not surprisingly, the controversy over the site continues unabated.

Radioactive waste management is not just an American problem. Indeed, the environmental legacy of nuclear weapons production is more severe in the former Soviet Union, which matched American production efforts without comparable social and political pressures to control emissions and contain wastes. Similarly, other nations are exploring ways to dispose of radioactive wastes from nuclear power plants, relying on interim storage practices until they can develop a permanent disposal site or strategy.

Conclusion

Nuclear technologies emerged as scientists and engineers learned more about the structure of the atom and the behavior of ionizing radiation in the late nineteenth century. Technological and medical applications of ionizing radiation developed along normal industrial lines during the first few decades of the twentieth century, and particular devices flourished and others failed in the consumer and medical marketplaces.

World War II fundamentally altered the nature and development of nuclear technologies. Massive government funding produced extraordinary developments, such as nuclear weapons, nuclear submarines, and nuclear power. The success of the Manhattan Project effectively married government direction and support with scientific research and the development of technological systems.

Nuclear weapons, submarines, and power reactors could not have emerged without the primary and ongoing support of large governments. No private entity possessed the financial resources to amass the technical expertise necessary for such development, nor could anything other than a large government assume the economic and human risks involved in developing the industrial infrastructure to support the programs.

The centrality of government illustrates the essential role that management plays in nuclear technology. Large, complex production systems support nuclear technologies, systems that require continual oversight and control to function properly. The systems produce deadly wastes that themselves need to be managed to minimize environmental and human health impacts as well as to prevent the proliferation of nuclear weapons.

Although the history of nuclear technology divides into the pre- and post-World War II eras, certain aspects of nuclear history bridge both time periods. For example, debates about the health effects of radiation exposure in the postwar period showed similar dynamics to those in earlier part of the twentieth century. The companies that employed the radium dial painters denied that occupational exposure was linked to any health problems, as did the US government when faced with accusations of employee and public health problems and offsite contamination caused by production and testing activities. Scientific and medical experts in both eras disagreed over the meaning of relevant data, and the interests of some of the health professionals who dismissed worker and public health concerns were intertwined with the success of the production activity.

The primary nuclear technology that bridged World War II, nuclear medicine, changed significantly due to increased government support for expanded research and production. Large facilities for producing isotopes, along with significant government funding for biomedical research and development, turned a niche medical field into a basic component of modern medical care. University research programs in atomic physics and related fields were similarly transformed by government funding in the postwar period. Prior to the war, the community of atomic physics was small and collegial, exploring the nature of the atom and the properties of atomic forces; in the post-war years, the field expanded dramatically with skyrocketing government funding and increasingly investigated questions of specific military interest.

Nuclear technologies have challenged the limits of human thinking. The destructive scale of nuclear war, the unlimited promise of nuclear power, and the extended timescales involved in radioactive waste management are all extraordinarily complex socio-technical issues. Like fire, nuclear technology can provide heat and light, and it can also burn and destroy. Learning to harness the power of nuclear technology without getting burned remains one of humanity's greatest challenges.

BIBLIOGRAPHY

Ackland, Len. *Making a Real Killing: Rocky Flats and the Nuclear West* (Albuquerque: University of New Mexico Press, 1999).

Balogh, Brian. *Chain Reaction: Expert Debate and Public Participation in American Commercial Nuclear Power, 1945–1975* (NYC: Cambridge University Press, 1991).

Boyer, Paul. *By the Bomb's Early Light: American Thought and Culture at the Dawn of the Atomic Age* (NYC: Pantheon, 1985).

Carlisle, Rodney and Joan Zenzen. *Building the Nuclear Arsenal: American Production Reactors, 1942–1992* (Baltimore: Johns Hopkins University Press, 1996).

Christman, Al. *Target Hiroshima: Deak Parsons and the Making of the Atomic Bomb* (Annapolis: Naval Institute Press, 1998).

Clark, Claudia. *Radium Girls: Women and Industrial Health Reform, 1910–1935* (Chapel Hill: University of North Carolina Press, 1997).

Dalton, Russell J., Garb, Paula, Lovrich, Nicholas, Pierce, John C., and Whiteley, John M. *Critical Masses: Citizens, Nuclear Weapons Production, and Environmental Destruction in the United States and Russia* (Cambridge, MA: MIT Press, 1999).

Divine, Robert A. *Blowing on the Wind: The Nuclear Test Ban Debate, 1954–1960* (NYC: Oxford University Press, 1978).

Duncan, Francis. *Rickover: The Struggle for Excellence* (Annapolis: Naval Institute Press, 2001).

Gerber, Michelle. *On the Home Front: The Cold War Legacy of the Hanford Nuclear Site* (Lincoln: University of Nebraska Press, 1992).

Hacker, Barton. *The Dragon's Tail: Radiation Safety in the Manhattan Project, 1942–1946* (Berkeley: University of California Press, 1984).

Hacker, Barton. *Elements of Controversy: The Atomic Energy Commission and Radiation Safety in Nuclear Weapons Testing, 1947–1974* (Berkeley: University of California Press, 1995).

Hales, Peter Bacon. *Atomic Spaces: Living on the Manhattan Project* (Urbana: University of Illinois Press, 1998).

Hecht, Gabrielle. *The Radiance of France* (Cambridge, MA: MIT Press, 1998).

Herken, Gregg. *The Winning Weapon: The Atomic Bomb in the Cold War, 1945–1950* (NYC: Vintage Books, 1982).

Herken, Gregg. *Cardinal Choices: Presidential Science Advising from the Atomic Bomb to SDI* (NYC: Oxford University Press, 1991).

Hewlett, Richard G. and Anderson, Oscar. *The New World, 1939–1946: Volume I, A History of the United States Atomic Energy Commission* (University Park: Pennsylvania State University Press, 1962).

Hewlett, Richard G. and Duncan, Francis. *Atomic Shield, 1947/1952: Volume II, A History of the United States Atomic Energy Commission* (University Park: Pennsylvania State University Press, 1969).

Hewlett, Richard G. and Duncan, Francis. *Nuclear Navy, 1946–1962* (Chicago: University of Chicago Press, 1974).

Hewlett, Richard G. and Holl, Jack M. *Atoms for Peace and War, 1953–1961: Volume III, A History of the United States Atomic Energy Commission* (Berkeley: University of California Press, 1989).

Holloway, David. *Stalin and the Bomb* (New Haven: Yale University Press, 1994).

Jacob, Gerald. *Site Unseen: The Politics of Siting a Nuclear Waste Repository* (Pittsburgh: University of Pittsburgh Press, 1990).

Jones, Vincent T. *Manhattan, the Army, and the Atomic Bomb* (Washington, DC: Center of Military History, US Army, 1985).

Kevles, Daniel. *The Physicists* (NYC: Knopf, 1978).

Makhijani, Arjun, Hu, Howard, and Yih, Katherine. *Nuclear Wastelands: A Global Guide to Nuclear Weapons Production and Its Health and Environmental Effects* (Cambridge, MA: MIT Press, 1995).

Mazuzan, George T. and Walker, J. Samuel. *Controlling the Atom: The Beginnings of Nuclear Regulation, 1946–1962* (Berkeley: University of California Press, 1985).

Norris, Robert S. *Racing for the Bomb: General Leslie R. Groves, the Manhattan Project's Indispensable Man* (South Royalton, VT: Steerforth Press, 2002).

Rhodes, Richard. *The Making of the Atomic Bomb* (NYC: Simon & Schuster, 1986).

Rhodes, Richard. *Dark Sun: The Making of the Hydrogen Bomb* (NYC: Simon & Schuster, 1995).

Rockwell, Theodore. *The Rickover Effect: How One Man Made a Difference* (Annapolis: Naval Institute Press, 1992).

Seaborg, Glenn T. *The Atomic Energy Commission Under Nixon: Adjusting to Troubled Times* (NYC: St Martin's Press, 1993).

Sherwin, Martin. *A World Destroyed: Hiroshima and the Origins of the Arms Race* (NYC: Vintage, 1987).

Smith, Alice Kimball. *A Peril and a Hope: The Scientists Movement in America, 1945–47* (Chicago: University of Chicago Press, 1965).

Walker, J. Samuel. *Containing the Atom: Nuclear Regulation in a Changing Environment, 1963–1971* (Berkeley: University of California Press, 1992).

Wellock, Thomas. *Critical Masses: Opposition to Nuclear Power in California, 1958–1978* (Madison: University of Wisconsin Press, 1998).

Winkler, Allan M. *Life Under a Cloud: American Anxiety about the Atom* (NYC: Oxford University Press, 1993).

Wolfson, Richard. *Nuclear Choices: A Citizen's Guide to Nuclear Technology* (Cambridge, MA: MIT Press, 1997).

CHAPTER SEVENTEEN

Television

DOUGLAS GOMERY

Although few deny the importance of television in the twentieth century, scholars are only now seriously engaging its technical invention, its innovation as a mass medium, and its diffusion into the most widely used in-home technology of the second half of the twentieth century. No technology has played a greater role in the lives of Americans than television, in a commitment of time, and an impact on its culture. Yet its invention took nearly the whole of the first half of the twentieth century.

Slow Invention: 1900–45

The invention of television goes back to the origins of electricity, the electromagnetic spectrum, the electron tube, the recording of sound and image, and the communication, via the air waves, of sounds and image. In 1900, the term "television" was coined by Constantin Perskyi at the International Electricity Congress, part of the Paris Exhibition. The creation of radio took center stage during the first two decades of the twentieth century, however. Television continued as an off-shoot of radio experiments until serious direct research commenced after World War I. Yet what was learned about radio technology proved the basis of television research (Abramson 1987).

During the 1920s, many individual inventors in the United States tinkered with TV, none more importantly than Charles Francis Jenkins (1867–1934). In 1921, he incorporated Jenkins Laboratories in Washington, DC for the sole purpose of "developing radio movies to be broadcast for entertainment in the home." By May 1922, Jenkins had achieved his first successful laboratory transmission; in October 1922, he gave his first public picture-only demonstration in Washington; by June 1925, he had achieved the first synchronized transmission of pictures and sound, using a 48-line mechanical system which Jenkins called "radiovision." On July 2, 1928, Jenkins optimistically began broadcasting regular telecasts designed to be received by public officials and local government engineers. He seemed to be headed, like Thomas Edison, to take control of a whole new medium of communication (Fisher and Fisher 1996).

But by then scientists employed by the Radio Corporation of America (RCA), and CBS – the two powers of radio broadcasting – had caught up technologically, and with the coming of the Great Depression had support, while Jenkins turned to making a living. In 1928, based upon the work of Russian emigre Alexander Zworykin (1889–1982) – a researcher for General Eletric which owned RCA at that point – began broadcasting of an all-electrically produced signal from experimental station W2XBS in New York City. While in the end an electronic system (such as RCA's) proved superior to the mechanical system Jenkins sponsored, in 1929 CBS first started W2XAB-TV from New York as a mechanical system. CBS started broadcasting seven-days-per-week, four hours per day, principally live pickups of sporting events and political rallies plus regular vaudeville airings. Early stars included New York Mayor James J. Walker, Kate Smith, George Gershwin, and dozens of long-forgotten college sports stars. It would be two years before NBC would place a TV transmitter atop the Empire State Building, and issue its first experimental tests – not regular programming – three days before Christmas 1931 (Abramson 1995).

Progress was slow, but steady through the depressed 1930s. In 1932, RCA demonstrated a new improved all-electronic television system, with greater clarity at 120 lines. Election day, November 8, 1932, CBS countered by televising reports on the presidential election to an estimated 3000 sets, principally found in the homes and offices of company employees. But this only proved to CBS owner William S. Paley that TV would not be going public soon, and so three months later he suspended television broadcasts. RCA continued its effort, and on June 29, 1936 transmitted a 343-line signal from atop the Empire State Building. On July 7, 1936 came NBC's first attempt at actual programming after six years of tests: a 30-minute variety show strictly for RCA licensees. On November 6, 1936, RCA displayed its 343-line system to the press as part of NBC's tenth anniversary of its radio network. The next spring, CBS conceded RCA was the clear leader and on April 1, 1937, it again initiated its experimental station by installing an RCA transmitter atop the Chrysler building (Paley 1979; Sobel 1986).

While both CBS and RCA experimented in New York City, Hollywood's Don Lee Broadcasting, Inc., a West Coast regional radio network, also experimented with "radio-movies." Beginning on March 10, 1933, Lee's W6XAO began full-scale broadcasting when an earthquake struck Los Angeles, broadcasting films of the damage the next day. Later, Lee's W6XAO was the first TV station to show a current full-length movie. Don Lee was making progress second only to RCA through the 1930s (Kisseloff 1995).

This steady activity caused the Federal Communications Commission (FCC) to take an interest. On October 13, 1937, the FCC adopted its first television spectrum allocations: 7 channels between 44 and 108 MHz, and 12 additional channels from 156–194 MHz. Invention proceeded slowly; it was another unplanned news event which seemed to spark action. On November 15, 1938. NBC's W2XBS telecast a fire, using a mobile unit that just happened to be in the vicinity of Ward's Island. There had been other broadcasts of live emergencies, but this broadcast to several thousand set owners in the largest city in the country caused a sensation. Radio covered the TV "reporters," and the next day newspapers commented on the sensational images. From then on, no one doubted TV's future (Lichty and Topping, 1975).

NBC staged the official beginning of TV in the country on April 30, 1939 when President Franklin D. Roosevelt and RCA head David Sarnoff spoke and appeared from the New York World's Fair. Three weeks later NBC telecast a Princeton–Columbia baseball game from Baker Field in New York City, and a whole new possibility for TV programming was opened up. NBC followed up later that summer with an August 1939 telecast of a major league baseball game, a double-header between the Cincinnati Reds and the Brooklyn Dodgers from Ebbets Field, Brooklyn. That fall NBC televised a college football game, and an NFL professional football game (Bilby 1986; Gomery 1997).

The FCC moved slowly to bring television out of its experimental phase, announcing in February 1940 that it would issue commercial licenses later that year. That spring, RCA cut the prices of television sets, and started a sales drive intended to put a minimum of 25,000 in homes in New York. CBS, and Don Lee, Inc. protested that RCA's sales efforts were really a backdoor attempt to freeze TV standards at specifications RCA preferred (Slotten 2000).

The FCC formed the National Television Standards Commission (NTSC) to cooperatively set technical standards. On March 8, 1941, the NTSC formally called for a 525-line, 30 frames per second, 4×3 dimensional screen, black and white system which few expected to last beyond the upcoming war. Yet except for the middle 1950s innovation of compatible color, this NTSC standard remained in place as the twenty-first century commenced. By May 1941, the Commission had approved and authorized commercial TV to begin on July 1, 1941 – with 10 stations granted commercial TV licenses requiring a minimum of 15 hours per week of broadcasting (Richie 1994).

NBC signed the Bulova Watch Company, the Sun Oil Company, Lever Bros., and Procter & Gamble to sponsor the first commercial telecasts on what was to be called WNBT (in the year 2000 named WNBC). On July 1, 1941, WNBT-TV initiated commercial television in the USA, based upon an advertising model developed through 15 years of radio experience, starting at 1:29 p.m. (Eastern time), with General Mills sponsoring a Brooklyn Dodgers verses Philadelphia Phillies professional baseball game, followed by the *Sunoco Newscast* with Lowell Thomas. That night, Ralph Edwards hosted *Truth Or Consequences*, simulcast on NBC radio and TV, and sponsored by Ivory Soap. CBS was less active as its New York station, WCBW-TV, went on the air on July 1, 1941 at 2:30 p.m. with only a test pattern. Rare shows included an afternoon broadcast of *Jack and the Beanstalk*, featuring live drawings by on-screen animator John Rupe. Seemingly the television age had begun, but all too soon the attack on Pearl Harbor halted all television technical progress, and turned electronics inventors to war activities such as perfecting radar (Bilby 1986).

Yet television continued as far-sighted pioneers looked to maintain their edge when the war would end. NBC and CBS – plus Hollywood's Don Lee, and a General Electric station based in Schenectady, NY – remained on the air a required minimum of 4 hours per week. Indeed, on January 6, 1942, about a month after the Japanese attack, the FCC was still granting licenses, in particular one to the Du Mont Laboratories to build a third commercial TV station for New York City. Typically stations broadcast newsreels about World War II, and local entertainment amateur shows. Balaban & Katz, the Chicago motion picture chain, also obtained a licence but ran their station by an all-female staff through the war. Indeed, the Commission did not issue a formal wartime license freeze until May 1942, so the five pioneers mentioned – plus a station in Philadelphia – kept on broadcasting through the war. Yet the urban based nature of TV broadcasting had been set in place even before most Americans had ever seen a broadcast.

Rapid Innovation of Black & White TV: 1946–60

After the August 1945 dropping of the atomic bombs on Japan, these pioneer six stations were still telecasting. An estimated 5,000 pre-war TV sets were in use, principally in labs and homes of corporate staff in and around New York City. The largest city in the country was the site for the greatest interest because there were three stations on the air. To innovate television in post-war America, at least three sets of decisions needed to be made:

1 The FCC had to allocate more licenses so television stations could go on air;
2 networks needed to be established among these stations to take advantage of economies of scale of programming;
3 sets had to be manufactured and sold so an audience could develop.

Radio station owners had the advantage as they knew the ways of the FCC. RCA led the way because it had dominating positions with its NBC division; CBS followed. Still, there were many new entrants, particularly newspapers, and electronics TV set manufacturers. The FCC, in September 1945, reported it would distribute licenses for 13 VHF (Very High Frequency) channels in each of 140 urban markets. This plan would go through five more revisions and iterations – until July 1, 1952 – when the Commission's Sixth Report & Order set in place the channel configuration that was still in place as the twentieth century ended. From the beginning, the FCC faced another problem of allocating adjacent channels. Big cities – such as Washington, DC, and Baltimore, and Philadelphia and New York – were simply too close to each other to easily accommodate many VHF stations in both locations. At first the FCC sought various forms of compromise to fashion an all-VHF world. But try as it did, by October 1948, the Commissioners threw up their hands, and declared a moratorium (in the trade called "the freeze") to study some other alternative. Still, for 3 years, wishing the problem would somehow go away, the Commission granted more than 100 "construction permits" which would turn into commercial licenses as soon as the station was built, and it began to air a minimum of 15 hours of programming per week.

In reality, during the fall of 1945 and well into 1946, the original six who had persisted through World War II were the only television stations "on the air". Scores of others were "experimenting," trying to decide if they wanted to invest the required hundreds of thousands of dollars. Most importantly, networking began on December 1, 1945 when AT&T cobbled together a coaxial cable plus microwave relay linkage connecting three stations in New York City, one in Philadelphia, one in Schenectady, and an experimental DuMont station in Washington, DC. The initial network telecast is still part of the schedule – the annual Army versus Navy football game. The camera situated at the 50-yard line captured President Truman entering the stadium, and offered a wide shot of the action. Two other cameras offered occasional close-ups. Networking clearly worked, but it would be 7 years before a TV nation would be created because of the multi-million investment in cable and relays by AT&T.

This successful network football broadcast fed heady days of anticipation. Applications piled up in the offices of the FCC in downtown Washington, DC. Early applicants included manufacturers of TV sets (RCA, DuMont, Philco, Raytheon, Westinghouse & Crosley), movie companies (Loew's MGM, Twentieth Century Fox, Disney, and Paramount), department stores like Macy's (which planned to sell sets), newspapers, radio stations and the leading radio networks – NBC, CBS, ABC, and Mutual.

All wanted licenses in America's biggest cities. Radio stations had made millions broadcasting to the vast population in and around New York, Chicago, and Philadelphia. Everyone wanted a TV license under the same circumstances where advertising demand would ensure high profits despite a relatively high capital investment that TV required. As the FCC only permitted one company to own as many as five television stations, and no more than one per city, and with no real TV sets actually for sale at Christmas of 1945; due to continuing war restrictions, many early applicants gave up. It was not a time for the faint of heart, only for those loving risk.

Still the more than 140 applications sat at the FCC as it began holding hearings to judge the first batch of applicants. The Commission decided to hold hearings first for four stations in Washington, DC to set a precedent. There were nine applicants: Bamberger Broadcasting Service (owner of WOR-AM radio in New York City), Capital Broadcasting Company (owner of WWDC-AM in Washington, DC), the DuMont manufacturer and broadcaster, the Evening Star Broadcasting Company (owner of the dominant newspaper and radio station WMAL-AM of Washington, DC), the Marcus Loew Booking Agency (then running WHN-AM in New York City and part of the Loew's MGM empire), NBC, Eleanor Patterson (owner of Washington, DC's Times-Herald newspaper), the Philco Radio & Television Corporation (a major TV set manufacturer and owner of the TV outlet in Philadelphia), and Scripps-Howard Radio (a radio station owner based in Cincinnati, also with major newspaper interests). This mixture of applicants – radio, newspaper, and movie interests – would prove typical (Lichty and Topping, 1975).

The whole of the new TV industry paid close attention to the hearings held that cold January of 1946. Testimony after testimony underscored that the cost to build and operate a station would require millions of dollars up-front before any profits could reasonably be expected. In early March 1946 the FCC announced its decision. The Commission underscored the importance of running a radio network and first awarded channel 4 to NBC. Then it signaled that owning the dominant local news-paper counted, and so awarded channel 7 to *The Evening Star*, which also was affiliated on its radio side with the ABC network. For channel 9, it again underscored radio experience and wealth by allocating this valuable spectrum space to Bamberger Broadcasting, long a powerful New York City radio station, and the dominant power in the Mutual radio network. The basic principle common among the three was that all were highly experienced broadcasters who could clearly afford to lose money while developing a television station. But if this support for the status quo was not a strong enough signal, potential outsiders were most disquieted when the FCC postponed making a decision for channel 5, and offered joint ownership to DuMont and Philco. The parties negotiated, Philco blinked, and set manufacturer DuMont took over channel 5 in June of 1946. (It would later operate the fourth network until 1955.)

DuMont quickly found a studio and tower location at the Hotel Harrington a half mile from the White House, and by the middle of April of 1946 TV was on the air from the nation's capital. NBC secured a studio at the Wardman Park hotel, and went on the air in June of 1947. The wealthy *Evening Star* newspaper began airing TV four months later. Only Bamberger – because of the lack of development of the Mutual TV network – got "cold feet," and sold to another wealthy local newspaper, *The Washington Post*, which started channel 9 in 1949, more than 3 years after the allocation decision had been made.

Two key precedents had been set. First, by rejecting Loew's, the FCC Commissioners recognized the ongoing anti-trust case by the Justice Department against the movie studios, and moved them to the bottom of any application ranking. The Hollywood movie business would have to look for other avenues to enter the TV business. Second, radio stations and local newspapers were favored, but the richer moved to the top of the heap. The less wealthy – such as Capital Broadcasting and *The Times-Herald* newspaper – were implicitly eliminated because the FCC Commissioners figured they could not afford to lose the necessary monies for the long run to make television last. Rich radio stations, and set manufacturers could.

Through the spring of 1946, the FCC began to meet in the largest cities in the country to duplicate the license allocation procedures that had worked for Washington, DC. The bigger the city, the more the stations. New Yorkers obtained the most – seven. Chicagoans obtained four stations. Los Angeles, booming after the war, and considered the leading city of the West also got seven. Other cities received three. Yet as this license allocation process methodically moved across the country, some 90 on-file applicants withdrew. Walt Disney withdrew his applications, for example, claiming he would wait for color, but like Twentieth Century-Fox, the cause lay in the realization that the anti-trust case would not be settled until May of 1948. All awaited action on the network front.

As more and more big cities came online, a network could and would be able to offer an advertiser access to the bulk of the nation's population. As evidenced by the first true December 1945 network broadcast of the Army-Navy game, sports broadcasting sparked early TV sales. Males took out their savings and purchased sets to see heavyweight boxing matches and baseball games. Looking back, we now know that obsession with TV began on a warm evening in New York City from Yankee stadium when on June 19, 1946 Joe Louis defeated Billy Conn for the heavyweight boxing championship. With stations connected from Washington, DC to Philadelphia to New York City to Schenectady, an estimated TV audience of 300,000 gathered to watch Louis defeat yet another "great white hope." TV sponsor Gillette hawked shaving razors and blades between rounds, and sales surged. Gillette, which had paid

$125,000 to reach male sports fans, celebrated, and television had found the first type of telecast which worked for station, advertiser, set manufacturer, and network. Those lucky Americans living within range of a big city could not wait to buy a TV set for Christmas 1946.

As stations came on, dealers in TV cities began joint promotions known as "T-Day" or "T-Week" – running specials in full-page newspaper advertisements, and regular radio spots in city after city. But it was in New York City area stores that sales soared as three stations were on the air, all network programs were shown, and the future of TV seemed very bright. Everyday was "T-Day" in New York City, with sports telecasts on weekends and evenings. NBC began its association with professional football on September 20, 1946 broadcasting the New York Giants versus Green Bay Packers football game from the Polo Grounds. Philco's Philadelphia station, which had been locally broadcasting University of Pennsylvania football games since 1939, began sending college and professional games onto the network, both from the University of Pennsylvania's Franklin Field. Baseball and boxing telecasts spurred the issuance of first advertising "rate card" by WBKB-TV in Chicago. DuMont announced it would televise all 1947 New York Yankees baseball games; CBS announced it would televise all 1947 Brooklyn Dodger baseball games (with Ford and General Foods as co-sponsors); and NBC announced it would telecast all 1947 games by baseball's New York Giants. The Goodyear Tire Corporation and Ford Motor signed deals with NBC and CBS for regular broadcasts of boxing.

By 1947, New York City was the locus of the television world with its headquarters of the networks: NBC, CBS, and DuMont – with ABC promising to open up shop soon. Pioneering network programmers all lived in New York, and took their feedback from the Madison Avenue advertising community. Reports of falling set prices were tempting homeowners and apartment dwellers by the thousands to acquire the then standard 8-inch set – on the installment plan – for between $100 and $200. Successful East Coast networking prompted the formation of a middle western network, centering in Chicago and extending to St Louis, Detroit, Milwaukee, and Cleveland. So great was the success in reaching males with sports that J. Walter Thompson advertising agency created "Kraft Television Theater" to "target" females. It premiered on the East Coast on the NBC network on May 7, 1947, the first regularly scheduled drama series on a network. Still males dominated purchasing decisions and viewing choices, so that the September 30, 1947 opening game of the World Series was carried jointly by the expanding NBC, CBS, and DuMont networks, and was seen by an estimated four million people.

In November 1947 the networks extended to Boston, and NBC's *Meet the Press* became the first network public affairs telecast. Milton Berle's initial appearance in the fall of 1948 is usually used to mark the beginning of television in America, yet his televised vaudeville came after great success with sports, drama, and news. Yet Berle did symbolize that TV was "hot," so much so that for the 1947 World Series, President Truman loaned his RCA TV set to the White House press corps to see if the Brooklyn Dodgers could finally beat the New York Yankees. New York and Washington symbolized the beginning of the TV nation. No one scoffed when RCA president David Sarnoff predicted there would TV sets in use in every major city within a year. With the AT&T coaxial cable hooking more cities, only the West Coast seemed underserved (Sarnoff 1968).

But all this 1947 prosperity was setting the stage for future problems. With all the success of televised sports, more and more applications for station licenses began to flow into the FCC offices, a new one each working day. Now entrepreneurs from smaller cities began to clamor for a place in this hot industry. But no one knew what to do with smaller cities located near larger ones, such as Trenton, New Jersey, located halfway between Philadelphia and New York City. Should New Yorkers or citizens of Philadelphia give up a new station so tiny Trenton could have one of its own? Engineers figured a Trenton allocation would cause interference for TV viewers in the two fastest growing TV cities in the USA – New York, and Philadelphia (Slotten 2000).

The Commission's concern was heightened as Christmas 1947 saw a TV set buying frenzy. Sales were so brisk that no one really knew how many sets were in place as 1947 ended. The official figure was 190,000; most industry insiders guessed the figure was far greater. Everyone knew one thing: New York City was showing a nation – principally in its Levittownesque suburbs – that there existed few better bargains for the dollar than buying a new TV set, even if it meant going into more debt. As the baby boom was in full swing, the TV set replaced the radio as the center of the living room. In 1948, TV signals suddenly seemed everywhere: Los Angeles, San Francisco, Atlanta, Chicago, Louisville, New Orleans, St Paul, Buffalo, Syracuse, Cincinnati, Cleveland, Toledo, Memphis, Fort Worth, Salt Lake City, Richmond, and Seattle.

By 1948, more than thirty companies were making TV sets – with more than 100 different models for sale. Many now saw their first TV image in a neighbor's home rather than at a bar, department, or appliance store. In 1948, manufacturers gave up on their original target demographic for sales – the rich – and began lowering prices for working-class families. By the end of 1948, 12-inch table model sets could be had for little more $100. The draw was so strong that sales surged during the Christmas 1948 shopping season, despite a recession beginning late in 1948 (Gomery 2001a).

Sports, dramas, and news were already staples; Milton Berle's popularity led to a plethora of new variety shows, none more popular than newspaper columnist Ed Sullivan's *Toast of the Town* on rival CBS. To impress the FCC, the networks in June of 1948 blanketed the two major political party conventions, both held in Philadelphia at the core of the Eastern network. Easterners saw the convention live; elsewhere, as with all forms of programming, the networks sent kinescope film recordings for next-day telecasts on not yet connected stations. More importantly, TV was beginning to reach a mass audience which advertisers took seriously. DuMont first telecast professional wrestling on its network on July 30, 1948 in prime-time. Because of TV's early big-city basis, "ethnic programming" – such as the January 10, 1949 premiere of *The Goldbergs* – premiered on CBS (MacDonald 1988).

Individual stations – by 1949 most often owned by radio stations and newspapers – spurred set sales through barrages of "free" publicity. So, for example, all of Chicago noticed in early April 1948 when *The Chicago Tribune* and its WGN-AM devoted space and time to the opening of *Tribune*'s new television station, WGN-TV. This second station in America's second city set off a buying frenzy on "T-Day." While much has been written about TV's presumed negative effect on radio listening and newspaper reading, in the real world of business, emerging media conglomerates like *The Tribune* were making more profits from TV than they lost through any declining radio, and/or newspaper advertising and circulation (Gomery 2001a).

On January 11, 1949 came an event which all labeled the equivalent of railroad's *Golden Spike* when the Eastern network, and the middle western network united. That night New Yorkers, the people of Richmond Virginia, those living in St Louis and Milwaukee – and millions in between – saw the programs. TV as a mass medium really began on that cold January night when the seven interconnected middle western TV stations linked up with eight East Coast stations. NBC counted 1.3 million TV sets in the USA, most in the East, but sales began rapidly equating the two regions in potential viewers. Overnight, the bulk of the US urban population had access to network TV. From then on, built on this base, with ever growing economies of scale, programmers could hire more expensive stars and producers, and more and more advertisers willingly anted up to reach this ever increasing mass of urban and suburban audience. Only one in eight households may have had a set, but the "Golden Spike" jettisoned the nay-sayers. A TV nation was coming; the only question was when would "everybody" have a TV set. Realistically, few expected that the answer would be: in less than a decade (Gomery 2001a).

Yet in the nation's capital the FCC was still in crisis: what to do with signal interference? Its solution was to call a halt to station licence allocation in October 1948, and announce a "Freeze." No more new construction permits would be issued. This freeze was expected to be short-lived, but would last until July 1952. Only 108 stations would make it on the air through that nearly four-year period, guaranteeing the pioneers continued profitability. Half the stations had no competition, "cream skimmed" the best that the three networks offered, and grew rich. Some major cities – like Denver, and Portland, Oregon – and most cities below the top-25 in population simply waited (Murray and Godfrey 1997).

Most importantly, the freeze meant that the trends in place, as of the close of 1948, would define the future of the use of the television technology for 30 years. Radio's NBC and CBS dominated, as did their long-standing network radio partners. Competing interests – led by ABC, DuMont, and Mutual – all started networks, with only ABC surviving. Indeed, in their corporate offices NBC and CBS executives actually breathed a sigh of relief as the freeze meant they could slow making network connections and thus lower short-run costs. They could – and did – plan a rational, profit maximizing national system to exclude most (that is ABC) as potential competitors for two generations. TV set sales never slowed a beat, because America was an urban nation. All the freeze did for rural and small town USA was fashion a pent up demand that would predictably explode once the moratorium was lifted.

During this period the TV set grew to dominate any home into which it was placed. Average screen size increased to 12 inches measured diagonally. In June

1949, Philco introduced the first built-in antenna. Motorola countered with easier-to-use volume and channel dials for its 1949 Christmas models. The average TV buyer earned from $40 to $100 per week, wages which placed the household firmly within the middle class. If the post-war era of the late 1940s has been symbolized by moving to a suburban home, and buying a sleek new automobile, purchasing a TV set – also on the installment plan – must be added to that late list (Spigel 1992).

TV viewing started after supper, peaked at 9:00 p.m. each evening, and ended with bedtime. Most TV sets were on 4–5 hours per day on average, simply because of the added hours tuned into sports on Saturdays and Sundays. Once the networks and local stations began adding afternoon (the soaps moving over from radio), and morning shows (led by NBC's "Today"), average set-use increased to 7 hours per day, and has remained remarkably constant since then. To use one well-studied example, the expanding TV programming day from the three Philadelphia stations was embraced by the whole metro area – from Allentown to the north down to Newark, Delaware south, from Reading on the west to southern New Jersey in the east. Thus Philadelphia's third place ABC affiliate, WFIL, channel 6, looked to fill its afternoon to rival NBC and CBS, and pioneered *American Bandstand* which quickly went network, and jump started rock music, proving TV could and would come to influence all aspects of American life (Allen 1985; Gomery 2001a).

As the 1940s ended, nearly 100 stations were on the air, able to reach two-thirds of the population of the USA. Advertisers of mass-market products were working to fit TV into their media plans, principally by substituting monies formerly spent for advertising on radio. Admiral, Philco and RCA were the leading makers of sets, offering vastly improved models for much less money, and watching sets fly off store shelves. The roof-top antenna installer was seen up and down the block thanks to brisk sales and high demand. All parties were making more and more profits, as the recession of 1949 was forgotten, and the boom of the 1950s commenced. As the calendar page flipped to January 1950 the television industry matrix was already in place, only awaiting a thaw by the FCC to liberate the rest of the country, to become part of the TV nation (Inglis 1990).

So strong was the demand that many Americans living just out of range of pioneering stations sought some way to be able to tune in. Dozens of smart technicians who owned local appliance dealerships erected a "community" antenna, and then for a minimal fee fed the unavailable signals to homes which, of course, had to purchase a set to gain this service. Thus was born in the mountains of Pennsylvania, blocked from Philadelphia and Pittsburgh stations, and valleys across the country, Community Antenna TV (or CATV). In the late 1940s, pioneering urban stations and their networks loved the added CATV viewers because they surveyed them, estimated their numbers, and charged advertisers higher rates. CATV entrepreneurs loved the fact that they only needed local permission to erect their tower, and run their wires, and did not have to apply to the FCC. Set manufacturers and their franchised appliance dealers loved the extra sales. But cable TV – born in 1948 and 1949 – was a reaction to an established broadcasting system in place and an urban-centric FCC policy (LeDuc 1973).

As the freeze dragged on, the networks – on September 4, 1951 – transmitted the first transcontinental TV network broadcast, featuring President Harry S. Truman. On September 22, 1951 came the first live sporting event seen coast-to-coast: a college football game between Duke and the University of Pittsburgh, on NBC. Two weeks later, a nation of urban dwellers settled in to watch the first live coast-to-coast network telecast of a World Series game. So popular was this Yankees versus Giants series, coming after Bobby Thompson's dramatic pennant winning home run, that Gillette sponsored it on both NBC, and CBS (Gomery 2001b).

That next spring – on April 14, 1952 – the FCC issued its Sixth Report and Order which mapped TV stations for the whole nation. The freeze was lifted formally as of July 1, 1952. Politicians loved it because all stations on the air at the time – save the single station in Albuquerque, New Mexico – were on the network, and their political conventions were aired to millions. Dwight D. Eisenhower benefited as his fabled smile led to a Fall Republican victory after 20 years of Democratic party presidents. As Ike was being sworn in, that same week on Monday January 19, 1953, a national mania arose as Lucille Ball gave birth to her second son the "same" night as fictional "Lucy Ricardo" on CBS's hit series "I Love Lucy" "gave birth" to "Little Ricky" on TV. With the lifting of the freeze, some 617 VHF and 1436 UHF stations, including 242 non-commercial educational stations, could come online. All wanted to become CBS affiliates as Lucy became TV's first true national TV star (see also Bogart 1956).

By 1960 most Americans had a TV set, more than had indoor plumbing. From a post-World War II figure of a penetration of 0.01 percent, the figure had climbed to over 95 percent. Some had no access to CATV, and thus were unable to access signals, principally in the mountainous West. No home technology had been more rapidly innovated; the final two-thirds of the twentieth century would simply take television in the home – and increasingly in more and more public spaces – as a given (Sterling 1984).

Color TV: Slower Innovation

But until the middle 1960s, television meant images in black and white. That technology drove the innovation; color TV would come more slowly. Its invention went back to 1929 when the first public demonstration of color TV was held at Bell Telephone Laboratories, using a form of the mechanical system CBS would later champion. A mechanical system was simpler, but not compatible with the NTSC system the FCC adopted in 1941. If the mechanical system was adopted, a set owner would require two units – one for color and another for black and white. Still CBS pushed its mechanical color system, starting even before World War II ended. On April 22, 1946, CBS transmitted a color television program successfully over 450-mile coaxial cable link from New York to Washington and back. Still the Commission waited (Paley 1979; Auletta 1991).

David Sarnoff reasoned CBS's incompatible system would never carry the day. On November 4, 1946, RCA demonstrated a crude all-electronic system for color TV.

Yet RCA engineers could never match the CBS system, and so on October 10, 1950, through William Paley's skillful political pressure, the FCC approved the CBS color proposal. Industry set manufacturers revolted, refusing to manufacture CBS-color sets. Sarnoff pushed his RCA researchers while RCA lawyers sued to overturn the FCC's pro-CBS ruling. The industry and the Commission waited, more absorbed with the realities of ending the freeze on new stations.

As set manufacturers and engineers denounced CBS-color incompatibility, dealers saw cheaper black and white sets selling briskly. It became harder for CBS to make the case that their system was technically superior, and once the FCC took up color after the freeze was settled, CBS conceded victory to RCA in the war over color TV standards. On August 30, 1953, NBC's *Kukla, Fran, and Ollie* children's show was broadcast experimentally in RCA compatible color; three months later, NBC heralded compatible color TV airing its popular *Colgate Comedy Hour* to the political elite in Washington. On December 17, 1953, the FCC officially reversed its earlier decision, and approved the RCA compatible, electronic color system as the standard. Thus the official first color broadcast came on January 1, 1954 as NBC televised the Rose Parade in color on 21 stations (Inglis 1990).

Still, 1950s Americans seemed satisfied with black & white sets at $100–$200 prices. Thousand-dollar-priced color sets – with only NBC network shows to watch – moved more slowly from dealers' show rooms. It would be a full decade before the majority of network programs would be in color. Early black and white set owners saw nothing wrong with their units; they spent time finding shows to please them. Finding a Lucille Ball or Arthur Godfrey to appeal to millions dominated the network's work, and no one could find a genre where color made so much of a difference that advertisers would pay extra.

Indeed, RCA made vast profits selling black and white sets to the working and middle class prior to 1960, and only then concentrated on selling color sets as replacements. Only when color sets came down in price in the early 1960s – as competitors offered cheaper color sets – did the nation turn to color TV. By 1972, more than half the homes in the USA had color sets. At that point the bible of the television listings, *TV Guide*, stopped tagging color program listings with a special symbol; instead *TV Guide* tagged black and white shows (Sobel 1986; Inglis 1990).

The Network Era: 1950–80

While technological battles drew interest within the industry, the TV audience settled in and watched three dominant TV networks. Here distribution economies and program monopolies trumped technology. Network economies led most stations to affiliate with NBC and CBS. Through the late 1940s, and into the early 1950s, DuMont and ABC competed to survive as the third network, with attempts by the Mutual radio system and Paramount Pictures of Hollywood never really ever getting off the ground. By 1960, CBS, NBC, and ABC defined television for most Americans, with their mixture of former radio comedies and dramas, soap operas, sports telecasts, and news broadcasts (Bliss 1991; Butsch 2000).

Most early 1950s shows were shown live. Gradually, during the 1950s, film replaced live broadcasting save for sports and news. Hollywood as film capital produced most prime-time entertainment by the late 1950s even as it owned no network and few stations. *I Love Lucy* pioneered Hollywood's entry as a TV's prime-time production capital. Later, feature films and made-for-TV movies became staples of nightly TV fare (Gomery 1992).

Television demanded new types of shows, and stars. It tried to take the best of radio and the movies, yet few could predict who might make an impact. Consider the case of CBS's first major star, Arthur Godfrey, who seemed to have no ostensible talent, but before the link to Hollywood started, Godfrey, more than single star, helped bring TV technology into American homes. At one point he had two shows in the top ten, dominating both Wednesday and Monday nights. Arthur Godfrey's *Talent Scouts* and *Arthur Godfrey and His Friends* proved so popular, that during the 1950s that they served as a cornerstone of the CBS-TV network's programming strategies (Smith 1990).

Arthur Godfrey ventured onto prime-time TV by simply permitting the televising of his radio hit, Arthur Godfrey's Talent Scouts. Fans embraced this amateur showcase, and during the 1951–2 TV season it reached number one in the ratings. Thereafter through the point where most Americans owned a set, Godfrey and Lucy made Monday night the most watched of the week. Godfrey pioneered cross-media synergy. He made the careers of Pat Boone, Tony Bennett, Eddie Fisher, Connie Francis, Leslie Uggams, Lenny Bruce, Steve Lawrence, Roy Clark, and Patsy Cline. His "discovery" of Patsy Cline on January 21, 1957 was typical in that the day before she was but another local talent scratching out a living in rural Virginia, the day after, her song "Walkin' After Midnight" shot up the music charts in both the pop and country categories. Though she sang a "country" song, recorded in Nashville, Godfrey insisted she not wear one of her trademark cowgirl outfits but appear in a cocktail dress. By the close of the twentieth century, Cline ranked a legendary country cross-over performer. Still Godfrey was fallible as he turned down both Elvis Presley and Buddy Holly!

For advertisers, Godfrey ranked as television's first great salesman. He blended a Southern folksiness with enough sophistication to convince Americans to buy almost anything. Godfrey frequently kidded his sponsors, but always "sold from the heart," only hawking products he had actually tried and/or regularly used. Godfrey made it sound like he was confiding to the viewer, and to the viewer alone, and early television viewers watched and listened to Godfrey's rich, warm, resonant descriptions and went out and purchased what he endorsed (Gomery 1997).

He also proved that any mistake made on television was magnified into a national scandal. He set off a furor on October 19, 1953 when he fired the then popular singer Julius La Rosa – on the air. The public did not read of this in a newspaper, but watched it happen live, and many never forgave Godfrey. Slowly he lost his fan base, and by 1960 was off the air completely. Even his apology, and freckled face grin, infectious chuckle, and unruly red hair – or being able to battle cancer and live – was not enough to throw off the image of the boss who humiliated his employees in public.

Through the 1950s, CBS, rather than technological pioneer NBC, proved the most watched TV network. William Paley pioneered *Gunsmoke*, and during the late 1950s set off a westerns craze. He stuck with *60 Minutes*, and made that news magazine show into TV's longest running hit. Paley's chief lieutenant, Frank Stanton, carried CBS to greater and greater earnings, based upon TV's most popular genre – the situation comedy. He ran some of the worst [*The Beverly Hillbillies*, and *Green Acres*] and some of the best [*The Dick Van Dyke Show*, and *The Phil Silvers Show.*] Indeed, looking back to when Silvers and his wacky platoon, based upon scripts written and directed by Nat Hiken, in 1956 knocked Milton Berle to second place in Berle's Tuesday time slot, we cannot deny that quality TV comedy became a part of the American Culture (Paley 1979; Campbell 1991; Everitt 2001).

NBC remained CBS's chief network rival. General David Sarnoff behind the scenes set the NTSC standard for black and white, and color, and RCA, NBC's parent company, sold the most TV sets until the 1970s when Sony's Trinitron (and Sarnoff's death) reduced RCA to just another network. Technologically NBC had all the advantages, but viewers watched programs, not caring about the technical advantages. Sarnoff was a greater technological leader, but not the showman Paley was, and so in the long run, frustratingly to him, year after year saw NBC follow CBS in the ratings. Try as he may, Sarnoff just could not make any advantage in programming popularity through RCA's technological leadership.

Sarnoff "failed," because throughout the 1950s, he did not embrace Hollywood and the star system as did Paley. Sports and live drama from New York worked, and Sarnoff stuck with them. His New York-based variety spectaculars competed with Lucy, and *Gunsmoke*, and consistently lost. It was not that Sarnoff was highbrow; it was he who had signed Milton Berle to a lifetime contract. Yet Berle and his vaudeville kind were not TV's future. As brilliant as *Sid Caesar* and *Imagine Coca* were, the future lay in filmed Hollywood series. Only in New York-based non-prime-time shows like *Today* and *Tonight* did NBC consistently top CBS. By the 1960s, NBC had become the pioneer in movies shown and made for TV, but CBS also quickly jumped on that bandwagon, and NBC lost any temporary advantage it may have had. David Sarnoff died in 1971, proud of RCA's technical triumphs, and disappointed at NBC's consistent second-place finishes (Bilby 1986).

The third dominant TV network, the American Broadcasting Company, struggled through the 1950s and 1960s, only gaining equality in the 1970s. Its rise, when compared to CBS and NBC, took far longer, and followed a far more rocky road. ABC as a company was begun, not by creative entrepreneurship, but by government order in 1943 when NBC, then the power in radio broadcasting, was ordered to give up one of its two radio networks. Edward J. Noble, famous as the father of Life Savers candy, purchased NBC Blue, the weaker of NBC's station lineups, for $8 million, and in 1945 he formally changed the name to the American Broadcasting Company.

The ABC television network came three years later, as Nobel and his aides scrambled to pick up affiliates in cities where NBC and CBS had already lined up the strongest television stations. Having fewer affiliates than NBC and CBS, ABC-TV started from a base of smaller audiences, and was thus perpetually at the short end of a new TV world. Two triumphs marked its beginning TV, merger with the United Paramount theater chain (a source of cash and leadership in Leonard Goldeneson), and its ability to out-draw and ultimately bury the DuMont network. The conditions set up by the FCC's *Sixth Report and Order* told ABC head, Leonard Goldenson, that only three networks would survive, and so only in 1955 when DuMont went under was ABC really set off on what would be its successful quest to catch up to industry leaders, CBS and NBC (Quinlan 1979; Goldenson 1991).

Goldenson and his able assistants looked for niche audiences not served by his two far larger rivals. For the next 20 years, ABC-TV sought out and cornered the youth market with such shows as *American Bandstand, Maverick,* and *The Mickey Mouse Club.* ABC-TV stars included Edd *Kookie* Byrnes and Ricky Nelson, both 1950s teen heartthrobs. It made deals with Walt Disney and Warner Bros studio to establish a link to Hollywood as strong as CBS. *The Wonderful World of Disney, Cheyenne, 77 Sunset Strip, Surfside 6,* and *Hawaiian Eye* all became relative hits, though never in the league with Lucy, Godfrey, or *Gunsmoke.* Through the 1950s and 1960s Goldenson and his staff experimented, and saw some success with *The Flintstones,* the first animated prime time television series, and *Mod Squad,* an inter-racial detective show. But it was not until the 1976–77 season which saw ABC finally rise to the top of the network ratings with the top three shows in prime time that season: *Happy Days, Laverne & Shirley,* and *Monday Night Football.* Leonard Goldenson is not as famous as David Sarnoff (who brought us NBC) or William S. Paley (who fashioned CBS), but ought to be. Starting in 1953, and taking 30 years, Goldenson created the modern ABC television network from no advantage of technological superiority (as NBC had with owner RCA) or talent (as CBS had). But he did (1) lure the big Hollywood movie studios into the TV production business (2) re-package sports and make it prime-time fare with Monday Night Football and Olympic coverage, and (3) led the networks into the era of movies made for TV and mini-series (Goldenson 1991).

By the late 1960s, critics were demanding an alternative to the networks. The Sixth Report & Order in 1952 had set aside specific slots for educational stations. On May 25, 1953, KUHT-TV Houston became the first non-commercial educational TV station. But money was scare, and the public voted to watch Lucy, Godfrey and company. It was not until the late 1960s that an fusion of federal, state, and local dollars created the Public Broadcasting network. PBS would produce many highly praised shows over the years, led by *Sesame Street* for children, but never would obtain a tenth of ratings of the "big three" during the network era. PBS was TV's step-child, praised by the educated elite, and tolerated by CBS, NBC, and ABC – because it absolved them of presenting educational (read: unprofitable shows). Yet PBS needs to be praised because it alone presented minority images to white Americans who grew up on *Leave It to Beaver,* and *Ozzie and Harriet* (Dates and Barlow 1993).

Technical Change: 1962–2000

The network era was not free of technical change. The first significant change came in distribution as landlines, and microwave relays were replaced by communications satellites. On July 9, 1962, the Telstar satellite was launched. That summer on July 23, 1962, a joint 3-network production was telecast to Europe featuring excerpts of a baseball game at Wrigley Field, Chicago, a live news conference by President John F. Kennedy, and a concert by the Mormon Tabernacle Choir, which had traveled to Mount Rushmore to perform. The host was Chet Huntley of NBC. High ratings came in October 1964 when NBC telecast live by Syncom III the opening ceremonies of the 1964 Summer Olympics in Tokyo. The early satellites rotated at different speeds than the earth, and it would be a decade before geo-synchronous satellites were in place, so that dishes could be aimed at "stationary" satellites. This made network transmission a third cheaper, and a fixed satellite system would provide the basis for CATV to become cable TV with its dozens of networks (Hudson 1990; Watson 1990).

Videotape recording replaced film and live production in all but sports. In April 1956, the Ampex corporation demonstrated the first practical videotape recorder; the three networks immediately placed orders, and on October 29, 1956, CBS provided the first use of videotape in network television programming, recording the East Coast evening news, and then running it later for viewers living in the Mountain and West Coast time zones. Previously, rebroadcasts had been done by kinescope film recordings. In November 1956, comic Jonathan Winters, at the time doing a 15-minute show two nights a week on NBC, used videotape to "play" two characters in the same skit. But the breakthrough came during the spring of 1957 when Arthur Godfrey taped his hit *Talent Scouts*, and ran "live on tape" shows while he was away in Africa. Tape would initiate the "instant replay" in sports, and "live on tape" versions of all studio shows, from *Tonight* to *All in the Family*. Here the Japanese led by Sony sold cheaper but high-quality apparatus, and by 1975 it had replaced RCA as the industry standard (Lardner 1987).

CATV had been extending broadcast signals for 25 years when in 1975, Atlanta-based entrepreneur Ted Turner and Time's Home Box Office (HBO) began to offer CATV re-runs from WTBS-The Superstation, and uncut, uninterrupted, uncensored movies of HBO. Soon suburbanites wanted this new service, and by 1980 the term CATV had given way to "cable TV." Turner made CNN world famous; other entrepreneurs aimed at niche markets under-served by the major networks and through the 1980s came dozens of new choices – such as MTV, A&E, ESPN, and BET. The three networks still dominated, but their grip on the market lessened as the cumulative audience of cable-only networks took away more and more of the former network absolute power. In reaction, Americans increased viewing to the point that the average household had a set on 8 hours per day – and it could be found in any room of the home (Whittemore 1990; Parsons 1998).

By the 1990s using television had become complicated. *TV Guide* became the size of a small-town telephone book. Remote controls made surfing through 50 or more channels easy, but as Larry King told *TV Guide*, he like most Americans "don't know how to work a VCR...I can't even reset the clock...It's always flashing '12:00' at me..." The VCR, initially thought to be used to watch popular shows at different times, in reality became a machine to play back pre-recorded movies. Most Americans found it far simpler just to drive to a video store, pick up a movie, slip it into the machine, and press "play." Hollywood prospered as never before (Compaine and Gomery 2000).

In 1994, General Motors – through its Hughes Electronics division – gave rural Americans the same multi-channel opportunities as their urban and suburban neighbors with television beamed directly to a home satellite dish. As the twentieth century ended, most Americans subscribed to either cable or satellite-delivered TV, and thus paid for what had once been a "free," advertiser-based service. But for this fee, they acquired access to about 50 channels instead of simply the big three networks and a PBS alternative. Nearly all Americans had a VCR, and video rentals and sales topped the box-office as Hollywood's source of revenues. A new "Golden Age" of TV choice had been set in motion (Compaine and Gomery 2000; Gomery 2000).

A Technical Triumph: 2000

As the twentieth century ended, young people quizzingly asked their elders: what was life like without television? What did you all do with all that "extra time?" The social and cultural implications of omnipresent TV touched and often changed all aspects of American life. Elections became TV specials and advertising blitzes, not whistle stop tours, and center square speeches. Presidents were judged by their performance on television. National scandals became "soap operas," as "news anchors" interpreted their every nuance. Trials staged as *Perry Mason*, gave way to Court TV. Constant sports telecasts created so much interest that new leagues – such as NBC's American Football League – were formed, and new sports – such as arena football – were invented (Compaine and Gomery 2000).

Television is the most successful communications and entertainment technology entertainment ever invented. Voting with their "free" time, Americans could not seem to get enough of what the tube offered, and seemed happy to feel "guilty" when asked about their attitude toward television, but when they got time to relax, invariably the first thing they did was grab the remote control, and begin surfing their favorite channels. Many found it amazing that children even before their first birthday learned to use a remote control, long before they learned to speak language, and long before they learned to write (Compaine and Gomery 2000).

All forms of childhood misbehavior were blamed on watching too much TV. And more and more television was blamed for all unexplainable evils in society, and the wasting away of any serious culture. By 1960 watching TV had become the nation's principle activity outside work (or school) and sleep. In 1961, when Newton Minow proclaimed television a "Vast Wasteland," most leaders and educators proclaimed agreement, while watching and enjoying their own favorite shows. The debate over the value of television as a positive or negative force continued as the twenty-first century commenced. Yet by 2000, anyone who looked, realized there were few spots one could escape the tube. TV was everywhere – in airports, restaurants, shopping malls, everywhere. The invention many doubted would make it in 1946 had become so much a part of American life, one had to plan how to escape from it (Boddy 1990; McCarthy 2001).

BIBLIOGRAPHY

Abramson, Albert. *The History of Television, 1880 to 1941* (Jefferson, North Carolina: McFarland, 1987).

Abramson, Albert. *Zworykin: Pioneer of Television* (Urbana: University of Illinois Press, 1995).

Allen, Robert C. *Speaking of Soap Operas* (Chapel Hill: University of North Carolina Press, 1985).

Auletta, Ken. *Three Blind Mice: How the Networks Lost Their Way* (New York: Random House, 1991).

Bilby, Kenneth. *The General: David Sarnoff* (New York: Harper & Row, 1986).

Bliss, Edward, Jr. *Now the News: The Story of Broadcast News* (New York: Columbia University Press, 1991).

Boddy, William. *Fifties Television: The Industry and Its Critics* (Urbana: University of Illinois Press, 1990).

Bogart, Leo. *The Age of Television* (New York: Ungar, 1956).

Butsch, Richard. *The Making of American Audiences: From Stage to Television, 1750–1990* (New York: Cambridge University Press, 2000).

Campbell, Richard. *60 Minutes and the News: A Mythology for Middle America* (Urbana: University of Illinois Press, 1991).

Compaine, Benjamin M. and Douglas Gomery. *Who Owns the Media?* (Mahwah, New Jersey: Lawrence Erlbaum Associates, 2000).

Dates, Janette L. and William Barlow, eds. *Split Image: African Americans in the Mass Media* (Washington, DC: Howard University Press, 1993).

Everitt, David. *King of the Half Hour* (Syracuse: Syracuse University Press, 2001).

Fisher, David E. and Marshall Jon Fisher. *Tube: The Invention of Television* (San Diego: Harcourt Brace, 1996).

Goldenson, Leonard H. *Beating the Odds* (New York: Charles Scribner's Sons, 1991).

Gomery, Douglas. *Shared Pleasures* (Madison: University of Wisconsin Press, 1992).

Gomery, Douglas. "Rethinking TV history," *Journalism & Mass Communication Quarterly*, 74/3 (Autumn 1997): 501–14.

Gomery, Douglas. "Once there were three, now there are seven," *Television Quarterly*, 31/3 (Spring 2000): 63–8.

Gomery, Douglas. "Finding TV's pioneering audiences," *Journal of Popular Film & Television*, 29/3 (Fall 2001a): 121–9.

Gomery, Douglas. "Television sweeps the nation," *Television Quarterly*, 32/2&3 (Summer/ Fall 2001b): 60–5.

Hudson, Heather E. *Communication Satellites: Their Development and Impact* (New York: The Free Press, 1990).

Inglis, Andrew F. *Behind the Tube: A History of Broadcasting Technology and Business* (Boston: Focal Press, 1990).

Kisseloff, Jeff. *The Box: An Oral History of Television, 1920–1961* (New York: Viking, 1995).

Lardner, James. *Fast Forward: Hollywood, the Japanese, and the VCR Wars* (New York: W.W. Norton & Company, 1987).

LeDuc, Don. *Cable Television and the FCC* (Philadelphia: Temple University Press, 1973).

Lichty, Lawrence W. and Malachi C. Topping, eds. *American Broadcasting: A Source Book on the History of Radio and Television* (New York: Hastings House, 1975).

McCarthy, Anna. *Ambient Television: Visual Culture and Public Space* (Durham: Duke University Press, 2001).

MacDonald, J. Fred. *One Nation Under Television* (New York: Pantheon, 1988).

Murray, Michael D. and Donald G. Godfrey, eds. *Television in America: Local Station History from Across the Nation* (Ames: Iowa State University Press, 1997).

Paley, William S. *As It Happened: A Memoir* (Garden City, New York: Doubleday, 1979).

Parsons, Patrick R. and Robert M. Frieden, *The Cable and Satellite Television Industries* (New York: Allyn & Bacon, 1998).

Quinlan, Sterling. *Inside ABC: American Broadcasting Company's Rise to Power* (New York: Hastings House, 1979).

Richie, Michael. *Please Stand By: A Prehistory of Television* (Woodstock: Overlook Press, 1994).

Sarnoff, David. *Looking Ahead* (New York: McGraw-Hill, 1968).

Slotten, Hugh R. *Radio and Television Regulation: Broadcast Technology in the United States, 1920–1960* (Baltimore: Johns Hopkins University Press, 2000).

Smith, Sally Bedell. *In All His Glory: The Life of William S. Paley* (New York: Simon & Schuster, 1990).

Sobel, Robert. *RCA* (New York: Stein & Day, 1986).

Spigel, Lynn. *Make Room for TV: Television and the Family Ideal in Postwar America* (Chicago: University of Chicago Press, 1992).

Sterling, Christopher. *Electronic Media* (New York: Praeger, 1984).

Watson, Mary Ann. *The Expanding Vista: American Television in the Kennedy Years* (New York: Oxford University Press, 1990).

Whittemore, Hank. *CNN* (Boston: Little, Brown, 1990).

CHAPTER EIGHTEEN

Computers and the Internet: Braiding Irony, Paradox, and Possibility

JEFFREY R. YOST

Irony has long had a place in the field of history, but all too frequently on the periphery of the narrative or analytic landscape – as an interesting aside rather than the main act. In the history of technology the focus on irony tends to be even less common, as paths of invention, innovation, and the rationalization of production dominate discourse and leave little room for exploring the ironic. Yet when irony does take center stage, as it did in Cowan's (1984) study of household technology, many topics typically in the background or even invisible, such as consumption, gender, politics, and evolving cultural meanings, come to the fore, illuminating various and often contradictory contexts, and lead the way to a more complex and meaningful understanding. In no area is this more evident than the history of computers, software, and networking.

Unlike myths and realities of various technologies where tinkering led to the invention of new devices with initially unforeseen uses, the history of the development and early applications of computers appears to be very systematic, rational and progressive in nature. Beginning in the mid-1940s, large government contracts funded leading scientists and engineers at top research universities and several companies in a concentrated effort to create machines that could rapidly calculate previously unsolvable mathematical equations. Digital computers had early success at such tasks and new models with ever-increasing memory and processing capabilities, coupled with advances in software, continually advanced the scientific, engineering, and soon, business applications of these machines. Within two decades, Gordon Moore proposed a simple formula, Moore's Law, that continues to predict with remarkable accuracy the rate of doubling of microchip capacity (every 18 months), and hence, computer processing power. Likewise, the development of the ARPANET, precursor to the Internet, seems to be a very orderly initiative led by the US Department of Defense (DoD) in collaboration with academe and industry. Despite the seemingly rational progression of a machine born by and for science, mathematics, and logic, the history of computing is characterized by much underlying irony and paradox.

The Prehistory of Digital Computing

In the second quarter of the nineteenth century British economist and mathematician Charles Babbage (1791–1871) designed the Analytical Engine, the first formal conceptualization of a calculating machine possessing many attributes of the modern day computer. Unlike the seventeenth-century calculating devices of Blaise Pascal (1623–66) and Gottfried Leibniz (1646–1716), the Analytical Engine was designed with programming capabilities (influenced by the Jacquard loom of 1802) and capacity for stored memory. As a result of inadequate financial resources, challenges of precision manufacturing, and Babbage's unwillingness to focus on just one design, the Analytical Engine was not built during his lifetime.

No evidence exists linking Babbage's ideas to development projects to design and build analog and digital computers in the 1930s and 1940s respectively. Instead, analog computing grew out of a long tradition of machines that used analogs or models to represent and understand physical phenomena. Conversely, digital computing borrowed ideas and equipment from mechanical business machines, including tabulators and punched card systems, combined this with World War II electronics research, and benefited from the federal government's continuing commitment to sponsor large-scale computer design projects.

Analog computing came of age during the interwar period, as such machines were used to measure physical elements and solve problems related to the design of dams, electrical networks, and other technologies. The leading figure in the creation and advancement of analog computing was Vannevar Bush (1890–1974), an electrical engineering instructor at MIT who invented the Differential Analyzer in the late 1920s. This machine, though easily the most significant computational device prior to digital computers, was specialized and limited to applications where models could be constructed.

Over the six decades preceding the advent of digital computers, technology fundamental to these electronic devices was developed in the US and European office machine industries. Hermann Hollerith (1860–1929), a young census clerk and inventor with greater business acumen than Babbage, saw an important opportunity to automate the tedious information processing work involved in the national census. In the 1880s, he developed a punched card tabulator capable of significantly enhancing the speed of compiling and processing data. Hollerith's tabulating machine beat out several others in competition for use on the 1890 US Census. Each of his more than 100 machines could replace the labor of 20 human computers.

Hollerith marketed his technology for a variety of business applications under a firm he founded in 1896, the Tabulating Machine Company. In 1911, through a merger, the firm became the Computer-Tabulator-Recording Company (C-T-R), and Hollerith retired a wealthy man. C-T-R would join a burgeoning group of firms representing the information processing segment of the international office machine trade. The United States took a leadership position in this industry by the early twentieth century through the success of C-T-R, National Cash Register (NCR), Burroughs Adding Machine Company, and Remington Rand, four firms that would all play a significant role in the post-World War II computer industry. During the interwar period these companies led the world in the manufacture of tabulators, cash registers, adding machines, and typewriters respectively. All four benefited from strong marketing and service operations and contributed to America's embracement of business machines, a critical story to the history of computing that historian James Cortada insightfully presents in *Before the Computer* (1993).

Computer-Tabulator-Recording Company, renamed International Business Machines (IBM) in 1924, would come to lead the business machine industry and dominate the computer trade by the late 1950s. A key component to the firm's success, however, lay with NCR. An NCR salesman, Thomas J. Watson (1874–1956), whom the firm's president John Patterson (1844–1922) had differences with and fired in 1911, would bring the strong sales and service know-how of his former employer to C-T-R later that year, soon becoming the firm's president and propelling it to unparalleled success.

The fact that punched card systems of the 1940s were simultaneously used to inform and organize New Deal initiatives, advance astronomical and other scientific research, and contribute to the Nazi war effort, and perhaps the Holocaust, indicates the range and moral disparity of applications. On a lighter note, as historian Lubar (1992) points out, the punched card ironically provided the legacy of a phrase printed on nearly all such cards after the early interwar period, "do not fold, spindle, or mutilate." Of perhaps greater irony than Lubar's primary point of culture (the phrase) outlasting technology (the artifact), the voting machines for the 2000 US Presidential Election demonstrated that punched cards were alive, if not well; and the phrase still existed as a real warning, not just part of our nation's vernacular.

ENIAC, EDVAC, and Creating a Whirlwind in Early Digital Computing

Notwithstanding several concomitant European computer projects of significance, ENIAC, EDVAC, and Whirlwind stand out as the most significant developments in early digital computing. The ENIAC (Electronic Numerical Integrator and Computer) is credited as the first electronic digital computer; the EDVAC (Electronic Discrete Variable Automatic Computer) defined the standard logical design or architecture of computers for years to come; and Project Whirlwind achieved advances in memory devices, and more importantly, real-time computing and timesharing.

From historian Stern's *From ENIAC to UNIVAC* (1981) and insider studies including Goldstine's *The Computer From Pascal to von Neumann* (1972) and Burks A. and Burks A.R. "The ENIAC: First General-Purpose Electronic Computer," (1981) to Campbell-Kelly and Aspray's *Computer: A History of the Information Machine* (1996) and Ceruzzi's *A History of Modern Computing* (1998), these developments are among the best documented in the history of information processing. The former three studies, along with the initiation of a dedicated journal, *Annals of the History of Computing,* and the launch of a computer history research center and archives, the Charles Babbage Institute, mark the origin of the history of modern computing as a subdiscipline in the late 1970s to early 1980s, while the latter two books, both synthetic studies, indicate the growing maturity of the field by the late 1990s. In the interim, some critical works furthered understanding of early developments and contexts, including two books by Flamm, *Creating the Computer* (1988) and *Targeting the Computer* (1987) and Aspray's *John von Neumann and the Origins of Modern Computing* (1990). These studies added depth to understanding early computer technology and its intellectual and institutional contexts, including the origin of computer science and the role of government funding in computer development.

The ENIAC was developed by J. Presper Eckert (1919–95) and John W. Mauchly (1907–1980) at the Moore School of Electrical Engineering (University of Pennsylvania) during World War II. The project, funded by US Army Ordnance, was designed in response to the Ballistic Research Laboratory's wartime need for computing hundreds of calculations for ballistic firing tables. The ENIAC, measuring 30×50 feet and costing $400,000, ironically, was not completed until months after the war. Nevertheless, the machine was of great significance as a general-purpose digital computer that set the stage for computing in the Cold War era. Its first major application was a mathematical model for the hydrogen bomb at Los Alamos National Laboratory.

The extent of prior influences on Eckert and Mauchly's computer is uncertain, particularly with regard to John Vincent Atanasoff (1903–95). In June 1940, Mauchly visited Atanasoff, a mathematician and physicist at Iowa State University. Antanasoff had been working on the design of a computer for several years. By 1942, he and Clifford Berry (1918–63) built the ABC, or Antansoff-Berry Computer. Before the ABC became fully operational, Antanasoff was recruited by the Naval Ordnance Laboratory, and never returned to the ABC project. Mauchly's visit undoubtedly heightened his interest in developing an ambitious computer for the Ballistic Research Laboratory, but beyond this, the impact of the ABC remains a mystery.

Even before the ENIAC was completed, its principal designers gave significant thought to its successor. The addition of John von Neumann (1903–57), a leading mathematician at Princeton University's Institute for Advanced Study, buoyed Eckert and Mauchly to follow through on a new project. Together they developed a new logic structure for a stored program computer. This critical feature allowed a program to treat its own instructions as data, setting the stage for programming languages and artificial intelligence. In June 1945 von Neumann wrote up his ideas and those of his colleagues in a report entitled, *The First Draft of a Report on the EDVAC*. This soon famous report had a much longer life than the machine it described, defining the logical structure of what came to be known as the von Neumann architecture.

Along with planning the EDVAC's architecture, the most significant computer development activity at the middle of the century ironically began as an entirely different project. In 1944, MIT initiated Project Whirlwind to produce an analog control device for a flight simulation system. Within 2 years, Whirlwind was redefined to develop a digital computer, in large part because of project leader Jay Forester's vision and skillful rhetoric in presenting Whirlwind. The challenges of moving beyond a batch processing machine to a real-time computer, and the escalating R&D costs, nearly killed Whirlwind during 1949. The project, however, was saved to produce what would become the central control computer for the Semi-Automatic Air Ground Environment (SAGE), a major command and control networked air defense system (Redmond and Smith 2000).

Strategic Air Ground Environment control centers initially were above ground at Semi-Automatic Air Command (SAC) centers, vulnerable to attack and severely limited for immediate air defense applications (Edwards 1996). Like the later Strategic Defense Initiative, SAGE had far more potential in an *offensive*, first strike scenario – when the system would only have to defend against a limited counterattack from surviving Soviet bombers and missiles. Of further irony, the originally state-of-the-art SAGE continued to operate with vacuum tubes decades after this technology was rendered obsolete in most realms by transistors and integrated circuits. Despite its limitations, SAGE was important in designing analog to digital conversion equipment, improving near-term computer reliability, and facilitating real-time computing, all of which would be utilized in scientific, medical, and other applications.

This pattern of large military expenditures on computing projects, failing to deliver fully on the original military objectives but having significant civilian applications, was common in the early history of computing. Even when computers were not directly involved in military applications, their rhetoric was critical to establishing and reinforcing dominant military ideological constructs. Historian Edwards, in an important monograph, *The Closed World* (1996), demonstrates how, politically, technologically, and ideologically, computers facilitated a closed world where all events were perceived within the context of the US and Soviet struggle of the Cold War.

The Birth of an Industry: From ERA and Eckert-Mauchly to IBM and the Seven Dwarfs

In spite of comments in the late 1940s by a number of computer insiders and business machine executives about the United States only needing a handful of computers in the foreseeable future, some individuals recognized the possibility of a significant scientific and business market for these machines. In 1946 Eckert and Mauchly left the University of Pennsylvania to form the Electronic Control Company, soon renamed the Eckert-Mauchly Computer Corporation. That same year, Engineering Research Associates (ERA) was formed, a company bringing together a number of individuals who had collaborated on electronics research during the war. ERA soon built several successful computers, including the Atlas, commissioned for the Navy, and a modified version for scientific applications, the ERA 1101.

Eckert-Mauchly concentrated on meeting existing demand for scientific computers as well as making inroads in the business applications market by developing the UNIVAC, or Universal Automatic Computer. This machine soon had dozens of installations and for much of the 1950s the name UNIVAC became synonymous with computer. Though Eckert-Mauchly and ERA had considerable technical success, they struggled financially. In the early 1950s, Remington Rand acquired both of these pioneering computer firms. In less than a decade, however, Remington Rand lost its apparent lead in the computer industry to IBM, a firm that by the late 1950s had solidified its position at the top of the international trade with the IBM 650 and later the IBM 1401 (the first computer having 10,000 installations).

Common implicit and explicit characterizations of IBM's late entry into the computing field and Remington Rand's failure to maintain its lead are problematic. From World War II forward, IBM was well aware of the future potential for digital computers and was developing technical know-how in electronics to compete. IBM's superior financial resources and internally built organizational capabilities in sales, service, and R&D infrastructure, placed them in an excellent position. For many years the historical literature, placing disproportional significance on IBM President Thomas J. Watson, Jr's reminiscences and other participant accounts, emphasized that IBM was caught off guard at the start of the computer industry. More recently, historians have begun to discredit these interpretations and show that IBM never played a catch-up role (Norberg 1993; Usselman 1993).

Conversely, Remington Rand's shortcomings highlight the difficulties established firms had with the transition to new technologies by acquiring and integrating firms, a development also demonstrated in the automobile and other trades. The IBM System/360 series of compatible computers in the early to mid-1960s was so named for the full-circle of price range and applications it provided. If the UNIVAC is analogous to Ford's Model T in its ability to capture attention and temporarily define a technology, the System/360 is similar to Alfred Sloan and General Motors' displacement of the standard by creating a range of price-differentiated products. Though it fell short of producing a computer for "every purse and purpose," the System/360 series further distanced IBM from Remington Rand, and its other six competitors in the computer trade — Burroughs, Control Data, Digital Equipment Corporation, NCR, RCA, and General Electric – companies that, despite producing many important computers, collectively became known as the "Seven Dwarfs." Not surprisingly, IBM has an extensive historiography, most notably, Pugh's (1995) superb study of the firm's technology and management, *Building IBM*, while the dwarfs typically have remained below historians' radar.

Computing Ideologies in the Mainframe Era

Outlining major development projects and shifts in the industry in the preceding sections gives some perspective on the ironic or unexpected occurrences or trajectories in the early history of computing. It also provides useful background to the area where far greater irony and paradox exist: the uses and cultural understanding of computer technology. In the following sections, a number of social and cultural issues will be explored within the context of the development and use of the discipline of artificial intelligence, software, minicomputing and supercomputing, personal computing, the ARPANET, the Internet, and the World Wide Web.

For most of the more than half-century history of electronic digital computers, most people in the United States did not have direct experience with these machines. In their first three decades of existence however, digital computers were significantly influencing many peoples' lives indirectly by: advancing possibilities for scientific and engineering computation; automating manufacturing processes; taking over accounting, payroll, and actuarial chores; helping to predict the weather; assisting in medical diagnosis; keeping national records of airline reservations in real-time; and many other applications. Despite computers often existing out of sight in their birth and adolescence, they were definitely not out of mind. While Bush's "As We May Think" (1945), Alan M. Turing's (1912–54) "Computing Machinery and Intelligence" (1950), Wiener's (1894–1964) *Cybernetics* (1948), and Berkeley's (1909–88) *Giant Brains or Machines That Think* (1949) were read and discussed within some circles, many more people were introduced to the basic ideas of these and other important early expressions of the achievements and future possibilities of computers from other sources.

In January 1950, *Time* published a cover illustration of an anthropomorphized computer wearing a Navy cap. At mid-century, whether with descriptions or imagery, journalistic accounts and advertisements created and perpetuated the metaphor of computers as giant brains. Two years after this cover article, many people saw video, for the first time, of what appeared to be an operating computer being utilized in association with CBS's coverage of the 1952 US Presidential Election returns. The televised UNIVAC computer contained flashing Christmas lights not involved with the use of the computer, which ironically was not even operational. These lights were attached so that viewers could see the computer "thinking." Meanwhile, a working UNIVAC backstage was processing data to project a winner. While the machine up front was presented as an expert, the UNIVAC backstage, being run by programmers and executives from Remington Rand, was predicting a landslide victory for Eisenhower over Stevenson. Remington Rand and CBS, however, did not trust the UNIVAC enough to publicize the projection, and instead reprogrammed the giant brain until it predicted a close race – what recent polls had indicated. It was not until enough returns came back to make the landslide victory obvious that the original projection of the computer was publicly disclosed.

Ever since the publication in 1936 of mathematician Alan Turing's seminal paper that defined his concept of a Universal Machine, computers' present or future role as thinking devices represented the most common presentation of the technology in popular media. As with other high-technologies, the computer has often been publicly understood more in terms of future expectations than current applications. By the early 1950s, pioneering research and the writings by computer insiders began to have a significant, though typically indirect, impact on societal perceptions of computing. Their work fueled popular articles on robotics and giant brains and dystopian works of fiction, most of which highlighted the threat computers posed to labor, human agency, or overall security. In one dystopia, Vonnegut Jr's *Player Piano* (1952), society is controlled by computers and engineers. As the narrative unfolds, an increasing number of the engineers come to share the fate of the manual laborers; as EPICAC (a play on ENIAC) automates intellectual work, the engineers too become superfluous and unemployable. More recently, *2001: A Space Odyssey* (1972), *AI* (2001) and other popular films, as well as novels, have presented computers as sophisticated thinking machines, often concentrating on the loss of control and threats posed to human beings.

In 1984 the scope of the history of automation and thinking machines was extended by two important studies, an intellectual history of real and conceptual computing machines, and a social history of computer applications in industry. In *Turing's Man*, Media scholar David Bolter shifts emphasis from Turing's popular question of whether or not machines could think, toward another of his ideas with more direct societal significance: have human's begun to think more like machines? Bolter argues that people have increasingly come to perceive themselves as processors of the information or data of the physical world. On the other hand, historian Noble (1984), in *Forces of Production*, emphasizes some fundamental incompatibilities between humans and computing machines. He provides a compelling social analysis of the introduction of computer numerical control technology to machine tools on the shop floor, emphasizing the resistance of laborers, and more generally, how computing technology has been delimited by social constraints.

Rhetoric and Responsibility in Artificial Intelligence Research

In the early to mid-1950s, Herbert Simon (1916–2001) and Allen Newell (1927–92) began pioneering research at Carnegie Institute of Technology, influenced in part by cybernetics (a term coined by MIT's Norbert Wiener to represent a new interdisciplinary field focused on communication and control) and more fundamentally by the theoretical work of Turing and von Neumann. Their work shifted away from cybernetics' focus on biological mechanisms and toward a concentration on symbolic systems. In 1955 Simon, Newell, and Clifford Shaw completed a mathematical theorem-proving computer program, the Logic Theorist, later credited as the first artificial intelligence (AI) program. Interested in similar work, John McCarthy of MIT organized a now famous conference in 1956 at Dartmouth and coined the term "artificial intelligence" for this new field.

Periodically, artificial intelligence research came under attack from those fearing displacement by the technology. More frequently, however, criticism of AI came from those believing the discipline was not achieving enough. From the field's origin, it became second nature for AI researchers to inflate accomplishments. In part a product of their enthusiasm and excitement for the field, it was also a conscious effort to maintain support from the Defense Advanced Research Projects Agency (DARPA) and other funding sources. Similar to the early years of Project Whirlwind, the rhetoric of grant proposals and informal meetings became critical for justifying DoD funding for projects that at best had modest or indirect defense applications.

A fundamental irony of the criticism that AI was failing to deliver was that the attacks from academics, journalists, and individuals in government heightened in the 1970s and early 1980s – a time when the field was making its first significant practical advances. Stanford University computer scientist Edward Feigenbaum, a former student of Herbert Simon, broke new ground in working with chemists and physicians to produce what he termed "expert systems." These computer programs used a database and inference engine to draw meaning from data. Feigenbaum and his physical and biological scientist collaborators completed DENDRAL in the early 1970s. This first expert system had important applications in organic chemistry. Expert systems fueled considerable criticism, within segments of the AI and cognitive science communities, from those believing biological models to create learning machines, rather than large databases and logic-based rules, represented the most meaningful area of research. This conflict escalated a more than decade old debate in AI research between those favoring generality and those favoring small discrete systems.

Looking at the trajectory of AI research more broadly, if Turing's ideas of machines imitating and one day meeting and exceeding human intelligence had been displaced as the dominant measure or paradigm during the 1960s or 1970s by J.C. Licklider (1915–90) or Douglas Engelbart's focus on the goal of computers augmenting human learning and thought, the development of artificial intelligence research and the nature of its applications likely would have been far different.

Software: Invisibility and Crisis

From the patched cord programming of the ENIAC to the simultaneous condemnation and embrace of Microsoft's operating systems and applications over the past decade, software has had a paradoxical existence. The neglect of software by executives at early mainframe computer companies is only matched by the lack of attention historians have given to software history. With the former, this was often to the detriment of mainframe companies and their customers, as inadequate resources for programming services and software products were often a bottleneck, or to use Thomas P. Hughes' influential terminology, a "reverse salient" of computing systems. Historians and software practitioners have produced narrative histories of the development of a small number of programming languages, including FORTRAN, COBOL, and ALGOL, but little on other aspects of software. Meanwhile, the reports by computer trade journals of the existence of a "software crisis" in the 1960s and 1970s were so common that the failure of software to keep up with advances in hardware seemed to be a chronic condition rather than a periodic outbreak.

Paradoxically, software coexisted in an invisible state, both literally and figuratively, and in a state of crisis. The invisibility of software in the eyes of computer engineers and executives sometimes led to or fueled a near-term or future state of crisis. The ultimate example of this was the Y2K problem, where a multi-decade machine-centered ethos led to a focus on the cost of computer time and storage devices, shortening code to a two-digit date, and ultimately became the most expensive single technological fix in history.

In the early years of computing, software was almost an afterthought in developing new computing systems. Even in the early 1960s, as IBM initiated their monumental System 360 project to develop a series of compatible computers, insufficient attention was paid to programming its operating system (OS/360). The System/360 was late in delivery, used far more memory than anticipated, had major cost overruns, and worked poorly in its early iterations. A decade later, Brooks, the OS/360 project manager, wrote *The Mythical Man-Month* (1975), a provocative series of essays on how the team interacted and more generally how large-scale programming projects take on a far different nature than their smaller counterparts. The fundamental paradox was that software development was, and continues to be, a craft enterprise, highly dependent on the creativity of individual programmers, while major projects, such as the writing of operating systems, required hundreds, if not thousands, of human years of labor. Throughout the 1960s and beyond, countless challenges were faced in managing and scaling up craft practices of programming. Today, the recognition of the uniqueness of software development is better understood and addressed in the combination of small specialty firms, and large companies such as Microsoft that are built more on an academic model, where individuality and creativity are encouraged and development centers are referred to as campuses. Other important software managerial techniques have also been developed over the past several decades. These include a series of industrial models, such as those designed by Barry Boehm for TRW in the 1970s and 1980s.

There are a number of identifiable factors that likely contributed to the neglect of software and its history. These include the propensity of historians of computing, and the computer industry, to focus on the supply side of machines rather than the demand side of applications software. Additionally, with regard to history, highly technical participant accounts have not garnered much of an audience, and have tended to sour scholars in the humanities and social sciences to the field.

Another important reason is the propensity of both engineers and historians to privilege technologies with a physical presence. The term "software engineering" came about in the late 1960s, as programmers tried to elevate their professional status, and as most computer engineers took little interest in programming. Even though most historians of technology have long viewed their discipline as one of the study of techniques, ideas, and know-how, such perspectives have typically taken a backseat to artifact-centered analysis. Software's invisibility (except for the medium to store/run/display code) has contributed to its neglect.

A further factor relates to the gender of its practitioners. Compared to computer engineers, there were more opportunities for women in software than hardware. This was an outgrowth of both its secondary status and the significant number of women who were human computers in the 1940s.

Despite fundamental contributions by women in software, such as Grace Murray Hopper's (1906–92) leadership in developing FLOW-MATIC and COBOL, much of the work by women in both programming and computer engineering, efforts that overcame great obstacles of male-dominated subcultures in the military and in university and government laboratories, have been underplayed if not completely ignored by historians. In the industry, presentations of women and computing in the 1960s and 1970s rarely emphasized accomplishments and perseverance, but instead, took the form of sexist promotional images where attractive young women, often models, were displayed as sexual ornaments to computing machinery, or in absurd "interactive" roles.

There are a small number of exceptions of participant and historical accounts of woman and computing and software. Ullman's fascinating memoir (1997) of her life as a software engineer provides meaningful insights on gender, a sobering account of how software is designed, and more broadly, a humanistic perspective on information technology and culture.

In the historical literature, communications scholar Jennifer Light (1999) details the role of early women programmers of the ENIAC. Light demonstrates that this work was placed in low-occupational classifications, despite the advanced knowledge that was required. Her article is a significant contribution, but additional research on women and programming, and more broadly, the gendering of the development, marketing, and use of information technology is needed.

Also needed is greater scholarly attention to other aspects of the social history of software, the history of software applications, and the history of the software industry. Some recent scholarship, however, is beginning to tackle these fundamental areas. Campbell-Kelly's study of the software trade is an important contribution to understanding both the early software business and its evolution into one of America's leading industries. Another pathbreaking study is MacKenzie's *Mechanizing Proof* (2001). MacKenzie, a pioneer in theorizing and writing on the social construction of technology, advances the history of mathematical proofs, software, and computing, and the relationship of these developments to notions of risk. Meanwhile, Ensmenger (2001) extends our knowledge of the labor history of software in a significant new article on efforts to professionalize programming in the 1950s and 1960s.

Processing and Prospering on the Periphery: Minicomputing and Supercomputing

The 360 series of computers helped perpetuate IBM's domination of mainframe computing in the 1960s and beyond. In the late 1950s, however, following upon the refinement of transistor technology that had been invented a decade earlier at Bell Laboratories by William Shockley (1919–89), John Bardeen (1908–91), and Walter Brattain (1902–87), new opportunities emerged for other companies at both the high and low end of the computer market. The reliability and cost effectiveness of transistors by the late 1950s and early 1960s allowed this technology to replace cumbersome vacuum tubes and core memories to advance the productivity of mainframe machines. Historian Bassett's *To the Digital Age* (2002), provides a valuable technical and institutional analysis of the development of semiconductor technology.

In 1957, William Norris and a small number of other key engineers left Sperry Rand to form the Control Data Corporation (CDC) and build powerful mainframe computers for advanced scientific applications. Within several years, buoyed by Seymour Cray, a former Sperry Rand engineer, CDC came out with the 1,604, by far the fastest computer in the world. Cray and his team followed this up in 1963 with the 6,600, a computer fifty times faster than its predecessor and the first machine referred to as a "supercomputer." Within a year, more than a hundred 6,600s were sold (at $8 million apiece) to government, universities, and corporations, and CDC had established itself as a leader in an important segment of the computer industry.

Following a trend common in computing and other high-technology industries, Cray left CDC in 1972 to start a new company, Cray Research. This firm would soon build the CRAY-1, and along with its spin-offs would dominate supercomputing for more than a decade.

Like CDC, Digital Equipment Corporation (DEC) formed in 1957 and quickly established a leadership position in a new niche of the computer industry. DEC, however, was not an outgrowth of an existing computer firm, but instead, a product of the microelectronics industry on the East Coast. The firm's first computer, PDP-1, was based on the TX-0 that Kenneth Olsen, the firm's founder, had worked on at MIT's Lincoln Laboratory. By 1965, DEC developed the PDP-8, a machine that had great success in both the business and scientific markets. Like supercomputers, minicomputers typically did not steal market share from the traditional mainframe business, but instead, led to greater proliferation of computing technology.

Another successful minicomputer company from Massachusetts was Data General, a firm formed by Edson DeCastro, formerly at DEC. Data General soon developed two important minicomputers, the NOVA and the ECLIPSE. Kidder's Pulitzer Prize-winning account of the ECLIPSE development team, *The Soul of a New Machine* (1981), demonstrates the excitement, commitment, and culture of engineers at Data General, and remains one of the more compelling narratives of technological development in the twentieth century.

The microelectronics industry of the East Coast would not only spawn a number of regional minicomputer manufacturers, but would also give rise to the West Coast microelectronics industry. William Shockley left Bell Laboratories several years after co-inventing the transistor to found Shockley Semiconductor in Sunnyvale, California, a location he chose to be nearby his mother. The importance of this firm was not in what it achieved, but in the engineers Shockley brought with him. Eight of these engineers would found Fairchild Semiconductor in 1957, now generally hailed as the firm that gave birth to Silicon Valley as the world's leading region of information technology development. In retrospect, the significance of Shockley's decision to move to California cannot be underestimated. Meanwhile, a technology that supposedly has rendered place inconsequential, ironically, has continued to concentrate its industry in one of the world's most expensive regions.

In August 1958, Jack Kilby, an engineer at Texas Instruments built the first integrated circuit (IC). Robert Noyce (1927–90) of Fairchild had been working on similar research and, the following year, proposed using silicon instead of the germanium wafer that Kilby had utilized for his IC. Silicon-integrated circuits made their way into many minicomputers by the mid-1960s. In 1968, Noyce, Gordon Moore, and a few other Fairchild engineers left to form the Intel Corporation. Within 3 years, this firm would create a revolutionary integrated circuit with the architecture of a general-purpose stored program computer, the microprocessor.

The microprocessor was developed by engineers at Intel for Busicom, a Japanese maker of hand-held calculators. Intel had always focused its attention on memory (DRAM) rather than logic chips, but the firm recognized how a logic chip could enable software routines to be retrieved from memory chips, and hence, boost the demand for the latter. Ironically, Intel's desire to build demand for an existing line led them into an area that they had consciously avoided since the company formed. Noyce negotiated a critical agreement in which the financially struggling Busicom received low unit prices for the calculator logic chips in exchange for Intel receiving rights to market them to non-calculator-producing customers; in doing so, he fundamentally redirected the company's primary product. While minicomputers had made desktop standalone computers a reality, Intel's microchips succeeded in placing the size, performance, and cost of computer-processing in a realm that made personal computers a possibility.

The Delayed Revolution of Personal Computing

The personal computer (PC) era began just over a quarter century ago with the development and marketing of the Altair 8800, an unassembled $400 computer kit (with the Intel 8080 microprocessor) that was first advertised in the January 1975 issue of *Popular Electronics*. Without the widespread enthusiasm of an electronic hobbyist subculture, the history of the personal computer would have likely been very different. The hobbyists showed the viability for inexpensive personal computers, for which existing computer manufacturers initially doubted there would be any perceived uses or demand. During 1977 the Apple II, Commodore, Tandy TRS-80, and other personal computers hit the market.

The Apple II, the first personal computer to have color graphics, propelled Apple Computer to industry leadership in the PC field by the late 1970s. The firm had been formed on April Fool's Day of 1976 by longtime friends Stephen Wozniak and Steven Jobs, both of whom were college dropouts and members of the Homebrew Computer Club. Wozniak, a talented computer designer, who had worked for Hewlett-Packard, led the way in developing the Apple II in their first headquarters, Job's garage. Job's in turn, assisted with design work, and more importantly, excelled at promoting the company. The setting of the firm's early work led to the famous "two men in a garage" motif, a corporate creation story retold by many journalists and an inspiring tale for future start-ups in Silicon Valley and elsewhere.

Anthropologist Pfaffenberger (1988) has presented how the early developers of the personal computer constructed necessary "meaning-frameworks" for the machine as a revolutionary technology capable of empowering students, blue-collar workers, and the elderly. Not only did the personal computer generally fail to achieve these early aims, and in Pfaffenberger's estimation constituted no revolution at all, but the machine's other common moniker, home computer, was also a bit of an exaggeration. Ironically, while some electronic hobbyists purchased the early kits, and a number of personal computers were sold for home use, most of the machines were making their way into corporate offices. IBM's introduction of the PC in 1981 fully legitimized and lent momentum to personal computers as standard office equipment in the 1980s and beyond.

In 1984, the well-known two-minute Orwellian television advertisement introducing the "revolutionary" Apple Macintosh personal computer was aired during the Super

Bowl. Both of the Macintosh's key innovations, the computer mouse and graphical user interface, had actually been developed years earlier in a slightly different form at the Xerox Palo Alto Research Center (PARC). The photocopier specialist, however, failed to capitalize on these technologies. The Macintosh's graphic interface, which recreated a desktop, and the mouse transformed personal computers into user-friendly machines, and led to substantial success for Apple. Soon after the Macintosh introduction, Microsoft, the firm supplying the operating system for the IBM PC, developed Windows, using similar graphics to Apple. This led Compaq and many other computer makers to build IBM-compatible personal computers incorporating Windows.

Apple's rhetoric aside, the advent of the personal computer was less than revolutionary. A hacker subculture emerged, which defined itself by infiltrating computer systems and leaving identifiers to inform administrators of vulnerabilities. The ethos of this subculture, however, was inquisitive and often benevolent, far from the destructive and threatening meaning the term "hacker" has evolved to represent. In the 1980s, computers were commonly used for word processing in offices, schools, and other environments; computer games, which grew far more complex than Atari's legendary Pong game (first introduced in 1971) extended their popularity; and spreadsheets were a godsend to accountants and business forecasters. Overall, however, the technology fell short of broadly changing education, work, or leisure. For this, the personal computer would have to go through a fundamental transformation from an information-processing device to a pervasive communication tool, a development dependent on the advent of the ARPANET, Internet, and World Wide Web.

From ARPANET to Internet

Like many of the early digital computer projects, the development of the ARPANET was a government-funded enterprise carried out by the DoD, private contractors, and academic scientists. It differed, however, in the range of individuals it brought together and the scale of ongoing cooperation it required. It was also unique in the level in which many of the participants on the project, including DoD administrators, computer scientists, graduate students, Bolt Beranek & Newman (BBN), and other contractors, were both the developers and principal users of the new technology, and in both roles participated in defining its structure, meaning, and future possibilities. The ARPANET would not have been possible without this broad participation, yet the project would not have begun without a few visionary leaders.

In 1958, immediately on the heels of Sputnik, the DoD initiated the Advanced Research Projects Agency (ARPA). Recognizing the fundamental importance of command-and-control systems to national defense, ARPA funded a special branch to concentrate on information technology, the Information Processing Techniques Office (IPTO). In an important technical, institutional, and policy history, Norberg and O'Neill (1996) detailed the role of this office and its visionary leaders in transforming the field of computing by projects in networking (ARPANET/Internet), graphics, time-sharing, and AI through the mid-1980s. Complementing this study, Roland and Shiman (2002) have contributed to our understanding of DARPA funded computer research from the mid-1980s through the mid-1990s.

The ARPANET project began when the third Director of the IPTO, Robert Taylor, brought Lawrence Roberts on as the project's manager in 1967, and the following year allocated $2.2 million toward the effort. The goal of the project was to construct a network connecting computers at ARPA-funded computer facilities across the nation to facilitate the sharing of resources among scientists. The potential use of the technology as a military communication system was also a major factor. This latter consideration was the force behind the most fundamental new technology of the system, several years before the project began. Paul Baran of the RAND Corporation became interested in and pioneered "packet switching" technology, or breaking of digital data into standard size packets to be sent across a network independently and later reassembled. This technique enhanced the reliability and efficiency in transferring information, and met Baran's goal of a redundant network capable of "military survivability" in the event of a nuclear war.

In 1969 Bolt Beranek and Newman (BBN), a Massachusetts electrical engineering firm with deep connections to MIT, was selected by the IPTO for the primary ARPANET contract. Over the next several years, BBN and scientists at leading ARPA-funded academic laboratories would design the ARPANET, establishing a cast of now well-known characters including Lawrence Roberts, Paul Baran, BBN's Robert Kahn, MIT's Wesley Clark, and UCLA's Leonard Kleinrock and Vinton Cerf. Many other individuals however, also contributed, including numerous scientists and graduate students of the Network Working Group (NWG), who used the developing system to communicate, and wrote most of its software. Historian Abbate (1998) details the culture within the NWG, and how a system designed for sharing scientific resources and for defense-related communications evolved into a human-centered communication tool with email ironically becoming the system's most common application by the early to mid-1970s.

The Internet, a network of networks including the ARPANET, was the brainchild of two principal designers of the earlier network system. In 1973, Robert Kahn and Vinton Cerf began work on a network of networks, and the two soon designed the host protocol, TCP, critical for the Internet. Like earlier computing technology, the Internet was not commercially viable at its onset, depending heavily on government funding. A concurrent federal government sponsored $200 million network, NSFNET, was created in the 1980s to link supercomputers nationwide. During 1983, the original ARPANET was split into a dedicated military-only network, MILNET, with the civilian network retaining the original name. Abbate convincingly argues that debates over design of the ARPANET and subsequent networks within and between diverse groups at the DoD, universities, and private firms resulted in a connected community that would ultimately produce a broad-based computer network infrastructure of greater appeal than overt commercial efforts. This appeal and widespread use became possible following Tim Berners-Lee's development of a hypertext system, the World Wide Web, at CERN (Organisation européenne pour la recherche nucléaire) in

Geneva, Switzerland, in 1990, and several years later, the design and distribution of browsers by Netscape and Microsoft. Berners-Lee has since led the effort to keep the Internet "free."

Critical scholarship on the development and early use of the Internet by Norberg and O'Neill and Abbate has been joined by a growing Internet historiography that includes ambitious and provocative efforts to understand networked computing and its use within fundamental economic and social structures. Historians Chandler and Cortada (2000); and Cortada (2002) have placed the Internet and World Wide Web within the broader context of American's fascination with information, and the evolving technologies of the past two centuries that have helped deliver it. In contrast, the entire world is Castells' stage in his monumental trilogy, *The Information Age: Economy, Society and Culture* (1996, 1997, 1998). Castells examines broad transformations of social structure into what he refers to as the network society. He describes how the revolution of information technology, the critique of culture, and the restructuring of the economy into a global information capitalism have collectively redefined the relationship of production, power, and experience, and in the process, displaced industrial capitalism and statism.

Continuities of cultural responses to events and circumstances predating digital computing are also evident in a number of important studies of earlier technologies. These include Marvin's (1988) and Douglas' (1987) insightful accounts of the early years of electricity consumption and radio broadcasting, in *When Old Technologies Were New* and *Inventing American Broadcasting, 1899–1922*, respectively. Marvin details the many ironic ideas, applications and marketing associated with imagined and real electronic devices at the advent of the consumer electronics trade, while Douglas reflects on a technology of freedom and possibility, rapidly transformed and increasingly controlled by mass entertainment and a corporate media system. Marvin's tale, focusing on the fluid and unstructured understanding of the electric light, telephone, and other electronic technologies, brings to mind rich analogies to claims for and beliefs in the possibilities of artificial intelligence and virtual reality. On the other hand, Douglas' account gives glimpses previewing the evolving economic, legal, and cultural structuring of the Internet through juxtaposing media representations and behind-the-scene struggles in radio, including the significant role of electronic hobbyists. In the end, early experiences with radio seem to foreshadow the contemporary and future world being ushered in by the structuring of the Internet, a world, as Rifkin (2000) argues, where life is increasingly becoming a "paid-for experience."

Productivity Paradox

The pervasive commercialization of the Internet is undeniable. In this regard, the similarities with radio and television are abundantly clear. The Internet, was created long before it came into one of its primary roles as a medium of commerce, entertainment and leisure, just as the digital computer was developed significantly prior to one of its most common uses, video games, came into play. Though early and sustained backing for computer development came from the federal government for national defense agendas, computers were soon commonly perceived as labor-saving devices that in time would add greatly to productivity.

Productivity, however, is perhaps the greatest paradox in the history of computing. Economists, computer scientists, and other scholars have devoted considerable attention to this question, and most have concluded that computers, at best, have had a modest positive impact on productivity in the post-World War II era, a return lower than investment in bonds, as pointed out by Landauer in his provocative book, *The Trouble with Computers* (1995). Ironically, while some government-sponsored projects with narrowly defined scientific or defense goals, such as the ARPANET, have led to broad opportunities and efficiencies, areas of great promise and continuous and substantial federal research funding, like artificial intelligence, have had minimal societal payoffs. Meanwhile, shortsightedness on a basic question such as representing the date in coding, has led to massive expenditures on Y2K compliance, and should, at least temporarily, put the productivity question to rest. The Y2K situation also points to a greater need for research on computers as infrastructure (Edwards 1998). Ironically, a focus on the future of computer technology comfortably coexists with blindness toward it, a phenomenon all too evident with regard to social possibilities and the Internet.

The Sands of Time: Social Responsibility in a Silicon World

The cultural construct of time has significantly shaped and, to a considerable degree, been shaped by computing technologies. The ever-advancing speed of digital computers and communication possibilities brought by computer networking have further fueled the compression of time and space, a worldwide development that began much earlier with various transportation and communication technologies. In the sciences, computers have reduced computational and data processing time, perhaps rendering these machines the most important scientific instrument of the second half of the twentieth century. In the world of business, journalists have frequently referred to "Internet Time," where time is so compressed that business models of the past are considered obsolete. These developments in scientific computing, and real and perceived business practices, have been more pronounced in the United States, but evident throughout the industrialized world.

Without question, the personal computer and World Wide Web appear to be prototypical postmodern technologies. Hypertext can change the way text is organized and read (privileging readers over writers); operating systems and applications allow the easy juxtaposing of text and images, and to different degrees, conceal underlying structure in preference of surface-level presentation and interaction. Scholars and journalists, however, often go further in making postmodern connections, presenting the Internet as a device that can lend ambiguity to self, render distance and place obsolete, and redefine the meaning of community – as the world develops into a "global village." While cyberspace has many real-world analogues such as chat rooms, bulletin boards, and neighborhoods, it is seen as very different from its real-world counterparts in the anonymity, safety, opportunity, and speed offered. Recent research into gender and Internet use by Susan Herring and others challenge many of these notions, demonstrating the prevalence of gendered power relations on the Internet. Herring demonstrates that language and etiquette quickly identify the gender of Internet users and that women are often harassed, stalked, or silenced by men in MUDs (Multiple User Domains/Dungeons), chat rooms, and listservs (Herring 1999). Like real neighborhoods, many cyber neighborhoods become unsafe, a point accentuated by the well-publicized LambdaMOO "virtual rape," where the control of several female characters created by women and "living" in a MUD were seized and sexually attacked. Computer communication has also been the basis for real-world stalking and many other types of crimes, as well as a fundamental tool for surveillance by law enforcement and intelligence agencies.

Of the postmodern theorists, historian Poster (2001) offers the most compelling analysis. Drawing on the theories of Baudrillard, Foucault, Derrida and others, Poster illustrates how new media, and particularly the Internet, might mediate the transformation of cultural figures and open possibilities for greater creativity and new social forms. Though acknowledging the role of traditional categories of race, class, and gender in giving rise to new media, he argues that these technologies enable practices that move beyond earlier complexes of domination, offering new possibilities for individual creativity and democracy. Alternatively, the scholarship of Herring and others tends to challenge such interpretations, indicating ways in which traditional social structures still apply to not just the development, but also the *use* of computers and the Internet. Likewise, the common framing of the Digital Divide demonstrates the continued significance of examining traditional social groups and institutional contexts.

As the Internet becomes an increasingly ubiquitous source for information and communication, the Digital Divide, or disparity between those with access and those without, has become a popular topic for journalists, politicians, and others. Journalists typically present the Digital Divide as a race issue with an easy solution: provide greater Internet access to African Americans or other underprivileged minorities. Though access is an important first step, it often draws attention away from more fundamental issues of power and culture in our society. Web surfing quickly turns to suffering for those who lack basic knowledge of the medium. Use of the World Wide Web as an effective informational tool and resource for developing knowledge is fundamentally an education issue that depends on the goals of the user, research skills, and critical thinking to evaluate large amounts of unmediated information. Furthermore, the history of computing has shown that developers and users have generally understood little of the subsequent evolution and social impacts of new technologies. The Internet promises to be no different, and presenting it as a technological fix to social problems is naïve and diversionary.

Without losing its irony, it seems appropriate that when Danny Hillis, the developer of massive parallel architectures for supercomputers and one of the most gifted intellects in computing, was asked to lead a project to build a machine to symbolize technology he chose a mechanical clock. The Clock of the Long Now, designed to keep time for the next 10,000 years, is being built to symbolize the importance of long-term perspectives and combat the short-sided thinking and policy-making that is a by-product of operating and thinking on Internet Time. Hillis' Long Now, the activities of Computer Professionals for Social Responsibility, and the past work of individuals such as Control Data's William Norris show a commitment to community involvement and making wise use of this powerful technology. Such work also hints at the great diversity of perspectives in both the academic and business computing community – an idea that tends to be overlooked in the common presentation of this community as homogeneous, whether they are shown as computer nerds (Turkle 1984), MUD dwellers (Turkle 1995) or as a nudist late-night computer programmer who came to symbolize the individualism and eccentricity of all of Silicon Valley in a popular recent book by journalist Bronson (1999).

Conclusion

As the development, structuring, and uses of computers, software, and networking rapidly evolve, they continue to be perceived simultaneously as sources of fascination, hope, consternation, and fear. These technologies, born and bred on defense ideologies, have become fundamental instruments of science, communication, information, work, and entertainment, opening up vast new possibilities while paradoxically undermining security by their very ubiquity. Cyberterrorism is increasingly spoken of in the same breath as biological, chemical, and nuclear weapons as great threats to American security. Alongside the risks, however, are many new opportunities in healthcare, education, commerce, and leisure. The ability to define goals for information technology, determine appropriate means, and carry them out in legislative and judicial chambers, corporate boardrooms, and equally important, classrooms, laboratories, offices, homes, and other environments becomes increasingly challenging. On one level, highlighting the history of computers and the Internet as ironic and paradoxical may appear to obscure more than inform, as the relationships between inputs of research and policymaking often differ markedly from the output of technological products and their plethora of uses. Such a focus, however, tends to redirect the attention away from simple cause-and-effect explanatory schemes and autonomous technology trappings, and toward a more complex understanding that begins to recognize the centrality of culture in defining policy alternatives, the trajectory of projects, and the widespread consumption and varied uses of computers. While it provides no easy solutions, attentiveness to irony and paradox can sometimes redirect our focus to ask different types of questions on developments, circumstances, and issues in computing, and more broadly, of our technological past.

Acknowledgments

The author is grateful for comments on earlier drafts provided by William Aspray, James Cortada, Paul Edwards, Philip Frana, David Hochfelder, Karin Matchett, and Arthur Norberg and Carroll Pursell.

BIBLIOGRAPHY

Abbate, Janet. *Inventing the Internet* (Cambridge, MA: MIT Press, 1998).

Aspray, William. *John von Neumann and the Origins of Modern Computing* (Cambridge, MA: MIT Press, 1990).

Bassett, Ross. *To the Digital Age: Research Labs, Start-Up Companies, and the Rise of Mos Technology* (Baltimore, MD: Johns Hopkins University Press, 2002).

Berkeley, Edmund. *Giant Brains or Machines That Think* (New York: Wiley, 1949).

Bolter, David. *Turing's Man: Western Culture in the Computer Age* (Chapel Hill, NC: University of North Carolina Press, 1984).

Bronson, Po. *The Nudist on the Late Shift* (New York: Random House, 1999).

Brooks, Frederick P., Jr. *The Mythical Man-Month: Essays on Software Engineering* (Reading, MA: Addison-Wesley Publishing Company, 1975).

Burks, Arthur W. and Alice R. Burks. "The ENIAC: first general-purpose electronic computer," *Annals of the History of Computing* 3:4 (October 1981): 310–99.

Bush, Vannevar. "As we may think," *The Atlantic Monthly* (July 1945).

Campbell-Kelly, Martin. *From Airline Reservations to Sonic the Hedgehog: A History of the Software Industry* (Cambridge, MA: MIT Press, 2003).

Campbell-Kelly, Martin and William Aspray. *Computer: A History of the Information Machine* (New York: Basic Books, 1996).

Castells, Manuel. *The Rise of the Network Society* (Oxford: Blackwell Publishers, 1996).

Castells, Manuel. *The Power of Identity* (Oxford: Blackwell Publishers, 1997).

Castells, Manuel. *End of the Millennium* (Oxford: Blackwell Publishers, 1998).

Ceruzzi, Paul. *A History of Modern Computing* (Cambridge, MA: MIT Press, 1998).

Chandler, Alfred D., Jr and James W. Cortada, eds. *A Nation Transformed by Information: How Information has Shaped the United States from Colonial Times to the Present* (Oxford: Oxford University Press, 2000).

Cortada, James W. *Before the Computer: IBM, NCR, Burroughs, and Remington Rand and the Industry They Created, 1865–1956* (Princeton, NJ: Princeton University Press, 1993).

Cortada, James W. *Making the Information Society: Experiences, Consequences, and Possibilities* (Upper Saddle River, NJ: Prentice-Hall, 2002).

Cowan, Ruth Schwartz. *More Work For Mother: The Ironies of Household Technology from the Open Hearth to the Microwave* (New York: Basic Books, 1984).

Douglas, Susan J. *Inventing American Broadcasting, 1899–1922* (Baltimore, MD: Johns Hopkins University Press, 1987).

Edwards, Paul. *The Closed World: Computers and the Politics of Discourse in Cold War America* (Cambridge, MA: MIT Press, 1996).

Edwards, Paul. "Y2K: Millennial reflections on computers as infrastructure." *History & Technology* 15 (1998): 7–29.

Ensmenger, Nathan. "The 'question of professionalism' in the computer fields," *IEEE Annals of the History of Computing* 23:4 (October–December 2001).

Flamm, Kenneth. *Targeting the Computer: Government Support and International Competition* (Washington, DC: Brookings Institution, 1987).

Flamm, Kenneth. *Creating the Computer: Government, Industry, and High Technology* (Washington, DC: Brookings Institution, 1988).

Goldstine, Herman H. *The Computer From Pascal to von Neumann* (Princeton, NJ: Princeton University Press, 1972).

Herring, Susan. "The rhetorical dynamics of gender harassment on-line." *The Information Society* 15:3 (1999): 151–67.

Kidder, Tracy. *The Soul of a New Machine* (New York: Avon Books, 1981).

Landauer, Thomas K. *The Trouble With Computers: Usefulness, Usability, and Productivity* (Cambridge, MA: MIT Press, 1995).

Light, Jennifer. "When computers were women." *Technology and Culture* 40:3 (July 1999): 455–83.

Lubar, Steven. "'Do not fold, spindle or mutilate': a cultural history of the punch card," *Journal of American Culture* 15:4 (Winter 1992): 43–55.

MacKenzie, Donald. *Mechanizing Proof* (Cambridge, MA: MIT Press, 2001).

Marvin, Carolyn. *When Old Technologies Were New: Thinking About Electronic Communication in the Late Nineteenth Century* (New York: Oxford University Press, 1988).

Noble, David F. *Forces of Production: A Social History of Automation* (New York: Oxford University Press, 1984).

Norberg, Arthur L. "New engineering companies and the evolution of the United States computer industry," *Business and Economic History* 22, Second series (Winter 1993): 181–93

Norberg, Arthur L. and Judy O'Neill. *Transforming Computer Technology: Information Processing for the Pentagon, 1962–1986* (Baltimore, MD: Johns Hopkins University Press, 1996).

Pfaffenberger, Bryan. "The social meaning of the personal computer: or, why the personal computer revolution was no revolution," *Anthropological Quarterly* 61:1 (January 1988): 39–47.

Poster, Mark. *What's the Matter With the Internet?* (Minneapolis, MN: University of Minnesota Press, 2001).

Pugh, Emerson. *Building IBM* (Cambridge, MA: MIT Press, 1995).

Redmond, Kent C. and Thomas M. Smith. *From Whirlwind to MITRE: The R&D Story of the SAGE Air Defense Computer* (Cambridge, MA: MIT Press, 2000).

Rifkin, Jeremy. *The Age of Access: The New Culture of Hypercapitalism Where All of Life is a Paid-For Experience* (New York: Penguin Putnam Inc., 2000).

Roland, Alex and Philip Shiman. *Strategic Computing: DARPA and the Quest for Machine Intelligence, 1983–1993* (Cambridge, MA: MIT Press, 2002).

Stern, Nancy. *From ENIAC to UNIVAC: An Appraisal of Eckert-Mauchly Computers* (Bedford, MA: Digital Press, 1981).

Turing, Alan M. "Computing machinery and intelligence." *Mind* 59 (1950): 433–60.

Turkle, Sherry. *The Second Self: Computers and the Human Spirit* (New York: Simon & Schuster, Inc., 1984).

Turkle, Sherry. *Life on the Screen: Identity in the Age of the Internet* (New York: Simon & Schuster, 1995).

Ullman, Ellen. *Close to the Machine: Technophilia and Its Discontents* (San Francisco: City Lights, 1997).

Usselman, Steven W. "IBM and its imitators," *Business and Economic History* 22:2 (Winter 1993): 1–35.

Vonnegut, Kurt. *Player Piano* (New York: Dell Publishing Company, 1952).

Wiener, Norbert. *Cybernetics or Control and Communication in the Animal and the Machine* (New York: Wiley, 1948).

PART V

PRODUCING AND READING
TECHNOLOGICAL CULTURE

CHAPTER NINETEEN

The Profession of Engineering in America

BRUCE SINCLAIR

Engineers seem such easy targets for cartoon humor. Scott Adams has made a living with his comic strip "Dilbert," by poking fun at socially inept, obtuse people, working in morally bankrupt jobs for dim-witted managers. And the fact that Adams has drawn on his own corporate work experience (as well as that of hundreds of other technical people who regularly e-mail him with real-life tales from the firms where they work) gives his material both authenticity and a wickedly funny bite.

We could dismiss this kind of comedy as an analytical category – once past "Dilbert," the multiple web pages devoted to jokes about engineers are, after all, pretty thin stuff – were it not for the fact that Americans have for so long thought of engineers and their abilities in such positive terms. For years, we celebrated technical accomplishment and the people responsible for it. We defined ourselves in terms of technical prowess. And not only did we think a talent for inventiveness the best emblem of our own culture, that conviction became a hallmark of our relations with other countries. Linked to democratic ideology, it served as one of the fundamentals of our foreign policy; if we helped less-advantaged people improve their technologies, and thus their economies, representative government would surely follow. The whole idea of Truman's Point IV program of technical assistance was captured by the uplifting image of a big, friendly American engineer working with local people in some distant, dusty part of the world to improve their agricultural production, water supply, or sanitary sewage facilities. And those in charge of the program explicitly meant him simultaneously to personify our technical competence, the virtues of our political system, and a generous national spirit. So, when did engineers become the stuff of cartoons? Or, to put it the other way around, when did they stop being our champions? Let's begin to answer that question by talking about a time when they clearly were.

Engaged in 1912 to build the elaborate, far-flung system that would bring water from the Sierra Nevada mountains down to San Francisco, City Engineer Michael Maurice O'Shaughnessy (1864–1934) soon became the most powerful public figure in the entire Bay Area, and one of the nation's best known civil engineers. A popular speaker before civic groups of all sorts, a man who wrote extensively for local papers as well as technical publications, and an imposing person widely and affectionately hailed as "The Chief," O'Shaughnessy exercised absolute command over his considerable empire, which, besides the Sierra water system, included the creation of a new

municipally owned street railway network, difficult tunnel construction projects to
open up areas of the city for development, sewage facilities, street paving and lighting,
parks, and indeed, everything else that remained to be done by way of rebuilding the
city in the years after the disastrous earthquake and fire of 1906.

For the new water supply, in particular, San Francisco's popular reform mayor
openly promised O'Shaughnessy absolute power over the project, free of any political
influence whatever. He would make all the contracts, hire the entire workforce,
design each structure, oversee its building, manage every cent of the money, and do
all that within a city government that had long been notorious for corrupt politics.
So he personified, simultaneously, the Progressive Era ideal of expertise in the service
of good government, and the engineering profession's dream of authoritative,
technocratic control over important public business.

It also tells us something about the man himself that at home in the evenings of
the first winter he was on the job, he read *The Winning of Barbara Worth*, a popular
romantic novel about an engineer who successfully brings water to the California
desert – a book soon to be a major motion picture, starring Ronald Coleman and the
lovely Vilma Banky, with Gary Cooper in a bit part. Those were the days when
engineers were the vigorous heroes of our popular culture. Over 50 feature films with
engineers as the male lead came out in the 1920s, and besides *The Winning of
Barbara Worth* (1911), best-selling novels like Zane Grey's *The U.P. Trail* (1918)
and John Fox's *Trail of the Lonesome Pine* (1908), also made into a movie (three
times, in fact), established an image of the ideal American male. Here's another piece
of fiction, a story called "A Girl of the Engineers," that appeared in the *Atlantic
Monthly* of 1906, in which the heroine describes the characteristics of such a person:

> they have been trained to stand alone, to talk little, never to
> complain, to bear dullness and monotony, some of them are
> dull and monotonous themselves. But they aren't petty; and
> in every one of them there is a strange need that drives them
> out into the deserts, a craving for movement and freedom and
> fresh new air that nothing can kill . . . It's what keeps them young;
> it's what makes them strong and exciting and different; it's
> What makes their gentleness so wonderfully gentle; it's what
> makes us love them.

We have a neat kind of symbiosis going on here. The authors of these enormously popular books tell us they found their inspiration in the actual triumphs of American engineers as they laid railroads across the continent, pulled useful materials up from the
earth, built dams in faraway places, and watered the deserts into flower. So they
described an idealized American type: rugged men of action who wore their knowledge
lightly, even as they brought it to bear on important work, builders, men of vision, too,
whose ideas and dedication made life better for others. And then the real engineers, the
models for those romantic novels, found such stories irresistible bedtime reading.

Historians like to argue that technologies only emerge from an inter-related array
of economic, political, and social circumstances. O'Shaughnessy's example strongly

suggests that the practitioners of technology are themselves the consequence of a similar sort of congruence. The next question we need to ask, then, is how did we get that apparently perfect match between popular fiction and real people? How did engineering come to be so attractive an occupation, and its work so closely identified with the nation's agenda?

These inquiries gain in importance when we reflect that at the country's beginning there was not anything even remotely like an engineering profession. There were no armies with military engineers, no patronage for the kinds of architect/engineers that graced French and Italian courts, nor any possibility for training up young men like them. Indeed, it was inevitable that the first European colonists in North America failed in their efforts to establish complex techniques and practices as they had known them in the old country. Iron-working on a European scale, whether in New France's Quebec or New England's Massachusetts, was never successfully transplanted. Neither was glass manufacture in Virginia, or any of the other seventeenth-century attempts to replicate in frontier settings the current levels of European technologies – with their sophisticated craft organizations, established markets, and financial resources. That is why emigre watchmakers went broke in the new world, and apprenticeship systems fell apart.

We can trace out the history that lies between these opposite conditions – the absence of an engineering profession and one in full throat – in two different though related ways. The first is through the literature that surrounds the practice of engineering in America, beginning in the late eighteenth century, and the second is through the historiography of efforts to create engineering's institutions of technical education and professional organization. In the first case, as time and circumstances required, people took on a few of the tasks that would subsequently be included within the engineer's brief. Millwrights channeled water to power grist- and saw-mills. Farmers used the tools and skills familiar to them from land clearing and barn construction to make simple bridges and rough roads. Men of some ambition, George Washington is only the best known example, learned surveying as an adjunct to land management. And in a country where the commodification of land assumed increasing importance, the determination of metes and bounds, the horizontal dimensions of property, became a matter of considerable interest. But by itself that knowledge did not an engineer make, or define a profession, and one instance of the difference became obvious when the design and construction of canals called for the ability to measure vertical distances accurately. In his book, *From Know-How to Nowhere*, Morison (1974) neatly captures the dilemma that confronted the projectors of the Middlesex Canal in late eighteenth-century Massachusetts when they realized none of them knew enough to run levels, design lock chambers, or most basically, just to keep the canal from leaking its water out through the bottom and sides. In their ignorance, they were forced to seek the advice of a traveling British engineer, William Weston, who like Benjamin Latrobe and other emigres, advised on nascent projects, took pupils into their offices in a kind of engineering apprenticeship, and helped Americans realize the need for expertise in complex ventures. It is at this juncture that we can begin to see the convergence of factors that would create an engineering profession in the US.

As in so many other ways, the War for Independence proved crucial. It brought European military engineers into Washington's army, and they created the impetus for a military academy, at West Point, New York, reorganized after 1816, along the lines of France's state-supported *Ecole Polytechnique*, to give engineering the highest prestige within the curriculum. That kind of training emphasized an education based on scientific theory, expressed in mathematical terms, the graduates of which – gentlemen by definition – would be entitled to social standing. And an engineering corps, given life by public funds, and authority for employment on civil projects by the General Survey Act of 1824, was obviously suited to work of national import – particularly in the creation of transportation systems. What remained to be determined was if this European model would serve private sector enterprise as well as projects of the state, and whether its graduates would be sufficient in number and flexible enough in outlook to meet the need for advanced technical knowledge employed to economic advantage.

The answer to that question of supply was definitely not, as Americans got caught up in a great enthusiasm for canals after the War of 1812, but before West Point had graduated many engineers. British canal building had already revealed the profitability of this transportation form, which was equally well-suited to the heavily indented Atlantic coastline of the US, and to the country's extensive web of rivers and lakes. The narrow, relatively flat strip of land separating the Delaware and Chesapeake bays where they almost come together at their northern ends, for example, seemed so obvious a place for a canal that it was imagined in the 1660s and surveyed in the 1760s. In other locations like that, where man-made waterways shortened shipping routes, overcame the difficulties of elevation, and greatly reduced the cost of transporting bulk goods, canals seemed obvious solutions to the problem of moving people and freight. And just as imperative as the sale of stock to fund such enterprises, their promoters rushed to secure expertise.

So compelling was that need, Calhoun argues in his original and important study *The American Civil Engineer: Origins and Conflict* (1960), that in scarcely a generation the canal and railroad building activities of the early nineteenth century had created a profession. There are interesting differences between the engineers who worked on early canal projects and those who worked on railroads. A very large number of the former, including some of the most prominent in their field, actually learned their profession right on the ground, working first as axe-men, in the case of John Jervis (1795–1885), or as surveyors, such as Benjamin Wright (1770–1842). And then, on large-scale engineering projects like the Erie Canal, they progressed up through the ranks of assistant and division engineers – acquiring practical knowledge at each step, often supplementing it with their own reading and observation. Their experience as engineers on the Erie led them afterwards to positions of authority in other engineering projects, and in numbers so large as to constitute a substantial majority of the profession at work in 1837. Conversely, academically educated engineers, especially from West Point, dominated early railroad construction, since the calculation of locomotive power requirements and the translation of that data to grade and curve characteristics went beyond the knowledge a bright young fellow might pick up by observation.

But while large organizations could give structure to an occupation, and provide training and identity to individuals within it, the relationship of engineers to boards of directors or commissioners – to management in other words – often proved problematic. Calhoun nicely outlines the conflicts inherent in the relation of technical expertise to financial authority. Often enough, the projectors of an improvement in transportation knew something in a general sense about the problems that required solution, but seldom did they know enough to sort out the particulars – how to design a lock chamber, with its associated apparatus for flooding and emptying the water in it, or how best to ballast the roadbed of a railway line. These tasks clearly belonged to the domain of the engineer, whose judgment was likewise sought to resolve disputes about the route of a transportation project, or to estimate the economic advantages of different forms of transportation. Engineering estimates of cost were also a form of knowledge usually beyond that possessed by businessmen, though they were crucial to a project's economic success and thus important in connecting technical expertise to considerations of finance.

The proprietors of transportation enterprises, however, usually reckoned that money management was their business, and they sought to limit engineers to issues of technical judgement, thus relegating them to a subordinate position, a bit like that of the contractor. West Point graduates, with a taste for both abstraction and authority, tended not to work well under those conditions. The fact that engineers sometimes also acted as contractors only complicated matters further. And confusion ran the other way, too. Sometimes engineers served as commissioners or directors, and frequently, once an improvement was completed, managed the enterprise. So while the engineer was specialized out of executive functions, as Calhoun says, circumstances often blurred the line between experts and managers.

It took some trial and error experimentation over time to sort out which tasks properly belonged to one group and which to the other. And it proved harder to do that in small-scale projects than in larger enterprises. But common to all of them, even in the early days of the engineering profession, the matter of control proved the rock upon which broad professional claims and aspirations most often foundered. Both at an instinctual level and as a basis for effective management, engineers looking to define themselves as independent professionals sought control over money as well as over design. As a practical matter, they asked, how could they certify the correctness of construction without the ability to withhold payments to contractors? Behind that apparently disingenuous question lay vital nuances of status and larger visions of authority.

It may seem wrong-headed to read backwards from the engineering population of the early twentieth-century characteristics that seem applicable to Calhoun's engineers of the early nineteenth century, but his descriptions of their failures and successes have a very familiar ring. It is clear, for example, that control is a central issue for engineers across the decades. They want to control the materials they work with and use, they want to control the conditions in which these materials are worked, and they also want to control the people who work the materials. This urge for jurisdiction has a lot to do with practice where, most of all, engineers value predictability – the certainty that materials and structures will function as designed. But throughout the nineteenth century, as engineers talked about their profession, it is clear that the aim to master their circumstances was also entangled with concerns about income and social position. At a personal level, control of data and of its correctness is crucial to reputation, but it often comes to seem to engineers that control over knowledge is the proper warrant for larger authority. Out of both these impulses, Calhoun's engineers wanted control over the labor force, over contractors, and the design process – as well as over the conception and management of the project itself. In those respects, they seem little different than the mechanical engineers of a century later who so earnestly believed they should command all the levers of power in modern industrial society.

Indeed, what Calhoun does for our understanding of engineers and engineering in America is to demonstrate how early the profession took on many of the characteristics it would have for another 150 years. The main issues got defined almost from the very beginning. Take the question of status, for instance, so allied to that of control – which would bedevil engineers for decades to come. Calhoun correctly identifies the early emergence of bureaucratic engineering structures, and the importance of organizational behavior. But despite the almost precocious realization that certain forms of organizational behavior might directly be related to personal success, the twin torments of professional independence and status anxiety persisted for 100 years and more, particularly in hard times. On any number of occasions, engineers rehearsed the old joke about doctors who buried their mistakes, and lawyers who argued cases they did not believe in, in order to claim for their profession that it was the only one true to itself. What this piece of humor reveals is that they felt themselves underappreciated, that they were in denial about the status differences conveyed by postgraduate education, and that while they might wish for the character of scientists, they worked in the culture of business. The rapid growth in the population of engineers during the period from 1880 to 1930, an increase of 3,000 percent, only made the tensions between professionalism and capital more explicit. Finally, the early history of engineering revealed another truth about its practice that would become increasingly apparent in time, and that was the relation of one's career to the scale of an engineering project. The fact that there may have been cranky, scratchy personalities in the first generation of American engineers, Calhoun calls them "individualists," shouldn't mask the reality that engineers have always depended on large-scale, corporate forms of support and allegiance. That is true whether thinking of Leonardo da Vinci or John Smeaton, whether the French engineers of the Canal du Midi, the army engineers of any nation from the fourteenth century onwards, and everyone whoever worked for Lockheed Martin. It is in the very nature of their work; they need patronage of one form or another, and scale is as essential to personal reputation as it is to public perception of the social value of engineering.

Despite whatever concerns early engineers may have had about professional ideals, and the relation of their work to them, there was never any doubt in the public mind about the grandeur of these enterprises. Or about their implications for the nation.

We won't discover that truth in the literature of engineering practice, but we will in the cultural productions of the era. The hopes Americans held out for systems of transportation and communication are clearly represented and intelligently analyzed in *The Railroad in American Art: Representations of Technological Change*, which Danly and Marx (1988) edited. Paintings as well as widely popular Currier & Ives prints celebrated the central role of railroads and the telegraph in what was depicted as America's destiny – the settlement of the continent, from coast to coast. In these images, the railroad proclaimed America's power as well as its beneficent intentions. Wilderness gave way to a pastoral vision that linked unleashed individual energies and a continent of untapped resources in an apparently harmonious union of nature and technology. And, in a different form of cultural expression, the prophetic character of these paintings and prints was reiterated in the language embedded in proposals for new kinds of higher education.

If we look at the historiography surrounding efforts to establish technical education in the US, we get an even clearer picture of the ways in which Americans framed their ideas about technical progress in terms of democratic reform and national purpose. Even before there were novels, movies, and actors to epitomize those stereotypical heroes of the early twentieth century, engineering had already been identified as the best kind of life for an American man. That's how Charles W. Eliot (1834–1926), then a faculty member at the newly created Massachusetts Institute of Technology described it, in an extended article he wrote for the *Atlantic Monthly* in 1869, called "The New Education." Subsequently Harvard's president, where his long tenure made him the country's most widely known educator, Eliot made two important claims in his article. First, he identified a different kind of occupational challenge. The dramatic economic developments of the previous 25 years, in manufacturing industry, in transportation, and in natural resource exploitation, had created an acute demand for men trained to manage these new enterprises. Calling that kind of work "the active life," Eliot meant not only to distinguish it from law, medicine, or theology, but to connect it to the robust spirit of the country itself. And, making his second point, he argued the importance of a correspondingly different kind of education for such occupations, one based on particularly American needs and experiences. It would be a university curriculum, but rather than the classics, one that concentrated on science, mathematics, engineering, and the analytic reasoning that went with those subjects – with all that instruction directed to the purposeful end of the country's material progress and its economic independence.

This habit of linking new occupations and forms of education to a larger national agenda actually began with the nineteenth century itself, and dominated the language surrounding most early experiments in technical education. All those urban mechanics' institutes of the 1820s and 1830s, for instance, sprang out of a reform movement that aimed to democratize educational opportunity and at the same time to encourage inventiveness and technological progress – the combination of which, their founders claimed, would realize the aspirations of the Declaration of Independence and the Bill of Rights. As it happened, these kinds of voluntary organizations, which pinned their hopes on elevating the working classes through evening lectures in "useful knowledge," were overtaken by events. Canal construction in the 1820s, and railroads in the decades that immediately followed – not to speak of the simultaneous emergence of large-scale textile manufacturing and machine-building – required more systematically acquired forms of expertise, and that problem got solved in two different ways.

Exemplifying one line of action, technical schools like Rensselaer Polytechnic Institute, founded at the same time and amidst rhetorical claims much like those of the mechanic institutes, evolved regular curricula in engineering. And by the 1840s a welter of institutions had emerged to provide the kind of training needed by those who would be managers in railroads, mines, mills, and manufacturing industry. Simultaneously, and as part of the same process, ambitious members of the middle class, who saw advantage in those rapid developments in manufacturing and the transportation industries, rose up to claim the new technical occupations upon which those economic activities depended.

We can see in the attempts to create new educational forms how the mechanics' institutes, with their hopes to raise working men into positions of authority and responsibility by programs of self-help, got left behind. Two examples illuminate the matter. In 1847, the same year the University of Pennsylvania established a School of Arts to teach the practical applications of science, and William Barton Rogers published his plan for what later became the Massachusetts Institute of Technology, the cotton textile magnate Abbott Lawrence urged upon Harvard University the importance of engineering education. He knew of promising young men who had been forced to go to Europe for their technical training, and argued that the full development of the country's mental resources was crucial to its future. So, with a large gift of money, he proposed that Harvard establish a school for those "who intend to enter upon an active life as engineers or chemists or, in general, as men of science applying their attainments to practical purposes." Here again, we see the connection drawn between adequate training for engineers and national prosperity, and also the argument that a democracy should present a complete spectrum of educational opportunities for its citizens. But in this case the citizens were those who could already afford to send their sons to university. Those were also just the people Charles W. Eliot had in mind when he wrote his piece on "The New Education," which explicitly addressed the concerns of the parent who imagined an "active life" for his boy, and in a world of higher education dominated by traditional subject matter, looked for the training appropriate to such a career. With Lawrence's money, Harvard said it would provide it, and the successful creation of university-based engineering education in the United States forever afterwards meant that technical training at any lower level in the system would be vocational in character.

Alfred Kennedy's efforts, in the early 1850s, to establish a technical school in Philadelphia along the lines of a European polytechnic institute, tell us a bit more about the social outcomes expected of the new education. The country wanted a place where students would be instructed "professionally," a term Kennedy used to emphasize the point that technical education could exist on the same intellectual plane as traditional collegiate studies. Furthermore, this different kind of school would create a new social stratum of "Professional Miners, Engineers, and Directors of farms and factories," that had not previously existed "as a class in this country" (Sinclair 1974). In the history of the engineering profession in America, occupation, education, and social standing were thus entangled from the very beginning, as engineering educators struggled to find a place under the sun for both their schools and their graduates.

We should notice a few things about the rise of the Polytechnics. One is that they reflected a new reality in the spectrum of technological activity, to wit, the emerging sub-specialties of mechanical, chemical, and mining engineering. A second point worth mention is that they oriented their instruction to fit graduates rather more for places in manufacturing and industrial organizations than for lives as independent consultants. And from their first appearance, polytechnics intended to offer what they described as a complete education, one unconnected to the curricula of established universities, and to anything like what would today be called non-technical electives. Thus, MIT's founders, particularly in their several nineteenth-century efforts to prevent the absorption of their school by Harvard, argued the necessity of a distinctly professional education for engineers, and sharply differentiated both its form and function from that of the university. Robert Thurston (1836–1902), long-time head of Cornell's Sibley College of Engineering and the first president of the American Society of Mechanical Engineers, subsequently became the most eloquent spokesman for that point of view.

As a result of a lengthy and comprehensive study of American engineering education that he made in1893, Thurston argued strongly that like medicine and law, engineering called for a separate and specialized education of its own. He did not mean that engineers should be the product of graduate education (Harvard tried that once, to its regret), and that weakened his proposal a little since the parallel to those other professions suggested it. But he did imagine a hierarchy of technical education that was breathtaking in its reach. It would begin with elementary level instruction in which spelling, reading and writing were to be taught using only language "peculiar to the trades, and methods of operation, and the technics of the industrial arts." Intermediate schools would provide vocational training, and the best students would then advance to a polytechnic university for "thoroughly scientific training and education." Besides turning out future engineers, Thurston intended his polytechnic to supply the country with gifted teachers and researchers as well as with talented administrators (Sinclair 1972). It would, in fact, serve as a national center of industrial research, coordinate the country's industrial policy, and advise the highest levels of government.

Like the emerald city of Oz, this elaborate vision of technical education and of the exalted place of engineers, fell wildly short of reality, whether with regard to trends in US higher education, or those of society's ordering. Land-grant universities grew substantially in number and size in the late nineteenth century, successfully integrating technical education into the university curriculum. By the beginning of the twentieth century they, and not the country's scattering of polytechnics, graduated the vast majority of engineers into the profession. But Thurston's ideas spoke to important shifts in his own work, the education of mechanical engineers, to the significance corporate industry had assumed by that time, and to the claims of Thorstein Veblen (1857–1929) and others that engineers should play a commanding role in modern industrial society.

But because educational change lagged behind the actual demands of the job market, most engineers in the first half of the nineteenth century learned their profession on the job, and that is the second way the problem of technical expertise got solved. Even though civil engineering existed as a distinct occupation by the late eighteenth century, and comprised a body of knowledge identifiable enough for inclusion in programs of academic education, it was not until the late nineteenth century that the number of formally educated engineers exceeded those trained on the job. Even more explicitly, mechanical engineering grew directly out of nineteenth-century craft practice and industrial work. Calvert (1967), in his *The Mechanical Engineer in America, 1830–1910*, described the evolution of this branch of the field from a shop culture dominated by on-the-job training, personal relationships, and proprietary interest, to a school culture characterized by formal education, upward mobility, and corporate employment. Thurston was not only instrumental in that transition, he also articulated a whole new set of possibilities that would flow from it, the most important of which was a human resources environment that continuously advanced the most capable to positions of responsibility and authority.

The engineering profession came to full maturity by the turn of the twentieth century. Formal degree programs in all branches of the field were well established at colleges and universities throughout the country, and prosperous New York-based national societies advanced the interests of practicing engineers across the entire range of specialization. Besides a swelling sense of their own value and importance, these technical people had become firmly persuaded that engineering should be a meritocracy and that talent ought to be rewarded. In the early years of the new century it was also possible to believe, along with the socialist and long-time G.E. research scientist Charles Steinmetz for one, that the corporation was an ideal form for the organization of human abilities into highly effective systems of production. From these propositions, it was a simple step to the conviction that efficiency rather than profit should be the guiding principle of industrial management, and that those who best understood how to maximize productivity ought to be running things. Beliefs like these harmonized comfortably with the spirit and convictions of Progressive era reformers, in a time that might well be described as the golden age of engineering professionalism. This conjunction of large-scale corporate industry, political ideology, and engineering self-awareness is also the period that has received most notice from historians, so it deserves our particular attention.

Progressivism, a middle-class urban reform movement, placed considerable emphasis on expertise as an antidote to the political corruption so rife in America's cities, since machine politics fed mostly off dishonesty in the contracting and management of public services like transportation, street paving, sewer construction, and the provision of utilities. Happily for engineers, this new attention to their value in matters of public importance came just at the time when the profession, its numbers substantially enlarged by a flood of graduates from recently developed programs of engineering education, needed more job opportunities. Connecting employment to reform made programs of civic improvement especially appealing. As a consequence, engineers in cities like Boston, St Louis, Philadelphia, and especially Cleveland, developed an array of committees in their local societies to fight corruption, to bring order to municipal services, and to provide objective technical judgment in contested issues. Some of these people went on to become even more active politically, pushing the national engineering societies toward issues of social responsibility, and creating alternative organizations when that effort failed. This movement also gave city engineers new stature and authority, and San Francisco's Michael O'Shaughnessy was only one example of that momentum.

"Progressivism" was allied to another movement of importance to engineers, and that was "Conservation." We capitalize these words because they represent an ideology, as well as a cast of characters, and a set of policies. The seemingly wanton destruction of America's forests, in the interest of quick profit and without regard for environmental consequences, called the Conservation Movement into existence. But the alternative that emerged was not preservation. Instead, in a response that matched Progressive ideas about solving problems through the application of expertise, people like Gifford Pinchot (1865–1946), came into prominence by arguing for the efficient management of the nation's natural resources. In its fully developed form, Conservation thought identified efficiency with maximization, with multiple-use strategies for resource exploitation. A supply of water, for instance, was most perfectly employed when it simultaneously created electric energy, watered the farmer's fields, served the drinking, cooking, and washing needs of city dwellers, met the requirements of industry, and incorporated recreation facilities into reservoirs constructed at sites of great natural beauty.

Just as urban reform gave purpose and job possibilities to engineers, so did this national campaign to protect forests against reckless destruction, to develop natural resources in ways that enhanced their value. And because of its support by Theodore Roosevelt, with his widely publicized enthusiasm for the outdoor life, the Conservationists also drew attention to nature and its wonders. So they offered, at one and the same time, a way to enjoy natural beauty and to maximize its utility. In the American west, especially, these ideas had real political and economic consequences. Among the most obvious and important for engineers were dozens of dam-building projects, not the least of which was the one built at Hetch Hetchy by Michael O'Shaughnessy. These huge structures – all of them part of elaborate water resource projects, made their engineers into important, public figures, and connected their profession to matters of vital national concern.

The Progressive movement in politics and the Conservation movement in natural resource policy coalesced with yet another crusade crucial to the professional ambitions of engineers, this one in the name of efficiency. Frederick Winslow Taylor (1856–1915) and his doctrine of scientific management emerged on the national stage early in the twentieth century, and out of some of the same circumstances as those other ideas for reform. Layton (1971), in his study *The Revolt of the Engineers: Social Responsibility and the American Engineering Profession*, caught the essence of Taylor's importance for the profession. What Taylor claimed to have discovered were scientific laws and methods for the management of both men and machines in industrial employment. The application of those principles and techniques, according to his experiments, resulted in enormous gains in worker productivity and consequently large savings for their employers. By themselves, those outcomes were striking enough, but Taylor's ambitions – and those of his zealous followers – went much further. In its crudest form, his system involved breaking a job down into its elementary parts, analyzing the worker's movements, and using time-and-motion studies – combined with an understanding of the physiology of fatigue – to determine the most efficient performance of a particular task. This "scientific" understanding of labor led Taylor to think he could determine what constituted a "fair day's work," and also to what he believed would be a fair rate of pay for it. Such was the basis for Taylor's claim that his management techniques could harmonize the competing interests of capital and labor, and thus end the strife so endemic to US industrial activity – and what first gained him national prominence.

Engineers felt an obvious interest in scientific management because it vested control over labor and labor processes in their hands. But Taylor's ideas proved even more compelling when extended to machine processes, factory layout, and to the entire arrangement of production. Not surprisingly, if one believes new technologies come out of a combination of factors, scientific management appeared just as corporate industry had assumed its modern form and scale, and the engineering profession had developed its own corporate form, its educational institutions, and a large number of practitioners. Furthermore, Layton shows that the increasing employment of engineers within big industrial organizations seriously undermined their chances for a clear professional identity, and also reduced their opportunities for entrepreneurship. Until Taylor, about the only way for them to improve their status and income potential was to enter the ranks of management. But his radical solution was to turn that world on its head by incorporating management within the engineer's job description. The most efficient use of labor, and to him most equitable, depended upon the most effective use of machines – an understanding that came to Taylor as a consequence of his revolutionary studies of high-speed metal-cutting. And it logically followed that, because of the intensely interconnected nature of the tools of manufacture, maximizing factory output required that engineers assume all responsibility for every element of the production system. So the rationalization of industry according to the principles of scientific management made technical knowledge the foundation of authority. This reorganization also replaced the traditional business hierarchy, in which power went up and down the line, with a set of parallel command centers, each with responsibility over a given function and each dependent upon particular kinds of information. Besides control over an enormously important enterprise, Taylor's plans created large new employment possibilities for engineers.

These ideas for changing the order of industrial activity, as well as the authority for it, proved especially attractive to Progressive-era thinkers, who imagined engineers to be an objective and essentially non-political force. As Veblen (1921) did in his *Engineers and the Price System*, they contrasted the impartial rationality of engineering thought with the greed of monopolies and their manipulation of productive resources for the sake of profit. But in fact, the engineering profession itself was politically divided and, some would say, far from impartial. The leadership of all the national engineering societies, headquartered in New York, proved essentially conservative in its outlook and more often than not corporate executives held the highest offices. Their tight grasp on policy and practice made younger engineers, especially those active in local engineering societies like the one in Cleveland, as much concerned to reform their own profession as they were keen to make engineering more responsive to major issues of the day – convictions that joined ideology to hopes of public esteem and career opportunity.

To many Progressive-era political reformers, the electric utility industry exemplified the problems of monopoly control over an important technology, and those engineers, who worried about the influence of business on the policies of professional societies, felt the same way. Electric utility executives like Detroit Edison's Alex Dow, or Chicago Edison's Alex Bailey dominated the governance of the American Society of Mechanical Engineers, for instance, and they used their power over annual meeting programs to forestall presentations of data inimical to their rate structures, and also to prevent the publication in society transactions of information like that, which public utility commissions might use in their regulatory function. Electrical systems do not emerge from some irresistible technical logic, or from a purely creative form of entrepreneurial system building and reformers like Morris L. Cooke (1872–1960) knew that.

Appointed director of public works for Philadelphia by the Progressive mayor Rudolph Blankenburg, known locally as "Old Dutch Cleanser," Cooke came into the job as a strong advocate of Taylor's scientific management, and he dedicated himself to the task of rooting out corruption by applying efficiency methods to city services. As a consequence of that process, he concluded that the Philadelphia Electric Company overcharged the city for electric streetlighting. Cooke then brought a suit against the company in a hearing before the public service commission, and won when testimony revealed the extent to which the company had overvalued its assets in establishing a rate for the city. Cooke found out in that action how difficult it was for cities to discover the actual cost of generating electricity, and he also learned that the most prominent consulting engineers, including those on the faculty of schools like MIT, were already in the pay of the utilities. City engineers in other places had that truth revealed to them, too. In Cleveland, the reform mayor Tom Johnson decided to outflank the Cleveland Electric Company by building a municipally owned electric generating plant, and had his city engineer, Frederick Ballard, subsequently elected president of the local engineering society, to design and construct the facility. Ballard had trouble getting General Electric and Westinghouse to bid on the machinery, and then real difficulty in presenting performance data from his plant to the technical community. Edison Company engineers prevented him from delivering a paper before the Boston Engineering Society, for example, and he faced very hostile reactions when Cooke smuggled him into an American Society of Mechanical

Engineers (ASME) session on the engineer in public service, where he showed that the municipal plant was profitably selling electricity at a third of the price the Cleveland Electric Company claimed it needed to charge.

Layton outlines in detail these Progressive-era efforts to redirect the engineering profession toward social responsibility, to make the public interest an engineer's first ethical obligation, as in law and medicine, rather than the interests of his employer. The reasons the reformers had only limited success in this crusade are not far to seek. By 1915 the vast majority of engineers worked for large corporate organizations, and the only difference between their circumstance and that of their counterparts 100 years earlier, was one of scale and what might be called density. Noble (1977) reveals the extent to which corporate influence had, by the first couple of decades of the twentieth century, shaped engineering education, engineering employment, engineering professionalism, and ultimately, the dominant ethos of most American technical people.

That is not to say they were all happy about it or that there were no more idealists in engineering, and several examples support that proposition. In a frank acknow-ledgment of the pressure that liberal-minded local engineering societies had put on them, the national engineering societies were forced to create geographic sections and give them representation within the organization. As Secretary of Commerce, Herbert Hoover reorganized the department to focus on the problem of waste in industry, the promulgation of industrial standards, and a campaign for national efficiency. These were all favorite issues for Progressive-minded engineers, who saw in Hoover, himself an engineer, a model of the ways in which they could shape public policy. And in the West, Ellison (2000) shows that Bureau of Reclamation engineers carried on an array of dam-building projects in the 1930s with Progressive ideals as their political foundation.

But the civil engineering projects of the Great Depression were one of the very few bright spots for engineers. For the first time, Americans raised serious questions about their vaunted technological abilities. There had been a lot of discussion during the 1920s about Machine Civilization – a catch phrase for the social and cultural implications of a new world of automatic machines, assembly line production, and depersonalized labor. The Depression gave that debate immediacy and specificity. The very machines and techniques that had promised such prosperity by saving the labor costs of manufacture now seemed the cause of massive unemployment. All the technological changes of the recent past, which engineers celebrated as their contri-butions to the nation's economic power, now appeared calamitous in their unanticipated consequences. Indeed, some critics called for reversing the direction of engineering, or redefining the meaning of progress. The sociologist Clarence Case argued the solution to the country's economic problems was "social engineering, not mechanical engineering." Roosevelt's Secretary of Agriculture, Henry Wallace, leveled even more pointed criticism at the profession for its wholesale adoption of business values and lack of regard for the social consequences of its work. As he put it, "no great harm would be done if a certain amount of technical efficiency in engineering were traded for a somewhat broader base in general culture (Pursell, 1974)."

Engineers in the mechanical and electrical branches of the profession felt these critiques with particular keenness, and some felt compelled to offer solutions to the crisis. Gerard Swope, trained in electrical engineering at MIT and head of G.E. was probably the best known of them because of his work with Roosevelt on the creation of the National Recovery Act (NRA). But mechanical engineers, who often said they were responsible for the country's industrial system, were also inclined toward analyses of the production system, and not surprisingly they tended to conclude that the problem was one of distribution. Dexter Kimball, dean of Cornell's engineering school and thus Robert Thurston's successor, admitted in a speech before the American Association for the Advancement of Science entitled "Social Effects of Mass Production," that mechanization contributed to some of the Depression's personal costs, and he imagined a future technology more appropriate in its scale and pace to humane outcomes. But Kimball was as exceptional in his willingness to explore unpleasant truths as he was misguided in his optimism. Most of the leading figures in the engineering profession, from whatever branch of it, wanted more technology, not less, and they openly opposed Roosevelt's policies. For his part, the president had equally little confidence in their abilities to understand the issues or to provide much help in their solution.

Engineers may have worried that a Depression-spawned crisis of technological confidence had ominous consequences for their profession. Most other Americans, however, continued to believe in the generative powers of invention as well as in the national talent for it. And they found in many of the era's publicly funded, large-scale engineering projects an exalted kind of reassurance. Nye (1996), in his *American Technological Sublime*, has helped us understand the emotional content of these structures. Hoover Dam became as popular a tourist destination as the Grand Canyon. One of those who came to see it wrote of his feelings, at the end, unconsciously choosing the same kind of language civil engineers used in describing the purposes of their profession: "Confronting this spectacle in the midst of emptiness and desolation first provokes fear, then wonderment, and finally a sense of awe and pride in man's skill in bending the forces of nature to his purpose." Dams like that symbolized abundance, prosperity, and a triumphant human spirit. Individual engineers were often lost in the scale of that kind of enterprise, but onlookers always recognized Hoover Dam as a transcendent engineering achievement – as they had before the Brooklyn Bridge and would later the Golden Gate Bridge.

The Allied victory in World War II, achieved with weapons not even in existence at the beginning of the conflict, proved a different kind of affirmation of technological competence. The weapons themselves went beyond the remarkable, of course, but the way in which technical and scientific expertise had been so effectively assembled was almost as impressive. The example that usually captures the most attention is the Manhattan Project because it depended on such an unparalleled concentration of intellectual resources to produce a weapon of such unmatched power. But to understand the long-term implications of wartime partnerships upon engineers and the engineering profession, the Office of Scientific Research and Development (OSRD) may be a better choice for analysis. We can see its roots in the response to those arguments of the 1930s calling for a moratorium on engineering and scientific research, and the reallocation of mental power to social issues. The most ardent voices raised against that challenge came from universities and industrial laboratories, among them that of Karl Compton, president of MIT, and the rhetoric he used then would come in handy later. A physicist with long alliances to industrial research, Compton also connected the Institute to government agencies when he became chair of the Science Advisory Board established by Roosevelt in 1933 (Pursell, 1965). That agency, formed to bring science and technology to problems of the Depression, did not last long, but it provided a direct precedent for the National Defense Research Council (NDRC), created in 1940 with Compton's second-in-command at MIT, the electrical engineer Vannevar Bush, at its head. And, in this sequence of correlated measures that created the postwar military/industrial/university complex, the NDRC was morphed into the Office of Scientific Research and Development 2 years later – with funding and authority for the development of the war's new weapons. Its most important decision, taken right at the start, and the thing that glued the three elements of that complex together, was to contract out research to the academy and to industry, paying for it with public funds. Bush, like Compton, consulted with industry from the beginning of his career, and OSRD used industrial research both as a model and point of departure. That put the operation in familiar hands, but amplified its effects a thousand fold with huge infusions of money, a highly coordinated workforce, and the exigencies of warfare. So, while what came out at the end of the war had antecedents in the prewar period, it was like nothing else that had ever existed before.

MIT was assuredly not the only school to benefit from government money during and in the years after the war, but it benefitted the most. Bush later admitted the creation of the NDRC was "an end run," and "a grab" by a small group to get great power, but he justified it by the needs of war. History seems to be on his side, in both cases, and it is certainly clear that MIT was transformed by the experience. So was engineering, and most dramatically in fields allied to radar, guided missile technology, and computing. In that postwar world, civil engineering lost much of its earlier glamour. In his autobiography, Meehan (1983) recalled that when it was time for him to select a major field of study, he picked civil engineering because the sign-up line was so short. Atomic power and rockets would take hold of the American imagination in the way bridges and dams used to, and those products of the integration of engineering, business, and science – the seamless linkage of new technologies and production processes – would replace engineers as the objects of public attention and affection.

Another of the war's effects was to more sharply differentiate the educational institutions that had received the greatest share of federal largesse from those receiving the least. By the 1950s, there was a huge difference in the usual career of an MIT graduate and that, say, of engineers graduated from schools like Oklahoma State. One group filled the offices of the new high-tech firms that sprang up after the war along Route 128 around Boston, and the other went off on foreign missions of technical assistance to Latin America, Asia, and the Middle East. Using only MIT to talk about American engineering obviously distorts the picture, and also leaves out important elements. But at the same time, institutions like Cal Tech and Georgia Tech, and engineering schools at U.C. Berkeley, the University of Illinois, Michigan or Stanford, were more like it than not – or they wanted to be – whether with respect to educational programs, supported research, or economic impact. So, there is some utility in looking at MIT and its efforts to remake itself after the war in order to gain insight into the education of American engineers, and thus the profession, too.

At MIT, all the old arrangements seemed quite out of balance after the war. Huge increases in sponsored research had called for large additions to the faculty, but many of them were now paid with soft money. By 1947, 28 percent of the faculty got their incomes from such sources. Furthermore, the indirect costs of research embedded in outside contracts distorted the school's budget, yielding almost $2 million, most of which disappeared into departments without a set of overall accounting procedures. Finally, this kind of work, which in dollar amount dwarfed the institute's entire educational budget, tended to splinter the faculty into small, independent units, and it also substantially increased the size of graduate programs, the funding of which also depended on sponsored research. So, notwithstanding a long emphasis on undergraduate instruction, one-third of MIT's student population that year were graduate students. These fundamental kinds of changes called into question the institution's basic practices and sense of purpose, and forced MIT's people to reconsider their own objectives. Warren K. Lewis, a professor of chemical engineering, chaired the committee charged with that task, and his report still looms large in the minds of those who think about the history of engineering education.

Lewis identified three central issues that needed resolution. Was MIT's focus to remain on undergraduate instruction? How could it balance scholarship that depended for its vitality on the open exchange of information, with the need for secrecy in research contracts for the Department of Defense? And, in what emerged as the most important question for his committee, did the postwar future call for an utterly different approach in the education of engineers? The institution's large engagement with graduate training (plus entirely novel fields of study, not to speak of the real need for research assistants) and the extent to which engineering education had become so fundamentally based on mathematics and science, suggested the possibility of an enlarged, less practical curriculum, as well as one that might extend beyond 4 years.

There were not any self doubts behind these questions, however. Instead, the Lewis committee laid out an aggressive and ambitious plan for the Institute, the central idea of which was that MIT's future lay in the education of leaders. In much the same way Britain's ancient universities confidently expected their graduates to fill the dominant positions in government, MIT's men explicitly characterized their school as a technological Oxbridge, and defined its mission in the same terms. In fact, it was not the first time the idea of such a comparison had occurred. John Ripley Freeman (1855–1932), class of '75, was an ardent exponent of a 1905 plan to create a new MIT campus on the banks of the Charles River opposite Harvard, imitating the architectural style of St Johns College, Cambridge, and expecting the look of the place to imbue engineering graduates with the culture suitable for a place in the boardrooms of major corporations. But the difference this time was real curricular change, not a set of cloisters. What made the Lewis plan distinct was that while it retained MIT's emphasis on a four-year professional training, it called for the creation of a new division of the institution devoted to education in the humanities and social sciences, with regular courses in those subjects required in every year of an undergraduate student's program, and he made that change the centerpiece of his report.

Lewis and his colleagues worried about a growing tendency in the country's institutions toward the concentration of authority and control, as well as towards the standardization of procedures and operations, because it seemed to threaten individual variation in interests and abilities. That concern reflects a sense of their own singular journeys – Lewis came off a farm in southern Delaware – but also the notion that MIT should nurture special and particular gifts in its students and, defending its costly tuition, that their school could better provide for such variation than large state-supported universities. Indeed, in the burgeoning postwar engineering enrolments in state universities, their research facilities also considerably enhanced by federal spending, one can see another reason for MIT to think hard about its future and to define itself out of that cohort.

The Lewis Report imagined lofty objectives for the then male-only institution – "intimate instruction to a restricted number of exceptionally able young men," conducted in a physical environment of "order, peace and beauty," and aimed at the fullest development of their characters as well as their intellectual abilities. It sounded very much like those British universities that were never very far from the minds of committee members, and reminiscent, too, of old hopes within the profession to create an elevated intellectual culture for engineering. But the report also recognized some worrisome realities. Large secret research projects seriously impaired "sound intellectual development," sponsored research threatened to undermine the school's purposes, and outside consulting that depended on a lot of travel took too much energy from teaching. Those were just the activities, of course, that knitted MIT faculty members and graduate students ever more tightly into the conjoined skeins of corporate industry and military contracting. In that context, as Noble (1984) has shown in his *Forces of Production*, the most valuable skills were how best to choose publicly funded projects with the greatest long-term research potential, and knowing how to spin off new start-up companies.

The subordination of professional independence to corporate necessities proved just as pronounced in professional engineering societies. To take only one example, all the major organizations – of civil engineers, mechanical engineers, chemical engineers, and electrical engineers – have for years engaged in formulating standards of all kinds. Standardizing the building materials of engineering allows for better inventory control, simplification in the design process, improved efficiency in manufacturing, and more precision in contractual negotiations. And the rationalization of all these elements was cast as an appealing form of public service, suggesting objective technical judgment brought to socially useful ends.

The development of a standard usually gathers together an engineering society sub-committee and the relevant stakeholders – a group that generally consists of trade and industry associations and the appropriate experts – who are practically always affiliated with the major firms whose interests are involved in the particular case, and whose companies generally provide the financial support for the work. Until recently, no one even suggested the importance or need for public representation on such bodies. Standards committees imagine they can insure impartiality by balancing their memberships with consumers and producers, on the theory that their competing interests will cancel each other out. But there is a tight correlation between technical knowledge and economic advantage, and standards are framed at that intersection. So, in the 1970s the ASME found itself embroiled in a lawsuit alleging conspiracy in restraint of trade, as a consequence of action by a sub-committee of its Boiler Code, and was fined just under $10 million when a US District Court ruled that the society was guilty of violating anti-trust statutes. Engineers like to think that standards embody "best practice," but Amy Slaton's research shows that besides encoding knowledge, standards order social relations and production processes. So besides, control over markets, they can be employed to shift jurisdictional boundaries in disputes with labor unions, and alter the design of work operations.

The ASME case was only one of the assaults on engineers and engineering in the latter years of the twentieth century. Ralph Nader's revelations of the authority corporate experts exercised in the regulation of the nuclear power industry, as well as his attack on the design and production of American cars in his book *Unsafe at Any Speed* (1972) seriously challenged the concept of professional integrity. The long and notorious collusion between General Electric and Westinghouse in the pricing of steam turbines, along with the publicity given to Carson's *Silent Spring* (1962), with its indictment of the apparently heedless use of industrial chemicals, helped foster an increasingly widespread assumption that engineers were simply organization men in ethically inert corporations. In this atmosphere of suspicion and mistrust, the corporate bodies of the engineering profession retreated to an essentially conservative emphasis in their programming, focusing on technical issues rather than activities that spoke to social concerns, whether of their members or the general public. Membership in these societies continues to increase, as the American population grows, and the number of foreign members swells at a greater rate, particularly in electrical and computer engineering. But most engineering organizations represent in their membership only a fraction of the total numbers of US engineers in practice; in any given year a good many of them do not renew their memberships; and all the societies are disturbed by the substantial numbers of student members who drop out after graduation.

Episodes like the Challenger disaster, and more recently that of the spaceship Columbia, throw into sharp contrast the difference between managerial agendas and the pointed efforts of engineers to prevent such calamities, but they also reveal the extent to which technical people are subordinated in the organization. No longer the subject of romantic novels or the heroes of motion pictures, engineers have almost disappeared in reality, too. Their professional societies seem little concerned with the

personal fortunes of their members or with their place in society, either. Furthermore, as mostly salaried employees of large business concerns, the terms of their
employment militate against concepts of professional individuality or independence,
let alone action of that sort. And even engineering education, as a distinct occupational specialty, threatens to vanish. In a recent article in *The Chronicle of Higher
Education* (January 24, 2003) entitled "Education for the Profession Formerly
Known as Engineering," Rosalind Williams, previously a Dean at MIT, argues that
the field is in a crisis of identity. Old definitions of its mission are no longer valid
because technological change itself has so completely transformed the issues and the
tools of that occupation. It used to be that engineering, both in the classroom and in
practice, rested on the fundamentals of physics and chemistry. Now, Williams says,
the critical problems of the field have to do with the "creation and management of
a self-made habitat," in which biology is the most essential science and the management
of information the most crucial skill. In the same way that the word "technology" is
commonly taken by most people today to mean computers and computing, in place
of its older all-encompassing definition, the traditional subdivisions of engineering
have been shouldered aside by a new kind of "technoscience," with its own operations
and forms of communication.

There is just a little bit of irony here. Against the face of nature, technical people
struggled to reduce the variables with which they worked, always hoping to render
everything consistent and predictable. Even in the design process, where novelty was
created, engineers cast and re-cast familiar elements "in the mind's eye," to use
Eugene Ferguson's apt expression. But this new instauration promises to end traditional boundaries of practice, as well as old categories in the ordering of knowledge.
Like a snake eating its own tail, technological change transforms the system that
produced it, though not by inner logic or by accident. Engineering is atomized into
smaller fragments that get mixed and re-mixed, diluting notions of professional
identity while keeping the locus of those things firmly in the sphere of corporate
influence. Even the history of engineering is increasingly submerged in interdisciplinary
approaches that seem a lot like reflections on technoscience, and that are more and
more presentist in their focus.

As if to exemplify the inexorable march of events, the old giving way to the new,
San Francisco's Sierra Nevada water supply system – Michael O'Shaughnessy's
triumphant creation – is now badly in need of repair. Bringing it up to date will
inevitably raise the question of making it larger, since the demand for water has
increased so much in the interval – calling for a work even more grand in scale and
daunting in its difficulties. Water, not oil, has become the truly scarce resource, and
that is why multinational firms, with their own engineers, now press for the privati-
zation of municipal supply systems. Addressing the problem will open up very difficult
and contentious political issues, besides all the technical ones. We lionized people
like O'Shaughnessy because they seemed so committed to the public interest. This
time around, just when we need it, we are less likely to have the benefit of unalloyed
confidence in the engineers who can do the job. And they will have little power to
shape the outcome.

BIBLIOGRAPHY

Carson, Rachael. *Silent Spring* (Boston: Houghton Mifflin, 1962).

Calhoun, Daniel C. *The American Civil Engineer: Origins and Conflict* (Cambridge: MIT Press, 1960).

Calvert, Monte A. *The Mechanical Engineer in America: Professional Cultures in Conflict, 1830–1910* (Baltimore: Johns Hopkins Press, 1967).

Cather, Willa. *Alexander's Bridge* (Boston: Houghton Mifflin, 1912).

Danly, Susan and Marx, Leo, eds. *The Railroad in American Art: Representations of Technological Change* (Cambridge: MIT Press, 1988).

Eliot, Charles W. "The new education," *Atlantic Monthly*, 23 (February and March 1869).

Ellison, Karin. *The Making of a Multiple Purpose Dam: Engineering Culture, the U.S. Bureau of Reclamation, and Grand Coulee Dam, 1917–1942*, PhD Dissertation (Massachusetts Institute of Technology, 2000).

Ferguson, Eugene S. *Engineering and the Mind's Eye* (Cambridge: MIT Press, 1992).

Hays, Samuel P. *Conservation and the Gospel of Efficiency: The Progressive Conservation Movement, 1890–1920* (Cambridge: Harvard University Press, 1959).

Layton, Edwin T. *The Revolt of the Engineers: Social Responsibility and the American Engineering Profession* (Cleveland: Press of the Case Western Reserve University, 1971).

[Lewis, Warren K.] *Report of the Committee on Educational Survey* (Cambridge: The Technology Press, 1949)

McMahon, Michal A. *The Making of a Profession: A Century of Electrical Engineering in America* (New York: IEEE, 1984)

Meehan, Richard. *Getting Sued and Other Tales from the Engineering Life* (Cambridge: MIT Press, 1983).

Merritt, Raymond H. *Engineering and American Society, 1830–1875* (Lexington: University of Kentucky Press, 1969).

Morison, Elting E. *From Know-How to Nowhere* (New York: New American Library, 1974).

Nader, Ralph. *Unsafe at Any Speed: The Designed in Dangers of the American Automobile* (New York: Grossman, 1972).

Noble, David F. *America by Design: Science, Technology, and the Rise of Corporate Capitalism* (New York: Alfred A. Knopf, 1977).

Noble, David F. *Forces of Production: A Social History of Industrial Automation* (New York: Knopf, 1984).

Nye, David. *American Technological Sublime* (Cambridge: MIT Press, 1996).

Pursell, Carroll W. "The Anatomy of a Failure: The Science Advisory Board, 1933–1935," *Proceedings of the American Philosophical Society*, 109 (December, 1965): 342–51.

Pursell, Carroll W. "A Savage Struck by Lightning: The Idea of a Research Moratorium, 1927–1937," *Lex et Sciencia*, 10 (Oct.–Dec., 1974): 146–61.

Reynolds, Terry, ed. *The Engineer in America: A Historical Anthology from Technology and Culture* (Chicago: University of Chicago Press, 1991).

Reynolds, Terry. *Seventy-Five Years of Progress: A History of the American Institute of Chemical Engineers* (New York: The Institute, 1983).

Seely, Bruce E. *Building the American Highway System: Engineers as Policy Makers* (Philadelphia: Temple University Press, 1987).

Sinclair, Bruce. "The promise of the future: technical education," in George Daniels, ed., *Nineteenth-Century American Science: A Reappraisal* (Evanston: Northwestern University Press, 1972).

Sinclair, Bruce. *Philadelphia's Philosopher Mechanics: A History of the Franklin Institute, 1824–1865* (Baltimore: Johns Hopkins University Press, 1974).

Sinclair, Bruce. *A Centennial History of the American Society of Mechanical Engineers, 1880–1980* (Toronto: University of Toronto Press, 1980).

Sinclair, Bruce. "Inventing a genteel tradition: MIT crosses the river," in Bruce Sinclair, ed., *New Perspectives on Technology and American Culture* (Philadelphia: American Philosophical Society, 1986).

Sinclair, Bruce. "Harvard, MIT, and the ideal technical education," in Clark A. Elliott and Margaret W. Rossiter, eds, *Science at Harvard University: Historical Perspectives* (Bethlehem: Lehigh University Press, 1992).

Veblen, Thorstein. *Engineers and the Price System* (New York: B.W. Huebsch, 1921).

Williams, Rosalind. *Retooling: A Historian Confronts Technological Change* (Cambridge: MIT Press, 2002).

Williams, Rosalind. "Education for the profession formerly known as engineering," *The Chronicle of Higher Education* (January 24, 2003).

Wright, Harold Bell. *The Winning of Barbara Worth* (Chicago: The Book Supply Company, 1911).

CHAPTER TWENTY

Popular Culture and Technology in the Twentieth Century

MOLLY W. BERGER

I've got a mule her name is Sal
Fifteen miles on the Erie Canal
She's a good old worker and a good old pal
Fifteen miles on the Erie Canal

We've hauled some barges in our day
Filled with lumber, coal, and hay
And we know every inch of the way
From Albany to Buffalo

Low bridge, everybody down
Low bridge, for we're coming to a town
And you'll always know your neighbor
You'll always know your pal
If you've ever navigated on the Erie Canal.

Each year, I look forward to the day when I teach early nineteenth-century transportation systems to those engineering students who find themselves in my history of American technology class. On that day, my students (or perhaps, at that moment, they consider themselves victims) hear me belt out "The Erie Canal Song," a relic that bubbles up uncontrollably from my days in the fifth grade at Severence Millikin Elementary School in Cleveland Heights, Ohio. The lyrics speak of hard work, the day-to-day activities along an unprecedented transportation system, the opening of national markets, and a rock solid relationship between a man and his mule. Billed as an "American Folk Song," post-World War II school music books tied the "Erie Canal Song" to a folk tradition that celebrated Yankee ingenuity and the promise that technology and technological systems held for a growing country. Through a popular song presumed to be well over one hundred years old, school music curriculum reinforced and addressed the twin Cold War anxieties of knowing both your technology and your neighbor.

Antebellum popular culture produced many songs about the Erie Canal, some fairly naughty that more often than not referred to a cook, rather than a mule, named Sal. But "The Erie Canal Song," described as a folk tune through generations of school music books, was actually written in 1905 by Tin Pan Alley composer, Theodore S. Allen. And thus, it serves as an interesting example of something created purposefully for a mass audience whose origins became obscured by cultural familiarity and evolved into something with an entirely different cultural meaning: a traditional American folk tune. This transformation points to the way in which the cultural products of industrial society not only represent the culture of everyday life, but also serve as ways through which people construct meanings of self and social identity. Composed to exploit a popular interest in the canal's resurgence and barge mechanization, "The Erie Canal Song" appealed to a nostalgia for simpler times, when technology like that of the canal was yet understandable and communities were only beginning to be transformed by them.

In the most elemental way, scholars define popular culture in opposition to high or learned culture. Popular culture is often linked to class, and if defined in an anthropological sense, more broadly to "the people." Historian Browne defines popular culture as everything in our everyday lives, save that 10 percent of so-called elite culture (Browne 2002, p. 24). This definition tends to regard "the people" and their culture as undifferentiated entities of coherent taste, their static list of things and activities as either "popular" or "unpopular." As the example of the "Erie Canal Song" demonstrates, groups of people can appropriate and recast things and activities as part of the ongoing transformation of culture over time. The song began as a popular entertainment, but once it found its way into school music books, it became an instrument of an educational ideology that sought to engage young American students with a romanticized pioneer history.

In his essay, "The Folklore of Industrial Society," Levine (1992) provides a useful way to both think about popular culture and connect it to ideas about technology. Moving beyond arguments that seek to validate popular culture as a valuable resource for discovery, Levine situates popular culture within the context of industrialization and capitalism. Popular culture is a product of mechanization and industrialization. In order for anything to be popular – widely accessible and widely accessed – it needs to be produced in large quantities and disseminated to large numbers of people. For example, in the seventeenth and eighteenth centuries, print technologies enabled the production of inexpensive stories, literature, and tracts known as chapbooks that peddlers and bookstores sold to a wide readership. Levine and others, though, regard the late nineteenth century as a watershed period, related to the structural transformation of industrial society of the late nineteenth and early twentieth centuries. As mass-produced commodities became the primary vehicles for cultural production, groups of people no longer produced culture themselves as in traditional folk culture, but worked with and expressed themselves through commercial products and technologically mediated entertainment. Thus, popular culture is linked to technology in a very fundamental way. The broad context of a capitalist industrial society frames the technological mediation of cultural forms such as books, radio, television, recordings, movies, and photographs and its dissemination through complex industries, markets, and technological systems. As sociologist Hall (1974) argues, popular culture is the ground on which culture is transformed, the site of a dialectical cultural re-working enacted by producers and consumers.

This essay's task is to discuss technology and popular culture in twentieth-century United States. Given Browne's (2002) definition, the possibilities are endless and so I have chosen an eclectic set of examples that move chronologically through the twentieth century. What binds them together, beyond my own interests, is that they each, in some way, offer a commentary on life in a technological society. Thus, they are not only made possible by a variety of technological media, but have technology as their subject, as well. The topics wend their way through early twentieth-century juvenile literature, Charlie Chaplin's classic film *Modern Times*, Disneyland's Tomorrowland, the *Jetsons* and the *Flintstones*, the *Star Wars* trilogy, Desert Storm trading cards, and the 1999 movie, *The Matrix*. Each of these offers a glimpse into a society that broadly embraced its technology and expressed its greatest hopes and fears through its popular culture. Together, they reveal technology as an arena through which ideas about power, morality, and progress are contested. Each of the examples, by virtue of being in the "popular" realm, also underscores the indivisible relationship between technology, popular culture, and the capitalist economic system that underpins them both.

To read the juvenile literature of the nineteen-teens and twenties, one would think the nation was overrun with touring cars filled with teens on mysterious adventures. The model for this mayhem was Tom Swift, boy inventor, who burst into the imaginations of young American readers in his 1910 debut novel, *Tom Swift and His Motor-Cycle, or, Fun and Adventures on the Road*. Grosset and Dunlap, Tom's publisher, introduced the series with the stated goal to "convey in a realistic way the wonderful advances in land and sea locomotion and to interest the boy of the present in the hope that he may be a factor in aiding the marvelous development that is coming in the future" (Deane 1990, p. 22). The publishers, through Tom's various adventures, sought to persuade young boys to think about becoming engineers. As a career choice, engineering not only served the public good, but, at least in adventure stories, presented a sure path to both excitement and financial reward. Tom was an inventor, and as such, inherited the mantle, not only of his father, Barton Swift (who "amassed a considerable fortune out of his many patents"), but of the generation of inventors and adventurers who inspired the authors of early twentieth-century juvenile literature with their real-life accomplishments and exploits. Indeed, several historians claim that Glenn Curtiss served as a model for Tom. Curtiss's career, for example, also began with bicycles and moved on through motorcycles and airplanes. Tom, like Curtiss, built his own aircraft in a furious burst of inventive activity, and went on to win a major air race as well as a handsome cash prize (Swift 1990, p. 28). Tom's adventures tapped into the nation's romance with engineers and the fantastic new technologies developed in the century's early decades.

In the 40 books that comprised the first Tom Swift series (1910–41), Tom encountered danger and skullduggery as he improved upon and perfected a long list of conveyances and inventions. Early books introduced readers to the excitement associated with Tom's motorcycle, motor boat, airship, submarine, electric runabout, and sky racer. Later stories centered on tantalizing technologies such as the wireless, electric rifle, wizard camera, searchlight, photo telephone, and giant cannon. In *Tom*

Swift and His War Tank, or, Doing His Bit for Uncle Sam (1918) and *Tom Swift and His Air Scout, or, Uncle Sam's Mastery of the Sky* (1919), Tom proved that superior technology could vanquish the enemy. After World War I, Tom intrigued young readers by circling the globe, dabbling with talking pictures, a house-on-wheels, giant magnet, television detector, and an ocean airport. Each of these stories followed a broad format through which Tom and an enduring and stereotyped cast of characters became embroiled in a contest between good and evil, whereby the combatants pitted competing versions of a technology against one another. That Tom's iteration ultimately proved superior was a given, but the persistent ongoing struggles demonstrated the moral responsibilities inherent in the development and ownership of modern technologies. If Tom were even a smidgen less clever, the bad men would triumph, subverting the promise of modern invention to nefarious and evil ends.

Despite their formulaic simplicity, stories such as these revealed the concerns and conflicts emerging from the process of industrialization and the development of a modern age. Each text gave instruction in the ways that technology worked, ensuring that young boys would not be left behind in the dust of emerging technological knowledge, while, at the same time, assuring them that this specialized knowledge was within their grasp. Ironically, at a time when engineers increasingly received formal training and accreditation through university programs and national engineering societies, Tom was a model of shop culture education and the power of the independent inventor, having rejected the idea of advanced schooling in favor of studying under his father's tutelage. The stories perpetuated the idea of the self-made man/inventor, honoring heroes such as Edison, Westinghouse, Ford, Curtiss, and the Wright Brothers. Both Barton Swift and the young Tom Swift earned an exceedingly comfortable living from patents and prizes, thus, firmly championing capitalism – at least an idealized form of capitalism – that prized honesty, industry, and patriotism. Inevitably, the villains were members of a "syndicate of wealthy men," unscrupulous in their methods and desires. Each Tom Swift novel was, therefore, a moral tale that differentiated between good and bad uses of money and reinforced the message that just rewards would accrue to those who adhered to a moral code, promoted technology for the public good, and courageously defended those values, no matter the danger.

Tom Swift lived in a man's world. Other than the housekeeper, Mrs. Baggert, and Mary Nestor, whom he courted for 19 years before finally marrying, all the characters, both good and bad, were boys and men. Adhering to a curious formula, many of the heroes and heroines of similar juvenile series of the time such as the Motor Girls, the Campfire Girls, or the Boy Inventors were motherless, as was Tom, whose mother died when he was an infant. Like the lost boys in *Peter Pan*, "they knew in what they called their hearts that one can get on quite well without a mother, and that it is only the mothers who think you can't" (Barrie 1911). Without mothers, the young boys and girls were liberated to pursue adventures no right-headed mother would allow. For example, in *Tom Swift and His Submarine Boat, or, Under the Ocean for Sunken Treasure* (1910) Tom sailed to the coast of Brazil in his submarine, where he fought off brown-skinned Brazilian natives, sharks, as well as the ever-present men from "the syndicate." Similarly, in *The Boy Inventors' Wireless*

Triumph (1912), the motherless cousins Jack Chadwick and Tom Jesson took command of a "Flying Road Racer" in the heart of the Yucatan jungle whilst in search of Jack's father. Not only did the absence of women, particularly mothers, strengthen and keep pure the relationship between men and technology, but it allowed the young heroes to keep at bay the middle-class curse of "overcivilization," which threatened to turn a whole generation of early twentieth-century young men into sissies. As historian Rotundo states, "the domestic realm meant restraint, dependence, confinement, and submission for a young man" (Rotundo 1993, p. 58). Unburdened by sentimental and restrictive influences, Tom and boy heroes like him immersed themselves wholeheartedly in a world of machines, tools, grease, and danger, emerging from each adventure more capable, manly, and richer than when they started.

In a 1926 library survey, 98 percent of public school children admitted reading juvenile series books, what librarians referred to as "trashy novels" (Chamberlain 2002, p. 198–9). The Tom Swift series alone was estimated to have sold thirty million copies by the late 1930s and thus their significance in shaping the ideas that young boys and girls held about technology cannot be underestimated (Prager 1976, p. 68). Yet the unabashed celebration of technology promulgated by these books existed alongside popular critiques of technology. In film, Fritz Lang's *Metropolis* (1927) questioned the concentration of capital and exploitive labor practices of industrial capitalism. In the United States, Charlie Chaplin tackled similar issues in his classic 1936 film, *Modern Times*.

Modern Times is one of the most widely-recognized critiques of modern technology and its effect on labor and society. The image of Chaplin caught in the gears of the factory machine is like no other in its ability to raise questions about the role of machines in human life. The context for understanding Chaplin's film is not only the severe economic depression and labor struggles of the 1930s, but also the decade-long change within the film industry as it shifted from silent film to talkies. Historians like to point out, too, that Chaplin began his film career in 1913, the same year that Henry Ford's moving assembly line began churning out Model-T automobiles in under 3 hours' time. As with other industries, film production had felt the pressures resulting from the application of scientific management principles. Chaplin's struggles against the hegemony of sound found their expression in *Modern Times*, as did his concerns about numbing labor practices of the modern factory. Historian Charles Musser explains the popularity of Chaplin's Tramp character as resonating with working-class audiences through its rejection of degrading work and appealing to middle-class audiences through its steadfast advocacy of individualism (Musser 1988, p. 48). The tramp could clobber his bosses in one comedic scene after another, yet survive to head off into the sunset for still another try at the good life. Even so, Chaplin's attempt at merging social consciousness and farce resulted in a disappointing box office. In a time of economic depression, several of the characters in *Modern Times* represented the needs of many who only wanted the opportunity to work, support themselves and their families, and participate in America's consumer society.

Modern Times begins with a long shot of a face of a clock, the quintessential icon of the factory critique. The challenge of a worker's day was as much the endless ticking of the clock as it was the repetitive and dehumanizing work on the assembly line. At the factory where the Tramp works, the company president takes a break from his jigsaw puzzle to order a speed-up of the factory line. He watches the factory floor on a large wall-mounted television screen and booms his orders to the shirtless foreman over a loud speaker. Away from the line for an all-too-short break, Chaplin continues to twitch violently in the motion of his bolt-tightening job. Back at his post, Chaplin is chosen to test a new invention, the Bellow's Feeding Machine, meant to enable a worker to continue on while being fed mechanically. In a reversal of roles, the machine becomes the comic and Chaplin the target (Stewart 1976, p. 301). Everything that can go wrong does, and Charlie is left covered with food, even forced to eat bolts that end up on his plate. By the end of the day, Charlie has a nervous breakdown, runs around the factory creating havoc, gets caught in the gears of the machine, and eventually is carted off to the hospital. Later in the movie, a similar scene echoes much of the action, with Charlie's boss getting caught in the machine, and Charlie feeding him in much the same manner as the Bellow's Feeding Machine, even using a whole chicken as a funnel for the hapless horizontal foreman's coffee.

Modern Times is a segmented narrative and it is only in the initial story line that Chaplin directly engages the themes of disparity of wealth, production-driven factory practices, and the stultifying monotony of routinized labor. While the film draws back from its initial indictment of industrial capitalism, it comments on the harsh realities of the Depression through Paulette Goddards' character, the gamine. The gamine's father dies in a brutal attack by unemployed workers and she is forced to steal to feed her younger sisters, who are taken away by juvenile authorities. Charlie's continuing mishaps further reveal the difficulties Americans had in finding and keeping work. The Tramp and gamine's Hooverville shack is in direct contrast to their middle-class dream life, where a cow stops at the kitchen door to deliver fresh milk for the happy couple. And their department store encounter with consumer capitalism – the gamine sleeps the night away in a "borrowed" white fur coat – serves to highlight the true nature of their desperate existence. Despite their inability to succeed, the Tramp and the gamine retain their faith in the system, head down a long country road, turning their backs on the city in search of a decent life somewhere off into the sunset.

Chaplin's social commentary runs parallel to another commentary on the introduction of sound to moving pictures. In his autobiography, Chaplin remembered the primitiveness of the first sound films and lamented the passing of silent film. He wrote, "A good silent picture had universal appeal to the intellectual and the rank and file. Now it was all to be lost" (Chaplin 1964, p. 325). Sound threatened Chaplin's art of pantomime and his highly successful style of comedy. Despite the overwhelming popularity of talkies, Chaplin persisted in producing silent films. *City Lights* (1931) employed a synchronized soundtrack and subtle sound effects but remained a non-dialogue picture. *Modern Times* was not only his first to use dialogue – a full 10 years after synchronized sound was introduced – but was the first in which audiences heard Chaplin's voice.

In addition to Chaplin's original score and gag-related sound effects, such as the gurgling stomachs in the prison office scene, Chaplin introduced some limited dialogue to what remained essentially a silent film. What is interesting, though, is that in every case, the spoken word is mediated through a technological device. Early on in the movie, the company president speaks to his foreman through the loudspeaker. The audience learns about the Bellows Feeding Machine through a phonograph record, and Charlie and the minister's wife listen to an advertisement about gastric distress over the radio (as their own tummies gurgle dismayingly). In each of these scenes, the pantomimed comedy remains the focal point, yet none would have succeeded without the sound effects. Finally, towards the end of the film, Chaplin makes the transition to full sound as he takes on the role of the singing waiter to an enthusiastic audience. Having lost the words to the song written on a wayward cuff, Chaplin gives voice to tuneful gibberish, thus conceding to the ascendancy of sound without relinquishing his hold on his physical comedic talent (Flom 1997, p. 97).

In 1981, IBM launched a $36 million advertising campaign to promote its new personal computer, the IBM-PC. The award-winning campaign leased the exclusive rights to use Chaplin's Tramp image as well as the words "modern times," and did so successfully for 6 years, describing its new computer as "a machine for modern times." One ad, for example, showed the Tramp pedaling away on a bicycle, his hat flying off, with a computer strapped to the back of the bike. The headline read, "How to move with modern times and take your PC with you." With stunning irony, the advertisements relied on readers and viewers associating Chaplin's character with the warm, human aspects of his character, and, by extension, transformed Big Blue into a friendly, human-scaled company peddling wares that even someone like Charlie could handle. The ads succeeded in negating the message that the movie had conveyed. As film historian Caputi notes, "IBM figuratively swallows him whole, thoroughly assimilates and converts him, effectively erasing his original message by producing a *doppelganger* who now befriends and promotes the machine and its order" (Caputi 1986, p. 79). In answering an angry charge against IBM's use of the *Modern Times* theme, the campaign's chief ad executive spinned, "By bringing Charlie into real modern times, we were able to show how he is finally able to conquer that frustration [with technology]. It is clear that technology is now on his side" (Maland 1989, p. 368). With a sense of presentism as his guiding principle, this executive implied that the 1930s were neither real nor modern, yet this kind of appropriation is precisely what enables popular culture to transform and recreate meaning, for better or worse.

The American century's technological juggernaut that gained speed during World War II culminated in the dramatic use of the atomic bomb and ushered in a period of technological rivalry between world superpowers. The era of the 1950s Cold War was one of competing cultural stories. Many Americans nostalgically recall the 1950s as "America's last happy time," with the perfect nuclear family of *Father Knows Best* and its comfortable suburban lifestyle standing in stark contrast to the turmoil of the 1960s and 1970s that followed. But the 1950s were also the decade of insidious anti-Communism, growing civil rights unrest, questions about whether America could maintain its technological preeminence, and worries about a rebellious new generation who worshipped James Dean, Elvis, and the Beats. These complexities were the context for Walt Disney's creation of Disneyland, his southern California theme park that opened on July 17, 1955 to a rapturous public and a national television audience. As early as 1958, screenwriter and novelist Halevy excoriated Disneyland, anticipating several decades of highbrow criticism when he claimed, "the whole world, the universe, and all man's striving for dominion over self and nature, have been reduced to a sickening blend of cheap formulas packaged to sell" (Halevy 1958, p. 511). Yet, more and more, scholars have begun to analyze the Disney parks for what they have to say about American sensibilities and belief systems. For example, King sees the parks as creative technological systems, part of the tradition of humanists such as Lewis Mumford and futurists such as Alvin Toffler, both of whom who believed that technology should serve, rather than dominate, humankind (King 1981, p. 117). While King looks to the parks more generally for evidence that documents Disney's "faith in the ultimate rightness of technological progress," Tomorrowland was the realm that overtly mediated between the past and the future.

As designed, visitors enter Disneyland through Main Street, USA, a romanticized 1890s reproduction of Disney's childhood town, Marceline, Missouri. Main Street, like many of the historical referents in the park, was "for those of us who remember those carefree times" (Disney 1963, p. 4). With Cinderella's castle as the prize at the end of Main Street, visitors reached a hub from which they could enter one of the four lands: Fantasyland, Frontierland, Adventureland, and Tomorrowland. Together these lands presented an amalgam of a selected past and an imagined future, both of which celebrated such American values as the frontier spirit, individualism, technological ingenuity and superiority, and the powerful myth of the nuclear family as the bulwark of democracy. Even before the park was completed, the four lands had become part of American culture through Disney's weekly television show, *Disneyland*, on which Disney gave viewers updates and guided tours building towards the park's opening. Frontierland and Tomorrowland in particular were what one television reporter called "tele-creations," in that neither drew on existing concepts within the Disney film and television archive. Thus, Disney's popular made-for-TV programs on space exploration, punctuated by commercials marketing the cars and appliances of American suburbia, introduced viewers to the promise of Tomorrowland (Marling 1991, pp. 204–5).

In the park's guidebook, Disney states, "Tomorrow can be wonderful age" (1963, p. 18). Of all the realms, Tomorrowland was the least cohesive thematically, bouncing between the past, the present, and the future. Tomorrowland served to highlight those values that promoted the advancement of American society through technology, and in the context of the Cold War, through technological superiority. Thus, Monsanto's all-plastic house of the future sat comfortably next to the Rocket to the Moon Ride, as the futuristic Disneyland-Alweg Monorail System, opened in 1959, whisked guests in silent comfort between the park and the Disneyland Hotel. Expressing the relentless problems Tomorrowland had keeping ahead of current practices, the guidebook claimed, "In Tomorrowland, you will actually experience what many of America's foremost men of science and industry predict for the world of tomorrow. And Tomorrowland has kept pace with today's rapid advances by continually adding new adventures based on man's latest achievements." Whether anticipating the future or keeping pace with the past, Tomorrowland promised a bright suburban future where youngsters could learn to drive, experience "liquid space," and travel from land to land by steam train, sky train, or monorail train.

When the park opened in 1955, Tomorrowland was the least developed area. As time and money began to run out, Disney nonetheless insisted that the Autopia ride be finished. Originally envisioned with miniature gas-powered automobiles circulating on freeways, cloverleafs, and overpasses, Disney anticipated that youngsters would actually learn to drive on the Autopia, thus preparing for their futures behind the wheel of the family car. While Disneyland's transportation systems recreated the age of both steam and the pedestrian, Autopia was one connection to Los Angeles and the car culture that it spawned. Even though Disneyland was infamously sited in the orange groves of Anaheim, a half-hour's drive south of Los Angeles, its future success depended on access via the half-completed Santa Ana Freeway. Before the park opened, youngsters brought in to "test-drive" the ride destroyed all but six of the automobiles, prompting engineers to encase the cars in bumpers and eventually install a track to keep young drivers under some control. At the wheel of the contemporary brightly colored finned automobiles, youngsters reversed roles with their parents, driving along the two-lane "freeway" through the lush green landscaping, as the sleek Monorail passed above their heads. Not an imagined or science-inspired future, the Autopia was, nonetheless, a future most children could anticipate with certainty.

When it opened, Tomorrowland included Autopia, the Matterhorn bobsled ride, the Circarama 360-degree film of *A Tour of the West*, and the Nautilus submarine ride based on Disney's recently released film version of Verne's 1870 *20,000 Leagues Under the Sea* (and the site of the purported adventure in "liquid space"). Yet, its overarching theme was that of space exploration. Young, white, good-looking college students served as guides through Tomorrowland wearing space-age costumes of shiny materials. The young men sported bubble-headed space helmets above their muscle-y trapunto-stitched space garb. The young women wore chic, swingy, short dresses and futuristic capes, their shapely bare legs accessorized with matching space/cowboy boots. The men's costumes covered them from head to toe, and included not just the over-sized helmet, but also a heavy utility belt and pants tucked into space/work boots, indicating just who would be doing the "real" work in space. A seventy-six-foot TWA (Trans World Airlines) "moonliner" beckoned visitors to the center of Tomorrowland, where, on the Rocket to the Moon ride, adventurers took a bumpy ride to the dark side of the moon, learning moon facts along the way. Nearby Astro-Jets allowed visitors to whirl around in their personal jets, controlling their craft's elevation as they circled above their earthbound friends.

The focus on space as the new frontier mostly dressed up the present in sleek new clothes.

As corporate partners, 32 companies sponsored rides and exhibits at Disneyland. Cultural critic Waldrep describes the Magic Kingdom as a "nationless place (the future) where companies replaced countries" (Waldrep 1993, p. 145). In Tomorrowland, corporate sponsors exhibited their products as they did at world's fairs. Monsanto's "House of the Future" featured picture telephones, plastic chairs, microwave ovens, speakerphones, and electric toothbrushes. The house itself, built at MIT, was constructed almost entirely of plastics. Years later, a giant wrecking ball brought in to demolish it bounced off its sturdy walls. Other somewhat less-compelling corporate exhibits included Dutch Boy Paints' "Color Gallery" and Kaiser Aluminum's "Hall of Aluminum Fame." Richland Oil sponsored the Autopia. In 1967, General Electric moved its 1964 New York World's Fair exhibit, the Carousel of Progress, to Disneyland. The Carousel featured a middle-class robot family who, in a series of four scenes, celebrated electric labor-saving devices dating from 1900, the 1920s, the 1940s, and the present. Not simply an extended commercial for General Electric, the exhibit also promoted the same ideals that Disney did throughout the park: a belief in technological progress, capitalism, family values, and the powerful ways they combined to buttress American ideology during a threatening period of time.

It is a short leap from Monsanto's "House of the Future" to the animated cartoon, *The Jetsons*. An academic database search for "Jetsons" turns up nearly 30 entries for articles about developing technologies that invariably refer to the early 1960s prime time cartoon. With opening lines like: "The world has been waiting for the Jetsons-like videophone for decades," or "It's not the Jetsons, but you'll be able to fly yourself to a community 'smartport' in an idiotproof miniplane," or "NASA designs for the Jetsons set with a habitation module for the International Space Station," these articles, dating from 1992–2002 in journals such as *Electronics Now*, *Science World*, *Telephony*, and *Technology Review*, use *The Jetsons* as the gold standard for measuring technological achievement. The 1962–3 animated series ran for 24 episodes during prime time, that early evening part of the television day dedicated to family viewing. Industry executives reserved prime time for shows that parents and children, especially teenagers, could watch together without being embarrassed by sexual innuendo or repulsed by violence. By 1960, 90 percent of American homes had at least one television, with the average person watching 5 hours per day. The challenge of marketing to and programming for mixed-age audiences was and continues to be a daunting one, but in the early 1960s, this challenge was surprisingly met by two animated (rather than live action) programs, *The Flintstones* and *The Jetsons*, both of which carried weighty messages about American family and consumer life and its relationship with technology.

The Flintstones premiered first, in 1960, and enjoyed a six-year prime time run. Based unabashedly on the highly successful situation comedy, *The Honeymooners*, *The Flintstones* featured Fred, his short sidekick Barney Rubble, their lovely wives Wilma and Betty, and their respective children, Pebbles and Bamm-Bamm. The Flintstones and Rubbles lived as neighbors in the working class but suburban-style Stone Age town of Bedrock. Much of the humor is based on sight gags and visual puns that played with 1960s consumer technologies re-interpreted in a Stone Age context. In the opening leader, Fred and the family jump into the family sedan, powered by Fred's frantically flapping feet, pick up the Rubble family, and arrive at the drive-in movie theater where Dino, the family pet snorkasaurus, pokes his long neck through the car's ragtop so that Pebbles and Bamm Bamm can get a good view of the screen. After the movie, and after the episode, they all stop at the Bronto-Burgers Drive-in for a late-night snack. The Flintstones and Rubbles, despite Fred and Barney's working-class jobs at the Slate Rock and Gravel Company, have all the accoutrements of a postwar middle-class lifestyle, including decorative indoor plumbing, an octopus dishwasher, built-in kitchen cupboards, electric-styled light fixtures sitting next to the upholstered sofas and easy chairs of a suburban (stone) bungalow. In Bedrock, a wooly mammoth's trunk provides water for shaving and showering, a bird beak becomes the hi-fi stylus, and a pterodactyl becomes an airplane.

Viewers can laugh at both Fred and Barney's impossibly henpecked lives, where, as is typical in many sitcoms, fathers are what historian Butsch calls "The White Male Working-Class Buffoon" (Wells 2002, p. 73). But the visual and verbal puns (imagine every possible play on the words rock, stone, and pebble) also remind viewers how wonderful it is to be living in a time and place where real dishwashers, not octopi, wash the dishes, and one's car runs on fuel, rather than foot power. Even though the Flintstones' and Rubbles' lives appropriate and satirize the middle-class suburban lifestyle, families watching their antics on the screen of their new television in the comfort of their family room can feel smug about actually having all the comforts that modern technologies provide.

At the other end of the time continuum, the Jetsons live a similar, but Space Age, middle-class life in the Sky Pad Apartments, multi-leveled circular buildings perched high in space atop long pylons with no distinct anchor to the ground. The family consists of George and Jane Jetson, their teenage daughter, Judy, and their precocious young son, Elroy. George works a two-hour-a-day, three-day-a-week job pushing buttons on a computer (R.U.D.I., Referential Universal Differential Indexer) at Cosmo Spaceley's Spacely Space Sprockets, Inc. In contrast to life in Bedrock, no one in the Jetsons does any kind of physical activity. Machines do everything imaginable. In the first episode, "Rosey the Robot," Jane is found doing finger exercises to a tele-vised exercise show because she is developing "push-button finger." George drives to work in a flying saucer car pod along "spaceways." He is delivered to his apartment via something resembling a vertical pneumatic tube and then further delivered to the living room via a moving sidewalk. Elroy gets washed in a shower that resembles a moving car wash. Jane cooks meals (before she hires Rosey the Robot to do the housework) on a "Food-a-Rack-a-Cycle," a push-button flat panel that delivers cooked food at the push of a button. Video phones, flat-panel display screens, a "toaster-style" bed that pops George up in the morning, flying suits, anti-gravity dance floors, talking wristwatches, wireless microphones, remote television broadcasts, ultrasound cleaning machines, and electronic pets all presage a future that is predictably recalled by those currently working and reporting on many of those same technologies.

Despite the life of limited and non-physical labor made possible by labor-saving devices, George is never quite happy. His technologies continually thwart him. Jane's "Food-a-Rack-a-Cycle" goes on the blink on the night Mr. Spacely comes to dinner. The hired robot maid, a used model ready to be sent to the junkyard, mouths off at Mr. Spacely and nearly costs George his job. George is continually caught up in space-way traffic jams that cause him to get ticketed for aggressive driving. George brings home an electronic "apartment-approved" dog, "Lectronimo," to satisfy his family's wish for a pet. On a test designed to determine the better pet, Lectronimo out scores Astro, the "real" dog that Elroy has brought home, but a technological glitch has Lectronimo mistaking George for a burglar, biting him in the "end," while Astro, through dumb luck, catches the burglar. George continually complains about being over-worked and tries every strategy to get another afternoon off. At the same time, Jane complains that housework gets her down.

Once again, viewers receive a lesson about technology. Does a life dominated by fickle machines really represent progress? Or do the unreliable machines invoke one more area over which people have no control? As media specialist Stockman argues, "the implication is that the future will be bleak, science-dominated and lonely. The machines have not made life easier, indeed their unpredictability causes more problems than they solve" (Stockman 1994, p. 36). Thus, as with the *Flintstones*, viewers are reassured that the times in which they live are far better than an imagined future or a primitive past. Forty years later, as many of the Jetson technologies become reality, the discourse about these technologies reveals the same balancing act between celebrating technology's promise and countering the unintended social consequences and vulnerabilities of a machine-dominated world.

I have box of 12 *Empire Strikes Back* drinking glasses in my attic from a 1980 Burger King giveaway. I have been saving them for 23 years, anticipating that, through their sale, I could finance my retirement. On a shelf above the glasses sits my 27-year-old son's Millennium Falcon, rebel cruiser, and his Darth Vader carrying case filled with *Star Wars* action figures. Up until the last flood several years ago, the basement bathroom was decorated with *Return of the Jedi* wallpaper. My grandson is sleeping on his uncles' *Star Wars* sheets. Just yesterday, in an online intersection of pop culture and pop psychology, I took a personality test to see which *Star Wars* figure I most resemble. Much to my dismay, it turned out to be the excruciatingly odd-looking Admiral Ackbar, the rebel admiral in *Return of the Jedi*, renowned for his great powers of organization, responsibility, and administration. All of this is to say that perhaps one of the most pervasive popular cultural phenomena of the twentieth century has been the release of George Lucas's *Star Wars Trilogy: Star Wars, A New Hope* (1977), *The Empire Strikes Back* (1980), and *The Return of the Jedi* (1983). By 1997, still running strong, the trilogy had brought in $1.3 billion in box office sales and another $3 billion in licensing fees – and I helped (Seabrook 1997, p. 191).

Together the three films tell a classic story of the battle between good and evil, of domination and rebellion, of a man's turn to the "dark side," and of his son's efforts to redeem him. It takes place "a long time ago, in a galaxy far, far away," and, despite its setting in the past, it is a future world that blends mythology, science fiction, technological environments, and narrative archetypes. While film critic Rosenbaum claims that the trilogy "doesn't seem to *mean* anything other than what it is: a well-crafted, dehumanized update of *Flash Gordon*," (Rosenbaum 1997, p. 106), psychomythic critic Mackey-Kallis believes that the films "manifest the clearest articulation of Perennial philosophy, Jungian psychology, and Zen Buddhism" (Mackey-Kallis 2001, p. 202). The characters are a cast of humans, alien creatures, robots (droids), and machines and it is often impossible to discern clear boundaries between any of the categories. Men act like and are machines, droids portray more emotion than the humans, the anthropomorphized creatures, like humans, are both good and evil. While the story is a archetypal one that could transpose to any time and place, *Star-Wars* has as its context multiple worlds transformed by and reliant upon technology. And for those fans whose lives have been transformed by its messages, who trust in "The Force," messages from the movies about technology inform their perspectives about right and wrong, perspectives not that different than those of Tom Swift's.

The story takes place in spaceships and on moons and planets other than Earth. The various spaceships are artificial environments, yet all seem to enjoy the benefits of gravity, in striking contrast to the images fed to the public of twentieth-century spacecraft with their cheerful astronauts bobbing about in microgravity. The giant Imperial Stardestroyer resembles an aircraft carrier gliding through the vast expanse of space. Still larger yet, the Death Star battlestation hovers menacingly. It is an enormous round armored space world constructed by the evil imperial forces, able to destroy whole planets with the blast of a single concentrated laser beam. In a demonstration of technological power, Darth Vader cruelly annihilates Princess Leia's home planet, Alderaan. By contrast, the rebel fleet is smaller, slower, less advanced, more likely to encounter technological failures. The rebel outposts are located on planets and moons with the harshest climates. Luke Skywalker and Ben Kenobi live on Tatooine, a desert wasteland where Luke helps his uncle "farm" for water with the aid of moisture vaporators. In *Empire Strikes Back*, the rebels establish a secret base on the ice world, Hoth. Reminiscent of an Antarctic research station, the rebels live in a protective steel dome that shields them from the frozen, nearly uninhabitable world outside. Each of these sites is earthlike, if severe, and they require sophisticated technological systems to support life. In contrast, the empire seems to be spacebound, with no grounded home and thus, completely dependent on its space stations and vehicles. Nearly every other setting is a technological one and the lesson is clear: at the least, the rebels required functional equipment and environments, yet they are "grounded." They persevere and are ultimately victorious due to their steadfast dedication to their humanistic cause. The empire, however, relies exclusively on its highly developed technology, depending on its strength to pursue evil imperial goals, but vulnerable to the rebels finding the one inevitable weakness in its systems.

In a parallel vein, opposing armies and characters reveal attitudes about the relationship between man and machine. Imperial stormtroopers are encased in white plastic-like armor from head to toe. Rebel forces wear ordinary clothes that are reminiscent of traditional mythological costumes. The armor affords no clear advantage other than to intimidate and appear machine-like. Stormtroopers fall as easily as the rebels under laser gun barrages. Darth Vader, cloaked from head to toe in menacing black, depends on a breath mask for life. A later battle with his son, Luke, reveals that he, like Luke, has a bionic hand. When Luke questions his spiritual guide, Obi-Wan Kenobi, as to whether there are any vestiges of good left in Darth Vader, Obi-Wan replies, "he is more machine now than man. Twisted and evil" (*Return of the Jedi*). The comment is not solely about the machine components that keep him alive, but refers as well to the absence of humanity that enables Vader to kill with precision and without remorse. Yet Darth Vader also possesses "the force," a spiritual power that Jedi knights draw from the "energy field of all living things . . . [that] binds the galaxy together" (*A New Hope*). Darth Vader, however, has gone over to "the dark side," and his attempts to lure Luke serve to demonstrate how easily that step can be taken. Their weapon, with which they wage battle against one another, is the lightsaber, the weapon of the Jedi knight. The lightsaber is both technological and spiritual and bridges the two antithetical worlds. Its metal handle hangs from the Jedi's belt, looking much like a sophisticated flashlight. Yet the Jedi's power releases its mystical light and only one's skill with "the force" can control it. While the battle between good and evil is clear, the characters and the technology are more complex. The overriding theme is one against technological determinism. Those with humanist ideals can use technology towards humanistic ends. Trusting in the force restores the power of the individual against what appears to be insurmountable technological power. It is the message that fuels a legion of loyal fans.

In the aftermath of September 11, 2001, my history of technology class brought up the subject of the "bubble gum" trading cards that were about to be released commemorating the terrorist attacks on New York City's World Trade Center. As I expressed dismay over what seemed to me to be a shockingly inappropriate way to profit from a national tragedy, one of my students mentioned that he had a complete set of Desert Storm trading cards that Topps, Inc. (the purveyor of, as one journalist describes, the "tougher-to-chew-than-asphalt-but-always-welcome slab of gum) had produced during the 1991 United States war with Iraq. My research subsequently revealed that war trading cards date back at least to the 1930s, building on a tradition of trading cards that, in the 1880s, began with natural history cards, continued with those depicting locomotives and steamships, and eventually led to the more familiar sports cards. Two anti-war industrialists, one an advertising executive, the other a confectionery mogul, sponsored the 1938–42 "Horrors of War" series with the hopes of directing youngsters towards "a favorable attitude toward peace" (Nelson 1997, p. 101). As the nation became drawn into World War II, these cards, rather than portraying the grisly details of battle, turned to depicting American and world weaponry, asking on each card, "Can America maintain peace with the World in Arms?" By 1941, the new series, National Defense, or Uncle Sam cards, urged a collective national readiness that even youngsters could influence through their support of the war effort. The widely available war cards served as a popular medium through which young children learned about world events. Once Topps, Inc.

went into the sports card business in the early 1950s, it offered a series on the Korean War, but refrained from issuing any on the Vietnam War.

The 1991 Gulf War, as author Kellner observed, was the first war "orchestrated for television," complete with a catchy title, war footage that resembled so many video games, and graphics that emulated the all-too-familiar Windows presentation. Thus, coverage, controlled by the State Department, became a form of compelling entertainment that manipulated a patriotic belief in the nation's moral and technological superiority (Carroll 2000, pp. 25–6). Topps, Inc.'s Desert Storm trading cards, produced in coordination with the Pentagon and the Navy, followed suit by portraying the United States and its allies as saviors, possessing 1,000 fold the talent and technology necessary to remind Iraq that it could not wrestle with Western interests. As with all stories that follow a triadic narrative of beginning, transformation, and resolution, when viewed in sequential order, the 264 cards nominally tell a story of war while educating youngsters about military technology and its ability to police an increasingly unruly world. The key players in this narrative are the bombers, aircraft carriers, tanks, hummvees, and assorted equipment that the allied combatants had at their disposal. In the card series, world leaders play an initial directorial role, setting events in motion, while brave servicemen and women use the technology under their command to turn back the infidels and destroy their pathetically inadequate equipment. The story ends happily as bunting-bedecked towns across the land welcome back their war heroes and parents and children reunite in happy embrace. Omitted from the story is any mention of war dead, either military or civilian, and any attempt to convey the complicated history that set up the war. As with the 2001 Enduring Freedom cards that show neither the destruction of the World Trade Center nor the devastating aftermath, Desert Storm cards display only the hardware, not the destruction and carnage that result from its use.

The first card in the first of three Desert Storm trading card series pictures President George Bush as Commander-in-Chief of the Armed Forces. The photo is a candid one of the President, who is wearing an air force flyer's jacket – a reminder of his World War II service – against a blurred military landscape. It contrasts greatly with the formal military headshots of his generals that follow and identifies him with the troops under his command. The card's text, however, distances the President from his role in securing a declaration of war, citing, "On January 16, 1991, Operation Desert Shield turned to Desert Storm as the US Military, supported by 27 other countries of the NATO alliance, mobilized to protect the sovereignty of Kuwait." Saddam Hussein and the country of Iraq are not mentioned as the military target until card number 28. Even in this brief – and only – explanation of events, the narrative does not explicitly state that Americans and their allies are bombing Iraq, only that Iraq ignored a deadline for withdrawal and that Desert Shield "changed" to Desert Storm. An occasional card shows distant bombs exploding, but only towards the end of the third series, when three cards narrate the Iraqi surrender with Iraqi troops "kissing the boots of American officers in thanks," is there any mention of Iraqi troops or people. The machines take center stage in a sanitized and context-free display. Indeed, a description of the F-117A Stealth Fighter/Bomber claims that bombs are dropped "for the purpose of disorienting, not killing, enemy soldiers" (Card #20).

Of the 264 cards, 226 of them depict military hardware. The jets, fighters, helicopters, ships, tanks, vehicles, missiles, bombs, and guns parade by in an overwhelming and seemingly endless display of military might. Their descriptions are matter-of-fact, listing capabilities and the advantages each brings to the conflict. For example, the F-18 Hornet is described as "the cutting edge warplane," with advanced features that include "small afterburning engines, large internal fuel capacity, and avionics" (Card #29). The second and third series were produced during and after the war and so some cards, but not many, refer to the equipment's role in the war, especially in its ability to withstand both heat and sand. The F-4G "Wild Weasel" jet fighters fired High Speed Anti-Radiation Missiles (HARMs), which, according to the narrative, "have proven so accurate during Desert Storm that enemy radar locations have often shut down, to avoid the risk of being destroyed" (Card #113). Conversely, the few cards that describe Iraqi armaments highlight their vulnerabilities. The infamous Scud missiles are described as being "for the most part, inaccurate" (Card #51). A second series Scud card claims that "most of the Scuds used by the Iraqis against the Allies have been intercepted by Operation Desert Storm Patriot missiles before targets were hit" (Card #101). A third series card shows an exploding Scud appearing like fireworks in the night sky and describes its demise at the hands of the Patriot missile (Card #223).

The cards echo in many ways the television coverage of the war. The focus on "smart bombs" that hit targets with mystifying accuracy enabled the State Department to create the impression of a "clean war" in which precise bombing avoided civilian casualties and high technology punished only the wicked (Burkhart 1997, p. 23). Moreover, few viewers could miss the connection between the "push-button, remote-controlled" war and the video games on which this generation of young soldiers had grown up (Carroll 2000, p. 25). Trading cards not only emphasized technological capabilities, but romanticized the exotic war theater through a series of pictures that silhouetted the hardware against magnificent desert sunsets. By collecting the cards, young boys and girls learned a great deal about planes, ships, missiles, and bombs, but almost nothing about oil, death, and the hardships of war. Indeed, if card number 189 were to be believed, "In the end, Hussein's actions left his nation devastated, without much influence in the Arab world and barely holding on to his leadership."

The Desert Storm trading cards conveyed a focused and uncomplicated message about technology to a generation primed to accept it without question, who has never known a world without personal computers and video games. By the end of the decade, however, a genre of films emerged that expressed fears about a world increasingly controlled by invisible and incomprehensible information technology systems. One of the most intriguing and popular of these was the 1999 film, *The Matrix*. Neo, the main character, discovers that the world he knows – the world of 1999 that we all know – is a computer-simulated world and that nearly everyone living in it is a projected animation of an enslaved person who is actually "living" in a human farm. There, endless rows of humans are suspended in artificial embryonic sacs, attached by cables to a power grid through which the ruling machines produce energy to run the "matrix" that they control. The "real" earth is a terrible dark wasteland, the product of a war between humans and the machines they created, whose artificial intelligence tipped the balance of power. In the war, it was the humans who, ignoring the possible ramifications of their technology, scorched the earth by obliterating the sun, thus enabling the takeover by the machines. While *The Matrix* reenacts 1999, the story takes place 200 years later, when only a small surviving band of free humans tend the flame of hope that they will be able to over-throw the machines. The story itself is an archetypal one of revelation and salvation. Neo proves himself to be "The One" who will save the human race.

While the messages about technology seem heavy-handed, they nonetheless represent a pervasive unease with the power of new information-based technologies. Shortly after the movie's release, Bill Joy, Sun Microsystem's Chief Scientist, published an article in *Wired* magazine entitled "Why the Future Doesn't Need Us." The article seriously questioned the wisdom of research programs whose goal was a future in which "humans gained near immortality by becoming one with robotic technology" (Joy 2000, p. 1). Joy outlines his and others' fears that, within a very few short decades, advances in self-replicating robotics, genetic engineering, and nanotechnology will result in no less than the destruction of the earth's biosphere. Even as he acknowledges these technologies' tremendous potential for improving human life, Joy warns that their danger lies not only in the frightening possibilities inherent in uncontrolled self-replication, but also in the fact that they are knowledge-based technologies, and thus, vulnerable to the motives of anyone with the know-ledge and a powerful computer. Joy cites the risk of human extinction as high as 30 to 50 percent. Suggestions that laws be enacted that only allow "nice" robots hardly allay his worries. The future he fears is one not that different than that portrayed by *The Matrix*. As one of the foremost inventors and spokespersons for computer technologies, his warning earned worldwide press coverage and generated scholarly responses such as a roundtable published in *New Perspectives Quarterly* (*NPQ* 2000). The dire warnings would have been easy enough to dismiss as so much Luddism coming from anyone other than Bill Joy, yet they remain largely unheeded.

An August 2003 front-page story announced a new action figure doll called "Elite Force Aviator. George W. Bush – US President and Naval Aviator." The doll is a like-ness of the President in the naval flight suit – complete with survival vest, parachute harness, helmet, and oxygen mask – that he wore during his dramatic May 1, 2003 tailhook landing in a Navy S-3B Viking jet aboard the aircraft carrier USS Abraham Lincoln (Dubya' Doll 2003). The President staged the event to make a major national address announcing the "end" of major combat operations in the 2003 war on Iraq. His father's trading card image wearing an Air Force flyer's jacket at least recalled Bush I's legitimate World War II service, where he flew fifty-eight attack missions earning the Distinguished Flying Cross and three Air Medals. The son's outfit recalled only a constructed moment in time. While George W. Bush learned to fly F-102 fighter jets during his stateside service with the Texas National Guard during the Vietnam War, an editorial in *The Nation* suggests he completed less than four of his six pledged years with the Guard, having beat the draft and then "gamed" the system (Corn 2003). A right-wing editorial commenting on the Democrat's excoriation of the carrier landing claimed that by "co-piloting that plane onto the aircraft carrier, Bush looked manly and strong" (Willmann 2003). The power of the doll lies in its ability to transform an absent without leave (AWOL) reservist into a member of the elite special forces, by virtue of its identification with the undeniable and considerable skill inherent in the tailhook landing and the sophisticated techno-logical power symbolized by the aircraft carrier. The irony lies with a child's ability to transform the doll through its deployment in service of his or her imagination, to which boxes of ubiquitous dismembered, undressed, and discarded action figures attest. The toy company's attempt to both capitalize on the President's popularity and convey support for the government's current war program is nonetheless subject to a child's interpretation. When the doll is re-discovered next summer in the bottom of the sandbox, one can only wonder whether its bedraggled condition will serve as a metaphor for a dangerously misguided foreign policy. This possibility attests to the ability that artifacts of popular culture hold to transform and rework cultural meaning as they escape the control of the culture elite.

This essay has wound its way through the twentieth century and into the twenty-first. Its subjects recount the remarkable technological changes that occurred from the early days of electricity and motor cars to a present characterized by digital technol-ogy and the complex capabilities of modern warfare. Popular culture proves itself to be a medium through which society explores both the excitement and anxieties generated by increasingly sophisticated technologies as they become socially and culturally embedded. Certain messages and concerns remain relatively constant, regardless of the time period or the nature of the technology. One theme that emerged through this study is the interconnectedness between technology and capitalism and the way in which popular culture supports and encourages that rela-tionship. Tom Swift's adventures demonstrate that technological innovation pays off, corporate sponsorships at Disneyland blend technology, economic enterprise, and entertainment into a seamless ideological whole, and the Star Wars movies, with their moral tale, are a huge economic empire unto themselves. Through the 1984 series of advertisements for IBM, even the film *Modern Times* is recast to advocate for corporate domination. A second theme sets technology and its use and control within a moral arena. Again, Tom Swift sets the stage, but each successive example in this essay raises questions about technological neutrality and the ways that individuals and institutions can use technology to serve morally charged interests. Finally, each of these examples has something to say about the relationship between technology and progress and how societies can use technology to advance towards social, economic, and political goals. These hugely significant discourses continue to manifest themselves in and be charted by the popular medium. As movies, songs, video games, novels, and television programs imprint themselves easily and indel-ibly on both young and adult minds, it seems particularly important to explore the messages they carry about technology and the people and institutions who control and manage it.

BIBLIOGRAPHY

Appleton, Victor. *Tom Swift and His Submarine Boat, or, Under the Ocean for Sunken Treasure* (New York: Grosset and Dunlap, 1910).

Barrie, J.M. *The Adventures of Peter Pan.* www.literature.org/authors/barrie-james-matthew/the-adventures-of-peter-pan/chapter-11.html.

Basalla, George. "Keaton and Chaplin: the silent film's response to technology," in *Technology in America: A History of Individuals and Ideas*, Carroll W. Pursell ed., 2nd edn (Cambridge: The MIT Press, 1990): pp. 227–36.

Bonner, Richard. *The Boy Inventors' Wireless Triumph* (New York: Hurst & Company, 1911).

Browne, Ray B. *Mission Underway: The History of the Popular Culture Association/American Culture Association and the Popular Culture Movement, 1967–2001* (Bowling Green, OH: Popular Culture Association/American Culture Association, 2002).

Burkhart, Julia. "The media in the Persian Gulf war: from carnival to crusade," in *The Gulf War as Popular Entertainment, An Analysis of the Military-Industrial Media Complex*, ed., Paul Leslie (Lewiston, NY: The Edwin Mellen Press, 1997): pp. 17–32.

Carroll, Michael Thomas. *Popular Modernity in America, Experience, Technology, Mythohistory* (Albany: State University of New York Press, 2000).

Chamberlain, Kathleen. " 'Wise censorship': cultural authority and the scorning of juvenile series books, 1890–1940," in *Scorned Literature: Essays on the History and Criticism of Popular Mass-Produced Fiction in America*, ed., Lydia Cushman Schuman and Deidre Johnson (Westport, CT: Greenwood Press, 2002): pp. 187–212.

Caputi, Jane. "Perspectives: On remembering and forgetting: Charlie Chaplin, IBM, and 1984," *Journal of Popular Film & Television* 14 (Summer 1986): 76–9.

Chaplin, Charles. *My Autobiography* (New York: Simon & Schuster, 1964).

Corn, David. "Capital Games, Bush's *Top Gun* Photo-Op" (2003) http://www.thenation.com/capitalgames/index.mhtml?bid=3&pid=633.

Deane, Paul. "Science and technology in the children's fiction series," *Lamar Journal of the Humanities*, 16 (1990): 20–32.

Dizer, John T. Jr. *Tom Swift & Company, "Boys' Books" by Stratemeyer and Others* (Jefferson, NC and London: McFarland and Company, 1982).

Dubya' Doll. *The Plain Dealer*, August 13, 2003.

Finnan, R.W. "The Unofficial Tom Swift Home Page," http://users.arczip.com/fwdixon/tomswift (1996–2003).

Flom, Eric L. *Chaplin in the Sound Era* (Jefferson, NC: McFarland and Company, 1997).

Halevy, Julian. "Disneyland and Las Vegas," *The Nation* 186 (June 7, 1958): 510–13.

Hall, Stuart. "Notes on Deconstructing 'The Popular'," *Journal of Social History* 7 (1974): 460–508.

Joy, Bill. "Why the future doesn't need us," *Wired* (August 4, 2000) http://www.wired.com/wired/archives/8.04/joy_pr.html.

King, Margaret J. "Disneyland and Walt Disney world: traditional values in futuristic form," *Journal of Popular Culture* 15 (Summer 1981): 116–56.

Levine, Lawrence. "The folklore of industrial society; popular culture and its audiences," *American Historical Review* 97 (December 1992): 1369–99.

Mackey-Kallis, Susan. *The Hero and the Perennial Journey Home in American Film* (Philadelphia: University of Pennsylvania Press, 2001).

Maland, Charles J. *Chaplin and American Culture* (Princeton: Princeton University Press, 1989).

Marling, Karal Ann. "Disneyland, 1955," *American Art* (Winter/Spring 1991): 169–207.

Musser, Charles. "Work, ideology and Chaplin's tramp," *Radical History Review* 41 (1988): 36–66.

Nelson, Murry R. "An alternative medium of social education – the 'Horrors of War' picture cards," *The Social Studies* 88 (May/June 1997): 101–7.

"Post-human history," *New Perspectives Quarterly* 17 (Summer 2000): 3–33.

Prager, Arthur. "Bless my collar button, if it isn't Tom Swift," *American Heritage*, 28 (1976): 64–75.

Rotundo, E. Anthony. *American Manhood: Transformations in Masculinity from the Revolution to the Modern Era* (New York: Basic Books, 1993).

Rosenbaum, Jonathan. *Movies as Politics* (Berkeley: University of California Press, 1997).

Seabrook, John. "Letters from skywalker ranch: why is the force still with us?," *The New Yorker* 72 (January 6, 1997); Reprinted in Sally Kline, ed.: *George Lucas Interviews* (Jackson, Miss.: University Press of Mississippi, 1991).

Stewart, Garrett. "Modern hard times: Chaplin and the cinema of self-reflection," *Critical Inquiry* 3 (Winter 1976): 295–314.

Stockman, Tina. "Discrediting the past, rubbishing the future – A critical comparison of the Flinstones and the Jetsons," *Journal of Educational Television* 20 (1994): 27–39.

Swift, Earl. "The perfect inventor," *American Heritage of Invention and Technology* 6 (1990): 24–31.

Topp's History. http://www.topps.com/AboutTopps/history.html.

Topp's Flashback. http://www.topps.com/Entertainment/Flashback/DesertStorm/desertstorm. html.

Waldrep, Sheldon. "The contemporary future of tomorrow," *The South Atlantic Quarterly* 92 (Winter 1993): 139–55.

Walt Disney's Guide to Disneyland, 8th edn (Walt Disney Productions, 1963).

Wells, Paul. "Tell me about your id, when you was just a kid, yah, animation and children's television culture," in David Buckingham, ed., *Small Screens: Television for Children* (London: Leicester University Press, 2002): pp. 61–95.

Willmann, Kevin. "Desperate Democrats Attack Bush's Carrier Landing" http://www. chronwatch.com/content/contentDisplay.asp?aid=2619.

SUGGESTED READING

Brooker, Will. Using the Force, Creativity, Community and *Star Wars* Fans (New York: Continuum, 2002).

Lipsitz, George. *Time Passages* (Minneapolis: University of Minneapolis Press, 1990).

Lynn, Kenneth S. *Charlie Chaplin and His Times* (New York: Simon & Schuster, 1997).

Mallory, Michael. *Hanna-Barbera Cartoons* (New York: Hugh Lauter Levin Associates, Inc., 1998).

Maltby, Richard, ed. *Dreams for Sale: Popular Culture in the Twentieth Century* (London: Harrap, 1989).

Oldenziel, Ruth. *Making Technology Masculine, Men, Women and Modern Machines in America, 1870–1945* (Amsterdam: Amsterdam University Press, 1999).

Ross, Andrew. *No Respect, Intellectuals and Popular Culture* (New York: Routledge, 1989).

Simon, Richard Keller. *Trash Culture, Popular Culture and the Great Tradition* (Berkeley: University of California Press, 1999).

Sorkin, Michael, ed. *Variations on a Theme Park: The New American City and the End of Public Space* (New York: Hill and Wang, 1992).

Spiegel, Lynn. *Make Room for TV: Television and Family Ideal in Postwar America* (Chicago: University of Chicago Press, 1992).

Stabile, Carol A. and Mark Harrison, eds. *Prime Time Animation, Television Animation and American Culture* (London: Routledge, 2003).

Tichi, Cecelia. *Shifting Gears, Technology, Literature, Culture in Modern America* (Chapel Hill: University of North Carolina Press, 1987).

Whitfield, Stephen J. *The Culture of the Cold War*, 2nd edn (Baltimore: Johns Hopkins University Press, 1996).

CHAPTER TWENTY-ONE

Art and Technology

HENRY ADAMS

Tools date back to prehistoric times; fairly complex machines, with gears and levers, existed in classical antiquity; mills, clocks, water-propelled toys, and other complex instruments existed in the middle ages. The development of new machines, however, greatly accelerated during the nineteenth century and has continued at a feverish pace to the present. At first most of this innovation involved mechanics – machines that worked with wheels, gears, and levers. Broadly speaking, this mechanical technology was used to increase production through the development of mills, factories, and mass production, or to speed up and reduce the cost of transport and travel, as in the development of the locomotive or the automobile. As this process of innovation continued, however, it led to more complex inventions, such as photography, sound recording, radio, television, and the computer. These new innovations continued to ingeniously exploit mechanical principles, but combined them with "invisible" forces, such as chemistry, electricity, and nuclear energy, to create processes increasingly remote from daily experience. In addition, as technology has grown more complex, machines have increasingly moved from performing highly repetitive tasks, to performing complex operations, such as mathematical calculations. In many instances, most notably the computer, the machine has moved from the realm of physical accomplishments, to mental ones, or to put this shift in slightly different language, we have gradually been moving from "The Mechanical Age" to "The Information Age," in which "information" is as much a product as a physical thing.

The task of describing how this process has affected "art" is complicated by the fact that "art" is a term with a variety of rather slippery meanings. Broadly speaking the term "art" is used in two different ways. On the one hand it applies to certain types of expression, such as painting, sculpture and architecture, to which our society awards special cultural significance and which it rates according to its value and rarity. A non-judgmental way of categorizing the distinction between art and non-art is simply to say that we tend to preserve works of art in art museums or to write about them in art books.

On the other hand, we use the term "art" to apply to anything done with a genius or skill that borders on magic. When we use the term in this way we may argue that some objects, generally viewed as art are not really art at all. Some paintings, for example, may not qualify as art because they are mechanical and unimaginative in execution. Some novels may not rate as works of art because they are dull. On the other hand, some activities not usually considered art, such as playing golf or baking apple pie, may reach the level of art when they are done with extraordinary flair. Similarly, an essentially utilitarian object, such as a chair or a bicycle, may meet the criterion of art when it is conceived and made with sufficient skill.

According to this second way of thinking, even technological innovation may qualify as "art" when it meets certain criteria. For example, Leonardo Da Vinci's drawings of flying machines may be considered "art" as well as "technology," because of the visionary imagination that they demonstrate, as well as because of their visual beauty. Viewed in this way, in fact, there is an interesting evolution from "art" to "technology" that can often be observed. The term "art" tends to apply to relatively open forms of creative play, in which creative choice is broad and in which "usefulness" plays a small role. As this play develops clear-cut rules and is turned towards a useful purpose, it tends to be described as scientific or technical rather than artistic.

When we view things in this way, it quickly becomes apparent that many forms of technology originated in "art" and in "play" rather than in a clear sense of what practical purpose an innovation would serve. Elaborate geared mechanisms, for example, were constructed in the early middle ages purely for purposes of amusement, for example to serve as table fountains. By the late middle ages it had become common to employ mechanisms of this type to serve as clocks. Only gradually did it dawn on society that these same mechanisms could perform practical tasks, such as grinding grain or weaving textiles, and the full development of the factory and mill did not occur until the early nineteenth century. In some peculiar way, it appears that for humans to devise useful objects, they often need to discard traditional notions of usefulness and to play without regard to any sensible purpose. Thus, in some instances, "art" and "technological invention and application" may not be clearly distinct activities, but simply different phases of the overall creative process.

The increasing significance of technology in shaping people's lives was vividly expressed in The Great Exhibition of 1851 in London, where, for the first time, products of industry, machines and inventions were displayed side by side with art. The very display space for this event, which attracted six million visitors, articulated the importance of new technology. The exhibition was held in The Crystal Palace, an iron and glass structure designed by Joseph Paxton, on the model of the greenhouse, which covered a ground area of eight hundred thousand square feet – about four times that of St Peter's. Due to its modular construction, it was erected in the brief time span of six months.

That technical marvels and machines of the sort displayed at the Great Exhibition would bring about a new way of thinking about beauty and artistic endeavor should have been self-evident, but in fact, it was not until four decades later that a writer posed the questions raised by this fact in clear-cut terms. At a later world fair, the World's Columbian Exposition of 1893, the historian Henry Adams, similarly confronted by displays that combined art with engines, was inspired to speculate that the energy previous societies had invested in art and religion had been concentrated into the machine. In "The Dynamo and the Virgin," the most famous chapter of his autobiography, *The Education of Henry Adams*, he declared that "the historian's business was to follow the track of energy," and speculated that whereas the medieval world had been ruled by the mystical power of The Virgin, the world of the future would be ruled by the Dynamo. Such a shift would entail major changes in the social order, not least the development of symbols, artworks and a mindset that focused on the beauty of the machine.

Artists trained to old way of thinking were fundamentally unsuited to this task. As Adams noted of such traditionally trained sculptors, painters and writers: "They felt a railway train a power; yet they, and all other artists, constantly complained that the power embodied in a railway train could never be embodied in art." Indeed, in art of the nineteenth century, it is remarkable how rarely one finds direct representations of industry or the machine. Thomas Anshutz in Philadelphia painted *Steelworkers Noontime* (1880; Fine Art Museums of San Francisco) and Adolf Menzel in Berlin created a large panorama of *The Iron Rolling Mill* (1875; National Gallery, Berlin), but on the whole it is odd how rarely one encounters images of this type. Not until the turn of the century did the machine become a popular subject for artists.

When artists finally began to focus on the machine, they focused on those very qualities that disrupted normal existence – that it was noisy, intrusive, and obnoxious. We see this, for example, in early renderings of the motorcar – among others, Toulouse-Lautrec's lithograph *The Motorist* (1896; Art Institute of Chicago), in which a demonic driver in goggles scatters sheep and people in his wake; or Umberto Boccioni's humorous tempera *Speeding Automobile* (1901; Automobile Club d'Italia, Rome) in which a fox escapes from a pack of hounds by jumping onto the back of a speeding car. Perhaps the first artistic movement to successfully seize on this theme of the noise, disruption and excitement of the machine was Italian Futurism, whose manifesto, penned by Marinetti, declared that "A roaring motorcar is more beautiful than the Victory of Samothrace."

As the Futurists sensed, capturing these new qualities of speed, disruption, and disorder seemed to demand a modern artistic language, outside the boundaries of academic art. Thus, for example, an elaborate carving of a prize-winning driver in his roadster, *Monument to Emile Levassor*, created by the academic sculptor Camille Lefebvre in 1907, seems fussy, decadent, immobile, and inappropriate to the subject. The tedious process of chipping details in marble seems out of tune with the very notion of speed and excitement. Cleverly, the Futurists borrowed the geometric clarity of Cubism and combined it with the motion studies of Eadward Muybridge, to create a new language for representing speed through the insistent repetition of geometrically powerful shapes. In fact, to a large degree the Futurists established the basic grammar of machine-age art, which has been adopted ever since. The principle elements of this grammar, in addition to the use of strongly geometric shapes that resemble levers and gears, include a delight in the fragmentation of forms, and the deployment of successive representations of an image to evoke motion. So successful were the Futurists that their visual language has descended to the popular realm. Their devices for representing action and movement are regularly used today in comic books.

Along with its noise and disruption, the machine brought other frightening social changes – above all, the drudgery of factory work, with its repetitive tasks and low wages. The idea that the machine turned men into machines became one of the nightmares of twentieth century art. On a popular level, this theme was explored in Charlie Chaplin's film *Modern Times* (1936), in which an industrial worker goes bezerk, and engages in senseless, repetitive, machine-like behavior, like that of the assembly line where he worked. The notion of men transformed into machines was also explored by a host of major twentieth-century sculptors and painters.

In America, Francis Picabia explored machinist subjects during his years in New York, for example, caricaturing the art dealer Alfred Stieglitz as a broken camera (1915; Metropolitan Museum of Art); Marcel Duchamp explored "machine eroticism" in a series of works, beginning with *The Bride* (1912; Philadelphia Museum of Art), which shows the bride as a well-oiled machine running on "love gasoline," and culminating in his *The Large Glass* (1915–23; Philadelphia Museum of Art), which contains a large cast of machine-like characters and is widely considered Duchamp's masterpiece. In Europe, Kasmir Mevich painted a knife-grinder as a machine-like robot, made up of grinding wheels (circa 1912; Yale University Art Gallery); and Jacob Epstein, in *The Rock Drill* (1913–14; Museum of Modern art), presented a miner as an insect like figure, who had come to resemble the drill in his hands. Linked with this nightmare of men becoming machines was the notion of machines losing control and taking human affairs in their hands, a nightmare explored in forms as various as Yves Tinguely's self-destroying machines and the renegade computer HAL in the novel (and film) *2001*, who attempts to take over his human handlers.

Such images of technology as disruptive and dehumanizing form a continuous tradition in twentieth-century art, and are still being created today. In the 1920s, however, an alternative tradition was developed for representing the impact of the machine, in part because the nature of technology changed. Early forms of technology were large in scale, such as factories, steel mills and railroads. In the 1920s, however, technology became smaller and cozier, and began to enter the average home in the form of such things as toasters, refrigerators and electric lights, all of which worked on electricity, a form of energy which was both invisible and silent. This led to a view of the machine world as white, pristine, and perfect. The 1920s also saw the glorification of the machine in the decorative style known as Art Deco, which was popularized through a great decorative arts exposition held in Paris in 1925. In contrast with Art Nouveau, which has stressed organic, sinuous forms, Art Deco stressed machine-like, angular ones. The style had many sources, ranging from Cubist collages to Aztec temples, but these sources were all absorbed into a machine-like style of drawing, which reduced all forms to either straight lines (like levers) or pure circular ones (like gears).

Some of the leading artists of the period celebrated the machine. In America, for example, Charles Sheeler, painted the new Ford Plant at River Rouge as a kind of Utopian city, while the French painters Louis Ozenfant and Pierre Janneret developed a style they termed Purism which was inspired by the precise and objective elegance of the machine. One fascinating figure, the American ex-patriate Gerald Murphy, even created large-scale paintings which glorified consumer objects, such as a watch and a safety razor. "Engineers are healthy, virile, active and useful, moral and happy," Le Corbusier wrote in *La Peinture Moderne* of 1925, implicitly declaring that engineers were the true artists of the modern world – an idea expressed more ironically by Marcel Duchamp, who declared that, "The only works of art America has given are her plumbing and her bridges."

The Russian constructivist Vladimir Tatlin pushed this idea towards its limit in his work. Tatlin believed that art could be formed by combining a program of clearly stated intentions with the pure and logical use of materials. His *Monument for the Third International* merges architecture and sculpture with moving mechanical elements. In the 1920s he began to construct aircraft – one man gliders. In such expressions, the line between the engineer and the artist becomes increasingly blurred. A logical extension of this approach was the argument that because of their beauty, machine already are works of art, a position that Marcel Duchamp took up and defended, with a blend of cold logic and ironic whimsy. In 1913, Duchamp began to create "ready-mades," functional objects such as a bicycle wheel, a bottle rack, or even a urinal, which became works of art because he declared them so. Duchamp's irony had two aspects: one was to declare that "art" consisted of any act of choice; the other was to point out that machine-made forms can be stunningly beautiful – often more beautiful than traditional paintings.

Finally, artists have devised a third means of responding to the machine – or at to the inner forces that propel it – through one of the most remarkable developments of twentieth-century art, abstract painting. In a world ruled by atomic energy and invisible electrical forces, conventional forms of visual representation came to seem inadequate as a picture of the world in which we live. Abstraction, which delves, or purports to delve, into a deeper level of reality, was a logical solution to this dilemma. In some cases, indeed, one can trace a direct relationship between Abstract styles and scientific investigations. As a child, for example, the painter Hans Hofmann won prizes for his work with electrical machines. As an adult he became a leading abstract painter, who created a world of floating shapes that push and pull against each other through forces of color. The world of Hofmann's abstractions clearly does not correspond with the world of daily life, in which solid objects respond to the forces of gravity. But it is strikingly similar to the subatomic world, in which fields of energy are controlled by positive and negative electrical charges. In some sense Hoffman's desire to create Abstract paintings seems to have been linked with his desire to understand the invisible world of electrical charges.

Art, Craft and the Machine

While the machine has been important as a subject for the twentieth-century artist, perhaps equally significant is the way in which every traditional mode of art has had its fundamental rules of operation significantly transformed by technology of some sort. The role of the machine has been particularly obvious and powerful in the realm of decorative arts and handicrafts. In the mid-nineteenth century, the ability of the machine to reproduce elaborate effects of carving or decoration quickly led to an overwhelming profusion of ornament in every imaginable historical style. This in turn led to a glut of the senses that led to the search for principles of reform. The most influential nineteenth-century reformer was William Morris, whose ideas of design were linked with an ideal of human brotherhood that led him to advocate socialism. Morris believed that simple handcrafted objects, like those of the Middle Ages, were virtuous in a way that modern machine-made objects were not. He sought to introduce more virtuous design both through more disciplined use of ornament and through a return to craft. Nonetheless, Morris recognized that handmade objects were too expensive for most people. Consequently, he reluctantly succumbed to the need for using machines, for example, using machines to produce his designs for wallpaper. William Morris had enormous influence not only in Britain but in America and on the continent. He was perhaps the central founding figure of the "Arts and Crafts movement," which strove to introduce a more virtuous and more handmade look into American and European interiors. Fundamentally, Morris was a Ludite, who hoped to go back to the simpler technologies of earlier periods. This tradition still continues in the realm of the arts and crafts, where evidence of handwork still carries connotations of spirituality and beauty. Paradoxically, this means that objects that are roughly formed are deemed superior to ones that are too perfect. Nonetheless, implicit in Morris's thinking was that beautiful things could be made by machine, so long as the machine was used "honestly," to produce machine-like effects, rather than being employed to fake the look of things made by hand.

During the latter part of the nineteenth century, and the early years of the twentieth however, a number of gifted designers challenged Morris's emphasis on handwork and argued that machine design could also be beautiful, if developed in its own unique terms. Finally, the influential Bauhaus School in Germany, led by the architect Walter Gropius, essentially codified the principles of proper machine design. Gropius and his faculty believed that the machine offered the opportunity to provide goods for everyone and relieve workers from tedious activities. Rather than seeking to conceal machine effects, the Bauhaus celebrated them.

Essentially, the Bauhuas eliminated all the rich ornament that Morris had so loved. It exploited the geometric clarity of machine-made objects; and stressed modern materials and immaculate surfaces. The Bauhaus made something of a fetish of using modern materials, for example, constructing chairs out of tubular steel rather than wood. It deliberately made objects look factory-made and mass-produced, even when in fact they had been made by hand at considerable expense. While the Bauhaus was closed by the Nazis after a few years, Gropius's theories had wide influence. He became Dean of the Architecture School at Harvard and his theories of design were promoted by the Museum of Modern Art in New York, which promoted them with reformist zeal.

In practice, it is difficult to follow either of these theories without compromise, although the ideals they represent have become issues that are evident in most examples of the arts and crafts. In practice, Morris found that handwork was too expensive even for his affluent clients. Consequently, he did often concede to the use of machines, so long as the hand element was prominent in the design. He was most successful, both commercially and artistically in ventures that openly used the machine, with products like wallpaper. In practice, the Bauhaus also never achieved its goal of mass production in great quantities. Indeed, many of the most famous Bauhaus objects were expensive hand-crafted objects, made to look as though they were mass-produced, and intended to serve as prototypes for mass production that never took place. As pushed by the Museum of Modern Art, the artists of the Bauhaus and their followers often ignored basic commercial realities.

Industrial Design

The challenge of designing for the machine created a new artistic profession, that of industrial designer. While there are precedents dating back to the nineteenth century, in the work of such figures as Christopher Dresser in Britain and Peter Behrens in Germany, through the 1920s, most products were conceived not by trained designers but by artisans or engineers within an industry. As late as 1931 a survey carried out by the magazine "Product Engineering" established that only 7 percent of its readers felt that the exterior design of a product was a crucial factor in its sales. This attitude changed fundamentally, however, in the 1930s, when the worldwide economic slump made manufacturers desperate for a means of improving sales.

The term "industrial design" was first used by Norman Bel Geddes in 1927, and its importance was dramatically illustrated in the same year when Henry Ford, who had resisted innovations in styling, finally gave in to competition from General Motors and halted production of the Ford Model T. The cost of closing down the factory and retooling to produce a more appealing car, the Model A, cost $18 million, and was described by one observer as "the most expensive art lesson in history." The birth of industrial design as a profession is often fixed at 1929 when Raymond Loewy took on his first major commission, the redesign of the Gestetner Duplicator. Loewy's work on this project essentially established the modern language of industrial design.

The phrase that "form follows function" has become a popular phrase for good architecture and design, but in fact, modern industrial design was founded on a different approach. In 1929, Sigmund Gestetner, a British manufacturer, commissioned Raymond Loewy to redesign his duplicating machines. Loewy then purchased one hundred dollars worth of Plasticine clay, spread a tarpaulin on the floor of his small living room, and covered the original machine with clay, reshaping it into a handsome cabinet that concealed all of the mechanisms except the operating controls. Loewy later applied the same principal to automobiles, appliances, cruise ships, and the locomotives of the Pennsylvania railroad, and his approach rapidly became the standard one for designing appliances. The essential idea was that appliances should be designed around the needs of the user rather than the needs of the machine. As a consequence, working parts can be enclosed and hidden. Not only is this more visually attractive, but in many instances it is safer and more practical, as it protects the user from becoming entangled in moving parts and protects the machine itself from damage.

The shape of this outer "skin" of an appliance is essentially arbitrary, but Loewy favored sleek, streamlined shapes, a preference that has continued in industrial design to the present day. In the case of automobiles and airplanes such shape does indeed reduce wind resistance and increase speed. But in the case of most industrial objects, such as refrigerators, typewriters and computers, the choice of rounded streamlined shapes is essentially symbolic. It creates a symbolic association with the power, speed, and modernity of objects such as rockets, ships and airplanes.

The buying public often liked streamlining in a flamboyant and ostentatious form, as in the finned cars that Harley Earl designed for General Motors. Highbrows, however, generally preferred a more restrained approach. Thus, when the Museum of Modern Art established a department of Design, it spurned the work of most American designers, favoring the simpler, more restrained look of the Bauhaus. The irony of this, however, is that most Bauhaus design is more expensive to produce and has never appealed to a mass audience. The Museum of Modern Art, consequently, became a showroom for products supposedly designed for the masses but affordable only to the elite. Moreover, in its quest for the pure application of design principles, the museum favored technologically simple objects, such as teacups, and avoided truly modern instruments, such as telephones or refrigerators. Paradoxically, whereas in previous centuries, ostentatious effects were considered proof of wealth and status, in the twentieth century, austerity has become the mark of affluence.

Modern Architecture

Among traditional art forms, technology had a particularly clear and pervasive influence on architecture, where new materials, such as steel and glass, made it possible to construct vast spans or to create buildings of remarkable height. To a large degree, the history of modern architecture is the history of the use of these new materials, and of the struggle to find an aesthetically pleasing manner of handling them.

At the end of the nineteenth century, American architecture tended to be divided into two parts. On the one hand were the buildings produced by the wealthy or for civic purposes, which tended to echo the architecture of the past and to contain historical ornament. On the other hand were purely utilitarian structures, such as factories and grain elevators, which employed modern materials such as steel girders and plate glass in a frank and unadorned manner. Such buildings, however, were viewed in a category separate from "fine" architecture, and in fact were often designed by engineers and builders rather than architects. The development of modern architecture might in large part be seen as an adaptation of this sort of functional building and its pervasive application for daily use. Indeed, in his influential book *Vers Une Architecture*, the French architect Le Corbusier illustrated his text with photographs of American grain elevators and factories, as well as ships, airplanes, and other frankly industrial objects. Nonetheless, modern architects did not simply employ these new materials in a strictly practical fashion – they consciously exploited their unusual aesthetic properties. For example, steel beams could be used to create a feeling of weightlessness, and to make a structure that seemed to defy normal concepts of physical support; glass could be used to open up walls and eliminate corners in a surprising fashion. The result was an architecture that broke out of the old-fashioned box in a surprising fashion.

The fundamental premise of modern architecture was that the appearance of the building should match the nature of its new materials and new forms of physical support. This often led to effects that look odd from a traditional standpoint, but became popular for precisely this reason. For example, traditional masonry walls serve a structural role, but in a steel-beam building the walls are essentially hung from the building. This means that walls and corners no longer needed to be solid, but could be opened up in unexpected ways. At the Fagus shoe factory in Germany, for example, Walter Gropius placed glass walls in the corners, effectively breaking open the box of traditional architecture, and creating a new sense of light and openness. Such open effects became one of the hallmarks of the modern look. Similarly, steel beams can support dramatic cantilevers, which could not be supported by traditional wood or masonry. These quickly became a signature of modern architects such as Frank Lloyd Wright. Wright's most dramatic residence, *Fallingwater*, cantilevers balconies over a stream in a way that seems to defy our normal conception of gravity.

The ways in which new technology transformed architectural design are dramatically illustrated through the evolution of the high-rise office building. After ten or twelve stories, masonry construction reaches a maximum possible height, since it runs into difficulties of compression and of inadequate lateral strength to combat wind sheer. Steel construction, on the other hand, can support a building of 50 or 100 stories without difficulty. Such buildings were so different from any previous form of architecture that they quickly acquired a new name – the skyscraper.

The basic practical purpose of skyscrapers was to maximize the rental property available on expensive real estate in order to maximize rental income. But to create usable high-rise buildings, a number of daunting technical challenges needed to be solved. One problem was that of getting people to the upper floors, since after five or six stories it becomes exhausting to climb stairs. Fortunately, the invention of the elevator, which was introduced by Elisha Graves Otis at the 1853 New York World's Fair, eliminated this problem.

Another difficulty was that of fire safety. Unprotected metal becomes soft when subjected to the heat of fire and collapses relatively quickly. (It melts at 2700 Fahrenheit, whereas major fires achieve temperatures of 3,000 degrees.) However, when a metal structure is encased in fire retardant materials, its vulnerability to fire is much decreased. In Chicago, a system was developed for wrapping the steel frame with fire-retardant terra cotta tile, which is both impervious to fire and relatively light. This was used both to encase the supporting members and to serve as flooring. Such a steel frame with hollow tile was three times lighter than masonry construction. Thus an eighteen-story building using the new system weighed no more than six stories in the former manner.

Resolving all these difficulties, and others of a similar nature, clearly went beyond the capability of a single individual, and required teams of gifted engineers and construction specialists, as well as highly developed systems of manufacture and mass production.

Given their novel nature, skyscrapers presented a new aesthetic challenge. What visual form should these new buildings take? Early skyscrapers often employed a variety of historical references, attempting to resemble famous historic buildings, such as Classical temples, Gothic churches, and Renaissance palaces, although they were differently proportioned. This procedure, however, came under attack almost immediately, since it seemed insincere to make a skyscraper in the guise of something else, and such ornament also entailed extra expense and was not useful.

The devastating Chicago Fire of 1871 made it necessary to rebuild a city of 200,000 people almost instantly, and encouraged a rapid acceleration of technical innovations. What became the standard program of skyscraper design was established by the Chicago architect Louis Sullivan and was first expressed in the Wainwright Building (St Louis). There the building takes a tripartite form: a base, extending up two or three stories, which houses the entryway of the building, and stores which are accessible from the street; a central column, where offices are located; and a top, which terminates the building, and suggest that this part of the building serves a different purpose, since it is generally used for housing machinery. This solution breaks the building up into visually readable parts in a fashion which is at once logical and aesthetically pleasing. Sullivan defended his solution with a phrase that has been widely repeated to justify a modern approach: "Form follows function."

While the upper portion of his building was almost plain, Sullivan employed elaborate Art Nouveau ornament on the base of the structure. The next step in the evolution of a Modern aesthetic was taken by the architects of the Bauhaus – Walter Gropius and Mies Van der Rohe – who eliminated such frills, creating buildings of unornamented metal and glass. While in Germany, Van der Rohe made visionary models of glass and steel skyscrapers, and he was finally able to execute them after he moved to the United States, notably in the Seagram Building in New York. His aesthetic dominated American architecture from the 1950s well into the 1970s.

To the uninformed eye, Van der Rohe's buildings seem like the pure expression of structure, since there is no decoration, only expanses of glass, girders, beams, and carefully placed rivets. Nonetheless, despite the dictum of "form follows function" that was used to justify this approach, what we see on the exterior of Van der Rohe's buildings is essentially a form of decoration, since the real structural elements were surrounded by fire-resistant material, and then covered with the exterior sheathing that we see. Indeed, skyscrapers in this "functional" mode show some variety in decorative treatment, since some architects chose to stress the vertical elements, other the horizontal, and different materials and proportions could create varied effects.

Advocates of modern architecture have often argued that it is morally superior to more historical and eclectic styles because it reflects the "truth" of how it is constructed. But in fact, the relationship of modern architecture to its actual structure is far from simple. "Form" does not so much "follow" function as "symbolize" function, and this function can be both visualized and symbolized in a great variety of ways.

So-called Post-Modern architecture was based on the realization that this decorative treatment of the exterior was essentially arbitrary and symbolic, and did not truly express the actual structure of the building. Consequently, Post-Modern architecture introduced forms of decorative treatment that were essentially playful and arbitrary, including elements based on historical sources, such as classical pediments and columns. As it happens, it is as easy to make complex forms by machine, such as pediments and columns, as it is to make simple steel beams and girders. Thus, the notion that one or another style of design expresses "truth" is clearly a fallacious one. As with industrial design, the best solution, within broad practical requirements, is clearly set by human needs rather than a fictitious concept of "function."

Photography as an Art Form

In the visual arts, photography brought about a fundamental transformation of vision. But photography itself has always presented curious problems of definition. Everyone agrees that photography was a new form of technology, but just when and under what circumstances should we regard photography as an art? Confusion about this issue has always made discussions of photography and art and particularly challenging undertaking.

Photography combines two principles, first that if a pin hole is made in a darkened room that it will cast an image on the opposite wall, and second, that certain substances darken when exposed to sunlight. The pin-hole camera, also known as a camera obscura, was described by Leonardo da Vinci in the Renaissance and was employed as an aid by the seventeenth-century Dutch painter Vermeer. The use of nitrate of silver to create images from sunlight was explored by Thomas Wedgewood, son of the British potter. To develop modern photography required solving a number of technical problems, most significantly how to halt the process of darkening, to create a permanent image. The first practical form of photography, the daguerreotype, was developed by Jean-Louis Daguerre, who produced unique images on a polished copper plate, and announced his discovery to the world in 1839. Simultaneously, a method of producing photographs on paper was developed in Britain by William Henry Fox Talbot. After several years of experiment, Talbot developed a technique known as the calotype or talbotype, which used a negative to make a print, and thus allowed the creation of multiple images.

Since the inventions of Daguerre and Talbot, photography has continued to develop in three ways. The first was to record the world more quickly and accurately; the second was to become easier to replicate; the third was to become easier to do. Early photographs required exposures as long as fifteen minutes, and in some cases those posing for portraits needed head clamps to stay in position so that they could be pictured without blurring. Better lenses and shorter exposures brought rapid improvement, but true action photography remained difficult, both because of long exposure times and the bulky apparatus. For example, a photograph of a Civil War battle by Timothy O'Sullivan shows smoke but no soldiers, since the soldiers moved too quickly to leave an image on film. Not until the development of the handheld Leica 25 millimeter camera in the 1930s, did it become possible to capture instantaneous effects, a possibility that was quickly seized by war reporters such as Robert Capa and photo-journalists such as Henri Cartier-Bresson.

The second was to make it possible to reproduce photographs more easily. Initially, photographs needed to be copied by hand through wood-engraving, but the development of photo-etching and engraving, and offset printing, made it possible to reproduce photographs directly. By the early twentieth-century, in fact, even drawings and paintings were reproduced photographically.

The third was to make photography easier for ordinary people. The great innovator here was George Eastman, who first marketed photography to the masses with the Brownie camera, introduced in 1888. This was based on two revolutionary insights. The first was that by using celluloid rather than glass, one could make a camera that was light and portable. The second was that by offering developing as a service that was free with the purchase of a roll of film, one could eliminate the most complicated part of the enterprise and make picture-taking a recreation for almost everyone.

Almost immediately after its invention, photography made inroads in many of the fields that traditionally had been served by painting. For example, the daguerreotype could produce portraits that were both more accurate and considerably less expensive than those produced by painters. In the early nineteenth century, large numbers of semi-trained painters pursued the portrait trade throughout the United States and Europe, but within a few years they had been pushed out of business by photographers.

The very ease of photography, however, raised questions about whether it should be considered a mechanical technique or an art form, particularly since many early portrait photographs were formulaic in their approach, consisting for the most part of frontal views of people sitting in chairs. This question persisted as photography grew more versatile, through the use of better lenses, shorter exposure times, and less cumbersome apparatus. Indeed, photography was generally used by practical-minded people who were interested in a straightforward record of a subject. For this reason, it was often regarded as less similar to creative art forms, such as painting, than to disciplines such as engineering. Curiously, film-making was never viewed as anything but an art form, even if an art form of a low type. Pie-throwing film actors might not be great artists, but since their profession resembled that of actors on the stage, their claim to be artists of some sort was never seriously questioned. Photography was so different than painting that it seemed to fit into a new category. Photographers who wished to be viewed as artists, needed to make a special case that they deserved this appellation.

Quite early in the development of the medium, some photographers very consciously attempted to treat photography as an art form by creating effects reminiscent of academic painting. One of the most ambitious of these figures was Oscar Rejlander, a Swede working in Britain, who used combination printing to create elaborate compositions of allegorical subjects. More artistically successful, at least to the modern eye, was Julia Margaret Cameron, who created both sentimental genre scenes and remarkable portraits of such luminaries as Darwin, Browning, and Tennyson. Such efforts, however, for the most part, were less appealing than actual paintings, since they lacked color, and contained no brushwork or direct evidence of the artist's touch. But just when this early school of art-photography was languishing, the cause of artistic photography was taken up by an British photographer, Peter Henry Emerson, who slightly shifted the terms of the debate. Basing his theories in part on the strictures of John Ruskin, Emerson argued that the purpose of art forms was to truthfully represent nature, and that photography could do this more successfully than almost any medium, since all it lacked was the color found in painting. What is more, Emerson acted on his principles, creating a strikingly beautiful portfolio of forty landscape photographs, titled *Life and Landscape on the Norfolk Broads*, published in 1886.

Ironically, Emerson himself eventually retreated from his claim that photography was an art. In a black-bordered pamphlet, *The Death of Naturalistic Photography*, published in 1891, he announced that photography was too technically limited to rank as a true art form. Emerson's publications and photographs, however, not only stirred up lively debate, but led to the creation of photography societies, devoted to exhibiting photography and promoting it as an art form.

Among the many inspired by his work was a young American, Alfred Stieglitz, who took up photography while studying at the University of Berlin in 1883. Stieglitz's first photographs were quite literal imitations of the academic and tonalist paintings of the period. He exhibited them widely and in the space of a decade garnered over 150 photography awards. On his return to America, Stieglitz became active in photographic societies, and also edited two successive journals devoted to photography, *Camera Notes* and *Camera Work*. At this time, Stieglitz and his followers used soft focus to endow their images with a sense of poetic mystery, reminiscent of the paintings of Whistler. Stieglitz also expanded his range of subject matter, focusing his camera on the modern life of New York, and exploring unusual weather effects, such as snow and rain, to create images that often are surprisingly parallel to the paintings of the Ash Can School. To promote the sale of photography, Stieglitz opened a commercial gallery, which soon became a forum not only for the work of the best contemporary photographers, but also for modern art of a daringly experimental nature by such figures as Picasso and Matisse. While promoting modern painting, Stieglitz also promoted the idea that photography could be marketed as a rare art form, and that a photographer's original prints could be as unique as those of a draftsman or etcher.

In 1917, he held an exhibition of the work of a young photographer named Paul Strand, which he also featured in the last two issues of *Camera Work*. Strand's work set a new direction for artistic photography. Rather than using soft focus, Strand produced images that were hard and clear, but which had an abstract quality because of their unusual viewpoints and emphasis on strong geometric patterns. Unlike earlier artistic photography, Strand did not crop or manipulate his images in the darkroom, but insisted that the image should take up the whole frame and should be complete in the artist's mind when he snapped the shutter. Unlike previous forms of artistic photography, which used painting as a reference point, Strand's work seems to find artistic qualities that were unique to photography as a medium. Strand's approach was soon taken up by other figures, such as Edward Steichen, Charles Sheeler, Edward Weston, Ansel Adams, and even Stieglitz himself. Even today it remains the principal mode of artistic photography.

Fundamentally, however, Stieglitz's artistically self-conscious approach, as refined by Paul Strand, with its emphasis on the control of the artist, runs against some of the most exciting qualities of photography as an art form. For one thing, the doctrine of "previsualization" promoted by "artistic" photographers (particularly Alfred Stieglitz and Edward Weston), seems to deny one of the most basic qualities of the medium, its ability to reveal the unexpected and unnoticed. The novelist Emile Zola, for example, who was a dedicated amateur photographer, told a reporter in 1900: "In my opinion you cannot say you have thoroughly seen anything until you have got a photograph of it, revealing a lot of points which otherwise would be unnoticed, and which in most cases could not be distinguished" (Newhall 1964, p. 94). Throughout the history of photography, amateurs, journalists, and individuals with practical goals, have often created memorable – even astonishing – images.

What is more, the modern power of photography derives largely from the fact that images can be reproduced in vast numbers at modest expense. While slow to be recognized as a true art form, the photojournalism of figures such as Dorothea Lange, Margaret Bourke-White, Walker Evans, or even the New York Post photographer Weegee (Arthur Felig), seems to more directly respond to the unique capabilities of photography as an art from, and those properties that are most unlike any other artistic medium.

Curiously, some of the ways in which photography has most transformed human vision have been viewed as mechanical achievements rather than artistic ones. For example, photography has dramatically transformed our understanding of animal locomotion – revealing, for example, how a horse's legs actually move, and eliminating an artistic convention for equine movement, with both fore and hind legs outstretched, that has persisted for centuries as the proper way of rendering a galloping horse. This accomplishment, however, has been widely considered a scientific accomplishment rather than an artistic one.

Painting

If photography presents complex challenges of interpretation, these become even more acute when we turn to painting. No one could question that photography and other technical developments have radically transformed the very nature of painting. But it is often difficult to articulate the nature of these changes and even more difficult to understand what factors may have prompted them.

Beginning in the nineteenth century, the development of new pigments encouraged artists to explore new effects. For example, in the 1850s the development of aniline pigments made possible a new group of color effects, with a glowing, fluorescent feeling. Soon after these pigments were introduced, artists recognized that their unique glowing qualities were ideally suited to sunsets. In the 1850s, a number of artists created dramatic sunset paintings, including Frederic Church, Sanford Gifford, Fitz

Hugh Lane, and others. Perhaps the culminating painting in this mode is Frederic Church's *Twilight in the Wilderness*, one of the most widely reproduced paintings of the nineteenth century. In the twentieth century the development of acrylic paints had a similar impact. While hard and durable like oil, acrylic has some of the flowing properties of watercolor. Since it does not contain oil, it also can be employed on unprimed canvas without deteriorating the surface. In the 1960s, soon after it was introduced, acrylic paint led to a whole new movement in abstract painting, Color Field Painting, in which artists such as Morris Louis and Kenneth Noland explored the impact of pouring pigment onto the canvas to create stained effects rather than applying pigment with a brush. The spray gun was first used for commercial purposes, such as painting automobiles, but it quickly made its way into fine Art. At the 1893 World's Columbian Exposition, the American painter Frank Millet boasted that he had used a spray gun to execute large areas of his murals. The full possibilities of the spray gun, however, were first explored in the 1960s by the color field painter Jules Olitski, who used the spray gun to eliminate brushstrokes and to create delicate mists of color.

Before the nineteenth century, painting outdoors was an arduous process. Pigments needed to be ground by hand and were stored in jars with thongs and membranes that kept the opening covered. The development of mass-produced eliminated a time-consuming aspect of the artist's preparations, and the development of the collapsable tin paint tube, by Connecticut inventor John Rand, made it possible for the first time to paint outdoors without difficulty. First marketed by Winsor-Newton in London in the 1840s, this invention played a major role in popularizing the practice of outdoor painting, a development which culminated in the creation of French Impressionism.

But the greatest effect of technology on painting surely occurred because of a separate invention, that challenged the traditional functions of the painter: the photograph. On being shown the new invention, the illustrious academic painter, Ernest Meissonier, declared: "From this moment, painting is dead!" In actual fact, Meissonier's statement proved incorrect. The century after photography was one of the greatest in the history of painting. But to survive, painting needed to move into new territories.

For centuries, the chief purpose of painting had been to reproduce the visible world, and in many respects painting could do this more quickly, more cheaply, and more accurately. In the field of portraiture, these qualities were particularly useful. During the 1820s, self-taught or modestly trained portrait painters plied their trade across the United States and Europe. Within a few decades, they had been almost entirely replaced by portrait studios. Nonetheless, for some time the painter could surpass the realism of the photograph in two respects: he could produce images that were larger, and he could produce images in color.

Loosely speaking, painters could compete with the photograph in two different ways: they could attempt to surpass its realism, or they could move into areas where realism no longer mattered, such as abstract painting. Much of late nineteenth-century painting can be seen as an effort to surpass the realism of the photograph.

Early cameras were limited in their ability to recreate reality, and consequently through much of the nineteenth-century painters were able to successfully compete with the camera on its own terms. Thus, for example, while early photographs created surprisingly realistic and detailed effects, they could not render an image in color, nor could they create an image of large scale. Landscape painters such as Frederic Church and Albert Bierstadt, therefore, were able to create paintings that were "photographic" in their realism, but achieved a scale and color not equaled by contemporary photographs. Significantly, both artists collected photographs as references for their work; Bierstadt's brothers were successful photographers, who like him specialized in views of the American west. As photography improved, it revealed aspects of the world that had not previously been visible to the eye. For example, the development of action photography revealed that the legs of horses fall into patterns entirely different from the spread-legged posture that had previously been the popular visual convention for a horse running at high speed. In America, painter Thomas Eakins, with the encouragement of the photographer and equestrian Fairman Rogers, spent approximately a year studying the gait of a trotting horse and then distilled his discoveries into a major painting, *A Spring Morning in the Park*, also known as *The Fairman Rogers Four-in-Hand* (1880; Philadelphia Museum of Art). Effects of waves, waterfalls, and water in motion were studied in the Renaissance by figures such as Leonardo da Vinci, but before the development of photography it was extremely difficult to freeze the appearance of a wave at a particular moment. The development of photography made it possible for painters to capture such effects. Painter Winslow Homer, for example, created a dramatic series of paintings focusing on breaking waves. Even in those instances where painters did not employ photographs directly, the fact that photography revealed new facts about such subjects encouraged painters to observe and record them with intensified interest.

The other direction was towards effects that looked handmade rather than photographic, and that emphasized the qualities of the human hand and mind. This direction stressed effects that moved increasingly away from a faithful representation of appearance, such as the Fauve style, which stressed arbitrary color, the Cubist style, which stressed arbitrary rearrangement of space, or purely abstract painting, which moved away from reality altogether. Pablo Picasso is said to have nightmares about the camera, and his ingenious stylistic inventions can be explained, at least in good part, as an attempt to find modes of visual expression which were ideally suited to the creation of the hand and eye, and could not be easily imitated with a camera. Even in realistic painting, artists stressed brushwork and facture – qualities of the human hand that the photograph could not duplicate. This move away from the photograph culminated in Abstract Expressionism, which was large, abstract, and brushy, and dramatized precisely those effects that stood out as different from the photographic image.

Like architecture and the decorative arts, painting has often explored a dialogue between the handmade and the machine made. Indeed, when we trace the succession of style, it appears that this dichotomy has often been a springboard for a new approach. Abstract Expressionism, for example, was a powerfully individual style, which stressed the unique, handmade qualities of every painting. Pop Art, which succeeded it, on the other hand, avoided handmade qualities, except as a reference to sloppiness and poor manufacture. Since forms of reproducing images mechanically were still limited in the 1960s, a major problem for the Pop Artists was to discover a means of reproducing images mechanically to retain their machine-made look. Robert Rauschenberg, for example, found that he could transfer images in newspaper by pouring lighter fluid on them and rubbing them onto a canvas. Andy Warhol initially copied cartoon and popular images by hand, but then discovered serigraphy, which allowed him to do so photographically and mechanically.

The Movies

At the time of this publication, movies and recorded music are the two largest American exports, far outstripping automobiles, appliances, or any other product. Both of these new media were invented just before the end of the nineteenth century, and their artistic development largely occurred in the twentieth century.

Film provides a particularly fascinating case of how art and technology can interact since artistic factors shaped the very invention of the medium. Movies, in fact, are not so much a new invention as a combination of existing inventions to serve a new purpose. Much of the challenge for the inventor lay in imaging what purpose would best be served.

The magic lantern, which projects slides on a wall or screen, dates back to the seventeenth century and was described by the British diarist, Samuel Pepys. The use of photography to record motion was pioneered by the British photographer, Eadward Muybridge, who used a battery of twenty or more cameras to record the successive stages of animal locomotion.

The idea of flipping rapidly through such photographs to create the illusion of movement was conceived by the French painter, Meissonier, who created a device for flipping from one photograph to another at a rapid pace. Thanks to a phenomenon known as "persistence of vision," the eye retains an after-image of each photograph for a fraction of a second, and consequently, at sufficient speed, the photographs create the illusion of unbroken movement.

Thomas Edison came up with the idea of using projected photographs, on the principle of a magic lantern, rather than mounted ones. He also recognized that celluloid, whose suitability for film had just been recognized by George Eastman, would make it possible to create long roles of film which could be projected. However, since celluloid is fragile, movie film tended to break. Consequently, it was necessary to develop a looping mechanism, which would allow a bit of slack, for both cameras and projectors. Moreover, Edison thought that moving pictures should take the form of a peep-show, with individuals looking into a slot. It was an assistant in his laboratory, William Dickson, who recognized that film could entertain an audience of people, and who joined forces with a group of theater owners to create the moving picture in its modern form.

As this summary suggests, while many of the problems were technical, much of the challenge of developing movies was to determine what form this new art should take, in particular, whether it should be a peepshow or a theatrical form.

Developing a narrative language for film proved equally complicated, since it quickly became apparent that film worked differently from any other artistic medium. Early film directors supposed that film is analogous to a theatrical production, and that consequently a fixed camera focused on a group of actors would produce a gripping story. They quickly discovered that a fixed camera produces dull movies. Film seems to require rapid movement from one scene to another through what is known as cutting.

The first films were 30 second shorts of ordinary events, such as people playing cards or a train pulling up to a station. But the novelty of such scenes wore off quickly. If film was ever to become a viable commercial medium, it was necessary to learn to tell a story. This proved more difficult than one might suppose, since film works differently than any other medium. People initially thought that stories could be created by photographing a stage play with a stationary camera. But this turned out to be dull. Remarkably, the human mind seems to read film in two different ways, simultaneously. On the one hand, we can imagine that the image is three-dimensional, with figures moving in deep space. But we also read movies like a stack of postcards. Cutting from one image to another is like flipping from one postcard to another in the stack. Film seems to work best when we jump abruptly from one scene to another.

The modern language of film was largely developed by David Wark Griffith. Before Griffith, movies were photographed in a stationary long shot. Griffith introduced what is now known as "classical cutting." Essentially, this involved quick jumps from one shot to another, constantly alternating long shots and close-ups and even developing a counterpoint of two or more narratives simultaneously. The key principal of this technique was to edit for dramatic intensity with emotional emphasis, rather than for purely physical reasons. While close-ups had been used before, Griffith realized that they could be used to increase the emotional intensity of a scene. In its most refined form, classical cutting involves some kind of psychological cause and effect. For example, you might move from a speaker, to an exchange of dialogue, to a reaction shot, to a medium shot of the two speakers, and finally to a close-up of another person.

Classic cutting breaks up the unity of space and time and allows us to follow a narrative through fragments and details. Thus, for example, in his masterwork, *The Birth of a Nation*, Griffith used multiple cameras to film the battle scenes. Thus, a scene that occurred in twenty minutes might produce an hour or two of film. This could then be trimmed down into an exciting sequence. Generally, Griffith would begin with a mastershot, which covered the whole scene from a distance, without cuts, and would then repeat the action with medium shots and close-ups. Near the end of *The Birth of a Nation*, Griffith cross-cuts between four different groups. He intensified the rhythm of the shots and the dramatic suspense by making the duration of the shots shorter and shorter as the scene moves towards its climax. To avoid monotony, he used long, medium and close shots, different angles, and even a moving camera that was mounted on a truck. In the famous last-minute rescue finale of the film, Griffith used 255 shots for about twenty minutes of screen time.

Griffith's approach was later intensified by the Russian filmmaker Sergei Eisenstein, who introduced the technique of montage – of jumping abruptly from one image to another in a fashion that eliminates normal concepts of continuity. His most famous use of this technique occurs in the film *Potemkin*, in a scene of Cossack soldiers slaughtering the townspeople of Odessa on a stairway leading down to the harbor. Eisenstein's overriding principle was kineticism – of jagged intense movement within the frame and rapid movement from one shot to another. To create a dramatic rhythm, Eisenstein juxtaposed light with dark, verticals with horizontals, lengthy shots with brief ones, close-ups with long shots, static set-ups with traveling shots, and so forth.

As it turned out, this new language of story-telling required new acting techniques. The great stage-actors of the late nineteenth century, such as Sarah Bernhardt, never successfully adjusted to film. Instead, film favored a bunch of newcomers who were ready to master its new language. This proved to have paradoxical aspects. On the one hand, the introduction of close-ups made possible a more subtle approach. An actor could communicate through subtle nuances of expression rather than by flailing their arms or tearing their hair. On the other hand, the most successful masters of the medium were generally masters of expressive motion and acrobatics, such as Charlie Chaplin, who came to film from vaudeville, Buster Keaton, who was a circus tumbler, and Douglas Fairbanks, who was essentially a dancer. The most successful of these figures worked in a highly intuitive and improvisatory fashion. Keaton's masterpiece, *The General*, for example, was shot without a script. He and his crew simply rented a train, went out and improvised scenes, and then went back to the cutting room and stitched together the individual scenes into a story.

Throughout its subsequent history, new technological developments have periodically shifted the nature of film, creating openings for newcomers. The development of sound, for example, instantly made most silent stars obsolete, opening the way for actors with vocal skills. The film often ranked as the greatest film of all time, *Citizen Kane* of 1941, was produced by a young upstart, Orson Welles, and included a number of innovative techniques, including overlapping dialogue, deep-focus cinematography, chiaroscuro lighting, unusual camera angles, and a film within a film.

The enormous expense of film made it a medium beyond the means of the individual artist. To produce film regularly required a form of mass production, which emerged in the so-called Studio System. By 1929, five major studios (Metro-Goldwyn-Mayer (MGM), Warners, Fox, Radio-Keith-Orpheum (RKO), and Paramount) had a virtual monopoly of the American market. They controlled the stars, the directors, the designers, the cinematographers and the technicians who worked backstage. They also owned the movie houses, which showed only films that they produced. They demanded "blind booking," even from independent theaters, requiring theaters to rent movies as a package, sight unseen, rather than individually. Such a system made it possible to produce movies quickly and efficiently. To make this easier, distinct genres were developed which operated with predictable formulas, such as the musical, the western, the gangster film, and the horror film.

Film-making, however, was fundamentally transformed in 1948, when the Federal Government successfully concluded an antitrust action that divested the five major companies of their theater chains. What is more, the advent of television siphoned off most of the so-called family audience, leaving behind only specialized groups, the largest of which was the so-called youth audience. This led to experiments with wide-screen and 3-D projection, and with stereophonic sound, which were intended to lure audiences away from the television sets to the theater. At the same time, the development of new equipment also encouraged shooting movies on location rather than in Hollywood studios and led to the creation of low budget pictures, such as *Easy Rider* (1969) which was produced for $375,000 and earned $50 million. In recent years, the business of film making has been profoundly affected by video and DVD, which provide a means of making a profit from a movie, even if it flops at the box office. At the same time, the increasing demand for costly special effects has made it more and more difficult to produce movies which make money on their first release.

Music

Unlike moving pictures, recordings of music were not a completely new art form. They simply provided a new vehicle for disseminating musical performance. But their impact on the nature of music was nearly equally great. For one thing, sound recordings made it easier to musicians in isolated places to reach a national market; and the availability of recordings of such musicians, brought about a great appreciation of regional musical styles. The size of the audience for recordings is enormously larger than that for live performance, since people can listen to music at all times of day and do not need to travel to a concert. Singing to a microphone also entails different technical challenges than singing in a concert hall, since sound projection is not an issue. The microphone thus encouraged a new kind of intimate singing style, while new electronic instruments encouraged a new kind of slightly metallic sound.

Perhaps even more significant, sound recording shifted the emphasis in music from the written score to the individual performance. In classical music, the performer is expected to faithfully follow the written score. Recorded music, on the other hand, encourages the performer to take liberties with the basic tune, in order to make it an expression of their own personality. Indeed, in purchased recordings, we tend to think less about the score than the performer – it is more important whether the performer is Duke Ellington or Ella Fitzgerald than who wrote the music.

One fascinating aspect of this is that performance often contains sounds and background noises not present in the musical score that add greatly to the effect. The first instance of this is a recording of a cakewalk by an anonymous group of musicians, made in 1900, which includes shouts and cries in the background like those of a spontaneous performance. Today it is not uncommon not only to include such background sounds, but also to include other noises, such as cars, motorcycles, seagulls, lapping water, and heartbeats, which merge with and add texture to the music. Through its willingness to depart from a fixed score, and to introduce a range of peculiar sound effects, recorded music has developed into virtually a new art form. In modern recordings, such effects are often added in layers of sound, mixing musical and non-musical sounds to create rich sound textures. The artistic possibilities of this were realized by Pop groups such as The Beatles, who created their effects not from a score but by improvising sounds in the recording studio, and then mixing tracks together in unusual combinations.

Conclusion

In closing this essay, two points about the relationship of art and technology need to be stressed. The first is that a brief essay cannot do justice to the complexity of this subject, since artists were quick to seize upon the possibilities of new technologies of all types. A good instance of this is the case of underwater painting. This was pioneered by Zarh Pritchard (1886–1956), an American born in India. During his school years, Pritchard read Charles Kingsley's fairy tale *The Water-Babies* (1863) and Jules Verne's science fiction adventure *Twenty Thousand Leagues Under the Sea* (1873), both of which featured human beings living freely on the ocean floor. When he became a painter, Pritchard became fascinated by the challenge of rendering the underwater world. At first he made dives without equipment and resurfaced between breaths to sketch above water. But with the invention of the diving suit and pumped air, it became possible for him to actually work underwater for as much as 2 hours at a time. Conventional paints would not work in this setting, but Pritchard solved this problem by sketching in oil crayons on oil-soaked paper taped to glass. Using this technique, he traveled extensively throughout the world, working for long periods underwater in locales as diverse as the kelp-filled caverns of Scotland and the coral lagoons of Tahiti. Between expeditions, Pritchard worked up his sketches into finished creations, recopying them in his studio onto large leather sheets that were stretched like canvas. Pritchard had no rivals, both because the machinery and assistance necessary to carry out underwater dives was expensive, and thus not available to most artists, and also because sketching underwater in the bulky diving apparatus of the period was extremely difficult.

While Pritchard's efforts do not occupy a major place in the history of art, they provide a stimulating example of how art and technology can interact to create unlikely new art forms. A new invention, the diving suit, made it possible for Pritchard to stay underwater for long periods. If he wished to paint underwater, however, he could not use traditional oils or watercolors but needed to find a medium (oil crayon) that would work in this setting. Once he made this choice, it affected the way he worked on land. If he had worked up his sketches in oil paint, it would have given them a look that removed them from his actual underwater sketches. Consequently, he made his studio works in crayon also. Finally, it should be noted that while the works he produced were based on first-hand experience, they also reflected the artistic movements of the period, particularly the American turn-of-the-century style known as Tonalism. The ultimate impulse for his effort can be traced back not simply to the invention of the diving suit but to the fairy-tales and science fiction that had excited him as a boy. The twentieth century is filled with such unusual examples of the interaction of art and technology. While sometimes individually of modest significance, considered cumulatively they mark a major transformation in man's relationship with the world.

The example of Pritchard also brings out another aspect of the relationship of art and technology, namely that it is complex – the result of a variety of factors coming together in unusual ways. This principle holds true not only for minor ventures such as Pritchard's, but for ventures which we now regard as seminal within the history of western art. A case in point is the development of French Impressionism, which according to one's viewpoint can be considered as a response to the collapsible paint tube, the railroad, or the camera. Before the nineteenth century, painting outdoors was an arduous process. Pigments needed to be ground by hand, with mortar and pestle, and were stored in jars with thongs and membranes that kept the opening covered. To paint outdoors with all this apparatus was difficult without a wheelbarrow. In the nineteenth century, however, the situation changed. First the development of mass-produced pigments made the task of starting a painting less arduous. Then the development of the collapsible paint tube, by the Connecticut inventor John Rand, greatly reduced the weight and bulk of the materials necessary to make a painting, and made it practical to carry them to a motif outdoors. It seems no accident that French Impressionism appeared within a few years of Rand's new paint tubes, which were first marketed by Winsor-Newton in London in the 1840s.

In addition, however, one can also see French Impressionism as a response to the railroad, which made it easy to get from the center of Paris to the seashore or the country in a short time. This in turn encouraged the development of leisure activities such as swimming, boating, and picnicking. The subject matter rendered by the Impressionists, the suburban landscape, would not have been available to them without the development of the railroad, and the same can be said of many of the activities within the landscape that they portrayed.

Finally, the Impressionists were surely influenced by the camera, albeit in seemingly contradictory ways. The camera encouraged painters to think of the retina as a flat surface which was sensitive to the impact of light and visual sensations. Thus, it inspired them to focus not on the world in geometric terms, as they knew it from the sense of touch, but as they knew it in purely optical terms, and to incorporate purely optical phenomena, such as glare, into their work. At the same time, the Impressionists were surely inspired by the limitations of the cameras of their time, which could photograph only in black-and-white and could not produce images of large scale. By creating large-sized colorful representations of the world, the Impressionists could surpass the abilities of the camera to transcribe natural appearances.

To date, most textbooks on art still speak of it as a self-contained entity, essentially insulated from the world around it. But many individual studies now exist that suggest the need for a new view of art history as a whole. Perhaps the time has come for a new art history, which will not only view art within a social context, but will examine its place within the context of the technologies that have transformed human society at an ever-accelerating pace over the last few centuries.

For most of human history, the past has been held up as superior to the present – and the figures of the past as wiser and more virtuous than those of the degraded modern age. In certain disciplines, such as government and law, this principle still serves as a fundamental basis of governance. In theory at least, law is based on precedent, and in theory, also, good government is based on principles laid down by "founding fathers."

The development of new technology upset this way of viewing things, since it made it quite evident that the graybeards of the past were not wiser but less wise than young upstarts in significant respects – less able to go fast, to build huge structures, to produce food and manufactured goods in huge quantities, or to perform other remarkable feats, such as flying or getting dead people to talk to us. The success of inventors in the practical sphere led artists to feel that "art" consisted less in mastering difficult skills, such as recording textures in paint, or rendering a human likeness, than in opening up new pathways and devising new forms of expression.

In many instances modern artists have had a superficial understanding of technology and machines, and of concepts such as "the fourth dimension." Nonetheless, the fact that technology was opening up new areas encourage them to attempt to do likewise. Throughout the twentieth century, scientists and inventors have provided an exciting model for creative breakthrough, a point suggestively illustrated by the fact that Picasso and Braque, the two inventors of Cubism, humorously referred to themselves by the nicknames of "Wilbur" and "Orville," after Wilbur and Orville Wright. It would be far-fetched to argue that one could trace close step-by-step parallels between the development of the airplane and the development of Cubism, but the fact that two bicycle mechanics had devised a new way of moving through and experiencing the world encouraged artists to attempt something equally revolutionary.

BIBLIOGRAPHY

Bel Geddes, Norman. *Horizons* (Boston: Little, Brown and Company, 1932).

Newhall, Beaumont. *The History of Photography*, The Museum of Modern Art (New York, 1964).

Giannetti, Louis, and Scott Eyman. *Flashback, A Brief History of Film*, Prentice-Hall, Upper addle River, New Jersey, fourth edition, 2001.

Giannetti, Louis. *Masters of the American Cinema*, Prentice-Hall, Inc., Englewood Cliffs, New Jersey, 1981.

Pontus-Hulten, K.G., *The Machine as Seen at the End of the Mechanical Age*, The Museum of Modern Art (New York, 1968).

Schonberger, Angela ed. *Raymond Loewy* (Prestel: Munich, 1990).

Wilson, Richard Guy, Dianne H. Pilgrim and Dickran Tashijan. *The Machine Age in America, 1918–1941*, The Brooklyn Museum, Harry N. Abrams, Publisher (New York, 1986).

CHAPTER TWENTY-TWO

Critics of Technology

DAVID E. NYE

Emergence of the Term "Technology"

While there are scattered criticisms of what we now call technology in ancient and medieval authors, sustained criticism can be traced only from the late eighteenth century until the present. In the 1950s the history of technology emerged as a professional discipline and began to refine and challenge the long pre-professional tradition, whose legacy was a set of still pertinent questions, including the following. Is technology inherently deterministic or is it inflected or even shaped by cultural differences?[1] Do technologies ensure abundance for all, for only certain groups, or for no one, because in the long term they will inadvertently destroy the environment? Do new technologies enhance freedom and democracy, or do they concentrate power and enable new forms of oppression? Does an increasingly technological life world expand mental horizons or encapsulate human beings in artifice?[2] After analyzing the origin of the term "technology," this essay will examine each of these questions in turn and through time.

Because "technology" is not an old word in English, considerable criticism addressing such questions developed before the word acquired its present meaning. During the seventeenth century "technology" emerged from modern Latin into English to describe a systematic study of one of the arts. By the early eighteenth century a characteristic definition was: "a description of the arts, especially the mechanical." The word was seldom used in the United States before the publication of *Elements of Technology* in 1832 by a Harvard University professor, Jacob Bigelow,[3] and as late as 1840 it is virtually impossible to find the term in use except as a citation of his work.[4] Leo Marx has observed, "At the time of the Industrial Revolution, and through most of the nineteenth century, the word *technology* primarily referred to a kind of book; except for a few lexical pioneers, it was not until the turn of this century that sophisticated writers like Thorstein Veblen began to use the word to mean the mechanic arts collectively. But that sense of the word did not gain wide currency until after World War I."[5] During the nineteenth century the term was embedded in the names of prominent educational institutions such as the Massachusetts Institute of Technology, but it had not become a common term in the discussion of industrialization. Instead, people spoke of "the mechanic arts" or the "useful arts" or "invention" or "science" in contexts where "technology" would now be used. For example, in 1859 Abraham Lincoln gave two lectures on discoveries and inventions without using the term.[6] Only in the twentieth century did "technology" come to mean entire systems of machines, and it can be an annoyingly vague abstraction that is taken to be at once both cause and effect, or both object and process. The word's unstable meaning was further complicated in the 1990s, when the mass media and stock market traders made "technology" a synonym for computers and information systems.

Thus "technology" is an unusually slippery term, with shifting meanings that are strongly inflected by ideology. Particularly in Great Britain, the term emerged into common use only after criticism of industrialization had become common. The poet William Blake (1757–1827) attacked the "dark Satanic mills" of the Midlands, and William Wordsworth (1770–1850) attacked the building of a railroad into this beloved Lake District: "Is there no nook of English ground secure/From rash assault?" And in a novel still resonant today, Mary Shelley's (1797–1851) *Frankenstein* (1818) evoked the possibility that scientists might create monsters that escaped their control. Without any need of the word "technology", Thomas Carlyle (1795–1881) made a full-scale critique of industrialization that contained many of the negative meanings that later would be poured into the term. Many saw what we would now call technology as a powerful shaping force, and machinery seemed to proliferate more rapidly than the political means to govern it. In 1839 Ralph Waldo Emerson (1803–1882) allowed that "the activity of the Engineer, of the railroad builder, &the manufacturer is real & inventive, &deserves regard."[7] But by 1853 Emerson succinctly concluded: "The age has an engine, but no engineer."[8] Were mechanical systems passing out of human control?

Technological Determinism

Like Emerson, many nineteenth-century critics saw machines and industry as the motor of change. The future, whether utopian or dystopian, was often seen as an outcome of mechanization. The phrase "industrial revolution" that gradually came into use after c. 1875, expressed a similar notion, that new technologies broke decisively with the past. While early socialists and free market capitalists might agree on little else, both saw industrialization as an unfolding of rationality. Even harsh early critics tended to assume that the machine itself was neutral, and focused their analysis on how it was being misused. Only in the twentieth century did many argue that technologies might be inherently dangerous. Accordingly, technological determinism, which often seemed beneficent in the nineteenth century, appeared more threatening thereafter.

Karl Marx (1818–1883) accepted the growth of corporations and the mechanization of society as part of an iron law of inevitable historical development.[9] In *The Critique of Political Economy* he argued that, "The mode of production of material life determines the general character of the social, political, and spiritual process of life."[10] Marx did not use the word "technology" in the first edition of *Kapital*,[11] but he made clear that the immediate results of industrialization were largely negative, notably the subdivision of labor, the loss of worker control over the time, the place, and the pace of work, the increasing control of the means of production by capital, the deskilling of work, and the growing polarization of the social classes. The collapse of capitalism, from Marx's point of view, was unavoidable, but not simply because inequalities would goad the workers to revolt. Rather, capitalism by its very nature created a series of economic crises whose intensity increased over time. These crises directly resulted from the growing investment in factories and machinery (fixed capital) that the capitalist substituted for wages (variable capital). As capital congealed into machines, wages correspondingly had to decrease for the capitalist to make a profit. Yet falling wages reduced demand, at the very time that the capitalist had more goods to sell. Thus, Marx argued, efficiency in production flooded the market with goods yet undermined demand. If a capitalist halted production while surpluses were sold off, that reduced demand still further. If he raised wages to stimulate demand, then profits fell. If he sought still greater efficiencies through mergers with rivals, this course of action only deferred the crisis, which became even more severe when it arrived. Marx's model seemed inevitable: greater mechanization produced greater surpluses yet impoverished more workers, causing increasingly severe economic crises. Thus mechanization of the means of production led to more than worker exploitation, social inequality, and class warfare. It led inevitably to collapse. To the extent that admiration for technology justified capitalism, it was merely part of false consciousness. The succeeding socialist regime would appropriate the means of production and build an egalitarian life of plenty for all. Thus Marxism developed a powerful critique of industrialization that included such concepts as alienation, deskilling, and reification, and yet ultimately it was not hostile to the machine as such. Evolutionary socialists agreed that technological systems ultimately would become the basis of a utopia.

Twentieth-century socialists also tended to identify new technologies with the inevitable decline of capitalism and the emergence of a better economic system. For example, German-born Charles Steinmetz (1865–1923), the leading scientist at General Electric in its first decades, expected socialism, or "industrial cooperation," to emerge along with a national electrical grid, because it was an inherently inter-dependent basis of economic and political reorganization. Electricity could not be stored efficiently and had to be consumed through large distribution systems as soon as it was produced. "The relation between the steam engine as a source of power and the electric motor is thus about the same as the relation between the individualist [capitalist] and the socialist...the one is independent of everything else, is self-contained, the other, the electric motor, is dependent on every other user in the system...the electric power is probably today the most powerful force tending towards coordination, that is cooperation [socialism]."[12] In Russia, Lenin famously declared that only when the Soviet Union had been completely electrified could full socialism be attained, and he vigorously pursued a ten-year plan of building generating plants and incorporating them into a national grid, with the goal of extending electrical service to every home.[13] As this example suggests, Marxists and socialists criticized how capitalists used technical systems, but seldom condemned industrialization itself.

In contrast, Werner Sombart (1863–1941) rejected determinism in *Technik und Kultur*, where he argued that cultures often shaped events more than technologies. For example, the failure of cultural and political institutions, and not technological change, accounted for the decline of ancient Rome. Sombart accorded technology an important role in history, particularly in modern times, but recognized the importance of institutional arrangements.

The Chicago School of sociology developed similar ideas in the United States. For example, when W.F. Ogburn (1886–1959) wrote about "the influence of invention and discovery," he denied that "mechanical invention is the source of all change" and pointed to such "social inventions" as "the city manager form of government... which have had great effects upon social customs. While many social inventions are only remotely connected with mechanical inventions, others appear to be precipitated by" them, such as "the trade union and the tourist camp." Yet the influence could flow in either direction. Social inventions could stimulate technical invention, "as in the 'safety first' campaigns..."[14] While Ogburn admitted that mechanization had a powerful effect on society, he also emphasized that "a social change is seldom the result of a single invention." Women's suffrage, for example, was the outcome of a great number of forces and converging influences, which included mass production, urbanization, birth control, the typewriter, improved education, and the theory of natural rights. Most important changes were the result of such a "piling up process." Making the distinction between social invention and technical invention also suggested the notion of a cultural lag. "There is often a delay or lag in the adaptive culture after the material culture has changed, and sometimes these lags are very costly, as was the case with workmen's compensation for industrial accidents."[15]

The idea that technologies developed more rapidly than society remained attractive to later theorists. During the 1960s Marshall McCluhan won a large following, as he argued that every major form of communication had reshaped the way human beings saw their world, causing changes in both public behavior and political institutions. Thus, the introduction of key innovations in communications, notably the printing press, radio, and television, had widespread, automatic effects. Alvin Toffler reworked such ideas into *Future Shock*, a bestseller that argued that technological change had accelerated to the point that human beings scarcely could cope with it, and *The Third Wave*, which argued that a new industrial revolution was occurring, driven by electronics, computers, and the space program.[16] Joshua Meyrowitz offered a more academic treatment of similar themes in *No Sense of Place: The Impact of Electronic Media on Social Behavior* (1985). In such studies, the word "impact" suggests that machines inexorably force their way into society. Meyrowitz concluded, "Television has helped change the deferential Negro into the proud Black... Television has given women an outside view of their incarceration in the home. Television has weakened visible authorities by destroying the distance and mystery that once enhanced their aura and prestige."[17]

Although the details of their analyses varied, McCluhan, Toffler, and Meyerwitz all made *externalist* arguments, in which new technologies are treated as autonomous forces that compel change. In *Being Digital* (1995), Nicholas Negroponte, of the

MIT Media Lab, made similar claims for the computer: "digital technology can be a natural force drawing people into greater world harmony."[18] The public has an appetite for proclamations that new technologies have beneficent "natural" effects with little government intervention or public planning. Such externalist arguments attribute to technology a dominant place within society, without focusing much on its invention or technical characteristics. Externalist studies of "technology transfer" often say little about machines and processes, such as firearms or textile factories, but a great deal about their "impact" on third-world countries.[19] The point of view is that of a third-person narrator who stands above and outside technical processes, looking at society. Such deterministic arguments seldom dwell on the often protracted difficulties in defining the technological object at the time of its invention and early diffusion. Such close analysis – common in the internalist approach that will be described presently – tends to undermine determinism, because it reveals the importance of particular individuals, accidents, chance, and local circumstances.

Many of the most influential critics of technology of the post-World War II era were determinists. Jacques Ellul paid little attention to the origins of individual inventions, but argued instead that an abstract "Technique" had permeated all aspects of society, and had become the new "milieu," and a substitute for Nature. Readers of Ellul's *The Technological Society* were told that Technique was an autonomous and unrelenting substitution of means for ends. Modern society's vast ensemble of techniques had become self-engendering and had accelerated out of humanity's control: "Technical progress tends to act, not according to an arithmetic, but according to a geometric progression."[20] In contrast, Ellul's later work, *The Ethics of Freedom* (1976), constructed a conservative Christian argument that defied the technological system, building upon the work of Søren Kierkegaard and existentialism, but it was little read.

Writers on the left found technology equally threatening, and here too the only possible antidote seemed to be a dramatic shift in consciousness. During the Berkeley student movement, Mario Savio called on supporters to "put your bodies on the machine and make it stop."[21] Herbert Marcuse, in such works as *One-Dimensional Man* (1964), attacked the technocratic state in both its capitalist and socialist formations. He called for revolutionary consciousness-raising as the preparation for a wholesale rejection of the managed system that everywhere was reducing human beings to unimaginative cogs in the machine of the state. Marcuse, who became popular with the student movements of the late 1960s, hoped that the New Left would spearhead the rejection of the technocratic regime. In *The Making of a Counter Culture* (1969) Theodore Roszak was equally critical, but less confrontational, arguing that reform of the technocratic state was impossible, and calling instead for the construction of alternative grass-roots institutions, such as those in the emerging hippie movement.[22]

As student radicalism faded during the 1970s, however, social revolution seemed less probable than technological domination, notably as analyzed in the work of Michel Foucault. He treated technology as the material expression of an overarching discourse that structured individual consciousness and shaped institutions, notably hospitals, asylums, and prisons.[23] Foucault conceived history according to epistemo-logical systems, each of which organized scientific thinking and social engineering over long periods of time. The individual, whether author, inventor, or citizen, was caught within, and scarcely aware of, structures of power deployed and naturalized throughout society.

Foucault, and later Francois Lyotard, authored academic bestsellers of the 1970s and 1980s, but their grand, deterministic theories found little favor in Science, Technology and Society programs. Leo Marx, for example, declared that postmodern theorists often ratify "the idea of the domination of life by large technological systems" and promote a "shrunken sense of the self."[24] The most sweeping rejection of tech-nological determinism, however, remains Langdon Winner's *Autonomous Technol-ogy* (1977), written in a spirit of "epistemological Luddism."[25] In dismantling all deterministic ideologies, Winner made it easier to think of technologies as being socially shaped, or constructed.

Recognizing the central role of culture in technological change, a trans-Atlantic group of sociologists, historians and philosophers worked together to define, what one book aptly labeled *The Social Construction of Technological Systems*.[26] Giving roughly equal weight to technical, social, economic and political factors, their case studies suggest how artifacts emerge as the concrete expression of social forces, personal needs, technical limits, and political maneuvering. They argue that not only the meanings ascribed to an artifact but also its actual design, is flexible during early stages until a design meets wide approval, which leads to closure. In the case of the bicycle, the danger of early high wheelers, while frightening to some riders, gave them a macho aura, and low bikes were for sissies. When Dunlop developed air ("balloon") tires to solve the problem of vibrations, these too were derided. However, bicycle design swiftly reached closure, when the low-wheeled models proved faster on the race track.

Just as bicycle form now varies far less than in the 1890s, the term "social construction" should not be taken to mean that industrial systems are infinitely malleable. If technologies are not powerful forces shaping history, they may still exercise a "soft determinism" once entire systems are in place. Established technical systems often become inflexible once they have achieved what Thomas P. Hughes calls "technological momentum," a concept useful for understanding large-scale systems, such as the electric grid or the railway. These have some flexibility when being defined in their initial phases, but as ownership, control, and technical specifi-cations are established, they become more rigid and less responsive to social pressures. Once railway track width has been made uniform and several thousand miles have been laid out, it is easy in theory but hard in practice to reconfigure the dimensions. Similarly, a society may initially choose to emphasize either mass transit or private automobiles, but later it is difficult to undo such a decision. The American commitment to the automobile has resulted in such massive infrastructure investments that in most of the United States it would be difficult to change the decision. Likewise, once it is built, an electrical grid is "less shaped by and more the shaper of its environment."[27] This may sound deterministic, but it is not, for human beings decided to build the grid and selected its components. The idea of "technological momentum" provides an explanation for the rigidities often mistaken for determinism.

As historians of technology have rejected determinism, their research has moved in two other directions. To use John Staudemaier's classification, the largest group are contextualists, but internalists also do much important work.[28] These are not so much opposed schools of thought as different emphases. Internalists reconstruct the history of machines and processes with an emphasis on the role of the inventor, laboratory practices, and the state of scientific knowledge at a particular time. They chart the sequence that leads from one physical object to the next. The approach has some affinities with art history,[29] but grew out of the history of science. An early synthesis was the five-volume *History of Technology* conceived in the 1950s by Charles Singer and his collaborators.[30] These volumes contain detailed histories of the development of industrial chemicals, textile machinery, steel making, and so forth. Internalists help to establish a bedrock of facts about individual inventors, their competition, their technical difficulties, and their solutions to particular problems. If many non-specialists believe that necessity is the mother of invention, internalists usually find that creativity is by no means an automatic process. A machine that is fervently desired cannot be ordered like a pizza. Edison spent years trying to invent a lightweight battery for the electric automobile that would hold a charge for a long time. He made some progress, but the problem still eludes complete solution today.[31] Money and talent can speed refinements along, but cannot always call an invention into being.

The internalist approach also emphasizes the alternate ways that problems were solved. For example, in the late nineteenth century the need for flexible power transmission over a distance was solved by a variety of devices, including compressed air, pressurized water, underground cables, pressurized steam, and electricity. These were not merely invented: by 1880 all were in commercial use.[32] The internalist makes clear the precise characteristics of such devices, and so helps us to understand, for example, the relative merits of the early steam-, electric-, and gasoline-powered automobiles. This is necessary (but not sufficient) knowledge to understand why Americans preferred the gasoline car. An internalist can be a feminist working on Madame Curie or a railroad historian anxious to understand the precise characteristics of different boxcars, but usually writes from the point of view of an insider looking over an inventor's shoulder. Such studies culminate at the moment when the new machine is created, and usually conclude just as it reaches the market.

Contextualists, in contrast, usually focus on machines as they become part of the larger social world.[33] In this approach machines are understood to be shaped by the concerns of society, yet at the same time they have a reciprocal, transformative effect. Technology is deeply embedded in a continual (re)construction of the world. A contextualist eschews the Olympian perspective, seeking to understand machines and technical processes as cultural practices that may develop in more than one way. Thus, the computer is not an implacable force moving through history (an externalist argument), but rather a system of machines and social practices that varies from one time period to another and from one culture to another. In the United States the computer was not a "thing" that came from outside society and had an "impact"; rather, it was shaped by its social context. Each technology is an extension of human lives: someone makes it, someone owns it, some oppose it, many use it, and all interpret it. The Internet was developed to facilitate communication among scientists, and partially funded with an eye to transmitting vital defense information in case of atomic attack. But these instrumental goals gradually gave way to a widespread demand for e-mail, the World Wide Web, and e-commerce. The Internet became an integral part of advertising, marketing, politics, news and entertainment. People used the Internet in unexpected and sometimes illegal ways. Surfing the Internet became a kind of tourism. The popular acceptance of the Internet also raised political issues. Who should own and control it? Did it threaten to destroy jobs by eliminating middlemen, or was it the basis of a new prosperity? Did it democratize access to information or create a digital divide between those on the net and those who could not afford it? Like every technology, the Internet implied several businesses, opened new social agendas, and raised political questions. It was not a thing in isolation, but an open-ended set of problems and possibilities.

If one takes this approach, then it appears fundamentally mistaken to think of "the home" or "the factory" or "the city" as passive, solid objects that undergo an abstract transformation when a new technology appears. Rather, every institution is a social space that incorporated the Internet at a certain historical juncture as part of its ongoing development. The Internet offers a series of choices based only partly on technical considerations. Its meaning must be looked for in the many contexts in which people decide how to use it. For example, in the 1990s many chose to buy books, videos, and CDs on the Internet, but fewer were ready for the online purchase of groceries. Most preferred the Internet to the fax machine, but use of the telephone continued to expand. People adapted the Internet in a wide range of social, political, economic, and aesthetic contexts, weaving them into the fabric of experience. It facilitated social transformations but it was incorporated into the structures of public life in somewhat different ways in different societies.

As this example suggests, a new technology will not have the same effect everywhere. The belief in technological determinism is more widespread among non-specialists than among historians of technology. Sweeping externalist histories, however popular with the general reader, clash with the research of both internalists and contextualists.

Technology as the Basis for Abundance?

Since the Renaissance, Western societies have been particularly successful at exploiting technologies to produce a surplus of food, goods and services. They have used new forms of transportation to breach geographical barriers and integrate most of the world into a single market, collapsing space and time. Yet in the long term, new technologies could conceivably lead to impoverishment. For example, building dams and irrigation systems in desert areas can increase food production, but after a few generations the land may become polluted and unproductive, because of salts and chemicals left behind by evaporating water. Likewise, burning coal produces not only electricity but also smoke containing sulfur dioxide that falls to the earth as acid rain, destroying plants, fish and wildlife. When such environmental effects are considered, technologies may be only a temporary basis of abundance. A few centuries of exploiting fossil fuels for transportation and production may lead to global warming, desertification, rising sea levels, and the collapse of agriculture in many areas.

In contrast, the common liberal capitalist view has long been that the greater efficiency of new machines produces prosperity for all, in the form of higher wages, less expensive goods, and timesaving innovations. Industrialization creates more wealth, more jobs, and more goods. In the antebellum period, Daniel Webster (1782–1852) and Edward Everett (1794–1865) were spokesmen for this viewpoint. Later, Robert Thurston (1839–1903), a specialist in textile production and president of the American Society of Mechanical Engineers, quantified the argument.[34] Between 1870 and 1890, he saw productivity rise almost 30 percent, while working hours dropped and real wages rose 20 percent. Similar gains throughout the nineteenth century had radically improved daily life, as people had more leisure time and more money to spend. Consumption of clothing, appliances, and home furnishings was rising rapidly, and Thurston drew graphs to express "the trend of our modern progress in all material civilization. Our mills, our factories, our workshops of every kind are mainly engaged in supplying our people with the comforts and the luxuries of modern life, and in converting crudeness and barbarism into cultured civilization. Measured by this gauge, we are 50 percent more comfortable than in 1880, sixteen times as comfortable as were our parents in 1850, and our children, in 1900 to 1910, will have twice as many luxuries and live twice as easy and comfortable lives."[35] With such optimistic arguments, in the early decades of the twentieth century, Americans made engineers into cultural heroes in popular novels and films.[36] When W. Sombart wrote his famous *Why Is There No Socialism in the United States?*, he observed that American workers had greater material well-being than their European counterparts.[37] They dressed better, ate better, and were more likely to own a home. As a result, they resented capitalism less than European workers did. The President of MIT wrote in 1911, "Our grandfathers, looking down upon us, would feel that they observed a new heaven and a new earth."[38]

Between 1851 and World War II, millions attended the many world's fairs held in the United States and Europe, all of which embodied the belief in material progress based on technology. These expositions displayed model homes, cities, and farms. Fairgoers glimpsed an improved technological future not as an abstraction, but materialized in models and demonstrations. They saw their first telephone at the Philadelphia Centennial Exposition in 1876; their first electrified cityscape at the Chicago Columbian Exposition of 1893, their first full-sized assembly line and first transcontinental telephone call at the San Francisco Panama Pacific Exposition in 1915, and their first television at the New York "World of Tomorrow" Exposition of 1939. Chicago's "Century of Progress" exposition of 1933 celebrated the growth of a small village into the second largest city in the United States. Its slogan was "Science Finds – Industry Applies – Man Conforms." Its exhibits were planned to "show you how

Man has come up from the caves of half a hundred thousand years ago, adapting himself to, being molded by, his environments, responding to each new thing discovered and developed. You see man's march upward to the present day...."[39]

Such technological optimism was common in the middle of the twentieth century. The upward march seemed to lead to a workweek of 30 hours or less, early retirement, and a life of leisure and comfort for all. In 1955, Congress was "told by union leaders that automation threatens mass unemployment and by business executives that it will bring unparalleled prosperity."[40] Most believed, however, that leisure could be properly managed, and the 1968 testimony "before a Senate subcommittee indicated that by 1985 people could be working just 22 hours a week, or 27 weeks a year, or they could retire at 38."[41] Some social scientists proclaimed that control of increasing amounts of energy was the measure of civilization. Thus the anthropologist Leslie White posited four stages in human history: hunting and gathering, agriculture, industrial steam-power, and the atomic age. Many expected atomic power to permit stupendous advances by reducing energy costs to a pittance.[42]

In the same years, Vannevar Bush urged Americans to see outer space as a new frontier that could be conquered through corporate research and development. Michael Smith has termed such thinking "commodity scientism."[43] The space program was justified by improved commodities it "spun-off" as by-products, such as new food concentrates, Teflon, and computer miniaturization. *The Los Angeles Herald-Examiner* editorialized: "America's moon program has benefited all mankind. It has brought better color television, water purification at less cost, new paints and plastics, improved weather forecasting, medicine, respirators, walkers for the handicapped, laser surgery, world-wide communications, new transportation systems, earthquake prediction systems and solar power."[44] If, during the 1960s, the space program seemed to create a technological cornucopia of goods, the personal computer and the Internet played the same role in the 1990s. Full computerization seemed to create a "new economy" that assured a permanent bull market on Wall Street.

However, the utopian sense that technologies endlessly open up new frontiers for expansion and development did not go unchallenged. Not only did the workweek fail to shrink as expected, but also many critics asked if the profits and the goods produced were fairly distributed. Nor was this a new concern. From the eighteenth century onwards, many workers feared technological unemployment, from the handloom weavers of early industrial Britain to the white-collar office workers of the 1990s, made redundant by computer software. In 1808, George Washington P. Custis declared a common view, that "expensive machines can only be erected by companies, which soon form monopolies. This prevents competition, which is the life of all infant establishments."[45] He thought it, "advisable in the commencement of manufactures to lessen the labor of machinery" and use more workers.[46] In Britain, similar concerns prompted the machine-breaking raids of the Luddites, supposed followers of Ned Ludd. Workers in every industrializing country have protested the transfer of their skilled work to machines. In recent decades, for example, typesetters, steel workers, telephone operators, and meatpackers have lost jobs to machines and new production techniques. For generations, witnesses to such change have warned that consumption would not be able to keep up with production, leading to massive unemployment. Thus an 1878 American pamphlet warned that the saturation point had been reached, and called for shorter working hours for all, to distribute the scarce work evenly. Likewise, during the 1930s, technology again seemed the central cause of unemployment and overproduction, and one Walter Pitkin (1878–1953) declared that the rate of consumption had entered a period of permanent stagnation. Because mass production had both lowered the cost of goods and increased their quality, consumer demand would fall and the number of jobs would decline.[47] Again, in the 1990s Jeremy Rifkin's *The End of Work*[48] predicted the inevitable disappearance of jobs in the global labor market. The only growth area appeared to be in the "knowledge sector" but it would not be able to absorb the millions displaced by computers, robots, and automated telecommunications. Yet, however, convincing such arguments seem in theory, for the last two hundred years employment has increased, primarily because of demand for new kinds of goods and services.

If technological unemployment has so far proved a sporadic, short-term problem, distribution of the surplus from production remains an issue. Early British industrialization, with its grimy cities and sharp class divisions was later replicated in Pennsylvanian coal towns, Chicago stockyards, and North Carolina mill towns, and later still in the low-wage sweatshops of Asia and Latin America. Income distribution has not marched automatically toward greater equality, but rather come only in some nations, usually after unionization and political conflict. In good part, because the United States had a low minimum wage and weak labor unions, between 1970 and 1995 the richest fifth of Americans increased their slice of the economic pie from 40.9 to 46.9 percent, while real wages actually declined for the rest of the workforce. If computers did not lead to mass unemployment, they were often used to increase income inequality.

Feminists have likewise argued that technological abundance has been unevenly shared. Numerous studies of housework have shown that the hours of domestic labor did not diminish once homes had electric vacuum cleaners, stoves, clothes-washers and dishwashers. Instead, men and children withdrew from domestic work, leaving mothers to do most of it alone, even as standards rose for child care, cuisine and cleanliness.[49] Outside the home, women's wages, pensions, and expected lifetime earnings remain lower than men's, not least because relatively few become chemists, engineers, computer programmers, or executives. If persisting inequality cannot be blamed on technology per se, it does strongly suggest that technologies are socially shaped to perpetuate pre-existing cultural values and male privilege.

The strongest challenges to technological abundance came not from labor unions or feminists but from ecologists, beginning with Henry David Thoreau and John Muir. Thoreau lived in a one-room house at Walden Pond in order to simplify his material life and make time for reading, reflection, and close study of nature. His *Walden* (1854) questioned the value of slicing life into segments governed by clock time and suggested that the railroad rode mankind rather than the reverse. Thoreau believed that human beings required contact with wilderness to understand their place in the universe, and advocated setting areas aside, to remain forever untouched.

Landscape painters such as Thomas Cole and historians such as Francis Parkman also encouraged nineteenth-century Americans to create national monuments, parks, and forests. Setting them aside was an implicit critique of industrial society, which spread to other nations.[50] This process culminated in 1972 with the creation of the United Nation's "World Heritage List." By that time the United States had created a special category of "wilderness areas" that permitted no roads, mines, hotels, or other human intrusions. There, all forms of technology were carefully controlled.

Thoreau, Muir, and other early environmentalists also inspired advocates of simpler living arrangements, who questioned the value of a clutter of technological gadgets. Some imitated their lives, by retreating from civilization into remote places to practice simple living. Helen and Scott Nearing, for example, left New York City to take up subsistence farming in the 1920s and for several generations provided living proof that one might have a good life with a minimum of technology. Thousands of others also quietly rejected technological abundance, as documented in David Shi's *The Simple Life*.[51] Inspired by such individuals and by works such as Paul Wachtel's *The Poverty of Affluence*, during the last decades of the twentieth century, new non-profit political organizations such as World Watch and Friends of the Earth appeared, lobbying against the ideology of growth. Beginning in the 1980s, World Watch issued yearly "State of the World" reports. Conventional economic theory assumes that the gross national product must continually grow, but such groups were convinced that increasing technological abundance both destroyed the environment and distracted human beings from helping one another. In this spirit, Alan Durning asked *How Much is Enough?* He pointed out that according to polls, Americans of the 1990s were no happier than they had been in 1957, even if the gross national product had doubled. Their work hours had increased while time spent with friends and family declined. Bombarded with thousands of advertisements a day, they over-consumed in a throwaway economy that impoverished the environment. Thus by the end of the twentieth century, virtually no one doubted the ability of new technologies to increase production, but a growing minority doubted the wisdom of the goal itself.

Technology and Freedom

What is the relationship between technology and the political system? In his late work, "The Laws," Plato suggested that a well-regulated state should study innovations carefully before permitting them.[52] He feared that new practices, even in children's games, could disrupt the body politic, just as new foods could disturb the human body. Such caution long persisted, and only in the Renaissance did many begin to encourage innovations. The new technology of printing, first used to produce Bibles, was soon used for political ends. The rise of newspapers coincided with increasing political activism among their middle-class readers. It became an axiom in political thought that a free press was essential in any working democracy. Similarly, each new form of communication, from the telegraph and telephone to radio, film, television and the Internet, has been heralded as a new guarantor of free speech and the free movement of ideas. Because modern communications give individuals a global reach, before their fall, Communist governments monopolized broadcasting, restricted ownership of short-wave radios, and in some cases even controlled access to typewriters.

Yet some critics have worried that modern communications may shape and dominate consciousness. Do they facilitate the exchange of ideas or enable new forms of hegemony? Television can transmit real-time images from anywhere in the world; media events can transfix millions of people. Do such broadcasts weaken the local community and cede power to distant authorities? A belief in autonomous technology would prevent such questions from being asked, but if machines and processes are social constructions, then it follows that people need to maximize their awareness of the choices available. The Amish people, for example, have cautiously allowed only some technologies into their farming communities. For example, they decided not to adopt tractors. Horses may not be as powerful, but they replace themselves and produce valuable manure. Tractors, gasoline and commercial fertilizers all take money out of the local community. The Amish prefer tools, transportation, and homes that they can build and repair themselves.

In contrast, most American and western European communities have few mechanisms to consider the social consequences of new technologies, whose acceptance or rejection they leave to "the market." The characteristic liberal view since the nineteenth century asserted technological advances were the mark of a free people. Only a nation freed of feudalism, guilds, royal monopolies and other artificial restraints on individual initiative were capable of making the most of new technologies. On July 4, 1830, Edward Everett declaimed at the new industrial town of Lowell, Massachusetts: "It is the spirit of a free country which animates and gives energy to its labor; which puts the mass in action, gives it motive and intensity, makes it inventive, sends it off in new directions, subdues to its command all the powers of nature, and enlists in its service an army of machines, that do all but think and talk." The proof of this argument was not theoretical but practical: "Compare a hand loom with a power loom; a barge, poled up against the current of a river, with a steamer breasting its force. The difference is not greater between them than between the efficiency of labor under a free or despotic government; in an independent state or a colony."[53] According to such thinking, it was no accident that industry thrived in Britain and the United States while languishing under despots. Closer to home, this argument seemed to explain why the slave South lagged behind the free-labor economy of the North.

Such thinking assumed a myriad small industries in laissez-faire competition. By the 1870s, however, the workings of the economy seemed to tell a different story. Horace Greeley (1811–72), a prominent newspaper editor, complained about the power of railroads, which were strongest at the local and state level. "The railway monopoly of New Jersey has for years held the political and financial control of that state, and levied an onerous tax upon all travel between the east and south."[54] Greeley noted that railroads controlled the shipment and pricing of the most important raw materials of the industrial economy, coal, iron, and steel. Pennsylvania, Maryland,

Massachusetts, "and various other states, east and west, find themselves today seemingly powerless in the grasp of railroad corporations their charters have called into being. With the growth of the principle of consolidation, the evil is increasing."[55] Populists made railroad regulation a central issue in state politics and in the presidential campaign of 1892.

Well before such attacks on monopolies, agrarian thinkers argued that only land provided real, long-term wealth. The physiocrats in France and Thomas Jefferson in America idealized farmers as the backbone of the state. The young Jefferson declared that America's workshops should remain in Europe, a position he modified somewhat after witnessing the embargoes and instabilities of the French Revolution and Napoleonic wars.[56] Yet Jefferson still wanted only enough manufacturing to serve domestic consumption, assuming that the predominance of agrarian communities was essential to assure political virtue. A Jeffersonian preference for rural life and decentralized power has remained the basis for a persistent American critique of industrialized society, notably in the writings of the Southern agrarians of the 1930s.[57]

As the number of farmers declined, agrarianism ceased to represent a numerous political constituency, but it remained a popular stance against industrialization. Novelist and critic Wendell Berry, who continued to farm using older methods, declared in 2000 that "the most critical difference" between "the industrial and the agrarian, the global and the local" was "knowledge. The global economy institutionalizes a global ignorance, in which producers and consumers cannot know or care about one another, and in which the histories of all products will be lost." As a result, consumers unwittingly participate in the destruction of ecological systems and exploitation of workers elsewhere. Berry called for "a revolt of local small producers and local consumers against the global industrialisation of the corporations."[58] As he wrote, such a revolt was underway, as thousands protested globalization in the streets of Seattle, Gothenburg, and Genoa.

Throughout the twentieth century, many worried that in an advanced technological society, men might become slaves to machines at work, and prisoners of technological systems that penetrated all aspects of their private life. Novelists have evoked the terror of living inside a society regulated and controlled through technological systems, including H.G. Wells (*When the Sleeper Wakes*), Aldous Huxley (*Brave New World*), and George Orwell (*1984*). Likewise, films such as Fritz Lang's *Metropolis* (1926) or Charlie Chaplin's *Modern Times* (1936) showed human beings trapped inside technological systems. Such systems tended to acquire intelligence and become malevolent in later films such as Stanley Kubrick's *2001* or *The Matrix*.

These fears had many sources, notably management's imposition of new forms of work organization. Frederick Winslow Taylor's *Principles of Scientific Management* (1911) sold widely in French, German, and Russian translations, and was praised by Lenin. At home Louis Brandeis and many later prominent in the New Deal lionized Taylor. He argued that there was "one best way" to do any job, which could be analyzed and broken into parts by an expert, stop-watch in hand. Taylor taught workers the most efficient sequences and movements and the correct pace for even the simplest task, such as shoveling. He also invented or modified tools, such as shovels of different sizes to handle materials with different weights. Individual tasks were organized into a rational sequence, so that work flowed more evenly. Workers who cooperated produced more. In return, managers were expected to pay them more, though not all employers remembered this part of his system. Labor leaders loathed Taylor's ideas, because they took all agency away from workers, and when his system was put into practice, it often provoked strikes. Taylor himself was subjected to hostile congressional hearings in 1912. Nevertheless, "Taylorism" had an enormous resonance beyond the factory in many areas, including home economics, education, and popular culture. Experts appeared in every area of life, proclaiming that they had discovered the "one best way" to lay out a kitchen, assemble an automobile, regulate traffic flow, or plan a community. In the neo-Marxist thought of Antonio Gramsci, Taylorism was an oppressive historical stage in the sequence that began with primitive accumulation and ended with the collapse of capitalism. In practice, however, Taylor was but one of many "experts" who attempted to dictate the rules for working and living.

After observing the rise of scientific management and the expansion of the engineering profession, Thorstein Veblen expected an end to capitalist control of the machine. Only the new class of technicians seemed to understand modern productive systems well enough to use them efficiently. From this perspective, not only workers but also capitalists had become incompetent, and the best form of government therefore would be a "technocracy." Such ideas found formal expression in the technocracy movement, and inspired some New Deal projects of the 1930s.

Even as scientific managers proliferated, Henry Ford's engineers developed the assembly line, which after 1913 quickly spread to many other companies. This form of continuous flow production drew on experience in the arms industry, slaughterhouses, and many other areas, but was considered to be such a startling innovation that thousands of tourists visited his factories to see it in operation. If the assembly line radically reduced the time needed to assemble a car, however, workers quickly found the repetitive labor mind-numbing. As factories adopted mass production, in many industries labor turnover rose to 10 percent a month, or more than 100 percent a year.[59] Workers were voting with their feet against hierarchical rigidity, against the accelerating pace of work, and against the anti-democratic control of the shop floor.

In part because of the assembly line, during the 1920s and after the German-based Frankfurt School of philosophy viewed technologies as the means of surveillance, social control, and hegemonic domination, that penetrated popular culture through publishing, radio, and film. In this view, the new forms of mass consumption were packaged and standardized, trivializing human complexities. Max Horkheimer complained to a colleague: "You will remember those terrible scenes in the movies when some years of a hero's life are pictured in a series of shots which take about one minute or two, just to show how he grew up or old, how a war started and passed by, and so on. This trimming of existence into some futile moments which can be characterized schematically symbolizes the dissolution of humanity into elements of administration."[60] From such a perspective, the standardization of the individual made democracy meaningless, as cultural power had apparently passed into the hands of the dream factories of Hollywood and the songsmiths of Tin Pan Alley.

During the ideological rigidities of the Cold War, such fears often seemed prescient, as the subdivision and control of information reached new heights. Lewis Mumford observed the obsessive secrecy that surrounded the Manhattan Project and the rest of the nuclear arms program, and warned, "The key to exercising arbitrary power is to restrict the communications of individuals and groups by subdividing information so that only a small part of the whole truth will be known to any single person."[61] In 1961, even President Dwight D. Eisenhower warned of the growing power of "the military industrial complex." Increasingly, it seemed, corporate and political leaders worked together, supported by teams of experts, so that when a technological issue arose, the debate was largely ritualized. Fluoridated water was deemed safe, interstate highways were preferable to mass transit, atomic power stations were a good idea, and genetically modified foods ought to be produced and sold. As Rick Sclove has argued in *Democracy and Technology*, when new technologies are adopted, lay citizens in the United States usually play a small role, often only after the most important decisions have been made.[62] When approving new products, the government seldom considers their cultural effects or political implications.

In contrast, the Dutch and the Danes have developed forums that give ordinary citizens the chance to interview "experts" and then to formulate advice on technological policy. Not every society gives the public the same chance to influence the social construction of its technological systems. Yet, as corporations use genetic engineering and new software to produce new life forms and increasingly intelligent machines, citizens are likely to demand more transparency and more debate in technological decision-making. If in the eighteenth century it seemed obvious that the free press ensured democracy, and if in the nineteenth century it seemed obvious that invention and discovery were the desirable result of laissez-faire economics, by the twenty-first century it was becoming obvious that new technologies, such as Microsoft's software, were too valuable and potentially too dangerous to be left unregulated in private hands.

Yet, have the technologies of communication been constructed to enhance such a debate? Jürgen Habermas has argued that public opinion is so thoroughly influenced by the mass media that the "communicative network of a public made up of rationally debating private citizens has collapsed; the public opinion once emergent from it has partly decomposed into the informal opinions of private citizens without a public and partly become concentrated" into expressions of institutions. The private person no longer operates in the public sphere known by Thomas Jefferson, but instead is "caught in the vortex of publicity that is staged for show or manipulation."[63] These words were written before the Internet emerged as a potential new public space, one which the United States government, with little public debate, opened to commercial interests in 1991.

Technology and the Changing Life World

Both Ralph Waldo Emerson and Thomas Carlyle worried that the machine would rob human beings of an organic relationship to nature. Carlyle observed in 1829: "Were we required to characterize this age of ours by any single epithet, we should be tempted to call it, not an Heroical, Devotional, Philosophical, or Moral Age, but above all others, the Mechanical Age." His critique also included the psychological effects of the reliance on machines: "Men are grown mechanical in head and in heart, as well as in hand. They have lost faith in individual endeavor, and in natural force of any kind. Not for internal perfection, but for external combinations and arrangements, for institutions, constitutions – for Mechanism of one sort or other, do they hope and struggle."[64]

One can trace a tradition from such nineteenth-century critics to Henry Adams (1838–1918), who judged the automobile to be "a nightmare at one hundred kilometers an hour, almost as destructive as the electric tram which was only 10 years older,"[65] and who in late life concluded that technology as a whole had accelerated out of control.[66] After the appalling destruction of World War I, Adams's autobiography sold briskly, and helped to convince "the lost generation" that technological civilization had produced what T.S. Eliot (1855–1965) called "the wasteland." Even modernists, who embraced the machine age, believed that a fundamental rupture had taken place, separating mankind from the natural world and putting in its place an artificial urban environment of skyscrapers and subways that ran day and night on electricity. Indeed, powerhouses became popular tourist attractions, and an architectural critic enthused, "there is a feeling of grandeur and of poetry and of beauty in the orderly assembly of this modern, efficient, and economical equipment."[67] During the 1920s and 1930s, many felt that such sites evoked a feeling of sublimity, as did the new experience of air travel.

In the second half of the twentieth century, however, advanced technologies were frequently depicted as agents of doom, as many critics feared technological annihilation. World War II graphically demonstrated the destructive potential of air power, rockets, radar, and, most ominously, the atom bomb. At the end of the war, Lewis Mumford warned in the *Saturday Review of Literature* that the US government was "carrying through a series of acts which will lead eventually to the destruction of mankind."[68] Atomic weapons undermined the sense that the natural world could be taken to be always, already there. As bombs proliferated, a "death world", empty of all forms of life emerged as the possible end of history. And as nuclear reactors spread due to the "Atoms for Peace" program, people began to realize that they also posed hazards. In 1953, Edward Teller said in a public address that "a runaway reactor can be relatively more dangerous than an atomic bomb."[69] Gradually, the public realized that inside a reactor, uranium-238 was transmuted into extremely lethal plutonium. A Brookhaven report in 1956 estimated that a reactor accident might cause damages as high as $1.5 billion. Yet much of the public remained only sporadically worried until awakened by the social activism of the 1960s and the energy crises of the 1970s.

Not all fears were nuclear. In *Silent Spring* (1962) Rachel Carson warned that the abuse of pesticides such as DDT poisoned the natural world and undermined the ecological system. An ever-larger chorus of critics identified advanced technology with atomic bombs, chemical pollution, biological mutants, malicious computers, or technical systems out of control. These dystopian fears recurred in science fiction, which often depicted a devastated future, where the remnants of humanity struggled to survive the wreckage of a third world war.

Some of the most interesting criticism has focused not upon such apocalyptic dangers, however, but rather upon the psychological effects of living within a technological life world, that wraps humanity in a cocoon of machines and conveniences. Philosophers have tended to emphasize not particular machines but rather whole systems that foster technocratic sensibilities. Notably, Martin Heidegger (1889–1976) argued that in the modern world technology provides a pre-theoretical "horizoning of experience." A child born after c. 1950 found it "natural" to use electric lights, watch television, drive an automobile, or use satellite communications. That child's grandparents regarded such things as remarkable innovations that had disrupted the "normal." As the pre-theoretical "horizon" of experience expands, one might argue that life becomes richer and fuller, but many recent philosophers of technology argue that "... as devices replaced practices, disenchantment set in."[70] As the technological domain encroaches upon or mediates all experience, it overtakes and delegitimizes not only traditional society but also older perceptions of the world. In place of the repetitive cycles of everyday life in a sustainable relationship with nature, "technological character is concentrated in its liberating powers to be anything, that is, to be new, to never repeat itself."[71] This apparent liberation comes at a cost. The penetration of technology into all aspects of being means, "Our new character is grounded in human-technology symbiosis. Prior to reflection, technology transforms character."[72] The transformation imposes itself on each child, becoming part of its social construction of what is "natural."

Building on Heidegger, Albert Borgman's *Technology and the Character of Contemporary Life* posited a division between engagement with things, such as a stove, and using devices, such as a furnace. Only things engage people in a world of physical action. For example, to use a stove, wood has to be sawed, carried, and burned, in rhythms shaped by the weather and food preparation. In contrast, a device, such as a furnace, makes few demands on skill, strength, or attention, and so becomes an unconscious element in daily life. Such devices create a sharp dichotomy between the surface and the increasingly unfamiliar machinery inside. Automatic heat becomes normal.

Once "normality" is defined by a web of devices and becomes more technologically complex with each generation, can mankind depart too far from nature? Are all forms of constructed "normality" psychologically viable? How malleable is "human nature"? Postmodernists emphasize how the acceleration of transportation and communication has shrunk space, sped up time, disconnected voice from presence, subverted social boundaries, intensified the circulation of information, and created a blizzard of representations. By the 1990s it began to seem self-evident that a postmodern self was organized to accommodate this new infrastructure. Steven Connor speculated that "the reconfiguration of the relations between the senses, especially of hearing, seeing and touch, promised by new communicative and representational technologies may allow for a transformation of the relations between feeling, thinking, and understanding...The sheer overload of sensory stimulus required to absorb by eye and ear results in a switching or referral of senses. These contemporary synesthesias make it appropriate for us to think in terms of visual cacophony and white noise...we must also expect a redistribution of the values previously sedimented in the senses of hearing, vision, taste, touch, and smell."[73]

The possible transformation of human psychology by technology was one central part of the problem of technology and the life world. In addition, there were questions about scale and appropriateness that assumed prominence once the energy crises of the 1970s revealed the vulnerability of western economies to oil and gas shortages. E.F. Schumacher's *Small is Beautiful* (1972) advocated that developing countries solve their own problems with simpler machines and small-scale workshops rather than complex, high-tech "solutions" that made them dependent upon foreign aid and imperial suppliers.[74] Such "low-tech" ideas also seemed appealing inside industrial nations, because they empowered individuals to select and construct many details of their technological life world. *The Whole Earth Catalogue* (1968) provided detailed information on where to buy and how to use a host of small-scale technologies to preserve food, generate power, build and insulate new forms of shelter such as geodesic domes, and generally escape from conventional consumption. By the middle 1970s, relying on passive solar heat or windmill-generated electricity became more than just a counter-culture interest. Amory Lovins, for example, attacked atomic energy as a brittle, centralized power delivery system that was costly, and created pollution with a half life of 100,000 years. In contrast, wind and solar power were flexible, de-centralized, non-polluting, and in the long term less expensive.[75] Atomic power was therefore deemed unsustainable, a conclusion seemingly confirmed by the accidents at Three Mile Island and Chernobyl. Afterwards, public opposition to nuclear plants became massive, since no one wanted to live within a hundred miles of one.

In most areas, however, the ideal of sustainability did not transform cultural practice. Notably, Americans continued their heavy reliance on automobiles, requiring huge energy outlays and encouraging sprawling land use. This is a less appropriate use of technology than the Dutch use of mass transit and bicycles to serve compact cities that include many row houses and apartments. Those born into either society think their lives are "normal," but the Dutch system produces an equally high standard of living while using only half the energy or land per capita. The life world of Holland may therefore be more technologically sustainable, than that of the United States.

The "life world" approach favored by many philosophers contrasts with the recent emphasis on "the consumer." Some business and social historians argue that machines do not shape consciousness but rather are shaped by those who purchase or use them. From this perspective, radio and television programming responds to listener interests, advertising constantly modifies itself to appeal to consumers, and products designed by engineers, such as early Pyrex cookware, do poorly in the marketplace unless and until the design is modified to accord with the customer's wishes.[76] Just as Henry Ford could not indefinitely convince the public to buy black cars without annual restyling, to hold market share every manufacturer eventually has to accede to market demands.

Yet, are consumers in control of their technologies? Some thoughtful critics argue that while new devices may not embody the deterministic powers once attributed to them, they may lead to unexpected and often unwanted results. For example, the computer was brought into many factories in order to impose more control on workers but in actual use it often undermined corporate hierarchies and democratized access to information.[77] Meanwhile, in offices computers also had unintended consequences: neck pains, eyestrain, and carpal tunnel syndrome.[78] In a related argument, Bruno Latour has shown that the French attempt to build a new mass transportation system in Paris was hardly a model of rationality. Rather than assume human beings are becoming more logical and machine-like, he asserts that "we have never really been modern."[79]

Overall, the technological life world may best be envisioned neither as a smothering blanket, nor as an autonomous realm self-consciously constructed by consumers, but rather as a contested and shifting terrain, whose contours human beings manage at times to shape to their will, but parts of which always remain elusively at the edge of consciousness.

Conclusions

In *Capitalism and Material Life* Fernand Braudel rejected technological determinism, as he reflected on the slowness of some societies to adopt new methods and techniques. He declared, "Technology is only an instrument and man does not always know how to use it."[80] Professional historians of technology seldom take the extreme positions on the four fundamental questions considered here. Few see new machines as coercive agents dictating social change, and most remain unpersuaded by externalist arguments. Instead, they operate in the middle ground. They may accept the possibility of "soft determinism," but they also vigilantly look for ironic or unintended outcomes. They read beyond the balance sheets showing increased productivity to ask whether technological abundance is unevenly distributed or has long-term ecological consequences. They recognize that new machines emerge from political and social contexts and can be used for hegemonic or subversive ends. They are concerned about the social and psychological implications of incorporating technologies into everyday life, but skeptical about claims that human nature is easily or radically altered. While increasingly aware of over-arching theories, historians of technology display little desire to escape from empiricism, perhaps because they constantly deal with stubborn artifacts as well as with texts.

NOTES

1   See Merritt Roe Smith and Leo Marx, eds. *Does Technology Drive History? The Dilemma of Technological Determinism* (Cambridge: MIT Press, 1994).

2   See Don Ihde, *Technology and the Lifeworld: From Garden to Earth* (Indiana University Press, 1990).

3   Jacob Bigelow, *The Useful Arts* (Boston: Thomas Webb, 1840).

4   This statement is based on a survey of 100,000 nineteenth-century journal articles in Cornell University's electronic archive, "Making of America" (http://moa.cit.cornell.edu/moa/index.html). Before 1840, there were only 34 uses of the term, and all but three were either in Bigelow or references to him. Two referred to curricula in German universities, and the last was an eccentric usage in a legal context that seems unrelated to machines. Even *Scientific American* seems to have had little use for the word before 1855. Between 1860 and 1870 the term appeared only 149 times, compared to 24,957 for "invention."

5   Leo Marx, "Technology: the emergence of a hazardous concept," *Social Research* vol. 64:3 (Fall 1997), pp. 966–7.

6   Abraham Lincoln, "Second lecture on discoveries and inventions," Roy P. Brasler, ed., *Collected Works of Abraham Lincoln* (New Brunswick: Rutgers University Press, 1953–5), vol. 3, pp. 357–8.

7   *The Journals and Miscellaneous Notebooks of Ralph Waldo Emerson*, ed. William H. Gilman, *et al.*, vol. VII (Cambridge: Harvard University Press, 1969), p. 436. See also p. 268.

8   Ralph Waldo Emerson, *Journals* VIII, p. 434.

9   For a summary and analysis of Marx, see Mulford Q. Sibley, *Political Ideas and Ideologies: A History of Political Thought* (New York: Harper & Row, 1970), pp. 461–82.

10 Karl Marx, *Selected Writings in Sociology and Social Philosophy*, trans, T.B. Bottomore and ed. T.B. Bottomore and Maximilien Rubel (New York: McGraw Hill, 1964), p. 64.

11 See Leo Marx, *op. cit.*, p. 975.

12 Charles Steinmetz citation from Ronald Kline, "Electricity and socialism: the career of Charles P. Steinmetz," conference paper, *History of Technology Colloquium*, University of Delaware, March 5, 1985, p. 9.

13 On Lenin's enthusiasm for electrification, see Thomas Hughes, *American Genesis* (New York: Viking Penguin, 1989), pp. 258–61.

14 W.F. Ogburn, "The influence of invention and discovery," in *Recent Social Trends in the United States* (New York: McGraw Hill, 1934) p. 124.

15 Ibid., p. 125.

16 Alvin Toffler, *Future Shock* (New York: Random House, 1970). These ideas were further developed in Toffler's *The Third Wave* (New York: Bantam Books, 1980).

17 Joshua Meyrowitz, *No Sense of Place: The Impact of Electronic Media on Social Behaviour* (Oxford: Oxford University Press, 1985), p. 309.

18 Nicholas Negroponte, *Being Digital* (New York: Vintage, 1995), p. 230.

19 See Gregory Clark, "Why isn't the whole world developed? lessons from the cotton mills," *Journal of Economic History* 47:1 (1987), pp. 141–73.

20 Cited in Langdon Winner, *Autonomous Technology: Technics-out-of Control as a Theme in Political Thought* (MIT Press, 1977), p. 61.

21 Savio cited in Leo Marx, "Afterword," *The Machine in the Garden* (New York: Oxford University Press, 2000), p. 384.

22 Theodore Roszak, *The Making of a Counter Culture* (New York: Doubleday, 1969).

23 Michel Foucault, *Discipline and Punish: The Birth of the Prison* (New York: Viking, 1977), *The Birth of the Clinic: An Archaeology of Medical Perception* (New York: Vintage Books, 1995).

24   Leo Marx, "The idea of technology and postmodern pessimism," in Yaron Ezrahi, Everett Mendelsohn, and Howard Segal, eds, *Technology, Pessimism, and Postmodernism* (Amherst, Mass.: University of Massachusetts Press, 1995), pp. 23–5.

25   Winner, *op. cit.*

26   Wiebe E. Bijker, Thomas P. Hughes, and Trevor Pinch, eds, *The Social Construction of Technological Systems: New Directions in the Sociology and History of Technology* (Cambridge: MIT Press, 1987).

27   Thomas P. Hughes, "Technological momentum," in Merritt Roe Smith and Leo Marx, *Does Technology Drive History? The Dilemma of Technological Determinism* (Cambridge: MIT Press, 1994), p. 108.

28   John M. Staudenmaier, "Rationality versus contingency in the history of technology," in Smith and Marx, pp. 260–73.

29   See George Kubler, *The Shape of Time: Remarks on the History of Things* (New Haven: Yale University Press, 1962).

30   Charles Singer, E.J. Holmyard, A.R. Hall, Trevor I. Williams *et al.*, *A History of Technology* (Oxford: Oxford University Press, 1951–8).

31   Paul Israel, *Edison, A Life of Invention* (New York: John Wiley & Sons, 1998), pp. 410–21.

32   Hunter, vol. 3, pp. 115–238.

33   Contextualists are the largest group of authors in SHOT's journal *Technology and Culture*.

34   Robert H. Thurston, "Our progress in mechanical engineering: the president's annual address," *Transactions of the American Society of Mechanical Engineers, 1881*. Copy in the Cornell University Library, pp. 7–8.

35   Robert H. Thurston, "The trend of national progress," *North American Review*, vol. 161, September 1895, p. 310.

36   Ibid., pp. 118–31.

37   Werner Sombart, *Why Is There No Socialism in the United States?* (White Plains, New York: M.E. Sharpe, 1976).

38   Cited in Cecelia Tichi, *Shifting Gears: Technology, Literature, Culture in Modernist America* (Chapel Hill: University of North Carolina Press, 1987), p. 122.

39   *Official Guide: Book of the Fair, 1933* (Chicago: A Century of Progress, 1933), p. 12.

40   A.H. Raskin, "Pattern for tomorrow's industry?" *New York Times Magazine*, December 18, 1955, p. 17.

41   Nancy Gibbs, "How America has run out of time," *Time Magazine* April 24, 1989, pp. 59–60.

42   Leslie A. White, *The Science of Culture* (New York: Grove Press, 1949), pp. 363–8.

43   Michael Smith, "Selling the moon: the US manned space program and the triumph of commodity scientism," in T.J. Jackson Lears and Richard Wightman Fox, eds, *The Culture of Consumption* (New York: Pantheon, 1983, pp. 175–209).

44   *Los Angeles Herald-Examiner*, July 20, 1969.

45   George W.P. Custis, "An address on the importance of encouraging agriculture and domestic manufactures (1808), Reprinted in Michael Brewster Folsom and Steven D. Lubar, *The Philosophy of Manufactures: Early Debates over Industrialization in the United States* (Cambridge: The MIT Press, 1982) p. 155.

46   Ibid., p. 155.

47   Walter B. Pitkin, *The Consumer: His Nature and Changing Habits* (New York: McGraw-Hill, 1932), p. 356.

48   Jeremy Rifkin, *The End of Work* (New York: Putnam Publishing Group, 1996).

49   Ruth Schwartz Cowan, *More Work for Mother* (New York: Basic Books, 1983).

50   See Roderick Nash, *Wilderness and the American Mind* (New Haven: Yale University Press, 1982, 3rd edn).

51 David Shi, *The Simple Life* (New York: Oxford University Press, 1985).

52 Edith Hamilton and Huntington Cairns, *The Collected Dialogues of Plato* (Princeton: Princeton University Press, 1963) "The Laws" Book 7, pp. 1369–70.

53 Edward Everett, "Address on fourth of July at Lowell," *Orations and Speeches of Edward Everett* (Boston: Charles C. Little and James Brown, 1850), vol. 2, pp. 52–3.

54 Horace Greeley, *The Great Industries of the United States.* (Reprint, New York: Garland Publishing, 1974), vol. 2, p. 1035.

55 Ibid., p. 1036.

56 Thomas Jefferson, *Notes on the State of Virginia* (New York: Harper Torchbook, 1964), p. 157.

57 Paul K. Conkin, *The Southern Agrarians* (Knoxville: University of Tennessee Press, 1988).

58 Weldell Berry, "Back to the land," from David Quammen, *The Best American Science and Nature Writing 2000* (Boston: Houghton Mifflin, 2000), p. 19.

59 Sumner L. Slichter, *The Turnover of Factory Labor* (Appleton, 1919). Paul F. Brissenden and Eli Frankel, *Labor Turnover in Industry: A Statistical Analysis* (London: Macmillan, 1922).

60 Quoted in Martin Jay, *The Dialectical Imagination* (Boston: Little, Brown, 1973), p. 214.

61 Lewis Mumford, *The Myth of the Machine: The Pentagon of Power* (New York: Harcourt, Brace, Jovanovich, 1979), p. 264.

62 Richard E. Sclove, *Democracy and Technology* (London: The Guilford Press, 1995).

63 Jürgen Habermas, *The Structural Transformation of the Public Sphere: An Inquiry into a Category of Bourgeois Society* (Cambridge: MIT Press, 1989), p. 247.

64 Thomas Carlyle, "Signs of the Times," *Edinburgh Review* 98 (1829), p. 265.

65 Henry Adams, *The Education of Henry Adams* (New York: Modern Library, 1931), p. 380.

66 See Chapter 11 of David E. Nye, *Second Creation: Technological Creation Stories in the United States* (Cambridge: MIT Press, 2003).

67 Donald Des Granges, "The designing of power stations," *Architectural Forum*, September 51, 1929, p. 362.

68 Lewis Mumford, "Gentlemen, you are mad!" *Saturday Review of Literature*, March 2, 1946.

69 Cited in Specer Weart, *Nuclear Fear* (Cambridge: Harvard University Press, 1988), p. 281.

70 Lawrence Haworth, "Focal things and focal practices," Eric Higgs *et al.*, *Technology and the Good Life?* (Chicago: University of Chicago Press, 2000), p. 59.

71 Carl Mitcham, "Of character and technology," in ibid., p. 144.

72 Ibid., p. 146.

73 Steven Connor, "Feel the noise: excess, affect and the acoustic," in Gerhard Hoffmann and Alfred Hornung, eds, *Emotion in Postmodernism*, (Heidelberg: Universitätsverlag C. Winter 1997), p. 162.

74 E.F. Schumacher, *Small is Beautiful: Economics as if People Mattered* (Harper & Row, 1973).

75 Amory Lovins, "Energy Strategy: The Road Not Taken," *Foreign Affairs*, October, 1976.

76 Regina Lee Blaszczyk, *Imagining Consumers: Design and Innovation from Wedgwood to Corning* (Baltimore: Johns Hopkins University Press, 2000).

77 Shoshana Zuboff, *In the Age of the Smart Machine: The Future of Work and Power* (New York: Basic Books, 1988).

78 For these and other "revenge effects" of new technologies, see Edward Tenner, *Why Things Bite Back: Technology and the Revenge of Unintended Consequences* (New York: Vintage, 1997), pp. 225–8 and passim.

79 Bruno Latour, *We Have Never Really Been Modern* (Cambridge: Harvard University Press, 1993), and *Aramis, or The Love of Technology* (Cambridge: Harvard University Press, 1996).

80 Fernand Braudel, *Capitalism and Material Life: 1400–1800* (New York: Harper Torchbooks, 1973), p. 274.

Index